GIVE ME LIBERTY!

AN AMERICAN HISTORY

Brief Sixth Edition

GIVE ME LIBERTY!

AN AMERICAN HISTORY

Brief Sixth Edition

VOLUME 1: TO 1865

ERIC FONER

W. W. Norton & Company
NEW YORK · LONDON

For my mother, Liza Foner (1909–2005), an accomplished artist
who lived through most of the twentieth century and into the twenty-first

W. W. Norton & Company has been independent since its founding in 1923, when William Warder Norton and Mary D. Herter Norton first published lectures delivered at the People's Institute, the adult education division of New York City's Cooper Union. The firm soon expanded its program beyond the Institute, publishing books by celebrated academics from America and abroad. By midcentury, the two major pillars of Norton's publishing program—trade books and college texts—were firmly established. In the 1950s, the Norton family transferred control of the company to its employees, and today—with a staff of five hundred and hundreds of trade, college, and professional titles published each year—W. W. Norton & Company stands as the largest and oldest publishing house owned wholly by its employees.

Editor: Steve Forman
Project Editor: Maura Gaughan
Assistant Editor: Lily Gellman
Managing Editor, College: Marian Johnson
Production Manager: Sean Mintus
Media Editor: Carson Russell
Associate Media Editors: Sarah Rose Aquilina and Alexander Lee
Media Project Editor: Rachel Mayer
Assistant Media Editor: Alexandra Malakhoff
Managing Editor, College Digital Media: Kim Yi

Ebook Production Manager: Danielle Lehmann
Marketing Manager, History: Sarah England Bartley
Design Director: Rubina Yeh
Designer: Chin-yee Lai / Lisa Buckley
Director of College Permissions: Megan Schindel
College Permissions Manager: Bethany Salminen
Photo Editor: Stephanie Romeo
Composition: Six Red Marbles
Illustrations: Mapping Specialists, Ltd.
Manufacturing: Transcontinental

Permission to use copyrighted material is included on page A-55.

The Library of Congress has cataloged an earlier edition as follows:

Names: Foner, Eric, 1943- author.
Title: Give me liberty! : an American history / Eric Foner.
Description: Sixth edition. | New York : W.W. Norton & Company, 2019. | Includes index.
Identifiers: LCCN 2019031048 | **ISBN 9780393675627 (hardcover)**
Subjects: LCSH: United States—History—Textbooks.
Classification: LCC E178 .F66 2019 | DDC 973—dc23
LC record available at https://lccn.loc.gov/2019031048

ISBN this edition: 978-0-393-41818-7

W. W. Norton & Company, Inc., 500 Fifth Avenue, New York, NY 10110
wwnorton.com
W. W. Norton & Company Ltd., 15 Carlisle Street, London W1D 3BS

2 3 4 5 6 7 8 9 0

ABOUT THE AUTHOR

ERIC FONER is DeWitt Clinton Professor Emeritus of History at Columbia University, where he earned his B.A. and Ph.D. In his teaching and scholarship, he focuses on the Civil War and Reconstruction, slavery, and nineteenth-century America. Professor Foner's publications include *Free Soil, Free Labor, Free Men: The Ideology of the Republican Party before the Civil War*; *Tom Paine and Revolutionary America*; *Nothing but Freedom: Emancipation and Its Legacy*; *Reconstruction: America's Unfinished Revolution, 1863–1877*; *The Story of American Freedom*; and *Forever Free: The Story of Emancipation and Reconstruction*. His history of Reconstruction won the *Los Angeles Times* Book Award for History, the Bancroft Prize, and the Parkman Prize. He has served as president of the Organization of American Historians and the American Historical Association. In 2006 he received the Presidential Award for Outstanding Teaching from Columbia University. His most recent books are *The Fiery Trial: Abraham Lincoln and American Slavery*, winner of the Bancroft and Lincoln Prizes and the Pulitzer Prize for History, *Gateway to Freedom: The Hidden History of the Underground Railroad*, winner of the New York Historical Society Book Prize, and *The Second Founding: How the Civil War and Reconstruction Remade the Constitution*.

CONTENTS

14. A NEW BIRTH OF FREEDOM: THE CIVIL WAR, 1861–1865 ... 395

DELIVERING

MAPS

TABLES AND FIGURES

PREFACE

G ive Me Liberty! An American History is a survey of American history from the earliest days of European exploration and conquest of the New World to the first decades of the twenty-first century. It offers students a clear, concise narrative whose central theme is the changing contours of American freedom.

I am extremely gratified by the response to the first five editions of *Give Me Liberty!,* which have been used in survey courses at many hundreds of two- and four-year colleges and universities throughout the country. The comments I have received from instructors and students encourage me to think that *Give Me Liberty!* has worked well in their classrooms. Their comments have also included many valuable suggestions for revisions, which I greatly appreciate. These have ranged from corrections of typographical and factual errors to thoughts about subjects that needed more extensive treatment. In making revisions for this Sixth Edition, I have tried to take these suggestions into account. I have also incorporated the findings and insights of new scholarship that has appeared since the original edition was written.

The most significant changes in this Sixth Edition involve heightened emphasis on a question as old as the republic and as current as today's newspapers: Who is an American?

Difference and commonality are both intrinsic parts of the American experience. Our national creed emphasizes democracy and freedom as universal rights, but these rights have frequently been limited to particular groups of people. The United States has long prided itself on being an "asylum for mankind," as Thomas Paine put it in *Common Sense*, his great pamphlet calling for American independence. Yet we as a people have long been divided by clashing definitions of "Americanness." The first Naturalization Act, adopted in 1790, limited the right to become a citizen when immigrating from abroad to white persons. And the right to vote was long denied to many Americans because of race, gender, property holding, a criminal record, or other reasons. Today, in debates over immigration and voting rights, the question of "Who is an American?" continues to roil our society.

In a nation resting, rhetorically at least, on the ideal of equality, the boundaries of inclusion and exclusion take on extreme significance. The greater the rights of American citizenship, the more important the definition of belonging. Groups like African-Americans and women, shut out from full equality from the beginning of the nation's history, have struggled to gain recognition as full and equal members of the society. The definition of citizenship itself and the rights that come with it have been subject to intense debate throughout American history. And the cry of "second-class citizenship" has provided a powerful language of social protest for those who feel themselves excluded. To be sure, not all groups have made demands for inclusion. In the colonial era and for much of the history of the American nation, many Native Americans have demanded recognition of their own national sovereignty.

There is stronger coverage of this theme throughout the book, and it is reinforced by a new primary-source feature, "Who Is an American?" The sixteen such features, distributed fairly evenly throughout the text, address the nature of American identity, the definition of citizenship, and controversies over inclusion and exclusion. These documents range from J. Hector St. John de Crèvecoeur's reflections on Americanness toward the end of the War of Independence and the Declaration of Sentiments of the Seneca Falls Convention to Frederick Douglass's great speech of 1869 in defense of Chinese immigration, "The Composite Nation," and Mary Church Terrell's poignant complaint about being treated as a stranger in her own country.

In the body of the text itself, the major additions that illuminate the history of this theme are as follows:

Chapter 3 contains a new discussion of the formation in colonial America of a British identity linked to a sense of difference from "others"—French and Spanish Catholics, Africans, and Native Americans. Chapter 4 discusses the development of a pan-Indian identity transcending the traditional rivalries between separate Native American nations. In Chapter 7, I have added an examination of how the U.S. Constitution deals with citizenship and how the lack of a clear definition made disagreement about its boundaries inevitable. A new subsection in Chapter 12 deals with claims by African-Americans before the Civil War to "birthright citizenship," the principle that anyone born in the country, regardless of race, national origin, or other characteristics, is entitled to full and equal citizenship. Chapter 15 expands the existing discussion of the constitutional amendments of the Reconstruction era to examine how they redrew the definition and boundaries of American citizenship.

In Chapter 17, I have expanded the section on the movement to restrict immigration. Chapter 18 contains a new discussion of Theodore Roosevelt's understanding of "Americanism" and whom it excluded. Chapter 19 examines the "science" of eugenics, which proposed various ways to "improve" the quality of the American population. Chapter 23 contains a new subsection on how the Cold War and the effort to root out "subversion" affected definitions of loyalty, disloyalty, and American identity. Immigration reform during the administration of Ronald Reagan receives additional attention in Chapter 26. Finally, Chapter 28 discusses the heated debates over immigration that helped elect Donald Trump in 2016, and how his administration in its first two years addressed the issue.

Other revisions, not directly related to the "Who Is an American?" theme, include a reorganization of the chapter on the Gilded Age (16) to give it greater clarity, a new subsection in Chapter 17 discussing the political and philosophical school known as pragmatism, and significant changes in Chapter 26 to take advantage of recent scholarship on modern conservatism. The final chapter (28) has been updated to discuss the election of 2016 and the first two years of the administration of Donald Trump. I have also added a number of new selections to Voices of Freedom to sharpen the juxtaposition of divergent concepts of freedom at particular moments in American history. And this edition contains many new images—paintings, photographs, broadsides, lithographs, and others.

Americans have always had a divided attitude toward history. On the one hand, they tend to be remarkably future-oriented, dismissing events of even the recent past as "ancient history" and sometimes seeing history as a burden to be overcome, a prison from which to escape. On the other hand, like many other peoples, Americans have always looked to history for a sense of personal or group identity and of national cohesiveness. This is why so many Americans devote time and energy to tracing their family trees and why they visit historical museums and National Park Service historical sites in ever-increasing numbers. My hope is that this book will convince readers with all degrees of interest that history does matter to them.

The novelist and essayist James Baldwin once observed that history "does not refer merely, or even principally, to the past. On the contrary, the great force of history comes from the fact that we carry it within us, . . . [that] history is literally present in all that we do." As Baldwin recognized, the force of history is evident in our own world. Especially in a political democracy like the United States, whose government is designed to rest on the consent of informed citizens, knowledge of the past is essential—not only for those of us whose profession is the teaching and writing of history, but for everyone. History, to be sure, does not offer simple lessons or immediate answers to current questions. Knowing the history of immigration to the United States, and all of the tensions, turmoil, and aspirations associated with it, for example, does not tell us what current immigration policy ought to be. But without that knowledge, we have no way of understanding which approaches have worked and which have not—essential information for the formulation of future public policy.

History, it has been said, is what the present chooses to remember about the past. Rather than a fixed collection of facts, or a group of interpretations that cannot be challenged, our understanding of history is constantly changing. There is nothing unusual in the fact that each generation rewrites history to meet its own needs, or that scholars disagree among themselves on basic questions like the causes of the Civil War or the reasons for the Great Depression. Precisely because each generation asks different questions of the past, each generation formulates different answers. The past thirty years have witnessed a remarkable expansion of the scope of historical study. The experiences of groups neglected by earlier scholars, including women, African-Americans, working people, and others, have received unprecedented attention from historians. New subfields—social history, cultural history, and family history among them—have taken their place alongside traditional political and diplomatic history.

Give Me Liberty! draws on this voluminous historical literature to present an up-to-date and inclusive account of the American past, paying due attention to the experience of diverse groups of Americans while in no way neglecting the events and processes Americans have experienced in common. It devotes serious attention to political, social, cultural, and economic history, and to their interconnections. The narrative brings together major events and prominent leaders with the many groups of ordinary people who make up American society. *Give Me Liberty!* has a rich cast of characters, from Thomas Jefferson to campaigners for woman suffrage, from Franklin D. Roosevelt to former slaves seeking to breathe meaning into emancipation during and after the Civil War.

Aimed at an audience of undergraduate students with little or no detailed knowledge of American history, *Give Me Liberty!* guides readers through the complexities of the subject without overwhelming them with excessive detail. The unifying theme of freedom that runs through the text gives shape to the narrative and integrates the numerous strands that make up the American experience. This approach builds on that of my earlier book, *The Story of American Freedom* (1998), although *Give Me Liberty!* places events and personalities in the foreground and is more geared to the structure of the introductory survey course.

Freedom, and the battles to define its meaning, have long been central to my own scholarship and undergraduate teaching, which focuses on the nineteenth century and especially the era of the Civil War and Reconstruction (1850–1877). This was a time when the future of slavery tore the nation apart and emancipation produced a national debate over what rights the former slaves, and all Americans, should enjoy as free citizens. I have found that attention to clashing definitions of freedom and the struggles of different groups to achieve freedom as they understood it offers a way of making sense of the bitter battles and vast transformations of that pivotal era. I believe that the same is true for American history as a whole.

No idea is more fundamental to Americans' sense of themselves as individuals and as a nation than freedom. The central term in our political language, freedom—or liberty, with which it is almost always used interchangeably—is deeply embedded in the record of our history and the language of everyday life. The Declaration of Independence lists liberty among mankind's inalienable rights; the Constitution announces its purpose as securing liberty's blessings. The United States fought the Civil War to bring about a new birth of freedom, World War II for the Four Freedoms, and the Cold War to defend the Free World. Americans' love of liberty has been represented by liberty poles, liberty caps, and statues of liberty, and acted out by burning stamps and burning draft cards, by running away from slavery, and by demonstrating for the right to vote. "Every man in the street, white, black, red, or yellow," wrote the educator and statesman Ralph Bunche in 1940, "knows that this is 'the land of the free' . . . 'the cradle of liberty.'"

The very universality of the idea of freedom, however, can be misleading. Freedom is not a fixed, timeless category with a single unchanging definition. Indeed, the history of the United States is, in part, a story of debates, disagreements, and struggles over freedom. Crises like the American Revolution, the Civil War, and the Cold War have permanently transformed the idea of freedom. So too have demands by various groups of Americans to enjoy greater freedom. The meaning of freedom has been constructed not only in congressional debates and political treatises, but on plantations and picket lines, in parlors and even bedrooms.

Over the course of our history, American freedom has been both a reality and a mythic ideal—a living truth for millions of Americans, a cruel mockery for others. For some, freedom has been what some scholars call a "habit of the heart," an ideal so taken for granted that it is lived out but rarely analyzed. For others, freedom is not a birthright but a distant goal that has inspired great sacrifice.

Give Me Liberty! draws attention to three dimensions of freedom that have been critical in American history: (1) the *meanings* of freedom; (2) the *social conditions* that make freedom possible; and (3) the *boundaries* of freedom that determine who is entitled to enjoy freedom and who is not. All have changed over time.

In the era of the American Revolution, for example, freedom was primarily a set of rights enjoyed in public activity—the right of a community to be governed by laws to which its representatives had consented and of individuals to engage in religious worship without governmental interference. In the nineteenth century, freedom came to be closely identified with each person's opportunity to develop to the fullest his or her innate talents. In the twentieth, the "ability to choose," in both public and private life, became perhaps the dominant understanding of freedom. This development was encouraged by the explosive growth of the consumer marketplace (a development that receives considerable attention in *Give Me Liberty!*), which offered Americans an unprecedented array of goods with which to satisfy their needs and desires. During the 1960s, a crucial chapter in the history of American freedom, the idea of personal freedom was extended into virtually every realm, from attire and "lifestyle" to relations between the sexes. Thus, over time, more and more areas of life have been drawn into Americans' debates about the meaning of freedom.

A second important dimension of freedom focuses on the social conditions necessary to allow freedom to flourish. What kinds of economic institutions and relationships best encourage individual freedom? In the colonial era and for more than a century after independence, the answer centered on economic autonomy, enshrined in the glorification of the independent small producer—the farmer, skilled craftsman, or shopkeeper—who did not have to depend on another person for his livelihood. As the industrial economy matured, new conceptions of economic freedom came to the fore: "liberty of contract" in the Gilded Age, "industrial freedom" (a say in corporate decision-making) in the Progressive era, economic security during the New Deal, and, more recently, the ability to enjoy mass consumption within a market economy.

The boundaries of freedom, the third dimension of this theme, have inspired some of the most intense struggles in American history. Although founded on the premise that liberty is an entitlement of all humanity, the United States for much of its history deprived many of its own people of freedom. Non-whites have rarely enjoyed the same access to freedom as white Americans. The belief in equal opportunity as the birthright of all Americans has coexisted with persistent efforts to limit freedom by race, gender, and class and in other ways.

Less obvious, perhaps, is the fact that one person's freedom has frequently been linked to another's servitude. In the colonial era and nineteenth century, expanding freedom for many Americans rested on the lack of freedom—slavery, indentured servitude, the subordinate position of women—for others. By the same token, it has been through battles at the boundaries—the efforts of racial minorities, women, and others to secure greater freedom—that the meaning and experience of freedom have been deepened and the concept extended into new realms.

Time and again in American history, freedom has been transformed by the demands of excluded groups for inclusion. The idea of freedom as a universal birthright owes much both to abolitionists who sought to extend the blessings of liberty to blacks and to immigrant groups who insisted on full recognition as American citizens. The principle of equal protection of the law without regard to race, which became a central element of American freedom, arose from the antislavery struggle and the Civil War and was reinvigorated by the civil rights revolution of the 1960s, which called itself the "freedom movement." The battle for the right of free speech by labor radicals and birth-control advocates in the first part of the twentieth century helped to make civil liberties an essential element of freedom for all Americans.

Although concentrating on events within the United States, *Give Me Liberty!* also situates American history in the context of developments in other parts of the world. Many of the forces that shaped American history, including the international migration of peoples, the development of slavery, the spread of democracy, and the expansion of capitalism, were worldwide processes not confined to the United States. Today, American ideas, culture, and economic and military power exert unprecedented influence throughout the world. But beginning with the earliest days of settlement, when European empires competed to colonize North America and enrich themselves from its trade, American history cannot be understood in isolation from its global setting.

Freedom is the oldest of clichés and the most modern of aspirations. At various times in our history, it has served as the rallying cry of the powerless and as a justification of the status quo. Freedom helps to bind our culture together and exposes the contradictions between what America claims to be and what it sometimes has been. American history is not a narrative of continual progress toward greater and greater freedom. As the abolitionist Thomas Wentworth Higginson noted after the Civil War, "revolutions may go backward." Though freedom can be achieved, it may also be taken away. This happened, for example, when the equal rights granted to former slaves immediately after the Civil War were essentially nullified during the era of segregation. As was said in the eighteenth century, the price of freedom is eternal vigilance.

In the early twenty-first century, freedom continues to play a central role in American political and social life and thought. It is invoked by individuals and groups of all kinds, from critics of economic globalization to those who seek to secure American freedom at home and export it abroad. I hope that *Give Me Liberty!* will offer beginning students a clear account of the course of American history, and of its central theme, freedom, which today remains as varied, contentious, and ever-changing as America itself. And I hope that it also enables students to understand the connections between past and current events, the historical context and antecedents of the social, political, cultural, and economic issues that the American people confront today.

Acknowledgments

All works of history are, to a considerable extent, collaborative books, in that every writer builds on the research and writing of previous scholars. This is especially true of a textbook that covers the entire American experience, over more than five centuries. My greatest debt is to the innumerable historians on whose work I have drawn in preparing this volume. The Suggested Reading list at the end of each chapter offers only a brief introduction to the vast body of historical scholarship that has influenced and informed this book. More specifically, however, I wish to thank the following scholars, who offered valuable comments, criticisms, and suggestions after generously reading portions of this work or using it in their classes.

Jennifer Hudson Allen, Brookhaven College
Joel Benson, Northwest Missouri State University
Lori Bramson, Clark College

Andrea Brinton-Sanches, Cedar Valley College
Monica L. Butler, Motlow State Community College
Tonia Compton, Columbia College
Adam Costanzo, Texas A&M University
Carl Creasman Jr., Valencia College
Ashley Cruseturner, McLennan Community College
Richard Driver, Northwest Vista College
Laura Dunn, Eastern Florida State College
Kathleen DuVal, University of North Carolina, Chapel Hill
Blake Ellis, Lone Star College—CyFair
Carla Falkner, Northeast Mississippi Community College
Robert Glen Findley, Odessa College
Amy L. Fluker, University of Mississippi
Van Forsyth, Clark College
Yvonne Frear, San Jacinto College
Beverly Gage, Yale University
Michael A. Gonzalez, El Paso Community College
Aram Goudsouzian, University of Memphis
Michael Harkins, Harper College
Peter D. Haro, San Diego City College
Sandra Harvey, Lone Star College—CyFair
Robert Hines, Palo Alto College
Traci Hodgson, Chemeketa Community College
Tamora Hoskisson, Salt Lake Community College
William Jackson, Salt Lake Community College
Alfred H. Jones, State College of Florida
Junko Isono Kato, Waseda University
David Kiracofe, Tidewater Community College
Jeremy Lehman, McLennan Community College
Brad Lookingbill, Columbia College
Jennifer Macias, Salt Lake Community College
Scott P. Marler, University of Memphis
Thomas Massey, Cape Fear Community College
Derek Maxfield, Genesee Community College
Lisa McGirr, Harvard University
Marianne McKnight, Salt Lake Community College
Jonson Miller, Drexel University
Ted Moore, Salt Lake Community College
Laura Murphy, Dutchess Community College
Nathan Perl-Rosenthal, University of Southern California
Christopher Phelps, University of Nottingham
Robert Pierce, Foothills College
Ernst Pinjing, Minot State University
Harvey N. Plaunt, El Paso Community College
Steve Porter, University of Cincinnati

John Putman, San Diego State University

R. Lynn Rainard, Tidewater Community College, Chesapeake Campus

Janet Rankin, Sierra College

Nicole Ribianszky, Georgia Gwinnett College

Nancy Marie Robertson, Indiana University—Purdue University Indianapolis

Anderson Rouse, University of North Carolina, Greensboro

Horacio Salinas Jr., Laredo Community College

John Shaw, Portland Community College

Christina Snyder, Pennsylvania State University

Wendy Soltz, Purdue University Fort Wayne

Danielle Swiontek, Santa Barbara Community College

Chris Tingle, Northwest Mississippi Community College

Richard M. Trimble, Ocean County College

Alan Vangroll, Central Texas College

Karine Walther, Georgetown University

Eddie Weller, San Jacinto College

Ashli White, Miami University

Andrew Wiese, San Diego State University

Matthew Zembo, Hudson Valley Community College

I am particularly grateful to my colleagues in the Columbia University Department of History: Pablo Piccato, for his advice on Latin American history; Evan Haefeli and Ellen Baker, who read and made many suggestions for improvements in their areas of expertise (colonial America and the history of the West, respectively); and Sarah Phillips, who offered advice on treating the history of the environment.

I am also deeply indebted to the graduate students at Columbia University's Department of History who helped with this project. For this edition, Michael "Mookie" Kideckel offered invaluable assistance in gathering material related to borderlands and Western history and on citizenship and identity for the current one. For previous editions, Theresa Ventura assisted in locating material for new sections placing American history in a global context, April Holm did the same for new coverage of the history of American religion and debates over religious freedom, James Delbourgo conducted research for the chapters on the colonial era, and Beverly Gage did the same for the twentieth century. In addition, Daniel Freund provided all-around research assistance. Victoria Cain did a superb job of locating images. I also want to thank my colleagues Elizabeth Blackmar and the late Alan Brinkley for offering advice and encouragement throughout the writing of this book. I am also grateful to the numerous students who, while using the textbook, pointed out to me errors or omissions that I have corrected.

Many thanks to Joshua Brown, director of the American Social History Project, whose website, History Matters, lists innumerable online resources for the study of American history. Thanks also to the instructors who helped build our robust digital resource and ancillary package. InQuizitive for History was revised by Cornelia Lambert (University of North Georgia), Jodie Steeley (Fresno City College), Jen Murray (Oklahoma State University), and Joel Tannenbaum (Community College of Philadelphia). The Coursepack Quizzes and Instructor's Manual were thoroughly updated by Jason Newman (Cosumnes River College). Allison Faber (Texas A&M University) revised the Lecture PowerPoint slides. And our Test Bank was revised to include new questions authored by Robert O'Brien (Lone Star College—CyFair), Emily Pecora, and Carolina Zumaglini, with accuracy checking help from Matt Zembo (Hudson Valley Community College) and Jim Dudlo (Brookhaven College).

At W. W. Norton & Company, Steve Forman was an ideal editor—patient, encouraging, and always ready to offer sage advice. I would also like to thank Steve's assistant editor Lily Gellman for her indispensable and always cheerful help on all aspects of the project; Ellen Lohman and Annie Beck for their careful copyediting and proofreading work; Stephanie Romeo and Donna Ranieri for their resourceful attention to the illustrations program; Leah Clark, Ted Szczepanski, and Debra Morton-Hoyt for splendid work on the covers for the Sixth Edition; Jennifer Barnhardt and Maura Gaughan for keeping the many threads of the project aligned and then tying them together; Sean Mintus for his efficiency and care in book production; Carson Russell for orchestrating the rich media package that accompanies the textbook and his colleagues Sarah Rose Aquilina and Alexandra Malakhoff; Sarah England Bartley, Steve Dunn, and Mike Wright for their alert reads of the U.S. survey market and their hard work in helping establish *Give Me Liberty!* within it; and Drake McFeely, Roby Harrington, and Julia Reidhead for maintaining Norton as an independent, employee-owned publisher dedicated to excellence in its work.

Many students may have heard stories of how publishing companies alter the language and content of textbooks in an attempt to maximize sales and avoid alienating any potential reader. In this case, I can honestly say that W. W. Norton allowed me a free hand in writing the book and, apart from the usual editorial corrections, did not try to influence its content at all. For this I thank them, while I accept full responsibility for the interpretations presented and for any errors the book may contain. Since no book of this length can be entirely free of mistakes, I welcome readers to send me corrections at ef17@columbia.edu.

My greatest debt, as always, is to my family—my wife, Lynn Garafola, for her good-natured support while I was preoccupied by a project that consumed more than its fair share of my time and energy, and my daughter, Daria, who while a ninth and tenth grader read every chapter of the First Edition as it was written, for a modest payment, and offered invaluable suggestions about improving the book's clarity, logic, and grammar.

Eric Foner
New York City
March 2019

GIVE ME LIBERTY! DIGITAL RESOURCES FOR STUDENTS AND INSTRUCTORS

W. W. Norton offers a robust digital package to support teaching and learning with *Give Me Liberty!* These resources are designed to make students more effective textbook readers, while at the same time developing their critical thinking and history skills.

RESOURCES FOR STUDENTS

All resources are available at digital.wwnorton.com/givemeliberty6brv1 with the access card at the front of this text.

NORTON INQUIZITIVE

InQuizitive is Norton's award-winning adaptive learning tool that enhances students' understanding of the key big-picture themes and objectives from each chapter using a series of highly visual and gamelike activities. The new Sixth Edition includes over 20 percent new or revised questions, including primary source document excerpts, maps and historical images from the text, interactive visual content, and new "Who Is an American?" videos featuring Eric Foner.

HISTORY SKILLS TUTORIALS

The History Skills Tutorials are interactive, online modules that provide students a framework for analyzing primary source documents, images, and maps. New to the Sixth Edition is a fourth tutorial, Analyzing Secondary Sources. All tutorials begin with author videos modeling the analysis process followed by interactive assessments that challenge students to apply what they have learned.

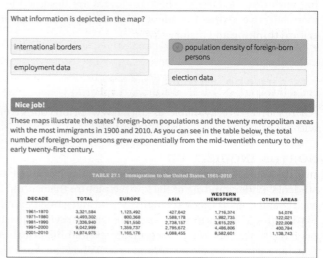

What information is depicted in the map?

- international borders
- employment data
- population density of foreign-born persons
- election data

Nice job!

These maps illustrate the states' foreign-born populations and the twenty metropolitan areas with the most immigrants in 1900 and 2010. As you can see in the table below, the total number of foreign-born persons grew exponentially from the mid-twentieth century to the early twenty-first century.

TABLE 27.1 Immigration to the United States, 1961–2010

DECADE	TOTAL	EUROPE	ASIA	WESTERN HEMISPHERE	OTHER AREAS
1961–1970	3,321,584	1,123,492	427,642	1,716,374	54,076
1971–1980	4,493,302	800,368	1,588,178	1,982,735	122,021
1981–1990	7,338,940	761,550	2,738,157	3,615,225	222,008
1991–2000	9,042,999	1,359,737	2,795,672	4,486,806	400,784
2001–2010	14,974,975	1,165,176	4,088,455	8,582,601	1,138,743

AUTHOR VIDEOS

In addition to the hundreds of author videos available through the ebook, student site, and InQuizitive, a new collection of videos featuring Eric Foner give students an in-depth look into the "Who Is an American?" book feature, and the issues of inclusion and exclusion as they have played out in American history. All videos are available with transcripts and closed captioning.

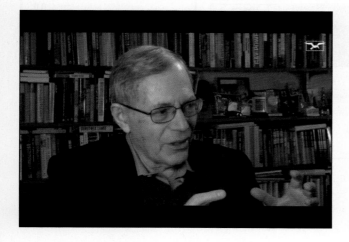

STUDENT SITE

The online Student Site offers additional resources for students to use outside of class. Resources include author videos in which Eric Foner explains the essential developments of each chapter, interactive iMaps study tools, and a comprehensive Online Reader with hundreds of additional primary sources, both textual and visual.

EBOOK

Norton Ebooks give students and instructors an enhanced reading experience at a fraction of the cost of a print textbook. Students are able to have an active reading experience and can take notes, bookmark, search, highlight, and even read offline. Instructors can add notes for students to see as they read the text. Features in *Give Me Liberty!* include enlargeable maps and art, embedded author videos that further explain key developments in the chapter, and pop-up key term definitions that give students useful context as they read. Norton Ebooks can be viewed on—and synced among—all computers and mobile devices.

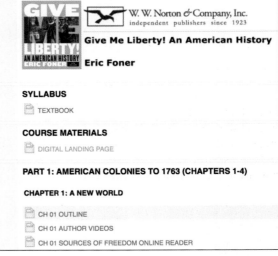

RESOURCES FOR INSTRUCTORS

All resources are available through wwnorton.com/instructors.

RESOURCES FOR YOUR LMS

Easily add high-quality Norton digital resources to your online, hybrid, or lecture course. Get started building your course with our easy-to-use coursepack files; all activities can be accessed right within your existing learning management system, and many components are customizable. Resources include InQuizitive, History Skills Tutorials, chapter outlines, review quizzes, flashcards, all of the resources from the Student Site, and more.

TEST BANK

The Test Bank features 30 percent new or revised questions, with more than 4,000 questions total—including multiple choice, true/false, matching, short answer, and essay questions—aligned with the chapter's Focus Questions. Classified according to level of difficulty and Bloom's Taxonomy, they provide multiple avenues for comprehension and skill assessment.

INSTRUCTOR'S MANUAL

The Instructor's Manual contains detailed Chapter Summaries, Chapter Outlines, Suggested Discussion Questions, Supplemental Web, Visual, and Print Resources, and new Interactive Instructor Activities.

LECTURE AND ART POWERPOINT SLIDES

The Lecture PowerPoints combine chapter review, art, and maps. Key topics to cover in class are sequentially arranged to follow the book, and new, robust lecture scripts, bulleted teaching points, and discussion questions fill the Notes section of each slide.

CHAPTER 1

A
NEW WORLD

★

Painted in 1718 by an unknown indigenous artist in modern-day Peru, *The Marriage of Captain Martin de Loyola to Beatriz Nusta* depicts the wedding, in 1572, of a daughter of the last ruler of the Inca empire and a nephew of Ignatius de Loyola, founder of the Jesuit order. With Inca royalty seated at the top left and Catholic saints in the center foreground, the work aims to legitimize Spain's colonial rule by assimilating into it the pre-conquest history of the Americas.

FOCUS QUESTIONS

- *What were the major patterns of Native American life in North America before Europeans arrived?*

- *How did Indian and European ideas of freedom differ on the eve of contact?*

- *What impelled European explorers to look west across the Atlantic?*

- *What happened when the peoples of the Americas came in contact with Europeans?*

- *What were the chief features of the Spanish empire in America?*

- *What were the chief features of the French and Dutch empires in North America?*

"The discovery of America," the British writer Adam Smith announced in his celebrated work *The Wealth of Nations* (1776), was one of "the two greatest and most important events recorded in the history of mankind." Historians no longer use the word "discovery" to describe the European exploration, conquest, and colonization of a hemisphere already home to millions of people. But there can be no doubt that when Christopher Columbus made landfall in the West Indian islands in 1492, he set in motion some of the most pivotal developments in human history. Immense changes soon followed in both the Old and New Worlds; the consequences of these changes are still with us today.

Human communities have interacted since the dawn of civilization. No society represents a single culture or people. For centuries before the conquest of the Americas, Europeans had intersected with Muslim populations in North Africa and Eurasia; indeed, the very idea of Europe as a distinct community arose out of such encounters. But since the voyages of Columbus, the interconnection of cultures and peoples has taken place on a global scale. The peoples of the American continents and Europe, previously unaware of each other's existence, were thrown into continuous interaction. Crops new to each hemisphere crossed the Atlantic, reshaping diets and transforming the natural environment. Because of centuries of lack of contact with peoples on other continents, the inhabitants of North and South America had developed no immunity to the germs that also accompanied the colonizers. As a result, they suffered a series of devastating epidemics, the greatest population catastrophe in human history. Within a decade of Columbus's voyage, a fourth continent—Africa—found itself drawn into the new transatlantic system of trade and population movement. In Africa, Europeans found a supply of unfree labor that enabled them to exploit the fertile lands of the Western Hemisphere. Indeed, of approximately 10 million men, women, and children who crossed from the Old World to the New between 1492 and 1820, the vast majority, about 7.7 million, were African slaves.

From the vantage point of 1776, the year the United States declared itself an independent nation, it seemed to Adam Smith that the "discovery" of America had produced both great "benefits" and great "misfortunes." To the nations of western Europe, the development of American colonies brought an era of "splendor and glory." Smith also noted, however, that to the "natives" of the Americas, the years since 1492 had been ones of "dreadful misfortunes" and "every sort of injustice." And for millions of Africans, the settlement of America meant a descent into the abyss of slavery.

Long before Columbus sailed, Europeans had dreamed of a land of abundance, riches, and ease beyond the western horizon. Europeans envisioned America as a religious refuge, a society of equals, a source of power and glory. They searched for golden cities and fountains of eternal youth. Some of these dreams would indeed be fulfilled. To many European settlers, America offered a far greater chance to own land and worship as they pleased than existed in Europe, with its rigid, unequal social order and official churches. Yet the New World also became the site of many forms of unfree labor, including indentured servitude, forced labor, and one of the most brutal and unjust systems, plantation slavery. The conquest and settlement of the Western Hemisphere opened new chapters in the long histories of both freedom and slavery.

THE FIRST AMERICANS

The Settling of the Americas

The residents of the Americas were no more a single group than Europeans or Africans. They spoke hundreds of different languages and lived in numerous kinds of societies. Most, however, were descended from bands of hunters and fishers who had crossed the Bering Strait via a land bridge at various times between 15,000 and 60,000 years ago—the exact dates are hotly debated by archaeologists.

Origins of settlement in the Americas

The New World was new to Europeans but an ancient homeland to those who already lived there. The hemisphere had witnessed many changes during its human history. First, the early inhabitants and their descendants spread across the two continents, reaching the tip of South America perhaps 11,000 years ago. As the climate warmed, they faced a food crisis as the immense animals they hunted, including woolly mammoths and giant bison, became extinct. Around 9,000 years ago, at the same time that agriculture was being developed in the Near East, it also emerged in modern-day Mexico and the Andes, and then spread to other parts of the Americas, making settled civilizations possible.

Emergence of agriculture

Indian Societies of the Americas

When Europeans arrived, North and South America contained cities, roads, irrigation systems, extensive trade networks, and large structures such as pyramid-temples whose beauty still inspires wonder. With a population close to 250,000, **Tenochtitlán**, the capital of the **Aztec** empire in what is now Mexico, was one of the world's largest cities. Farther south lay the Inca kingdom, centered in modern-day Peru. Its population of

Roads, irrigation systems, and trade networks

THE FIRST AMERICANS

A map illustrating the probable routes by which the first Americans settled the Western Hemisphere at various times between 15,000 and 60,000 years ago.

A modern visualization of Cahokia in the Mississippi River Valley, the largest Native American urban center in what is now the United States.

perhaps 12 million was linked by a complex system of roads and bridges that extended 2,000 miles along the Andes mountain chain.

Indian civilizations in North America had not developed the scale, grandeur, or centralized organization of the Aztec and Inca societies to their south. North American Indians lacked the technologies Europeans had mastered, such as metal tools and machines, gunpowder, and the scientific knowledge necessary for long-distance navigation. Their "backwardness" became a central justification for European conquest. But Indian societies had perfected techniques of farming, hunting, and fishing, developed structures of political power and religious belief, and engaged in far-reaching networks of trade and communication.

Justification for conquest

Mound Builders of the Mississippi River Valley

Remarkable physical remains still exist from some of the early civilizations in North America. Around 3,500 years ago, before Egyptians built the pyramids, Native Americans constructed a large community centered on a series of giant semicircular mounds on a bluff overlooking the Mississippi River in present-day Louisiana. Known today as Poverty Point, it was a commercial and governmental center whose residents established trade routes throughout the Mississippi and Ohio River valleys.

More than a thousand years before Columbus sailed, Indians of the Ohio River valley, called "mound builders" by eighteenth-century settlers who encountered the large earthen burial mounds they created, traded across half the continent. After their decline, another culture flourished in the Mississippi River valley, centered on the city of Cahokia

Cahokia

THE FIRST AMERICANS 5

A modern aerial photograph of the ruins of Pueblo Bonita, in Chaco Canyon in present-day New Mexico. The rectangular structures are the foundations of dwellings, and the circular ones are *kivas*, or places of religious worship.

Pueblo Indians

near present-day St. Louis, a fortified community with between 10,000 and 30,000 inhabitants in the year 1200. It stood as the largest settled community in what is now the United States until surpassed in population by New York and Philadelphia around 1800. The remains can still be visited today.

Western Indians

In the arid northeastern area of present-day Arizona, the Hopi and Zuni and their ancestors engaged in settled village life for over 3,000 years. During the peak of the region's culture, between the years 900 and 1200, these peoples built great planned towns with large multiple-family dwellings in local canyons, constructed dams and canals to gather and distribute water, and conducted trade with groups as far away as central Mexico and the Mississippi valley. The largest of their structures, Pueblo Bonita, in Chaco Canyon, New Mexico, stood five stories high and had over 600 rooms. Not until the 1880s was a dwelling of comparable size constructed in the United States.

After the decline of these communities, probably because of drought, survivors moved to the south and east, where they established villages and perfected the techniques of desert farming. These were the people Spanish explorers called the Pueblo Indians (because they lived in small villages, or *pueblos*, when the Spanish first encountered them in the sixteenth century). On the Pacific coast, another densely populated region, hundreds of distinct groups resided in independent villages and lived primarily by fishing, hunting sea mammals, and gathering wild plants and nuts.

Indians of Eastern North America

In eastern North America, hundreds of tribes inhabited towns and villages scattered from the Gulf of Mexico to present-day Canada. They lived on corn, squash, and beans, supplemented by fishing and hunting deer, turkeys, and other animals. Indian trade routes crisscrossed the eastern part of the continent. Tribes frequently warred with one another to obtain goods, seize captives, or take revenge for the killing of relatives. They conducted diplomacy and made peace. Little in the way of centralized authority existed until, in the fifteenth century, various leagues or confederations emerged in an effort to bring order to local regions. In the Southeast, the Choctaw, Cherokee, and

Chickasaw each united dozens of towns in loose alliances. In present-day New York and Pennsylvania, five Iroquois peoples—the Mohawk, Oneida, Cayuga, Seneca, and Onondaga—formed a **Great League of Peace**, bringing a period of stability to the area.

The most striking feature of Native American society at the time Europeans arrived was its sheer diversity. Each group had its own political system and set of religious beliefs, and North America was home to literally hundreds of mutually unintelligible languages. Indians did not think of themselves as a single people, an idea invented by Europeans and only many years later adopted by Indians themselves. Indian identity centered on the immediate social group—a tribe, village, chiefdom, or confederacy. When Europeans first arrived, many Indians saw them as simply one group among many. The sharp dichotomy between Indians and "white" persons did not emerge until later in the colonial era.

Diversity of Native American society

Native American Religion

Nonetheless, the diverse Indian societies of North America did share certain common characteristics. Their lives were steeped in religious ceremonies often directly related to farming and hunting. Spiritual power, they believed, suffused the world, and sacred spirits could be found in all kinds of living and inanimate things—animals, plants, trees, water,

The Village of Secoton, by John White, an English artist who spent a year on the Outer Banks of North Carolina in 1585–1586 as part of an expedition sponsored by Sir Walter Raleigh. A central street links houses surrounded by fields of corn. In the lower part, dancing Indians take part in a religious ceremony.

THE FIRST AMERICANS | 7

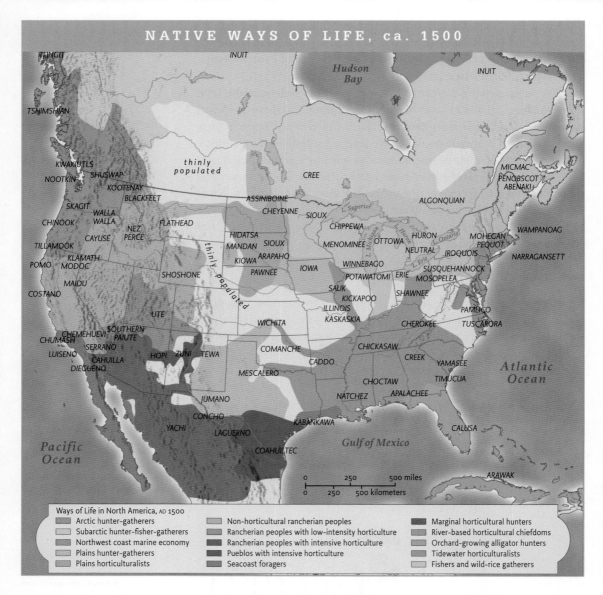

NATIVE WAYS OF LIFE, ca. 1500

TLINGIT
INUIT
Hudson Bay
INUIT
TSHIMSHIAN
KWAKIUTLS
NOOTKIN SHUSWAP
thinly populated
CREE
MICMAC
PENOBSCOT
ABENAKI
KOOTENAY
BLACKFEET
ASSINIBOINE
ALGONQUIAN
SKAGIT
WALLA WALLA
CHEYENNE
SIOUX
L. Superior
CHINOOK
CAYUSE
NEZ PERCE
FLATHEAD
CHIPPEWA
WAMPANOAG
TILLAMOOK
KLAMATH
HIDATSA
MANDAN SIOUX
MENOMINEE OTTAWA
HURON
NEUTRAL
MOHEGAN
PEQUOT
POMO MODOC
KIOWA ARAPAHO
IROQUOIS
NARRAGANSETT
MAIDU
SHOSHONE
PAWNEE
IOWA
WINNEBAGO
POTAWATOMI ERIE
SUSQUEHANNOCK
MOSOPELEA
COSTANO
SAUK
KICKAPOO
SHAWNEE
PAMLICO
thinly populated
UTE
ILLINOIS
KASKASKIA
CHEROKEE
TUSCARORA
CHEMEHUEVI
SOUTHERN PAIUTE
WICHITA
CHUMASH
SERRANO
COMANCHE
CHICKASAW
CREEK
YAMASEE
LUISENO
CAHUILLA
HOPI ZUNI TEWA
CADDO
DIEGUENO
MESCALERO
CHOCTAW
TIMUCUA
Atlantic Ocean
JUMANO
NATCHEZ
APALACHEE
CONCHO
KABANKAWA
CALUSA
YACHI
LAGUERNO
COAHUILTEC
Gulf of Mexico
Pacific Ocean
ARAWAK

| | 0   250   500 miles |
| | 0   250   500 kilometers |

Ways of Life in North America, AD 1500

- Arctic hunter-gatherers
- Subarctic hunter-fisher-gatherers
- Northwest coast marine economy
- Plains hunter-gatherers
- Plains horticulturalists
- Non-horticultural rancherian peoples
- Rancherian peoples with low-intensity horticulture
- Rancherian peoples with intensive horticulture
- Pueblos with intensive horticulture
- Seacoast foragers
- Marginal horticultural hunters
- River-based horticultural chiefdoms
- Orchard-growing alligator hunters
- Tidewater horticulturalists
- Fishers and wild-rice gatherers

The native population of North America at the time of first contact with Europeans consisted of numerous tribes with their own languages, religious beliefs, and economic and social structures. This map suggests the numerous ways of life existing at the time.

and wind. Through religious ceremonies, they aimed to harness the aid of powerful supernatural forces to serve human interests. Indian villages also held elaborate religious rites, participation in which helped to define the boundaries of community membership. In all Indian societies, those who seemed to possess special abilities to invoke supernatural

Rituals

powers—shamans, medicine men, and other religious leaders—held positions of respect and authority.

In some respects, Indian religion was not that different from popular spiritual beliefs in Europe. Most Indians held that a single Creator stood atop the spiritual hierarchy. Nonetheless, nearly all Europeans arriving in the New World quickly concluded that Indians were in dire need of being converted to a true, Christian faith.

Land and Property

Generally, village leaders assigned plots of land to individual families to use for a season or more, and tribes claimed specific areas for hunting. Unclaimed land remained free for anyone to use. Families "owned" the right to use land, but they did not own the land itself. Indians saw land as a common resource, not an economic commodity. There was no market in real estate before the coming of Europeans.

Land as a common resource

Nor were Indians devoted to the accumulation of wealth and material goods. Especially east of the Mississippi River, where villages moved every few years when soil or game became depleted, acquiring numerous possessions made little sense. However, status certainly mattered in Indian societies. Tribal leaders tended to come from a small number of families, and chiefs lived more splendidly than average members of society. But their reputation often rested on their willingness to share goods with others rather than hoarding them for themselves.

A Catawba map illustrates the differences between Indian and European conceptions of landed property. The map depicts not possession of a specific territory, but trade and diplomatic connections between various native groups and with the colony of Virginia, represented by the rectangle on the lower right. The map, inscribed on deerskin, was originally presented by Indian chiefs to Governor Francis Nicholson of South Carolina in 1721. This copy, the only version that survives, was made by the governor for the authorities in London. It added English labels that conveyed what the Indians had related orally with the gift.

A detail from a seventeenth-century map of English North America shows Native Americans hunting whales off of Long Island.

Generosity was among the most valued social qualities, and gift giving was essential to Indian society. Trade, for example, meant more than a commercial transaction—it was accompanied by elaborate ceremonies of gift exchange that bound different groups in webs of mutual obligation. "There are no beggars among them," reported the English colonial leader Roger Williams of New England's Indians.

Gender Relations

The system of gender relations in most Indian societies also differed markedly from that of Europe. Membership in a family defined women's lives, but they openly engaged in premarital sexual relations and could even choose to divorce their husbands. Most, although not all, Indian societies were matrilineal—that is, centered on clans or kinship groups in which children became members of the mother's family, not the father's. Under English law, a married man controlled the family's property and a wife had no independent legal identity. In contrast, Indian women owned dwellings and tools, and a husband generally moved to live with the family of his wife. Because men were frequently away on the hunt, women took responsibility not only for household duties but for most agricultural work as well.

European Views of the Indians

Europeans tended to view Indians in extreme terms. They were regarded either as "noble savages," gentle, friendly, and superior in some ways to Europeans, or as uncivilized barbarians. Over time, however, negative images of Indians came to overshadow positive ones. Early European descriptions of North American Indians as barbaric centered on three areas—religion, land use, and gender relations. Whatever their country of origin, European newcomers concluded that Indians lacked genuine religion, or in fact worshiped the devil. Whereas the Indians saw nature as a world of spirits and souls, the Europeans viewed it as a collection of potential commodities, a source of economic opportunity.

Europeans invoked the Indians' distinctive pattern of land use and ideas about property to answer the awkward question raised by a British minister at an early stage of England's colonization: "By what right or warrant can we enter into the land of these Savages, take away their rightful inheritance from them, and plant ourselves in their places?" While the Spanish claimed title to land in America by right of conquest and papal authority, the English, French, and Dutch came to rely on the idea that Indians had not actually "used" the land and thus had no claim to it. Despite the Indians' highly developed agriculture and well-established towns, Europeans frequently described them as nomads without settled communities.

In the Indians' gender division of labor and matrilineal family structures, Europeans saw weak men and mistreated women. Hunting and fishing, the primary occupations of Indian men, were considered leisure activities in much of Europe, not "real" work. Because Indian women worked in the fields, Europeans often described them as lacking freedom. Europeans insisted that by subduing the Indians, they were actually bringing them freedom—the freedom of true religion, private property, and the liberation of both men and women from uncivilized and unchristian gender roles.

Indian women planting crops while men break the sod. An engraving by Theodor de Bry, based on a painting by Jacques Le Moyne de Morgues. Morgues was part of an expedition of French Huguenots to Florida in 1564; he escaped when the Spanish destroyed the outpost in the following year.

A seventeenth-century engraving by a French Jesuit priest illustrates many Europeans' view of Indian religion. A demon hovers over an Iroquois longhouse, suggesting that Indians worship the devil.

INDIAN FREEDOM, EUROPEAN FREEDOM

Indian Freedom

Although many Europeans initially saw Indians as embodying freedom, most colonizers quickly concluded that the notion of "freedom" was alien to Indian societies. European settlers reached this conclusion in part because

Indians did not appear to live under established governments or fixed laws, followed their own—not European—definitions of authority, and lacked the kind of order and discipline common in European society. Indians also did not define freedom as individual autonomy or tie it to the ownership of property—two attributes important to Europeans.

Freedom in the group

What were the Indians' ideas of freedom? The modern notion of freedom as personal independence had little meaning in most Indian societies, but individuals were expected to think for themselves and did not always have to go along with collective decision making. Far more important than individual autonomy were kinship ties, the ability to follow one's spiritual values, and the well-being and security of one's community. In Indian culture, group autonomy and self-determination, and the mutual obligations that came with a sense of belonging and connectedness, took precedence over individual freedom. Ironically, the coming of Europeans, armed with their own language of liberty, would make freedom a preoccupation of American Indians, as part and parcel of the very process by which they were reduced to dependence on the colonizers.

Christian Liberty

On the eve of colonization, Europeans held numerous ideas of freedom. Some were as old as the city-states of ancient Greece, others arose during the political struggles of the early modern era. Some laid the foundations for modern conceptions of freedom, others are quite unfamiliar today. Freedom was not a single idea but a collection of distinct rights and privileges, many enjoyed by only a small portion of the population.

Freedom as a spiritual condition

One conception common throughout Europe understood freedom less as a political or social status than as a moral or spiritual condition. Freedom meant abandoning the life of sin to embrace the teachings of Christ. "Christian Liberty," however, had no connection to later ideas of religious toleration, a notion that scarcely existed anywhere on the eve of colonization. In the premodern world, religion was not simply a matter of spiritual doctrines and practices, but systems of belief that permeated every aspect of people's lives. Religious beliefs were therefore inseparable from what would later be considered "secular" matters, such as who enjoyed basic rights. A person's religion was closely tied to his or her economic, political, and social position.

Every nation in Europe had an established church that decreed what forms of religious worship and belief were acceptable. Dissenters faced persecution by the state as well as condemnation by church authorities. Religious uniformity was thought to be essential to public order; the modern idea that a person's religious beliefs and practices are a matter of private choice, not legal obligation, was almost unknown.

Freedom and Authority

In its secular form, the equating of liberty with devotion to a higher authority suggested that freedom meant obedience to law. The identification of freedom with the rule of law did not, though, mean that all subjects of the crown enjoyed the same degree of freedom. Early modern European societies were extremely hierarchical, with marked gradations of social status ranging from the king and hereditary aristocracy down to the urban and rural poor. Inequality was built into virtually every social relationship.

Hierarchy in the family

Within families, men exercised authority over their wives and children. According to the legal doctrine known as "coverture," when a woman married she surrendered her legal identity, which became "covered" by that of her husband. She could not own property or sign contracts in her own name, control her wages if she worked, write a separate will, or, except in the rarest of circumstances, go to court seeking a divorce. The husband had the exclusive right to his wife's "company," including domestic labor and sexual relations.

Everywhere in Europe, family life depended on male dominance and female submission. Indeed, political writers of the sixteenth century explicitly compared the king's authority over his subjects with the husband's over his family. Both were ordained by God.

Liberty and Liberties

In this hierarchical society, liberty came from knowing one's social place and fulfilling the duties appropriate to one's rank. Most men lacked the freedom that came with economic independence. Property qualifications and other restrictions limited the electorate to a minuscule part of the adult male population. The law required strict obedience of employees, and breaches of labor contracts carried criminal penalties.

Hierarchy in society

European ideas of freedom still bore the imprint of the Middle Ages, when "liberties" meant formal, specific privileges such as self-government, exemption from taxation, or the right to practice a particular trade, granted to individuals or groups by contract, royal decree, or purchase. Only those who enjoyed the "freedom of the city," for example, could engage in certain economic activities. Numerous modern civil liberties did not exist. The law decreed acceptable forms of religious worship. The government regularly suppressed publications it did not like, and criticism of authority could

Limited civil liberties

lead to imprisonment. Nonetheless, every European country that colonized the New World claimed to be spreading freedom—for its own population and for Native Americans.

THE EXPANSION OF EUROPE

Sea route to the East

It is fitting that the second epochal event that Adam Smith linked to Columbus's voyage of 1492 was the discovery by Portuguese navigators of a sea route from Europe to Asia around the southern tip of Africa. The European conquest of America began as an offshoot of the quest for a sea route to India, China, and the islands of the East Indies, the source of the silk, tea, spices, porcelain, and other luxury goods on which international trade in the early modern era centered. For centuries, this commerce had been conducted across land, from China and South Asia to the Middle East and the Mediterranean region. Profit and piety—the desire to eliminate Islamic middlemen and win control of the lucrative trade for Christian western Europe—combined to inspire the quest for a direct route to Asia.

Chinese and Portuguese Navigation

Zheng He's voyages

At the beginning of the fifteenth century, one might have predicted that China would establish the world's first global empire. Between 1405 and 1433, Admiral Zheng He led seven large naval expeditions in the Indian Ocean. The first convoy consisted of 62 ships that were larger than those of any European nation, along with 225 support vessels and more than 25,000 men. On his sixth voyage, Zheng explored the coast of East Africa. Had his ships continued westward, they could easily have reached North and South America. But as a wealthy land-based empire, China did not feel the need for overseas expansion, and after 1433 the government ended support for long-distance maritime expeditions.

New techniques of sailing and navigation

It fell to Portugal, far removed from the overland route to Asia, to begin exploring the Atlantic. Taking advantage of new long-distance ships known as **caravels** and new navigational devices such as the compass and quadrant, the Portuguese showed that it was possible to sail down the coast of Africa and return to Portugal. Until 1434, no European sailor had seen the coast of Africa below the Sahara. But in that year, a Portuguese ship brought a sprig of rosemary from West Africa, proof that one could sail beyond the desert and return.

Little by little, Portuguese ships moved farther down the coast. In 1485, they reached Benin, an imposing city whose craftsmen produced bronze sculptures that still inspire admiration for their artistic beauty and superb casting techniques. The Portuguese established fortified trading

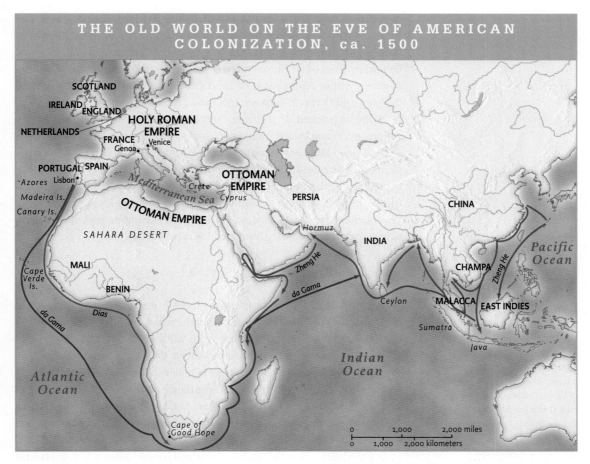

THE OLD WORLD ON THE EVE OF AMERICAN COLONIZATION, ca. 1500

posts on the western coast of Africa. The profits reaped by these Portuguese "factories"—so named because merchants were known as "factors"—inspired other European powers to follow in their footsteps.

Portugal also began to colonize Madeira, the Azores, and the Canary and Cape Verde Islands, which lie in the Atlantic off the African coast. The Portuguese established plantations on the Atlantic islands, eventually replacing the native populations with thousands of slaves shipped from Africa—an ominous precedent for the New World.

In the fifteenth century, the world known to Europeans was limited to Europe, parts of Africa, and Asia. Explorers from Portugal sought to find a sea route to the East in order to circumvent the Italian city-states and Middle Eastern rulers who controlled the overland trade.

Freedom and Slavery in Africa

Slavery in Africa long predated the coming of Europeans. Traditionally, African slaves tended to be criminals, debtors, and captives in war. They worked within the households of their owners and had well-defined rights, such as possessing property and marrying free persons. It was not uncommon for African slaves to acquire their freedom. Slavery was one of several forms of labor, not the basis of the economy as it would become in large parts of the New World. The coming of the Portuguese, soon followed by traders from other European nations, accelerated the buying and selling of slaves within Africa. At least 100,000 African slaves were transported to Spain and Portugal between 1450 and 1500.

Having reached West Africa, Portuguese mariners pushed their explorations ever southward along the coast. Bartholomeu Dias reached the Cape of Good Hope at the continent's southern tip in 1487. In 1498, Vasco da Gama sailed around it to India, demonstrating the feasibility of a sea route to the East. With a population of under 1 million, Portugal established a vast trading empire, with bases in India, southern China, and Indonesia. But six years before da Gama's voyage, Christopher Columbus had, he believed, discovered a new route to China and India by sailing west.

The Voyages of Columbus

A seasoned mariner and fearless explorer from Genoa, a major port in northern Italy, Columbus had for years sailed the Mediterranean and North Atlantic, studying ocean currents and wind patterns. Like nearly all navigators of the time, Columbus knew the earth was round. But he drastically underestimated its size. He believed that by sailing westward he could relatively quickly cross the Atlantic and reach Asia. No one in Europe knew that two giant continents lay 3,000 miles to the west. The Vikings, to be sure, had sailed from Greenland to Newfoundland around the year 1000 and established a settlement, Vinland. But this outpost was abandoned after a few years and had been forgotten, except in Norse legends.

Columbus's Landfall, an engraving from *La lettera dell'isole* (Letter from the Islands). This 1493 pamphlet reproduced, in the form of a poem, Columbus's first letter describing his voyage of the previous year. Under the watchful eye of King Ferdinand of Spain, Columbus and his men land on a Caribbean island, while local Indians flee.

For Columbus, as for other figures of the time, religious and commercial motives reinforced one another. Along with developing trade with the East, he hoped to convert Asians to Christianity and enlist them in a crusade to redeem Jerusalem from Muslim control.

Columbus sought financial support throughout Europe for the planned voyage. He relied on a number of sources for his estimate of the size of the globe, including Marco Polo's account of his visit by land to China in the thirteenth century and, as a devout Catholic, the Bible. Eventually, King Ferdinand and Queen Isabella of Spain agreed to become sponsors. Their marriage in 1469 had united the warring kingdoms of Aragon and Castile. In 1492, they completed the ***reconquista***—the "reconquest" of Spain from the Moors, African Muslims who had occupied part of the Iberian Peninsula for centuries. With Spain's territory united, Ferdinand and Isabella—like the rulers of the Italian city-states—were anxious to circumvent the Muslim stranglehold on eastern trade. It is not surprising, then, that Columbus set sail with royal letters of introduction to Asian rulers, authorizing him to negotiate trade agreements.

CONTACT

Columbus in the New World

On October 12, 1492, after only thirty-three days of sailing from the Canary Islands, where he had stopped to resupply his three ships, Columbus and his expedition arrived at the Bahamas. Soon afterward, he encountered the far larger islands of Hispaniola (today the site of Haiti and the Dominican Republic) and Cuba. When one of his ships ran aground, he abandoned it and left thirty-eight men behind on Hispaniola. But he found room to bring ten inhabitants of the island back to Spain for conversion to Christianity.

In the following year, 1493, Columbus returned with seventeen ships and more than 1,000 men to explore the area and establish a Spanish outpost. Columbus's settlement on the island of Hispaniola, which he named La Isabella, failed, but in 1502 another Spanish explorer, Nicolás de Ovando, arrived with 2,500 men and established a permanent base, the first center of the Spanish empire in America. Columbus went to his grave believing that he had discovered a westward route to Asia. The explorations of another Italian, Amerigo Vespucci, along the coast of South America between 1499 and 1502 made plain that a continent entirely unknown to Europeans had been encountered. The New World would come to bear not Columbus's name but one based on Vespucci's—America. Vespucci also realized that the native inhabitants were distinct peoples, not residents of the East Indies as Columbus had believed, although the name "Indians," applied to them by Columbus, has endured to this day.

Exploration and Conquest

Thanks to Johannes Gutenberg's invention of the printing press in the 1430s, news of Columbus's achievement traveled quickly, at least among the educated minority in

Engravings, from the *Florentine Codex*, of the forces of Cortés marching on Tenochtitlán and assaulting the city with cannon fire. The difference in military technology between the Spanish and Aztecs is evident. Indians who allied with Cortés had helped him build vessels and carry them in pieces over mountains to the city. The codex (a volume formed by stitching together manuscript pages) was prepared under the supervision of a Spanish missionary in sixteenth-century Mexico.

EUROPE

Vinland

Cabot (1497)

NORTH
AMERICA

NEWFOUNDLAND

Columbus (1492)

Columbus (1493)

Columbus (1502)

AFRICA

Balboa (1513)

Atlantic
Ocean

Columbus (1498)

Magellan (1519–1522)

Vespucci (1501–1502)

Cabral (1500)

Pacific
Ocean

SOUTH
AMERICA

Magellan (1519–1522)

| 0 | 1,000 | 2,000 miles |
| 0 | 1,000 | 2,000 kilometers |

Christopher Columbus's first Atlantic crossing, in 1492, was soon followed by voyages of discovery by English, Portuguese, Spanish, and Italian explorers.

Europe. Other explorers were inspired to follow in his wake. John Cabot, a Genoese merchant who had settled in England, reached Newfoundland in 1497. Soon, scores of fishing boats from France, Spain, and England were active in the region. Pedro Cabral claimed Brazil for Portugal in 1500.

But the Spanish took the lead in exploration and conquest. Inspired by a search for wealth, national glory, and the desire to spread Catholicism, Spanish **conquistadores**, often accompanied by religious missionaries and carrying flags emblazoned with the sign of the cross, radiated outward from Hispaniola. In 1513, Vasco Núñez de Balboa trekked across the isthmus of Panama and became the first European to gaze upon the Pacific Ocean. Between 1519 and 1522, Ferdinand Magellan led the first expedition to sail around the world, encountering Pacific islands and peoples previously unknown to Europe.

Spreading Catholicism

The first explorer to encounter a major American civilization was Hernán Cortés, who in 1519 arrived at Tenochtitlán, the nerve center of the Aztec empire, whose wealth and power rested on domination of numerous subordinate peoples nearby. The Aztecs were violent warriors who engaged in the ritual sacrifice of captives and others, sometimes thousands at a time. This practice thoroughly alienated their neighbors.

With only a few hundred European men, Cortés conquered the Aztec city, relying on superior military technology such as iron weapons and gunpowder. He shrewdly enlisted the aid of some of the Aztecs' subject peoples, who supplied him with thousands of warriors, without whose aid he could not have succeeded. His most powerful ally, however, was disease—a smallpox epidemic that devastated Aztec society. A few years later, Francisco Pizarro conquered the great Inca kingdom centered in modern-day Peru. Pizarro's tactics were typical of the *conquistadores*. He captured the Incan king, demanded and received a ransom, and then killed the king anyway. Soon, treasure fleets carrying cargoes of gold and silver from the mines of Mexico and Peru were traversing the Atlantic to enrich the Spanish crown.

Hernán Cortés and Francisco Pizarro

The Demographic Disaster

The transatlantic flow of goods and people is sometimes called the **Columbian Exchange**. Plants, animals, and cultures that had evolved independently on separate continents were now thrown together. Products introduced to Europe from the Americas included corn, tomatoes, potatoes, peanuts, and

TABLE 1.1 Estimated Regional Populations: The Americas, ca. 1500

North America	3,800,000
Mexico	17,200,000
Central America	5,625,000
Hispaniola	1,000,000
The Caribbean	3,000,000
The Andes	15,700,000
South America	8,620,000
Total	54,945,000

TABLE 1.2 Estimated Regional Populations: The World, ca. 1500	
India	110,000,000
China	103,000,000
Other Asia	55,400,000
Western Europe	57,200,000
The Americas	55,000,000
Russia and Eastern Europe	34,000,000
Sub-Saharan Africa	38,300,000
Japan	15,400,000
World Total	467,300,000

tobacco, while people from the Old World brought wheat, rice, sugarcane, horses, cattle, pigs, and sheep to the New. But Europeans also carried germs previously unknown in the Americas.

No one knows exactly how many people lived in the Americas at the time of Columbus's voyages—current estimates range between 50 and 90 million, most of whom lived in Central and South America. In 1492, the Indian population within what are now the borders of the United States was between 2 and 5 million. The Indian populations of the Americas suffered a catastrophic decline because of contact with Europeans. Never having encountered diseases like smallpox, influenza, and measles, Indians had not developed antibodies to fight them. The result was devastating. The population of Mexico would fall by more than 90 percent in the sixteenth century, from perhaps 20 million to under 2 million. As for the area that now forms the United States, its Native American population fell continuously. It reached its lowest point around 1900, at only 250,000.

Overall, the death of perhaps 80 million people—close to one-fifth of humankind—in the first century and a half after contact with Europeans represents the greatest loss of life in human history. The causes were numerous—not only disease but other consequences of European colonization, including wars using advanced military technology, enslavement, forced conversion to Christianity, and destruction of long-established communities. All these enabled Europeans to conquer the Americas.

Young Woman with a Harpsichord, a colorful painting from Mexico in the early 1700s, depicts an upper-class woman. Her dress, jewelry, fan, the cross around her neck, and the musical instrument all emphasize that while she lives in the colonies she embodies the latest in European fashion and culture.

THE SPANISH EMPIRE

By the middle of the sixteenth century, Spain had established an immense empire that reached from Europe to the Americas and Asia. The Atlantic and Pacific oceans, once barriers separating different parts of the world, now became highways for the exchange of goods and the movement of people. Spanish galleons carried gold and silver from Mexico and Peru eastward to Spain and westward to Manila in the Philippines and on to China.

Stretching from the Andes Mountains of South America through present-day Mexico and the Caribbean and eventually into Florida and the southwestern United States, Spain's empire exceeded in size the Roman empire of the ancient world. Its center was Mexico City, a magnificent capital built on the ruins of the Aztec city of Tenochtitlán that boasted churches, hospitals, monasteries, government buildings, and the New World's first university. Unlike the English and French New World empires, Spanish America was essentially an urban civilization. For centuries, its great cities, notably Mexico City, Quito, and Lima, far outshone any urban centers in North America and most of those in Europe.

An image from the *Tlaxcala Codex*, which chronicles events in a region of central Mexico in the sixteenth century. Aztec warriors dressed in eagle and jaguar costumes dance before Spanish officials and priests.

Governing Spanish America

At least in theory, the government of Spanish America reflected the absolutism of the newly unified nation at home. Authority originated with the king and flowed downward through the Council of the Indies—the main body in Spain for colonial administration—and then to viceroys in Mexico and Peru and other local officials in America. The Catholic Church also played a significant role in the administration of Spanish colonies, frequently exerting its authority on matters of faith, morals, and treatment of the Indians.

Successive kings kept elected assemblies out of Spain's New World empire. Royal officials were generally appointees from Spain, rather than *criollos*, or **creoles**, as persons born in the colonies of European ancestry were called. But as Spain's power declined in Europe beginning in the seventeenth century, the local elite came to enjoy more and more effective authority over colonial affairs.

Colonists and Indians in Spanish America

Despite the decline in the native population, Spanish America remained populous enough that, with the exception of the West Indies and a few cities, large-scale importations of African slaves were unnecessary. Instead, the Spanish forced tens of thousands of Indians to work in gold and silver mines, which supplied the empire's wealth, and on large-scale farms, or ***haciendas***, controlled by Spanish landlords. In Spanish America, unlike other New World empires, Indians performed most of the labor.

The opportunity for social advancement drew numerous colonists from Spain—225,000 in the sixteenth century and a total of 750,000 in the three

Social mobility in Spanish America

centuries of Spain's colonial rule. Eventually, a significant number came in families, but at first the large majority were young, single men, many of them laborers, craftsmen, and soldiers. Many also came as government officials, priests, professionals, and minor aristocrats, all ready to direct the manual work of Indians, since living without having to labor was a sign of noble status. The most successful of these colonists enjoyed lives of luxury similar to those of the upper classes at home.

Unlike in the later British empire, Indian inhabitants always outnumbered European colonists and their descendants in Spanish America, and large areas remained effectively under Indian control for many years. Spanish authorities granted Indians certain rights within colonial society and looked forward to their eventual assimilation. The Spanish crown ordered wives of colonists to join them in America and demanded that single men marry. But with the population of Spanish women remaining low, the intermixing of the colonial and Indian peoples soon began. As early as 1514, the Spanish government formally approved of such marriages, partly as a way of bringing Christianity to the native population. By 1600, *mestizos* (persons of mixed origin) made up a large part of the urban population of Spanish America. Over time, Spanish America evolved into a hybrid culture, part Spanish, part Indian, and in some areas part African, but with a single official faith, language, and governmental system.

A hybrid culture

Justifications for Conquest

The Europeans who crossed the Atlantic in the wake of Columbus's voyage had immense confidence in the superiority of their own cultures to those they encountered in America. They expected these societies to abandon their own beliefs and traditions and embrace those of the newcomers. Failure to do so reinforced the conviction that these people were uncivilized "heathens" (non-Christians). In addition, Europeans brought with them a long history of using violence to subdue their foes and a missionary zeal to spread the benefits of their own civilization to others, while reaping the benefits of empire. Spain was no exception.

Religious motivation

To further legitimize Spain's claim to rule the New World, a year after Columbus's first voyage Pope Alexander VI divided the non-Christian world between Spain and Portugal. The line was subsequently adjusted to give Portugal control of Brazil, with the remainder of the Western Hemisphere falling under Spanish authority. Its missionary purpose in colonization was already familiar because of the long holy war against Islam within Spain itself and Spain's 1492 order that all Muslims and Jews had to convert to Catholicism or leave the country. But missionary zeal was powerfully reinforced in the sixteenth century, when the Protestant Reformation divided the Catholic Church. In 1517, Martin Luther, a German priest, posted

Spanish *conquistadores* murdering Indians at Cuzco, in Peru. The Dutch-born engraver Theodor de Bry and his sons illustrated ten volumes about New World exploration published between 1590 and 1618. A Protestant, de Bry created vivid images that helped to spread the Black Legend of Spain as a uniquely cruel colonizer.

his ***Ninety-Five Theses***, which accused the church of worldliness and corruption. Luther wanted to cleanse the church of abuses such as the sale of indulgences (official dispensations forgiving sins). He insisted that all believers should read the Bible for themselves, rather than relying on priests to interpret it for them. His call for reform led to the rise of new Protestant churches independent of Rome and plunged Europe into more than a century of religious and political strife.

Spain, the most powerful bastion of orthodox Catholicism, redoubled its efforts to convert the Indians to the "true faith." Spain insisted that the primary goal of colonization was to save the Indians from heathenism and prevent them from falling under the sway of Protestantism. Religious orders established missions throughout the empire, and over time millions of Indians were converted to Catholicism. On the other hand, Spanish rule, especially in its initial period, decimated the Indian population and subjected Indians to brutal labor conditions. The *conquistadores* and subsequent governors, who required conquered peoples to acknowledge the Catholic Church and provide gold and silver, saw no contradiction between serving God and enriching themselves. Others, however, did.

Converting Indians

As early as 1537, Pope Paul III, who hoped to see Indians become devout subjects of Catholic monarchs, outlawed Indians' enslavement (an edict never extended to apply to Africans). Fifteen years later, the Dominican priest **Bartolomé de Las Casas** published an account of the decimation of the Indian population with the compelling title *A Very Brief Account of the Destruction of the Indies*.

Las Casas's writings denounced Spain for causing the death of millions of innocent people and for denying Indians their freedom. He narrated in shocking detail the "strange cruelties" carried out by "the Christians," including the burning alive of men, women, and children and the imposition of forced labor. "The entire human race is one," he proclaimed, and while he continued to believe that Spain had a right to rule in America, largely on religious grounds, he called for Indians to enjoy "all guarantees of liberty and justice" from the moment they became subjects of Spain. Las Casas also suggested, however, that importing slaves from Africa would help to protect the Indians from exploitation.

Spain's "strange cruelties"

Reforming the Empire

Largely because of Las Casas's efforts, Spain in 1542 promulgated the New Laws, commanding that Indians no longer be enslaved. In 1550, Spain abolished the *encomienda* system, under which the first settlers had been granted authority over conquered Indian lands with the right to extract forced labor from the native inhabitants. In its place, the government established the ***repartimiento* system**, whereby residents of Indian villages remained legally free and entitled to wages, but were still required to perform a fixed amount of labor each year. The Indians were not slaves—they had access to land, were paid wages, and could not be bought and sold. But since the requirement that they work for the Spanish remained the essence of the system, it still allowed for many abuses by Spanish landlords and by priests who required Indians to toil on mission lands as part of the conversion process.

Indian labor

Over time, Spain's brutal treatment of Indians improved somewhat. The Spanish established their domination not just through violence and disease but by bringing education, medical care, and European goods, and because many Indians embraced Christianity. But Las Casas's writings, translated almost immediately into several European languages, contributed to the spread of the **Black Legend**—the image of Spain as a uniquely brutal and exploitative colonizer. This image would provide a potent justification for other European powers to challenge Spain's predominance in the New World.

Exploring North America

While the Spanish empire centered on Mexico, Peru, and the West Indies, the hope of finding a new kingdom of gold soon led Spanish explorers into new territory. In 1508, Spain established the first permanent colony in what is now the United States. That first colony was not, as many people believe, at Jamestown, Virginia, or St. Augustine, Florida, but on the island of Puerto Rico, now a U.S. "commonwealth." Unlike many other European settlements that followed it, Puerto Rico had gold; Juan Ponce de León, who

New colonies

EARLY SPANISH CONQUESTS AND EXPLORATIONS IN THE NEW WORLD

By around 1600, New Spain had become a vast empire stretching from the modern-day American Southwest through Mexico and Central America and into the former Inca kingdom in South America. This map shows early Spanish exploration, especially in the present-day United States, Mexico, and Peru.

led the colony, sent a considerable amount to Spain, while keeping some for himself. In 1513, Ponce embarked for Florida, in search of wealth, slaves, and a fountain of eternal youth, only to be repelled by local Indians.

In the late 1530s and 1540s, Juan Rodriguez Cabrillo explored the Pacific coast as far north as present-day Oregon, and expeditions led by Hernando de Soto, Cabeza de Vaca, Francisco Vásquez de Coronado, and others marched through the Gulf region and the Southwest, fruitlessly searching for another Mexico or Peru. These expeditions, really mobile communities with hundreds of adventurers, priests, potential settlers, slaves, and livestock, spread disease and devastation among Indian communities. De Soto's was particularly brutal. His men tortured, raped, and enslaved countless Indians and transmitted deadly diseases. When Europeans in the seventeenth century returned to colonize the area traversed by de Soto's party, little remained of the societies he had encountered.

Hernando De Soto

Spain in Florida and the Southwest

Nonetheless, these explorations established Spain's claim to a large part of what is now the American South and Southwest. The first region to be colonized within the present-day United States was Florida. Spain hoped to establish a military base there to combat pirates who threatened the treasure fleet that each year sailed from Havana for Europe loaded with gold and silver from Mexico and Peru. Spain also wanted to forestall French incursions in the area. In 1565, Philip II of Spain authorized the nobleman Pedro Menéndez de Avilés to lead a colonizing expedition to Florida. Menéndez destroyed a small outpost at Fort Caroline, which a group of Huguenots (French Protestants) had established in 1562 near present-day Jacksonville. Menéndez and his men went on to establish Spanish forts on St. Simons Island, Georgia, and at St. Augustine, Florida. The latter remains the oldest site in the continental United States continuously inhabited by European settlers and their descendants. In general, though, Florida failed to attract settlers, remaining an isolated military settlement, in effect a fortified outpost of Cuba. As late as 1763, Spanish Florida had only 4,000 inhabitants of European descent.

Florida as military base

Spain took even longer to begin the colonization of the American Southwest. It was not until 1598 that Juan de Oñate led a group of 400 soldiers, colonists, and missionaries north from Mexico to establish a permanent settlement. While searching for fabled deposits of precious metals, Oñate's nephew and fourteen soldiers were killed by inhabitants of Acoma, the "sky city" located on a high bluff in present-day New Mexico.

Juan de Oñate in New Mexico

Oñate decided to teach the local Indians a lesson. After a two-day siege, his forces scaled the seemingly impregnable heights and destroyed Acoma, killing more than 800 of its 1,500 or so inhabitants, including 300 women. Of the 600 Indians captured, the women and children were consigned to servitude in Spanish families, while adult men were punished by the cutting off of one foot. Oñate's message was plain—any Indians who resisted Spanish authority would be crushed. In 1606, however, Oñate was ordered home and punished for his treatment of New Mexico's Indians. In 1610, Spain established the capital of New Mexico at Santa Fe, the first permanent European settlement in the Southwest.

The Pueblo Revolt

In 1680, New Mexico's small and vulnerable colonist population numbered fewer than 3,000. Relations between the Pueblo Indians and colonial authorities had deteriorated throughout the seventeenth century, as governors, settlers, and missionaries sought to exploit the labor of an Indian population that declined from about 60,000 in 1600 to some 17,000 eighty years later. Franciscan friars worked relentlessly to convert Indians to Catholicism, often using intimidation and violence. As the Inquisition—the persecution of non-Catholics— became more and more intense in Spain, so did the friars' efforts to stamp out traditional religious ceremonies in New Mexico. At the same time, the Spanish assumed that the Indians could never unite against the colonizers. In August 1680, they were proven wrong.

St. Anthony and the Infant Jesus, painted on a tanned buffalo hide by a Franciscan priest in New Mexico in the early eighteenth century. This was not long after the Spanish reconquered the area, from which they had been driven by the Pueblo Revolt.

Little is known about the life of Popé, who became the main organizer of an uprising that aimed to drive the Spanish from the colony and restore the Indians' traditional autonomy. Under Popé's leadership, New Mexico's Indians joined in a coordinated uprising. Ironically, because the Pueblos spoke six different languages, Spanish became the revolt's "lingua franca" (a common means of communication among persons of different linguistic backgrounds). Some 2,000 warriors destroyed isolated farms and missions, killing 400 colonists, including 21 Franciscan missionaries. Most of the Spanish survivors, accompanied by several hundred Christian Indians, made their way south out of New Mexico. Within a few weeks, a century of colonization in the area had been destroyed.

The **Pueblo Revolt** was the most complete victory for Native Americans over Europeans and the only wholesale expulsion of settlers in the history of North America. Cooperation among the Pueblo peoples, however, soon evaporated. By the end of the 1680s, warfare had broken out among several villages, even as Apache and Navajo raids continued. Popé died around 1690. In 1692, the Spanish launched an invasion that reconquered New Mexico.

VOICES OF FREEDOM

From Bartolomé de Las Casas,
History of the Indies (1528)

Las Casas was the Dominican priest who condemned the treatment of Indians in the Spanish empire. His widely disseminated *History of the Indies* helped to establish the Black Legend of Spanish cruelty.

The Indians [of Hispaniola] were totally deprived of their freedom and were put in the harshest, fiercest, most horrible servitude and captivity which no one who has not seen it can understand. Even beasts enjoy more freedom when they are allowed to graze in the fields. But our Spaniards gave no such opportunity to Indians and truly considered them perpetual slaves, since the Indians had not the free will to dispose of their persons but instead were disposed of according to Spanish greed and cruelty, not as men in captivity but as beasts tied to a rope to prevent free movement. When they were allowed to go home, they often found it deserted and had no other recourse than to go out into the woods to find food and to die. When they fell ill, which was very frequently because they are a delicate people unaccustomed to such work, the Spaniards did not believe them and pitilessly called them lazy dogs and kicked and beat them; and when illness was apparent they sent them home as useless. . . . They would go then, falling into the first stream and dying there in desperation; others would hold on longer but very few ever made it home. I sometimes came upon dead bodies on my way, and upon others who were gasping and moaning in their death agony, repeating "Hungry, hungry." And this was the freedom, the good treatment and the Christianity the Indians received.

About eight years passed under [Spanish rule] and this disorder had time to grow; no one gave it a thought and the multitude of people who originally lived on the island . . . was consumed at such a rate that in these eight years 90 per cent had perished. From here this sweeping plague went to San Juan, Jamaica, Cuba and the continent, spreading destruction over the whole hemisphere.

From "Declaration of Josephe"
(December 19, 1681)

Josephe was a Spanish-speaking Indian questioned by a royal attorney in Mexico City investigating the Pueblo Revolt. The revolt of the Indian population, in 1680, temporarily drove Spanish settlers from present-day New Mexico.

Asked what causes or motives the said Indian rebels had for renouncing the law of God and obedience to his Majesty, and for committing so many of crimes, [he answered] the causes they have were alleged ill treatment and injuries received from [Spanish authorities], because they beat them, took away what they had, and made them work without pay. Thus he replies.

Asked if he has learned if it has come to his notice during the time that he has been here the reason why the apostates burned the images, churches, and things pertaining to divine worship, making a mockery and a trophy of them, killing the priests and doing the other things they did, he said that he knows and had heard it generally stated that while they were besieging the villa the rebellious traitors burned the church and shouted in loud voices, "Now the God of the Spaniards, who was their father, is dead, and Santa Maria, who was their mother, and the saints, who were pieces of rotten wood," saying that only their own god lived. Thus they ordered all the temples and images, crosses and rosaries burned, and their function being over, they all went to bathe in the rivers, saying that they thereby washed away the water of baptism. For their churches, they placed on the four sides and in the center of the plaza some small circular enclosures of stone where they went to offer flour, feathers, and the seed of maguey [a local plant], maize, and tobacco, and performed other superstitious rites, giving the children to understand that they must all do this in the future. The captains and the chiefs ordered that the names of Jesus and Mary should nowhere be uttered. . . . He has seen many houses of idolatry which they have built, dancing the dance of the cachina [part of a traditional Indian religious ceremony], which this declarant has also danced. Thus he replies to the question.

QUESTIONS

1. *Why does Las Casas, after describing the ill treatment of Indians, write, "And this was the freedom, the good treatment and the Christianity the Indians received"?*

2. *What role did religion play in the Pueblo Revolt?*

3. *What ideas of freedom are apparent in the two documents?*

Some communities welcomed them back as a source of military protection. But Spain had learned a lesson. In the eighteenth century, colonial authorities adopted a more tolerant attitude toward traditional religious practices and made fewer demands on Indian labor.

THE FRENCH AND DUTCH EMPIRES

If the Black Legend inspired a sense of superiority among Spain's European rivals, the precious metals that poured from the New World into the Spanish treasury aroused the desire to match Spain's success. The establishment of Spain's American empire transformed the balance of power in the world economy. The Atlantic replaced the overland route to Asia as the major

Shifts in global trade

axis of global trade. During the seventeenth century, the French, Dutch, and English established colonies in North America. England's mainland colonies, to be discussed in the next chapter, consisted of agricultural settlements with growing populations whose hunger for land produced incessant conflict with native peoples. New France and New Netherland were primarily commercial ventures that never attracted large numbers of colonists. Because French and Dutch settlements were more dependent than the English on Indians as trading partners and military allies, Native Americans exercised more power and enjoyed more freedom in their relations with these settlements.

French Colonization

The first of Spain's major European rivals to embark on New World explorations was France. The explorer Samuel de Champlain, sponsored by a French fur-trading company, founded Quebec in 1608. In 1673, the Jesuit priest Jacques Marquette and the fur trader Louis Joliet located the Mississippi River, and by 1681 René-Robert Cavelier, Sieur de La Salle, had descended to the Gulf of Mexico, claiming the entire Mississippi River valley for France. New France eventually formed a giant arc along the St. Lawrence, Mississippi, and Ohio rivers.

Settlement in New France

By 1700, the number of white inhabitants of New France had risen to only 19,000. With a far larger population than England, France sent many fewer emigrants to the Western Hemisphere. The government at home feared that significant emigration would undermine France's role as a European great power and might compromise its effort to establish trade and good relations with the Indians. Unfavorable reports about America circulated widely in France. Canada was widely depicted as an icebox, a land of savage Indians, a dumping ground for criminals. Most French who left their homes during these years preferred to settle in the Netherlands, Spain, or the West Indies. The revocation in 1685 of the Edict of Nantes,

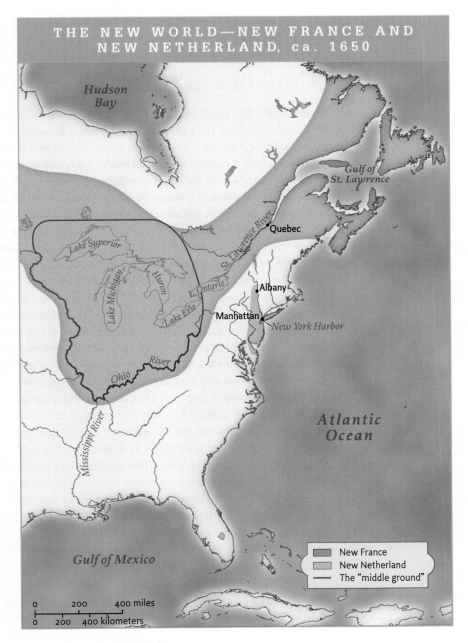

THE NEW WORLD—NEW FRANCE AND
NEW NETHERLAND, ca. 1650

Hudson
Bay

Gulf of
St. Lawrence

Lake Superior

Lake Michigan

Huron

L. Ontario

Lake Erie

St. Lawrence River

•Quebec

•Albany

Manhattan•

New York Harbor

Ohio River

Mississippi River

Atlantic
Ocean

Gulf of Mexico

New France
New Netherland
The "middle ground"

0   200   400 miles
0   200   400 kilometers

New France and New Netherland.

which had extended religious toleration to French Protestants, led well over 100,000 Huguenots to flee their country. But they were not welcome in New France, which the crown desired to remain an outpost of Catholicism.

New France and the Indians

Alliances with Indians

With its small white population and emphasis on the fur trade rather than agricultural settlement, the viability of New France depended on friendly relations with local Indians. The French prided themselves on adopting a more humane policy than their imperial rivals. "Only our nation," declared one French writer, "knows the secret of winning the Indians' affection." The French worked out a complex series of military, commercial, and diplomatic connections, the most enduring alliances between Indians and settlers in colonial North America. Samuel de Champlain, the intrepid explorer who dominated the early history of New France, denied that Native Americans were intellectually or culturally inferior to Europeans. Although he occasionally engaged in wars with local Indians, he dreamed of creating a colony based on mutual respect between diverse peoples. The Jesuits, a missionary religious order, did seek, with some success, to convert Indians to Catholicism. Unlike Spanish missionaries in early New Mexico, they allowed Christian Indians to retain a high degree of independence and much of their traditional social structure, and they did not seek to suppress all traditional religious practices.

Jesuits

Like other colonists throughout North America, however, the French brought striking changes in Indian life. Contact with Europeans was inevitably followed by the spread of disease. Participation in the fur trade drew natives into the burgeoning Atlantic economy, introducing new goods and transforming hunting from a search for food into a quest for marketable commodities. Indians were soon swept into the rivalries among European empires.

The middle ground

As in the Spanish empire, New France witnessed considerable cultural exchange and intermixing between colonial and native populations. On the "middle ground" of the Great Lakes region in French America, Indians and whites encountered each other for many years on a basis of relative equality. And *métis*, or children of marriages between Indian women and French traders and officials, became guides, traders, and interpreters. Like the Spanish, the French seemed willing to accept Indians as part of colonial society. Indians who converted to Catholicism were promised full citizenship. In fact, however, it was far rarer for natives to adopt French ways than for French settlers to become attracted to the "free" life of the Indians.

Movement between societies

The Dutch Empire

In 1609, Henry Hudson, an Englishman employed by the Dutch East India Company, sailed into New York Harbor searching for a Northwest Passage to Asia. Hudson and his crew became the first Europeans to sail up the

This engraving, which appears in Samuel de Champlain's 1613 account of his voyages, is the only likeness of the explorer from his own time. Champlain, wearing European armor and brandishing an arquebus (an advanced weapon of the period), stands at the center of this pitched battle between his Indian allies and the hostile Iroquois.

river that now bears his name. Hudson did not find a route to Asia, but he did encounter abundant fur-bearing animals and Native Americans more than willing to trade furs for European goods. He claimed the area for the Netherlands, and his voyage planted the seeds of what would eventually become a great metropolis, New York City. In 1624, the Dutch West India Company, which had been awarded a monopoly of Dutch trade with America, settled colonists on Manhattan Island.

Henry Hudson

These ventures formed one small part in the rise of the Dutch overseas empire. In the early seventeenth century, the Netherlands dominated international commerce, and Amsterdam was Europe's foremost shipping and banking center. The small nation had entered a golden age of rapidly accumulating wealth and stunning achievements in painting, philosophy, and the sciences. With a population of only 2 million, the Netherlands established a far-flung empire that reached from Indonesia to South Africa and the Caribbean and temporarily wrested control of Brazil from Portugal.

An engraving of the Huron town Hochelaga, site of modern-day Montreal, from a book about voyages of discovery by Giovanni Battista Ramusio, an Italian geographer, published in 1556.

Dutch Freedom

The Dutch prided themselves on their devotion to liberty. Indeed, in the early seventeenth century they enjoyed two freedoms not recognized elsewhere in Europe—freedom of the press and of private religious practice. Amsterdam became a haven for persecuted Protestants from all over Europe and for Jews as well.

Despite the Dutch reputation for cherishing freedom, New Netherland was hardly governed democratically. New Amsterdam, the main population center, was essentially a fortified military outpost controlled by appointees of the West India Company. Although the governor called on prominent citizens for advice from time to time, neither an elected assembly nor a town council, the basic unit of government at home, was established.

In other ways, however, the colonists enjoyed more liberty than their counterparts elsewhere in North America. Even their slaves possessed

rights. Some enjoyed "half-freedom"—they were required to pay an annual fee to the company and work for it when called upon, but they were given land to support their families. Settlers employed slaves on family farms or for household or craft labor, not on large plantations as in the West Indies.

Women in the Dutch settlement enjoyed far more independence than in other colonies. According to Dutch law, married women retained their

separate legal identity. They could go to court, borrow money, and own property. Men were used to sharing property with their wives.

New Netherland attracted a remarkably diverse population. As early as the 1630s, at least eighteen languages were said to be spoken in New Amsterdam, whose residents included not only Dutch settlers but also Africans, Belgians, English, French, Germans, Irish, and Scandinavians.

The Dutch and Religious Toleration

The Dutch long prided themselves on being uniquely tolerant in religious matters compared to other European nations and their empires. It would be wrong, however, to attribute modern ideas of religious freedom to either the Dutch government and company at home or the rulers of New Netherland. Both Holland and New Netherland had an official religion, the Dutch Reformed Church, one of the Protestant national churches to emerge from the Reformation. The Dutch commitment to freedom of conscience extended to religious devotion exercised in private, not public worship in nonestablished churches.

When Jews, Quakers, Lutherans, and others demanded the right to practice their religion openly, Governor Petrus Stuyvesant adamantly refused, seeing such diversity as a threat to a godly, prosperous order. Twenty-three Jews arrived in New Amsterdam in 1654 from Brazil and the Caribbean. Referring to them as "members of a deceitful race," Stuyvesant ordered the newcomers to leave. But the company overruled him, noting that Jews at home had invested "a large amount of capital" in its shares.

Nonetheless, it is true that the Dutch dealt with religious pluralism in ways quite different from the practices common in other New World empires. Religious dissent was tolerated as long as it did not involve open

Coastal Native Americans were adept mariners. This detail from the earliest known engraving of New Amsterdam (1627) depicts Dutch and Indian boats in the harbor.

and public worship. No one in New Netherland was forced to attend the official church, nor was anyone executed for holding the wrong religious beliefs (as would happen in Puritan New England).

Settling New Netherland

During the seventeenth century, the Netherlands sent 1 million people overseas (many of them recent immigrants who were not in fact Dutch) to populate and govern their far-flung colonies. Very few, however, made North America their destination. By the mid-1660s, the European population of New Netherland numbered only 9,000. New Netherland remained a tiny backwater in the Dutch empire. So did an even smaller outpost near present-day Wilmington, Delaware, established in 1638 by a group of Dutch merchants. To circumvent the West India Company's trade monopoly, they claimed to be operating under the Swedish flag and called their settlement New Sweden. Only 300 settlers were living there when New Netherland seized the colony in 1655.

Sparse European settlement in New Netherland

New Netherland and the Indians

The Dutch came to North America to trade, not to conquer. Mindful of the Black Legend of Spanish cruelty, the Dutch determined to treat the native inhabitants more humanely. Having won their own independence from Spain after the longest and bloodiest war of sixteenth-century Europe, many Dutch identified with American Indians as fellow victims of Spanish oppression.

Dutch treatment of American Indians

From the beginning, Dutch authorities recognized Indian sovereignty over the land and forbade settlement in any area until it had been

The seal of New Netherland, adopted by the Dutch West India Company in 1630, suggests the centrality of the fur trade to the colony's prospects. Surrounding the beaver is *wampum*, a string of beads used by Indians in religious rituals and as currency.

purchased. But they also required tribes to make payments to colonial authorities. Near the coast, where most newcomers settled, New Netherland was hardly free of conflict with the Indians. With the powerful Iroquois Confederacy of the upper Hudson Valley, however, the Dutch established friendly commercial and diplomatic relations.

Borderlands and Empire in Early America

A **borderland**, according to one historian, is "a meeting place of peoples where geographical and cultural borders are not clearly defined." Numerous such places came into existence during the era of European conquest and settlement, including the "middle ground" of the Great Lakes region in New France. Boundaries between empires, and between colonists and native peoples, shifted constantly, overlapping claims to authority abounded, and hybrid cultures developed. As Europeans consolidated their control in some areas, the power of native peoples weakened. But at the edges of empire, power was always unstable, and overlapping cultural interactions at the local level defied any single pattern. European conquest was not a simple story of expanding domination over either empty space or powerless peoples, but of a continual struggle to establish authority. The Spanish, French, and Dutch empires fought each other for dominance in various parts of the continent, and Indians often wielded both economic and political power, pitting European empires against each other. Despite laws restricting commerce between empires, traders challenged boundaries, traversing lands claimed by both Europeans and Indians. People of European and Indian descent married and exchanged cultural attributes.

Shared features of the Spanish, French, and Dutch empires

Thus, before the planting of English colonies in North America, other European nations had established various kinds of settlements in the New World. Despite their differences, the Spanish, French, and Dutch empires shared certain features. All brought Christianity, new forms of technology and learning, new legal systems and family relations, and new forms of economic enterprise and wealth creation. They also brought savage warfare and widespread disease. These empires were aware of one another's existence. They studied and borrowed from one another, each lauding itself as superior to the others.

From the outset, dreams of freedom—for Indians, for settlers, for the entire world through the spread of Christianity—inspired and justified colonization. It would be no different when, at the beginning of the seventeenth century, England entered the struggle for empire in North America.

CHAPTER REVIEW AND ONLINE RESOURCES

REVIEW QUESTIONS

1. Describe why the "discovery" of America was one of the "most important events recorded in the history of mankind," according to Adam Smith.

2. Describe the different global economies that Europeans participated in or created during the European age of expansion.

3. One of the most striking features of Indian societies at the time of the encounter with Europeans was their diversity. Support this statement with several examples.

4. Compare and contrast European values and ways of life with those of the Indians. Consider addressing religion, views about ownership of land, gender relations, and notions of freedom.

5. What were the main factors fueling the European age of expansion?

6. Compare the different economic and political systems of Spain, Portugal, the Netherlands, and France in the age of expansion.

7. Compare the political, economic, and religious motivations behind the French and Dutch empires with those of New Spain.

8. How would European settlers explain their superiority to Native Americans and justify both the conquest of native lands and terminating their freedom?

9. Why did Native Americans exercise more power in their relations with the Dutch and French than with the English?

KEY TERMS

Tenochtitlán (p. 3)
Aztec (p. 3)
Great League of Peace (p. 7)
caravels (p. 14)
reconquista (p. 16)
conquistadores (p. 19)
Columbian Exchange (p. 19)
creoles (p. 21)
haciendas (p. 21)
mestizos (p. 22)
Ninety-Five Theses (p. 23)
Bartolomé de Las Casas (p. 23)
repartimiento system (p. 24)
Black Legend (p. 24)
Pueblo Revolt (p. 27)
métis (p. 32)
borderland (p. 36)

Go to 🐰 INQUIZITIVE

To see what you know—and learn what you've missed—with personalized feedback along the way.

Visit the *Give Me Liberty!* **Student Site** for primary source documents and images, interactive maps, author videos featuring Eric Foner, and more.

CHAPTER 2

BEGINNINGS OF ENGLISH AMERICA

★

1607–1660

The artist John White spent a year on the Outer Banks of North Carolina in 1785–86 as part of an expedition sponsored by Sir Walter Raleigh. In this drawing, he depicts an Indian village surrounded by a stockade.

On April 26, 1607, three small ships carrying colonists from England sailed into the mouth of Chesapeake Bay. After exploring the area for a little over two weeks, they chose a site sixty miles inland on the James River for their settlement, hoping to protect themselves from marauding Spanish warships. Here they established Jamestown (named for the king of England) as the capital of the colony of Virginia (named for his predecessor, Elizabeth I, the "virgin queen"). But despite these bows to royal authority, the voyage was sponsored not by the English government, which in 1607 was hard-pressed for funds, but by the **Virginia Company**, a private business organization whose shareholders included merchants, aristocrats, and members of Parliament, and to which the queen had given her blessing before her death in 1603.

When the three ships returned home, 104 settlers remained in Virginia. All were men, for the Virginia Company had more interest in searching for gold and in other ways exploiting the area's natural resources than in establishing a functioning society. Nevertheless, Jamestown became the first permanent English settlement in the area that is now the United States. The settlers were the first of tens of thousands of Europeans who crossed the Atlantic during the seventeenth century to live and work in North America. They led the way for new empires that mobilized labor and economic resources, reshaped societies throughout the Atlantic world, and shifted the balance of power at home from Spain and Portugal to the nations of northwestern Europe.

English North America in the seventeenth century was a place where entrepreneurs sought to make fortunes, religious minorities hoped to worship without governmental interference and to create societies based on biblical teachings, and aristocrats dreamed of re-creating a vanished world of feudalism. For ordinary men and women, emigration offered an escape from lives of deprivation and inequality. "No man," wrote John Smith, an early leader of Jamestown, "will go from [England] to have less freedom" in America. The settlers of English America came to enjoy greater rights than colonists of other empires, including the power to choose members of elected assemblies, protections of the common law such as the right to trial by jury, and access to land, the key to economic independence. In some colonies, though by no means all, colonists enjoyed considerably more religious freedom than existed in Europe.

Many degrees of freedom coexisted in seventeenth-century North America, from the slave, stripped completely of liberty, to the independent landowner, who enjoyed a full range of rights. The settlers' success, however, rested on depriving Native Americans of their land and, in some colonies, on importing large numbers of African slaves as laborers. Freedom and lack of freedom expanded together in seventeenth-century America.

FOCUS QUESTIONS

- *What were the main contours of English colonization in the seventeenth century?*

- *What challenges did the early English settlers face?*

- *How did Virginia and Maryland develop in their early years?*

- *What made the English settlement of New England distinctive?*

- *What were the main sources of discord in early New England?*

- *How did the English Civil War affect the colonies in America?*

ENGLAND AND THE NEW WORLD

Unifying the English Nation

Mary I, the queen who tried to restore Catholicism in England, as painted in 1554 by Antonis Mor, a Dutch artist who made numerous portraits of European royalty. He depicts her as a woman of firm determination. During her brief reign (1553–1558), nearly 300 Protestants were burned at the stake.

As the case of Spain suggests, early empire building was, in large part, an extension of the consolidation of national power in Europe. But during the sixteenth century, England was a second-rate power wracked by internal disunity. Henry VIII, crowned in 1509, launched the Reformation in England. When the Pope refused to annul his marriage to Catherine of Aragon, Henry severed the nation from the Catholic Church. In its place he established the Church of England, or **Anglican Church**, with himself at the head. Decades of religious strife followed, as did considerable persecution of Catholics under Henry's successor, Edward VI. In 1553, Edward's half sister Mary became queen. She temporarily restored Catholicism as the state religion and executed a number of Protestants. Mary's successor, Elizabeth I (reigned 1558–1603), restored the Anglican ascendancy and executed more than 100 Catholic priests.

England and Ireland

Subduing Ireland

England's long struggle to conquer and pacify Ireland, which lasted well into the seventeenth century, absorbed money and energy that might have been directed toward the New World. In subduing Ireland, whose Catholic population was deemed a threat to the stability of Protestant rule in England, the government employed a variety of approaches, including military conquest, the slaughter of civilians, the seizure of land and introduction of English economic practices, and the dispatch of large numbers of settlers. Rather than seeking to absorb the Irish into English society, the English excluded the native population from a territory of settlement known as the Pale, where the colonists created their own social order.

The methods used in Ireland anticipated policies England would undertake in America. Some sixteenth-century English writers directly compared the allegedly barbaric "wild Irish" with American Indians.

England and North America

Not until the reign of Elizabeth I did the English turn their attention to North America, although sailors and adventurers still showed more interest in raiding Spanish cities and treasure fleets in the Caribbean than establishing settlements. The government granted charters (grants of exclusive rights and privileges) to Sir Humphrey Gilbert and Sir Walter

Raleigh, authorizing them to establish colonies in North America at their own expense.

With little or no support from the crown, both ventures failed. Gilbert, who had earned a reputation for brutality in the Irish wars by murdering civilians and burning their crops, established a short-lived settlement on Newfoundland in 1582. Three years later, Raleigh dispatched a fleet of five ships with some 100 colonists to set up a base on Roanoke Island, off the North Carolina coast. But the colonists, mostly young men under military leadership, abandoned the venture in 1586 and returned to England. A second group of 100 settlers, composed of families who hoped to establish a permanent colony, was dispatched that year. Their fate remains a mystery. When a ship bearing supplies arrived in 1590, the sailors found the **Roanoke colony** abandoned. Raleigh, by now nearly bankrupt, lost his enthusiasm for colonization. To establish a successful colony, it seemed clear, would require more planning and economic resources than any individual could provide.

The Roanoke colony

Spreading Protestantism

As in the case of Spain, national glory, profit, and religious mission merged in early English thinking about the New World. The Reformation heightened the English government's sense of Catholic Spain as its mortal enemy

The Armada Portrait of Queen Elizabeth I, by the artist George Gower, commemorates the defeat of the Spanish Armada in 1588 and appears to link it with English colonization of the New World. England's victorious navy is visible through the window, while the queen's hand rests on a globe, with her fingers pointing to the coast of North America.

ENGLAND AND THE NEW WORLD | 41

(a belief reinforced in 1588 when a Spanish naval armada unsuccessfully attempted to invade the British Isles). By the late sixteenth century, anti-Catholicism had become deeply ingrained in English popular culture.

Although atrocities were hardly confined to any one nation—as England's own conduct in Ireland demonstrated—the idea that the empire of Catholic Spain was uniquely murderous and tyrannical enabled the English to describe their own imperial ambitions in the language of freedom. In *A Discourse Concerning Western Planting*, written in 1584, the Protestant minister and scholar Richard Hakluyt listed twenty-three reasons that Queen Elizabeth I should support the establishment of colonies. Among them was the idea that English settlements would form part of a divine mission to rescue the New World and its inhabitants from the influence of Catholicism and tyranny.

Richard Hakluyt

But bringing freedom to Indians was hardly the only motivation Hakluyt and other writers advanced. National power and glory, they argued, could be achieved through colonization. England, a relatively minor power at the end of the sixteenth century, could come to rival great nations like Spain and France.

Yet another motivation was that colonists could enrich the mother country and themselves by providing English consumers with goods now supplied by foreigners and opening a new market for English products. Unlike early adventurers such as Raleigh, who thought of wealth in terms of deposits of gold, Hakluyt insisted that trade would be the basis of England's empire.

The Social Crisis

Equally important, America could be a refuge for England's "surplus" population, benefiting mother country and emigrants alike. The late sixteenth century was a time of social crisis in England, with economic growth unable to keep pace with the needs of a population that grew from 3 million in 1550 to about 4 million in 1600. In the sixteenth and seventeenth centuries, landlords sought profits by raising sheep for the expanding trade in wool and introducing more modern farming practices such as crop rotation. They evicted small farmers and fenced off "commons" previously open to all.

Population growth

While many landlords, farmers, and town merchants benefited from the **enclosure movement**, as this process was called, thousands of persons were uprooted from the land. Many flooded into England's cities. Others, denounced by authorities as rogues, vagabonds, and vagrants, wandered the roads in search of work. "All our towns," wrote the Puritan leader John Winthrop in 1629, shortly before leaving England for Massachusetts, "complain of the burden of poor people and strive by all means to rid any such as they have." England, he added somberly, "grows weary of her inhabitants."

For years, the government struggled to deal with this social crisis, sometimes resorting to extreme measures, such as whipping or hanging the unemployed or forcing them to accept any job offered to them. Another solution was to encourage the unruly poor to leave for the New World. As colonists, they could become productive citizens, contributing to the nation's wealth.

From poverty to emigration

Masterless Men

Although authorities saw wandering or unemployed "masterless men" as a danger to society, popular attitudes viewed economic dependence as lack of freedom. Only those who controlled their own labor could be regarded as truly free. Indeed, popular tales and ballads romanticized the very vagabonds, highwaymen, and even beggars denounced by the propertied and powerful, since despite their poverty they at least enjoyed freedom from wage work.

The New World as a land of opportunity

The image of the New World as a unique place of opportunity, where the English laboring classes could regain economic independence by acquiring land and where even criminals would enjoy a second chance, was deeply rooted from the earliest days of settlement. John Smith had scarcely landed in Virginia in 1607 when he wrote that in America "every man may be the master and owner of his own labor and land." The main lure for emigrants from England to the New World was not so much riches in gold and silver as the promise of independence that followed from owning land. Economic freedom and the possibility of passing it on to one's children attracted the largest number of English colonists.

A pamphlet published in 1609 promoting emigration to Virginia.

THE COMING OF THE ENGLISH

English Emigrants

Seventeenth-century North America was an unstable and dangerous environment. Diseases decimated Indian and settler populations alike. Without sustained immigration, most settlements would have collapsed. With a population of between 4 million and 5 million, about half that of Spain and a quarter of that of France, England produced a far larger number of men, women, and children willing to brave the dangers of emigration to the New World. In large part, this was because economic conditions in England were so bad.

Between 1607 and 1700, more than half a million people left England. North America was not the destination of the majority of these emigrants. Approximately 180,000 settled in Ireland, and about the same number migrated to the West Indies, where the introduction of sugar cultivation promised riches for those who could obtain land. Nonetheless, the population of England's mainland colonies quickly outstripped that of their rivals. The Chesapeake area, where the tobacco-producing colonies of Virginia and Maryland developed a constant demand for cheap labor, received about 120,000 settlers. New England attracted 21,000 immigrants, nearly all of them arriving before 1640. In the second part of the seventeenth century, the Middle Colonies (New York, New Jersey, and Pennsylvania) attracted about 23,000 settlers. Although the arrivals to New England and the Middle Colonies included many families, the majority of newcomers were young, single men from the bottom rungs of English society, who had little to lose by emigrating.

Demographics of colonists

Indentured Servants

Settlers who could pay for their own passage—government officials, clergymen, merchants, artisans, landowning farmers, and members of the lesser nobility—arrived in America as free persons. Most quickly acquired land. In the seventeenth century, however, nearly two-thirds of English settlers came as **indentured servants**, who voluntarily surrendered their freedom for a specified time (usually five to seven years) in exchange for passage to America.

Slavery and indentured servitude

Like slaves, servants could be bought and sold, could not marry without the permission of their owner, were subject to physical punishment, and saw their obligation to labor enforced by the courts. But, unlike slaves, servants could look forward to a release from bondage. Assuming they survived their period of labor, servants would receive a payment known as "freedom dues" and become free members of society.

Given the high death rate, many servants did not live to the end of their terms. Many servants found the reality of life in the New World less appealing than they had anticipated. Employers constantly complained of servants running away, not working diligently, or being unruly, all manifestations of what one commentator called their "fondness for freedom."

Land and Liberty

Landownership as the basis of liberty

Land, English settlers believed, was the basis of liberty. Owning land gave men control over their own labor and, in most colonies, the right to vote. The promise of immediate access to land lured free settlers, and freedom dues that included land persuaded potential immigrants to sign contracts as indentured servants. Land in America also became a way for the king to reward relatives and allies. Each colony was launched with a huge grant of land from the crown, either to a company or to a private individual known as a proprietor. Some grants, if taken literally, stretched from the Atlantic Ocean to the Pacific.

Without labor, however, land would have little value. Since immigrants did not come to America intending to work the land of others (except temporarily in the case of indentured servants), the very abundance of "free" land eventually led many property owners to turn to slaves as a workforce.

Englishmen and Indians

Land in North America, of course, was already occupied. And the arrival of English settlers presented the native inhabitants of eastern North America with the greatest crisis in their history. Unlike the Spanish, English colonists were chiefly interested in displacing the Indians and settling on their land, not intermarrying with them, organizing their labor, or making them subjects of the crown. The English exchanged goods with the native population, and Indians often traveled through colonial settlements. Fur traders on the frontiers of settlement sometimes married Indian women, partly as a way of gaining access to native societies and the kin networks essential to economic relationships. Most English settlers, however, remained obstinately separate from their Indian neighbors.

The only known contemporary portrait of a New England Indian, this 1681 painting by an unknown artist was long thought to represent Ninigret II, a leader of the Narragansetts of Rhode Island. It has been more recently identified as Robin Cassacinamon, an influential Pequot leader and friend of John Winthrop II, a governor of colonial Connecticut, who originally owned the painting. Apart from the wampum beads around his neck, everything the Indian wears is of English manufacture.

Despite their insistence that Indians had no real claim to the land since they did not cultivate or improve it, most colonial authorities acquired land by purchase, often in treaties forced upon Indians after they had suffered military defeat. To keep the peace, some colonial governments tried to prevent the private seizure or purchase of Indian lands, or they declared certain areas off-limits to settlers. But these measures were rarely enforced and ultimately proved ineffective. New settlers and freed servants sought land for themselves, and those who established families in America needed land for their children.

The seventeenth century was marked by recurrent warfare between colonists and Indians. These conflicts generated a strong feeling of superiority among the colonists and left them intent on maintaining the real and imagined boundaries separating the two peoples. Over time the English displaced the original inhabitants more thoroughly than any other European empire.

The Transformation of Indian Life

Many eastern Indians initially welcomed the newcomers, or at least their goods, which they appreciated for their practical advantages. Items like woven cloth, metal kettles, iron axes, fishhooks, hoes, and guns were quickly integrated into Indian life. Indians also displayed a great desire for goods like colorful glass beads and copper ornaments that could be incorporated into their religious ceremonies.

Changes in Indian farming, hunting, and cooking practices

As Indians became integrated into the Atlantic economy, subtle changes took place in Indian life. European metal goods changed their farming, hunting, and cooking practices. Men devoted more time to hunting beaver for fur trading. Later observers would describe this trade as one in which Indians exchanged valuable commodities like furs and animal skins for worthless European trinkets. In fact, both Europeans and Indians gave up goods they had in abundance in exchange for items in short supply in their own society. But as the colonists achieved military superiority over the Indians, the profits of trade mostly flowed to colonial and European merchants.

Environmental changes

As settlers fenced in more and more land and introduced new crops and livestock, the natural environment changed in ways that undermined

Another drawing by the artist John White shows seventeen male and female Secotan Indians dancing around a circle of posts in a religious ritual in modern-day North Carolina. White was a careful observer of their clothing and body markings and the objects used in the ceremony.

traditional Indian agriculture and hunting. Pigs and cattle roamed freely, trampling Indian cornfields and gardens. The need for wood to build and heat homes and export to England depleted forests on which Indians relied for hunting. The rapid expansion of the fur trade diminished the population of beaver and other animals. In short, Indians' lives were powerfully altered by the changes set in motion in 1607 when English colonists landed at Jamestown.

SETTLING THE CHESAPEAKE

The Jamestown Colony

The early history of Jamestown was, to say the least, not promising. The colony's leadership changed repeatedly, its inhabitants suffered an extraordinarily high death rate, and, with the Virginia Company seeking a quick profit, supplies from England proved inadequate. The first settlers were "a quarrelsome band of gentlemen and servants." They included few farmers and laborers and numerous sons of English gentry who preferred to prospect for gold rather than farm.

Disease and lack of food took a heavy toll. By the end of the first year, the original population of 104 had fallen by half. New arrivals (including the first two women, who landed in 1608) brought the numbers up to 400 in 1609, but by 1610, after a winter long remembered as the "starving time," only 65 settlers remained alive. At one point, the survivors abandoned Jamestown and sailed for England, only to be intercepted and persuaded to return to Virginia by ships carrying a new governor, 250 colonists, and supplies.

Only rigorous military discipline held the colony together. **John Smith**, one of the colony's first leaders, imposed a regime of forced labor on company lands. "He that will not work, shall not eat," Smith declared.

By 1640, English settlement in the Chesapeake had spread well beyond the initial colony at Jamestown, as tobacco planters sought fertile land near navigable waterways.

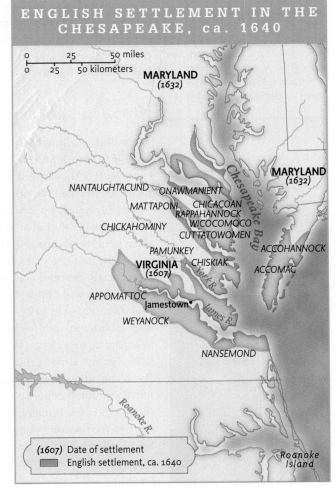

ENGLISH SETTLEMENT IN THE CHESAPEAKE, ca. 1640

0   25   50 miles
0   25   50 kilometers

MARYLAND
(1632)

MARYLAND
(1632)

NANTAUGHTACUND   ONAWMANIENT
MATTAPONI   CHICACOAN
RAPPAHANNOCK
CHICKAHOMINY   WICOCOMOCO
CUTTATOWOMEN
ACCOHANNOCK
PAMUNKEY   CHISKIAK   ACCOMAC
VIRGINIA   CHISKIAK
(1607)
APPOMATTOC
Jamestown•
WEYANOCK   James R.

NANSEMOND

Roanoke R.

Chesapeake Bay

York R.

(1607) Date of settlement
English settlement, ca. 1640

Roanoke Island

POWHATAN
Held this state & fashion when Capt: Smith
was delivered to him prisoner
1607

Powhatan, the most prominent Indian leader in the original area of English settlement in Virginia. This image, showing Powhatan and his court, was engraved on John Smith's map of Virginia and included in Smith's *General History of Virginia*, published in 1624.

The only portrait of Pocahontas during her lifetime was engraved by Simon van de Passe in England in 1616. This is a later copy by an unknown artist. After converting to Christianity, she took the name Rebecca.

Smith's autocratic mode of governing alienated many of the colonists. After being injured in an accidental gunpowder explosion in 1609, he was forced to return to England. But his immediate successors continued his iron rule.

The Virginia Company slowly realized that for the colony to survive it would have to abandon the search for gold, grow its own food, and find a marketable commodity. It would also have to attract more settlers. With this end in view, it announced new policies in 1618. Instead of retaining all the land for itself, the company introduced the **headright system**, awarding fifty acres of land to any colonist who paid for his own or another's passage. Thus, anyone who brought in a sizable number of servants would immediately acquire a large estate. In place of the governor's militaristic regime, a "charter of grants and liberties" was issued, including the establishment of a **House of Burgesses**. When it convened in 1619, this became the first elected assembly in colonial America. Also in 1619, the first twenty Africans arrived in Virginia on a Dutch vessel. These events laid the foundation for a society that would one day be dominated economically and politically by slaveowning planters.

Powhatan and Pocahontas

When the English arrived at Jamestown, they landed in an area inhabited by some 15,000 to 25,000 Indians living in numerous small agricultural villages. Most acknowledged the rule of Wahunsonacock, a shrewd and forceful leader who had recently consolidated his authority over the region and collected tribute from some thirty subordinate tribes. Called Powhatan by the settlers after the Indian word for both his tribe and his title of paramount chief, he quickly realized the advantages of trade with the newcomers.

In the first two years of Jamestown's existence, relations with Indians were mostly peaceful and based on a fairly equal give-and-take. At one point, Smith was captured by the Indians and threatened with execution by Powhatan, only to be rescued by Pocahontas, reputedly the favorite among his many children by dozens of wives. The incident has come down in legend as an example of a rebellious, love-struck teenager defying her father. In fact, it was probably part of an elaborate ceremony designed by Powhatan to demonstrate his power over the colonists and incorporate them into his realm. Pocahontas subsequently became an intermediary between the two peoples, bringing food and messages to Jamestown. In 1614, she married the English colonist John Rolfe. Two years later, she accompanied her husband to England, where she caused a sensation in the court of James I as a symbol of Anglo-Indian harmony and missionary success. But she succumbed to disease in 1617. Her father died the following year.

The Uprising of 1622

Once it became clear that the English were interested in establishing a permanent and constantly expanding colony, not a trading post, conflict with local Indians was inevitable. In 1622, Powhatan's brother and successor, Opechancanough, led a brilliantly planned surprise attack that in a single day wiped out one-quarter of Virginia's settler population of 1,200. The surviving 900 colonists organized themselves into military bands, which then massacred scores of Indians and devastated their villages. By going to war, declared Governor Francis Wyatt, the Indians had forfeited any claim to the land. Virginia's policy, he continued, must now be nothing less than the "expulsion of the savages to gain the free range of the country."

Opechancanough

The unsuccessful **Uprising of 1622** fundamentally shifted the balance of power in the colony. The settlers' supremacy was reinforced in 1644 when a last desperate rebellion led by Opechancanough, now said to be 100 years old, was crushed after causing the deaths of some 500 colonists. Virginia forced a treaty on the surviving coastal Indians, who now numbered fewer than 2,000, that acknowledged their subordination to the government at Jamestown and required them to move to tribal reservations to the west and not enter areas of European settlement without permission. Settlers spreading inland into the Virginia countryside continued to seize Indian lands.

The destruction caused by the Uprising of 1622 was the last in a series of blows suffered by the Virginia Company. Two years later, it surrendered its charter and Virginia became the first royal colony, its governor now appointed by the crown. Investors had not turned a profit, and although the company had sent 6,000 settlers to Virginia, its white population numbered only 1,200 when the king assumed control. The government in London for years paid little attention to Virginia. Henceforth, the local elite, not a faraway company, controlled the colony's development. And that elite was growing rapidly in wealth and power thanks to the cultivation of a crop introduced from the West Indies by John Rolfe—tobacco.

The first royal colony

A Tobacco Colony

King James I considered tobacco "harmful to the brain and dangerous to the lungs" and issued a spirited warning against its use. But increasing numbers of Europeans enjoyed smoking and believed the tobacco plant had medicinal benefits. Tobacco became Virginia's substitute for gold. It enriched an emerging class of tobacco planters, as well as members of the colonial government who assigned good land to themselves. The crown

An advertisement for tobacco includes images of slaves handling barrels and tobacco plants.

profited from customs duties (taxes on tobacco that entered or left the kingdom). The spread of tobacco farming produced a dispersed society with few towns and inspired a frenzied scramble for land. By the middle of the seventeenth century, a new influx of immigrants with ample financial resources—sons of merchants and English gentlemen—had taken advantage of the headright system and governmental connections to acquire large estates along navigable rivers. They established themselves as the colony's social and political elite.

The expansion of tobacco cultivation also led to an increased demand for field labor, met for most of the seventeenth century by young, male indentured servants. Despite harsh conditions of work in the tobacco fields, a persistently high death rate, and laws mandating punishments from whipping to an extension of service for those who ran away or were unruly, the abundance of land continued to attract migrants. Of the 120,000 English immigrants who entered the Chesapeake region during the seventeenth century, three-quarters came as servants. Virginia's white society increasingly came to resemble that of England, with a wealthy landed gentry at the top; a group of small farmers, mostly former indentured servants who had managed to acquire land, in the middle; and an army of poor laborers—servants and landless former indentured servants—at the bottom.

Women and the Family

Virginia, however, lacked one essential element of English society—stable family life. Given the demand for male servants to work in the tobacco fields, men in the Chesapeake outnumbered women for most of the seventeenth century by four or five to one. The vast majority of women who immigrated to the region came as indentured servants. Since they usually had to complete their terms of service before marrying, they did not begin to form families until their mid-twenties. The high death rate, unequal ratio between the sexes, and late age of marriage retarded population growth.

Slow population growth

In the colonies as in England, a married woman possessed certain rights before the law, including a claim to **dower rights** of one-third of her husband's property in the event that he died before she did. When the widow died, however, the property passed to the husband's male heirs. (English law was far less generous than in Spain, where a woman could hold independently any property inherited from her parents, and a man and wife owned jointly all the wealth accumulated during a marriage.)

Women's lives

Social conditions in the colonies, however, opened the door to roles women rarely assumed in England. A widow or one of the few women who never married could sometimes take advantage of her legal status as a *feme sole* (a "woman alone," who enjoyed an independent legal iden-

Processing tobacco was as labor intensive as caring for the plant in the fields. Here slaves and female indentured servants work with the crop after it has been harvested.

tity denied to married women) to make contracts and conduct business. Margaret Brent, who arrived in the Chesapeake in 1638, acquired land, managed her own plantation, and acted as a lawyer in court. But because most women came to Virginia as indentured servants, they could look forward only to a life of hard labor in the tobacco fields and early death.

The Maryland Experiment

The second Chesapeake colony, Maryland, followed a similar course of development. As in Virginia, tobacco came to dominate the economy and tobacco planters the society. But in other ways, Maryland's history was strikingly different.

Maryland was established in 1632 as a proprietary colony, that is, a grant of land and governmental authority to a single individual. This was Cecilius Calvert, the son of a recently deceased favorite of King Charles I. The charter granted him "full, free, and absolute power," including control of trade and the right to initiate all legislation, with an elected assembly confined to approving or disapproving his proposals. Although Calvert disliked representative institutions, the charter guaranteed to colonists "all privileges, franchises, and liberties" of Englishmen. While these were not spelled out, they undoubtedly included the idea of a government limited by the law. Here was a recipe for conflict, and Maryland had more than its share during the seventeenth century.

Proprietary colony

Religion in Maryland

Further aggravating instability in the colony was the fact that Calvert, a Catholic, envisioned Maryland as a refuge for his persecuted coreligionists, especially the younger sons of Catholic gentry who had few economic or political prospects in England. In Maryland, he hoped, Protestants and Catholics could live in a harmony unknown in Europe. Most appointed officials were Catholic, including relatives of the proprietor. But Protestants always formed a majority of the settlers. Most, as in Virginia, came as indentured servants.

Maryland as a refuge for persecuted Catholics

As in Virginia, the death rate remained very high. Almost 70 percent of male settlers in Maryland died before reaching the age of fifty, and half the children born in the colony did not live to adulthood. But at least initially, Maryland seems to have offered servants greater opportunity for landownership than Virginia. Unlike in the older colony, freedom dues in Maryland included fifty acres of land. As tobacco planters engrossed the best land later in the century, however, the prospects for landless men diminished.

THE NEW ENGLAND WAY

The Rise of Puritanism

As Virginia and Maryland evolved toward societies dominated by a small aristocracy ruling over numerous bound laborers, a very different social order emerged in seventeenth-century New England. The early history of that region is intimately connected to the religious movement known as "Puritanism," which arose in England late in the sixteenth century. The term was initially coined by opponents to ridicule those not satisfied with the progress of the Protestant Reformation in England. **Puritans** differed among themselves on many issues. But all shared the conviction that the Church of England retained too many elements of Catholicism in its religious rituals and doctrines. Puritans saw elaborate church ceremonies, the rule that priests could not marry, and ornate church decorations as vestiges of "popery." Many rejected the Catholic structure of religious authority descending from a pope or king to archbishops, bishops, and priests. Only independent local congregations, they believed, should choose clergymen and determine modes of worship. These Puritans were called "Congregationalists."

Puritanism and the Protestant Reformation in England

Puritans considered religious belief a complex and demanding matter and urged believers to seek the truth by reading the Bible and listening to sermons by educated ministers, rather than devoting themselves to sacraments administered by priests and to what Puritans considered formulaic prayers. The sermon was the central rite of Puritan practice. In the course of a lifetime, according to one estimate, the average Puritan listened to some 7,000 sermons. In their religious beliefs, Puritans followed the ideas of the French-born Swiss theologian John Calvin. The world, Calvin taught, was divided between the elect and the damned, but no one knew who was destined to be saved, which had already been determined by God. Nevertheless, leading a good life and prospering economically might be indications of God's grace, whereas idleness and immoral behavior were sure signs of damnation.

John Calvin

Moral Liberty

Puritanism was characterized by a zeal that alienated many who held differing religious views. A minority of Puritans (such as those who settled in Plymouth Colony) became separatists, abandoning the Church of England entirely to form their own independent churches. Most, however, hoped to purify the church from within. But in the 1620s and 1630s, as Charles I seemed to be moving toward a restoration of Catholic ceremonies and the Church of England dismissed Puritan ministers and censored their writings, many Puritans decided to emigrate. When Puritans emigrated to New England, they hoped to escape what they believed to be the religious and worldly corruptions of English society. They would establish a "city set upon a hill," a Bible Commonwealth whose influence would flow back across the Atlantic and rescue England from godlessness and social decay.

"City set upon a hill"

Like so many other immigrants to America, Puritans came in search of liberty, especially the right to worship and govern themselves in what they deemed a truly Christian manner. Freedom certainly did not mean unrestrained action, improper religious practices, or sinful behavior, of which, Puritans thought, there were far too many examples in England. In a 1645 speech to the Massachusetts legislature explaining the Puritan conception of freedom, **John Winthrop**, the colony's governor, distinguished sharply between two kinds of liberty. "Natural" liberty, or acting without restraint, suggested "a liberty to do evil." This was the false idea of freedom supposedly adopted by the Irish, Indians, and bad Christians generally. Genuine "moral" liberty meant "a liberty to that only which is good." It was quite compatible with severe restraints on speech, religion, and personal behavior. True freedom, Winthrop insisted, depended on "subjection to authority," both religious and secular; otherwise, anarchy was sure to follow. To Puritans, liberty meant that the elect had a right

"Natural liberty" and "moral liberty"

to establish churches and govern society, not that others could challenge their beliefs or authority.

The Pilgrims at Plymouth

The first Puritans to arrive in America were a group of separatists known as the **Pilgrims**. They had already fled to the Netherlands in 1608. A decade later, fearing that their children were being corrupted by the surrounding culture, they decided to emigrate to Virginia. In September 1620, the *Mayflower*, carrying 150 settlers and crew (among them many non-Puritans), embarked from England. Blown off course, they landed not in Virginia but hundreds of miles to the north, on Cape Cod. Here the 102 who survived the journey established the colony of Plymouth. Before landing, the Pilgrim leaders drew up the **Mayflower Compact**, in which the forty-one adult men going ashore agreed to obey "just and equal laws" enacted by representatives of their own choosing. This was the first written frame of government in what is now the United States. Men not normally signatories to such documents—printers, carpenters, even indentured servants—were among those who affixed their names. (This was over 200 years before most working-class men were allowed to vote in Great Britain.)

 The Pilgrims arrived in an area whose native population had recently been decimated by smallpox. They established Plymouth on the site of an abandoned Indian village whose fields had been cleared before the

The Mayflower

An early seventeenth-century engraving shows the English explorer Bartholomew Gosnold encountering Native Americans. Gosnold landed at Cape Cod in 1602 and then established a small outpost on nearby Cuttyhunk Island. The region's Indians had much experience with Europeans before Pilgrims settled there.

epidemic and were ready for cultivation. Nonetheless, the settlers arrived six weeks before winter without food or farm animals. Half died during the first winter. The remaining colonists survived only through the help of local Indians. In the autumn of 1621, the Pilgrims invited their Indian allies to a harvest feast celebrating their survival, the first Thanksgiving.

The Pilgrims hoped to establish a society based on the lives of the early Christian saints. Their government rested on the principle of consent, and voting was not restricted to church members. All land was held in common until 1627, when it was divided among the settlers. Plymouth survived as an independent colony until 1691, but it was soon overshadowed by Massachusetts Bay to its north.

The Great Migration

Chartered in 1629, the Massachusetts Bay Company was founded by a group of London merchants who hoped to further the Puritan cause and turn a profit through trade with the Indians. The first five ships sailed from England in 1629, and by 1642 some 21,000 Puritans had immigrated to Massachusetts, a flow of population long remembered as the **Great Migration**. After 1640, migration to New England virtually ceased, and in some years more colonists left the region than arrived. Nonetheless, the Great Migration established the basis for a stable and thriving society.

In many ways, the settling of New England was unique. Although servants represented about one-quarter of the Great Migration, most settlers arrived in Massachusetts in families. Compared with colonists in Virginia and Maryland, they were older and more prosperous, and the number of men and women more equally balanced. Because of the even sex ratio and New England's healthier climate, the population grew rapidly, doubling every twenty-seven years. By 1700 New England's white population of 91,000 outnumbered that of both the Chesapeake and the West Indies.

The Puritan Family

Whatever their differences with other Englishmen on religious matters, Puritans shared with the larger society a belief in male authority within the household as well as an adherence to the common-law tradition that severely limited married women's legal and economic rights. Male authority was especially vital because in a farming society without large numbers of slaves or servants, control over the labor of one's family was essential to a man's economic success.

To be sure, Puritans deemed women to be the spiritual equals of men, and women were allowed to become full church members. Although

Seal of the Massachusetts Bay Colony. The Indian's scanty attire suggests a lack of civilization. His statement "Come Over and Help Us," based on an incident in the Bible, illustrates the English conviction that they were liberating the native population, rather than exploiting them as other empires had.

A migration of families

Male authority in the household

THE NEW ENGLAND WAY | 55

The Savage Family, a 1779 painting by the New England artist Edward Savage, depicts several generations of a typically numerous Puritan family.

all ministers were men, the Puritan belief in the ability of believers to interpret the Bible opened the door for some women to claim positions of religious leadership. The ideal Puritan marriage was based on reciprocal affection and companionship, and divorce was legal. Yet within the household, the husband's authority was virtually absolute.

Family and society

The family was the foundation of strong communities, and unmarried adults seemed a danger to the social fabric. The typical New England woman married at twenty-two, a younger age than her English counterparts, and gave birth seven times. Because New England was a far healthier environment than the Chesapeake, more children survived infancy. Thus, much of a woman's adult life was devoted to bearing and rearing children.

Government and Society in Massachusetts

Since Puritans feared excessive individualism and lack of social unity, the leaders of Massachusetts organized the colony in self-governing towns. Groups of settlers received a land grant from the colony's government and then subdivided it, with residents awarded house lots in a central area and land on the outskirts for farming. Much land remained in commons, either for collective use or to be divided among later settlers or the sons of the town's founders. Each town had its own Congregational Church. Each, according to a law of 1647, was required to establish a school, since the ability to read the Bible was central to Puritan belief. To train an educated ministry, Harvard College was established in 1636

The New England town

(nearly a century after the Royal University of Mexico, founded in 1551), and two years later the first printing press in English America was established in Cambridge.

Wishing to rule the colony without outside interference and to prevent non-Puritans from influencing decision making, the eight shareholders of the Massachusetts Bay Company emigrated to America, taking the charter with them and transforming a commercial document into a form of government. In 1634, a group of deputies elected by freemen (landowning church members) was added to form a single ruling body, the General Court. Ten years later, company officers and elected deputies were divided into two legislative houses. Unlike Virginia, whose governors were appointed first by a faraway company and, after 1624, by the crown, or Maryland, where authority rested with a single proprietor, the freemen of Massachusetts elected their governor.

The Massachusetts Bay Charter

The principle of consent was central to Puritanism. Churches were formed by voluntary agreement among members, who elected the minister. No important church decision was made without the agreement of the male members. Towns governed themselves, and local officials, delegates to the General Court, and the colonial governor were all elected. Puritans, however, were hardly believers in equality. Church membership, a status that carried great prestige and power, was a restrictive category. Anyone could worship at a church, but to be a full member

Church membership

An embroidered banner depicting the main building at Harvard, the first college established in the English colonies. It was probably made by a Massachusetts woman for a husband or son who attended Harvard.

required demonstrating that one had experienced divine grace and could be considered a "visible saint," usually by testifying about a conversion experience. Voting in colony-wide elections was limited to men who had been accepted as full church members. Puritan democracy was for those within the circle of church membership; those outside the boundary occupied a secondary place in the Bible Commonwealth.

Church and State in Puritan Massachusetts

Seventeenth-century New England was a hierarchical society in which socially prominent families were assigned the best land and the most desirable seats in church. Ordinary settlers were addressed as "goodman" and "goodwife," while the better sort were called "gentleman" and "lady" or "master" and "mistress." When the General Court in 1641 issued a Body of Liberties outlining the rights and responsibilities of Massachusetts colonists, it adopted the traditional understanding of liberties as privileges that derived from one's place in the social order. While some liberties applied to all inhabitants, there were separate lists of rights for freemen, women, children, and servants. The Body of Liberties also allowed for slavery. The first African slave appears in the records of Massachusetts Bay in 1640.

The Body of Liberties

Massachusetts forbade ministers to hold office so as not to interfere with their spiritual responsibilities. But the law required each town to establish a church and to levy a tax to support the minister. Massachusetts prescribed the death penalty for, among other things, worshiping "any god, but the lord god," practicing witchcraft, or committing blasphemy.

Like many others in the seventeenth century, Puritans believed that religious uniformity was essential to social order. Puritans did not believe in religious toleration—there was one truth, and their faith embodied it. Religious liberty meant the liberty to practice this truth. But the principle of autonomy for local congregations soon clashed with the desire for religious uniformity.

Religious uniformity

NEW ENGLANDERS DIVIDED

Modern ideas of individualism, privacy, and personal freedom would have struck Puritans as quite strange. They considered too much emphasis on the "self" dangerous to social harmony and community stability. In the closely knit towns of New England, residents carefully monitored one another's behavior and chastised or expelled those who violated communal norms. Towns banished individuals for such offenses as criticiz-

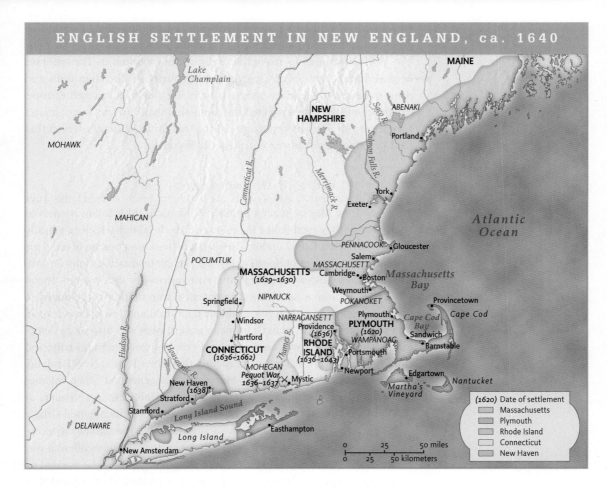

ENGLISH SETTLEMENT IN NEW ENGLAND, ca. 1640

By the mid-seventeenth century, English settlement in New England had spread well inland and up and down the Atlantic coast.

ing the church or government, complaining about the colony in letters home to England, or, in the case of one individual, Abigail Gifford, being "a very burdensome woman." Tolerance of difference was not high on the list of Puritan values.

Roger Williams

Differences of opinion about how to organize a Bible Commonwealth, however, emerged almost from the founding of Massachusetts. With its emphasis on individual interpretation of the Bible, Puritanism contained the seeds of its own fragmentation. The first sustained criticism of the existing order came from the young minister Roger Williams, who arrived in Massachusetts in 1631 and soon began to insist that its congregations withdraw from the Church of England and that church and state

Roger Williams, New England's most prominent advocate of religious toleration.

be separated. Williams believed that any law-abiding citizen should be allowed to practice whatever form of religion he chose.

Williams aimed to strengthen religion, not weaken it. The embrace of government, he insisted, corrupted the purity of Christian faith and drew believers into endless religious wars like those that racked Europe. Furthermore, Williams rejected the conviction that Puritans were an elect people on a divine mission to spread the true faith. Williams denied that God had singled out any group as special favorites.

Rhode Island and Connecticut

Banished from Massachusetts in 1636, Williams and his followers moved south, where they established the colony of Rhode Island, which eventually received a charter from London. Rhode Island became a beacon of religious freedom. It had no established church, no religious qualifications for voting until the eighteenth century, and no requirement that citizens attend church. It became a haven for **Dissenters** (Protestants who belonged to denominations other than the established church) and Jews persecuted in other colonies. Rhode Island's frame of government was also more democratic. The assembly was elected twice a year, the governor annually, and town meetings were held more frequently than elsewhere in New England.

Religious disagreements in Massachusetts generated other colonies as well. In 1636, the minister Thomas Hooker established a settlement at Hartford. Its system of government, embodied in the Fundamental Orders of 1639, was modeled on that of Massachusetts—with the significant exception that men did not have to be church members to vote. Quite different was the colony of New Haven, founded in 1638 by immigrants who wanted an even closer connection between church and state. In 1662, Hartford and New Haven received a royal charter that united them as the colony of Connecticut.

Connecticut

The Trial of Anne Hutchinson

Another threat to the Puritan establishment, because of both her gender and her influential following, was Anne Hutchinson. A midwife and the daughter of a clergyman, Hutchinson, wrote John Winthrop, was "a woman of a ready wit and bold spirit." Hutchinson began holding meetings in her home, where she led discussions of religious issues among men and women, including a number of prominent merchants and public officials. In Hutchinson's view, salvation was God's direct gift to the elect and could not be earned by good works, devotional practices, or other human effort. Most Puritans shared this belief. What set Hutchinson apart was her charge that nearly all the ministers in Massachusetts were guilty of

Hutchinson's criticisms of Puritan leaders

faulty preaching for distinguishing "saints" from the damned on the basis of activities such as church attendance and moral behavior rather than an inner state of grace.

Critics denounced Hutchinson for Antinomianism (a term for putting one's own judgment or faith above both human law and the teachings of the church). In 1637, she was tried in civil court for sedition (expressing opinions dangerous to authority). An articulate woman, Hutchinson ably debated her university-educated accusers during her trial. But when she said God spoke to her directly rather than through ministers or the Bible, she violated Puritan doctrine and sealed her own fate. Such a claim, the colony's leaders felt, posed a threat to organized churches—and, indeed, to all authority. Hutchinson and a number of her followers were banished.

Hutchinson's trial

Anne Hutchinson lived in New England for only eight years, but she left her mark on the region's religious culture. As in the case of Roger Williams, her career showed how the Puritan belief in individual interpretation of the Bible could easily lead to criticism of the religious and political establishment. It would take many years before religious toleration—which violated the Puritans' understanding of "moral liberty" and social harmony—came to Massachusetts.

Significance of Anne Hutchinson

Puritans and Indians

Along with disruptive religious controversies, New England, like other colonies, had to deal with the difficult problem of relations with Indians. The native population of New England numbered perhaps 100,000 when the Puritans arrived. But because of recent epidemics, the migrants encountered fewer Indians near the coast than in other parts of eastern North America. In areas of European settlement, colonists quickly outnumbered the native population. Some settlers, notably Roger Williams, sought to treat the Indians with justice. Williams insisted that the king had no right to grant land already belonging to someone else. No town, said Williams, should be established before its site had been purchased. John Winthrop, on the other hand, believed uncultivated land could legitimately be taken. Although he recognized the benefits of buying land rather than simply seizing it, he insisted that such purchases require Indians to submit to English authority and pay tribute to the colonists.

Treating Indians with justice

To New England's leaders, the Indians represented both savagery and temptation. They enjoyed freedom but of the wrong kind—what Winthrop condemned as undisciplined "natural liberty." Puritans feared that Indian society might attract colonists who lacked the proper moral fiber. In 1642, the Connecticut General Court set a penalty of three years at hard labor for any colonist who abandoned "godly society" to live

VOICES OF FREEDOM

From "The Trial of Anne Hutchinson" (1637)

Anne Hutchinson began holding religious meetings in her home in Massachusetts in 1634. She attracted followers who believed that most ministers were not adhering strictly to Puritan theology. In 1637, she was placed on trial for sedition. In her defense, she claimed to be inspired by a revelation from God, a violation of Puritan beliefs. The examination of Hutchinson is a classic example of the clash between established power and individual conscience.

GOV. JOHN WINTHROP: Mrs. Hutchinson, you are called here as one of those that have troubled the peace of the commonwealth and the churches here; you are known to be a woman that hath had a great share in the promoting and divulging of those opinions that are the cause of this trouble, . . . and you have maintained a meeting and an assembly in your house that hath been condemned by the general assembly as a thing not tolerable nor comely on the sight of God nor fitting for your sex. . . .

MRS. ANNE HUTCHINSON: That's matter of conscience, Sir.

GOV. JOHN WINTHROP: Your conscience you must keep, or it must be kept for you. . . . Your course is not to be suffered for. Besides we find such a course as this to be greatly prejudicial to the state. . . . And besides that it will not well stand with the commonwealth that families should be neglected for so many neighbors and dames and so much time spent. We see no rule of God for this. We see not that any should have authority to set up any other exercises besides what authority hath already set up. . . .

MRS. ANNE HUTCHINSON: I bless the Lord, he hath let me see which was the clear ministry and which the wrong. . . . Now if you do condemn me for speaking what in my conscience I know to be truth I must commit myself unto the Lord.

MR. NOWEL (ASSISTANT TO THE COURT): How do you know that was the spirit?

MRS. ANNE HUTCHINSON: By an immediate revelation.

DEP. GOV. THOMAS DUDLEY: How! An immediate revelation. . . .

GOV. JOHN WINTHROP: Mrs. Hutchinson, the sentence of the court you hear is that you are banished from out of our jurisdiction as being a woman not fit for our society, and are to be imprisoned till the court shall send you away.

From John Winthrop, Speech to the Massachusetts General Court (July 3, 1645)

John Winthrop, governor of the Massachusetts Bay Colony, describes two very different definitions of liberty in this speech.

The great questions that have troubled the country, are about the authority of the magistrates and the liberty of the people. . . . Concerning liberty, I observe a great mistake in the country about that. There is a twofold liberty, natural (I mean as our nature is now corrupt) and civil or federal. The first is common to man with beasts and other creatures. By this, man, as he stands in relation to man simply, hath liberty to do what he lists; it is a liberty to do evil as well as to [do] good. This liberty is incompatible and inconsistent with authority, and cannot endure the least restraint of the most just authority. The exercise and maintaining of this liberty makes men grow more evil, and in time to be worse than brute beasts. . . . This is that great enemy of truth and peace, that wild beast, which all the ordinances of God are bent against, to restrain and subdue it.

The other kind of liberty I call civil or federal, it may also be termed moral. . . . This liberty is the proper end and object of authority, and cannot subsist without it; and it is a liberty to that only which is good, just, and honest. . . . This liberty is maintained and exercised in a way of subjection to authority; it is of the same kind of liberty wherewith Christ hath made us free. The woman's own choice makes . . . a man her husband; yet being so chosen, he is her lord, and she is to be subject to him, yet in a way of liberty, not of bondage; and a true wife accounts her subjection her honor and freedom, and would not think her condition safe and free, but in her subjection to her husband's authority. Such is the liberty of the church under the authority of Christ.

QUESTIONS

1. *To what extent does Hutchinson's being a woman play a part in the accusations against her?*

2. *Why does Winthrop consider "natural" liberty dangerous?*

3. *How do Hutchinson and Winthrop differ in their understanding of religious liberty?*

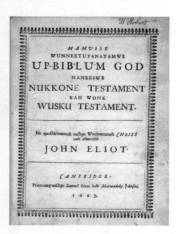

The title page of a translation of the Bible into the Massachusett Indian language, published by John Eliot in 1663.

with the Indians. To counteract the attraction of Indian life, the leaders of New England also encouraged the publication of **captivity narratives** by those captured by Indians. The most popular was *The Sovereignty and Goodness of God* by Mary Rowlandson, who was seized with other settlers and held for three months until ransomed during an Indian war in the 1670s. Rowlandson acknowledged that she had been well treated and suffered "not the least abuse or unchastity," but her book's overriding theme was her determination to return to Christian society.

Puritans announced that they intended to bring Christian faith to the Indians, but they did nothing in the first two decades of settlement to accomplish this. They generally saw Indians as an obstacle to be pushed aside.

The Pequot War

Indians in New England lacked a paramount chief like Powhatan in Virginia. Coastal Indian tribes, their numbers severely reduced by disease, initially sought to forge alliances with the newcomers to enhance their own position against inland rivals. But as the white population expanded and new towns proliferated, conflict with the region's Indians became unavoidable. The turning point came in 1637 when a fur trader was killed by Pequots—a powerful tribe who controlled southern New England's fur trade and exacted tribute from other Indians. A force of Connecticut and Massachusetts soldiers, augmented by Narragansett allies, surrounded the main Pequot fortified village at Mystic and set it ablaze, killing those who tried to escape. Over 500 men, women, and children lost their lives in the massacre. By the end of the **Pequot War** a few months later, most of the Pequots had been exterminated or sold into Caribbean slavery. The treaty that restored peace decreed that their name be wiped from the historical record.

Massacre at Mystic

The colonists' ferocity shocked their Indian allies, who considered European military practices barbaric. But to most Puritans, the defeat of a "barbarous nation" by "the sword of the Lord" offered further proof that Indians were unworthy of sharing New England with the visible saints of the church.

The New England Economy

The leaders of the New England colonies prided themselves on the idea that religion was the primary motivation for emigration. But economic motives were hardly unimportant. One promotional pamphlet of the 1620s spoke of New England as a place "where religion and profit jump together."

Economic motivation for emigrants

Most Puritans came from the middle ranks of society and paid for their family's passage rather than indenturing themselves to labor. They sought in New England not only religious liberty but also economic

An engraving from John Underhill's *News from America*, published in London in 1638, shows the destruction of the Pequot village on the Mystic River in 1637. The colonial forces, firing guns, are aided by Indian allies with bows and arrows.

advancement—if not riches, then at least a "competency," the economic independence that came with secure landownership or craft status.

Lacking a marketable staple like sugar or tobacco, New Englanders turned to fishing and timber for exports. With very few slaves in seventeenth-century New England, most households relied on the labor of their own members, including women in the home and children in the fields. Sons remained unmarried into their mid-twenties, when they could expect to receive land from their fathers, from local authorities, or by moving to a new town.

Fish and timber exports

The Merchant Elite

Per capita wealth in New England lagged far behind that of the Chesapeake, but it was much more equally distributed. A majority of New England families owned their own land, the foundation for a comfortable independence. Nonetheless, as in the Chesapeake, economic development produced some social inequalities. For example, on completing their terms, indentured servants rarely achieved full church membership or received grants of land. Most became disenfranchised wage earners.

Social inequalities

New England assumed a growing role within the British empire based on trade. As early as the 1640s, New England merchants shipped and marketed the staples of other colonies to markets in Europe and Africa. They

Mrs. Elizabeth Freake and Baby Mary. Painted by an anonymous artist in the 1670s, this portrait depicts the wife and daughter of John Freake, a prominent Boston merchant and lawyer. To illustrate the family's wealth, Mrs. Freake wears a triple strand of pearls, a garnet bracelet, and a gold ring, and her child wears a yellow silk dress.

"Jeremiads"

engaged in a particularly profitable trade with the West Indies, whose growing slave plantations they supplied with fish, timber, and agricultural produce gathered at home. Especially in Boston, a powerful class of merchants arose who challenged some key Puritan policies, including the subordination of economic activity to the common good. As early as the 1630s, when the General Court established limits on prices and wages and gave a small group of merchants a monopoly on imports from Europe, others protested. Some left Boston to establish a new town at Portsmouth, in the region eventually chartered as the royal colony of New Hampshire. Others remained to fight, with increasing success, for the right to conduct business as they pleased. By the 1640s, Massachusetts had repealed many of its early economic regulations. Eventually, the Puritan experiment would evolve into a merchant-dominated colonial government.

Some Puritan leaders were understandably worried about their society's growing commercialization. By 1650, less than half the population of Boston had become full church members, which forced Puritan leaders to deal with the religious status of the third generation. Should they uphold the rigorous admission standards of the Congregational Church, thus limiting its size? Or should they make admission easier and remain connected to more people? The **Half-Way Covenant** of 1662 tried to address this problem by allowing for the baptism of and a kind of "half-way" membership for grandchildren of those who arrived during the Great Migration. But church membership continued to stagnate.

By the 1660s and 1670s, ministers were regularly castigating the people for selfishness and a "great backsliding" from the colony's original purposes. These warnings, called "jeremiads" after the ancient Hebrew prophet Jeremiah, interpreted crop failures and disease as signs of divine disapproval and warned of further punishment to come if New Englanders did not mend their ways. Yet hard work and commercial success had always been central Puritan values. In this sense, the commercialization of New England was as much a fulfillment of the Puritan mission in America as a betrayal.

RELIGION, POLITICS, AND FREEDOM

The Rights of Englishmen

Even as English emigrants began the settlement of colonies in North America, England itself became enmeshed in political and religious conflict, in which ideas of liberty played a central role. By 1600, the traditional definition of "liberties" as a set of privileges confined to one or another social group still persisted, but alongside it had arisen the idea that certain

The execution of Charles I in 1649, a central event of the English Civil War.

"rights of Englishmen" applied to all within the kingdom. This tradition rested on the Magna Carta (or Great Charter) of 1215. An agreement between King John and a group of barons, the Magna Carta listed a series of "liberties" granted by the king to "all the free men of our realm," a restricted group at the time, since many residents of England were serfs. The liberties mentioned in the Magna Carta included protection against arbitrary imprisonment and the seizure of one's property without due process of law.

The Magna Carta

Over time, the document came to be seen as embodying the idea of **"English liberty"**—that the king was subject to the rule of law, and that all persons should enjoy security of person and property. These rights were embodied in the common law, whose provisions, such as habeas corpus (a protection against being imprisoned without a legal charge), the right to face one's accuser, and trial by jury came to apply to all free subjects of the English crown. As serfdom slowly disappeared, the number of Englishmen considered "freeborn," and therefore entitled to these rights, expanded enormously. The belief in freedom as the common heritage of all Englishmen and the conception of the British empire as the world's guardian of liberty helped to legitimize English colonization in the Western Hemisphere and to cast imperial wars against Catholic France and Spain as struggles between freedom and tyranny.

Rights of "freeborns"

The English Civil War

At the beginning of the seventeenth century, when English immigrants began arriving in the New World, "freedom" still played only a minor role in England's political debates. But the political upheavals of that century elevated the notion of "English freedom" to a central place. The struggle for political supremacy between Parliament and the Stuart monarchs James I and Charles I culminated in the English Civil War of the 1640s and early 1650s.

Meeting of the General Council of the Army at Putney, scene of the debate in 1647 over liberty and democracy between Levellers and more conservative army officers.

The leaders of the House of Commons (the elective body that, along with the hereditary aristocrats of the House of Lords, made up the English Parliament) accused the Stuart kings of endangering liberty by imposing taxes without parliamentary consent, imprisoning political foes, and leading the nation back toward Catholicism. Civil war broke out in 1642, resulting in a victory for the forces of Parliament. In 1649, Charles I was beheaded, the monarchy abolished, and England declared "a Commonwealth and Free State"—a nation governed by the will of the people. Oliver Cromwell, the head of the victorious Parliamentary army, ruled for almost a decade after the execution of the king. In 1660, the monarchy was restored and Charles II assumed the throne. But by then, the breakdown of authority had stimulated intense discussions of liberty, authority, and what it meant to be a "freeborn Englishman."

England's Debate over Freedom

The idea of freedom suddenly took on new and expanded meanings between 1640 and 1660. The writer John Milton called for freedom of speech and of the press. New religious sects sprang up, demanding religious toleration for all Protestants as well as the end of public financing and special privileges for the Anglican Church. The Levellers, history's first democratic political movement, proposed a written constitution, the Agreement of the People, which began by proclaiming "at how high a rate we value our just freedom," and went on to list inalienable rights Parliament could not infringe upon. Although "democracy" was still widely equated with anarchy, the document proposed to abolish the monarchy and House of Lords and to greatly expand the right to vote.

The Levellers offered a glimpse of the modern definition of freedom as a universal entitlement in a society based on equal rights, not a function of social class. Another new group, the Diggers, went even further, hoping to give freedom an economic underpinning through the common ownership of land. Gerard Winstanley, the Diggers' leader, said that true freedom applied equally "to the poor as well as the rich"; all were entitled to "a comfortable livelihood in this their own land." Some of the ideas of liberty that flourished during the 1640s and 1650s would be carried to America by English immigrants.

The Diggers

The Civil War and English America

The Civil War, accompanied by vigorous discussions of the rights of freeborn Englishmen, inevitably reverberated in England's colonies, dividing them from one another and internally. Most New Englanders sided with

WHO IS AN AMERICAN?

From Henry Care, *English Liberties, Or, The Free-Born Subject's Inheritance* (1680).

Before the United States existed as an independent nation, settlers in Britain's North American colonies shared a sense of identity linked with the idea that liberty was a unique possession of Englishmen. Care was a British journalist and writer on politics. His book was an influential example of how seventeenth-century identities rested, in part, on negative images of other nations. Well into the eighteenth century, it was widely reprinted in the colonies as well as the mother country.

The Constitution of our English government (the best in the world) is no arbitrary tyranny like the Turkish Grand Seignior's, or the French Kings, whose wills (or rather lusts) dispose of the lives and fortunes of their unhappy subjects; nor an Oligarchy where the great men (like fish in the ocean) prey upon, and live by devouring the lesser at their pleasure. Nor yet a Democracy or popular State, much less an Anarchy, where all confusedly are hail fellows well met, but a most excellently mixt or qualified Monarchy, where the King is vested with large prerogatives sufficient to support majesty; and restrained only from power of doing himself and his people harm, which would be contrary to the end of all government, . . . the nobility adorned with privileges to be a screen to majesty, and a refreshing shade to their inferiors, and the commonality, too, so guarded in their persons and properties by the fence of law, [which] renders them Freemen, not Slaves.

In France and other nations the mere will of the prince is law, his word takes off any . . . head, imposes taxes, or seizes any man's estate, when, how, and as often as he wishes. . . . But in England, the law is both the measure and the bond of every subject's duty and allegiance, each man having a fixed fundamental right born with him as to the freedom of his person and property in his estate, which he cannot be deprived of, but either by his consent, or some crime for which the law has imposed . . . a penalty. . . .

This original happy frame of government is truly and properly called an Englishman's liberty, a privilege not to [be] exempt from the law, but to be freed in person and estate, from arbitrary violence and oppression.

QUESTIONS

1. *Why does Care consider the English system of "balanced" government the best in the world?*

2. *How does his view of other countries affect his pride in being English?*

Parliament in the Civil War of the 1640s. Some returned to England to join the Parliamentary army or take up pulpits to help create a godly commonwealth at home. But Puritan leaders were increasingly uncomfortable as the idea of religious toleration for Protestants gained favor in England.

The Quakers

Meanwhile, a number of followers of Anne Hutchinson became Quakers, one of the sects that sprang up in England during the Civil War. Quakers held that the spirit of God dwelled within every individual, not just the elect, and that this "inner light," rather than the Bible or teachings of the clergy, offered the surest guidance in spiritual matters. When Quakers appeared in Massachusetts, colonial officials had them whipped, fined, and banished. In 1659 and 1660, four Quakers who returned from exile were hanged. When Charles II, after the restoration of the monarchy in 1660, reaffirmed the Massachusetts charter, he ordered the colony to recognize the "liberty of conscience" of all Protestants.

In Maryland, the combination of the religious and political battles of the Civil War, homegrown conflict between Catholic and Protestant settlers, and anti-proprietary feeling produced a violent civil war within the colony, later recalled as the "plundering time." Indeed, Maryland in the 1640s verged on total anarchy, with a pro-Parliament force assaulting those loyal to Charles I.

Religious freedom in Maryland

After years of struggle between the Protestant planter class and the Catholic elite, Maryland in 1649 adopted an **Act Concerning Religion (or Maryland Toleration Act)**, which institutionalized the principle of toleration that had prevailed from the colony's beginning. All Christians were guaranteed the "free exercise" of religion. Although the Act did not grant this right to non-Christians, it did, over time, bring some political stability to Maryland. The law was also a milestone in the history of religious freedom in colonial America.

England's colonial expansion

By the middle of the seventeenth century, several English colonies existed along the Atlantic coast of North America. Established as part of an ad hoc process rather than arising under any coherent national plan, they differed enormously in economic, political, and social structure. The seeds had been planted, in the Chesapeake, for the development of plantation societies based on unfree labor, and in New England, for settlements centered on small towns and family farms. Throughout the colonies, many residents enjoyed freedoms they had not possessed at home, especially access to land and the right to worship as they desired. Others found themselves confined to unfree labor for many years or an entire lifetime.

The next century would be a time of crisis and consolidation as the population expanded, social conflicts intensified, and Britain moved to exert greater control over its flourishing North American colonies.

CHAPTER REVIEW AND ONLINE RESOURCES

REVIEW QUESTIONS

1. Compare and contrast settlement patterns, treatment of Indians, and religion of the Spanish and English in the Americas.

2. For English settlers, land was the basis of independence and liberty. Explain the reasoning behind that concept and how it differed from the Indians' conception of land.

3. Describe the factors promoting and limiting religious freedom in the New England and Chesapeake colonies.

4. Describe who chose to emigrate to North America from England in the seventeenth century and explain their reasons.

5. In what ways did the economy, government, and household structure differ in New England and the Chesapeake colonies?

6. The English believed that, unlike the Spanish, their motives for colonization were pure, and that the growth of empire and freedom would always go hand in hand. How did the expansion of the British empire affect the freedoms of Native Americans, the Irish, and even many English citizens?

7. Considering politics, social tensions, and debates over the meaning of liberty, how do the events and aftermath of the English Civil War demonstrate that the English colonies in North America were part of a larger Atlantic community?

8. How did the tobacco economy draw the Chesapeake colonies into the greater Atlantic World?

9. How did the idea of freedom help legitimize English colonization?

KEY TERMS

Virginia Company (p. 39)
Anglican Church (p. 40)
Roanoke colony (p. 41)
enclosure movement (p. 42)
indentured servants (p. 44)
John Smith (p. 47)
headright system (p. 48)
House of Burgesses (p. 48)
Uprising of 1622 (p. 49)
dower rights (p. 50)
Puritans (p. 52)
John Winthrop (p. 53)
Pilgrims (p. 54)
Mayflower Compact (p. 54)
Great Migration (p. 55)
Dissenters (p. 60)
captivity narratives (p. 64)
Pequot War (p. 64)
Half-Way Covenant (p. 66)
English liberty (p. 67)
Act Concerning Religion (or Maryland Toleration Act) (p. 70)

Go to 🐇 INQUIZITIVE

To see what you know—and learn what you've missed—with personalized feedback along the way.

Visit the *Give Me Liberty! Student Site* for primary source documents and images, interactive maps, author videos featuring Eric Foner, and more.

CHAPTER 3

CREATING ANGLO-AMERICA

★

1660–1750

A View of Bethlehem, One of the Brethren's Principal Settlements in Pennsylvania, a lithograph produced in London in 1757, depicts a prosperous Moravian community, one of numerous settlements established by religious groups who emigrated from Europe to Britain's American colonies. In the left foreground, with a roof made of tiles from a local workshop, is the Crown Inn, which stood for over a century until razed to make way for a railroad. To its right is a large barn, with animals grazing nearby.

In the last quarter of the seventeenth century, a series of crises rocked the European colonies of North America. Social and political tensions boiled over in sometimes ruthless conflicts between rich and poor, free and slave, settler and Indian, and members of different religious groups. At the same time, struggles within and between European empires echoed in the colonies.

The bloodiest and most bitter conflict occurred in southern New England, where in 1675 an Indian alliance launched attacks on farms and settlements that were encroaching on Indian lands. It was the most dramatic and violent warfare in the region in the entire seventeenth century.

New Englanders described the Wampanoag leader **Metacom** (known to the colonists as King Philip) as the uprising's mastermind, although in fact most tribes fought under their own leaders. By 1676, Indian forces had attacked nearly half of New England's ninety towns. Twelve in Massachusetts were destroyed. As refugees fled eastward, the line of settlement was pushed back almost to the Atlantic coast. Some 1,000 settlers, out of a population of 52,000, and 3,000 of New England's 20,000 Indians perished in the fighting.

In mid-1676, the tide of battle turned and a ferocious counterattack broke the Indians' power once and for all. Although the uprising united numerous tribes, others remained loyal to the colonists. The role of the Iroquois in providing essential military aid to the colonists helped to solidify their developing alliance with the government of New York. Together, colonial and Indian forces inflicted devastating punishment on the rebels. Metacom was executed, Indian villages were destroyed, and captives were killed or sold into slavery in the West Indies. Both sides committed atrocities in this merciless conflict, but in its aftermath the image of Indians as bloodthirsty savages became firmly entrenched in the New England mind.

In the long run, **King Philip's War** produced a broadening of freedom for white New Englanders by expanding their access to land. But this freedom rested on the final dispossession of the region's Indians.

FOCUS QUESTIONS

- *How did the English empire in America expand in the mid-seventeenth century?*

- *How was slavery established in the Western Atlantic world?*

- *What major social and political crises rocked the colonies in the late seventeenth century?*

- *What were the directions of social and economic change in the eighteenth-century colonies?*

- *How did patterns of class and gender roles change in eighteenth-century America?*

GLOBAL COMPETITION AND THE EXPANSION OF ENGLAND'S EMPIRE

The Mercantilist System

By the middle of the seventeenth century, it was apparent that the colonies could be an important source of wealth for England. According to the prevailing theory known as **mercantilism**, governments should regulate economic activity so as to promote national power. They should encourage manufacturing and commerce by special bounties, monopolies, and other measures. Above all, trade should be controlled so that more gold and silver flowed into countries than left them. That is, exports of goods, which generated revenue from abroad, should exceed imports, which required paying foreigners for their products. In the mercantilist outlook, the role

The role of colonies

of colonies was to serve the interests of the mother country by producing marketable raw materials and importing manufactured goods from home. "Foreign trade," declared an influential work written in 1664 by a London merchant, formed the basis of "England's treasure." Commerce, not territorial plunder, was the foundation of empire.

Parliament in 1651 passed the first **Navigation Act**, which aimed to wrest control of world trade from the Dutch, whose merchants profited from free trade with all parts of the world and all existing empires. Additional measures followed in 1660 and 1663. According to the Navigation laws, cer-

"Enumerated" goods

tain "enumerated" goods—essentially, the most valuable colonial products, such as tobacco and sugar—had to be transported in English ships and sold initially in English ports, although they could then be re-exported to foreign markets. Similarly, most European goods imported into the colonies had to be shipped through England, where customs duties were paid. This enabled English merchants, manufacturers, shipbuilders, and sailors to reap the benefits of colonial trade, and the government to enjoy added income from taxes. As members of the empire, American colonies would profit as well, since their ships were considered English. Indeed, the Navigation Acts stimulated the rise of New England's shipbuilding industry.

The Conquest of New Netherland

The restoration of the English monarchy when Charles II assumed the throne in 1660 sparked a new period of colonial expansion. The govern-

Colonial expansion

ment chartered new trading ventures, notably the Royal African Company, which was given a monopoly of the slave trade. Within a generation, the number of English colonies in North America doubled.

First to come under English control was New Netherland, seized in 1664 during an Anglo-Dutch war that also saw England gain control of Dutch trading posts in Africa. Charles II awarded the colony to his younger brother James, the duke of York, with "full and absolute power" to govern as

English rule in New York

he pleased. (Hence the colony's name became New York.) English rule transformed this minor military base into an important imperial outpost, a seaport trading with the Caribbean and Europe, and a launching pad for military operations against the French. New York's European population, around 9,000 when the English assumed control, rose to 20,000 by 1685.

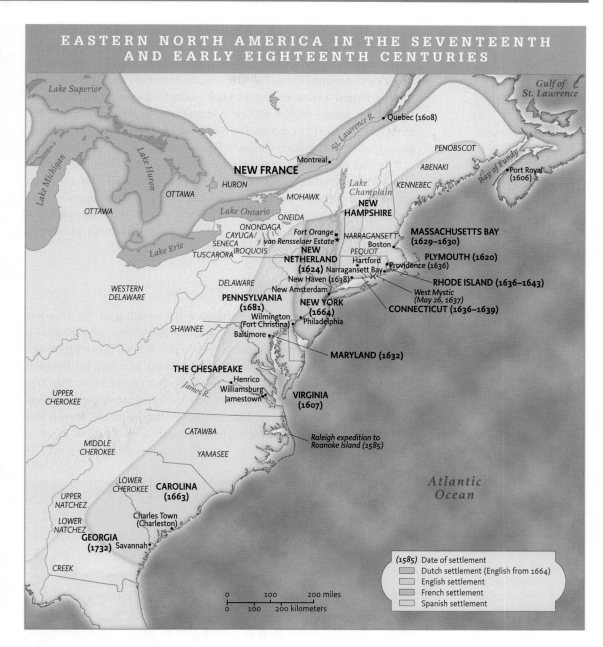

EASTERN NORTH AMERICA IN THE SEVENTEENTH AND EARLY EIGHTEENTH CENTURIES

By the early eighteenth century, numerous English colonies populated eastern North America, while the French had established their own presence to the north and west.

English rule expanded the freedom of some New Yorkers, while reducing that of others. The terms of surrender guaranteed that the English would respect the religious beliefs and property holdings of the colony's many ethnic communities. But English law ended the Dutch tradition by which married women conducted business in their own name. There had been many female traders in New Amsterdam, but few remained by the end of the seventeenth century. The English, in a reversal of Dutch practice, also expelled free blacks from many skilled jobs.

English rule and blacks

Others benefited enormously from English rule. The duke of York and his appointed governors continued the Dutch practice of awarding immense land grants to favorites. By 1700, nearly 2 million acres of land were owned by only five New York families who intermarried regularly, exerted considerable political influence, and formed one of colonial America's most tightly knit landed elites.

New York and the Indians

Initially, English rule also strengthened the position of the Iroquois Confederacy of upstate New York. Sir Edmund Andros, who had been appointed governor of New York after fighting the French in the Caribbean, formed an alliance known as the **Covenant Chain**, in which the imperial ambitions of the English and Indians reinforced one another. The Five (later Six) Iroquois Nations assisted Andros in clearing parts of New York of rival tribes and helped the British in attacks on the French and their Indian allies. Andros, for his part, recognized the Iroquois claim to

The Iroquois Nations

An engraving representing the Grand Council of the Iroquois Nations of the area of present-day upstate New York. From a book about American Indians published in Paris by a Jesuit missionary, who depicts the Indians in the attire of ancient Romans. Note the prevalence of wampum belts in the image, in the foreground and in the hand and at the feet of the central figure. Wampum was used to certify treaties and other transactions.

authority over Indian communities in the vast area stretching to the Ohio River. But beginning in the 1680s, Indians around the Great Lakes and Ohio Valley regrouped and with French aid attacked the Iroquois, pushing them to the east. By the end of the century, the Iroquois Nations adopted a policy of careful neutrality, seeking to play the European empires off one another while continuing to profit from the fur trade.

The Charter of Liberties

Many New York colonists, meanwhile, began to complain that they were being denied the "liberties of Englishmen," especially the right to consent to taxation. In 1683, the duke of York agreed to call an elected assembly, whose first act was to draft a Charter of Liberties and Privileges. The charter required that elections be held every three years among male property owners and the freemen of New York City; it also reaffirmed traditional English rights such as trial by jury and security of property, as well as religious toleration for all Protestants.

English rights

The Founding of Carolina

For more than three decades after the establishment of Maryland in 1632, no new English settlement was planted in North America. Then, in 1663, Charles II awarded to eight proprietors the right to establish a colony to the north of Florida, as a barrier to Spanish expansion. Not until 1670 did the first settlers arrive to found Carolina. In its early years, Carolina was the "colony of a colony," an offshoot of the tiny island of Barbados. In the mid-seventeenth century, Barbados was the Caribbean's richest plantation economy, but a shortage of available land led wealthy planters to seek opportunities in Carolina for their sons. At first, Carolinians armed friendly Indians, employing them on raids into Spanish Florida, and enslaved others, shipping them to other mainland colonies and the West Indies. Between 1670 and 1720, the number of Indian slaves exported from Charleston was larger than the number of African slaves imported. In 1715, the Yamasee and Creek rebelled, but the **Yamasee uprising** was crushed, and most of the remaining Indians were enslaved or driven out of the colony into Spanish Florida.

Carolina as a barrier to Spanish expansion

The Fundamental Constitutions of Carolina, issued by the proprietors in 1669, proposed to establish a feudal society with a hereditary nobility, serfs, and slaves. Needing to attract settlers quickly, however, the proprietors also provided for an elected assembly and religious toleration—by now recognized as essential to enticing migrants to North America. They also instituted a generous headright system, offering 150 acres for each

The Fundamental Constitutions of Carolina

member of an arriving family (in the case of indentured servants, of course, the land went to the employer) and 100 acres to male servants who completed their terms.

Rights of slaveholders

The proprietors instituted a rigorous legal code that promised slave-owners "absolute power and authority" over their human property and included imported slaves in the headright system. This allowed any persons who settled in Carolina and brought with them slaves instantly to acquire large new landholdings. In its early days, however, the economy centered on cattle raising and trade with local Indians. Carolina grew slowly until planters discovered the staple—rice—that would make them the wealthiest elite in English North America and their colony an epicenter of mainland slavery.

The Holy Experiment

The last English colony to be established in the seventeenth century was Pennsylvania in 1681. The proprietor, William Penn, envisioned it as a place where those facing religious persecution in Europe could enjoy spiritual freedom, and colonists and Indians would coexist in harmony.

William Penn

A devout member of the **Society of Friends (Quakers)**, Penn was particularly concerned with establishing a refuge for his coreligionists, who faced increasing persecution in England. He had already assisted a group of English Quakers in purchasing half of what became the colony of New Jersey from Lord John Berkeley, who had received a land grant from the duke of York. Penn was largely responsible for the frame of government announced in 1677, the West Jersey Concessions, which created an elected assembly with a broad suffrage and established religious liberty.

A Quaker Meeting, a painting by an unidentified British artist, dating from the late eighteenth or early nineteenth century. It illustrates the prominent place of women in Quaker gatherings.

Like the Puritans, Penn considered his colony a "holy experiment," but of a different kind—"a free colony for all mankind that should go hither." He hoped that Pennsylvania could be governed according to Quaker principles, among them the equality of all persons (including women, blacks, and Indians) before God and the primacy of the individual conscience. To Quakers, liberty was a universal entitlement, not the possession of any single people—a position that would eventually make them the first group of whites to repudiate slavery. Penn also treated Indians with a consideration unique in the colonial experience, purchasing land before reselling it to colonists and offering refuge to tribes driven out of other colonies by warfare. Since Quakers were pacifists who came to America unarmed and did not even organize a militia until the 1740s, peace with the native population was essential.

Religious freedom was Penn's most fundamental principle. His Charter of Liberty, approved by the assembly in 1682, offered "Christian liberty" to all who affirmed a belief in God and did not use their freedom to promote "licentiousness." There was no established church in Pennsylvania, and attendance at religious services was entirely voluntary, although Jews were barred from office by a required oath affirming belief in the divinity of Jesus Christ. At the same time, the Quakers upheld a strict code of personal morality. Penn's Frame of Government prohibited swearing, drunkenness, and adultery. Not religious uniformity but a virtuous citizenry would be the foundation of Penn's social order.

Penn and religious liberty

Land in Pennsylvania

Given the power to determine the colony's form of government, Penn established an appointed council to originate legislation and an assembly elected by male taxpayers and "freemen" (owners of 100 acres of land for free immigrants and 50 acres for former indentured servants). These rules made a majority of the male population eligible to vote. Penn owned all the colony's land and sold it to settlers at low prices, which helped the colony prosper. Pennsylvania's religious toleration, healthy climate, and inexpensive land, along with Penn's aggressive efforts to publicize the colony's advantages, soon attracted immigrants from all over western Europe.

Pennsylvania's elected government

Ironically, the freedoms Pennsylvania offered to European immigrants contributed to the deterioration of freedom for others. The colony's successful efforts to attract settlers would eventually come into conflict with Penn's benevolent Indian policy. And the opening of Pennsylvania caused fewer indentured servants to choose Virginia and Maryland, a development that did much to shift those colonies toward reliance on slave labor.

Freedoms in Pennsylvania

ORIGINS OF AMERICAN SLAVERY

The incessant demand for workers spurred by the spread of tobacco cultivation eventually led Chesapeake planters to turn to the transatlantic trade in slaves. Compared with indentured servants, slaves offered planters many advantages. As Africans, they could not claim the protections of English common law. Slaves' terms of service never expired, and they therefore did not become a population of unruly landless men. Their children were slaves, and their skin color made it more difficult for them to

The turn to slavery

escape into the surrounding society. African men, moreover, unlike their Native American counterparts, were accustomed to intensive agricultural labor, and they had encountered many diseases known in Europe and developed resistance to them, so were less likely to succumb to epidemics.

Englishmen and Africans

English views of alien peoples

The English had long viewed alien peoples with disdain, including the Irish, Native Americans, and Africans. They described these strangers in remarkably similar language as savage, pagan, and uncivilized. "Race"—the idea that humanity is divided into well-defined groups associated with skin color—is a modern concept that had not fully developed in the seventeenth century. Nor had "racism"—an ideology based on the belief that some races are inherently superior to others and entitled to rule over them.

Nonetheless, anti-black stereotypes flourished in seventeenth-century England. Africans were seen as so alien—in color, religion, and social practices—that they were "enslavable" in a way that poor Englishmen were not. Most English also deemed Indians to be uncivilized. But the Indian population declined so rapidly, and it was so easy for Indians, familiar with the countryside, to run away, that Indian slavery never became viable in the Atlantic colonies.

In *Free Women of Color with Their Children and Servants in a Landscape*, Agostino Brunias, an Italian artist who was sent to the West Indies by the British government in the 1760s to paint the local population, portrays an outing of fashionable free women with their children and slaves, some dressed in livery. Although the scene depicted is in the Caribbean, the work resembles numerous paintings of the leisure activities of the well-to-do in Britain. The painting reflects the three-race system that developed in the British Caribbean—the free women are light-skinned but not white. The woman at the center looks directly at the viewer, emphasizing her aristocratic bearing.

Slavery in History

Slavery has existed for nearly the entire span of human history. It was central to the societies of ancient Greece and Rome. In the Mediterranean world, a slave trade in Slavic peoples survived into the fifteenth century. (The English word "slavery" derives from "Slav.") In West Africa, as noted in Chapter 1, slavery and a slave trade predated the coming of Europeans, and small-scale slavery existed among Native Americans. But slavery in nearly all these instances differed greatly from the institution that developed in the New World.

In the Americas, slavery was based on the **plantation**, an agricultural enterprise that brought together large numbers of workers under the control of a single owner. This imbalance magnified the possibility of slave resistance and made it necessary to police the system rigidly. Labor on slave plantations was far more demanding than the household slavery common in Africa, and the death rate among slaves much higher. In the New World, slavery would come to be associated with race, a concept that drew a permanent line between whites and blacks.

Slavery in the West Indies

A sense of Africans as alien and inferior made their enslavement by the English possible. But prejudice by itself did not create North American slavery. For this institution to take root, planters and government authorities had to be convinced that importing African slaves was the best way to solve their persistent shortage of labor. During the seventeenth century, the shipping of slaves from Africa to the New World became a major international business. By 1600, huge sugar plantations worked by slaves from Africa had made their appearance in Brazil, a colony of Portugal. In the seventeenth century, England, Holland, Denmark, and France joined Spain as owners of West Indian islands.

Sugar plantations

With the Indian population having been wiped out by disease, and with the white indentured servants unwilling to do the back-breaking, monotonous work of sugar cultivation, the massive importation of slaves from Africa began. On Barbados, for example, the slave population increased from 20,000 to more than 80,000 between 1660 and 1670. By the end of the seventeenth century, huge sugar plantations manned by hundreds of slaves dominated the West Indian economy, and on most of the islands the African population far outnumbered that of European origin.

Sugar was the first crop to be mass-marketed to consumers in Europe. Before its emergence, international trade consisted largely of precious metals like gold and silver, and luxury goods aimed at an elite market, like the spices and silks imported from Asia. Sugar was by far the most important product of the British, French, and Portuguese empires, and New World sugar plantations produced immense profits. Saint Domingue, today's Haiti, was the jewel of the French empire. In 1660, Barbados generated more trade than all the other English colonies combined.

Compared with its rapid introduction in Brazil and the West Indies, slavery developed slowly in North America. Slaves cost more than indentured servants, and the high death rate among tobacco workers

Cutting Sugar Cane, an engraving from *Ten Views in Antigua*, published in 1823. Male and female slaves harvest and load the sugar crop while an overseer on horseback addresses a slave. During the eighteenth century, sugar was the chief crop produced by Western Hemisphere slaves.

made it economically unappealing to pay for a lifetime of labor. As late as 1680, there were only 4,500 blacks in the Chesapeake, a little over 5 percent of the region's population. The most important social distinction in the seventeenth-century Chesapeake was not between black and white but between the white plantation owners who dominated politics and society and everybody else—small farmers, indentured servants, and slaves.

Slavery and the Law

Centuries before the voyages of Columbus, Spain had enacted a series of laws granting slaves certain rights relating to marriage, the holding of property, and access to freedom. These laws were transferred to Spain's American empire. They were often violated but nonetheless gave slaves opportunities to claim rights under the law. The law of slavery in English North America would become far more repressive than in the Spanish empire, especially on the all-important question of whether avenues existed by which slaves could obtain freedom.

For much of the seventeenth century, however, the legal status of Chesapeake blacks remained ambiguous and the line between slavery and freedom more permeable than it would later become. The first Africans, twenty in all, arrived in Virginia in 1619. Although the first black arrivals were almost certainly treated as slaves, it appears that at least some managed to become free after serving a term of years. To be sure, racial distinctions were enacted into law from the outset. As early as the 1620s, the law barred blacks from serving in the Virginia militia. In 1643, a poll tax (a tax levied on individuals) was imposed on African but not white women. In

both Virginia and Maryland, however, free blacks could sue and testify in court, and some even managed to acquire land and purchase white servants or African slaves. Blacks and whites labored side by side in the tobacco fields, sometimes ran away together, and established intimate relationships.

The Rise of Chesapeake Slavery

Not until the 1660s did the laws of Virginia and Maryland refer explicitly to slavery. As tobacco planting spread and the demand for labor increased, the condition of black and white servants diverged sharply. Authorities sought to improve the status of white servants, hoping to counteract the widespread impression in England that Virginia was a death trap. At the same time, access to freedom for blacks receded.

A Virginia law of 1662 provided that in the case of a child one of whose parents was free and one slave, the status of the offspring followed that of the mother. (This provision not only reversed the European practice of defining a child's status through the father but also made the sexual abuse of slave women profitable for slaveholders, since any children that resulted remained the owner's property.) In 1667, the Virginia House of Burgesses decreed that religious conversion did not release a slave from bondage. Thus, Christians could own other Christians as slaves. Authorities also defined all offspring of interracial relationships as illegitimate. By 1680, even though the black population was still small, notions of racial differ-ence were well entrenched in the law. In British North America, unlike the Spanish empire, no distinctive mulatto, or mixed-race, class existed; the law treated everyone with African ancestry as black.

Black slavery

Bacon's Rebellion: Land and Labor in Virginia

Virginia's shift from white indentured servants to African slaves as the main plantation labor force was accelerated by one of the most dramatic confrontations of this era, **Bacon's Rebellion** of 1676. Governor William Berkeley had for thirty years run a corrupt regime in alliance with an inner circle of the colony's wealthiest tobacco planters. He rewarded his followers with land grants and lucrative offices. But as tobacco farming spread inland, planters connected with the governor engrossed the best lands, leaving freed servants (a growing population, since Virginia's death rate was finally fall-ing) with no options but to work as tenants or to move to the frontier. By the 1670s, poverty among whites had reached levels reminiscent of England.

Sir William Berkeley, governor of colonial Virginia, 1641–1652 and 1660–1677, in a portrait by Sir Peter Lely. Berkeley's authoritarian rule helped to spark Bacon's Rebellion.

In addition, the right to vote, previously enjoyed by all adult men, was confined to landowners in 1670. Governor Berkeley maintained peaceful relations with Virginia's remaining native population. His refusal to allow white settlement in areas reserved for Indians angered many land-hungry colonists.

Long-simmering social tensions coupled with widespread resentment against the injustices of the Berkeley regime erupted in Bacon's Rebellion. In 1676, after a minor confrontation between Indians and colo-nists on Virginia's western frontier, settlers demanded that the governor authorize the extermination or removal of the colony's Indians, to open more land for whites. When Berkeley refused, a series of Indian massacres quickly grew into a full-fledged rebellion.

To some extent, Bacon's Rebellion was a conflict within the Virginia elite—between Berkeley's men and the backers of Nathaniel Bacon, a wealthy and ambi-tious planter who disdained Berkeley's cronies. But

VOICES OF FREEDOM

Maryland Act Concerning Negroes and Other Slaves (1664)

Like Virginia, Maryland in the 1660s enacted laws to clarify questions arising from the growing importance of slavery. This law made all black servants in the colony slaves for life, and required any white woman who married a slave to serve her husband's owner until the slave's death.

Be it enacted by the Right Honorable the Lord Proprietary by the advice and consent of the upper and lower house of this present General Assembly, that all Negroes or other slaves already within the province, and all Negroes and other slaves to be hereafter imported into the province, shall serve durante vita [for life]. And all children born of any Negro or other slave shall be slaves as their fathers were, for the term of their lives.

And forasmuch as divers freeborn English women, forgetful of their free condition and to the disgrace of our nation, marry Negro slaves, by which also divers suits may arise touching the issue [children] of such women, and a great damage befalls the masters of such Negroes for prevention whereof, for deterring such freeborn women from such shameful matches. Be it further enacted by the authority, advice, and consent aforesaid, that whatsoever freeborn woman shall marry any slave from and after the last day of this present Assembly shall serve the master of such slave during the life of her husband. And that all the issue of such freeborn women so married shall be slaves as their fathers were. And be it further enacted, that all the issues of English or other freeborn women that have already married Negroes shall serve the masters of their parents till they be thirty years of age and no longer.

From Letter by a Female Indentured Servant (September 22, 1756)

Only a minority of emigrants from Europe to British North America were fully free. Indentured servants were men and women who surrendered their freedom for a specified period of time in exchange for passage to America. The letter by Elizabeth Springs from Maryland to her father in England expresses complaints voiced by many indentured servants.

Honored Father,

My being forever banished from your sight, will I hope pardon the boldness I now take of troubling you with these. My long silence has been purely owing to my undutifulness to you, and well knowing I had offended in the highest degree, put a tie on my tongue and pen, for fear I should be extinct from your good graces and add a further trouble to you. . . .

O Dear Father, believe what I am going to relate the words of truth and sincerity and balance my former bad conduct [to] my sufferings here, and then I am sure you'll pity your distressed daughter. What we unfortunate English people suffer here is beyond the probability of you in England to conceive. Let it suffice that I am one of the unhappy number, am toiling almost day and night, and very often in the horse's drudgery, . . . and then tied up and whipped to that degree that you now serve an animal. Scarce any thing but Indian corn and salt to eat and that even begrudged nay many Negroes are better used, almost naked no shoes nor stockings to wear, and the comfort after slaving during master's pleasure, what rest we can get is to wrap ourselves up in a blanket and lie upon the ground. This is the deplorable condition your poor Betty endures, and now I beg if you have any bowels of compassion left show it by sending me some relief. Clothing is the principal thing wanting, which if you should condescend to, may easily send them to me by any of the ships bound to Baltimore town, Patapsco River, Maryland. And give me leave to conclude in duty to you and uncles and aunts, and respect to all friends. . . . Elizabeth Sprigs.

QUESTIONS

1. *What does the Maryland law tell us about how the consolidation of slavery affected ideas about racial difference?*

2. *Why does Elizabeth Sprigs compare her condition unfavorably to that of blacks?*

3. *What do these documents suggest about the limits of freedom in early colonial America?*

Bacon's call for the removal of all Indians from the colony, a reduction of taxes at a time of economic recession, and an end to rule by "grandees" rapidly gained support from small farmers, landless men, indentured servants, and even some Africans. The bulk of his army consisted of discontented men who had recently been servants.

Bacon's supporters

Bacon promised freedom (including access to Indian lands) to all who joined his ranks. In 1676, Bacon gathered an armed force for an unauthorized and indiscriminate campaign against those he called the governor's "protected and darling Indians." He marched on Jamestown, burning it to the ground. The governor fled, and Bacon became the ruler of Virginia. Only the arrival of a squadron of warships from England restored order.

The specter of a civil war among whites greatly frightened Virginia's ruling elite, who took dramatic steps to consolidate their power and improve their image after Bacon's death in October 1676. They restored property qualifications for voting, which Bacon had rescinded, and reduced taxes. They also adopted a more aggressive Indian policy, opening western areas to small farmers, many of whom prospered from a rise in tobacco prices after 1680. To avert the further growth of a rebellious population of landless former indentured servants, Virginia's authorities accelerated the shift to slaves (who would never become free) on the tobacco plantations.

Effects of Bacon's Rebellion

A Slave Society

Between 1680 and 1700, slave labor began to supplant indentured servitude on Chesapeake plantations. Bacon's Rebellion contributed to this development, but so did other factors. As the death rate began to fall, it became more economical to purchase a laborer for life. Moreover, the Royal Africa Company's monopoly on the English slave trade ended, thus opening the door to other traders and reducing the price of imported African slaves.

The spread of slavery

By 1700, blacks constituted more than 10 percent of Virginia's population. Fifty years later, they made up nearly half. Recognizing the growing importance of slavery, the House of Burgesses in 1705 enacted a new slave code. Slaves were property, completely subject to the will of their masters and, more generally, of the white community. They could be bought and sold, leased, fought over in court, and passed on to one's descendants. Henceforth, blacks and whites were tried in separate courts. No black, free or slave, could own arms, strike a white man, or employ a white servant. Virginia had changed from a "society with slaves," in which slavery was one system of labor among others, to a "slave society," where slavery stood at the center of the economic process.

Slave code of 1705

A scene from King Philip's War, included on a 1675 map of New England.

Throughout history, slaves have run away and in other ways resisted bondage. Colonial newspapers were filled with advertisements for runaway slaves. These notices described the appearance and skills of the fugitive and included such comments as "He has great notions of freedom."

Runaway slaves

COLONIES IN CRISIS

King Philip's War of 1675–1676 and Bacon's Rebellion the following year coincided with disturbances in other colonies. In Maryland, where the proprietor, Lord Baltimore, in 1670 suddenly restricted the right to vote to owners of fifty acres of land or a certain amount of personal property, a Protestant uprising unsuccessfully sought to oust his government and restore the suffrage for all freemen. In several colonies, increasing settlement on the frontier led to resistance by alarmed Indians. The Pueblo Revolt of 1680 (discussed in Chapter 1) indicated that the crisis of colonial authority was not confined to the British empire.

Uprisings

The Glorious Revolution

Turmoil in England also reverberated in the colonies. In 1688, the long struggle for domination of English government between Parliament and the crown reached its culmination in the **Glorious Revolution**, which established parliamentary supremacy once and for all and secured the

Parliamentary supremacy

Protestant succession to the throne. When Charles II died in 1685, he was succeeded by his brother James II (formerly the duke of York), a practicing Catholic and a believer that kings ruled by divine right. In 1687, James decreed religious toleration for both Protestant Dissenters and Catholics. The following year, the birth of James's son raised the alarming prospect of a Catholic succession. A group of English aristocrats invited the Dutch nobleman William of Orange, the husband of James's Protestant daughter Mary, to assume the throne in the name of English liberties. As the landed elite and leaders of the Anglican Church rallied to William's cause, James II fled and the revolution was complete.

Unlike the broad social upheaval that marked the English Civil War of the 1640s, the Glorious Revolution was in effect a coup engineered by a group of aristocrats in alliance with an ambitious Dutch prince. But the overthrow of James II entrenched more firmly than ever the notion that liberty was the birthright of all Englishmen and that the king was subject to the rule of law. To justify the ouster of James II, Parliament in 1689 enacted an **English Bill of Rights**, which listed parliamentary powers such as control over taxation as well as rights of individuals, including trial by jury. In the same year, the Toleration Act allowed Protestant Dissenters (but not Catholics) to worship freely, although only Anglicans could hold public office.

Liberty as the birthright of all Englishmen

As always, British politics were mirrored in the American colonies. After the Glorious Revolution, Protestant domination was secured in most of the colonies, while Catholics and Dissenters suffered various forms of discrimination. Throughout English America the Glorious Revolution powerfully reinforced among the colonists the sense of sharing a proud legacy of freedom and Protestantism with the mother country.

Effects of the Glorious Revolution

The Glorious Revolution in America

The Glorious Revolution exposed fault lines in colonial society and offered local elites an opportunity to regain authority that had recently been challenged. Until the mid-1670s, the North American colonies had essentially governed themselves, with little interference from England. Governor Berkeley ran Virginia as he saw fit; proprietors in New York, Maryland, and Carolina governed in any fashion they could persuade colonists to accept; and New England colonies elected their own officials and openly flouted trade regulations. In 1675, however, England established the **Lords of Trade** to oversee colonial affairs. Three years later, the Lords questioned the Massachusetts government about its compliance with the Navigation Acts. They received the surprising reply that since the colony had no representatives in Parliament, the acts did not apply to it unless the Massachusetts General Court approved.

English oversight

In the 1680s, England moved to reduce colonial autonomy. Shortly before his death, James II between 1686 and 1689 combined Connecticut, Plymouth, Massachusetts, New Hampshire, Rhode Island, New York, and East and West Jersey into a single super-colony, the **Dominion of New England**. It was ruled by the former New York governor Sir Edmund Andros, who did not have to answer to an elected assembly. These events reinforced the impression that James II was an enemy of freedom.

English authority and colonial autonomy

In 1689, news of the overthrow of James II triggered rebellions in several American colonies. In April, the Boston militia seized and jailed Edmund Andros and other officials, whereupon the New England colonies reestablished the governments abolished when the Dominion of New England was created. In May, a rebel militia headed by Captain Jacob Leisler established a Committee of Safety and took control of New York. Two months later, Maryland's Protestant Association overthrew the government of the colony's Catholic proprietor, Lord Baltimore.

Rebellions in American colonies

All of these new regimes claimed to have acted in the name of English liberties and looked to London for approval. But the degrees of success of these coups varied markedly. Concluding that Lord Baltimore had mismanaged the Maryland colony, William revoked his charter (although the proprietor retained his land and rents) and established a new, Protestant-dominated government. In 1715, after the Baltimore family had converted to Anglicanism, proprietary power was restored. But the events of 1689 transformed the ruling group in Maryland and put an end to the colony's unique history of religious toleration.

The outcome in New York was far different. Although it was not his intention, Jacob Leisler's regime divided the colony along ethnic and economic lines. Members of the Dutch majority reclaimed local power after more than two decades of English rule, while bands of rebels ransacked the homes of wealthy New Yorkers. William refused to recognize Leisler's authority and dispatched a new governor, backed by troops. Many of Leisler's followers were imprisoned, and he himself was executed. For generations, the rivalry between Leisler and anti-Leisler parties polarized New York politics.

Turmoil in New York

The New England colonies, after deposing Governor Andros, lobbied hard in London for the restoration of their original charters. Most were successful, but Massachusetts was not. In 1691, the crown issued a new charter that absorbed Plymouth into Massachusetts and transformed the political structure of the Bible Commonwealth. Town government remained intact, but henceforth property ownership, not church membership, would be the requirement to vote in elections for the General Court. The governor was now appointed in London rather than elected. Massachusetts became a royal colony, the majority of whose voters were no

Political change in Massachusetts

longer Puritan "saints." Moreover, it was required to abide by the **English Toleration Act** of 1690—that is, to allow all Protestants to worship freely.

These events produced an atmosphere of considerable tension in Massachusetts, exacerbated by raids by French troops and their Indian allies on the northern New England frontier. The advent of religious toleration heightened anxieties among the Puritan clergy, who considered other Protestant denominations a form of heresy. Indeed, not a few Puritans thought they saw the hand of Satan in the events of 1690 and 1691.

The Salem Witch Trials

Belief in witchcraft

Belief in magic, astrology, and witchcraft was widespread in seventeenth-century Europe and America, existing alongside the religious beliefs sanctioned by the clergy and churches. Witches were individuals, usually women, who were accused of having entered into a pact with the devil to obtain supernatural powers, which they used to harm others or to interfere with natural processes. When a child was stillborn or crops failed, many believed that witchcraft was at work.

In Europe and the colonies, witchcraft was punishable by execution. It is estimated that between the years 1400 and 1800, more than 50,000 people were executed in Europe after being convicted of witchcraft. Witches were, from time to time, hanged in seventeenth-century New England. Most were women beyond childbearing age who were outspoken, economically independent, or estranged from their husbands, or who in other ways violated traditional gender norms.

Until 1692, the prosecution of witches had been sporadic. But in that year, a series of trials and executions took place in Salem, Massachusetts, that made its name to this day a byword for fanaticism and persecution. The **Salem witch trials** began when several young girls began to suffer fits and nightmares, attributed by their elders to witchcraft. Soon, three "witches" had been named, including Tituba, an Indian from the Caribbean who was a slave in the home of one of the girls. Since the only way to avoid prosecution was to confess and name others, accusations of witchcraft began to snowball. By the middle of 1692, hundreds of residents of Salem had come forward to accuse their neighbors. Although many of the accused confessed to save their lives, fourteen women and five men were hanged, protesting their innocence to the end.

An engraving from Ralph Gardiner's *England's Grievance Discovered*, published in 1655, depicts women hanged as witches in England. The letters identify local officials: A is the hangman, B the town crier, C the sheriff, and D a magistrate.

As accusations and executions multiplied, it became clear that something was seriously wrong with the colony's system of justice. The governor of Massachusetts dissolved the Salem court and ordered the remaining prisoners released. The events in Salem discredited the tradition of prosecuting witches and encouraged prominent colonists to seek scientific explanations for natural events such as comets and illnesses, rather than attribute them to magic.

THE GROWTH OF COLONIAL AMERICA

As stability returned after the crises of the late seventeenth century, English North America experienced an era of remarkable growth. Between 1700 and 1770, crude backwoods settlements became bustling provincial capitals. The hazards of disease among colonists diminished, agricultural settlement pressed westward, and hundreds of thousands of newcomers arrived from the Old World. Thanks to a high birthrate and continuing immigration, the population of England's mainland colonies, 265,000 in 1700, grew nearly tenfold, to over 2.3 million seventy years later. (It is worth noting, however, that because of the decline suffered by the Indians, the North American population was considerably lower in 1770 than it had been in 1492.)

Population increase

A Diverse Population

Probably the most striking characteristic of colonial American society in the eighteenth century was its sheer diversity. In 1700, the colonies were essentially English outposts. In the eighteenth century, African and non-English European arrivals skyrocketed, while the number emigrating from England declined.

African and non-English arrivals surge

About 40 percent of European immigrants to the colonies during the eighteenth century continued to arrive as bound laborers who had temporarily sacrificed their freedom to make the voyage to the New World. But as the colonial economy prospered, poor indentured migrants were increasingly joined by professionals and skilled craftsmen—teachers, ministers, weavers, carpenters—whom England could ill afford to lose. This brought to an end official efforts to promote English emigration.

End of official English emigration efforts

Nevertheless, the government in London remained convinced that colonial development enhanced the nation's power and wealth. To bolster the Chesapeake labor force, nearly 50,000 convicts were sent to work in the tobacco fields. Officials also encouraged Protestant immigration from

TABLE 3.1   Origins and Status of Migrants to British North American Colonies, 1700–1775

	TOTAL	SLAVES	INDENTURED SERVANTS	CONVICTS	FREE
Africa	278,400	278,400	—	—	—
Ireland	108,600	—	39,000	17,500	52,100
Germany	84,500	—	30,000	—	54,500
England/Wales	73,100	—	27,200	32,500	13,400
Scotland	35,300	—	7,400	2,200	25,700
Other	5,900	—	—	—	5,900
Total	585,800	278,400	103,600	52,200	151,600

the non-English parts of the British Isles and from the European continent, promising newcomers access to land and the right to worship freely.

Among eighteenth-century migrants from the British Isles, the 70,000 English newcomers were considerably outnumbered by 145,000 from Scotland and Ulster, the northern part of Ireland, where many Scots had settled as part of England's effort to subdue the island. Mostly Presbyterians, they added significantly to religious diversity in North America.

The German Migration

Germans the largest group of newcomers from Europe

Germans, 85,000 in all, formed the largest group of newcomers from the European continent. In the eighteenth century, Germany was divided into numerous small states, each with a ruling prince who determined the official religion. Those who found themselves worshiping the "wrong" religion—Lutherans in Catholic areas, Catholics in Lutheran areas, and everywhere, followers of small Protestant sects such as Mennonites, Moravians, and Dunkers—faced persecution. Many decided to emigrate. Other migrants were motivated by persistent agricultural crises and the difficulty of acquiring land.

English and Dutch merchants created a well-organized system whereby **redemptioners** (as indentured families were called) received passage in exchange for a promise to work off their debt in America. Most settled in frontier areas—rural New York, western Pennsylvania, and the southern backcountry—where they formed tightly knit farming communities in which German remained the dominant language.

German settlements

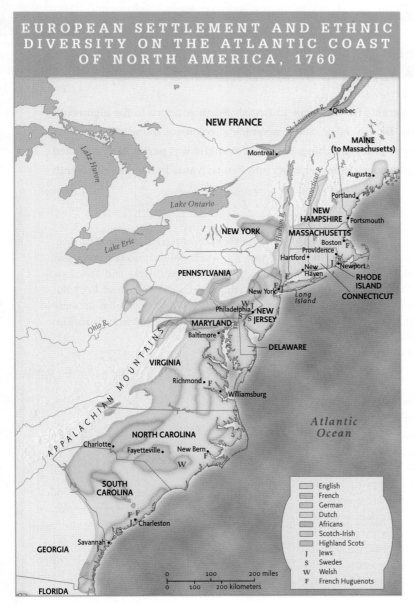

EUROPEAN SETTLEMENT AND ETHNIC DIVERSITY ON THE ATLANTIC COAST OF NORTH AMERICA, 1760

Among the most striking features of eighteenth-century colonial society was the racial and ethnic diversity of the population (except in New England). This resulted from increased immigration from the non-English parts of the British Isles and from mainland Europe, as well as the rapid expansion of the slave trade from Africa.

Religious Diversity

Eighteenth-century British America was not a "melting pot" of cultures. Ethnic groups tended to live and worship in relatively homogeneous communities. But outside of New England, which received few immigrants and retained its overwhelmingly English ethnic character, American society

American society more diverse than Britain

From Benjamin Franklin, *Observations Concerning the Increase of Mankind* (1751)

Only a minority of immigrants from Europe to British North America in the eighteenth century came from the British Isles. Some prominent colonists found the growing diversity of the population quite disturbing. Benjamin Franklin was particularly troubled by the large influx of newcomers from Germany into Pennsylvania in the mid-eighteenth century.

Why should the Palatine [German] boors be suffered to swarm into our settlements, and by herding together establish their language and manners to the exclusion of ours? Why should Pennsylvania, founded by the English, become a Colony of *Aliens*, who will shortly be so numerous as to Germanize us instead of our Anglifying them, and will never adopt our language or customs, any more than they can acquire our complexion?

Which leads me to add one remark: That the number of purely white people in the world is proportionably very small. All Africa is black or tawny. Asia chiefly tawny. America (exclusive of the newcomers) wholly so. And in Europe, the Spaniards, Italians, French, Russians and Swedes, are generally of what we call a swarthy complexion; as are the Germans also, the Saxons only excepted, who with the English, make the principal body of white people on the face of the earth. I could wish their numbers were increased. And while we are, as I may call it, *scouring* our planet, by clearing America of woods, and so making this side of our globe reflect a brighter light to the eyes of inhabitants in Mars or Venus, why should we . . . darken its people? Why increase the sons of Africa, by planting them in America, where we have so fair an opportunity, by excluding all Blacks and Tawneys, of increasing the lovely White and Red? But perhaps I am partial to the complexion of my country, for such kind of partiality is natural to mankind.

QUESTIONS

1. *What is Franklin's objection to the growing German presence?*

2. *What does Franklin's characterization of the complexions of various groups suggest about the reliability of his perceptions of non-English peoples?*

had a far more diverse population than Britain. Nowhere was this more evident than in the practice of religion.

Apart from New Jersey (formed from East and West Jersey in 1702), Rhode Island, and Pennsylvania, the colonies did not adhere to a modern separation of church and state. Nearly every colony levied taxes to pay the salaries of ministers of an established church, and most barred Catholics and Jews from voting and holding public office. But increasingly, de facto toleration among Protestant denominations flourished. By the mid-eighteenth century, dissenting Protestants in most colonies had gained the right to worship as they pleased and own their churches, although many places still barred them from holding public office and taxed them to support the official church. A visitor to Pennsylvania in 1750 described the colony's religious diversity: "We find there Lutherans, Reformed, Catholics, Quakers, Menonists or Anabaptists, Herrnhuters or Moravian Brethren, Pietists, Seventh Day Baptists, Dunkers, Presbyterians, . . . Jews, Mohammedans, Pagans."

Protestants

Indian Life in Transition

The tide of newcomers, who equated liberty with secure possession of land, threatened to engulf the surviving Indian populations. By the eighteenth century, Indian societies that had existed for centuries had disappeared, the victims of disease and warfare, and the communities that remained were well integrated into the British imperial system. Indeed, Indian warriors did much of the fighting in the century's imperial wars. Few Indians chose to live among whites rather than in their own communities. But they had become well accustomed to using European products such as knives, hatchets, needles, kettles, and firearms. Alcohol introduced by traders created social chaos in many Indian communities. One Cherokee told the governor of South Carolina in 1753, "The clothes we wear, we cannot make ourselves. . . . We use their ammunition with which we kill deer. . . . Every necessary thing we must have from the white people."

Indians and European empire

While traders saw in Indian villages potential profits and British officials saw allies against France and Spain, farmers and planters viewed Indians as little more than an obstacle to their desire for land. They expected Indians to give way to white settlers. In Pennsylvania, for example, the flood of German and Scotch-Irish settlers into the backcountry upset the relatively peaceful Indian–white relations constructed by William Penn. The infamous **Walking Purchase** of 1737 brought the fraudulent dealing so common in other colonies to Pennsylvania. The Lenni Lanape Indians agreed to cede a tract of land bounded by the distance a man could walk in thirty-six hours. To their amazement, Governor James Logan hired a team of swift runners, who marked out an area far in excess of

America was often depicted as a Native American in the colonial era, as in this print from the first half of the eighteenth century.

AMERICA.

William Penn's Treaty with the Indians. Penn's grandson, Thomas, the proprietor of Pennsylvania, commissioned this romanticized painting from the artist Benjamin West in 1771, by which time harmony between Indians and colonists had long since turned to hostility. In the nineteenth century, many reproductions of this image circulated, reminding Americans that Indians had once been central figures in their history.

what the Indians had anticipated. By 1760, when Pennsylvania's population, a mere 20,000 in 1700, had grown to 220,000, Indian-colonist relations, initially the most harmonious in British North America, had become poisoned by suspicion and hostility.

Regional Diversity

By the mid-eighteenth century, the different regions of the British colonies had developed distinct economic and social orders. Small farms tilled by family labor and geared primarily to production for local consumption predominated in New England and the new settlements of the **backcountry** (the area stretching from central Pennsylvania southward through the Shenandoah Valley of Virginia and into upland North and South Carolina). The backcountry was the most rapidly growing region in North America. By the eve of the American Revolution, it contained one-quarter of Virginia's population and half of South Carolina's. Most were farm families raising grain and livestock.

In the older portions of the Middle Colonies of New York, New Jersey, and Pennsylvania, farmers were more oriented to commerce than on the frontier. They grew grain both for their own use and for sale abroad and supplemented the work of family members by employing wage laborers, tenants, and in some instances slaves. With its fertile soil, favorable climate, initially peaceful Indian relations, generous governmental land distribution policy, and rivers that facilitated long-distance trading, Pennsylvania came to be known as "the best poor man's country." Ordinary colonists there enjoyed a standard of living unimaginable in Europe.

The Consumer Revolution

Inexpensive consumer goods

During the eighteenth century, Great Britain eclipsed the Dutch as the leading producer and trader of inexpensive consumer goods, including colonial products like coffee and tea, and such manufactured goods as linen, metalware, pins, ribbons, glassware, ceramics, and clothing. Trade integrated the British empire. The American colonies shared in the era's consumer revolution. In port cities and small inland towns, shops proliferated and American newspapers were filled with advertisements for British goods.

Consumerism in a modern sense—the mass production, advertising, and sale of consumer goods—did not exist in colonial America. Nonetheless, even modest farmers and artisans owned books, ceramic plates, metal cutlery, and items made of imported silk and cotton. Tea, once a luxury enjoyed only by the wealthy, became virtually a necessity of life.

Colonial Cities

Colonial cities like Boston, New York, Philadelphia, and Charleston were quite small by the standards of Europe or Spanish America. In 1700, when the population of Mexico City stood at 100,000, Boston had 6,000 residents and New York 4,500.

English American cities were mainly gathering places for agricultural goods and for imported items to be distributed to the countryside. Nonetheless, the expansion of trade encouraged the rise of port cities, home to a growing population of colonial merchants and artisans (skilled craftsmen) as well as an increasing number of poor. In 1770, with some 30,000 inhabitants, Philadelphia was "the capital of the New World," at least its British component, and, after London and Liverpool, the empire's third busiest port. The financial, commercial, and cultural center of British America, Philadelphia founded its growth on economic integration with the rich agricultural region nearby. Philadelphia merchants organized the collection of farm goods, supplied rural storekeepers, and extended credit to consumers. They exported flour, bread, and meat to the West Indies and Europe.

The rise of port cities

The city was also home to a large population of furniture makers, jewelers, and silversmiths serving wealthier citizens, and hundreds of lesser artisans like weavers, blacksmiths, coopers, and construction workers. The typical artisan owned his own tools and labored in a small workshop, often his home, assisted by family members and young journeymen and apprentices learning the trade. The artisan's skill gave him a far greater degree of economic freedom than those dependent on others for a livelihood.

Despite the influx of British goods, American craftsmen benefited from the expanding consumer market. Most journeymen enjoyed a reasonable chance of rising to the status of master and establishing workshops of their own.

American craftsmen and the expanding consumer market

An Atlantic World

People, ideas, and goods flowed back and forth across the Atlantic, knitting together the empire and its diverse populations and creating webs of interdependence among the European empires. As trade expanded, the North American and West Indian colonies became the major overseas market for British manufactured goods. Although most colonial output was consumed at home, North Americans shipped farm products to Britain, the West Indies, and, with the exception of goods like tobacco "enumerated" under the Navigation Acts, outside the empire. Virtually the entire Chesapeake tobacco crop was marketed in Britain, with most of it then

Trade in the Atlantic world

re-exported to Europe by British merchants. Most of the bread and flour exported from the colonies was destined for the West Indies. African slaves there grew sugar that could be distilled into rum, a product increasingly popular among both North American colonists and Indians, who obtained it by trading furs and deerskins that were then shipped to Europe. The mainland colonies carried on a flourishing trade in fish and grains with southern Europe. Ships built in New England made up one-third of the British empire's trading fleet.

Membership in the empire had many advantages for the colonists. Most Americans did not complain about British regulation of their trade because commerce enriched the colonies as well as the mother country and lax enforcement of the Navigation Acts allowed smuggling to flourish. In a dangerous world, moreover, the Royal Navy protected American shipping. Eighteenth-century English America drew closer to, and in some ways became more similar to, the mother country across the Atlantic.

SOCIAL CLASSES IN THE COLONIES

The Colonial Elite

Most free Americans benefited from economic growth, but as colonial society matured an elite emerged that, while neither as powerful nor as wealthy as the aristocracy of England, increasingly dominated politics and society. In New England and the Middle Colonies, expanding trade made possible the emergence of a powerful upper class of merchants, often linked by family or commercial ties to great trading firms in London. By 1750, the Chesapeake and Lower South were dominated by slave plantations producing **staple crops**, especially tobacco and rice, for the world market. Here great planters accumulated enormous wealth. The colonial elite also included the rulers of proprietary colonies like Pennsylvania and Maryland.

America had no titled aristocracy as in Britain. But throughout British America, men of prominence controlled colonial government. In Virginia, the upper class was so tightly knit and intermarried so often that the colony was said to be governed by a "cousinocracy." Nearly every Virginian of note achieved prominence through family connections. Thomas Jefferson's grandfather was a justice of the

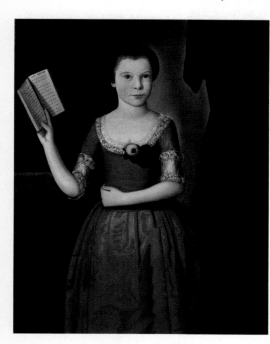

This portrait of Jane Beekman—daughter of James Beekman, one of the wealthiest colonists—was painted by the artist John Durand in 1767. It is unusual in depicting a young girl with a book (a collection, in Latin, of the works of the Renaissance scholar Erasmus), rather than simply emphasizing fashionable attire. The Beekman family was of Dutch and French Huguenot heritage, and both cultures emphasized the importance of education, including education for women.

peace (an important local official), militia captain, and sheriff, and his father a member of the House of Burgesses. George Washington's father, grandfather, and great-grandfather had been justices of the peace. The Virginia gentry used its control of provincial government to gain possession of large tracts of land as western areas opened for settlement.

The richest group of mainland colonists were South Carolina planters. Like their Virginia counterparts, South Carolina grandees lived a lavish lifestyle amid imported furniture, fine wines, silk clothing, and other items from England. Their wealth enabled them to spend much of their time enjoying the social life of Charleston, the only real urban center south of Philadelphia and the richest city in British North America.

New World Cultures

Before the American Revolution, there was no real "American" identity. In the seventeenth century, the term "Americans" tended to be used to describe Indians rather than colonists. Europeans often depicted the colonies pictorially with an image of a Native American. Many European immigrants maintained traditions, including the use of languages other than English, from their home countries. Some cultures mixed more than others: intermarriage with other groups was more common among Huguenots (French Protestants) than among Jews, for example. Those from the British Isles sought to create a dominant "English" identity in the New World. This involved convincing Britons that the colonists were like themselves.

Many in Great Britain, however, saw the colonists as a collection of convicts, religious dissidents, and impoverished servants. This, in turn, inspired many colonists to assert a claim to Britishness more strongly. They insisted that British identity meant allegiance to certain values, among them free commerce and "English liberty." Yet many colonists saw some people, including American Indians and Africans, as unable to wield the responsibilities of liberty due to their place of birth, culture, or inborn traits. They must be ruled over, not take part in governance.

British identity in the colonies was defined, in part, in opposition to others, including Spanish and French Catholics, Africans, and Native Americans. As early as the late sixteenth century, in his writings on colonization, Richard Hakluyt wrote that there was "no greater glory" than "to conquer the barbarian, to recall the savage and the pagan to civility, to

Robert "King" Carter of Virginia, painted by an unknown artist around 1720. Carter was one of the wealthiest and most influential men in the colonies. At his death he owned 300,000 acres of land and over 700 slaves. He served twice as Speaker of the House of Burgesses and once as governor. He is dressed in the attire of an English gentleman.

Fashionably dressed twelve-year-old Ralph Izard, painted in 1754 by Jeremiah Theus, just before Izard's departure to receive an education in England. The boy had recently inherited a large plantation in South Carolina, upon the death of his parents.

draw the ignorant within the orbit of reason, and to fill with reverence for divinity the godless and the ungodly." But since most Indians preferred to maintain their own cultures and religions, the colonists did not include them in a collective colonial identity. This was a major difference with the Spanish and French New World Empires, where, as noted in Chapter 1, intermarriage and culture exchange between settlers and Indians were far more common.

Anglicization

For much of the eighteenth century, the American colonies had more regular trade and communications with Britain than among themselves. Rather than thinking of themselves as distinctively American, they became more and more English—a process historians call "Anglicization."

Wealthy Americans tried to model their lives on British etiquette and behavior. Somewhat resentful at living in provincial isolation—"at the end of the world," as one Virginia aristocrat put it—they sought to demonstrate their status and legitimacy by importing the latest London fashions and literature, sending their sons to Britain for education, and building homes equipped with fashionable furnishings modeled on the country estates and town houses of the English gentry.

Throughout the colonies, elites emulated what they saw as England's balanced, stable social order. Liberty, in their eyes, meant, in part, the power to rule—the right of those blessed with wealth and prominence to dominate others. They viewed society as a hierarchical structure in which some men were endowed with greater talents than others and were destined to govern. Each place in the hierarchy carried with it different responsibilities, and one's status was revealed in dress, manners, and the splendor of one's home. On both sides of the Atlantic, elites viewed work as something reserved for common folk and slaves. Freedom from labor was the mark of the gentleman.

Poverty in the Colonies

At the other end of the social scale, poverty emerged as a visible feature of eighteenth-century colonial life. Although not considered by most colonists part of their society, the growing number of slaves lived in impoverished conditions. Among free Americans, poverty was hardly as widespread as in Britain, where in the early part of the century between one-quarter and one-half of the people regularly required public assistance. But as the colonial population expanded, access to land diminished rapidly, especially in long-settled areas, forcing many propertyless males to seek work in their region's cities or in other colonies. In colonial cities, the number of propertyless wage earners subsisting at the poverty line steadily increased. Taking the colonies as a whole, half of the wealth at mid-century was concentrated in the hands of the richest 10 percent of the population.

Increase in poverty in eighteenth-century colonies

Attitudes and policies toward poverty in colonial America mirrored British precedents. The better-off colonists generally viewed the poor as lazy, shiftless, and responsible for their own plight. To minimize the burden on taxpayers, poor persons were frequently set to labor in workhouses, where they produced goods that reimbursed authorities for part of their upkeep.

The Middle Ranks

The large majority of free Americans lived between the extremes of wealth and poverty. Along with racial and ethnic diversity, what distinguished the mainland colonies from Europe was the wide distribution of land and the economic autonomy of most ordinary free families. Altogether, perhaps two-thirds of the free male population were farmers who owned their own land.

By the eighteenth century, colonial farm families viewed landownership almost as a right, the social precondition of freedom. They strongly resented efforts, whether by Native Americans, great landlords, or colonial governments, to limit their access to land. A dislike of personal dependence and an understanding of freedom as not relying on others for a livelihood sank deep roots in British North America.

This portrait of the Cheney family by an unknown late-eighteenth-century artist illustrates the high birthrate in colonial America and suggests how many years of a woman's life were spent bearing and raising children.

Women and the Household Economy

In the household economy of eighteenth-century America, the family was the center of economic life. The independence of the small farmer depended in considerable measure on the labor of dependent women and children. "He that hath an industrious family shall soon be rich," declared one colonial saying, and the high birthrate in part reflected the need for as many hands as possible on colonial farms.

As the population grew and the death rate declined, family life stabilized and more marriages became lifetime commitments. Free women were expected to devote their lives to being good wives and mothers. As colonial society became more structured, opportunities that had existed for women in the early period receded. In Connecticut, for example, the courts were informal and unorganized in the seventeenth century, and women often represented themselves. In the eighteenth century, it became necessary to hire a lawyer as one's spokesman in court. Women, barred from practicing as attorneys, disappeared from judicial proceedings. Because of the desperate need for labor in the seventeenth century, men and women both did various kinds of work. In the eighteenth century, the division of labor along gender lines solidified. Women's work was clearly defined, including cooking, cleaning, sewing, making butter, and assisting with agricultural chores. Even as the consumer revolution reduced the demands on many women by making available store-bought goods previously produced at home, women's work seemed to increase. Lower infant mortality meant more time spent in child care and domestic chores.

Division of labor along gender lines

North America at Mid-Century

By the mid-eighteenth century, the area that would become the United States was home to a remarkable diversity of peoples and different kinds of social organization, from Pueblo villages of the Southwest to tobacco plantations of the Chesapeake, towns and small farms of New England, and fur-trading outposts of the northern and western frontier. Elites tied to imperial centers of power dominated the political and economic life of nearly every colony. But large numbers of colonists enjoyed far greater opportunities for freedom—access to the vote, prospects of acquiring land, the right to worship as they pleased, and an escape from oppressive government—than existed in Europe. The colonies' economic growth contributed to a high birthrate, long life expectancy, and expanding demand for consumer goods.

Opportunities for freedom

Yet many others found themselves confined to the partial freedom of indentured servitude or to the complete absence of freedom in slavery. Both timeless longings for freedom and new and unprecedented forms of unfreedom had been essential to the North American colonies' remarkable development.

Freedom and unfreedom

CHAPTER REVIEW AND ONLINE RESOURCES

REVIEW QUESTIONS

1. Both the Puritans and William Penn viewed their colonies as "holy experiments." How did they differ?

2. The textbook states, "Prejudice by itself did not create North American slavery." Examine the economic forces, events, and laws that shaped the experiences of enslaved people.

3. How did English leaders understand the place and role of the American colonies in England's empire?

4. How did King Philip's War, Bacon's Rebellion, and the Salem witch trials illustrate a widespread crisis in British North America in the late seventeenth century?

5. The social structure of the eighteenth-century colonies was growing more open for some but not for others. Consider the statement with respect to men and women, whites and blacks, and rich and poor.

6. By the end of the seventeenth century, commerce was the foundation of empire and the leading cause of competition between European empires. Explain how the North American colonies were directly linked to Atlantic commerce by laws and trade.

7. If you traveled from New England to the South, how would you describe the diversity you saw between the different colonies?

8. What impact did the family's being the center of economic life have on gender relations and the roles of women?

9. Why did the colonists identify themselves as British through the mid-eighteenth century?

KEY TERMS

Metacom (p. 73)
King Philip's War (p. 73)
mercantilism (p. 73)
Navigation Act (p. 74)
Covenant Chain (p. 76)
Yamasee uprising (p. 77)
Society of Friends (Quakers) (p. 78)
plantation (p. 80)
Bacon's Rebellion (p. 83)
Glorious Revolution (p. 87)
English Bill of Rights (p. 88)
Lords of Trade (p. 88)
Dominion of New England (p. 89)
English Toleration Act (p. 90)
Salem witch trials (p. 90)
redemptioners (p. 92)
Walking Purchase (p. 95)
backcountry (p. 96)
staple crops (p. 98)

Go to 🐰 INQUIZITIVE

To see what you know—and learn what you've missed—with personalized feedback along the way.

Visit the *Give Me Liberty!* **Student Site** for primary source documents and images, interactive maps, author videos featuring Eric Foner, and more.

CHAPTER 4

SLAVERY, FREEDOM, AND THE STRUGGLE FOR EMPIRE

★

TO 1763

A MAP of the moſt INHABITED part of VIRGINIA containing the whole PROVINCE of MARYLAND with Part of PENSILVANIA, NEW JERSEY and NORTH CAROLINA. Drawn by Joshua Fry & Peter Jefferson in 1775.

he Right Honourable, George Dunk Earl of Halifax Firſt Lor the Reſt of the Right Honourable and Honourable Commiſsioners, for TRAD This Map is moſt humbly Inſcribed to their Lordſhip By their Lordſhip's

A detail from a 1768 map of Virginia and Maryland depicts a tobacco wharf. A planter negotiates with a merchant or sea captain, while slaves go about their work.

Sometime in the mid-1750s, Olaudah Equiano, the eleven-year-old son of a West African village chief, was kidnapped by slave traders. He soon found himself on a ship headed for Barbados. Equiano was sold to a plantation owner in Virginia and then purchased by a British sea captain, who renamed him Gustavus Vassa. While still a slave, he enrolled in a school in England where he learned to read and write, and then enlisted in the Royal Navy. In 1763, however, Equiano was sold once again and returned to the Caribbean. Three years later, he purchased his freedom. He went on to experience shipwrecks, a colonizing venture in Central America, and even an expedition to the Arctic Circle. Equiano eventually settled in London, and in 1789 he published *The Interesting Narrative of the Life of Olaudah Equiano, or Gustavus Vassa, the African*, which he described as a "history of neither a saint, a hero, nor a tyrant," but of a victim of slavery who through luck or fate ended up more fortunate than most of his people. He condemned the idea that Africans were inferior to Europeans and therefore deserved to be slaves. The book became the era's most widely read account by a slave of his own experiences. Equiano died in 1797.

Recent scholars have suggested that Equiano may have been born in the New World rather than Africa. In either case, while his life was no doubt unusual, it illuminates broad patterns of eighteenth-century American history. As noted in the previous chapter, this was a period of sustained development for British North America. Compared with England and Scotland—united to create Great Britain by the Act of Union of 1707—the colonies were growing much more rapidly.

Ideas, people, and goods flowed back and forth across the ocean. Even as the colonies' populations became more diverse, they were increasingly integrated into the British empire. Their laws and political institutions were extensions of those of Britain, their ideas about society and culture reflected British values, their economies were geared to serving the empire's needs.

Equiano's life also underscores the greatest irony in the history of the eighteenth century—the simultaneous expansion of freedom and slavery. This was the era when the idea of the "freeborn Englishman" became powerfully entrenched in the outlook of both colonists and Britons. More than any other principle, liberty was seen as what made the British empire distinct. Yet the eighteenth century was also the height of the Atlantic slave trade, a commerce increasingly dominated by British merchants and ships. Slavery existed in every colony of British North America. And unlike Equiano, very few slaves were fortunate enough to gain their freedom.

FOCUS QUESTIONS

• How did African slavery differ regionally in eighteenth-century North America?

• What factors led to distinct African-American cultures in the eighteenth century?

• What were the meanings of British liberty in the eighteenth century?

• What concepts and institutions dominated colonial politics in the eighteenth century?

• How did the Great Awakening challenge the religious and social structure of British North America?

• How did the Spanish and French empires in America develop in the eighteenth century?

• What was the impact of the Seven Years' War on imperial and Indian–white relations?

SLAVERY AND EMPIRE

Olaudah Equiano;
or
GUSTAVUS VASSA,
the African?

The frontispiece of Olaudah Equiano's account of his life, the best-known narrative by an eighteenth-century slave. The portrait of Equiano in European dress and holding a Bible challenges stereotypes of blacks as "savages" incapable of becoming civilized.

Of the Africans transported to the New World between 1492 and 1820, more than half arrived between 1700 and 1800. The **Atlantic slave trade** would later be condemned by statesmen and general opinion as a crime against humanity. But in the eighteenth century, it was a regularized business in which European merchants, African traders, and American planters engaged in complex bargaining over human lives, all with the expectation of securing a profit. The slave trade was a vital part of world commerce.

In the British empire of the eighteenth century, free laborers working for wages were atypical and slavery was the norm. The first mass consumer goods in international trade were produced by slaves—sugar, rice, coffee, and tobacco. The rising demand for these products fueled the rapid growth of the Atlantic slave trade.

Atlantic Trade

In the eighteenth century, the Caribbean remained the commercial focus of the British empire and the major producer of revenue for the crown. A series of triangular trading routes crisscrossed the Atlantic, carrying British manufactured goods to Africa and the colonies, colonial products to Europe, and slaves from Africa to the New World. Most colonial vessels, however, went back and forth between cities like New York, Charleston, and Savannah, and to ports in the Caribbean. Merchants in New York, Massachusetts, and Rhode Island participated actively in the slave trade, shipping slaves from Africa to the Caribbean or southern colonies. The slave economies of the West Indies were the largest market for fish, grain, livestock, and lumber exported from New England and the Middle Colonies. In Britain itself, the profits from slavery and the slave trade stimulated the rise of ports such as Liverpool and Bristol and the growth of banking, shipbuilding, and insurance. They also helped to finance the early industrial revolution.

With slavery so central to Atlantic commerce, it should not be surprising that for large numbers of free colonists and Europeans, freedom meant in part the power and right to enslave others. And as slavery became more and more entrenched, so too, as the Quaker abolitionist John Woolman commented in 1762, did "the idea of slavery being connected with the black color, and liberty with the white."

Entrenchment of slavery

Africa and the Slave Trade

A few African societies, like Benin for a time, opted out of the Atlantic slave trade, hoping to avoid the disruptions it inevitably caused. But most African

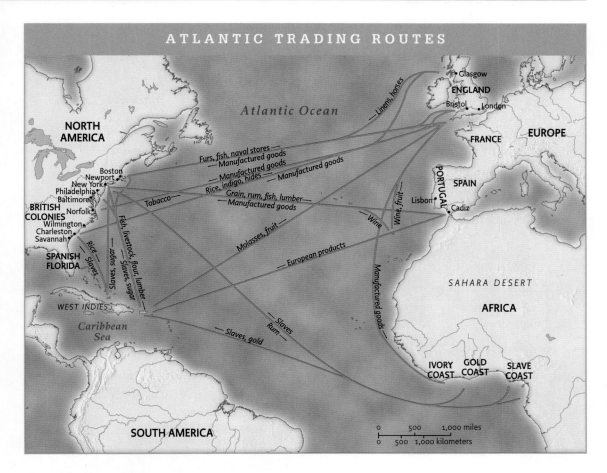

ATLANTIC TRADING ROUTES

rulers took part, and they proved quite adept at playing the Europeans off against one another, collecting taxes from foreign merchants, and keeping the capture and sale of slaves under their own control. Few Europeans ventured inland from the coast. Traders remained in their "factories" and purchased slaves brought to them by African rulers and dealers.

From a minor institution, slavery grew to become more and more central to West African society, a source of wealth for African merchants and of power for newly emerging African kingdoms. But the loss every year of tens of thousands of men and women in the prime of their lives to the slave trade weakened and distorted West Africa's society and economy.

A series of trading routes crisscrossed the Atlantic, bringing manufactured goods to Africa and Britain's American colonies, slaves to the New World, and colonial products to Europe.

The Middle Passage

For slaves, the voyage across the Atlantic—known as the **Middle Passage** because it was the second, or middle, leg in the triangular trading routes linking Europe, Africa, and America—was a harrowing experience. Men,

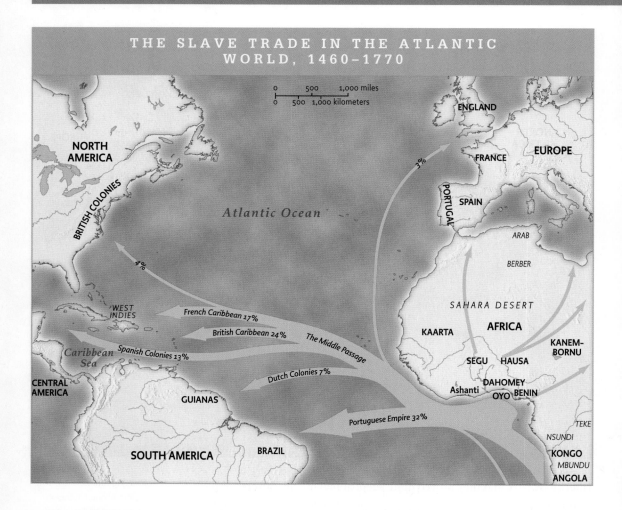

THE SLAVE TRADE IN THE ATLANTIC WORLD, 1460–1770

The Atlantic slave trade expanded rapidly in the eighteenth century. The mainland colonies received only a tiny proportion of the Africans brought to the New World, most of whom were transported to Brazil and the West Indies.

Slave population

women, and children were crammed aboard vessels as tightly as possible to maximize profits. Equiano, who later described "the shrieks of the women and the groans of the dying," survived the Middle Passage, but many Africans did not. Diseases such as measles and smallpox spread rapidly, and about one slave in five perished before reaching the New World. Ship captains were known to throw the sick overboard in order to prevent the spread of epidemics.

Only a small proportion (less than 5 percent) of slaves carried to the New World were destined for mainland North America. The vast majority landed in Brazil or the West Indies, where the high death rate on the sugar plantations led to a constant demand for new slave imports. Overall, the area that was to become the United States imported between 400,000 and 600,000 slaves. By 1770, due to the natural reproduction of the slave

PLAN, PROFIL, ET DISTRIBUTION DU NAVIRE LA MARIE SERAPHIQUE
DE NANTES, ARMÉ PAR M. GRÙEL, POUR ANGOLE, SOUS LE COMMANDEMENT DE GAUGY, QUI A TRAITÉ A LOANGUE,
DONT LA VUE EST CY DESSOUS, LA QUANTITÉ DE 307 CAPTIFS DIVERS, EN 3 MOIS 2 6 JOURS, PARTY LE 31 DÉCEMBRE 1769. AYANT EN CALLE, SUR LE PONT, ET DANS LA
CHALOUPE 3 V. BARIQUES D'EAU SUIVANT LES PLANS CY DESSOUS.

PLANS DE LA CALLE.   L'ENTRE-PONT.   LE PONT.
PREMIER PLAN.   SECOND PLAN.

This image, made by a sailor in 1769 for the ship's owner, a merchant in Nantes, France, depicts the interior of a slave-trading vessel, the *Marie-Séraphique*. The cargo carried in barrels, generally guns, cloth, and metal goods, was to be traded for slaves. The third image from the left depicts the conditions under which slaves endured the Middle Passage across the Atlantic. The ship carried over 300 slaves. The broadside also included a calculation of the profit of the voyage.

population, around one-fifth of the estimated 2.3 million persons (not including Indians) living in the English colonies of North America were Africans and their descendants.

Chesapeake Slavery

By the mid-eighteenth century, three distinct slave systems were well entrenched in Britain's mainland colonies: tobacco-based plantation slavery in the Chesapeake, rice-based plantation slavery in South Carolina and Georgia, and nonplantation slavery in New England and the Middle Colonies. The largest and oldest of these was the plantation system of the Chesapeake, where more than 270,000 slaves resided in 1770, nearly half of the region's population. Virginia and Maryland were as closely tied to Britain as any other colonies, and their economies were models of mercantilist policy (described in Chapter 3).

Tobacco-based plantation slavery

As Virginia expanded westward, so did slavery. By the eve of the American Revolution, the center of gravity of slavery in the colony had shifted from the Tidewater (the region along the coast) to the Piedmont farther inland. Most Chesapeake slaves, male and female, worked in the tobacco fields, but thousands labored as teamsters, as boatmen, and in skilled crafts. Numerous slave women became cooks, seamstresses, dairy maids, and personal servants. Slavery was common on small farms as well

Types of slave labor

as plantations; nearly half of Virginia's white families owned at least one slave in 1770.

Hierarchy of Chesapeake society

Slavery transformed Chesapeake society into an elaborate hierarchy of degrees of freedom. At the top stood large planters, below them numerous lesser planters and landowning yeomen, and at the bottom a large population of convicts, indentured servants, tenant farmers, and slaves. Violence lay at the heart of the slave system. Even a planter like Landon Carter, who prided himself on his concern for the well-being of his slaves, noted casually in his diary, "They have been severely whipped day by day."

Race as a line of social division

Race took on more and more importance as a line of social division. Whites increasingly considered free blacks dangerous and undesirable. Free blacks lost the right to employ white servants and to bear arms, were subjected to special taxes, and could be punished for striking a white person, regardless of the cause. In 1723, Virginia revoked the voting privileges of property-owning free blacks. Because Virginia law required that freed slaves be sent out of the colony, free blacks remained only a tiny part of the population—less than 4 percent in 1750.

The Rice Kingdom

As in early Virginia, frontier conditions allowed leeway to South Carolina's small population of African-born slaves, who farmed, tended livestock, and were initially allowed to serve in the militia to fight the Spanish and Indians. And as in Virginia, the introduction of a marketable staple crop, in this case rice, led directly to economic development, the large-scale importation of slaves, and a growing divide between white and black. In the 1740s, another staple, indigo (a crop used in producing blue dye), was developed. Like rice, indigo required large-scale cultivation and was grown by slaves.

Staple crops

Since rice production requires considerable capital investment to drain swamps and create irrigation systems, it is economically advantageous for rice plantations to be as large as possible. Thus, South Carolina planters owned far more land and slaves than their counterparts in Virginia. Moreover, since mosquitoes bearing malaria (a disease to which Africans had developed partial immunity) flourished in the watery rice fields, planters tended to leave plantations under the control of overseers and the slaves themselves.

Large-scale rice plantations

In the Chesapeake, field slaves worked in groups under constant supervision. Under the "task" system that developed in eighteenth-century South Carolina, individual slaves were assigned daily jobs, the completion of which allowed them time for leisure or to cultivate crops of their own.

The task system

In 1762, one rice district had a population of only 76 white males among 1,000 slaves. By 1770, the number of South Carolina slaves had reached 75,000, well over half the colony's population.

The Georgia Experiment

Rice cultivation also spread into Georgia. The colony was founded in 1732 by a group of philanthropists led by James Oglethorpe, a wealthy reformer who sought to improve conditions for imprisoned debtors and abolish slavery. Oglethorpe hoped to establish a haven where the "worthy poor" of England could enjoy economic opportunity. The government in London supported the creation of Georgia to protect South Carolina against the Spanish and their Indian allies in Florida.

James Oglethorpe

Initially, the proprietors banned liquor and slaves, leading to continual battles with settlers, who desired both. By the 1740s, Georgia offered the spectacle of colonists pleading for the "English liberty" of self-government so that they could enact laws introducing slavery. In 1751, the proprietors surrendered the colony to the crown. The colonists quickly won the right to an elected assembly, which met in Savannah. It repealed the ban on slavery (and liquor), as well as an early measure that had limited landholdings to 500 acres. Georgia became a miniature version of South Carolina. By 1770, as many as 15,000 slaves labored on its coastal rice plantations.

Slavery in the North

Unlike in the plantation regions, slavery was less central to the economies of New England and the Middle Colonies, where small farms predominated. Slaves made up only a small percentage of these colonies' populations, and it was unusual for families to own more than one or two slaves. Nonetheless, slavery was not marginal to northern colonial life. Slaves worked as farm hands, in artisan shops, as stevedores loading and unloading ships, and as personal servants. With slaves so small a part of the population that they seemed to pose no threat to the white majority, laws were

TABLE 4.1 Slave Population as Percentage of Total Population of Original Thirteen Colonies, 1770

COLONY	SLAVE POPULATION	PERCENTAGE
Virginia	187,600	42%
South Carolina	75,168	61
North Carolina	69,600	35
Maryland	63,818	32
New York	19,062	12
Georgia	15,000	45
New Jersey	8,220	7
Connecticut	5,698	3
Pennsylvania	5,561	2
Massachusetts	4,754	2
Rhode Island	3,761	6
Delaware	1,836	5
New Hampshire	654	1

A portrait of Ayuba Diallo, a Muslim merchant in Senegal who became a victim of the slave trade in 1731 and was transported to Maryland. He escaped in 1733 and with the help of wealthy patrons regained his freedom. Because of Diallo's unusual talents—he knew both English and Arabic and could relate the Koran from memory—he became a celebrity in England, which he visited in 1733. He sat for two portraits by the noted artist William Hoare. This is the earliest known painting of an African who experienced slavery in Britain's North American colonies. Diallo returned to his homeland in 1734.

less harsh than in the South. In New England, where in 1770 the 15,000 slaves represented less than 3 percent of the region's population, slave marriages were recognized in law; the severe physical punishment of slaves was prohibited; and slaves could bring suits in court, testify against whites, and own property and pass it on to their children—rights unknown in the South.

Slavery had been present in New York from the earliest days of Dutch settlement. As New York City's role in the slave trade expanded, so did slavery in the city. In 1746, its 2,440 slaves amounted to one-fifth of the city's total population. Most were domestic workers, but slaves worked in all sectors of the economy. In 1770, about 27,000 slaves lived in New York and New Jersey, 10 percent of their total population. Slavery was also a significant presence in Philadelphia, although the institution stagnated after 1750 as artisans and merchants relied increasingly on wage laborers, whose numbers were augmented by population growth and the completion of the terms of indentured servants.

SLAVE CULTURES AND SLAVE RESISTANCE

Becoming African-American

The nearly 300,000 Africans brought to the mainland colonies during the eighteenth century were not a single people. They came from different cultures, spoke different languages, and practiced many religions. Slavery threw together individuals who would never otherwise have encountered one another and who had never considered their color or residence on a single continent a source of identity or unity. Their bond was not kinship, language, or even "race," but slavery itself. By the nineteenth century, slaves no longer identified themselves as Ibo, Ashanti, Yoruba, and so on, but as African-Americans. In music, art, folklore, language, and religion, their cultural expressions emerged as a synthesis of African traditions, European elements, and new conditions in America.

For most of the eighteenth century, the majority of American slaves were African by birth. Advertisements seeking information about runaways often described them by African origin ("young Gambia Negro," "new Banbara Negro fellow"). Indeed, during the eighteenth century, black life in the colonies was "re-Africanized" as the earlier Creoles (slaves born in the New World) came to be outnumbered by large-scale importations from Africa.

Slave imports

African Religion in Colonial America

No experience was more wrenching for African slaves in the colonies than the transition from traditional religions to Christianity. Although African religions varied as much as those on other continents, they shared some elements, especially belief in the presence of spiritual forces in nature and a close relationship between the sacred and secular worlds. In the religions of West Africa, the region from which most slaves brought to British North America originated, there was no hard and fast distinction between the secular and spiritual worlds. Nature was suffused with spirits, and the dead could influence the living.

Although some slaves came to the colonies familiar with Christianity or Islam, the majority of North American slaves practiced traditional African religions (which many Europeans deemed superstition or even witchcraft) well into the eighteenth century. When they did adopt Christian practices, many slaves merged them with traditional beliefs, adding the Christian God to their own pantheon of lesser spirits, whom they continued to worship.

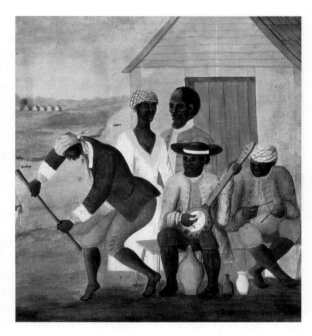

The Old Plantation, a late-eighteenth-century watercolor, depicts slaves dancing in a plantation's slave quarters, perhaps at a wedding. The musical instruments and pottery are African in origin, while much of the clothing is of European manufacture, indicating the mixing of African and white cultures among the era's slaves. The artist has been identified as John Rose, owner of a rice plantation near Beaufort, South Carolina.

African-American Cultures

By the mid-eighteenth century, the three slave systems in British North America had produced distinct African-American cultures. In the Chesapeake, because of a more healthful climate, the slave population began to reproduce itself by 1740. Because of the small size of most plantations and the large number of white **yeoman farmers**, slaves here were continuously exposed to white culture. They soon learned English, and many were swept up in the religious revivals known as the Great Awakening, discussed later in this chapter.

In South Carolina and Georgia, two very different black societies emerged. On the rice plantations, slaves lived in extremely harsh conditions and had a low birthrate throughout the eighteenth century, making rice production dependent on continued slave imports from Africa. The slaves seldom came into contact with whites. They constructed African-style houses, chose African names for their children, and spoke Gullah, a language that mixed various African roots and was unintelligible to most whites. In Charleston and Savannah, however, the experience

This portrait of William Duguid, a Boston textile merchant, was painted in 1773 by Prince Demah Barnes. It depicts Duguid wearing imported clothing with an elaborate floral pattern. What makes the painting unique, however, is that Barnes was a slave, whose owner, a Massachusetts merchant, encouraged what he called Barnes's "natural genius" and took him on a brief visit to London for training. Still a slave, Barnes enlisted in the Massachusetts militia in 1777 after his Loyalist owners fled the state. He died of smallpox in 1778.

Slave rebellions

of slaves who labored as servants or skilled workers was quite different. They assimilated more quickly into Euro-American culture, and sexual liaisons between white owners and slave women produced the beginning of a class of free mulattos.

In the northern colonies, where slaves represented a smaller part of the population, a distinctive African-American culture developed more slowly. Living in close proximity to whites, slaves enjoyed more mobility and access to the mainstream of life than their counterparts farther south. But they had fewer opportunities to create stable family life or a cohesive community.

Resistance to Slavery

The common threads that linked these regional African-American cultures were the experience of slavery and the desire for freedom. Throughout the eighteenth century, blacks risked their lives in efforts to resist enslavement. Colonial newspapers, especially in the southern colonies, were filled with advertisements for runaway slaves. In South Carolina and Georgia, they fled to Florida, to uninhabited coastal and river swamps, or to Charleston and Savannah, where they could pass for free. In the Chesapeake and Middle Colonies, fugitive slaves tended to be familiar with white culture and therefore, as one advertisement put it, could "pretend to be free."

What Edward Trelawny, the colonial governor of Jamaica, called "a dangerous spirit of liberty" was widespread among the New World's slaves. The eighteenth century's first slave uprising occurred in New York City in 1712, when a group of slaves set fire to houses on the outskirts of the city and killed the first nine whites who arrived on the scene. During the 1730s and 1740s, continuous warfare involving European empires and Indians opened the door to slave resistance. In 1731, a slave rebellion in Louisiana, where the French and the Natchez Indians were at war, temporarily halted efforts to introduce the plantation system in that region.

Slaves seized the opportunity for rebellion offered by the War of Jenkins' Ear, which pitted England against Spain. In September 1739, a group of South Carolina slaves, most of them recently arrived from Kongo where some had been soldiers, seized a store containing numerous weapons at the town of Stono. Beating drums to attract followers, the armed band marched southward toward Florida, burning houses and barns, killing whites they encountered, and shouting "Liberty." The **Stono Rebellion** took the lives of more than two dozen whites and as many as 200 slaves. Some slaves managed to reach Florida, where in 1740 they were armed by the Spanish to help repel an attack by a force from Georgia.

In 1741, a panic (which some observers compared to the fear of witches in Salem in the 1690s) swept New York City. Rumors spread that slaves, with some white allies, planned to burn part of the city, seize weapons, and either turn New York over to Spain or murder the white population. More than 150 blacks and 20 whites were arrested, and 34 alleged conspirators, including 4 white persons, were executed. Historians still disagree as to how extensive the plot was or whether it existed at all. In eighteenth-century America, dreams of freedom knew no racial boundary.

RUN AWAY

THE 18th Inftant at Night from the Subfcriber, in the City of New-York, four Negro Men, Viz. LESTER, about 40 Years of Age, had on a white Flannel Jacket and Drawers, Duck Trowfers and Home-fpun Shirt. CÆSAR, about 18 Years of Age, cloth-ed in the fame Manner. ISAAC, aged 17 Years cloathed in the fame Manner, except that his Breeches were Leather; and MINGO, 15 Years of Age, with the the fame Clothing as the 2 firft, all of them of a middling Size, Whoever delivers either of the faid Negroes to the Subfcriber, fhall receive TWENTY SHILLINGS Reward for each befide all reafon-able Charges. If any perfon can give Intelligence of their being harbour'd, a reward of TEN POUNDS will be paid upon conviction of the Offender. All Mafters of Veffels and others are forewarn'd not to Tranfport them from the City, as I am refolved to profecute as far as the Law will allow. WILLIAM BULL.
N. B. If the Negroes return, they fhall be pardon'd. - 88

An advertisement seeking the return of four runaway slaves from New York City.

AN EMPIRE OF FREEDOM

British Patriotism

Despite the centrality of slavery to its empire, eighteenth-century Great Britain prided itself on being the world's most advanced and freest nation. It was not only the era's greatest naval and commercial power but also the home of a complex governmental system, with a powerful Parliament representing the interests of a self-confident landed aristocracy and mer-chant class. For much of the eighteenth century, Britain found itself at war with France, which had replaced Spain as its major continental rival. This situation led to a large military, high taxes, and the creation of the Bank of England to help finance the conflicts. For both Britons and colonists, war helped to sharpen a sense of national identity against foreign foes.

British power

British patriotic sentiment became more assertive as the eighteenth century progressed. Symbols of British identity proliferated: the songs "God Save the King" and "Rule, Britannia," and even the modern rules of cricket, the national sport. Especially in contrast to France, Britain saw itself as a realm of widespread prosperity, individual liberty, the rule of law, and the Protestant faith. Wealth, religion, and freedom went together.

British identity

The British Constitution

Central to this sense of British identity was the concept of liberty. Eighteenth-century Britons believed power and liberty to be natural antagonists. To mediate between them, advocates of British freedom

British liberty

A 1770 engraving from the *Boston Gazette* by Paul Revere illustrates the association of British patriotism and liberty. Britannia sits with a liberty cap and her national shield, and releases a bird from a cage.

celebrated the rule of law, the right to live under legislation to which one's representatives had consented, restraints on the arbitrary exercise of political authority, and rights such as trial by jury enshrined in the common law. Until the 1770s, most colonists believed themselves to be part of the freest political system mankind had ever known.

These ideas sank deep roots not only within the "political nation"—those who voted, held office, and engaged in structured political debate—but also far more broadly in British and colonial society. Ordinary persons challenged efforts by merchants to raise the cost of bread above the traditional "just price" and the Royal Navy's practice of "impressment"—kidnapping poor men on the streets for maritime service.

Republican Liberty

Liberty was central to two sets of political ideas that flourished in the Anglo-American world. One is termed by scholars **republicanism**, which celebrated active participation in public life by economically independent citizens as the essence of liberty. Republicans assumed that only property-owning citizens possessed "virtue"—defined in the eighteenth century not simply as a personal moral quality but as the willingness to subordinate self-interest to the pursuit of the public good.

Moral and economic ideas of liberty

In eighteenth-century Britain, this body of thought about freedom was most closely associated with a group of critics known as the "Country Party" because much of their support arose from the landed gentry. In Britain, Country Party writings had little impact, but they were eagerly devoured in the American colonies, whose elites were attracted to the emphasis on the political role of the independent landowner and their warnings against the tendency of political power to infringe on liberty.

The "Country Party"

Liberal Freedom

The second set of eighteenth-century political ideas celebrating freedom came to be known as **liberalism** (although its meaning was quite different from what the word suggests today). Whereas republican liberty had a public and social quality, liberalism was essentially individual and private. The leading philosopher of liberalism was John Locke, whose *Two Treatises of*

Locke's treatises

Government, written around 1680, had limited influence in his own lifetime but became extremely well known in the next century. Government, he wrote, was formed by a mutual agreement among equals (the parties being male heads of households, not all persons). In this "social contract," men surrendered a part of their right to govern themselves in order to enjoy the benefits of the rule of law. They retained, however, their natural rights, whose existence predated the establishment of political authority. Protecting the security of life, liberty, and property required shielding a realm of private life and personal concerns—including family relations, religious preferences, and economic activity—from interference by the state. During the eighteenth century, Lockean ideas—individual rights, the consent of the governed, the right of rebellion against unjust or oppressive government—would become familiar on both sides of the Atlantic.

Like other Britons, Locke spoke of liberty as a universal right yet seemed to exclude many persons from its full benefits. The free individual in liberal thought was essentially the propertied white man. Nonetheless, by proclaiming that all individuals possess natural rights that no government may violate, Lockean liberalism opened the door to the poor, women, and even slaves to challenge limitations on their own freedom.

In the eighteenth century, republicanism and liberalism often reinforced each other. Both political outlooks could inspire a commitment to constitutional government and restraints on despotic power. Both emphasized the security of property as a foundation of freedom. Both traditions were transported to eighteenth-century America and would eventually help to divide the empire.

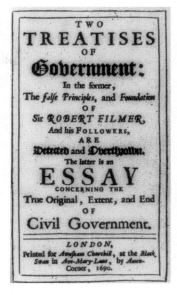

The title page of John Locke's *Two Treatises of Government*, which traced the origins of government to an original state of nature and insisted that political authorities must not abridge mankind's natural rights.

THE PUBLIC SPHERE

Colonial politics for most of the eighteenth century was considerably less tempestuous than in the seventeenth, with its bitter struggles for power and frequent armed uprisings. Political stability in Britain coupled with the maturation of local elites in America made for more tranquil government.

The Right to Vote

In many respects, politics in eighteenth-century America had a more democratic quality than in Great Britain. Suffrage requirements varied from colony to colony, but as in Britain the linchpin of voting laws was the property qualification. Its purpose was to ensure that men who possessed an economic stake in society and the independence of judgment that

Property and the vote

supposedly went with it determined the policies of the government. Slaves, servants, tenants, adult sons living in the homes of their parents, the poor, and women all lacked a "will of their own" and were therefore ineligible to vote. The wide distribution of property in the colonies, however, meant that a far higher percentage of the population enjoyed voting rights than in the Old World. It is estimated that between 50 and 80 percent of adult white men could vote in eighteenth-century colonial America, as opposed to fewer than 5 percent in Britain.

Limits on voting

Colonial politics, however, was hardly democratic in a modern sense. Voting was almost everywhere considered a male prerogative. In some colonies, Jews, Catholics, and Protestant Dissenters like Baptists and Quakers could not vote. Propertied free blacks, who enjoyed the franchise in Virginia, South Carolina, and Georgia in the early days of settlement, lost that right during the eighteenth century. In the northern colonies, although the law did not bar blacks from voting, local custom often did. Native Americans were generally prohibited from voting.

Political Cultures

Despite the broad electorate among white men, "the people" existed only on election day. Between elections, members of colonial assemblies remained out of touch with their constituents. Strongly competitive elections were the norm only in the Middle Colonies. Considerable power in colonial politics rested with those who held appointive, not elective, office. Governors and councils were appointed by the crown in the nine royal colonies and by the proprietors of Pennsylvania and Maryland. Moreover, laws passed by colonial assemblies could be vetoed by governors or in London. In New England, most town officers were elected, but local officials in other colonies were appointed by the governor or by powerful officials in London.

Appointive office

Qualifications for voting and office

Property qualifications for officeholding were far higher than for voting. In South Carolina, for example, nearly every free adult white male could meet the voting qualification of fifty acres of land or payment of twenty shillings in taxes, but to sit in the assembly one had to own 500 acres of land and ten slaves or town property worth £1,000. As a result, throughout the eighteenth century nearly all of South Carolina's legislators were planters or wealthy merchants.

Democracy and deference

In some colonies, an ingrained tradition of "deference"—the assumption among ordinary people that wealth, education, and social prominence carried a right to public office—sharply limited effective choice in elections. Virginia politics, for example, combined political democracy for white men with the tradition that voters should choose among candidates from the gentry. Aspirants for public office actively sought to ingratiate themselves with ordinary voters, distributing food and liquor freely at the courthouse where balloting took place. In Thomas Jefferson's first campaign for the House of Burgesses in 1768, his expenses included hiring two men "for bringing up rum" to the polling place. Even in New England, with its larger number of elective positions, town leaders were generally the largest property holders.

The Rise of the Assemblies

In the seventeenth century, the governor was the focal point of political authority, and colonial assemblies were weak bodies that met infrequently. But preoccupied with events in Europe and imperial rivalries, successive British governments during the first half of the eighteenth century adopted a policy of **salutary neglect**, leaving the colonies largely to govern themselves. As economic development enhanced the power of American elites, the assemblies they dominated became more and more assertive. Their leaders insisted that assemblies possessed the same rights and powers in local affairs as the House of Commons enjoyed in Britain. The most successful governors were those who accommodated the rising power of the assemblies and used their appointive powers and control of land grants to win allies among assembly members.

Colonial governors

Many of the conflicts between governors and elected assemblies stemmed from the colonies' economic growth. To deal with the scarcity of gold and silver coins, the only legal form of currency, some colonies printed paper money, although this was strongly opposed by the governors, authorities in London, and British merchants who did not wish to be paid in what they considered worthless paper. Numerous battles also took place over land policy (sometimes involving divergent attitudes toward

Conflicts between governors and assemblies

This 1765 engraving depicting an election in Pennsylvania suggests the intensity of political debate in the Middle Colonies, as well as the social composition of the electorate. Those shown arguing outside the Old Court House in Philadelphia include physicians (with wigs and gold-topped canes), ministers, and lawyers. A line of men wait on the steps to vote.

the remaining Indian population) and the level of rents charged to farmers on land owned by the crown or proprietors.

In their negotiations and conflicts with royal governors, leaders of the assemblies drew on the writings of the English Country Party, whose emphasis on the constant tension between liberty and political power and the dangers of executive influence over the legislature made sense of their own experience. Of the European settlements in North America, only the British colonies possessed any considerable degree of popular participation in government.

Popular participation in British colonial government

Politics in Public

The language of liberty reverberated outside the relatively narrow world of elective and legislative politics. The "political nation" was dominated by the American gentry, whose members addressed each other in letters, speeches, newspaper articles, and pamphlets filled with references to classical learning. But especially in colonial cities, the eighteenth century witnessed a considerable expansion of the "public sphere"—the world of political organization independent of the government, where an informed citizenry openly discussed questions that had previously been the preserve of officials.

The public sphere

In Boston, New York, and Philadelphia, clubs proliferated where literary, philosophical, scientific, and political issues were debated. Such groups were generally composed of men of property, but some drew ordinary citizens into discussions of public affairs. Colonial taverns and coffeehouses also became important sites for political debates. In Philadelphia, one clergyman commented, "the poorest laborer thinks himself entitled to deliver his sentiments in matters of religion or politics with as much freedom as the gentleman or scholar."

Taverns and coffeehouses

The Colonial Press

Neither the Spanish possessions of Florida and New Mexico nor New France possessed a printing press, although missionaries had established one in Mexico City in the 1530s. In British North America, however, the press expanded rapidly during the eighteenth century. So did the number of political broadsides and pamphlets published, especially at election time. By the eve of the American Revolution, some three-quarters of the free adult male population in the colonies (and more than one-third of the women) could read and write, and a majority of American families owned at least one book. Circulating libraries appeared in many colonial cities and towns, making possible a wider dissemination of knowledge at

Literacy in colonial America

a time when books were still expensive. The first, the Library Company of Philadelphia, was established by Benjamin Franklin in 1731.

The first continuously published colonial newspaper, the *Boston News-Letter*, appeared in 1704. There were twenty-five colonial newspapers by 1765, mostly weeklies with small circulations—an average of 600 sales per issue. Probably the best-edited was the *Pennsylvania Gazette*, established in 1728 in Philadelphia and purchased the following year by Benjamin Franklin. At its peak, the *Gazette* attracted 2,000 subscribers. By the 1730s, political commentary was widespread in the American press.

Newspapers

Freedom of Expression and Its Limits

The public sphere thrived on the free exchange of ideas. But freedom of expression was not generally considered one of the ancient rights of Englishmen. The phrase "freedom of speech" originated in Britain during the sixteenth century. A right of legislators, not ordinary citizens, it referred to the ability of members of Parliament to express their views without fear of reprisal, on the grounds that only in this way could they effectively represent the people. Outside of Parliament, free speech had no legal protection. A subject could be beheaded for accusing the king of failing to hold "true" religious beliefs, and language from swearing to criticism of the government exposed a person to criminal penalties.

Freedom of speech

As for freedom of the press, governments on both sides of the Atlantic viewed this as extremely dangerous. Until 1695, when a British law requiring the licensing of printed works before publication lapsed, no newspaper, book, or pamphlet could legally be printed without a government license. After 1695, the government could not censor newspapers, books, and pamphlets before they appeared in print, but it continued to try to manage the press by direct payments to publishers and journalists. Authors and publishers could still be prosecuted for "seditious libel"— a crime that included defaming government officials—or punished for contempt.

Freedom of the press

Elected assemblies, not governors, most frequently discouraged freedom of the press in colonial America. Dozens of publishers were hauled before assemblies and forced to apologize for comments regarding one or another member. Colonial newspapers vigorously defended freedom of the press as a central component of liberty, insisting that the citizenry had a right to monitor the workings of government and subject public officials to criticism. But since government printing contracts were crucial for economic success, few newspapers attacked colonial governments unless financially supported by an opposition faction.

The Trial of Zenger

The most famous colonial court case involving freedom of the press demonstrated that popular sentiment opposed prosecutions for criticism of public officials. This was the 1735 trial of John Peter Zenger, a German-born printer who had immigrated to New York as a youth. Financed by wealthy opponents of Governor William Cosby, Zenger's newspaper, the *Weekly Journal*, lambasted the governor for corruption, influence peddling, and "tyranny." New York's council ordered four issues burned and had Zenger himself arrested and tried for seditious libel. Zenger's attorney, Andrew Hamilton, urged the jury to judge not the publisher but the governor. If they decided that Zenger's charges were correct, they must acquit him, and, Hamilton proclaimed, "every man who prefers freedom to a life of slavery will bless you."

Zenger was found not guilty. The case sent a warning to prosecutors that libel cases might be very difficult to win, especially in the superheated atmosphere of New York politics. The outcome demonstrated that the idea of free expression was becoming ingrained in the popular imagination.

John Peter Zenger

Benjamin West's depiction of Benjamin Franklin, painted in 1816, twenty-six years after his subject's death, emphasizes his scientific work rather than his political career. Franklin conducted pioneering experiments in 1752 that demonstrated the electrical nature of lightning. West shows him seated on clouds, surrounded by angelic assistants.

The American Enlightenment

During the eighteenth century, many educated Americans began to be influenced by the outlook of the European **Enlightenment**. This philosophical movement, which originated among French thinkers and soon spread to Britain, sought to apply the scientific method of careful investigation based on research and experiment to political and social life. Enlightenment ideas crisscrossed the Atlantic along with goods and people. Enlightenment thinkers insisted that every human institution, authority, and tradition be judged before the bar of reason. The self-educated Benjamin Franklin's wide range of activities—establishing a newspaper, debating club, and library; publishing the widely circulated *Poor Richard's Almanack*; and conducting experiments to demonstrate that lightning is a form of electricity—exemplified the

Enlightenment spirit and made him probably the best-known American in the eighteenth-century world.

Enlightenment thinkers hoped that "reason," not religious enthusiasm, could govern human life. During the eighteenth century, many prominent Americans moved toward the position called Arminianism, which taught that reason alone was capable of establishing the essentials of religion. Others adopted **Deism**, a belief that God essentially withdrew after creating the world, leaving it to function according to scientific laws without divine intervention. Belief in miracles, in the revealed truth of the Bible, and in the innate sinfulness of mankind were viewed by Arminians, Deists, and others as outdated superstitions that should be abandoned in the modern age.

Deism

In the seventeenth century, the English scientist Isaac Newton had revealed the natural laws that governed the physical universe. Here, Deists believed, was the purest evidence of God's handiwork. Deists concluded that the best form of religious devotion was to study the workings of nature, rather than to worship in organized churches or appeal to divine grace for salvation. By the late colonial era, a small but influential group of leading Americans, including Benjamin Franklin and Thomas Jefferson, could be classified as Deists.

THE GREAT AWAKENING

Like freedom of the press, religion was another realm where the actual experience of liberty outstripped its legal recognition. Religion remained central to eighteenth-century American life. Sermons, theological treatises, and copies of the Bible were by far the largest category of material produced by colonial printers.

Religious Revivals

Many ministers were concerned that westward expansion, commercial development, the growth of Enlightenment rationalism, and lack of individual engagement in church services were undermining religious devotion. These fears helped to inspire the revivals that swept through the colonies beginning in the 1730s. Known as the **Great Awakening**, the revivals were less a coordinated movement than a series of local events united by a commitment to a "religion of the heart," a more emotional and personal Christianity than that offered by existing churches.

A more personal Christianity

Religious fundamentalism

The eighteenth century witnessed a resurgence of religious fundamentalism in many parts of the world, in part a response to the rationalism of the Enlightenment and a desire for greater religious purity. In the Middle East and Central Asia, where Islam was widespread, followers of a form of the religion known as Wahabbism called for a return to the practices of the religion's early days. Methodism and other forms of enthusiastic religion were flourishing in Europe. Like other intellectual currents of the time, the Great Awakening was a transatlantic movement.

Jonathan Edwards

During the 1720s and 1730s, the New Jersey Dutch Reformed clergyman Theodore Frelinghuysen, his Presbyterian neighbors William and Gilbert Tennent, and the Massachusetts Congregationalist minister Jonathan Edwards pioneered an intensely emotional style of preaching. Edwards's famous sermon *Sinners in the Hands of an Angry God* portrayed sinful man as a "loathsome insect" suspended over a bottomless pit of eternal fire by a slender thread that might break at any moment. Only a "new birth"—immediately acknowledging one's sins and pleading for divine grace—could save men and women from eternal damnation.

The Preaching of Whitefield

More than any other individual, the English minister George Whitefield, who declared "the whole world his parish," sparked the Great Awakening. For two years after his arrival in America in 1739, Whitefield brought his highly emotional brand of preaching to colonies from Georgia to New England. God, Whitefield proclaimed, was merciful. Rather than being predestined for damnation, men and women could save themselves by repenting of their sins. Whitefield appealed to the passions of his listeners, powerfully sketching the boundless joy of salvation and the horrors of damnation.

George Whitefield, the English evangelist who helped to spark the Great Awakening in the colonies. Painted around 1742 by John Wollaston, who had immigrated from England to the colonies, the work depicts Whitefield's powerful effect on male and female listeners. It also illustrates Whitefield's eye problem, which led critics to dub him "Dr. Squintum."

Tens of thousands of colonists flocked to Whitefield's sermons, which were widely reported in the American press, making him a celebrity and helping to establish the revivals as the first major intercolonial event in North American history. In Whitefield's footsteps, a host of traveling preachers or "evangelists" (meaning, literally, bearers of good news) held revivalist meetings, often to the alarm of established ministers.

The Awakening's Impact

By the time they subsided in the 1760s, the revivals had changed the religious configuration of the colonies and enlarged the boundaries of liberty. Whitefield inspired the emergence of numerous Dissenting churches. Congregations split into factions headed by Old Lights (traditionalists) and New Lights (revivalists), and new churches proliferated—Baptist, Methodist, Presbyterian, and others. Many of these new churches began to criticize the colonial practice of levying taxes to support an established church; they defended religious freedom as one of the natural rights government must not restrict.

The Great Awakening threw into question many forms of authority and inspired criticism of aspects of colonial society. Revivalist preachers frequently criticized commercial society, insisting that believers should make salvation, not profit, "the one business of their lives." Preaching to the small farmers of the southern backcountry, Baptist and Methodist revivalists criticized the worldliness of wealthy planters and attacked as sinful activities such as gambling, horse racing, and lavish entertainments on the Sabbath. A few preachers explicitly condemned slavery. Especially in the Chesapeake, the revivals brought numerous slaves into the Christian fold, an important step in their acculturation as African-Americans.

Critique of commercial society

The revivals encouraged many colonists to trust their own views rather than those of established elites. In listening to the sermons of self-educated preachers, forming Bible study groups, and engaging in intense religious discussions, ordinary colonists asserted the right to independent judgment. Although the revivalists' aim was spiritual salvation, the independent frame of mind they encouraged would have significant political consequences.

IMPERIAL RIVALRIES

Spanish North America

The rapid growth of Britain's North American colonies took place at a time of increased jockeying for power among European empires. But the colonies of England's rivals, although covering immense territories, remained thinly populated and far weaker economically. The Spanish empire encompassed an area that stretched from the Pacific coast and New Mexico into the Great Plains and eastward through Texas and Florida. After 1763, it also included Louisiana, which Spain obtained from France. On paper a vast territorial empire, Spanish North America actually consisted of a few isolated urban clusters, most prominently St. Augustine in Florida, San Antonio in Texas, and Santa Fe and Albuquerque in New Mexico.

In the second half of the century, the Spanish government made a concerted effort to reinvigorate its empire north of the Rio Grande River. It sought to stabilize relations with Indians, especially the nomadic Comanche and Apache, who controlled much of the land claimed by Spain

A rare map by a Comanche artist depicts the Battle of Sierra Blanca of July 30, 1787, between Comanche and Apache warriors in modern-day New Mexico. It was presented to the Spanish governor, who had recently formed an alliance with the Comanche. The battle was a resounding victory for the Comanche, who suffered only one dead and four wounded, while killing four Apache and capturing thirty-five. The letters on the map refer to an accompanying key, including A: the Comanche commander; B: Comanche warriors; D: Apache prisoners; and E: 16 captured horses—an indication of the importance of horses to southwestern Indians by this time.

This illustration of friars preaching, from an eighteenth-century work by the missionary Pablo de Beaumont, depicts demons dispatched by the devil as an ever-present threat to the missionaries' efforts to convert Native Americans.

and whose raids on mines and ranches, settled Indian communities, and each other wreaked havoc. Spain was also alarmed by the growing number of French merchants who made their way into the region from Louisiana.

During the reigns of Carlos II and Carlos III, Spanish reformers, like other Enlightenment figures, hoped that applying scientific methods to society would bring about progress, but at the same time they aimed to preserve the absolutist monarchy and Spain's American empire. Reformers condemned Spain's past treatment of Indians and called for more humane policies. They pointed out that despite the Black Legend of unique Spanish cruelty, Indians comprised well over half of the inhabitants of New Spain, but now amounted to less than 6 percent of the population of the mainland English colonies. But no coherent policy was adopted. In 1776, Spain put the region, previously governed from Mexico City, under a local military commander, who used a combination of coercion, gifts, and trade to woo unconquered Indians. These tactics to some extent strengthened Spain's hold on the northern part of its American empire, but did not succeed in eliminating Indian power in the area.

Spain's problem stemmed in large part from the small size of the settler population. New Mexico in 1765 had only 20,000 inhabitants, with Pueblo Indians slightly outnumbering persons of European descent. Although ranching expanded, the economy of New Mexico essentially rested on trading with and extracting labor from the surviving Indian population. Moreover, the manpower demands of wars in Europe made it impossible for the Spanish government to meet local military commanders' requests for more troops. The powerful Comanche and Apache continued to dominate large parts of northern New Spain.

Texas colonization

Similar problems existed in Texas. Spain began the colonization of Texas at the beginning of the eighteenth century, partly as a buffer to prevent French commercial influence, then spreading in the Mississippi Valley, from intruding into New Mexico. The Spanish established complexes consisting of religious missions and *presidios* (military outposts) at Los Adaes, La Bahía, and San Antonio. But the region attracted few settlers. Texas had only 1,200 Spanish colonists in 1760. Florida stagnated as well.

The Spanish in California

The clash of empires also took place on the Pacific Coast. In the mid-eighteenth century, empire builders in Moscow dreamed of challenging the Spanish for control of the region's fur trade, minerals, and ports. Russian traders established a series of forts in Alaska and then moved southward toward modern-day California. As late as 1812, Russians founded Fort Ross, only 100 miles north of San Francisco.

Even though only a small number of Russians actually appeared in California, the alarmed Spanish in 1769 launched the "Sacred Experiment" to take control of the coast north of San Diego to prevent its occupation by foreigners. In 1774, Juan Bautista de Anza, an explorer and military officer, led an expedition that discovered a usable overland route to California from northern Mexico. But a Native American uprising in 1781 wrested control of the overland route from the Spanish. Given the distance and difficulties of communication, authorities in Mexico City decided to establish missions in California, run by the Franciscan religious order, rather than sending colonists. The friars would set up ranching and farming activities and convert Indians into loyal Spaniards.

A string of Spanish missions and *presidios* soon dotted the California coastline, from San Diego to Los Angeles, Santa Barbara, Monterey, San Francisco, and Sonoma. Born on the Spanish Mediterranean island of Mallorca, **Father Junípero Serra** became one of the most controversial figures in California's early history. He founded the first California mission, in San Diego, in 1769 and administered the mission network until his death in 1784. Serra was widely praised in Spain for converting thousands of Indians to Christianity. In 2015, he was elevated to sainthood by the Catholic Church. But forced labor and disease took a heavy toll among Indians who lived at the missions Serra directed. Many ran away, and the friars responded with whippings and imprisonment. "Naturally we want our liberty," one fugitive from the missions remarked.

Present-day California was a densely populated area, with a native population of perhaps 250,000 when Spanish settlement began. But as in other regions, the coming of soldiers and missionaries proved a disaster for the Indians. More than any other Spanish colony, California was a mission frontier. These outposts served simultaneously as religious institutions and centers of government and labor. Father Serra and other missionaries hoped to convert the natives to Christianity and settled farming, although Serra accommodated native traditions such as dancing and traditional healing. The missions also relied on forced Indian labor to grow grain, work in orchards and vineyards, and tend cattle. By 1821, when Mexico won its independence from Spain, California's native population had declined by

Although painted in the twentieth century, this portrait of Father Junípero Serra is based on one that dates from the eighteenth century, when Serra conducted missionary work in present-day California.

California missions

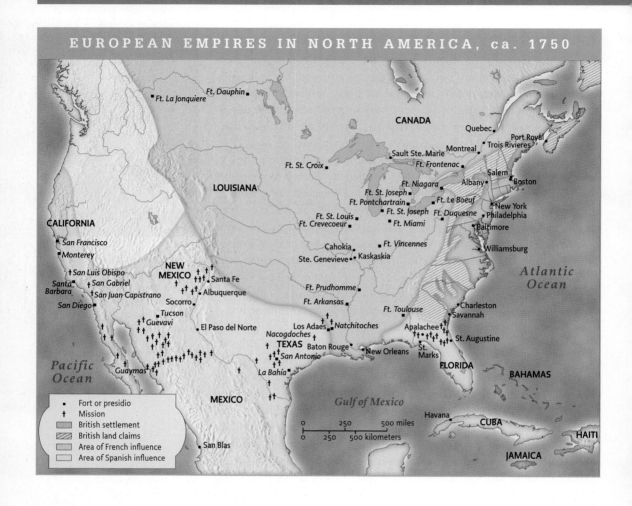

EUROPEAN EMPIRES IN NORTH AMERICA, ca. 1750

Legend:
- Fort or presidio
- † Mission
- British settlement
- British land claims
- Area of French influence
- Area of Spanish influence

Three great empires—the British, French, and Spanish—competed for influence in North America for much of the eighteenth century.

more than one-third. But the area had not attracted Spanish settlers. When Spanish rule came to an end in 1821, twenty missions were operating, with an average population of over 1,000 Indians, but *Californios* (California residents of Spanish descent) numbered only 3,200.

The French Empire

French expansion

Indians retained far more power in Spanish North America than in areas of English settlement. The same was true when it came to a greater rival to British power in North America—as well as in Europe and the Caribbean—France. During the eighteenth century, the population and economy of Canada expanded. At the same time, French traders pushed into the Mississippi River valley southward from the Great Lakes and northward from Mobile, founded in 1702, and New Orleans, established in 1718. In the St. Lawrence River valley of French Canada, prosperous farming communities developed. By 1750, the area had a population of about 55,000 colonists. Another 10,000 (about half Europeans, half African-American slaves) resided in Louisiana.

Nonetheless, the population of French North America continued to be dwarfed by the British colonies. Prejudice against emigration to North America remained widespread in France because many there viewed the French colony as a place of cruel exile for criminals and social outcasts. Nonetheless, by claiming control of a large arc of territory and by establishing close trading and military relations with many Indian tribes, the French empire posed a real challenge to the British. French forts and trading posts ringed the British colonies. The French were a presence on the New England and New York frontiers and in western Pennsylvania.

French and British empires

BATTLE FOR THE CONTINENT

For much of the eighteenth century, the western frontier of British North America was the flashpoint of imperial rivalries. The Ohio Valley became caught up in a complex struggle for power involving the French, British, rival Indian communities, and settlers and land companies pursuing their own interests. On this **middle ground**, a borderland between the French and British empires and Indian sovereignty, villages sprang up where members of numerous tribes lived side by side, along with European traders and the occasional missionary.

The Ohio Valley

By the mid-eighteenth century, Indians had learned that direct military confrontation with Europeans meant suicide, and that an alliance with a single European power exposed them to danger from others. The Indians of the Ohio Valley sought (with some success) to play the British and French empires off against one another and to control the lucrative commerce with whites. The Iroquois were masters of balance-of-power diplomacy.

This hand-colored engraving from around 1720 depicts the mouth of the Mississippi River and the city of New Orleans, then quite small. On the left and right are Native American villages surrounded by stockades.

In 1750, few white settlers inhabited the Ohio Valley. The area was known more by rumor than by observation, and contemporary maps bore little resemblance to the actual geography. Nonetheless, many prominent colonists dreamed of establishing a new "empire" in what was then the West. Many others saw the West as a place where they could easily acquire land, and the freedom that went with it. In 1749, the government of Virginia awarded an immense land grant—half a million acres—to the Ohio Company. The company's members included the colony's royal governor, Robert Dinwiddie, and the cream of Virginia society—Lees, Carters, and the young George Washington. The land grant sparked the French to bolster their presence in the region. It was the Ohio Company's demand for French recognition of its land claims that inaugurated the **Seven Years' War** (known in the colonies as the **French and Indian War**), the first of the century's imperial wars to begin in the colonies and the first to result in a decisive victory for one combatant. It permanently altered the global balance of power.

The Seven Years' War

Only in the eighteenth century, after numerous wars against its great rivals France and Spain, did Britain emerge as the world's leading empire and its center of trade and banking. By the 1750s, British possessions and trade reached around the globe. The existence of global empires implied that warfare among them would also be global.

What became a worldwide struggle for imperial domination began in 1754 with British efforts to dislodge the French from forts in western Pennsylvania. In the previous year, George Washington, then only twenty-one years old, had been dispatched by the colony's governor on an unsuccessful mission to persuade French soldiers to abandon a fort they were building on lands claimed by the Ohio Company. In 1754, Washington returned to the area with two companies of soldiers. After an ill-considered attack on a larger French and Indian force, resulting in the loss of one-third of his men, Washington was forced to surrender. Soon afterward, an expedition led by General Edward Braddock against Fort Duquesne (today's Pittsburgh) was ambushed by French and Indian forces, leaving Braddock and two-thirds of his 3,000 soldiers dead or wounded.

For two years, the war went against the British. The southern backcountry was ablaze with fighting among British forces, colonists, and Indians. Inhumanity flourished on all sides. Indians killed hundreds of colonists in western Pennsylvania and pushed the line of settlement all the way back to Carlisle, only 100 miles west of Philadelphia. In Nova Scotia, the British rounded up 5,000 local French residents, called Acadians, confiscated their land, and expelled them from the region, selling their farms to settlers from New England. Some of those expelled ended up as far away as Louisiana, where their descendants came to be known as Cajuns.

As the British government under Secretary of State William Pitt, who took office in 1757, raised huge sums of money and poured men and naval forces into the war, the tide of battle turned. By 1759, Britain—with colonial

Benjamin Franklin produced this famous cartoon in 1754, calling on Britain's North American colonies to unite against the French.

and Indian soldiers playing a major role—had captured the pivotal French outposts Forts Duquesne, Ticonderoga (north of Albany), and Louisbourg on Cape Breton Island, which guarded the mouth of the St. Lawrence River. In September of that year, a French army was defeated on the Plains of Abraham near Quebec. British forces also seized nearly all the islands in the French Caribbean and established control of India.

A World Transformed

Britain's victory fundamentally reshaped the world balance of power. In the Peace of Paris in 1763, France ceded Canada to Britain, receiving back in return the sugar islands of Guadeloupe and Martinique (far more lucrative colonies from the point of view of French authorities). Spain ceded Florida to Britain in exchange for the return of the Philippines and Cuba (seized by the British during the war). Spain also acquired from France the vast Louisiana colony. France's 200-year-old North American empire had come to an end. The entire continent east of the Mississippi River was now in British hands.

The global balance of power

Eighteenth-century warfare, conducted on land and sea across the globe, was enormously expensive. The Seven Years' War put strains on all the participants. The war's cost produced a financial crisis in France that almost three decades later would help to spark the French Revolution. The British would try to recoup part of the cost of war by increasing taxes on their American colonies.

The costs of war

New Indian Identities

Among other consequences, the Seven Years' War helped lay the foundation for the emergence of a distinct Native American identity. American Indians had traditionally identified most strongly along lines of kinship, shared language, and common geographical residence, including towns and confederacies. Like early colonists, they did not have well-formed ideas about nation and race. The violence directed against Indians by soldiers and settlers during the war led many Indian leaders to envision both stronger allegiance to tribal "nationhood" and pan-Indian identity more broadly. A religious movement that emerged during the Seven Years' War saw different prophets urge Indians toward a sense of themselves based on shared conflict with Anglo-America. Some even developed racial theories, arguing that Indians, whites, and Africans constituted the primary division of peoples in North America. Not all Indians, however, embraced this message. Many rejected the idea of a single Native American identity. Serious debates took place among Indians about the best way to secure their individual and collective independence.

Pan-Indian identity

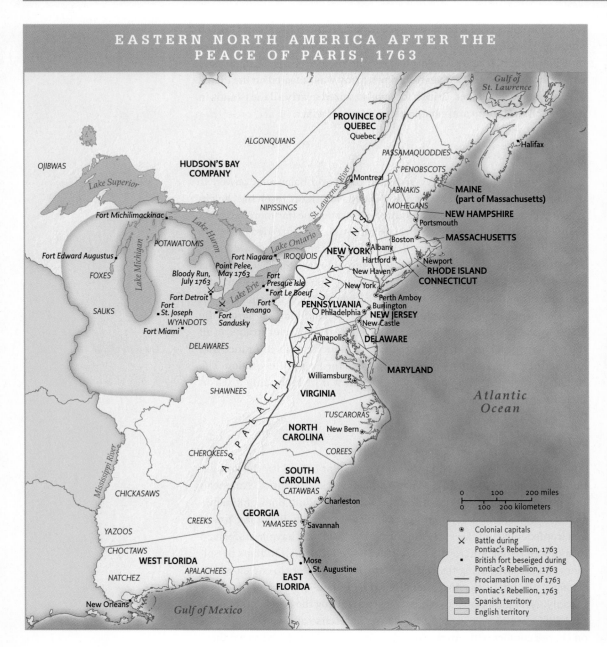

EASTERN NORTH AMERICA AFTER THE PEACE OF PARIS, 1763

OJIBWAS

Lake Superior

Fort Michilimackinac

POTAWATOMIS

Fort Edward Augustus

FOXES

Lake Michigan

Lake Huron

NIPISSINGS

Fort Niagara

Point Pelee,
May 1763

Bloody Run,
July 1763

Fort Detroit

Fort
St. Joseph

WYANDOTS

Fort Miami

SAUKS

Fort
Sandusky

Fort
Presque Isle

Fort
Le Boeuf

Fort
Venango

Lake Erie

Lake Ontario

IROQUOIS

DELAWARES

SHAWNEES

CHEROKEES

CHICKASAWS

CREEKS

YAZOOS

CHOCTAWS

NATCHEZ

APALACHEES

CATAWBAS

COREES

TUSCARORAS

ALGONQUIANS

HUDSON'S BAY
COMPANY

PROVINCE OF
QUEBEC
Quebec

Montreal

St. Lawrence River

*Gulf of
St. Lawrence*

Halifax

PASSAMAQUODDIES

PENOBSCOTS

ABNAKIS

MOHEGANS

MAINE
(part of Massachusetts)

NEW HAMPSHIRE

Portsmouth

NEW YORK

Albany

Boston

MASSACHUSETTS

Hartford

New Haven

Newport

RHODE ISLAND
CONNECTICUT

New York

Perth Amboy

Burlington

PENNSYLVANIA

Philadelphia

NEW JERSEY

New Castle

DELAWARE

Annapolis

MARYLAND

Williamsburg

VIRGINIA

New Bern

NORTH
CAROLINA

SOUTH
CAROLINA

Charleston

GEORGIA

YAMASEES

Savannah

WEST FLORIDA

Mose

St. Augustine

EAST
FLORIDA

New Orleans

Gulf of Mexico

*Atlantic
Ocean*

A P P A L A C H I A N   M O U N T A I N S

Mississippi River

| 0 | 100 | 200 miles |
| 0 | 100 | 200 kilometers |

⊕ Colonial capitals
✕ Battle during
Pontiac's Rebellion, 1763
▪ British fort beseiged during
Pontiac's Rebellion, 1763
— Proclamation line of 1763
☐ Pontiac's Rebellion, 1763
☐ Spanish territory
☐ English territory

The Peace of Paris, which ended the Seven Years' War, left all of North America east of the Mississippi in British hands, ending the French presence on the continent.

Throughout eastern North America, the abrupt departure of the French in the aftermath of the Seven Years' War eliminated the balance-of-power diplomacy that had enabled groups like the Iroquois to maintain a significant degree of autonomy. Without consulting them, the French had ceded land Indians claimed as their own to British control. The Treaty of Paris left Indians more dependent than ever on the British and ushered in a period of confusion over land claims, control of the fur trade, and tribal relations in general.

Effect on Indians

In 1763, in the wake of the French defeat, Indians of the Ohio Valley and Great Lakes launched a revolt against British rule. Although known among the colonists as **Pontiac's Rebellion** after an Ottawa war leader, the rebellion owed at least as much to the teachings of **Neolin**, a Delaware religious prophet. During a religious vision, the Master of Life instructed Neolin that his people must reject European technology, free themselves from commercial ties with whites and dependence on alcohol, clothe themselves in the garb of their ancestors, and drive the British from their territory (although friendly French inhabitants could remain). Neolin combined this message with the relatively new idea of pan-Indian identity. All Indians, he preached, were a single people, and only through cooperation could they regain their lost independence.

Neolin's message

The Proclamation Line

In the spring and summer of 1763, Ottawas, Hurons, and other Indians besieged Detroit, then a major British military outpost, seized nine other forts, and killed hundreds of white settlers who had intruded onto Indian lands. British forces soon launched a counterattack, and over the next few years the tribes one by one made peace. But the uprising inspired the government in London to issue the **Proclamation of 1763**, prohibiting further colonial settlement west of the Appalachian Mountains. These lands were reserved exclusively for Indians. Moreover, the proclamation banned the sale of Native American lands to private individuals.

Proclamation of 1763

The British aim was less to protect the Indians than to stabilize the situation on the colonial frontier and to avoid being dragged into an endless series of border conflicts. But the proclamation enraged both settlers and speculators hoping to take advantage of the expulsion of the French to consolidate their claims to western lands. They ignored the new policy. George Washington himself ordered his agents to buy up as much Indian land as possible, while keeping the transactions "a profound secret" because of their illegality. Failing to offer a viable solution to the question of westward expansion, the Proclamation of 1763 ended up further exacerbating settler–Indian relations.

VOICES OF FREEDOM

From Scarouyady, Speech to Pennsylvania Provincial Council (1756)

The outbreak of the Seven Years' War inflamed relations between Native Americans and white settlers in the Pennsylvania backcountry. Scarouyady, an Oneida leader who wished to maintain harmony, told the colony's leaders that he approved of war against hostile tribes and hoped that a fort could be built to protect friendly Indians and keep armed whites in check. But the middle ground was rapidly disappearing.

You have . . . tried all amicable means with [the Delaware Indians] and with the Six Nations, but as all have proved ineffectual, you do right to strike them. You have had a great deal of patience; other people on losing a single man, would have armed and drove off the foe; but you have sat still while numbers of your people have been and now are murdered. . . . Your enemies have got great advantage by your inactivity; show them you are men.

You told us that you must now build a Fort at Shamokin; we are glad to hear it; it is a good thing. . . . The Fort at Shamokin is not a thing of little consequence; it is of the greatest importance to us as well as you. Your people are foolish; for want of this Fort, the Indians, who are your friends, can be of no service to you, having no place to go to where they can promise themselves protection. They cannot be called together; they can do nothing for you; they are not secure any where. At present your people cannot distinguish foes from friends; they think every Indian is against them; they blame us all without distinction, because they see nobody appear for them; the common people to a man entertain this notion, and insult us wherever we go. We bear their ill usage, though very irksome; but all this will be set right when you have built the Fort, and you will see that we in particular are sincere, and many others will come to your assistance. We desire when the fort is built, you will put into the command of so important a place some of your people; grave, solid, and sensible men, who are in repute amongst you, and in whom we can place a Confidence. . . . Do yourselves and us Justice, and bring your Enemies to a due Sense of themselves, and to offer just Terms, and then, and not till then, think of a Peace. This is our Advice.

From Pontiac, Speeches
(1762 and 1763)

Pontiac was a leader of the pan-Indian resistance to English rule known as Pontiac's Rebellion, which followed the end of the Seven Years' War. Neolin was a Delaware religious prophet who helped to inspire the rebellion.

Englishmen, although you have conquered the French, you have not yet conquered us! We are not your slaves. These lakes, these woods, and mountains were left to us by our ancestors. They are our inheritance; and we will part with them to none. Your nation supposes that we, like the white people, cannot live without bread and pork and beef! But you ought to know that He, the Great Spirit and Master of Life, has provided food for us in these spacious lakes, and on these woody mountains.

[The Master of Life has said to Neolin:]

I am the Maker of heaven and earth, the trees, lakes, rivers, and all else. I am the Maker of all mankind; and because I love you, you must do my will. The land on which you live I have made for you and not for others. Why do you suffer the white man to dwell among you? My children, you have forgotten the customs and traditions of your forefathers. Why do you not clothe yourselves in skins, as they did, use bows and arrows and the stone-pointed lances, which they used? You have bought guns, knives, kettles and blankets from the white man until you can no longer do without them; and what is worse, you have drunk the poison firewater, which turns you into fools. Fling all these things away; live as your wise forefathers did before you. And as for these English—these dogs dressed in red, who have come to rob you of your hunting-grounds, and drive away the game—you must lift the hatchet against them. Wipe them from the face of the earth, and then you will win my favor back again, and once more be happy and prosperous.

QUESTIONS

1. *What aspects of white behavior does Scarouyady object to?*

2. *What elements of Indian life does Neolin criticize most strongly?*

3. *How do Scarouyady and Pontiac differ in the ways they address white audiences?*

Pennsylvania and the Indians

Frontier tensions

The Seven Years' War not only redrew the map of the world but produced dramatic changes within the American colonies as well. In Pennsylvania, the conflict shattered the decades-old rule of the Quaker elite and dealt the final blow to the colony's policy of accommodation with the Indians. During the war, with the frontier ablaze with battles between settlers and French and Indian warriors, western Pennsylvanians demanded that colonial authorities adopt a more aggressive stance. When the governor declared war on hostile Delawares, raised a militia, and offered a bounty for Indian scalps, many of the assembly's pacifist Quakers resigned their seats, effectively ending their control of Pennsylvania politics.

The town of Paxton

In December 1763, while Pontiac's Rebellion still raged, a party of fifty armed men, mostly Scotch-Irish farmers from the vicinity of the Pennsylvania town of Paxton, destroyed the Indian village of Conestoga and then marched on Philadelphia, intending to attack Moravian Indians who resided near the city. The governor ordered the expulsion of much of the Indian population. By the 1760s, Pennsylvania's Holy Experiment was at an end and with it William Penn's promise of "true friendship and amity" between colonists and the native population.

Colonial Identities

Before the war, the colonies had been largely isolated from one another. Outside of New England, more Americans probably traveled to England than from one colony to another. The **Albany Plan of Union** of 1754, drafted by Benjamin Franklin at the outbreak of the Seven Years' War, envisioned the creation of a Grand Council composed of delegates from each colony, with the power to levy taxes and deal with Indian relations and the common defense. Rejected by the colonial assemblies, whose powers Franklin's proposal would curtail, the plan was never sent to London for approval.

The war and American identity

Participation in the Seven Years' War created greater bonds among the colonies. But the war also strengthened colonists' pride in being members of the British empire. It has been said that Americans were never more British than in 1763. The defeat of the Catholic French reinforced the equation of British nationality, Protestantism, and freedom.

But soon, the American colonists would come to believe that membership in the empire jeopardized their liberty. When they did, they set out on a road that led to independence.

CHAPTER REVIEW AND ONLINE RESOURCES

REVIEW QUESTIONS

1. How did Great Britain's position in North America change relative to the other European powers during the first three-quarters of the eighteenth century?

2. How did the ideas of republicanism and liberalism differ in eighteenth-century British North America?

3. Three distinct slave systems were well entrenched in Britain's mainland colonies. Describe the main characteristics of each system.

4. How and why did the colonists' sense of a collective British identity change during the years before 1764?

5. What ideas generated by the American Enlightenment and the Great Awakening prompted challenges to religious, social, and political authorities in the British colonies?

6. How were colonial merchants in British America involved in the Atlantic economy, and what was the role of the slave trade in that economy?

7. We often consider the impact of the slave trade only on the United States, but its impact extended much further. How did it affect West African nations and society, other regions of the New World, and the nations of Europe?

8. How was an African-American collective identity created in these years, and what role did slave rebellions play in that process?

9. How did a distinct Native American identity start to emerge after the Seven Years' War?

KEY TERMS

Atlantic slave trade (p. 106)
Middle Passage (p. 107)
yeoman farmers (p. 113)
Stono Rebellion (p. 114)
republicanism (p. 116)
liberalism (p. 116)
salutary neglect (p. 119)
Enlightenment (p. 122)
Deism (p. 123)
Great Awakening (p. 123)
Father Junípero Serra (p. 127)
middle ground (p. 129)
Seven Years' War (p. 130)
French and Indian War (p. 130)
Pontiac's Rebellion (p. 133)
Neolin (p. 133)
Proclamation of 1763 (p. 133)
Albany Plan of Union (p. 136)

Go to 🐰 INQUIZITIVE

To see what you know—and learn what you've missed—with personalized feedback along the way.

Visit the *Give Me Liberty!* **Student Site** for primary source documents and images, interactive maps, author videos featuring Eric Foner, and more.

CHAPTER 5

THE AMERICAN REVOLUTION

★

1763–1783

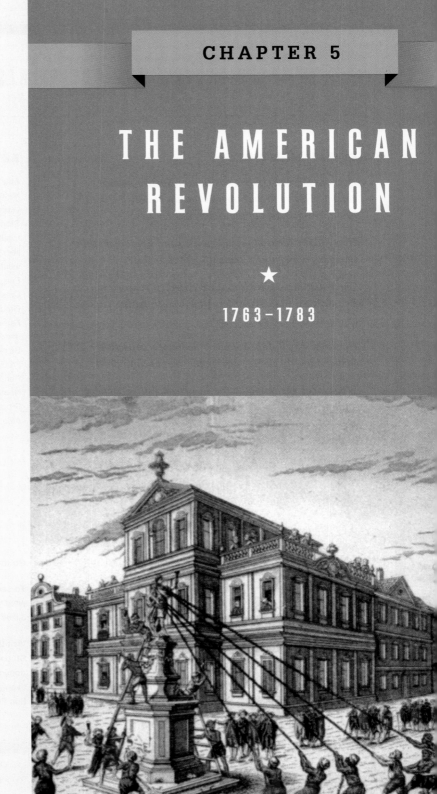

A French engraving depicts New Yorkers tearing down the statue of King George III in July 1776, after the approval of the Declaration of Independence. Slaves are doing the work, while whites look on. The statue was later melted down to make bullets for the Continental army.

On the night of August 26, 1765, a violent crowd of Bostonians assaulted the elegant home of Thomas Hutchinson, chief justice and lieutenant governor of Massachusetts. Hutchinson and his family barely had time to escape before the crowd broke down the front door and proceeded to destroy or carry off most of their possessions, including paintings, furniture, silverware, and notes for a history of Massachusetts Hutchinson was writing. By the time the crowd departed, only the outer walls of the home remained standing.

The immediate cause of the riot was the **Stamp Act**, a recently enacted British tax that many colonists felt violated their liberty. Only a few days earlier, Hutchinson had helped to disperse a crowd attacking a building owned by his relative Andrew Oliver, a merchant who had been appointed to help administer the new law. Both crowds were led by Ebenezer Mackintosh, a shoemaker who enjoyed a wide following among Boston's working people.

The riot of August 26 was one small episode in a series of events that launched a half-century of popular protest and political upheaval throughout the Western world. The momentous era that came to be called the Age of Revolution began in British North America, spread to Europe and the Caribbean, and culminated in the Latin American wars for independence. In all these struggles, "Liberty" emerged as the foremost rallying cry for popular discontent. Rarely has the idea played so central a role in political debate and social upheaval.

If the attack on Hutchinson's home demonstrated the depths of feeling aroused by Britain's efforts to impose greater control over its empire, it also revealed that revolution is a dynamic process whose consequences no one can anticipate. The crowd's fury expressed resentments against the rich and powerful quite different from colonial leaders' objections to Parliament's attempt to tax the colonies. The Stamp Act crisis inaugurated not only a struggle for colonial liberty in relation to Great Britain but also a multisided battle to define and extend liberty within the new nation.

FOCUS QUESTIONS

- *What were the roots and significance of the Stamp Act controversy?*

- *What key events sharpened the divisions between Britain and the colonists in the late 1760s and early 1770s?*

- *What key events marked the move toward American independence?*

- *How were American forces able to prevail in the Revolutionary War?*

THE CRISIS BEGINS

Consolidating the Empire

When George III assumed the throne of Great Britain in 1760, no one on either side of the Atlantic imagined that within two decades Britain's American colonies would separate from the empire. Having treated the colonists as allies during the Seven Years' War, Britain reverted in the mid-1760s to seeing them as subordinates whose main role was to enrich

According to the doctrine of "virtual representation," the House of Commons represented all residents of the British empire, whether or not they could vote for members. In this 1775 cartoon criticizing the idea, a blinded Britannia, on the far right, stumbles into a pit. Next to her, two colonists complain of being robbed by British taxation. In the background, according to an accompanying explanation of the cartoon, stand the "Catholic" city of Quebec and the "Protestant town of Boston," the latter in flames.

the mother country. During this period, the government in London concerned itself with the colonies in unprecedented ways, hoping to make British rule more efficient and systematic and to raise funds to help pay for the war and to finance the empire. Nearly all British political leaders supported the new laws that so enraged the colonists. To fight the Seven Years' War, Britain had borrowed from banks and individual investors more than £150 million (the equivalent of tens of trillions of dollars in today's money). It seemed only reasonable that the colonies should help pay this national debt, foot part of the bill for continued British protection, and stop cheating the treasury by violating the Navigation Acts.

Nearly all Britons, moreover, believed that Parliament represented the entire empire and had a right to legislate for it. Millions of Britons, including the residents of major cities like Manchester and Birmingham, had no representatives in Parliament. But according to the widely accepted theory of **virtual representation**—which held that each member represented the empire, not just his own district—the interests of all who lived under the British crown were supposedly taken into account. When Americans began to insist that because they were unrepresented in Parliament, the British government could not tax the colonies, they won little support in the mother country.

The British government had already alarmed many colonists by issuing **writs of assistance** to combat smuggling. These were general search warrants that allowed customs officials to search anywhere they chose for smuggled goods. In a celebrated court case in Boston in 1761, the lawyer James Otis insisted that the writs were "an instrument of arbitrary power, destructive to English liberty, and the fundamental principles of the [British] Constitution," and that Parliament therefore had no right to authorize them. ("American independence was then and there born," the Boston lawyer John Adams later remarked—a considerable exaggeration.) Many colonists were also outraged by the Proclamation of 1763 (mentioned in the previous chapter), which barred further settlement on lands west of the Appalachian Mountains.

Outrage in the colonies

Taxing the Colonies

The Sugar Act of 1764

In 1764, the **Sugar Act**, introduced by Prime Minister George Grenville, reduced the existing tax on molasses imported into North America from the French West Indies from six pence to three pence per gallon. But the act also established a new machinery to end widespread smuggling by colonial merchants. And to counteract the tendency of colonial juries to acquit merchants charged with violating trade regulations, it strengthened the admiralty courts, where accused smugglers could be judged without benefit of a jury trial. Thus, colonists saw the measure not as a welcome reduction in taxation but as an attempt to get them to pay a levy they would otherwise have evaded. At the same time, the Currency Act reaffirmed the earlier ban on colonial assemblies' issuing paper as "legal tender"—that is, money that individuals are required to accept in payment of debts.

The Sugar Act was an effort to strengthen the long-established (and long-evaded) Navigation Acts. The Stamp Act of 1765 was a new departure in imperial policy. For the first time, Parliament attempted to raise money from direct taxes in the colonies rather than through the regulation of trade. The act required that all sorts of printed material produced in the colonies—such as newspapers, books, court documents, commercial papers, land deeds, and almanacs—carry a stamp purchased from authorities. Its purpose was to help finance the operations of the empire, including the cost of stationing British troops in North America, without seeking revenue from colonial assemblies.

The Stamp Act of 1765

Whereas the Sugar Act had mainly affected residents of colonial ports, the Stamp Act managed to offend virtually every free colonist—rich and poor, farmers, artisans, and merchants. It was especially resented by members of the public sphere who wrote, published, and read books and newspapers and followed political affairs. The prospect of a British army permanently stationed on American soil also alarmed many colonists. And by imposing the stamp tax without colonial consent, Parliament directly challenged the authority of local elites who, through the assemblies they controlled, had established their power over the raising and spending of money. They were ready to defend this authority in the name of liberty.

Opposition to the Stamp Act was the first great drama of the revolutionary era and the first major split between colonists and Great Britain over the meaning of freedom. Nearly all colonial political leaders opposed the act. They invoked the rights of the freeborn Englishman, which, they insisted, colonists should also enjoy. Liberty, they insisted, could not be secure where property was "taken away without consent."

Opposition to the Stamp Act

Taxation and Representation

At stake were clashing ideas of the British empire itself. American leaders viewed the empire as an association of equals in which free inhabitants overseas enjoyed the same rights as Britons at home. Colonists in other

This teapot protesting the Stamp Act was produced in England and marketed in colonial America, illustrating the close political and economic connections between the two.

Stamp Act repeal

outposts of the empire, such as India, the West Indies, and Canada, echoed this outlook. All, in the name of liberty, claimed the right to govern their own affairs. The British government and its appointed representatives in America, by contrast, saw the empire as a system of unequal parts in which different principles governed different areas, and all were subject to the authority of Parliament. To surrender the right to tax the colonies would set a dangerous precedent for the empire as a whole.

Some opponents of the Stamp Act distinguished between "internal" taxes like the stamp duty, which they claimed Parliament had no right to impose, and revenue legitimately raised through the regulation of trade. But more and more colonists insisted that Britain had no right to tax them at all, since Americans were unrepresented in the House of Commons. **"No taxation without representation"** became their rallying cry. Virginia's House of Burgesses approved four resolutions offered by the fiery orator Patrick Henry. They insisted that the colonists enjoyed the same "liberties, privileges, franchises, and immunities" as residents of the mother country and that the right to consent to taxation was a cornerstone of "British freedom." (The House rejected as too radical three other resolutions, including Henry's call for outright resistance to unlawful taxation, but these were also reprinted in colonial newspapers.)

In October 1765, the Stamp Act Congress, with twenty-seven delegates from nine colonies, including some of the most prominent men in America, met in New York and endorsed Virginia's position. Its resolutions began by affirming the "allegiance" of all colonists to the "Crown of Great Britain" and their "due subordination" to Parliament. But they went on to insist that the right to consent to taxation was "essential to the freedom of a people." Soon, merchants throughout the colonies agreed to boycott British goods until Parliament repealed the Stamp Act. This was the first major cooperative action among Britain's mainland colonies. By seeking to impose uniformity on the colonies rather than dealing with them individually as in the past, Parliament had inadvertently united America.

The Stamp Act crisis, however, did not lead inevitably to revolution. Nearly all the British colonies in the Western Hemisphere protested the tax, but only about half eventually decided to strike for independence. At this point, most colonists continued to believe that their liberties and material interests were safer inside the British empire than outside it.

Liberty and Resistance

No word was more frequently invoked by critics of the Stamp Act than "liberty." Throughout the colonies, opponents of the new tax staged mock funerals in which liberty's coffin was carried to a burial ground, only to have the occupant miraculously revived at the last moment, whereupon the assembled crowd repaired to a tavern to celebrate. As the crisis continued, symbols of liberty proliferated. A large elm tree came to be known as the Liberty Tree. Its image soon appeared in prints and pamphlets throughout the colonies.

The Liberty Tree

Colonial leaders resolved to prevent the new law's implementation, and by and large they succeeded. Even before the passage of the Stamp Act, a **Committee of Correspondence** in Boston communicated with other colonies to encourage opposition to the Sugar and Currency Acts. Now, such committees sprang up in other colonies, exchanging ideas and information about resistance. Initiated by colonial elites, the movement against the Stamp Act quickly drew in a far broader range of Americans. The act, wrote John Adams, had inspired "the people, even to the lowest ranks," to become "more attentive to their liberties, more inquisitive about them, and more determined to defend them, than they were ever before known."

Organized resistance

Opponents of the Stamp Act, however, did not rely solely on debate. Even before the law went into effect, crowds forced those chosen to administer it to resign and destroyed shipments of stamps. In 1765, New York City residents were organized by the newly created **Sons of Liberty**, who led protest processions, posted notices reading "Liberty, Property, and No Stamps," and enforced the boycott of British imports.

Stunned by the ferocity of American resistance and pressured by London merchants and manufacturers who did not wish to lose their American markets, the British government retreated. In 1766, Parliament repealed the Stamp Act. But this concession was accompanied by the Declaratory Act, which rejected Americans' claims that only their elected representatives could levy taxes. Parliament, proclaimed this measure, possessed the power to pass laws for "the colonies and people of America . . . in all cases whatsoever." Since the debt-ridden British government continued to need money raised in the colonies, passage of the Declaratory Act promised further conflict.

The Declaratory Act

The Regulators

The Stamp Act crisis was not the only example of violent social turmoil during the 1760s. Many colonies experienced contentious internal divisions as well. As population moved westward, the conflicting land claims of settlers, speculators, colonial governments, and Indians sparked fierce disputes. As in the Stamp Act crisis, "Liberty" was the rallying cry, but in this case liberty had less to do with imperial policy than with secure possession of land.

Beginning in the mid-1760s, a group of wealthy residents of the South Carolina backcountry calling themselves **Regulators** protested the under-representation of western settlements in the colony's assembly and the legislators' failure to establish local governments that could regularize land titles and suppress bands of outlaws.

Backcountry tensions

A parallel movement in North Carolina mobilized small farmers, who refused to pay taxes, kidnapped local officials, assaulted the homes of land speculators, merchants, and lawyers, and disrupted court proceedings. Here, the complaint was not a lack of government, but corrupt county authorities. Demanding the democratization of local government, the Regulators condemned the "rich and powerful" (the colony's elite) who used their political authority to prosper at the expense of "poor industrious" farmers. At their peak, the Regulators numbered around 8,000 armed farmers. The region remained in turmoil until 1771, when, in the "battle of Alamance," the farmers were suppressed by the colony's militia.

Social divisions and politics

The emerging rift between Britain and America eventually super-imposed itself on conflicts within the colonies. But the social divisions revealed in the Stamp Act riots and backcountry uprisings made some members of the colonial elite fear that opposition to British measures might unleash turmoil at home. As a result, they were more reluctant to challenge British authority when the next imperial crisis arose.

THE ROAD TO REVOLUTION

The Townshend Crisis

In 1767, the government in London decided to impose a new set of taxes on Americans, known as the **Townshend Acts**. They were devised by the Chancellor of the Exchequer (the cabinet's chief financial minister), Charles Townshend. In opposing the Stamp Act, some colonists had seemed to suggest that they would not object if Britain raised revenue by regulating trade. Taking them at their word, Townshend persuaded Parliament to impose new taxes on goods imported into the colonies and to create a new board of customs commissioners to collect them and suppress smuggling. Although many merchants objected to the new enforcement procedures, opposition to the Townshend duties developed more slowly than in the case of the Stamp Act. Leaders in several colonies nonetheless decided in 1768 to reimpose the ban on importing British goods.

Reliance on American rather than British goods, on homespun clothing rather than imported finery, became a symbol of American resistance. It also reflected, as the colonists saw it, a virtuous spirit of self-sacrifice as compared with the self-indulgence and luxury many Americans were coming to associate with Britain. Women who spun and wove at home so as not to purchase British goods were hailed as Daughters of Liberty.

Homespun clothing as resistance

The idea of using homemade rather than imported goods especially appealed to Chesapeake planters, who found themselves owing increasing amounts of money to British merchants. Nonimportation, wrote George Washington, gave "the extravagant man" an opportunity to "retrench his expenses" by reducing the purchase of British luxuries, without having to advertise to his neighbors that he might be in financial distress.

Nonimportation

Urban artisans, who welcomed an end to competition from imported British manufactured goods, strongly supported the boycott. Philadelphia and New York merchants at first were reluctant to take part, although they eventually agreed to go along. As had happened during the Stamp Act crisis, the streets of American cities filled with popular protests against the duties imposed by Parliament. Extralegal local committees attempted to enforce the boycott of British goods.

The Boston Massacre

Boston once again became the focal point of conflict. Royal troops had been stationed in the city in 1768 after rioting that followed the British seizure of the ship *Liberty* for violating trade regulations. The soldiers, who competed for jobs on Boston's waterfront with the city's laborers, became more and more unpopular. On March 5, 1770, a fight between a snowball-throwing crowd and British troops escalated into an armed confrontation that left five Bostonians dead. One of those who fell in what came to be called the **Boston Massacre** was **Crispus Attucks,** a sailor of mixed Indian-African-white ancestry. The commanding officer and eight soldiers were put on trial in Massachusetts. Ably defended by John Adams, who viewed lower-class crowd actions as a dangerous method of opposing British policies, seven were found not guilty, while two were convicted of manslaughter. But Paul Revere, a member of the Boston Sons of Liberty and a silversmith and engraver, helped to stir up indignation against the British army by producing a widely circulated (and quite inaccurate) print of the Boston Massacre depicting a line of British soldiers firing into an unarmed crowd.

Royal troops in Boston

By 1770, as merchants' profits shriveled and many members of the colonial elite found they could not do without British goods, the

The Boston Massacre. Less than a month after the Boston Massacre of 1770, in which five colonists died, Paul Revere produced this engraving of the event. Although it inaccurately depicts what was actually a disorganized brawl between residents of Boston and British soldiers, this image became one of the most influential pieces of political propaganda of the revolutionary era.

nonimportation movement was collapsing. British merchants, who wished to remove a possible source of future interruption of trade, pressed for repeal of the Townshend duties. When the British ministry agreed, leaving in place only a tax on tea, and agreed to remove troops from Boston, American merchants quickly abandoned the boycott.

Once again, an immediate crisis had been resolved. Nonetheless, many Americans concluded that Britain was succumbing to the same pattern of political corruption and decline of liberty that afflicted other countries. In addition, rumors circulated in the colonies that the Anglican Church in England planned to send bishops to America. Among members of other Protestant denominations, the rumors—strongly denied in London—sparked fears that bishops would establish religious courts like those that had once persecuted Dissenters.

The Tea Act

The next crisis underscored how powerfully events in other parts of Britain's global empire affected the American colonies. The East India Company, a giant trading monopoly, effectively governed recently acquired British possessions in India. Numerous British merchants, bankers, and other individuals had invested heavily in its stock. A classic speculative bubble ensued, with the price of stock in the company rising sharply and then collapsing. To rescue the company and its investors, the British government decided to help it market its enormous holdings of Chinese tea in North America.

To further stimulate its sales and bail out the East India Company, the British government, now headed by Frederick Lord North, offered the company a series of rebates and tax exemptions. These enabled it to dump low-priced tea on the American market, undercutting both established merchants and smugglers.

The tax on tea was not new. But many colonists insisted that to pay it on this large new body of imports would acknowledge Britain's right to tax the colonies. As tea shipments arrived, resistance developed in the major ports. On December 16, 1773, a group of colonists disguised as Indians boarded three ships at anchor in Boston Harbor and threw more than 300 chests of tea into the water. The event became known as the **Boston Tea Party**. The loss to the East India Company was around £10,000 (the equivalent of more than $4 million today).

The Intolerable Acts

The British government, declared Lord North, must now demonstrate "whether we have, or have not, any authority in that country." Its response to the Boston Tea Party was swift and decisive. Parliament closed the port of Boston to all trade until the tea was paid for. It radically altered the Massachusetts Charter of 1691 by curtailing town meetings and authorizing the governor to appoint members to the council—positions previously filled by election. Parliament also empowered military commanders to lodge soldiers in private homes. These measures, called the Coercive or **Intolerable Acts** by Americans, united the colonies in opposition to what was widely seen as a direct threat to their political freedom.

At almost the same time, Parliament passed the Quebec Act. This extended the southern boundary of that Canadian province to the Ohio River and granted legal toleration to the Roman Catholic Church in Canada. The act not only threw into question land claims in the Ohio country but also persuaded many colonists that the government in London was conspiring to strengthen Catholicism— dreaded by most Protestants—in its American empire.

An Attempt to Land a Bishop in America, an engraving from a London magazine published in 1769. A crowd of New Englanders prevents a ship carrying a bishop dispatched by the Church of England from landing. The crowd carries the works of political philosopher John Locke and a banner proclaiming "Liberty and Freedom of Conscience," and hurls the writings of Protestant theologian John Calvin at the bishop.

THE COMING OF INDEPENDENCE

The Continental Congress

Opposition to the Intolerable Acts now spread to small towns and rural areas that had not participated actively in previous resistance. In September 1774, in the town of Worcester, Massachusetts, 4,600 militiamen from thirty-seven towns (half the adult male population of the entire county) lined both sides of Main Street as the British-appointed officials walked between them. That month, a convention of delegates from Massachusetts towns approved a series of resolutions (called the Suffolk Resolves for the county in which Boston is located) that urged Americans to refuse obedience to the new laws, withhold taxes, and prepare for war.

Suffolk Resolves

To coordinate resistance to the Intolerable Acts, a **Continental Congress** convened in Philadelphia, bringing together the most prominent political leaders of twelve mainland colonies (Georgia did not take part). From Massachusetts came the "brace of Adamses"—John and his more radical cousin Samuel. Virginia's seven delegates included George Washington, Richard Henry Lee, and the renowned orator Patrick Henry. "The distinctions between Virginians, Pennsylvanians, New Yorkers, and New Englanders," Henry declared, "are no more. I am not a Virginian, but an American." In March 1775, Henry concluded a speech urging a Virginia convention to begin military preparations with a legendary credo: "Give me liberty, or give me death!"

Leaders of the Congress

The Continental Association

Before it adjourned at the end of October 1774, the Congress endorsed the Suffolk Resolves and adopted the Continental Association, which called for an almost complete halt to trade with Great Britain and the West Indies (at South Carolina's insistence, exports of rice to Europe were exempted). Congress authorized local Committees of Safety to implement its mandates and to take action against "enemies of American liberty," including businessmen who tried to profit from the sudden scarcity of goods.

The Committees of Safety

The Committees of Safety began the process of transferring effective political power from established governments whose authority derived from Great Britain to extralegal grassroots bodies reflecting the will of the people. By early 1775, some 7,000 men were serving on local committees throughout the colonies, a vast expansion of the "political nation." The committees became training grounds where small farmers, city artisans, propertyless laborers, and others who had heretofore had little role in government discussed political issues and exercised political power. When the New York assembly refused to endorse the Association, local committees continued to enforce it anyway.

The Sweets of Liberty

By 1775, talk of liberty pervaded the colonies. The past few years had witnessed an endless parade of pamphlets with titles like *A Chariot of Liberty* and *Oration on the Beauties of Liberty*. (The latter, a sermon delivered in Boston by Joseph Allen in 1772, became the most popular public address of the years before independence.) Sober men spoke longingly of the "sweets of liberty." Commented a British immigrant who arrived in Maryland early in 1775: "They are all liberty mad."

As the crisis deepened, Americans increasingly based their claims not simply on the historical rights of Englishmen but on the more abstract language of natural

rights and universal freedom. The First Continental Congress defended its actions by appealing to the "principles of the English constitution," the "liberties of free and natural-born subjects within the realm of England," and the "immutable law of nature." John Locke's theory of natural rights offered a powerful justification for colonial resistance, as did Thomas Jefferson in *A Summary View of the Rights of British America*, written in 1774. Americans, Jefferson declared, were "a free people claiming their rights, as derived from the laws of nature, and not as the gift of their chief magistrate."

In March 1776, James Pike, a soldier in the Massachusetts militia, carved this scene on his powder horn to commemorate the battles of Lexington and Concord. At the center stands the Liberty Tree.

The Outbreak of War

By the time the Second Continental Congress convened in May 1775, war had broken out between British soldiers and armed citizens of Massachusetts. On April 19, a force of British soldiers marched from Boston toward the nearby town of Concord to seize arms being stockpiled there. Riders from Boston, among them Paul Revere, warned local leaders of the troops' approach. Militiamen took up arms and tried to resist the British advance. Skirmishes between Americans and British soldiers took place, known as the **Battles of Lexington and Concord**. By the time the British retreated to the safety of Boston, some forty-nine Americans and seventy-three members of the Royal Army lay dead.

Lexington and Concord

What the philosopher Ralph Waldo Emerson would later call "the shot heard 'round the world" began the American War of Independence. In May 1775, Ethan Allen and the Green Mountain Boys from Vermont, together with militiamen from Connecticut led by Benedict Arnold, surrounded Fort Ticonderoga in New York and forced it to surrender. The following winter, Henry Knox, George Washington's commander of artillery, arranged for some of the Ticonderoga cannon to be dragged hundreds of miles to the east to reinforce the siege of Boston, where British forces were ensconced. On June 17, 1775, two months after Lexington and Concord, the British had dislodged colonial militiamen from Breed's Hill, although only at a heavy cost in casualties. (The battle came to be named the **Battle of Bunker Hill**, after the nearby Bunker Hill.) But the arrival of American cannon in March 1776 and their entrenchment above the city made the British position in Boston untenable. The British army under the command of Sir William Howe was forced to abandon the city. Before leaving, Howe's forces cut down the original Liberty Tree.

The Second Continental Congress

Meanwhile, the Second Continental Congress authorized the raising of a **Continental army**, printed money to pay for it, and appointed George Washington its commander. In response, Britain declared the colonies in a state of rebellion, dispatched thousands of troops, and ordered the closing of all colonial ports.

Independence?

By the end of 1775, the breach with Britain seemed irreparable. But many colonists shied away from the idea of independence. Pride in membership in the British empire was still strong, and many political leaders, especially in colonies that had experienced internal turmoil, feared that a complete break with the mother country might unleash further conflict.

The Dunmore proclamation

Such fears affected how colonial leaders responded to the idea of independence. The elites of Massachusetts and Virginia, who felt supremely confident of their ability to retain authority at home, tended to support a break with Britain. Southern leaders not only were highly protective of their political liberty but also were outraged by a proclamation issued in November 1775 by Lord Dunmore, the British governor and military commander in Virginia. **Lord Dunmore's proclamation** offered freedom to any slave who escaped to his lines and bore arms for the king.

Fear of domestic turmoil

In New York and Pennsylvania, however, the diversity of the population made it difficult to work out a consensus on how far to go in resisting British measures. Many established leaders drew back from further resistance. Joseph Galloway, a Pennsylvania leader and delegate to the Second Continental Congress who worked to devise a compromise between British and colonial positions, warned that independence would be accompanied by constant disputes within America. He even predicted a war between the northern and southern colonies.

Common Sense

As 1776 dawned, America presented the unusual spectacle of colonists at war against the British empire but still pleading for their rights within it. Ironically, it was a recent emigrant from England, not a colonist from a family long established on American soil, who grasped the inner logic of the situation and offered a vision of the broad significance of American independence. Thomas Paine had emigrated to Philadelphia late in 1774. He quickly became associated with a group of advocates of the American cause, including John Adams and Dr. Benjamin Rush, a leading Philadelphia physician. It was Rush who suggested to Paine that he write a pamphlet supporting American independence.

Common Sense appeared in January 1776. The pamphlet began not with a recital of colonial grievances but with an attack on the "so much boasted Constitution of England" and the principles of hereditary rule and monarchical government. Rather than being the most perfect system of government in the world, Paine wrote, the English monarchy was headed by "the royal brute of England," and the English constitution was composed in large part of "the base remains of two ancient tyrannies . . . monarchical tyranny in the person of the king [and] aristocratical tyranny in the persons of the peers."

Paine on monarchy and aristocracy

Turning to independence, Paine drew on the colonists' experiences to make his case. "There is something absurd," he wrote, "in supposing a Continent to be perpetually governed by an island." With independence, moreover, the colonies could for the first time trade freely with the entire world and insulate themselves from involvement in the endless imperial wars of Europe. Membership in the British empire, Paine insisted, was a burden to the colonies, not a benefit.

Toward the close of the pamphlet, Paine moved beyond practical considerations to outline a breathtaking vision of the historical importance of the American Revolution. "The cause of America," he proclaimed in stirring language, "is in great measure, the cause of all mankind." The new nation would become the home of freedom, "an asylum for mankind."

The cover of *Common Sense*, Thomas Paine's influential pamphlet denouncing the idea of hereditary rule and calling for American independence.

Few of Paine's ideas were original. What made *Common Sense* unique was his mode of expressing them and the audience he addressed. Previous political writings had generally been directed toward the educated elite. Paine, however, pioneered a new style of political writing, one designed to expand dramatically the public sphere where political discussion took place. He wrote clearly and directly, and he avoided the complex language and Latin phrases common in pamphlets aimed at educated readers. *Common Sense* quickly became one of the most successful and influential pamphlets in the history of political writing, selling, by Paine's estimate, some 150,000 copies. Paine directed that his share of the profits be used to buy supplies for the Continental army.

In the spring of 1776, scores of American communities adopted resolutions calling for a separation from Britain. Only six months elapsed between the appearance of *Common Sense* and the decision by the Second Continental Congress to sever the colonies' ties with Great Britain.

The Declaration of Independence

Colonial grievances

On July 2, 1776, the Congress formally declared the United States an independent nation. Two days later, it approved the **Declaration of Independence**, written by Thomas Jefferson and revised by the Congress before approval. (See the Appendix for the full text.) Most of the Declaration consists of a lengthy list of grievances directed against King George III, ranging from quartering troops in colonial homes to imposing taxes without the colonists' consent. One clause in Jefferson's draft, which condemned the inhumanity of the slave trade and criticized the king for overturning colonial laws that sought to restrict the importation of slaves, was deleted by the Congress at the insistence of Georgia and South Carolina.

Jefferson's preamble

The Declaration's enduring impact came not from the complaints against George III but from Jefferson's preamble, especially the second paragraph, which begins, "We hold these truths to be self-evident, that all men are created equal, that they are endowed by their Creator with certain unalienable Rights, that among these are Life, Liberty, and the pursuit of Happiness." By "unalienable rights," Jefferson meant rights so basic, so rooted in human nature itself, that no government could take them away.

Jefferson then went on to justify the breach with Britain. Government, he wrote, derives its powers from "the consent of the governed." When a government threatens its subjects' natural rights, the people have the authority "to alter or to abolish it." The Declaration of Independence is ultimately an assertion of the right of revolution.

The Declaration and American freedom

The Declaration also changed forever the meaning of American freedom. It completed the shift from the rights of Englishmen to the rights of mankind as the object of American independence. No longer a set of specific rights, no longer a privilege to be enjoyed by a corporate body or people in certain social circumstances, liberty had become a universal entitlement.

When Jefferson substituted the "pursuit of happiness" for property in the familiar triad that opens the Declaration, he tied the new nation's star to an open-ended, democratic process whereby individuals develop their own potential and seek to realize their own life goals. Individual self-fulfillment, unimpeded by government, would become a central element of American freedom. Tradition would no longer rule the present, and Americans could shape their society as they saw fit.

An Asylum for Mankind

A distinctive definition of nationality resting on American freedom was born in the Revolution. From the beginning, the idea of "American exceptionalism"—the belief that the United States has a special mission to be a refuge from tyranny, a symbol of freedom, and a model for the rest of the world—has occupied a central place in American nationalism. The new nation declared itself, in the words of Virginia leader James Madison, the "workshop of liberty to the Civilized World." Unburdened by the institutions—monarchy, aristocracy, hereditary privilege—that oppressed the peoples of the Old World, America and America alone was the place where the principle of universal freedom could take root. This was why Jefferson addressed the Declaration to "the opinions of mankind," not just the colonists themselves or Great Britain.

First to add his name to the Declaration of Independence was the Massachusetts merchant John Hancock, president of the Second Continental Congress, with a signature so large, he declared, according to legend, that King George III could read it without his spectacles.

America as a Symbol of Liberty, a 1775 engraving from the cover of the *Pennsylvania Magazine*, edited by Thomas Paine soon after his arrival in America. The shield displays the colony's coat of arms. The female figure holding a liberty cap is surrounded by weaponry of the patriotic struggle, including a cartridge box marked "liberty," hanging from a tree (*right*).

The Global Declaration of Independence

Even apart from the Declaration of Independence, 1776 was a momentous year in North America. Spain established Mission Dolores, the first European settlement at San Francisco, in an effort to block Russian advances on the Pacific coast. In San Diego, local Indians rebelled, unsuccessfully, against Spanish rule. The Lakota Sioux, migrating westward from Minnesota, settled in the Black Hills of North Dakota, their homeland for the next century. All these places and peoples would eventually become part of the United States, but, of course, no one knew this in 1776.

Meanwhile, the struggle for independence reverberated around the globe. The American colonists were less concerned with securing human rights for all mankind than with winning international recognition in their struggle for independence from Britain. But Jefferson hoped that this rebellion would become "the signal of arousing men to burst the chains . . . and to assume the blessings and security of self-government." The Declaration quickly appeared in French and German translations, although not, at first, in Spanish, since the government feared it would inspire dangerous ideas among the peoples of Spain's American empire.

In the years since 1776, numerous anticolonial movements have modeled their own declarations of independence on America's. Today more than half the countries in the world, in places as far-flung as China (issued

Legacy of the Declaration

VOICES OF FREEDOM

From Samuel Seabury, An Alarm to the
Legislature of the Province in New-York (1775)

An Anglican minister and graduate of Yale College, Samuel Seabury was a devoted Loyalist who in 1774 and 1775 published several pamphlets opposing the revolutionary movement. He remained in the United States after the War of Independence and became the new nation's first Episcopal bishop.

The unhappy contention we have entered into with our parent state, would inevitably be attended with many disagreeable circumstances, with many and great inconveniences to us, even were it conducted on our part, with propriety and moderation. What then must be the case, when all proper and moderate measures are rejected? . . . When every scheme that tends to peace, is branded with ignominy; as being the machination of slavery! When nothing is called FREEDOM but SEDITION! Nothing LIBERTY but REBELLION! . . .

A Committee, chosen in a tumultuous, illegal manner, usurped the most despotic authority over the province. They entered into contracts, compacts, combinations, treaties of alliance, with the other colonies, without any power from the legislature of the province. They agreed with the other Colonies to send Delegates to meet in convention at Philadelphia, to determine upon the rights and liberties of the good people of this province.

The state to which the Grand Congress, and the subordinate Committees, have reduced the colonies, is really deplorable. They have introduced a system of the most oppressive tyranny that can possibly be imagined;—a tyranny, not only over the actions, but over the words, thoughts, and minds, of the good people of this province. People have been threatened with the vengeance of a mob, for speaking in support of order and good government. . . .

Behold, Gentlemen, behold the wretched state to which we are reduced! A foreign power is brought in to govern this province. Laws made at Philadelphia, by factious men from New-England, New-Jersey, Pennsylvania, Maryland, Virginia, and the Carolinas, are imposed upon us by the most imperious menaces. Money is levied upon us without the consent of our representatives. . . . Mobs and riots are encouraged, in order to force submission to the tyranny of the Congress.

From Thomas Paine, *Common Sense* (1776)

A recent emigrant from England, Thomas Paine in January 1776 published *Common Sense*, a highly influential pamphlet that in stirring language made the case for American independence.

In the following pages I offer nothing more than simple facts, plain arguments, and common sense. . . .

Male and female are the distinctions of nature, good and bad the distinctions of heaven; but how a race of men came into the world so exalted above the rest, and distinguished like some new species, is worth enquiring into, and whether they are the means of happiness or of misery to mankind. . . . One of the strongest *natural* proofs of the folly of hereditary right in kings, is, that nature disapproves it, otherwise she would not so frequently turn it into ridicule, by giving mankind an *ass for a lion*. . . .

The sun never shined on a cause of greater worth. 'Tis not the affair of a city, a country, a province, or a kingdom, but of a continent—of at least one eighth part of the habitable globe. 'Tis not the concern of a day, a year, or an age; posterity are virtually involved in the context, and will be more or less affected, even to the end of time, by the proceedings now. Now is the seed time of continental union, faith and honor. . . .

I challenge the warmest advocate for reconciliation to show a single advantage that this continent can reap by being connected with Great Britain. . . . But the injuries and disadvantages which we sustain by that connection, are without number. . . . Any submission to, or dependence on, Great Britain, tends directly to involve this Continent in European wars and quarrels, and set us at variance with nations who would otherwise seek our friendship, and against whom we have neither anger nor complaint.

O ye that love mankind! Ye that dare oppose, not only the tyranny, but the tyrant, stand forth! Every spot of the old world is overrun with oppression. Freedom hath been hunted round the globe. Asia, and Africa, have long expelled her. Europe regards her like a stranger, and England hath given her warning to depart. O! Receive the fugitive, and prepare in time an asylum for mankind.

QUESTIONS

1. *Why does Seabury believe the Continental Congress and local committees are undermining Americans' liberties?*

2. *What does Paine see as the global significance of the American struggle for independence?*

3. *How do the two writers differ in their view of the main threats to American freedom?*

after the revolution of 1911) and Vietnam (1945), have such declarations, though few of them include a list, like Jefferson's, of the rights of citizens that their governments cannot abridge.

But even more than the specific language of the Declaration, the principle that legitimate political authority rests on the will of "the people" has been adopted around the world. The idea that "the people" possess rights was quickly internationalized. Slaves in the Caribbean, colonial subjects in India, and indigenous inhabitants of Latin America could all speak this language, to the dismay of those who exercised power over them.

The will of "the people"

SECURING INDEPENDENCE

The Balance of Power

Declaring Americans independent was one thing; winning independence another. The newly created American army confronted the greatest military power on earth. Viewing the Americans as traitors, Britain resolved to crush the rebellion. On the surface, the balance of power seemed heavily weighted in Britain's favor. It had a well-trained army (supplemented by hired soldiers from German states such as Hesse), the world's most powerful navy, and experienced military commanders. Americans had to rely on local militias and an inadequately equipped Continental army.

On the other hand, American soldiers were fighting on their own soil for a cause that inspired devotion and sacrifice. During the eight years of war from 1775 to 1783, some 200,000 men bore arms in the American army (whose soldiers were volunteers) and militias (where service was required of every able-bodied man unless he provided a substitute). The patriots suffered dearly for the cause. Of the colonies' free white male population aged sixteen to forty-five, one in twenty died in the War of Independence, the equivalent of nearly 2 million deaths in today's population. But so long as the Americans maintained an army in the field, the idea of independence remained alive no matter how much territory the British occupied.

Despite British power, to conquer the thirteen colonies would be an enormous and expensive task, and it was not at all certain that the

The Yankee Doodle Intrenchments near Boston, a 1776 British cartoon depicting the American revolutionaries as unimposing citizen soldiers egged on—according to the accompanying text—by a thieving commander and a reckless Puritan minister. The British greatly underestimated Americans' fighting ability in the War of Independence. One member of Parliament in 1775 claimed the colonists "were neither soldiers, nor could be made so," as they were naturally cowardly and "incapable of any sort of order or discipline."

public at home wished to pay the additional taxes that a lengthy war would require. Moreover, European rivals, notably France, welcomed the prospect of a British defeat. If the Americans could forge an alliance with France, a world power second only to Britain, it would go a long way toward equalizing the balance of forces.

Blacks in the Revolution

To American slaves, the War of Independence offered an unprecedented opportunity to seize their own freedom. Many pursued this goal by fighting in one of the opposing armies. At the war's outset, George Washington refused to accept black recruits. But he changed his mind after Lord Dunmore's 1775 proclamation, which offered freedom to slaves who joined the British cause. Some 5,000 blacks enlisted in state militias and the Continental army and navy. Since individuals drafted into the militia were allowed to provide a substitute, slaves suddenly gained considerable bargaining power. Not a few acquired their freedom by agreeing to serve in place of an owner or his son. In 1778, Rhode Island formed a black regiment and promised freedom to slaves who enlisted, while compensating the owners for their loss of property. Blacks who fought under George Washington and in other state militias did so in racially integrated companies (although invariably under white officers). They were the last black American soldiers to do so officially until the Korean War.

Except for South Carolina and Georgia, the southern colonies also enrolled free blacks and slaves to fight. They were not explicitly promised freedom, but many received it individually after the war ended.

Fighting on the side of the British also offered opportunities for freedom. Before his forces were expelled from Virginia, 800 or more slaves had escaped from their owners to join Lord Dunmore's Ethiopian Regiment, wearing, according to legend, uniforms that bore the motto "Liberty to Slaves." Other escaped slaves served the Royal Army as spies, guided their troops through swamps, and worked as military cooks, laundresses, and construction workers. George Washington himself saw seventeen of his slaves flee to the British, some of whom signed up to fight the colonists. "There is not a man of them, but would leave us, if they believed they could make their escape," his cousin Lund Washington reported. "Liberty is sweet."

American Foot Soldiers, Yorktown Campaign, a 1781 watercolor by a French officer, includes a black soldier from the First Rhode Island Regiment, an all-black unit of 250 men.

Dunmore's regiment

The First Years of the War

Had the British commander, Sir William Howe, prosecuted the war more vigorously at the outset, he might have nipped the rebellion in the bud by destroying Washington's army. But although Washington suffered numerous defeats in the first years of the war, he generally avoided direct confrontations with the British and managed to keep his army intact. Having abandoned Boston, Howe attacked New York City in the summer of 1776. Washington's army had likewise moved from Massachusetts to Brooklyn to defend the city. Howe pushed American forces back and almost cut off Washington's retreat across the East River.

British ships landing sailors on the New Jersey side of the Hudson River in November 1776. They quickly scaled the palisades and began pursuing George Washington's retreating army.

Battles of New Jersey

Howe pursued the American army but never managed to inflict a decisive defeat. Demoralized by successive failures, however, many American soldiers simply went home. Once 28,000 men, Washington's army dwindled to fewer than 3,000. To restore morale and regain the initiative, he launched successful surprise attacks on **Hessian** soldiers at Trenton, New Jersey, on December 26, 1776, and on a British force at Princeton on January 3, 1777. Shortly before crossing the Delaware River to attack the Hessians, Washington had Thomas Paine's inspiring essay *The American Crisis* read to his troops. "These are the times that try men's souls," Paine wrote. "The summer soldier and the sunshine patriot will, in this crisis, shrink from the service of their country; but he that stands it *now*, deserves the love and thanks of man and woman."

The Battle of Saratoga

In the summer of 1777, a second British army, led by General John Burgoyne, advanced south from Canada, hoping to link up with Howe and isolate New England. But in July, Howe instead moved his forces from New York City to attack Philadelphia. In September, the Continental Congress fled to Lancaster in central Pennsylvania, and Howe occupied the City of Brotherly Love. Not having been informed of Burgoyne's plans, Howe had unintentionally abandoned him. American forces blocked Burgoyne's way, surrounded his army, and on October 17, 1777, forced him to surrender at the **Battle of Saratoga**. The victory provided a significant boost to American morale.

Howe and Burgoyne

During the winter of 1777–1778, the British army, now commanded by Sir Henry Clinton, was quartered in Philadelphia. (In the Revolution,

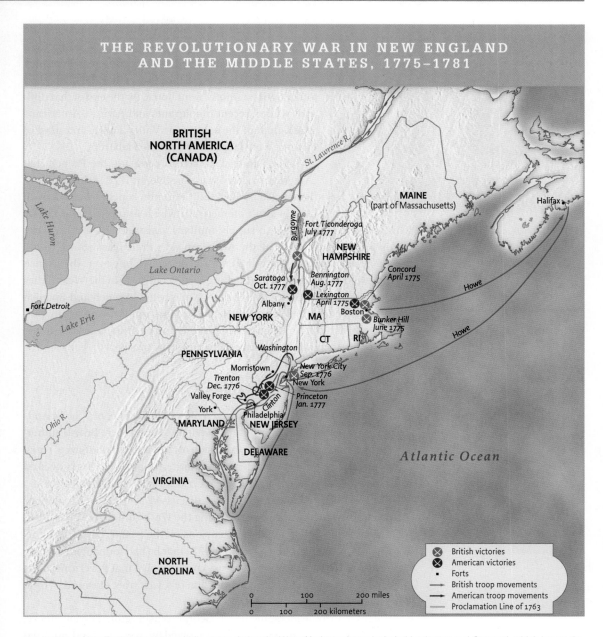

THE REVOLUTIONARY WAR IN NEW ENGLAND AND THE MIDDLE STATES, 1775–1781

BRITISH NORTH AMERICA (CANADA)

St. Lawrence R.

MAINE (part of Massachusetts)

Halifax

Lake Huron

Burgoyne

Fort Ticonderoga July 1777

NEW HAMPSHIRE

Concord April 1775

Howe

Lake Ontario

Saratoga Oct. 1777

Bennington Aug. 1777

Lexington April 1775

Albany

Boston

Bunker Hill June 1775

Howe

Fort Detroit

Lake Erie

NEW YORK

MA

CT   RI

PENNSYLVANIA

Washington

Morristown

New York City Sep. 1776

New York

Trenton Dec. 1776

Clinton

Princeton Jan. 1777

Valley Forge

York

Philadelphia

NEW JERSEY

Ohio R.

MARYLAND

DELAWARE

Atlantic Ocean

VIRGINIA

NORTH CAROLINA

| 0 | 100 | 200 miles |
| 0 | 100 | 200 kilometers |

⊗ British victories
⊗ American victories
▪ Forts
→ British troop movements
→ American troop movements
— Proclamation Line of 1763

Key battles in New England and the middle states during the War of Independence included Lexington and Concord, which began the armed conflict; the campaign in New York and New Jersey; and Saratoga, sometimes called the turning point of the war.

Benjamin Franklin designed this three-dollar bill for the new nation. It depicts an eagle fighting a crane with a Latin motto meaning "the outcome is in doubt."

as in most eighteenth-century wars, fighting came to a halt during the winter.) Meanwhile, Washington's army remained encamped at Valley Forge, where they suffered terribly from the frigid weather. Men who had other options simply went home. By the end of that difficult winter, recent immigrants and African-Americans made up half the soldiers at Valley Forge, and most of the rest were landless or unskilled laborers.

But Saratoga helped to persuade the French that American victory was possible. In 1778, American diplomats led by Benjamin Franklin concluded a Treaty of Amity and Commerce in which France recognized the United States and agreed to supply military assistance. Soon afterward, Spain also joined the war on the American side. French assistance would play a decisive part in the war's end. At the outset, however, the French fleet showed more interest in attacking British outposts in the West Indies than in directly aiding the Americans. Nonetheless, French and Spanish entry transformed the War of Independence into a global conflict. By putting the British on the defensive in places ranging from Gibraltar to the West Indies, it greatly complicated their military prospects.

The War in the Borderlands

In the trans-Appalachian West, the war took on the character of a borderlands conflict as much as a struggle for independence. Here, where British authority remained weak even after the expulsion of the French in the Seven Years' War and Indians enjoyed considerable authority, the patriots' victory marked a decisive shift of power away from native tribes and toward white settlers.

Despite the Proclamation of 1763, discussed in Chapter 4, colonists had continued to move westward during the 1760s and early 1770s, leading Indian tribes to complain of intrusions on their land. Lord Dunmore, Virginia's royal governor, observed in 1772 that he had found it impossible "to restrain the Americans. . . . They do not conceive that government has any right to forbid their taking possession of a vast tract of country" or to force them to honor treaties with Indians.

Indian lands in the West

Many patriot leaders, including George Washington, Patrick Henry, and Thomas Jefferson, were deeply involved in western land speculation. Washington himself had acquired more than 60,000 acres of land in western Pennsylvania after the Seven Years' War by purchasing land vouchers (a form of soldiers' wages) from his men at discount rates.

About 200,000 Native Americans lived east of the Mississippi River in 1790. Like white Americans, Indians divided in allegiance during the

War of Independence. Indians chose the side they felt would advance their own ideas of liberty. Some, like the Stockbridge tribe in Massachusetts, suffered heavy losses fighting the British. Many tribes tried to maintain neutrality, only to see themselves break into pro-American and pro-British factions. Most of the Iroquois nations sided with the British, but the Oneida joined the Americans. Despite strenuous efforts to avoid conflict, members of the Iroquois Confederacy for the first time faced each other in battle. (After the war, the Oneida submitted to Congress claims for losses suffered during the war, including sheep, hogs, kettles, frying pans, plows, and pewter plates—evidence of how fully they had been integrated into the market economy.) In the South, younger Cherokee leaders joined the British while older chiefs tended to favor the Americans.

Choosing sides

Among the grievances listed by Jefferson in the Declaration of Independence was Britain's enlisting "savages" to fight on its side. But in the war that raged throughout the western frontier, savagery was not confined to either combatant. In the Ohio country, the British encouraged Indian allies to burn frontier farms and settlements. For their part, otherwise humane patriot leaders ignored the traditional rules of warfare when it came to Indians. William Henry Drayton, a leader of the patriot cause in South Carolina and the state's chief justice in 1776, advised officers marching against the Cherokees to "cut up every Indian cornfield, burn every Indian town," and enslave all Indian captives. Three years later, Washington dispatched an expedition, led by General John Sullivan, against hostile Iroquois, with the aim of "the total destruction and devastation of their settlements and the capture of as many prisoners of every age and sex as possible." After his campaign ended, Sullivan reported that he had burned forty Indian towns, destroyed thousands of bushels of corn, and uprooted a vast number of fruit trees and vegetable gardens. Many Iroquois communities faced starvation. The destruction of the "middle ground" would not be completed until after the War of 1812, but it received a major impetus from American independence.

Savage warfare

The War in the South

In 1778, the focus of the war shifted to the South. Here the British hoped to exploit the social tensions between backcountry farmers and wealthy planters that had surfaced in the Regulator movements, to enlist the support of the numerous colonists in the region who remained loyal to the crown, and to disrupt the economy by encouraging slaves to escape. In December 1778, British forces occupied Savannah, Georgia. In May 1780, Clinton captured Charleston, South Carolina, and with it an American army of 5,000 men.

British occupation in the South

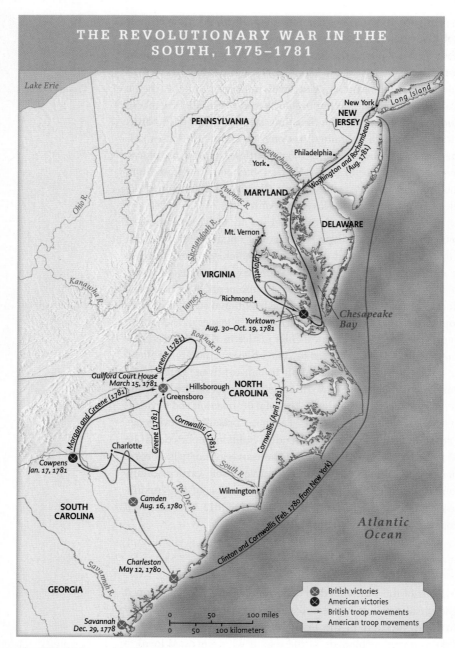

THE REVOLUTIONARY WAR IN THE SOUTH, 1775–1781

Lake Erie

PENNSYLVANIA

New York
NEW JERSEY
Long Island

Philadelphia

York

Susquehanna R.

Washington and Rochambeau (Aug. 1781)

MARYLAND

DELAWARE

Ohio R.

Potomac R.

Mt. Vernon

Shenandoah R.

Lafayette

VIRGINIA

Kanawha R.

James R.

Richmond

Yorktown
Aug. 30–Oct. 19, 1781

Chesapeake Bay

Roanoke R.

Greene (1781)

Guilford Court House
March 15, 1781

Hillsborough
NORTH CAROLINA

Greensboro

Morgan and Greene (1781)

Greene (1781)

Cornwallis (1781)

Cornwallis (April 1781)

Cowpens
Jan. 17, 1781

Charlotte

South R.

Wilmington

SOUTH CAROLINA

Pee Dee R.

Camden
Aug. 16, 1780

Clinton and Cornwallis (Feb. 1780 from New York)

Atlantic Ocean

Savannah R.

Charleston
May 12, 1780

GEORGIA

Savannah
Dec. 29, 1778

0   50   100 miles
0   50   100 kilometers

⊗ British victories
⊗ American victories
→ British troop movements
→ American troop movements

After 1777, the focus of the War of Independence shifted to the South, where it culminated in 1781 with the British defeat at Yorktown.

The year 1780 was arguably the low point of the struggle for independence. Congress was essentially bankrupt, and the army went months without being paid. The British seemed successful in playing on social conflicts within the colonies, as thousands of southern Loyalists joined up with British forces (fourteen regiments from Savannah alone) and tens of thousands of slaves sought freedom by fleeing to British lines. In August, Lord Charles Cornwallis routed an American army at Camden, South Carolina. The following month one of Washington's ablest commanders, **Benedict Arnold**, defected and almost succeeded in turning over to the British the important fort at West Point on the Hudson River.

THE HORSE AMERICA, *throwing his Master*.

A British cartoon from 1779, *The Horse America Throwing His Master*, lampoons King George III for being unable to keep control of the colonies. In the background, a French officer carries a flag adorned with the fleur-de-lis, a symbol of that country, the colonists' ally. Powerful satirical attacks on public authorities, including the king, were commonplace in eighteenth-century Britain.

But the British failed to turn these advantages into victory. British commanders were unable to consolidate their hold on the South. Wherever their forces went, American militias harassed them. A bloody civil war engulfed North and South Carolina and Georgia, with patriot and Loyalist militias inflicting retribution on each other and plundering the farms of their opponents' supporters.

Victory at Last

In January 1781, American forces under Daniel Morgan dealt a crushing defeat to British forces at Cowpens, South Carolina. Two months later, at Guilford Courthouse, North Carolina, General Nathanael Greene, while conducting a campaign of strategic retreats, inflicted heavy losses on Cornwallis, the British commander in the South. Cornwallis moved into Virginia and encamped at Yorktown, located on a peninsula that juts into Chesapeake Bay. Brilliantly recognizing the opportunity to surround Cornwallis, Washington rushed his forces, augmented by French troops under the Marquis de Lafayette, to block a British escape by land. Meanwhile, a French fleet controlled the mouth of the Chesapeake, preventing supplies and reinforcements from reaching Cornwallis's army.

Yorktown

Imperial rivalries had helped to create the American colonies. Now, the rivalry of European empires helped to secure American independence. Taking land and sea forces together, more Frenchmen than Americans participated in the decisive **Battle of Yorktown**. On October 19, 1781, Cornwallis surrendered his army of 8,000 men. When the news reached London, public support for the war evaporated and peace negotiations soon began.

Two years later, in September 1783, American and British negotiators concluded the **Treaty of Paris**. The American delegation—John Adams,

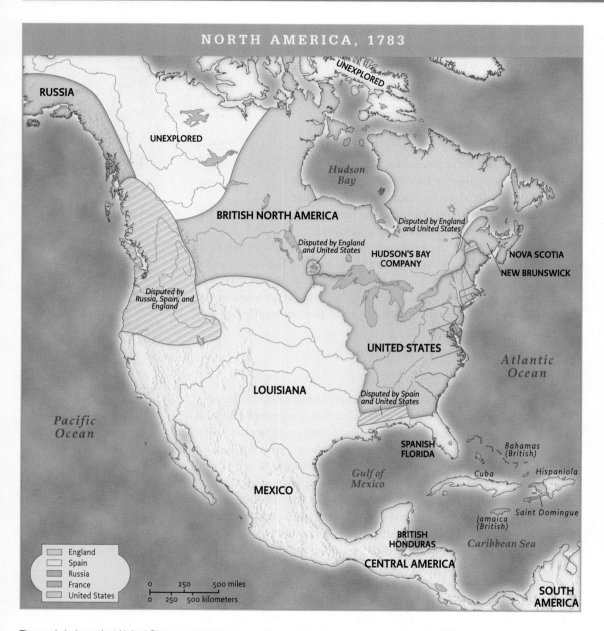

NORTH AMERICA, 1783

RUSSIA

UNEXPLORED

UNEXPLORED

Hudson
Bay

BRITISH NORTH AMERICA

Disputed by England
and United States

Disputed by England
and United States

HUDSON'S BAY
COMPANY

NOVA SCOTIA

NEW BRUNSWICK

Disputed by
Russia, Spain, and
England

UNITED STATES

Atlantic
Ocean

LOUISIANA

Pacific
Ocean

Disputed by Spain
and United States

SPANISH
FLORIDA

Bahamas
(British)

Cuba

Hispaniola

Gulf of
Mexico

MEXICO

Saint Domingue

Jamaica
(British)

BRITISH
HONDURAS

Caribbean Sea

CENTRAL AMERICA

SOUTH
AMERICA

England
Spain
Russia
France
United States

0   250   500 miles
0   250   500 kilometers

The newly independent United States occupied only a small part of the North American continent in 1783.

Benjamin Franklin, and John Jay—achieved one of the greatest diplomatic triumphs in the country's history. They not only won recognition of American independence but also gained control of the entire region between Canada and Florida east of the Mississippi River and the right of Americans to fish in Atlantic waters off of Canada (a matter of considerable importance to New Englanders). At British insistence, the Americans agreed that colonists who had remained loyal to the mother country would not suffer persecution and that Loyalists' property that had been seized by local and state governments would be restored.

Territorial gains

Until independence, the thirteen colonies had formed part of Britain's American empire, along with Canada and the West Indies. But Canada rebuffed repeated calls to join the War of Independence, and leaders of the West Indies, fearful of slave uprisings, also remained loyal to the crown. With the Treaty of Paris, the United States of America became the Western Hemisphere's first independent nation. Its boundaries reflected not so much the long-standing unity of a geographical region, but the circumstances of its birth.

CHAPTER REVIEW AND ONLINE RESOURCES

REVIEW QUESTIONS

1. *How important was the Stamp Act crisis in bringing about the American Revolution?*

2. *Patrick Henry proclaimed that he was not a Virginian, but rather an American. What unified the colonists and what divided them at the time of the Revolution?*

3. *Discuss the ramifications of using slaves in the British and Continental armies. Why did the British authorize the use of slaves? Why did the Americans? How did the slaves benefit?*

4. *Why did the colonists reach the conclusion that membership in the empire threatened their freedoms, rather than guaranteed them?*

5. *How did new ideas of liberty contribute to tensions between the social classes in the American colonies?*

6. *Why did people in other countries believe that the American Revolution (or the Declaration of Independence) was important to them or their own countries?*

7. *Summarize the difference of opinion between British officials and colonial leaders over the issues of taxation and representation.*

8. *How did the actions of the British authorities help to unite the American colonists during the 1760s and 1770s?*

KEY TERMS

Stamp Act (p. 139)
virtual representation (p. 140)
writs of assistance (p. 140)
Sugar Act (p. 140)
"no taxation without representation" (p. 142)
Committee of Correspondence (p. 143)
Sons of Liberty (p. 143)
Regulators (p. 144)
Townshend Acts (p. 144)
Boston Massacre (p. 145)
Crispus Attucks (p. 145)
Boston Tea Party (p. 147)
Intolerable Acts (p. 147)
Continental Congress (p. 148)
Battles of Lexington and Concord (p. 149)
Battle of Bunker Hill (p. 150)
Continental army (p. 150)
Lord Dunmore's proclamation (p. 150)
Common Sense (p. 151)
Declaration of Independence (p. 152)
Hessian (p. 158)
Battle of Saratoga (p. 158)
Benedict Arnold (p. 163)
Battle of Yorktown (p. 163)
Treaty of Paris (p. 163)

Go to 🐰 INQUIZITIVE

To see what you know—and learn what you've missed—with personalized feedback along the way.

Visit the *Give Me Liberty!* **Student Site** for primary source documents and images, interactive maps, author videos featuring Eric Foner, and more.

CHAPTER 6

THE REVOLUTION WITHIN

★

Liberty Displaying the Arts and Sciences. This 1792 painting by Samuel Jennings is one of the few visual images of the early republic explicitly linking slavery with tyranny and liberty with abolition. The female figure offers books to newly freed slaves. Other forms of knowledge depicted include a globe and an artist's palette. Beneath her left foot lies a broken chain. In the background, freed slaves enjoy some leisure time. By this time, allegorical representations of America as a woman in classical clothing, with a cap of liberty, had mostly replaced America as a Native American.

- *How did equality become
  a stronger component of
  American freedom after
  the Revolution?*

- *How did the expansion
  of religious liberty after
  the Revolution reflect the
  new American ideal of
  freedom?*

- *How did the definition of
  economic freedom change
  after the Revolution, and
  who benefited from the
  changes?*

- *How did the Revolution
  diminish the freedoms of
  both Loyalists and Native
  Americans?*

- *What was the impact of the
  Revolution on slavery?*

- *How did the Revolution
  affect the status of women?*

Born in Massachusetts in 1744, Abigail Adams became one of the revolutionary era's most articulate and influential women. At a time when educational opportunities for girls were extremely limited, she taught herself by reading books in the library of her father, a Congregational minister. In 1764, she married John Adams. During the War of Independence, with her husband away in Philadelphia and Europe serving the American cause, she stayed behind at their Massachusetts home, raising their four children and managing the family's farm. The letters they exchanged form one of the most remarkable correspondences in American history. A keen observer of public affairs, she kept her husband informed of events in Massachusetts and offered opinions on political matters. Later, when Adams served as president, he relied on her for advice more than on members of his cabinet.

In March 1776, a few months before the Second Continental Congress declared American independence, Abigail Adams wrote her best-known letter to her husband. She began by commenting indirectly on the evils of slavery. How strong, she wondered, could the "passion for Liberty" be among those "accustomed to deprive their fellow citizens of theirs"? She went on to urge Congress, when it drew up a "Code of Laws" for the new republic, to "remember the ladies." All men, she warned, "would be tyrants if they could."

It was the leaders of colonial society who initiated resistance to British taxation. But as Abigail Adams's letter illustrates, the struggle for American liberty emboldened other colonists to demand more liberty for themselves. At a time when so many Americans—slaves, indentured servants, women, Indians, apprentices, propertyless men—were denied full freedom, the struggle against Britain threw into question many forms of authority and inequality.

Abigail Adams accepted the prevailing belief that a woman's primary responsibility was to her family. But she resented the "absolute power" husbands exercised over their wives. Her letter is widely remembered today. Less familiar is John Adams's response, which illuminated how the Revolution had unleashed challenges to all sorts of inherited ideas of deference and authority: "We have been told that our struggle has loosened the bands of government everywhere; that children and apprentices were disobedient; that schools and colleges were grown turbulent; that Indians slighted their guardians, and negroes grew insolent to their masters." To John Adams, this upheaval, including his wife's claim to greater freedom, was an affront to the natural order of things. To others, it formed the essence of the American Revolution.

DEMOCRATIZING FREEDOM

The Dream of Equality

The American Revolution took place at three levels simultaneously. It was a struggle for national independence, a phase in a century-long global battle among European empires, and a conflict over what kind of nation an independent America should be.

The Revolution unleashed public debates and political and social struggles that enlarged the scope of freedom and challenged inherited structures of power within America. In rejecting the crown and the principle of hereditary aristocracy, many Americans also rejected the society of privilege, patronage, and fixed status that these institutions embodied. The idea of liberty became a revolutionary rallying cry, a standard by which to judge and challenge homegrown institutions as well as imperial ones.

Jefferson's seemingly straightforward assertion in the Declaration of Independence that "all men are created equal" announced a radical principle whose full implications no one could anticipate. In both Britain and its colonies, a well-ordered society was widely thought to depend on obedience to authority—the power of rulers over their subjects, husbands over wives, parents over children, employers over servants and apprentices, slaveholders over slaves. Inequality had been fundamental to the colonial social order; the Revolution challenged it in many ways. Henceforth, American freedom would be forever linked with the idea of equality—equality before the law, equality in political rights, equality of economic opportunity, and, for some, equality of condition. "Whenever I use the words *freedom* or *rights*," wrote Thomas Paine, "I desire to be understood to mean a perfect equality of them. . . . The floor of Freedom is as level as water."

Abigail Adams, a portrait by Gilbert Stuart, painted over several years beginning in 1800. Stuart told a friend that, as a young woman, Adams must have been a "perfect Venus."

The Revolution and equality

Expanding the Political Nation

In political, social, and religious life, previously marginalized groups challenged the domination by a privileged few. In the end, the Revolution did not undo the obedience to which male heads of household were entitled from their wives and children, and, at least in the southern states, their slaves. For free men, however, the democratization of freedom was dramatic. Nowhere was this more evident than in challenges to the traditional limitation of political participation to those who owned property.

In the political thought of the eighteenth century, "democracy" had several meanings. One, derived from the writings of Aristotle, defined democracy as a system in which the entire people governed directly.

Political participation

Democracy

However, this was thought to mean mob rule. In the wake of the American Revolution, the term came into wider use to express the popular aspirations for greater equality inspired by the struggle for independence.

Throughout the colonies, election campaigns became freewheeling debates on the fundamentals of government. Universal male suffrage, religious toleration, and even the abolition of slavery were discussed not only by the educated elite but also by artisans, small farmers, and laborers, now emerging as a self-conscious element in politics. In many colonies-turned-states, members of the militia demanded the right to elect all their officers and to vote for public officials whether or not they met age and property qualifications. They thereby established the tradition that service in the army enabled excluded groups to stake a claim to full citizenship.

The public and politics

The Revolution in Pennsylvania

The Revolution's radical potential was more evident in Pennsylvania than in any other state. Nearly the entire prewar elite opposed independence, fearing that severing the tie with Britain would lead to rule by the "rabble" and to attacks on property. The vacuum of political leadership opened the door for the rise of a new pro-independence grouping, based on the artisan and lower-class communities of Philadelphia, and organized in extralegal committees and the local militia.

Staunch advocates of equality, Pennsylvania's radical leaders particularly attacked property qualifications for voting. "God gave mankind freedom by nature," declared the anonymous author of the pamphlet *The People the Best Governors*, "and made every man equal to his neighbors." The people, therefore, were "the best guardians of their own liberties," and every free man should be eligible to vote and hold office. Three months after independence, Pennsylvania adopted a new state constitution that sought to institutionalize democracy by concentrating power in a one-house legislature elected annually by all men over age twenty-one who paid taxes. It abolished the office of governor, dispensed with property qualifications for officeholding, and provided that schools with low fees be established in every county. It also included clauses guaranteeing "freedom of speech, and of writing," and religious liberty.

The New Constitutions

Like Pennsylvania, every state adopted a new constitution in the aftermath of independence. Nearly all Americans now agreed that their governments must be **republics**, meaning that their authority rested on the consent of the governed, and that there would be no king or hereditary aristocracy.

A pewter mug, made by William Will, an important craftsman in Philadelphia, in the late 1770s, depicts Captain Peter Ickes, a Pennsylvania militia officer, with the popular slogan "Liberty or Death."

In part to counteract what he saw as Pennsylvania's excessive radicalism, John Adams in 1776 published *Thoughts on Government*, which insisted that the new constitutions should create balanced governments whose structure would reflect the division of society between the wealthy (represented in the upper house) and ordinary men (who would control the lower). A powerful governor and judiciary would ensure that neither class infringed on the liberty of the other. Adams's call for two-house legislatures was followed by every state except Pennsylvania, Georgia, and Vermont. But only his own state, Massachusetts, gave the governor an effective veto over laws passed by the legislature. Americans had long resented efforts by appointed governors to challenge the power of colonial assemblies. They preferred power to rest with the legislature.

The Right to Vote

The issue of requirements for voting and officeholding proved far more contentious. To John Adams, as conservative on the internal affairs of America as he had been radical on independence, freedom and equality were opposites. Men without property, he believed, had no "judgment of their own," and the removal of property qualifications, therefore, would "confound and destroy all distinctions, and prostrate all ranks to one common level."

Democracy gained the least ground in the southern states, whose highly deferential political traditions enabled the landed gentry to retain their control of political affairs. In Virginia and South Carolina, the new constitutions retained property qualifications for voting and authorized the gentry-dominated legislature to choose the governor.

The most democratic new constitutions moved much of the way toward the idea of voting as an entitlement rather than a privilege, but they generally stopped short of universal **suffrage**, even for free men. Pennsylvania's constitution no longer required ownership of property, but it retained the taxpaying qualification. As a result, it enfranchised nearly all of the state's free male population but still barred a small number, mainly paupers and domestic servants, from voting. Nonetheless, even with the taxpaying requirement, it was a dramatic departure from the colonial practice of restricting the suffrage to those who could claim to be economically independent. It elevated "personal liberty," in the words of one essayist, to a position more important than property ownership in defining the boundaries of the political nation.

By the 1780s, except in Virginia, Maryland, and New York, a large majority of the adult white male population could meet voting requirements. New Jersey's new state constitution of 1776 granted the suffrage to all "inhabitants" who met a property qualification. Until the state added the word "male" (along with "white") in 1807, property-owning women, mostly

John Dickinson's copy of the Pennsylvania constitution of 1776, with handwritten proposals for changes. Dickinson, one of the more conservative advocates of independence, felt the new state constitution was far too democratic. He crossed out a provision that all "free men" should be eligible to hold office, and another declaring the people not bound by laws that did not promote "the common good."

Freedom and the right to vote

widows, did cast ballots. In the popular language of politics, if not in law, freedom and an individual's right to vote had become interchangeable. Who should vote remains controversial to this day.

TOWARD RELIGIOUS TOLERATION

Religious pluralism

As remarkable as the expansion of political freedom was the Revolution's impact on American religion. Religious toleration, declared one Virginia patriot, was part of "the common cause of Freedom." We have already seen that Rhode Island and Pennsylvania had long made a practice of toleration. But freedom of worship before the Revolution arose more from the reality of religious pluralism than from a well-developed theory of religious liberty. Most colonies supported religious institutions with public funds and discriminated in voting and officeholding against Catholics, Jews, and even dissenting Protestants. On the very eve of independence, Baptists who refused to pay taxes to support local Congregational ministers were still being jailed in Massachusetts. "While our country are pleading so high for liberty," the victims complained, "yet they are denying of it to their neighbors."

Catholic Americans

The War of Independence weakened the deep tradition of American anti-Catholicism. When the Second Continental Congress decided on an ill-fated invasion of Canada, it invited the inhabitants of predominantly Catholic Quebec to join in the struggle against Britain, assuring them

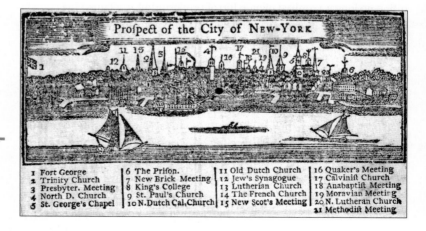

A 1771 image of New York City lists some of the numerous churches visible from the New Jersey shore, illustrating the diversity of religions practiced in the city.

Prospect of the City of New-York

1 Fort George	6 The Prison.	11 Old Dutch Church	16 Quaker's Meeting
2 Trinity Church	7 New Brick Meeting	12 Jew's Synagogue	17 Calvinist Church
3 Presbyter. Meeting	8 King's College	13 Lutherian Church	18 Anabaptist Meeting
4 North D. Church	9 St. Paul's Church	14 The French Church	19 Moravian Meeting
5 St. George's Chapel	10 N.Dutch Cal,Church	15 New Scot's Meeting	20 N. Lutheran Church
			21 Methodist Meeting

that Protestants and Catholics could readily cooperate. In 1778, the United States formed an alliance with France, a Catholic nation. The indispensable assistance provided by France to American victory strengthened the idea that Catholics had a role to play in the newly independent nation. This was a marked departure from the traditional notion that the full rights of Englishmen applied only to Protestants. When America's first Roman Catholic bishop, John Carroll of Maryland, visited Boston in 1791, he received a cordial welcome.

Separating Church and State

Many of the leaders of the Revolution considered it essential for the new nation to shield itself from the unruly passions and violent conflicts that religious differences had inspired during the past three centuries. Men like Thomas Jefferson, John Adams, James Madison, and Alexander Hamilton viewed religious doctrines through the Enlightenment lens of rationalism and skepticism. They believed in a benevolent Creator but not in supernatural interventions into the affairs of men.

The drive to separate church and state brought together Deists like Jefferson, who hoped to erect a "wall of separation" that would free politics and the exercise of the intellect from religious control, with members of evangelical sects, who sought to protect religion from the corrupting embrace of government.

The movement toward religious freedom received a major impetus during the revolutionary era. Throughout the new nation, states disestablished their established churches—that is, deprived them of public funding and special legal privileges—although in some cases they appropriated money for the general support of Protestant denominations. The seven state constitutions that began with declarations of rights all declared a commitment to "the free exercise of religion."

To be sure, every state but New York—whose constitution of 1777 established complete religious liberty—kept intact colonial provisions barring Jews from voting and holding public office. Massachusetts retained its Congregationalist establishment well into the nineteenth century. It would not end public financial support for religious institutions until

In Side of the Old Lutheran Church in 1800, York, Pa. A watercolor by a local artist depicts the interior of one of the numerous churches that flourished after independence. While the choir sings, a man chases a dog out of the building and another man stokes the stove. The institutionalization of religious liberty was one of the most important results of the American Revolution.

Disestablishing churches

Limits to religious freedom

1833. Throughout the country, however, Catholics gained the right to worship without persecution.

Jefferson and Religious Liberty

In Virginia, Thomas Jefferson drew up a **Bill for Establishing Religious Freedom**, which was introduced in the House of Burgesses in 1779 and adopted, after considerable controversy, in 1786. Jefferson's bill, whose preamble declared that God "hath created the mind free," eliminated religious requirements for voting and officeholding and government financial support for churches, and barred the state from "forcing" individuals to adopt one or another religious outlook. Late in life, Jefferson would list this measure, along with the Declaration of Independence and the founding of the University of Virginia, as the three accomplishments (leaving out his two terms as president) for which he wished to be remembered.

Definition of "rights"

Religious liberty became the model for the revolutionary generation's definition of "rights" as private matters that must be protected from governmental interference. In an overwhelmingly Christian (though not necessarily churchgoing) nation, the separation of church and state drew a sharp line between public authority and a realm defined as "private." It also offered a new justification for the idea of the United States as a beacon of liberty. In successfully opposing a Virginia tax for the general support of Christian churches, James Madison insisted that one reason for the complete separation of church and state was to reinforce the principle that the new nation offered "asylum to the persecuted and oppressed of every nation and religion."

Religious denominations

The Revolution did not end the influence of religion on American society—quite the reverse. Thanks to religious freedom, the early republic witnessed an amazing proliferation of religious denominations. The most well-established churches—Anglican, Presbyterian, and Congregationalist—found themselves constantly challenged by upstarts like Free-Will Baptists and Universalists. Today, even as debate continues over the proper relationship between spiritual and political authority, more than 1,300 religions are practiced in the United States.

Christian Republicanism

Despite the separation of church and state, colonial leaders were not hostile to religion. Indeed, religious and secular language merged in the struggle for independence, producing an outlook scholars have called Christian Republicanism. Proponents of evangelical religion and of republican government both believed that in the absence of some kind of moral restraint (provided by religion and government), human nature was likely to succumb to corruption and vice. Samuel Adams, for example, believed the new nation would become a "Christian Sparta," in which Christianity and personal self-discipline underpinned both personal and national progress. American religious leaders interpreted the American Revolution as a divinely sanctioned event, part of God's plan to promote the development of a good society. Rather than being so sinful that it would have to be destroyed before Christ returned, as many ministers had previously preached, the world, the Revolution demonstrated, could be perfected.

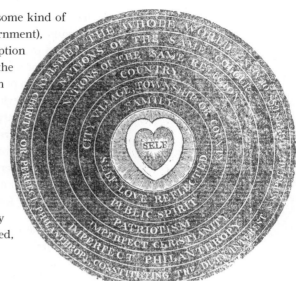

A Virtuous Citizenry

Patriot leaders worried about the character of future citizens, especially how to encourage the quality of "virtue," the ability to sacrifice self-interest for the public good. Some, like Jefferson, John Adams, and Benjamin Rush, put forward plans for the establishment of free, state-supported public schools. These would instruct future citizens in what Adams called "the principles of freedom," equipping them for participation in the now-expanded public sphere and for the wise election of representatives. A broad diffusion of knowledge was essential for a government based on the will of the people to survive. No nation, Jefferson wrote, could "expect to be ignorant and free."

Circle of the Social and Benevolent Affections, an engraving in *The Columbian Magazine*, 1789, illustrates various admirable qualities radiating outward from the virtuous citizen, including love for one's family, community, nation, and all humanity. Affection only for those of the same religion or "colour" is labeled "imperfect."

DEFINING ECONOMIC FREEDOM

Toward Free Labor

In economic as well as political and religious affairs, the Revolution rewrote the definition of freedom. In colonial America, slavery was one part of a broad spectrum of kinds of unfree labor. In the generation after independence, with the rapid decline of indentured servitude and apprenticeship and the transformation of paid domestic service into an occupation for blacks and white females, the halfway houses between slavery and freedom disappeared, at least for white men.

Unfree labor

The lack of freedom inherent in apprenticeship and servitude increasingly came to be seen as incompatible with republican citizenship. In 1784, a group of "respectable" New Yorkers released a newly arrived shipload of indentured servants on the grounds that their status was "contrary to . . . the idea of liberty this country has so happily established." By 1800, indentured servitude had all but disappeared from the United States. This development sharpened the distinction between freedom and slavery, and between a northern economy relying on what would come to be called "free labor" (that is, working for wages or owning a farm or shop) and a southern economy ever more heavily dependent on the labor of slaves.

Decline in indentured servitude

The Soul of a Republic

Americans of the revolutionary generation were preoccupied with the social conditions of freedom. Could a republic survive with a sizable dependent class of citizens? "A general and tolerably equal distribution of landed property," proclaimed the educator and newspaper editor Noah Webster, "is the whole basis of national freedom." "Equality," he added, was "the very soul of a republic." At the Revolution's radical edge, some patriots believed that government had a responsibility to limit accumulations of property in the name of equality. To most free Americans, however, "equality" meant equal opportunity, rather than equality of condition. Many leaders of the Revolution nevertheless assumed that in the exceptional circumstances of the New World, with its vast areas of available land and large population of independent farmers and artisans, the natural workings of society would produce justice, liberty, and equality.

Equal opportunity rather than equality of condition

Like many other Americans of his generation, Thomas Jefferson believed that to lack economic resources was to lack freedom. Among his achievements included laws passed by Virginia abolishing entail

View from Bushongo Tavern, an engraving from *The Columbian Magazine*, 1788, depicts the landscape of York County, Pennsylvania, exemplifying the kind of rural independence many Americans thought essential to freedom.

(the limitation of inheritance to a specified line of heirs to keep an estate within a family) and primogeniture (the practice of passing a family's land entirely to the eldest son). These measures, he believed, would help to prevent the rise of a "future aristocracy."

Abolishing entail and primogeniture

The Politics of Inflation

The Revolution thrust to the forefront of politics debates over whether local and national authorities should take steps to bolster household indepen-dence and protect Americans' livelihoods by limiting price increases. To finance the war, Congress issued hundreds of millions of dollars in paper money. Coupled with wartime disruption of agriculture and trade and the hoarding of goods by some Americans hoping to profit from shortages, this produced an enormous **inflation** as prices rapidly rose.

Between 1776 and 1779, more than thirty incidents took place in which crowds confronted merchants accused of holding scarce goods off the market. Often, they seized stocks of food and sold them at the traditional "just price," a form of protest common in eighteenth-century England. In one such incident, a crowd of 100 Massachusetts women accused an "eminent, wealthy, stingy merchant" of hoarding coffee, opened his warehouse, and carted off the goods. "A large concourse of men," wrote Abigail Adams, "stood amazed, silent spectators of the whole transaction."

Responses to wartime inflation

The Debate over Free Trade

In 1779, with inflation totally out of control (in one month, prices in Philadelphia jumped 45 percent), Congress urged states to adopt measures to fix wages and prices. This request reflected the belief that the task of republican government was to promote the public good, not individuals' self-interest. But when a Committee of Safety tried to enforce price controls, it met spirited opposition from merchants and other advocates of a free market.

Against the traditional view that men should sacrifice for the public good, believers in **free trade** argued that economic development arose from economic self-interest. Adam Smith's great treatise on economics, ***The Wealth of Nations***, published in England in 1776, was beginning to become known in the United States. Smith's argument that the "invisible hand" of the free market directed economic life more effectively and fairly than governmental intervention offered intellectual justification for those who believed that the economy should be left to regulate itself.

Smith's "invisible hand"

Advocates of independence had envisioned America, released from the British Navigation Acts, trading freely with all the world.

Committee-Room.

May 28. 1779.

RESOLVED,

THAT the Retail Prices of the underwritten Articles on the firſt Day of May were as follows----

Coffee,	- per pound,	£ 0 : 17 : 6	
Bohea Tea,	ditto,	4 : 15 : 0	
Loaf Sugar,	ditto,	2 : 15 : 0	
Muſcovado Sugar,	ditto,	from 0 : 18 : 9 to £1 : 5 : 0 according to Quality.	
Weſt India Rum,	by gallon or quart,	7 : 0 : 0	
Country Rum,	by do. or do.	5 : 5 : 0	
Whiſkey,	by do.	2 : 0 : 0	
Rice,	per pound,	0 : 3 : 0	

And as it is abſolutely neceſſary, that Dry Goods, and all other Commodities, whether imported or the Produce of the Country, ſhould fall in Price as well as thoſe Articles which are already Publiſhed; therefore,

Reſolved, That this Committee do earneſtly requeſt and expect, that no Perſon do ſell any Commodity whatever, at a Higher Price than the ſame was ſold for on the firſt Day of this Month.

By Order of the Committee,
WILLIAM HENRY, CHAIRMAN.

A broadside printed by the extralegal Philadelphia price control committee, setting the retail prices of various goods. Advocates of a free market strongly opposed the committee's efforts.

Social bases of loyalism

Opponents of price controls advocated free trade at home as well. "Natural liberty" would regulate prices. Here were two competing conceptions of economic freedom—one based on the traditional view that the interests of the community took precedence over the property rights of individuals, the other insisting that unregulated economic freedom would produce social harmony and public gain. After 1779, state and federal efforts to regulate prices ceased. But the clash between these two visions of economic freedom would continue long after independence had been achieved.

THE LIMITS OF LIBERTY

Colonial Loyalists

Not all Americans shared in the democratization of freedom brought on by the American Revolution. **Loyalists**—those who retained their allegiance to the crown—experienced the conflict and its aftermath as a loss of liberty. Many leading Loyalists had supported American resistance in the 1760s but drew back at the prospect of independence and war. Altogether, an estimated 20 to 25 percent of free Americans remained loyal to the British, and nearly 20,000 fought on their side.

There were Loyalists in every colony, but they were most numerous in New York, Pennsylvania, and the backcountry of the Carolinas and Georgia. Some were wealthy men whose livelihoods depended on close working relationships with Britain—lawyers, merchants, Anglican ministers, and imperial officials. Many feared anarchy in the event of an American victory.

The struggle for independence heightened existing tensions between ethnic groups and social classes within the colonies. Some Loyalist ethnic minorities, like Highland Scots in North Carolina, feared that local majorities would infringe on their cultural autonomy. In the South, many backcountry farmers who had long resented the domination of public affairs by wealthy planters sided with the British, as did numerous slaves, who hoped an American defeat would bring them freedom.

The Loyalists' Plight

The War of Independence was in some respects a civil war among Americans. The new state governments, or crowds of patriots, suppressed newspapers thought to be loyal to Britain. Pennsylvania arrested and seized the property of Quakers, Mennonites, and Moravians—pacifist denominations who refused to bear arms because of their religious beliefs. With the approval of Congress, many states required residents to take oaths of allegiance to the new nation. Those who refused were denied the right to vote and in many cases forced into exile. Some wealthy Loyalists saw their land confiscated and sold at auction.

A 1780 British cartoon commenting on the "cruel fate" of American Loyalists. Pro-independence colonists are likened to savage Indians.

When the war ended, as many as 60,000 Loyalists were banished from the United States or emigrated voluntarily—mostly to Britain, Canada, or the West Indies—rather than live in an independent United States. But for those who remained, hostility proved to be short-lived. In the Treaty of Paris of 1783, as noted in Chapter 5, Americans pledged to end the persecution of Loyalists by state and local governments and to restore property seized during the war. Loyalists who did not leave the country were quickly reintegrated into American society, although confiscated Loyalist property was not returned.

White Freedom, Indian Freedom

Independence created governments democratically accountable to voters who coveted Indian land. But liberty for whites meant loss of liberty for Indians. Independence offered the opportunity to complete the process of dispossessing Indians of their rich lands in upstate New York, the Ohio Valley, and the southern backcountry. The only hope for the Indians, Jefferson wrote, lay in their "removal beyond the Mississippi."

Dispossession of Indian lands

American independence, a group of visiting Indians told the Spanish governor of St. Louis, was "the greatest blow that could have been dealt us." The Treaty of Paris marked the culmination of a century in which the balance of power in eastern North America shifted away from the Indians and toward white Americans. In the treaty, the British abandoned their Indian allies, agreeing to recognize American sovereignty over the entire region east of the Mississippi River, completely ignoring the Indian presence. In

The Treaty of Paris and Indian peoples

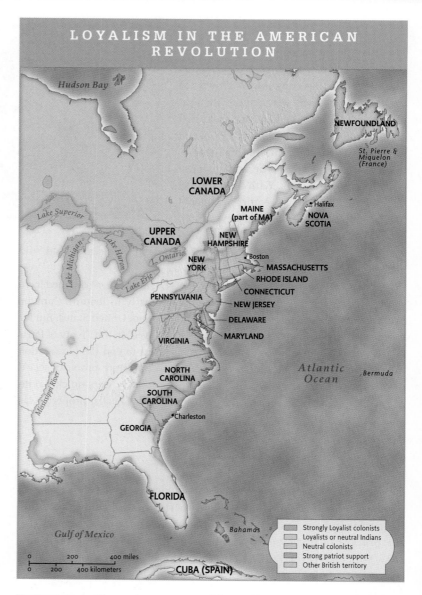

LOYALISM IN THE AMERICAN REVOLUTION

Hudson Bay

NEWFOUNDLAND

St. Pierre &
Miquelon
(France)

LOWER
CANADA

MAINE
(part of MA)

Halifax

NOVA
SCOTIA

Lake Superior

UPPER
CANADA

NEW
HAMPSHIRE

Lake Michigan

Lake Huron

L. Ontario

NEW
YORK

Boston

MASSACHUSETTS

Lake Erie

RHODE ISLAND

CONNECTICUT

PENNSYLVANIA

NEW JERSEY

DELAWARE

MARYLAND

VIRGINIA

Atlantic
Ocean

Bermuda

Mississippi River

NORTH
CAROLINA

SOUTH
CAROLINA

Charleston

GEORGIA

FLORIDA

Bahamas

Gulf of Mexico

	Strongly Loyalist colonists
	Loyalists or neutral Indians
	Neutral colonists
	Strong patriot support
	Other British territory

0   200   400 miles
0   200   400 kilometers

CUBA (SPAIN)

The Revolutionary War was, in some ways, a civil war within the colonies. There were Loyalists in every colony; they were most numerous in New York and North and South Carolina.

the end there seemed to be no permanent place for the descendants of the continent's native population in a new nation bent on creating an empire in the West.

SLAVERY AND THE REVOLUTION

Although Indians experienced American independence as a real threat to their own liberty, African-Americans saw in the ideals of the Revolution and the reality of war an opportunity to claim freedom. When the United States declared its independence in 1776, the slave population had grown to 500,000, about one-fifth of the new nation's inhabitants.

The Language of Slavery and Freedom

Slavery played a central part in the language of revolution. Apart from "liberty," it was the word most frequently invoked in the era's legal and political literature. In debates over British rule, slavery was primarily a political category, shorthand for the denial of one's personal and political rights by arbitrary government. Those who lacked a voice in public affairs, declared a 1769 petition demanding an expansion of the right to vote in Britain, were "enslaved."

The meaning of slavery

    The presence of hundreds of thousands of slaves powerfully affected the meaning of freedom for the leaders of the American Revolution. In a famous speech to Parliament warning against attempts to intimidate the colonies, the British statesman Edmund Burke suggested that familiarity with slavery made colonial leaders unusually sensitive to threats to their own liberties. Where freedom was a privilege, not a common right, he observed, "those who are free are by far the most proud and jealous of their freedom." On the other hand, many British observers could not resist pointing out the colonists' apparent hypocrisy. "How is it," asked Dr. Samuel Johnson, "that we hear the loudest yelps for liberty from the drivers of negroes?"

Advertisement for newly arrived slaves, in a Savannah newspaper, 1774. Even as colonists defended their own liberty against the British, the buying and selling of slaves continued.

Obstacles to Abolition

The contradiction between freedom and slavery seems so self-evident that it is difficult today to appreciate the power of the obstacles to **abolition**. At the time of the Revolution, slavery was already an old institution in America. It existed in every colony and formed the basis of the economy and social

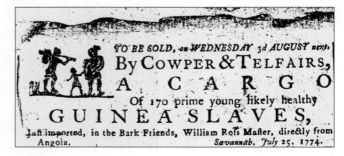

TO BE SOLD, on WEDNESDAY 3d AUGUST next,
By COWPER & TELFAIRS,
A CARGO
Of 170 prime young likely healthy
GUINEA SLAVES,
Jaſt imported, in the Bark Friends, William Roſs Maſter, directly from Angola.
Savannah, July 25, 1774.

structure from Maryland southward. Virtually every founding father owned slaves at one point in his life, including not only southern planters but also northern merchants, lawyers, and farmers. (John Adams and Tom Paine were notable exceptions.) Thomas Jefferson owned more than 100 slaves when he wrote of mankind's unalienable right to liberty, and everything he cherished in his own manner of life, from lavish entertainments to the leisure that made possible the pursuit of arts and sciences, ultimately rested on slave labor.

Slavery amid freedom

Some patriots, in fact, argued that slavery for blacks made freedom possible for whites. Owning slaves offered a route to the economic autonomy widely deemed necessary for genuine freedom, a point driven home by a 1780 Virginia law that rewarded veterans of the War of Independence with 300 acres of land—and a slave.

The Cause of General Liberty

Freedom as universal

Nonetheless, by imparting so absolute a value to liberty and defining freedom as a universal entitlement rather than a set of rights specific to a particular place or people, the Revolution inevitably raised questions about the status of slavery in the new nation. Before independence, there had

Excelsior (Latin for "Ever Upward"), a large oil painting by an unknown artist, is probably an early representation of the coat of arms of New York, adopted in 1778 as one part of the transition from colony to state. It contains numerous symbols of liberty, independence, and optimism for the future including a cap of liberty, the sunrise, an eagle atop a world globe, Justice with her scales, and an olive branch of peace.

been little public discussion of the institution, even though enlightened opinion in the Atlantic world had come to view slavery as morally wrong and economically inefficient, a relic of a barbarous past.

Samuel Sewall, a Boston merchant, published *The Selling of Joseph* in 1700, the first antislavery tract printed in America. All "the sons of Adam," Sewall insisted, were entitled to "have equal right unto liberty." During the course of the eighteenth century, antislavery sentiments had spread among Pennsylvania's Quakers, whose belief that all persons possessed the divine "inner light" made them particularly receptive.

Antislavery sentiments

But it was during the revolutionary era that slavery for the first time became a focus of public debate. The Pennsylvania patriot Benjamin Rush in 1773 called on "advocates for American liberty" to "espouse the cause of . . . general liberty" and warned that slavery was one of those "national crimes" that one day would bring "national punishment."

Petitions for Freedom

The Revolution inspired widespread hopes that slavery could be removed from American life. Most dramatically, slaves themselves appreciated that by defining freedom as a universal right, the leaders of the Revolution had devised a weapon that could be used against their own bondage. The language of liberty echoed in slave communities, North and South. The most insistent advocates of freedom as a universal entitlement were African-Americans, who demanded that the leaders of the struggle for independence live up to their self-proclaimed creed.

The first concrete steps toward emancipation in revolutionary America were **freedom petitions**—arguments for liberty presented to New England's courts and legislatures in the early 1770s by enslaved African-Americans. How, one such petition asked, could America "seek release from English tyranny and not seek the same for disadvantaged Africans in her midst?" The turmoil of war offered other avenues to freedom. Many slaves ran away from their masters and tried to pass as freeborn. The number of fugitive-slave advertisements in colonial newspapers rose dramatically in the 1770s and 1780s. As one owner put it in accounting for his slave Jim's escape, "I believe he has nothing in view but freedom."

In 1776, the year of American independence, **Lemuel Haynes**, a black member of the Massachusetts militia and later a celebrated minister, urged Americans to "extend" their conception of freedom. If liberty were truly "an innate principle" for all mankind, Haynes insisted, "even an African [had] as equally good a right to his liberty in common with Englishmen." Like Haynes, many black writers and leaders sought to make white Americans understand slavery as a concrete reality—the denial of all the

A portrait of the poet Phillis Wheatley (1753–1784).

essential elements of freedom—not a metaphor for lack of political representation, as many whites used the word.

Most slaves of the revolutionary era were only one or two generations removed from Africa. They did not need the ideology of the Revolution to persuade them that freedom was a birthright—their experience and that of their parents and grandparents suggested as much. "My love of freedom," wrote the black poet Phillis Wheatley in 1783, arose from the "cruel fate" of being "snatch'd from Afric's" shore. Yet when blacks invoked the Revolution's ideology of liberty to demand their own rights and defined freedom as a universal entitlement, they demonstrated how American they had become.

British Emancipators

As noted in the previous chapter, some 5,000 slaves fought for American independence, and many thereby gained their freedom. Yet far more slaves obtained liberty from the British. Lord Dunmore's proclamation of 1775, and the Philipsburg Proclamation of General Henry Clinton issued four years later, offered sanctuary to slaves, except those owned by Loyalists, who escaped to British lines. All told, tens of thousands of slaves, including one-quarter of all the slaves in South Carolina and one-third of those in Georgia, deserted their owners and fled to British lines. This was by far the largest exodus from the plantations until the outbreak of the Civil War.

Miss Breme Jones, a late eighteenth-century watercolor depicting a South Carolina slave. The inscription on the left, based on a passage from John Milton's *Paradise Lost*, reads: "Grave in her steps / Heaven in her eyes / And all her movement / Dignity and Love." The work was commissioned by Jones's owner John Rose, possibly as recognition of how she helped him raise his two small children after the death of his wife.

Some of these escaped slaves were recaptured as the tide of battle turned in the patriots' favor. But at the war's end, more than 15,000 black men, women, and children accompanied the British out of the country. They ended up in Nova Scotia, England, and Sierra Leone, a settlement for former slaves from the United States established by the British on the coast of West Africa. Some were re-enslaved in the West Indies.

The issue of compensation for the slaves who departed with the British poisoned relations between Britain and the new United States for decades to come. Finally, in 1827, Britain agreed to make payments to 1,100 Americans who claimed they had been improperly deprived of their slave property.

Voluntary Emancipations

For a brief moment, the revolutionary upheaval appeared to threaten the continued existence of slavery. During the War of Independence, nearly every state prohibited or discouraged the further importation of slaves from Africa. The war left much of the plantation South in ruins. During the 1780s and 1790s, a considerable number of slaveholders, especially in Virginia and Maryland, voluntarily emancipated their slaves. In 1796, for example, Richard Randolph, a member of a prominent Virginia family, drafted a will that condemned slavery as an "infamous practice," provided for the freedom of about ninety slaves, and set aside part of his land for them to own. Farther south, however, voluntary emancipation never got under way. Even during the war, when South Carolina needed more troops, the colony's leaders rejected the idea of emancipating some blacks to aid in the fight against the British. They would rather lose the war than lose their slaves.

Voluntary emancipations in the South

Abolition in the North

Between 1777 (when Vermont drew up a constitution that banned slavery) and 1804 (when New Jersey acted), every state north of Maryland took steps toward emancipation, the first time in recorded history that legislative power had been invoked to eradicate slavery. But even here, where slavery was not central to the economy, the method of abolition reflected how property rights impeded emancipation. Generally, abolition laws did not free living slaves. Instead, they provided for the liberty of any child born in the future to a slave mother, but only after he or she had served the mother's master until adulthood as compensation for the owner's future economic loss.

Legislation against slavery

Because of these legal provisions, abolition in the North was a slow, drawn-out process. The first national census, in 1790, recorded 21,000 slaves still living in New York and 11,000 in New Jersey. New Yorker John Jay, chief justice of the United States, owned five slaves in 1800. As late as 1830, the census revealed that there were still 3,500 slaves in the North.

Slow process of abolition

This engraving depicts a parade welcoming George Washington and the Continental army into New York City on November 25, 1783, shortly after British forces evacuated the city, which they had occupied for almost the entire War of Independence. Women take part in the celebration alongside men. But the crowd is shown as entirely white—even though many blacks and some Native Americans resided in the city.

VOICES OF FREEDOM

From their home in Massachusetts, Abigail Adams maintained a lively correspondence with her husband while he was in Philadelphia serving in the Continental Congress. In this letter, she suggests some of the limits of the patriots' commitment to liberty.

I wish you would write me a letter half as long as I write you, and tell me if you may where your fleet have gone? What sort of defense Virginia can make against our common enemy? Whether it is so situated as to make an able defense? . . . I have sometimes been ready to think that the passion for Liberty cannot be equally strong in the breasts of those who have been accustomed to deprive their fellow creatures of theirs. Of this I am certain, that it is not founded upon that generous and Christian principle of doing to others as we would that others should do unto us. . . .

I long to hear that you have declared an independency, and by the way in the new Code of Laws which I suppose it will be necessary for you to make I desire you would Remember the Ladies, and be more generous and favorable to them than your ancestors. Do not put such unlimited power into the hands of the husbands. Remember all men would be tyrants if they could. If particular care and attention is not paid to the Ladies we are determined to foment a Rebellion, and will not hold ourselves bound by any such laws in which we have no voice, or representation.

That your sex are naturally tyrannical is a truth so thoroughly established as to admit of no dispute, but such of you as wish to be happy willingly give up the harsh title of Master for the more tender and endearing one of Friend. Why then, not put it out of the power of the vicious and the lawless to use us with cruelty and indignity with impunity? Men of sense in all ages abhor those customs which treat us only as the vassals of your sex. Regard us then as beings placed by providence under your protection and in imitation of the Supreme Being make use of that power only for our happiness.

From Petitions of Slaves to the Massachusetts Legislature (1773 and 1777)

Many slaves saw the struggle for independence as an opportunity to assert their own claims to freedom. Among the first efforts toward abolition were petitions by Massachusetts slaves to their legislature.

The efforts made by the legislative of this province in their last sessions to free themselves from slavery, gave us, who are in that deplorable state, a high degree of satisfaction. We expect great things from men who have made such a noble stand against the designs of their *fellowmen* to enslave them. We cannot but wish and hope Sir, that you will have the same grand object, we mean civil and religious liberty, in view in your next session. The divine spirit of *freedom*, seems to fire every breast on this continent. . . .

* * *

Your petitioners apprehend that they have in common with all other men a natural and unalienable right to that freedom which the great parent of the universe hath bestowed equally on all mankind and which they have never forfeited by any compact or agreement whatever but [they] were unjustly dragged by the hand of cruel power from their dearest friends and . . . from a populous, pleasant, and plentiful country and in violation of laws of nature and of nations and in defiance of all the tender feelings of humanity brought here . . . to be sold like beast[s] of burden . . . among a people professing the mild religion of Jesus. . . .

In imitation of the laudable example of the good people of these states your petitioners have long and patiently waited the event of petition after petition by them presented to the legislative body. . . . They cannot but express their astonishment that it has never been considered that every principle from which America has acted in the course of their unhappy difficulties with Great Britain pleads stronger than a thousand arguments in favor of your petitioners [and their desire] to be restored to the enjoyment of that which is the natural right of all men.

> ## QUESTIONS
>
> 1. *What does Abigail Adams have in mind when she refers to the "unlimited power" husbands exercise over their wives?*
>
> 2. *How do the slaves employ the principles of the Revolution for their own aims?*
>
> 3. *What do these documents suggest about the boundaries of freedom in the era of the American Revolution?*

Free Black Communities

All in all, the Revolution had a contradictory impact on American slavery and, therefore, on American freedom. Gradual as it was, the abolition of slavery in the North drew a line across the new nation, creating the dangerous division between free and slave states. Abolition in the North, voluntary manumissions in the Upper South, and the escape of thousands from bondage created, for the first time in American history, a sizable population of **free blacks** (many of whose members took new family names like Freeman or Freeland).

On the eve of independence, virtually every black person in America had been a slave. Now, free communities, with their own churches, schools, and leaders, came into existence. They formed a standing challenge to the logic of slavery, a haven for fugitives, and a springboard for further efforts at abolition. From 1776 to 1810, the number of free blacks residing in the United States grew from 10,000 to nearly 200,000, and many free black men, especially in the North, enjoyed the right to vote under new state constitutions.

Nonetheless, the stark fact is that slavery survived the War of Independence and, thanks to the natural increase of the slave population, continued to grow. The national census of 1790 revealed that despite all those who had become free through state laws, voluntary emancipation, and escape, the number of slaves in the United States had grown to 700,000—200,000 more than in 1776.

A photograph from around 1851 of Caesar, who had been a slave in New York State until the institution was finally ended in 1827.

The Life and Adventures of a FEMALE SOLDIER.

HANNAH SNELL, was born in *Fryer-Street* in the Parish of St. *Hellen's*, in the city of *Worcester*, in *England*, on the

A woodcut widely reprinted during the War of Independence shows Hannah Snell, who allegedly joined the British army in 1745 disguised as a man. It suggests that women could take up arms in their country's cause.

DAUGHTERS OF LIBERTY

Revolutionary Women

The revolutionary generation included numerous women who contributed to the struggle for independence. Deborah Sampson, the daughter of a poor Massachusetts farmer, disguised herself as a man and in 1782, at age twenty-one, enlisted in the Continental army. Ultimately, her commanding officer learned her secret but kept it to himself, and she was honorably discharged at the end of the war. Years later, Congress awarded her a soldier's pension. Other patriotic women participated in crowd actions against unscrupulous merchants, raised funds to assist soldiers, contributed homespun goods to the army, and passed along information about British army movements.

Within American households, women participated in the political discussions unleashed by independence. "Was not every fireside," John Adams later recalled, "a theater of politics?" Gender formed a boundary limiting those entitled to the full blessings of American freedom. The principle of **coverture** (described in Chapter 1) remained intact in the new nation. The husband still held legal authority over the person, property, and choices of his wife. Despite the expansion of democracy, politics remained overwhelmingly a male realm.

For men, political freedom meant the right to self-government, the power to consent to the individuals and political arrangements that ruled over them. For women, however, the marriage contract superseded the social contract. A woman's relationship to the larger society was mediated through her relationship with her husband. In both law and social reality, women lacked the essential qualification of political participation—autonomy based on ownership of property or control of one's own person. Overall, the republican citizen was, by definition, male.

Republican Motherhood

According to the ideology of **republican motherhood** that emerged as a result of independence, women played an indispensable role by training future citizens. Even though republican motherhood ruled out direct female involvement in politics, it encouraged the expansion of educational opportunities for women, so that they could impart political wisdom to their children. Women, wrote Benjamin Rush, needed to have a "suitable education," to enable them to "instruct their sons in the principles of liberty and government."

The idea of republican motherhood reinforced the trend, already evident in the eighteenth century, toward the idea of "companionate" marriage, a voluntary union held together by affection and mutual dependency rather than male authority. In her letter to John Adams quoted above, Abigail Adams recommended that men should willingly give up "the harsh title of Master for the more tender and endearing one of Friend."

The structure of family life itself was altered by the Revolution. In colonial America, those living within the household often included indentured servants, apprentices, and slaves. After independence, southern slaves remained, rhetorically at least, members of the owner's "family." In the North, however, with the rapid decline of various forms of indentured servitude and apprenticeship, a more modern definition of the household as consisting of parents and their children took hold. Hired workers, whether domestic servants or farm laborers, were not considered part of the family.

Portrait of John and Elizabeth Lloyd Cadwalader and Their Daughter Anne. This 1772 portrait of a prominent Philadelphia businessman and his family by the American artist Charles Willson Peale illustrates the emerging ideal of the "companionate" marriage, which is based on affection rather than male authority.

Keep Within the Compass, a late eighteenth-century engraving, illustrates the happiness of a "virtuous woman" if she remains within the world of home and family and some of the "troubles" awaiting her if she ventures outside. The woman appears in a space marked off by a compass, an instrument for drawing a circle.

Two pages from *The New England Primer*, first published in Boston around 1690 and reissued in numerous editions throughout the eighteenth century. The book taught the alphabet to young children by referring to moral principles and stories from the Bible. Schoolbooks of the era emphasized both learning and religious devotion.

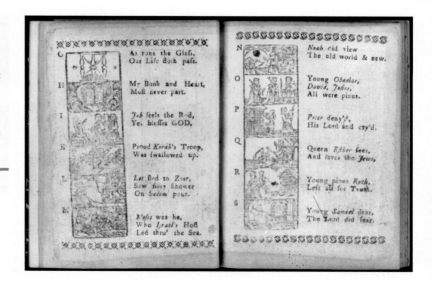

The Arduous Struggle for Liberty

The Revolution changed the life of virtually every American. As a result of the long struggle against British rule, the public sphere, and with it the right to vote, expanded markedly. Bound labor among whites declined dramatically, religious groups enjoyed greater liberty, blacks mounted a challenge to slavery in which many won their freedom, and women in some ways enjoyed a higher status. On the other hand, for Indians, many Loyalists, and the majority of slaves, American independence meant a deprivation of freedom.

The winds of change were sweeping across the Atlantic world. The year 1776 saw not only Paine's *Common Sense* and Jefferson's Declaration but also the publication in England of Adam Smith's *Wealth of Nations*, which attacked the British policy of closely regulating trade, and Jeremy Bentham's *Fragment on Government*, which criticized the nature of British government. Moreover, the ideals of the American Revolution helped to inspire countless subsequent struggles for social equality and national independence, from the French Revolution, which exploded in 1789, to the uprising that overthrew the slave system in Haiti in the 1790s, to the Latin American wars for independence in the early nineteenth century, and numerous struggles of colonial peoples for nationhood in the twentieth. But within the new republic, the debate over who should enjoy the blessings of liberty would continue long after independence had been achieved.

CHAPTER REVIEW AND ONLINE RESOURCES

REVIEW QUESTIONS

1. For the lower classes, colonial society had been based on inequality, deference, and obedience. How did the American Revolution challenge that social order?

2. Why did the Revolution cause more radical changes in Pennsylvania than elsewhere, and how was this radicalism demonstrated in the new state constitution?

3. How did ideas of political freedom affect people's ideas about economic rights and relationships?

4. What role did the founders foresee for religion in American government and society?

5. What was the impact of the American Revolution on Native Americans?

6. What were the most important features of the new state constitutions?

7. How did popular views of property rights prevent slaves from enjoying all the freedoms of the social contract?

8. How did revolutionary America see both improvements and limitations in women's roles and rights?

KEY TERMS

republics (p. 170)

suffrage (p. 171)

Bill for Establishing Religious Freedom (p. 174)

inflation (p. 177)

free trade (p. 177)

The Wealth of Nations (p. 177)

Loyalists (p. 178)

abolition (p. 181)

freedom petitions (p. 183)

Lemuel Haynes (p. 183)

free blacks (p. 188)

coverture (p. 189)

republican motherhood (p. 189)

Go to 🐰 INQUIZITIVE

To see what you know—and learn what you've missed—with personalized feedback along the way.

Visit the *Give Me Liberty!* **Student Site** for primary source documents and images, interactive maps, author videos featuring Eric Foner, and more.

CHAPTER 7

FOUNDING A NATION

★

1783–1791

The Federal Ship Hamilton, an engraving depicting the centerpiece of the Grand Federal Procession in New York City in 1788 that celebrated the ratification of the Constitution. The ship carried over thirty seamen and fired several thirteen-gun salutes during the parade, one for each state. Alexander Hamilton was one of the era's key nationalists and an author of *The Federalist*, which made the argument for ratification.

During June and July of 1788, civic leaders in cities up and down the Atlantic coast organized colorful pageants to celebrate the ratification of the U.S. Constitution. For one day, Benjamin Rush commented of Philadelphia's parade, social class "forgot its claims," as thousands of marchers—rich and poor, businessman and apprentice—joined in a common public ceremony. The parades testified to the strong popular support for the Constitution in the nation's cities. Elaborate banners and floats gave voice to the hopes inspired by the new structure of government. "May commerce flourish and industry be rewarded," declared Philadelphia's mariners and shipbuilders.

Throughout the era of the Revolution, Americans spoke of their nation as a "rising empire." Whereas Europe's empires were governed by force, America's would be different. In Jefferson's phrase, it would be "an empire of liberty," bound together by a common devotion to the principles of the Declaration of Independence. Already, the United States exceeded in size Great Britain, Spain, and France combined. As a new nation, it possessed many advantages, including physical isolation from the Old World (a significant asset between 1789 and 1815, when European powers were almost constantly at war), a youthful population certain to grow much larger, and a broad distribution of property ownership and literacy among white citizens.

On the other hand, the nation's prospects at the time of independence were not entirely promising. Control of its vast territory was by no means secure. Nearly all of the 3.9 million Americans recorded in the first national census of 1790 lived near the Atlantic coast. Large areas west of the Appalachian Mountains remained in Indian hands. The British retained military posts on American territory near the Great Lakes.

Away from navigable waterways, communication and transportation were primitive. The population consisted of numerous ethnic and religious groups and some 700,000 slaves, making unity difficult to achieve. No republican government had ever been established over so vast a territory or with so diverse a population. "We have no Americans in America," commented John Adams. It would take time for consciousness of a common nationality to sink deep roots.

Profound questions needed to be answered. What course of development should the United States follow? How could the competing claims of local self-government, sectional interests, and national authority be balanced? Who should be considered full-fledged members of the American people, entitled to the blessings of liberty? These issues became the focus of heated debate as the first generation of Americans sought to consolidate their new republic.

FOCUS QUESTIONS

- *What were the achievements and problems of the Confederation government?*

- *What major compromises molded the final content of the Constitution?*

- *How did Anti-Federalist concerns raised during the ratification process lead to the creation of the Bill of Rights?*

- *How did the definition of citizenship in the new republic exclude Native Americans and African-Americans?*

AMERICA UNDER THE CONFEDERATION

The Articles of Confederation

The first written constitution of the United States was the **Articles of Confederation**, drafted by Congress in 1777 and ratified by the states four years later. The Articles sought to balance the need for national coordination of the War of Independence with widespread fear that centralized political power posed a danger to liberty. It explicitly declared the new national government to be a "perpetual union." But it resembled less a blueprint for a common government than a treaty for mutual defense. Under the Articles, the thirteen states retained their individual "sovereignty, freedom, and independence." The national government consisted of a one-house Congress, in which each state, no matter how large or populous, cast a single vote. There was no president to enforce the laws and no judiciary to interpret them. Major decisions required the approval of nine states rather than a simple majority.

Limitations of the Articles

The only powers specifically granted to the national government by the Articles of Confederation were those essential to the struggle for independence—declaring war, conducting foreign affairs, and making treaties with other governments. Congress had no real financial resources. It could coin money but lacked the power to levy taxes or regulate commerce. Its revenue came mainly from contributions by the individual states. To amend the Articles required the unanimous consent of the states, a formidable obstacle to change.

Accomplishments under the Articles

But Congress in the 1780s did not lack for accomplishments. The most important was establishing national control over land to the west of the thirteen states and devising rules for its settlement. Citing their original royal charters, which granted territory running all the way to the "South Sea" (the Pacific Ocean), states such as Virginia, the Carolinas, and Connecticut claimed immense tracts of western land. Land speculators, politicians, and prospective settlers from states with clearly defined boundaries insisted that such land must belong to the nation at large. Only after the land-rich states, in the interest of national unity, ceded their western claims to the central government did the Articles win ratification.

Congress, Settlers, and the West

Establishing rules for the settlement of this national domain—the area controlled by the federal government, stretching from the western boundaries of existing states to the Mississippi River—was critical. Although some Americans spoke of it as if it were empty, over 100,000 Indians inhabited the region. Congress took the position that by aiding the British, Indians had forfeited the right to their lands. But little distinction was made among tribes that had sided with the enemy, aided the patriots, or played no part in the war at all. At peace conferences at Fort Stanwix, New York, in 1784 and Fort McIntosh near Pittsburgh the following year, American representatives demanded and received large surrenders of Indian land north of the Ohio River. Similar treaties soon followed with the Cherokee, Choctaw, and Chickasaw tribes in the South.

When it came to disposing of western land and regulating its settlement, the Confederation government faced conflicting pressures. Many leaders believed that the economic health of the new republic required that farmers have access to land in the West. But they also saw land sales as a potential source of revenue.

The arrival of peace triggered a large population movement from settled parts of the original states into frontier areas like upstate New York and across the Appalachian Mountains into Kentucky and Tennessee. To settlers, the right to take possession of western lands was an essential element of American freedom. When a group of Ohioans petitioned Congress in 1785, assailing landlords and speculators who monopolized available acreage and asking that preference in land ownership be given to "actual settlements," their motto was "Grant us Liberty."

At the same time, however, like British colonial officials before them, many leaders of the new nation feared that an unregulated flow of population across the Appalachian Mountains would provoke constant warfare with Indians. Moreover, they viewed frontier settlers as disorderly and lacking in proper respect for authority.

A design for the Great Seal of the United States produced by a committee of Congress in 1782 includes symbols of liberty, war, and peace, a shield with thirteen stars, and an eagle, all below a Latin phrase meaning "In Defense of Liberty." On the reverse (illustrated at upper right) is an unfinished pyramid with thirteen steps and the Eye of Providence.

Frontier fears

The Land Ordinances

A series of measures approved by Congress during the 1780s defined the terms by which western land would be marketed and settled. Drafted by Thomas Jefferson, the **Ordinance of 1784** established stages of self-government for the West. The region would be divided into districts initially governed by Congress and eventually admitted to the Union as member states. By a single vote, Congress rejected a clause that would have prohibited slavery throughout the West. A second resolution, the **Ordinance of 1785**, regulated land sales in the region north of the Ohio

Western settlement and self-government

The creation of a nationally controlled public domain from western land ceded by the states was one of the main achievements of the federal government under the Articles of Confederation.

River, which came to be known as the Old Northwest. Land would be surveyed by the government and then sold in "sections" of a square mile (640 acres) at $1 per acre. In each township, one section would be set aside to provide funds for public education.

Like the British before them, American officials found it difficult to regulate the thirst for new land. The minimum purchase price of $640, however, put public land out of the financial reach of most settlers. They generally ended up buying smaller parcels from speculators and land companies. For many years, actual and prospective settlers pressed for a reduction in the price of government-owned land, a movement that did not end until the Homestead Act of 1862 offered free land in the public domain.

Price of land

A final measure, the **Northwest Ordinance of 1787**, called for the eventual establishment of from three to five states north of the Ohio River and east of the Mississippi. Thus was enacted the basic principle of what Jefferson called the **empire of liberty**—rather than ruling over the West as a colonial power, the United States would admit the area's population as equal members of the political system. Territorial expansion and self-government would grow together.

Territorial expansion and self-government

The Northwest Ordinance pledged that "the utmost good faith" would be observed toward local Indians and that their land would not be taken without consent. "It will cost much less," one congressman noted, "to conciliate the good opinion of the Indians than to pay men for destroying them." But national land policy assumed that whether through purchase, treaties, or voluntary removal, the Indian presence would soon disappear. The ordinance also prohibited slavery in the Old Northwest, a provision that would have far-reaching consequences when the sectional conflict between North and South developed. But for years, owners brought slaves into the area, claiming that they had voluntarily signed long-term labor contracts.

Slavery prohibited

The Confederation's Weaknesses

Whatever the achievements of the Confederation government, in the eyes of many influential Americans they were outweighed by its failings. Both the national government and the country at large faced worsening economic problems. To finance the War of Independence, Congress had borrowed large sums of money by selling interest-bearing bonds and paying soldiers and suppliers in notes to be redeemed in the future. Lacking a secure source of revenue, it found itself unable to pay either interest or the debts themselves. With the United States now outside the British empire, American ships were barred from trading with the West

WESTERN ORDINANCES, 1784–1787

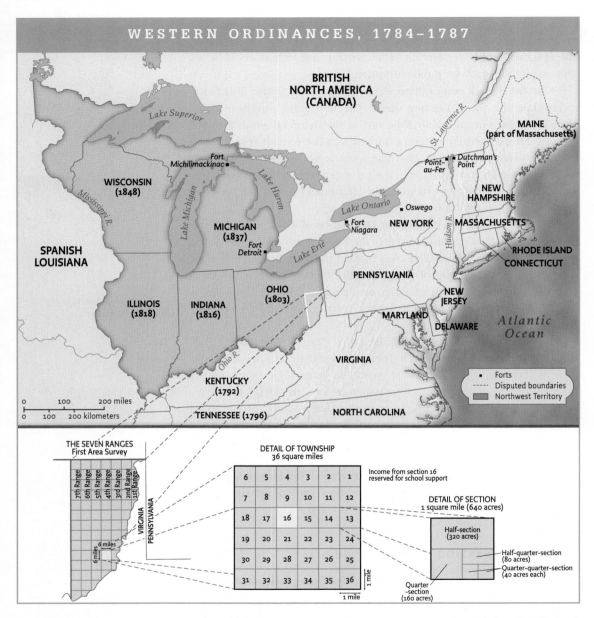

A series of ordinances in the 1780s provided for both the surveying and sale of lands in the public domain north of the Ohio River and the eventual admission of states carved from the area as equal members of the Union.

Indies. Imported goods, however, flooded the market, undercutting the business of many craftsmen, driving down wages, and draining money out of the country.

Some American businessmen looked for new areas with which to trade. In 1784, the *Empress of China* set sail for Canton, the first ship to do so flying the American flag. It carried furs, wine, Spanish silver dollars, and American ginseng. It returned the following year with silk, tea, and Chinese porcelain. The investors turned a large profit. The voyage demonstrated the feasibility of trade with Asia, but for the moment, this could not compensate for the loss of nearby markets in the British West Indies.

With Congress unable to act, the states adopted their own economic policies. Several imposed tariff duties on goods imported from abroad. In order to increase the amount of currency in circulation and make it easier for individuals to pay their debts, several states printed large sums of paper money. Others enacted laws postponing debt collection. Creditors considered such measures attacks on their property rights.

A Bankruptcy Scene. Creditors repossess the belongings of a family unable to pay its debts, while a woman weeps in the background. Popular fears of bankruptcy led several states during the 1780s to pass laws postponing the collection of debts.

Shays's Rebellion

In late 1786 and early 1787, crowds of debt-ridden farmers closed the courts in western Massachusetts to prevent the seizure of their land for failure to pay taxes. The uprising came to be known as **Shays's Rebellion**, a name affixed to it by its opponents, after Daniel Shays, one of the leaders and a veteran of the War of Independence. The participants in Shays's Rebellion modeled their tactics on the crowd activities of the 1760s and 1770s and employed liberty trees and liberty poles as symbols of their cause. They received no sympathy from Governor James Bowdoin, who dispatched an army headed by the former Revolutionary War general Benjamin Lincoln. The rebels were dispersed in January 1787.

Uprising in Massachusetts

Observing Shays's Rebellion from Paris where he was serving as ambassador, Thomas Jefferson refused to be alarmed. "A little rebellion now and then is a good thing," he wrote to a friend. "The tree of liberty must be refreshed from time to time with the blood of patriots and tyrants." But the uprising was the culmination of a series of events in the 1780s that persuaded an influential group of Americans that the national government must be strengthened so that it could develop uniform economic policies and protect property owners from infringements on their rights by local majorities.

Among proponents of stronger national authority, liberty had lost some of its luster. The danger to individual rights, they came to believe,

"Abuses of liberty"

now arose not from a tyrannical central government, but from the people themselves. "Liberty," declared James Madison, "may be endangered by the abuses of liberty as well as the abuses of power." To put it another way, private liberty, especially the secure enjoyment of property rights, could be endangered by public liberty—unchecked power in the hands of the people.

James Madison, "father of the Constitution," in a miniature portrait painted by Charles Willson Peale in 1783. Madison was only thirty-six years old when the Constitutional Convention met.

Nationalists of the 1780s

Madison, a diminutive Virginian and the lifelong disciple and ally of Thomas Jefferson, thought deeply about the nature of political freedom. He was among the group of talented and well-organized men who spearheaded the movement for a stronger national government. Another was Alexander Hamilton, who had come to North America from the West Indies as a youth. Hamilton was perhaps the most vigorous proponent of an "energetic" government that would enable the new nation to become a powerful commercial and diplomatic presence in world affairs. Men like Madison and Hamilton were nation builders. They came to believe during the 1780s that the country's future greatness depended on enhancing national authority.

Alexander Hamilton, another youthful leader of the nationalists of the 1780s, was born in the West Indies in 1755. This life-size portrait was commissioned by five New York merchants and painted by John Trumbull in 1792, when Hamilton was Secretary of the Treasury.

The concerns voiced by critics of the Articles found a sympathetic hearing among men who had developed a national consciousness during the Revolution. Nationalists included army officers, members of Congress accustomed to working with individuals from different states, and diplomats who represented the country abroad. Influential economic interests also desired a stronger national government. Among these were bondholders who despaired of being paid so long as Congress lacked a source of revenue, urban artisans seeking tariff protection from foreign imports, merchants desiring access to British markets, and all those who feared that the states were seriously interfering with property rights.

In September 1786, delegates from six states met at Annapolis, Maryland, to consider ways for better regulating interstate and international commerce. The delegates proposed another gathering, in Philadelphia, to amend the Articles of Confederation. Every state except Rhode Island, which had gone the furthest in developing its own debtor-relief and trade policies, sent delegates to the Philadelphia convention. When they assembled in May 1787, they decided to scrap the Articles of Confederation entirely and draft a new constitution for the United States.

A NEW CONSTITUTION

The fifty-five men who gathered for the **Constitutional Convention** included some of the most prominent Americans. Thomas Jefferson and John Adams, serving as diplomats in Europe, did not take part. But among the delegates were George Washington (whose willingness to serve as presiding officer was an enormous asset) and Benjamin Franklin (now eighty-one years old). John Adams described the convention as a gathering of men of "ability, weight, and experience." He might have added, "and wealth." They earned their livings as lawyers, merchants, planters, and large farmers. Nearly half, including a number of Northerners, owned slaves. Washington owned over two hundred, three of whom he brought to Philadelphia.

At a time when fewer than one-tenth of 1 percent of Americans attended college, more than half the delegates had college educations. Their shared social status and political experiences bolstered their common belief in the need to strengthen national authority and curb what one called "the excesses of democracy." To ensure free and candid debate, the deliberations took place in private. Madison, who believed the outcome would have great consequences for "the cause of liberty throughout the world," took careful notes. They were not published, however, until 1840, four years after he became the last delegate to pass away.

Elite convention delegates

The Structure of Government

It quickly became apparent that the delegates agreed on many points. The new constitution would create a legislature, an executive, and a national judiciary. Congress would have the power to raise money without relying on the states. States would be prohibited from infringing on the rights of property. And the government would represent the people. Most delegates hoped to find a middle ground between the despotism of monarchy and aristocracy and what they considered the excesses of popular self-government. "We had been too democratic," observed George Mason of Virginia, but he warned against the danger of going to "the opposite extreme." The key to stable, effective republican government was finding a way to balance the competing claims of liberty and power.

Legislature, executive, and national judiciary

Differences quickly emerged over the proper balance between the federal and state governments and between the interests of large and small states. Early in the proceedings, Madison presented what came to be called the **Virginia Plan**. It proposed the creation of a two-house legislature with a state's population determining its representation in each. Smaller states, fearing that populous Virginia, Massachusetts, and Pennsylvania would dominate the new government, rallied behind the **New Jersey Plan**.

Competing interests

This called for a single-house Congress in which each state cast one vote, as under the Articles of Confederation. In the end, a compromise was reached—a two-house Congress consisting of a Senate in which each state had two members, and a House of Representatives apportioned according to population. Senators would be chosen by state legislatures for six-year terms. They were thus insulated from sudden shifts in public opinion. Representatives were to be elected every two years directly by the people.

The Limits of Democracy

Under the Articles of Confederation, no national official had been chosen by popular vote. Thus, the mode of choosing the House of Representatives signaled an expansion of democracy. The Constitution, moreover, imposed neither property nor religious qualifications for voting.

Overall, however, the new structure of government was less than democratic. The delegates sought to shield the national government from the popular enthusiasms that had alarmed them during the 1780s and to ensure that the right kind of men held office. The delegates assumed that the Senate would be composed of each state's most distinguished citizens. They made the House of Representatives quite small (initially 65 members, at a time when the Massachusetts assembly had 200), on the assumption that only prominent individuals could win election in large districts.

Less-than-democratic structure

Nor did the delegates provide for direct election of either federal judges or the president. Members of the Supreme Court would be appointed by the president for life terms. The president would be chosen either by members of an electoral college or by the House of Representatives. A state's electors would be chosen either by its legislature or by popular vote.

The actual system of election seemed a recipe for confusion. Each elector was to cast votes for two candidates for president, with the second-place finisher becoming vice president. If no candidate received a majority of the electoral ballots—as the delegates seem to have assumed would normally be the case—the president would be chosen from among the top three finishers by the House of Representatives, with each state casting one vote. The Senate would then elect the vice president. The delegates devised this extremely cumbersome system of indirect election because they did not trust ordinary voters to choose the president and vice president directly.

This portrait of George Washington, painted in the early 1790s by Charles Peale Polk, is based on one executed in 1787 by Polk's uncle, Charles Willson Peale. It depicts Washington as he looked when he presided over the Constitutional Convention in Philadelphia.

The Division and Separation of Powers

Hammered out in four months of discussion and compromise, the Constitution is a document of only 4,000 words that provides only the briefest outline of the new structure of government. (See the Appendix for the full text.) It embodies two basic political principles—**federalism**, sometimes called the **division of powers**, and the system of **checks and balances** between the different branches of the national government, also known as the **separation of powers**.

"Federalism" refers to the relationship between the national government and the states. Compared with the Articles of Confederation, the Constitution significantly strengthened national authority. It charged the president with enforcing the law and commanding the military. It empowered Congress to levy taxes, borrow money, regulate commerce, declare war, deal with foreign nations and Indians, and promote the "general welfare." The Constitution also included strong provisions to prevent the states from infringing on property rights. They were barred from issuing paper money, impairing contracts, interfering with interstate commerce, and levying their own import or export duties. On the other hand, most day-to-day affairs of government, from education to law enforcement, remained in the hands of the states. This principle of divided sovereignty was a recipe for debate, which continues to this day, over the balance of power between the national government and the states.

Federalism

The separation of powers, or the system of checks and balances, refers to the way the Constitution seeks to prevent any branch of the national government from dominating the other two. To prevent an accumulation of power dangerous to liberty, authority within the government is diffused and balanced against itself. Congress enacts laws, but the president can veto them, and a two-thirds majority is required to pass legislation over his objection. Federal judges are nominated by the president and approved by the Senate, but to ensure their independence, the judges then serve for life. The president can be impeached by the House and removed from office by the Senate for "high crimes and misdemeanors."

Checks and balances

The Debate over Slavery

The structure of government was not the only source of debate at the Constitutional Convention. As Madison recorded, "the institution of slavery and its implications" divided the delegates at many sessions.

The words "slave" and "slavery" do not appear in the original Constitution—a concession to the sensibilities of delegates who feared they would "contaminate the glorious fabric of American liberty." Nonetheless, the document contained strong protections for slavery. It prohibited Congress from abolishing the importation of slaves from abroad for twenty years. It required states to return to their owners fugitives from bondage.

This advertisement by a slave-trading company appeared in a Richmond, Virginia, newspaper only a few months after the signing of the Constitution. The company seeks to buy 100 slaves to sell to purchasers in states farther south. Slavery was a major subject of debate at the Constitutional Convention.

And the **three-fifths clause** provided that three-fifths of the slave population would be counted in determining each state's representation in the House of Representatives and its electoral votes for president.

South Carolina's influence

South Carolina's delegates had come to Philadelphia determined to defend slavery, and they had a powerful impact on the final document. They originated the fugitive slave clause and the electoral college. They insisted on strict limits on the power of Congress to levy taxes within the states, fearing future efforts to raise revenue by taxing slave property. Gouverneur Morris, one of Pennsylvania's delegates, declared that he was being forced to decide between offending the southern states and doing injustice to "human nature." For the sake of national unity, he said, he would choose the latter.

Nonetheless, the Constitution did provide a basis for later antislavery political movements. Many of the framers, including slaveholders from the Upper South, hoped that the institution would eventually die out, and they successfully resisted efforts to place an explicit national recognition of property in human beings in the document. Slavery remained an institution created by state, not national, law. This opened the door to efforts to bar slavery in places of national jurisdiction, especially the western territories.

Slavery in the Constitution

The Constitution's slavery clauses were compromises, efforts to find a middle ground between the institution's critics and defenders. Taken together, however, they embedded slavery more deeply than ever in American life and politics. The slave trade clause allowed a commerce condemned by civilized society—one that had been suspended during the War of Independence—to continue until 1808. On January 1, 1808, the first day that Congress was allowed under the Constitution, it prohibited the further importation of slaves. But in the interim, partly to replace slaves who had escaped to the British and partly to provide labor for the expansion of slavery to fertile land away from the coast, some 170,000 Africans were brought to the new nation as slaves.

Slave trade clause

Fugitive slave clause

The fugitive slave clause accorded slave laws "extraterritoriality"—that is, the condition of bondage remained attached to a person even if he or she escaped to a state where slavery had been abolished. Nonetheless, the clause was strikingly ambiguous. It did not say who was responsible for apprehending a fugitive slave or what judicial procedures would be employed to return him or her to bondage. As time went on, these questions would become a major source of conflict between the North and the South. And the three-fifths clause allowed the white South to exercise far greater power in national affairs than

Three-fifths clause

the size of its free population warranted. Of the first sixteen presidential elections, between 1788 and 1848, all but four placed a southern slaveholder in the White House.

Nevertheless, some slaveholders detected a potential threat buried in the Constitution. Patrick Henry, who condemned slavery but feared abolition, warned that, in time of war, the new government might take steps to arm and liberate the slaves. "May Congress not say," he asked, "that every black man must fight?" What Henry could not anticipate was that the war that eventually destroyed slavery would be launched by the South itself to protect the institution.

Threat to slavery

The Final Document

Gouverneur Morris put the finishing touches on the final draft of the new Constitution, trying to make it, he explained, "as clear as our language would permit." For the original preamble, which began, "We the people of the States of New Hampshire, Massachusetts," etc., he substituted the far more powerful "We the people of the United States." He added a statement of the Constitution's purposes, including to "establish justice," promote "the general welfare," and "secure the blessings of liberty"—things the Articles of Confederation, in the eyes of most of the delegates, had failed to accomplish.

The last session of the Constitutional Convention took place on September 17, 1787. Benjamin Franklin urged the delegates to put aside individual objections and approve the document, whatever its imperfections.

The Preamble

The Signing of the Constitution, by mid-nineteenth-century American artist Thomas Prichard Rossiter, depicts the conclusion of the Constitutional Convention of 1787. Among the founding fathers depicted are James Wilson, signing the document at the table in the center, and George Washington, presiding from the dais with an image of the sun behind him.

Of the forty-five delegates who remained in Philadelphia, thirty-nine signed the Constitution. It was then sent to the states for ratification.

The Constitution created a new framework for American development. It made possible a national economic market. It created national political institutions, reduced the powers of the states, and sought to place limits on popular democracy. The ratification process, however, unleashed a nationwide debate over the best means of preserving American freedom.

THE RATIFICATION DEBATE AND THE ORIGIN OF THE BILL OF RIGHTS

The Federalist

Even though the Constitution provided that it would go into effect when nine states, not all thirteen as required by the Articles of Confederation, had given their approval, ratification was by no means certain. Each state held an election for delegates to a special ratifying convention. A fierce public battle ensued, producing hundreds of pamphlets and newspaper articles and spirited campaigns to elect delegates. To generate support, Hamilton, Madison, and John Jay composed a series of eighty-five essays

For ratification: Alexander Hamilton, James Madison, John Jay

This satirical engraving by Amos Doolittle depicts some of the issues in the debate over the ratification of the Constitution. The wagon in the center is carrying Connecticut and sinking into the mud under the weight of debts and paper money as "Federals" and "Antifederals" try to pull it out. Federals call for the state to "comply with Congress" (that is, to pay money requisitioned by the national government); the Antifederals reply, "Tax luxury" and "Success to Shays," a reference to Shays's Rebellion. Underneath the three merchant ships is a phrase criticizing the tariffs that states were imposing on imports from one another (which the Constitution prohibited).

that appeared in newspapers under the pen name Publius and were gathered as a book, **The Federalist**, in 1788. Today, the essays are regarded as among the most important American contributions to political thought. At the time, however, they were only one part of a much larger national debate over ratification.

Again and again, Hamilton and Madison repeated that rather than posing a danger to Americans' liberties, the Constitution in fact protected them. Any government, Hamilton insisted, could become oppressive, but with its checks and balances and division of power, the Constitution made political tyranny almost impossible. At the New York ratifying convention, Hamilton assured the delegates that the Constitution had created "the perfect balance between liberty and power."

Protecting American liberties

"Extend the Sphere"

Madison, too, emphasized how the Constitution was structured to prevent abuses of authority. But in several essays, especially *Federalist* nos. 10 and 51, he moved beyond such assurances to develop a strikingly new vision of the relationship between government and society in the United States. Madison identified the essential dilemma, as he saw it, of the new republic—government must be based on the will of the people, yet the people had shown themselves susceptible to dangerous enthusiasms. The problem of balancing democracy and respect for property would only grow in the years ahead because, he warned, economic development would inevitably increase the numbers of poor. What was to prevent them from using their political power to secure "a more equal distribution" of wealth by seizing the property of the rich?

Madison's Federalist nos. 10 and 51

In this late eighteenth-century engraving, Americans celebrate the signing of the Constitution beneath a temple of liberty.

The answer, Madison explained, lay not simply in the way power balanced power in the structure of government, but in the nation's size and diversity. Previous republics had existed only in small territories—the Dutch republic or the Italian city-states of the Renaissance. But, argued Madison, the very size of the United States was a source of stability, not, as many feared, weakness. "Extend the sphere," he wrote. In a nation as large as the United States, so many distinct interests—economic, regional, and political—would arise that no single one would ever be able to take over the government and oppress the rest.

Madison's writings did much to shape the early nation's understanding of its new political institutions. In arguing that the size of the republic helped to secure Americans' rights, they reinforced the tradition that saw continuous westward expansion as essential to freedom.

The Anti-Federalists

Opponents of ratification, called **Anti-Federalists**, insisted that the Constitution shifted the balance between liberty and power too far in the direction of the latter. Anti-Federalists lacked the coherent leadership of the Constitution's defenders. They included state politicians fearful of seeing their influence diminish, among them such revolutionary heroes as Samuel Adams, John Hancock, and Patrick Henry. Small farmers, many of whom supported the state debtor-relief measures of the 1780s that the Constitution's supporters deplored, also saw no need for a stronger central government. Some opponents of the Constitution denounced the document's protections for slavery; others warned that the powers of Congress were so broad that it might enact a law for abolition.

Anti-Federalists repeatedly predicted that the new government would fall under the sway of merchants, creditors, and others hostile to the interests of ordinary Americans. Popular self-government, they claimed, flourished best in small communities, where rulers and ruled interacted daily. The result of the Constitution, warned Melancton Smith of New York, a member of Congress under the Articles of Confederation, would be domination of the "common people" by the "well-born."

"Liberty" was the Anti-Federalists' watchword. America's happiness, they insisted, "arises from the freedom of our institutions and the limited nature of our government," both threatened by the new Constitution. To the vision of the United States as an energetic great power, Anti-Federalists counterposed a way of life grounded in local, democratic institutions. Anti-Federalists also pointed to the Constitution's lack of a **Bill of Rights**, which left unprotected rights such as trial by jury and freedom of speech and the press.

In general, pro-Constitution sentiment flourished in the nation's cities and in rural areas closely tied to the commercial marketplace. The Constitution's most energetic supporters were men of substantial property. But what George Bryan of Pennsylvania, a supporter of ratification, called the "golden phantom" of prosperity also swung urban artisans, laborers, and sailors behind the movement for a government that would use its "energy and power" to revive the depressed economy. Anti-Federalism drew its support from small farmers in more isolated rural areas such as the Hudson Valley of New York, western Massachusetts, and the southern backcountry.

In the end, the supporters' energy and organization, coupled with their domination of the colonial press, carried the day. Ninety-two news-

Against ratification: Samuel Adams, John Hancock, Patrick Henry

Rule by the "well-born"

Social bases of support and opposition

papers and magazines existed in the United States in 1787. Of these, only twelve published a significant number of Anti-Federalist pieces. Madison also won support for the new Constitution by promising that the first Congress would enact a Bill of Rights. By mid-1788, the required nine states had ratified. Only Rhode Island and North Carolina voted against ratification, and they subsequently had little choice but to join the new government. Anti-Federalism died. But as with other movements in American history that did not immediately achieve their

goals—for example, the Populists of the late nineteenth century—some of the Anti-Federalists' ideas eventually entered the political mainstream. To this day, their belief that a too-powerful central government is a threat to liberty continues to influence American political culture.

The Bill of Rights

Ironically, the parts of the Constitution Americans most value today—the freedoms of speech, the press, and religion; protection against unjust criminal procedures; equality before the law—were not in the original document. All of these but the last (which was enshrined in the Fourteenth Amendment after the Civil War) were contained in the first ten amendments, known as the Bill of Rights. Madison believed a Bill of Rights "redundant or pointless." "Parchment barriers" to the abuse of authority, he observed, would prove least effective when most needed. Madison's prediction would be amply borne out at future times of popular hysteria, such as during the Red Scare following World War I and the McCarthy era of the 1950s, when all branches of government joined in trampling on freedom of expression.

Nevertheless, every new state constitution contained some kind of declaration of citizens' rights, and large numbers of Americans—Federalist and Anti-Federalist alike—believed the new national Constitution should also have one. Madison presented to Congress a series of amendments that became the basis of the Bill of Rights, which was ratified by the states in 1791. The First Amendment prohibited Congress from legislating with regard to

Banner of the Society of Pewterers. A banner carried by one of the many artisan groups that took part in New York City's Grand Federal Procession of 1788 celebrating the ratification of the Constitution. The banner depicts artisans at work in their shop and some of their products. The words "Solid and Pure," and the inscription at the upper right, link the quality of their pewter to their opinion of the new frame of government and hopes for the future. The inscription reads:

The Federal Plan Most Solid and Secure / Americans Their Freedom Will Endure / All Arts Shall Flourish in Columbia's Land / And All Her Sons Join as One Social Band

First Amendment rights

VOICES OF FREEDOM

From David Ramsay, *The History of the American Revolution* (1789)

A member of the Continental Congress from South Carolina, David Ramsay published his history of the Revolution the year after the Constitution was ratified. In this excerpt, he lauds the principles of representative government and the right of future amendment, embodied in the state constitutions and adopted in the national one, as unique American political principles and the best ways of securing liberty.

The world has not hitherto exhibited so fair an opportunity for promoting social happiness. It is hoped for the honor of human nature, that the result will prove the fallacy of those theories that mankind are incapable of self government. The ancients, not knowing the doctrine of representation, were apt in their public meetings to run into confusion, but in America this mode of taking the sense of the people, is so well understood, and so completely reduced to system, that its most populous states are often peaceably convened in an assembly of deputies, not too large for orderly deliberation, and yet representing the whole in equal proportion. These popular branches of legislature are miniature pictures of the community, and from their mode of election are likely to be influenced by the same interests and feelings with the people whom they represent. . . .

In no age before, and in no other country, did man ever possess an election of the kind of government, under which he would choose to live. The constituent parts of the ancient free governments were thrown together by accident. The freedom of modern European governments was, for the most part, obtained by concessions, or liberality of monarchs, or military leaders. In America alone, reason and liberty concurred in the formation of constitutions. . . . In one thing they were all perfect. They left the people in the power of altering and amending them, whenever they pleased. In this happy peculiarity they placed the science of politics on a footing with the other sciences, by opening it to improvements from experience, and the discoveries of future ages. By means of this power of amending American constitutions, the friends of mankind have fondly hoped that oppression will one day be no more.

From James Winthrop, Anti-Federalist Essay Signed "Agrippa" (1787)

A local official in Middlesex, Massachusetts, James Winthrop published sixteen public letters between November 1787 and February 1788 opposing ratification of the Constitution.

It is the opinion of the ablest writers on the subject, that no extensive empire can be governed upon republican principles, and that such a government will degenerate into a despotism, unless it be made up of a confederacy of smaller states, each having the full powers of internal regulation. This is precisely the principle which has hitherto preserved our freedom. No instance can be found of any free government of considerable extent which has been supported upon any other plan. Large and consolidated empires may indeed dazzle the eyes of a distant spectator with their splendor, but if examined more nearly are always found to be full of misery. . . . It is under such tyranny that the Spanish provinces languish, and such would be our misfortune and degradation, if we should submit to have the concerns of the whole empire managed by one empire. To promote the happiness of the people it is necessary that there should be local laws; and it is necessary that those laws should be made by the representatives of those who are immediately subject to [them]. . . .

It is impossible for one code of laws to suit Georgia and Massachusetts. They must, therefore, legislate for themselves. Yet there is, I believe, not one point of legislation that is not surrendered in the proposed plan. Questions of every kind respecting property are determinable in a continental court, and so are all kinds of criminal causes. The continental legislature has, therefore, a right to make rules in all cases. . . . No rights are reserved to the citizens. . . . This new system is, therefore, a consolidation of all the states into one large mass, however diverse the parts may be of which it is composed. . . .

A bill of rights . . . serves to secure the minority against the usurpation and tyranny of the majority. . . . The experience of all mankind has proved the prevalence of a disposition to use power wantonly. It is therefore as necessary to defend an individual against the majority in a republic as against the king in a monarchy.

QUESTIONS

1. *Why does Ramsay feel that the power to amend the Constitution is so important a political innovation?*

2. *Why does Winthrop believe that a Bill of Rights is essential in the Constitution?*

3. *How do Ramsay and Winthrop differ concerning how the principle of representation operates in the United States?*

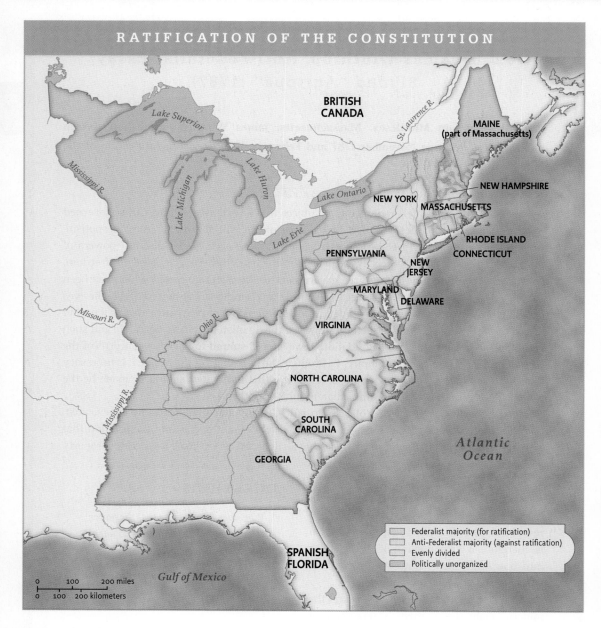

RATIFICATION OF THE CONSTITUTION

BRITISH CANADA

MAINE
(part of Massachusetts)

Lake Superior

Mississippi R.

Lake Michigan

Lake Huron

Lake Ontario

NEW YORK

NEW HAMPSHIRE

MASSACHUSETTS

Lake Erie

RHODE ISLAND

PENNSYLVANIA

CONNECTICUT

Missouri R.

Ohio R.

NEW JERSEY

MARYLAND

DELAWARE

St. Lawrence R.

VIRGINIA

Mississippi R.

NORTH CAROLINA

Atlantic
Ocean

SOUTH
CAROLINA

GEORGIA

Federalist majority (for ratification)
Anti-Federalist majority (against ratification)
Evenly divided
Politically unorganized

SPANISH
FLORIDA

Gulf of Mexico

0   100   200 miles
0   100   200 kilometers

Federalists—those who supported the new Constitution—tended to be concentrated in cities and nearby rural areas, whereas backcountry farmers were more likely to oppose the new frame of government.

religion or infringing on freedom of speech, freedom of the press, or the right of assembly. The Second upheld the people's right to "keep and bear arms" in conjunction with "a well-regulated militia." Others prohibited abuses such as arrests without warrants and forcing a person accused of a crime to testify against himself, and reaffirmed the right to trial by jury.

Although the roots and even the specific language of some parts of the Bill of Rights lay far back in English history, other provisions reflected the changes in American life brought about by the Revolution. The most remarkable of these was constitutional recognition of religious freedom. Unlike the Declaration of Independence, which invokes the blessing of divine providence, the Constitution is a purely secular document that contains no reference to God and bars religious tests for federal officeholders. The First Amendment prohibits the federal government from legislating on the subject of religion—a complete departure from British and colonial precedent. Under the Constitution it was and remains possible, as one critic complained, for "a papist, a Mohomatan, a deist, yea an atheist" to become president of the United States. Madison was so adamant about separating church and state that he even opposed the appointment of chaplains to serve Congress and the military.

Constitutional recognition of religious freedom

The Bill of Rights aroused little enthusiasm on ratification and for decades was all but ignored. Not until the twentieth century would it come to be revered as an indispensable expression of American freedom. Nonetheless, the Bill of Rights subtly affected the language of liberty. Applying only to the federal government, not the states, it reinforced the idea that concentrated national power posed the greatest threat to freedom. And it contributed to the long process whereby freedom came to be discussed in the vocabulary of rights.

Legacy of the Bill of Rights

Among the most important rights were freedom of speech and the press, vital building blocks of a democratic public sphere. Once an entitlement of members of Parliament and colonial assemblies, free speech came to be seen as a basic right of citizenship.

"WE THE PEOPLE"

Who Belongs? The Constitution and American Citizenship

A nation, in one scholar's famous phrase, is more than a political entity or a specific piece of territory—it is also "an imagined political community," whose borders are as much intellectual as geographic. The creation of the United States required creating "Americans," that is, people who considered themselves members of the new nation, not simply of individual states. But who qualified as an American citizen? The Constitution did not say.

In British law, the American colonists, like persons in Great Britain, were "subjects" of the crown, entitled to protection and required to provide allegiance and, if male, to take up arms when called upon by the government. Independence transformed British subjecthood into American citizenship but did little to clarify its definition and rights. The word "citizen" appears several times in the Constitution, but no definition is given. One provision, known as the "comity" clause, prohibits states from discriminating between the "privileges and immunities" of their own citizens and those of other states. In other words, a person who moves from New York to Illinois must enjoy the same rights as those already in Illinois. This language assumes that the rights of citizens are determined by the states, not the federal government.

"Citizen"

Derivation of citizenship

The Constitution does require the president to be a "natural born citizen," that is, a person born in the country. This suggests, but does not explicitly state, that citizenship derives either from birth in the United States or, for immigrants from abroad (ineligible to become president), from a "naturalization" process. On occasion, the federal government created American citizens by purchasing the land on which they lived, for example, the Louisiana Territory acquired from France in 1803, or via conquest, as in the Mexican-American War. In both cases, residents of territory acquired by the United States could choose to become American citizens if they so desired (although whether this applied to Native Americans living under tribal sovereignty remained unclear).

Despite the enormous prestige that the idea of citizenship acquired in the first half of the nineteenth century, there was no commonly agreed-upon understanding of the rights that went with it or the role of the federal government in defining and guaranteeing those rights. Whites, male and female, born in the United States were commonly assumed to be citizens, but white women lacked basic rights enjoyed by men. Slaves were not American citizens, nor were Indians, but the status of free black Americans born in the United States remained highly controversial. Blacks voted in elections that chose delegates to the state conventions that ratified the Constitution. In the 1790s, the federal government issued certificates affirming the citizenship of black sailors, to prevent them from being seized by the British and "impressed" into the Royal Navy. Yet as time went on, the slave states placed increasingly severe restrictions on the lives of free blacks and refused to recognize them as citizens. Some northern states did, however, and all of the northern states accorded African-Americans basic rights such as property ownership, trial by jury, and the ability to hold public meetings, publish newspapers, and establish their own churches. But nowhere did they enjoy full equality before the law. One judge referred to free blacks as "quasi citizens." Not until the Reconstruction era that followed the Civil War was a clear statement added to the Constitution that affirmed the principle of "birthright citizenship"—that anyone born in the United States, no matter his or her race, language, religion, national origin, or the legal situation of one's parents, is an American citizen and is entitled to the equal protection of the laws.

"Birthright citizenship"

National Identity

The Constitution opens with the words "We the People." Although one might assume that the "people" of the United States included all those living within the nation's borders, the text made clear that this was not the case. The Constitution identifies three populations inhabiting the United States: Indians, treated as members of independent tribes and not part of the American body politic; "other persons"—that is, slaves; and the "people." Only the third were entitled to American freedom.

Exclusion of Indians and slaves

Indians in the New Nation

The early republic's policies toward Indians and African-Americans illustrate the conflicting principles that shaped American nationality. American leaders agreed that the West should not be left in Indian hands, but they disagreed about the Indians' ultimate fate. The government hoped to encourage the westward expansion of white settlement, which implied one of three things: the removal of the Indian population to lands even farther west, their total disappearance, or their incorporation into white "civilization" with the expectation that they might one day become part of American society.

Indian tribes had no representation in the new government. The treaty system gave them a unique status within the American political system. But despite this recognition of their sovereignty, treaties were essentially ways of transferring land from Indians to the federal government or the states.

Political status of Indian tribes

Open warfare continued in the Ohio Valley after ratification. In 1791, Little Turtle, leader of the Miami Confederacy, inflicted a humiliating defeat on American forces led by Arthur St. Clair, the American governor of the Northwest Territory. With 630 dead, this was the costliest loss ever suffered by the U.S. Army at the hands of Indians. In 1794, 3,000 American troops under Anthony Wayne defeated Little Turtle's forces at the Battle of Fallen Timbers. This led directly to the **Treaty of Greenville** of 1795,

The signing of the Treaty of Greenville of 1795, painted by an unknown member of General Anthony Wayne's staff. In the treaty, a group of tribes ceded most of the area of the current states of Ohio and Indiana, along with the site that became the city of Chicago, to the United States.

in which twelve Indian tribes ceded most of Ohio and Indiana to the federal government. The treaty also established the **annuity system**—yearly grants of federal money to Indian tribes that institutionalized continuing government influence in tribal affairs and gave outsiders considerable control over Indian life.

Many prominent figures, however, rejected the idea that Indians were innately inferior to white Americans. Thomas Jefferson believed that Indians merely lived at a less advanced stage of civilization. Indians could become full-fledged members of the republic by abandoning communal landholding and hunting in favor of small-scale farming.

To pursue the goal of assimilation, Congress in the 1790s authorized President Washington to distribute agricultural tools and livestock to Indian men and spinning wheels and looms to Indian women. To whites, the adoption of American gender norms, with men working the land and women tending to their homes, would be a crucial sign that the Indians were becoming "civilized." But the American notion of civilization required so great a transformation of Indian life that most tribes rejected it. To Indians, freedom meant retaining tribal autonomy and identity, including the ability to travel widely in search of game. "Since our acquaintance with our brother white people," declared a Mohawk speaker at a 1796 treaty council, "that which we call freedom and liberty, becomes an entire stranger to us." There was no room for Indians who desired to retain their traditional way of life in the American empire of liberty.

Blacks and the Republic

By 1790, the 700,000 African-Americans far exceeded the Indian population within the United States. The status of free blacks was somewhat indeterminate. The North's **gradual emancipation** acts assumed that former slaves would remain in the country, not be colonized abroad. During the era of the Revolution, free blacks enjoyed at least some of the legal rights accorded to whites, including, in most states, the right to vote. The large majority of blacks, of course, were slaves, and slavery rendered them all but invisible to those imagining the American community.

Many white Americans excluded blacks from their conception of the American people. The Constitution empowered Congress to create a uniform system by which immigrants became citizens, and the Naturalization Act of 1790 offered the first legislative definition of American nationality. With no debate, Congress restricted the process of becoming a citizen from abroad to "free white persons." The word "white" in this act excluded a large majority of the world's population from emigrating to the "asylum for

Naturalization Act of 1790

WHO IS AN AMERICAN?

From J. Hector St. John de Crèvecoeur, *Letters from an American Farmer* (1782)

In the era of the Revolution, many foreigners celebrated the United States as not only an independent nation but a new society, in which individuals could enjoy opportunities unknown in the Old World and where a new nationality was being forged from the diverse populations of Europe. No one promoted this image of America more enthusiastically than J. Hector St. John de Crèvecoeur, a Frenchman who had settled in New York, married the daughter of a prominent landowner, and later returned to Europe and wrote about his experiences in America.

[The European who comes to the United States] beholds fair cities, substantial villages, extensive fields, an immense country filled with decent houses, good roads, orchards, meadows, and bridges, where an hundred years ago all was wild, woody and uncultivated. . . . A modern society offers itself to his contemplation, different from what he had hitherto seen. It is not composed, as in Europe, of great lords who possess every thing and of a herd of people who have nothing. Here are no aristocratical families, no courts, no kings, no bishops, no ecclesiastical dominion. . . . We have no princes, for whom we toil, starve, and bleed: we are the most perfect society now existing in the world. Here man is free; as he ought to be. . . .

The next wish of this traveler will be to know whence came all these people? They are a mixture of English, Scotch, Irish, French, Dutch, Germans, and Swedes. From this promiscuous breed, that race now called Americans have arisen. . . . In this great American asylum, the poor of Europe have by some means met together. . . . Urged by a variety of motives, here they came. . . .

What then is the American, this new man? He is either an European, or the descendant of an European, hence that strange mixture of blood, which you will find in no other country. . . . He is an American, who leaving behind him all his ancient prejudices and manners, receives new ones from the new mode of life he has embraced, the new government he obeys, and the new rank he holds. . . . Here individuals of all nations are melted into a new race of men.

QUESTIONS

1. *What characteristics of American life does Crèvecoeur believe unite people of different origins in the United States into one people?*

2. *What aspects of society, and what parts of the American people, are left out of his description?*

TABLE 7.1 Total Population and Black Population of the United States, 1790

STATE	TOTAL POPULATION	SLAVES	FREE BLACKS
New England:			
New Hampshire	141,899	158	630
Vermont*	85,341	0	271
Massachusetts	378,556	0	5,369
Connecticut	237,655	2,764	2,771
Rhode Island	69,112	948	3,484
Maine**	96,643	0	536
Middle States:			
New York	340,241	21,324	4,682
New Jersey	184,139	11,423	2,762
Pennsylvania	433,611	3,737	6,531
South:			
Delaware	59,096	8,887	3,899
Maryland	319,728	103,036	8,043
Virginia	747,610	292,627	12,866
North Carolina	395,005	100,572	5,041
South Carolina	249,073	107,094	1,801
Georgia	82,548	29,264	398
Kentucky*	73,677	12,430	114
Tennessee*	35,691	3,417	361
Total	3,929,625	697,624	59,557

*Vermont, Kentucky, and Tennessee were territories that had not yet been admitted as states.

**Maine was part of Massachusetts in 1790.

mankind" and partaking in the blessings of American freedom. For eighty years, no non-white immigrant could become a naturalized citizen. Africans were allowed to do so in 1870, but not until the 1940s did persons of Asian origin become eligible. (Native Americans were granted American citizenship in 1924.)

Jefferson, Slavery, and Race

Man's liberty, John Locke had written, flowed from "his having reason." To deny liberty to those who were not considered rational beings did not seem to be a contradiction. White Americans increasingly viewed blacks as permanently deficient in the qualities that made freedom possible—the capacity for self-control, reason, and devotion to the larger community. These were the characteristics that Jefferson, in a famous comparison of the races in his book ***Notes on the State of Virginia***, published in 1785, claimed blacks lacked, partly due to natural incapacity and partly because the bitter experience of slavery had (quite understandably, he felt) rendered them disloyal to the nation.

Jefferson was obsessed with the connection between heredity and environment, race and intelligence. His belief that individuals' abilities and achievements are shaped by social conditions inclined him to hope that no group was fixed permanently in a status of inferiority. In the case of blacks, however, he could not avoid the "suspicion" that nature had permanently deprived them of the qualities that made republican citizenship possible. Benjamin Banneker, a free African-American from Maryland who had taught himself the principles of mathematics, sent Jefferson a copy of an astronomical almanac he had published, along with a plea for the abolition of slavery. Jefferson replied, "Nobody wishes more than I do to see such proofs as you exhibit, that nature has given to our black brethren, talents equal to the other colors of men." To his friend Joel Barlow, however, Jefferson suggested that a white person must have helped Banneker with his calculations.

"Nothing is more certainly written in the book of fate," wrote Jefferson, "than that these people are to be free." Yet he felt that America should have a homogeneous citizenry with common experiences, values, and inborn abilities. These contradictions in Jefferson reflected the divided mind of his generation. Some prominent Virginians assumed that blacks could become part of the American nation. Edward Coles, an early governor of Illinois, brought his slaves from Virginia, freed them, and settled them on farms. Washington, who died in 1799, provided in his will that his 277 slaves would become free after the death of his wife, Martha. Believing the slave trade immoral, Jefferson tried to avoid selling slaves to pay off his mounting debts. But his will provided for the freedom of only five, all relatives of his slave Sally Hemings, with whom he appears to have fathered one or more children.

Principles of Freedom

Even as the decline of apprenticeship and indentured servitude narrowed the gradations of freedom among the white population, the Revolution widened the divide between free Americans and those who remained in slavery. Race, one among many kinds of legal and social inequality in colonial America, now emerged as a convenient justification for the existence of slavery in a land that claimed to be committed to freedom. Blacks' "natural faculties," Alexander Hamilton noted in 1779, were "probably as good as ours." But the existence of slavery, he added, "makes us fancy many things that are founded neither in reason nor experience."

"We the people" increasingly meant only white Americans. "Principles of freedom, which embrace only half mankind, are only half systems," declared the anonymous author of a Fourth of July speech in Hartford, Connecticut, in 1800. "Declaration of Independence," he wondered, "where art thou now?" The answer came from a Richmond newspaper: "Tell us not of principles. Those principles have been annihilated by the existence of slavery among us."

This portrait from around 1825 depicts Euphemia Toussaint, the New York–born niece of Pierre Toussaint, a slave who had been brought to the city by his owner from the French colony Saint Domingue (modern-day Haiti) around 1787. Toussaint gained his freedom in 1807 and renamed himself in honor of the leader of the Haitian Revolution of the 1790s. He became a successful hairdresser and contributor to various charities in the city. Born in 1815, Euphemia died at the age of fourteen.

An advertisement seeking the return of Ona Judge, a domestic slave of Martha Washington, who escaped in 1796 while the family was in Philadelphia, where George Washington served as president. She made her way to New Hampshire, and evaded efforts to recapture her.

Ten Dollars Reward.

ABSCONDED from the houſehold of the Preſident of the United States, on Saturday afternoon, ONEY JUDGE, a light Mulatto girl, much freckled, with very black eyes, and buſhy black hair—She is of middle ſtature, but ſlender and delicately made, about 20 years of age. She has many changes of very good clothes of all ſorts, but they are not ſufficiently recollected to deſcribe.

CHAPTER REVIEW AND ONLINE RESOURCES

REVIEW QUESTIONS

1. How did the limited central government created by the Articles of Confederation reflect the issues behind the Revolution and fears for individual liberties?

2. What were the ideas and motivations that pushed Americans to expand west?

3. What events and ideas led to the belief in 1786 and 1787 that the Articles of Confederation were not working well?

4. The Constitution has been described as a "bundle of compromises." Which compromises were the most significant in shaping the direction of the new nation and why?

5. What were the major arguments in support of the Constitution given by the Federalists?

6. What were the major arguments against the Constitution put forth by the Anti-Federalists?

7. How did the Constitution address the status of American slavery?

8. How did the Constitution address the question of who is an American citizen?

9. How did the idea of citizenship change in the first half of the nineteenth century?

KEY TERMS

Articles of Confederation (p. 194)
Ordinance of 1784 (p. 195)
Ordinance of 1785 (p. 195)
Northwest Ordinance of 1787 (p. 197)
empire of liberty (p. 197)
Shays's Rebellion (p. 199)
Constitutional Convention (p. 201)
Virginia Plan (p. 201)
New Jersey Plan (p. 201)
federalism (p. 203)
division of powers (p. 203)
checks and balances (p. 203)
separation of powers (p. 203)
three-fifths clause (p. 204)
The Federalist (p. 207)
Anti-Federalists (p. 208)
Bill of Rights (p. 208)
Treaty of Greenville (p. 215)
annuity system (p. 216)
gradual emancipation (p. 216)
Notes on the State of Virginia (p. 218)

Go to INQUIZITIVE

To see what you know—and learn what you've missed—with personalized feedback along the way.

Visit the *Give Me Liberty!* **Student Site** for primary source documents and images, interactive maps, author videos featuring Eric Foner, and more.

CHAPTER 8

SECURING THE REPUBLIC

★

1791–1815

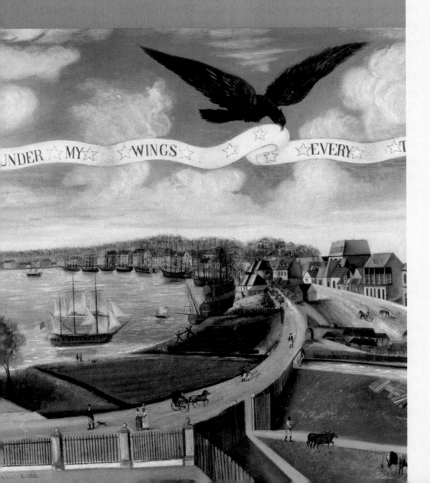

New Orleans in 1803, at the time of the Louisiana Purchase. The painting shows a view of the city from a nearby plantation. The town houses of merchants and plantation owners line the broad promenade along the waterfront. At the lower center, a slave goes about his work. An eagle holds aloft a banner that suggests the heady optimism of the young republic: Under My Wings Every Thing Prospers.

- *What issues made the politics of the 1790s so divisive?*

- *How did competing views of freedom and global events promote the political divisions of the 1790s?*

- *What were the achievements and failures of Jefferson's presidency?*

- *What were the causes and significant results of the War of 1812?*

O n April 30, 1789, in New York City, the nation's temporary capital, George Washington became the first president under the new Constitution. All sixty-nine electors had awarded him their votes. Dressed in a plain suit of "superfine American broad cloth" rather than European finery, Washington took the oath of office on the balcony of Federal Hall before a large crowd that reacted with "loud and repeated shouts" of approval. He then retreated inside to deliver his inaugural address before members of Congress and other dignitaries.

Washington's speech expressed the revolutionary generation's conviction that it had embarked on an experiment of enormous historical importance, whose outcome was by no means certain. "The preservation of the sacred fire of liberty and the destiny of the republican model of government," Washington proclaimed, depended on the success of the American experiment in self-government.

American leaders believed that maintaining political harmony was crucial to this success. They were especially anxious to avoid the emergence of organized political parties, which had already appeared in several states. Parties were considered divisive and disloyal. "They serve to organize faction," Washington would later declare, and to substitute the aims of "a small but artful" minority for the "will of the nation." The Constitution makes no mention of political parties, and the original method of electing the president assumes that candidates would run as individuals, not on a party ticket (otherwise, the second-place finisher would not have become vice president). Nonetheless, national political parties quickly arose. Originating in Congress, they soon spread to the general populace. Instead of harmony, the 1790s became, in the words of one historian, an "age of passion." Political rhetoric became inflamed because the stakes seemed so high—nothing less than the legacy of the Revolution, the new nation's future, and the survival of American freedom.

POLITICS IN AN AGE OF PASSION

Washington's first administration

President Washington provided a much-needed symbol of national unity. He brought into his cabinet some of the new nation's most prominent political leaders, including Thomas Jefferson as secretary of state and Alexander Hamilton to head the Treasury Department. He also appointed a Supreme Court of six members, headed by John Jay of New York. But harmonious government proved short-lived.

Hamilton's Program

Political divisions first surfaced over the financial plan developed by Hamilton in 1790 and 1791. His immediate aims were to establish the nation's financial stability, bring to the government's support the country's most powerful financial interests, and encourage economic development. His long-term purpose was to make the United States a major commercial and military power. The goal of national greatness, he believed, could never be realized if the government suffered from the same weaknesses as under the Articles of Confederation.

Hamilton's program had five parts. The first step was to establish the new nation's credit-worthiness—that is, to create conditions under which persons would loan money to the government by purchasing its bonds, confident that they would be repaid. Hamilton proposed that the federal government assume responsibility for paying off at its full face value the national debt inherited from the War of Independence, as well as outstanding debts of the states. Second, he called for the creation of a new national debt. The old debts would be replaced by new interest-bearing bonds issued to the government's creditors. This would give men of economic substance a stake in promoting the new nation's stability, because the stronger and more economically secure the federal government, the more likely it would be to pay its debts.

The third part of Hamilton's program called for the creation of a **Bank of the United States**, modeled on the Bank of England, to serve as the nation's main financial agent. A private corporation rather than a branch of the government, it would hold public funds, issue bank notes that would serve as currency, and make loans to the government when necessary, all the while returning a tidy profit to its stockholders. Fourth, to raise revenue, Hamilton proposed a tax on producers of whiskey. Finally, in a Report on Manufactures delivered to Congress in December 1791, Hamilton called for the imposition of a tariff (a tax on imported foreign goods) and government subsidies to encourage the development of factories that could manufacture products currently purchased from abroad.

Liberty and Washington, painted by an unknown artist around 1800, depicts a female figure of liberty placing a wreath on a bust of the first president. She carries an American flag and stands on a royal crown, which has been thrown to the ground. In the background is a liberty cap. Washington had died in 1799 and was now immortalized as a symbol of freedom, independence, and national pride.

The Emergence of Opposition

Hamilton's vision of a powerful commercial republic won strong support from American financiers, manufacturers, and merchants. But it alarmed those who believed the new nation's destiny lay in charting a different path of development. Hamilton's plans hinged on close ties with Britain, America's main trading partner. To James Madison and Thomas Jefferson,

Support for Hamilton's plan

the future lay in westward expansion, not connections with Europe. Their goal was a republic of independent farmers marketing grain, tobacco, and other products freely to the entire world. Jefferson and Madison quickly concluded that the greatest threat to American freedom lay in the alliance of a powerful central government with an emerging class of commercial capitalists, such as Hamilton appeared to envision.

Opposition to Hamilton's plan

To Jefferson, Hamilton's system "flowed from principles adverse to liberty, and was calculated to undermine and demolish the republic." Hamilton's plans for a standing army seemed to his critics a bold threat to freedom. The national bank and assumption of state debts, they feared, would introduce into American politics the same corruption that had undermined British liberty, and enrich the wealthy at the expense of ordinary Americans. During the 1780s, speculators had bought up at great discounts (often only a few cents on the dollar) government bonds and paper notes that had been used to pay those who fought in the Revolution or supplied the army. Under Hamilton's plan, speculators would reap a windfall by being paid at face value while the original holders received nothing. Because transportation was so poor, moreover, many backcountry farmers were used to distilling their grain harvest into whiskey, which could then be carried more easily to market. Hamilton's whiskey tax seemed to single them out unfairly in order to enrich bondholders.

The Jefferson–Hamilton Bargain

At first, opposition to Hamilton's program arose almost entirely from the South, the region that had the least interest in manufacturing development. It also had fewer holders of federal bonds than the Middle States and New England. Because Hamilton insisted that all his plans were authorized by the Constitution's broad "general welfare" clause, many southerners who had supported the new Constitution now became "strict constructionists," who insisted that the federal government could exercise only powers specifically listed in the document. Jefferson believed the new national bank unconstitutional, because the right of Congress to create a bank was not mentioned in the Constitution.

"Strict constructionists"

Opposition in Congress threatened the enactment of Hamilton's plans. Behind-the-scenes negotiations followed. They culminated at a famous dinner in 1790 at which Jefferson brokered an agreement whereby southerners accepted Hamilton's fiscal program (with the exception of subsidies to manufacturers) in exchange for the establishment of the permanent national capital on the Potomac River between Maryland and Virginia. Major Pierre-Charles L'Enfant, a French-born veteran of the War of Independence, designed a grandiose plan for

A bargain struck

The national capital

the "federal city" modeled on the great urban centers of Europe, with wide boulevards, parks, and fountains. When it came to constructing public buildings in the nation's new capital, most of the labor was performed by slaves.

The Impact of the French Revolution

Political divisions deepened in response to events in Europe. When it began in 1789, nearly all Americans welcomed the French Revolution, inspired in part by the example of their own rebellion. But in 1793, the revolution took a more radical turn with the execution of King Louis XVI along with numerous aristocrats and other foes of the new government, and war broke out between France and Great Britain.

War between France and Great Britain

Events in France became a source of bitter conflict in America. Jefferson and his followers believed that despite its excesses the revolution marked a historic victory for the idea of popular self-government, which must be defended at all costs. Enthusiasm for France inspired a rebirth of symbols of liberty. Liberty poles and caps reappeared on the streets of American towns and cities. To Washington, Hamilton, and their supporters, however, the revolution raised the specter of anarchy.

The rivalry between Britain and France did much to shape early American politics. The "permanent" alliance between France and the United States, which dated to 1778, complicated the situation. No one advocated that the United States should become involved in the European war, and Washington in April 1793 issued a proclamation of American neutrality. Meanwhile, the British seized hundreds of American ships trading with the French West Indies and resumed the hated practice of **impressment**—kidnapping sailors, including American citizens of British origin, to serve in their navy. Sent to London to present objections, while still serving as chief justice, John Jay negotiated an agreement in 1794 that produced the greatest public controversy of Washington's presidency. **Jay's Treaty** contained no British concessions on impressment or the rights of American shipping. Britain did agree to abandon outposts on the western frontier, which it was supposed to have done in 1783. Critics of the administration charged that it aligned the United States with monarchical Britain in its conflict with republican France. Jay's Treaty sharpened political divisions in the United States and led directly to the formation of an organized opposition party.

In the 1790s, the French Revolution set Great Britain and France on the path to war. Yet British merchants, aware of the enthusiasm for revolutionary France in the United States, produced items for sale to Americans that celebrated the bonds between "the two great republics." This pitcher is adorned with the flags of the two countries and a cap of liberty.

Political Parties

By the mid-1790s, two increasingly coherent parties had appeared in Congress, calling themselves **Federalists and Republicans**. (The latter had no connection with today's Republican Party, which was founded in the 1850s.) Both parties laid claim to the language of liberty, and each accused its opponent of engaging in a conspiracy to destroy it.

The Federalists, supporters of the Washington administration, favored Hamilton's economic program and close ties with Britain. Prosperous merchants, farmers, lawyers, and established political leaders (especially outside the South) tended to support the Federalists. Their outlook was generally elitist, reflecting the traditional eighteenth-century view of society as a fixed hierarchy and of public office as reserved for men of economic substance—the "rich, the able, and the well-born," as Hamilton put it. Freedom, Federalists insisted, did not mean the right to stand up in opposition to the government. Federalists feared that the "spirit of liberty" unleashed by the American Revolution was degenerating into anarchy and "licentiousness."

The Federalists may have been the only major party in American history forthrightly to proclaim democracy and freedom dangerous in the hands of ordinary citizens. The **Whiskey Rebellion** of 1794, which broke out when backcountry Pennsylvania farmers sought to block collection of the new tax on distilled spirits, reinforced this conviction. The "rebels" invoked the symbols of 1776, displaying banners reading "Liberty or Death." But Washington dispatched 13,000 militiamen to western Pennsylvania (a larger force than he had commanded during the Revolution). He accompanied them part of the way, the only time in American history that a president has actually commanded an army in the field. The "rebels" offered no resistance.

The Republican Party

Republicans, led by Madison and Jefferson, were more sympathetic to France than the Federalists and had more faith in democratic self-government. They drew their support from an unusual alliance of wealthy southern planters and ordinary farmers throughout the country. Enthusiasm for the French Revolution increasingly drew urban artisans into Republican ranks as well. Republicans were far more critical than the

A 1794 painting by the Baltimore artist and sign painter Frederick Kemmelmeyer depicting President George Washington as commander-in-chief of the army dispatched to put down the Whiskey Rebellion.

Venerate the Plough, a medal of the Philadelphia Society for the Promotion of Agriculture, 1786. Americans such as Jefferson and Madison believed that farmers were the most virtuous citizens and therefore agriculture must remain the foundation of American life.

Federalists of social and economic inequality, and more accepting of broad democratic participation as essential to freedom.

Political language became more and more heated. Federalists denounced Republicans as French agents, anarchists, and traitors. Republicans called their opponents monarchists. Each charged the other with betraying the principles of American freedom. Washington himself received mounting abuse. When he left office, a Republican newspaper declared that his name had become synonymous with "political iniquity" and "legalized corruption."

A print shop in the early republic. The increasing number of newspapers played a major role in the expansion of the public sphere.

An Expanding Public Sphere

The debates of the 1790s produced not only one of the most intense periods of partisan warfare in American history but also an enduring expansion of the public sphere and with it the democratic content of American freedom. More and more citizens attended political meetings and became avid readers of pamphlets and newspapers. The establishment of nearly 1,000 post offices made possible the wider circulation of personal letters and printed materials. The era witnessed the rapid growth of the American press—the number of newspapers rose from around 100 to 260 during the 1790s, and reached nearly 400 by 1810.

This piece of needlework woven in 1808 by twenty-year-old Lucina Hudson of South Hadley, Massachusetts, depicts a young woman holding an American flag topped by a liberty cap. "Liberty needlework" was quite popular in the early nineteenth century.

Inspired by the Jacobin clubs of Paris, supporters of the French Revolution and critics of the Washington administration in 1793 and 1794 formed nearly fifty **Democratic-Republican societies**. The Republican press publicized their meetings, replete with toasts to French and American liberty. Federalists saw the societies as another example of how liberty was getting out of hand. The government, not "self-created societies," declared the president, was the authentic voice of the American people. Forced to justify their existence, the societies developed a defense of the right of the people to debate political issues and organize to affect public policy. To the societies, political liberty meant not simply voting in elections but constant involvement in public affairs. Blamed by Federalists for helping to inspire the Whiskey Rebellion, the societies disappeared by the end of 1795.

VOICES OF FREEDOM

From Judith Sargent Murray,
"On the Equality of the Sexes" (1790)

A prominent writer of plays, novels, and poetry, Judith Sargent Murray of Massachusetts was one of the first women to demand equal educational opportunities for women.

Is it upon mature consideration we adopt the idea, that nature is thus partial in her distributions? Is it indeed a fact, that she hath yielded to one half of the human species so unquestionable a mental superiority? I know that to both sexes elevated understandings, and the reverse, are common. But, suffer me to ask, in what the minds of females are so notoriously deficient, or unequal. . . .

Are we deficient in reason? We can only reason from what we know, and if an opportunity of acquiring knowledge hath been denied us, the inferiority of our sex cannot fairly be deduced from thence. . . . Will it be said that the judgment of a male of two years old, is more sage than that of a female's of the same age? I believe the reverse is generally observed to be true. But from that period what partiality! How is the one exalted, and the other depressed, by the contrary modes of education which are adopted! The one is taught to aspire, and the other is early confined and limited. As their years increase, the sister must be wholly domesticated, while the brother is led by the hand through all the flowery paths of science. Grant that their minds are by nature equal, yet who shall wonder at the *apparent* superiority. . . . At length arrived at womanhood, the uncultivated fair one feels a void, which the employments allotted her are by no means capable of filling. . . . She herself is most unhappy; she feels the want of a cultivated mind. . . . Should it . . . be vociferated, "Your domestic employments are sufficient"—I would calmly ask, is it reasonable, that a candidate for immortality, for the joys of heaven, an intelligent being, who is to spend an eternity in contemplating the works of Deity, should at present be so degraded, as to be allowed no other ideas, than those which are suggested by the mechanism of a pudding, or the sewing the seams of a garment? . . .

Yes, ye lordly, ye haughty sex, our souls are by nature *equal* to yours.

From Address of the Democratic-Republican Society of Pennsylvania (December 18, 1794)

The creation of around fifty Democratic-Republican societies in 1793 and 1794 reflected the expansion of the public sphere. The Pennsylvania society issued an address defending itself against critics who questioned its right to criticize the administration of George Washington.

The principles and proceedings of our Association have lately been caluminated [tarred by malicious falsehoods]. We should think ourselves unworthy to be ranked as Freemen, if awed by the name of any man, however he may command the public gratitude for past services, we could suffer in silence so sacred a right, so important a principle, as the freedom of opinion to be infringed, by attack on Societies which stand on that constitutional basis.

Freedom of thought, and a free communication of opinions by speech through the medium of the press, are the safeguards of our Liberties. . . . By the freedom of opinion, cannot be meant the right of thinking merely; for of this right the greatest Tyrant cannot deprive his meanest slave; but, it is freedom in the communication of sentiments [by] speech or through the press. This liberty is an imprescriptable [unlimitable] right, independent of any Constitution or social compact; it is as complete a right as that which any man has to the enjoyment of his life. These principles are eternal— they are recognized by our Constitution; and that nation is already enslaved that does not acknowledge their truth. . . .

If freedom of opinion, in the sense we understand it, is the right of every Citizen, by what mode of reasoning can that right be denied to an assemblage of Citizens? . . . The Society are free to declare that they never were more strongly impressed with . . . the importance of associations . . . than at the present time. The germ of an odious Aristocracy is planted among us—it has taken root. . . . Let us remain firm in attachment to principles. . . . Let us be particularly watchful to preserve inviolate the freedom of opinion, assured that it is the most effectual weapon for the protection of our liberty.

QUESTIONS

1. *How does Murray answer the argument that offering education to women will lead them to neglect their "domestic employments"?*

2. *Why does the Democratic-Republican Society insist on the centrality of "free communication of opinions" in preserving American liberty?*

3. *How do these documents reflect expanding ideas about who should enjoy the freedom to express one's ideas in the early republic?*

An engraving from *The Lady's Magazine and Repository of Entertaining Knowledge*, published in Philadelphia in 1792. A woman identified as the "Genius of the Ladies Magazine" kneels before Liberty, presenting a petition for the "Rights of Women." In the foreground are symbols of the arts, science, and literature—knowledge that should be available to women as well as men.

But much of their organization and outlook was absorbed into the emerging Republican Party. They helped to legitimize the right of "any portion of the people," regardless of station in life, to express political opinions and take an active role in public life.

The Rights of Women

The democratic ferment of the 1790s inspired renewed discussion about women's rights. In 1792, Mary Wollstonecraft published in England her extraordinary pamphlet *A Vindication of the Rights of Woman*. Wollstonecraft did not directly challenge traditional gender roles. Her call for greater access to education and to paid employment for women rested on the idea that this would enable single women to support themselves and married women to perform more capably as wives and mothers. But she did "drop a hint," as she put it, that women "ought to have representation" in government. Within two years, American editions of Wollstonecraft's work had appeared, signaling new opportunities for women in the public sphere. Increasing numbers began expressing their thoughts in print. **Judith Sargent Murray**, one of the era's most accomplished American women, wrote essays for the *Massachusetts Magazine* under the pen name "The Gleaner."

Women were contributing new ideas, but were they part of the new body politic? There was nothing explicitly limiting the rights in the Constitution to men. The Constitution's use of the word "he" to describe officeholders, however, reflected the widespread assumption that politics was a realm for men. The time had not yet come for a broad assault on gender inequality.

The men who wrote the Constitution did not envision the active and continuing involvement of ordinary citizens in affairs of state. But the rise of political parties seeking to mobilize voters in hotly contested elections, the emergence of the "self-created societies," the stirrings of women's political consciousness, and even armed uprisings such as the Whiskey Rebellion broadened and deepened the democratization of public life set in motion by the American Revolution.

THE ADAMS PRESIDENCY

In 1792, Washington won unanimous reelection in the electoral college. Four years later, he decided to retire from public life, in part to establish the precedent that the presidency is not a life office. In his Farewell Address (mostly drafted by Hamilton and published in the newspapers rather than delivered orally; see the Appendix for excerpts from the speech), Washington defended his administration against criticism, warned against the party spirit, and advised his countrymen to steer clear of international power politics by avoiding "permanent alliances with any portion of the foreign world."

The Election of 1796

George Washington's departure unleashed fierce party competition over the choice of his successor. In this, the first contested presidential election, two tickets presented themselves: John Adams, with Thomas Pinckney of South Carolina for vice president, representing the Federalists, and Thomas Jefferson, with Aaron Burr of New York, for the Republicans. Adams received seventy-one electoral votes to Jefferson's sixty-eight. Because of factionalism among the Federalists, Pinckney received only fifty-nine votes, so Jefferson, the leader of the opposition party, became vice president. Voting fell almost entirely along sectional lines: Adams carried New England, New York, and New Jersey, while Jefferson swept the South, along with Pennsylvania.

The first contested presidential election

In 1797, John Adams assumed leadership of a divided nation. His presidency was beset by crises. On the international front, the country was nearly dragged into the ongoing European war. As a neutral nation, the United States claimed the right to trade nonmilitary goods with both Britain and France, but both countries seized American ships with impunity. In 1797, American diplomats were sent to Paris to negotiate a treaty to replace the old alliance of 1778. French officials presented them with a demand for bribes before negotiations could proceed. When Adams made public the envoys' dispatches, the French officials were designated by the last three letters of the alphabet. This **XYZ affair** poisoned America's relations with its former ally. By 1798, the United States and France were engaged in a "quasi-war" at sea. But despite pressure from Hamilton, who desired a declaration of war, Adams in 1800 negotiated peace with France.

XYZ affair

Adams was less cautious in domestic affairs. Unrest continued in many rural areas. In 1799, farmers in southeastern Pennsylvania obstructed the assessment of a tax on land and houses that Congress had imposed to help fund an expanded army and navy. A crowd led by John Fries, a local militia leader and auctioneer, released arrested men from prison. The army arrested Fries for treason and proceeded to terrorize his supporters, tear down liberty poles, and whip Republican newspaper editors.

The "Reign of Witches"

But the greatest crisis of the Adams administration arose over the **Alien and Sedition Acts** of 1798. Confronted with mounting opposition, some of it voiced by immigrant pamphleteers and editors, Federalists moved to silence their critics. A new Naturalization Act extended from five to four-teen years the residency requirement for immigrants seeking American citizenship. The Alien Act allowed the deportation of persons from abroad deemed "dangerous" by federal authorities. The Sedition Act (which was set to expire in 1801, by which time Adams hoped to have been reelected) authorized the prosecution of virtually any public assembly or publication critical of the government. The new law meant that opposition editors could be jailed for almost any political comment they printed.

The passage of these measures launched what Jefferson—recalling events in Salem, Massachusetts, a century earlier—termed a "reign of witches." Eighteen individuals, including several Republican newspaper editors, were charged under the Sedition Act. Ten were convicted of spreading "false, scandalous, and malicious" information about the government. Matthew Lyon, a member of Congress from Vermont and editor of a Republican newspaper, *The Scourge of Aristocracy*, received a sentence of four months in prison and a fine of $1,000. In Massachusetts, authorities indicted several men for erecting a liberty pole bearing the inscription "No Stamp Act, no Sedition, no Alien Bill, no Land Tax; Downfall to the Tyrants of America."

Matthew Lyon

The Virginia and Kentucky Resolutions

Opposition to the Sedition Act

The Sedition Act thrust freedom of expression to the center of discus-sions of American liberty. Madison and Jefferson mobilized opposition, drafting resolutions adopted by the Virginia and Kentucky legislatures. The **Virginia and Kentucky resolutions** attacked the Sedition Act as an unconstitutional violation of the First Amendment. Virginia's, writ-ten by Madison, called on the federal courts to protect free speech. The original version of Jefferson's Kentucky resolution went further, asserting that states could nullify laws of Congress that violated the Constitution—that is, states could unilaterally prevent the enforcement of such laws within their borders. The legislature deleted this passage.

"Freedom of discussion"

No other state endorsed the Virginia and Kentucky resolutions. Many Americans, including many Republicans, were horrified by the idea of state action that might endanger the Union. But the "crisis of freedom" of the late 1790s strongly reinforced the idea that "freedom of discussion" was an indispensable attribute of American liberty and of democratic government. Free speech, as the Massachusetts Federalist Harrison Gray Otis noted, had become the people's "darling privilege."

The "Revolution of 1800"

"Jefferson and Liberty" became the watchword of the Republican campaign of 1800. By this time, Republicans had developed effective techniques for mobilizing voters, such as printing pamphlets, handbills, and newspapers and holding mass meetings to promote their cause. The Federalists, who viewed politics as an activity for a small group of elite men, found it difficult to match their opponents' mobilization. Nonetheless, they still dominated New England and enjoyed considerable support in the Middle Atlantic states. Jefferson triumphed, with seventy-three electoral votes to Adams's sixty-five.

Before assuming office, Jefferson was forced to weather an unusual constitutional crisis. Each party arranged to have an elector throw away one of his two votes for president, so that its presidential candidate would come out a vote ahead of the vice presidential. But the designated Republican elector failed to do so. As a result, both Jefferson and his running mate, Aaron Burr, received seventy-three electoral votes. With no candidate having a majority, the election was thrown into the House of Representatives that had been elected in 1798, where the Federalists enjoyed a slight majority. For thirty-five ballots, neither man received a majority of the votes. Finally, Hamilton intervened. He disliked Jefferson but believed him enough of a statesman to recognize that the Federalist financial system could not be dismantled.

Detail of an 1800 campaign banner, with a portrait of Thomas Jefferson and the words "John Adams is no more."

Hamilton's support for Jefferson tipped the balance. To avoid a repetition of the crisis, Congress and the states soon adopted the Twelfth Amendment to the Constitution, requiring electors to cast separate votes for president and vice president. The election of 1800 also set in motion a chain of events that culminated four years later when Burr killed Hamilton in a duel.

The events of the 1790s demonstrated that a majority of Americans believed ordinary people had a right to play an active role in politics, express their opinions freely, and contest the policies of their government. To their credit, Federalists never considered resistance to the election result. Adams's acceptance of defeat established the vital precedent of a peaceful transfer of power from a defeated party to its successor.

Slavery and Politics

Lurking behind the political battles of the 1790s lay the divisive issue of slavery. Jefferson, after all, received every one of the South's forty-one electoral votes. He always referred to his victory as the **Revolution of 1800** and saw it not simply as a party success but as a vindication of American freedom. Yet the triumph of "Jefferson and Liberty" would not have been possible without slavery. Had

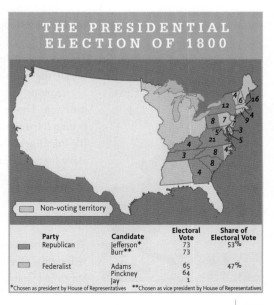

THE PRESIDENTIAL ELECTION OF 1800

Non-voting territory

Party	Candidate	Electoral Vote	Share of Electoral Vote
Republican	Jefferson*	73	53%
	Burr**	73	
Federalist	Adams	65	47%
	Pinckney	64	
	Jay	1	

*Chosen as president by House of Representatives   **Chosen as vice president by House of Representatives three-fifths of the slaves not been counted in apportionment of electoral votes among the states, John Adams would have been reelected in 1800.

The issue of slavery would not disappear. The very first Congress under the new Constitution received petitions calling for emancipation. One bore the weighty signature of Benjamin Franklin, who in 1787 had agreed to serve as president of the Pennsylvania Abolition Society. The blessings of liberty, Franklin's petition insisted, should be available "without distinction of color to all descriptions of people." Congress avoided the issue of emancipation. But in 1793, to implement the Constitution's fugitive slave clause, it enacted a law providing for local officials to facilitate the return of escaped slaves.

The Haitian Revolution

Events during the 1790s underscored how powerfully slavery defined and distorted American freedom. The same Jeffersonians who hailed the French Revolution as a step in the universal progress of liberty reacted in horror at the slave revolution that began in 1791 in Saint Domingue, the jewel of the French overseas empire situated not far from the southern coast of the United States. Toussaint L'Ouverture, an educated slave on a sugar plantation, forged the rebellious slaves into an army able to defeat British forces seeking to seize the island and then an expedition hoping to reestablish French authority. The slave uprising led to the establishment of Haiti as an independent nation in 1804.

Although much of the country was left in ruins by years of warfare, the **Haitian Revolution** affirmed the universality of the revolutionary era's creed of liberty. It inspired hopes for freedom among slaves in the United States. Throughout the nineteenth century, black Americans would celebrate the winning of Haitian independence.

Among white Americans, the response to the Haitian Revolution was different. Thousands of refugees from Haiti poured into the United States, fleeing the upheaval. Many spread tales of the massacres of slaveowners and the burning of their plantations, which reinforced white Americans' fears of slave insurrection at home. When Jefferson became president, he sought to quarantine and destroy the hemisphere's second independent republic.

Toussaint L'Ouverture, leader of the slave revolution in Saint Domingue (modern-day Haiti). Painted in 1800 as part of a series of portraits of French military leaders, it depicts him as a courageous general.

Gabriel's Rebellion

The momentous year of 1800 witnessed not only the "revolution" of Jefferson's election but also an attempted real one, a plot by slaves in Virginia to gain their freedom. It was organized by a Richmond blacksmith,

Gabriel, and his brothers Solomon, also a blacksmith, and Martin, a slave preacher. The conspirators planned to march on the city from surrounding plantations. They would kill some white inhabitants and hold the rest, including Governor James Monroe, hostage until their demand for the abolition of slavery was met. The plot was soon discovered and the leaders arrested. Twenty-six slaves, including Gabriel, were hanged and dozens more transported out of the state.

Blacks in 1800 made up half of Richmond's population. One-fifth were free. A black community had emerged in the 1780s and 1790s, and **Gabriel's Rebellion** was rooted in its institutions. In cities like Richmond, many skilled slave craftsmen, including Gabriel himself, could read and write and enjoyed the privilege of hiring themselves out to employers— that is, negotiating their own labor arrangements, with their owner receiving their "wages." Their relative autonomy helps account for slave artisans' prominent role in the conspiracy.

The black community in Richmond

Like other Virginians, the participants in the conspiracy spoke the language of liberty forged in the American Revolution and reinvigorated during the 1790s. "We have as much right," one conspirator declared, "to fight for our liberty as any men." After the rebellion, however, the Virginia legislature tightened controls over the black population—making it illegal for them to congregate on Sundays without white supervision—and severely restricted the possibility that masters could voluntarily free their slaves. Any slave freed after 1806 was required to leave Virginia or be sold back into slavery. The door to manumission, thrown open during the American Revolution, had been slammed shut.

Tightening control over blacks in Virginia

JEFFERSON IN POWER

The first president to begin his term in Washington, D.C., Jefferson assumed office on March 4, 1801. The city, with its unpaved streets, impoverished residents, and unfinished public buildings, scarcely resembled L'Enfant's grand plan. At one point, part of the roof of the Capitol collapsed, narrowly missing the vice president.

Jefferson's inaugural address was conciliatory toward his opponents. "Every difference of opinion," he declared, "is not a difference of principle. . . . We are all Republicans, we are all Federalists." He went on to expound the policies his administration would follow—economy in government, unrestricted trade, freedom of religion and the press, friendship to all nations but "entangling alliances" with none. America, "the world's best hope," would flourish if a limited government allowed its citizens to be "free to regulate their own pursuits."

Jefferson's inauguration

Dismantling the Federalist system

Jefferson hoped to dismantle as much of the Federalist system as possible. Among his first acts as president was to pardon all those imprisoned under the Sedition Act. During his eight years as president, he reduced the number of government employees and slashed the army and navy. He abolished all taxes except the tariff, including the hated tax on whiskey, and paid off part of the national debt. His policies ensured that the United States would not become a centralized state on a European model, as Hamilton had envisioned.

Judicial Review

Nonetheless, as Hamilton predicted, it proved impossible to uproot national authority entirely. Jefferson distrusted the unelected judiciary. But during his presidency, and for many years thereafter, the Federalist John Marshall headed the Supreme Court. A strong believer in national supremacy, Marshall established the Court's power to review laws of Congress and the states.

The Marshall court

The first landmark decision of the Marshall Court came in 1803, in the case of ***Marbury v. Madison***. On the eve of leaving office, Adams had appointed a number of justices of the peace for the District of Columbia. Madison, Jefferson's secretary of state, refused to issue commissions (the official documents entitling them to assume their posts) to these "midnight judges." Four, including William Marbury, sued for their offices. Marshall's decision declared unconstitutional the section of the Judiciary Act of 1789 that allowed the courts to order executive officials to deliver judges' commissions. It exceeded the power of Congress as outlined in the Constitution and was therefore void. Marbury, in other words, may have been entitled to his commission, but the Court had no power under the Constitution to order Madison to deliver it. The Supreme Court had assumed the right to determine whether an act of Congress violates the Constitution—a power known as "judicial review."

John Marshall, who served as Chief Justice from 1801 to 1835, in an 1810 portrait by Cephas Thompson.

Seven years later, in *Fletcher v. Peck*, the Court extended judicial review to state laws. In 1794, four land companies had paid nearly every member of the state legislature, Georgia's two U.S. senators, and a number of federal judges to secure their right to purchase land in present-day Alabama and Mississippi claimed by Georgia. Two years later, many of the corrupt lawmakers were defeated for reelection, and the new legislature rescinded the land grant and subsequent sales. Whatever the circumstances of the legislature's initial action, Marshall declared, the Constitution prohibited Georgia from taking any action that impaired a contract. Therefore, the individual purchasers could keep their land, and the legislature could not repeal the original grant.

The Louisiana Purchase

But the greatest irony of Jefferson's presidency involved his greatest achievement, the **Louisiana Purchase** of 1803. This resulted not from astute American diplomacy but because the rebellious slaves of Saint Domingue defeated forces sent by the ruler of France, Napoleon Bonaparte, to reconquer the island. Moreover, to take advantage of the sudden opportunity to purchase Louisiana, Jefferson had to abandon his conviction that the federal government was limited to powers specifically mentioned in the Constitution, because the document said nothing about buying territory from a foreign power.

Jefferson's ideological compromise

This vast Louisiana Territory, which stretched from the Gulf of Mexico to Canada and from the Mississippi River to the Rocky Mountains, had been ceded by France to Spain in 1762 as part of the reshuffling of colonial possessions at the end of the Seven Years' War. France secretly reacquired it in 1800. Soon after taking office, Jefferson learned of the arrangement. He had long been concerned about American access to the port of New Orleans, which lay within Louisiana at the mouth of the Mississippi River. The right to trade through New Orleans, essential to western farmers, had been acknowledged in the Treaty of San Lorenzo (also known as Pinckney's Treaty) of 1795 between the United States and Spain. But Jefferson feared that the far more powerful French might try to interfere with American commerce. Needing money for military campaigns in Europe and with his dreams of American empire in ruins because of his inability to reestablish control over Saint Domingue, Napoleon offered to sell the entire Louisiana Territory. The cost, $15 million (the equivalent of perhaps $250 million in today's money), made the Louisiana Purchase one of history's greatest real estate bargains.

Reasons for the Louisiana Purchase

In a stroke, Jefferson had doubled the size of the United States. Jefferson admitted that he had "done an act beyond the Constitution." But he believed the benefits justified his transgression. Farmers, Jefferson had written, were "the chosen people of God," and the country would remain "virtuous" as long as it was "chiefly agricultural." Now, Jefferson believed, he had ensured the agrarian character of the United States and its political stability for centuries to come.

Effects of the Purchase

Lewis and Clark

Within a year of the purchase, Jefferson dispatched an expedition led by Meriwether Lewis and William Clark, two Virginia-born veterans of Indian wars in the Ohio Valley, to explore the new territory. Their objectives were both scientific and commercial—to study the area's plants, animal life, and geography, and to discover how the region could be exploited economically.

Scientific and commercial objectives

A page from William Clark's journal of the Lewis and Clark expedition, depicting a salmon. Among their tasks was to record information about the West's plants, animal life, and geography.

Louisiana slavery

The first war fought by the U.S.

Jefferson hoped the **Lewis and Clark expedition** would establish trading relations with western Indians and locate a water route to the Pacific Ocean.

In the spring of 1804, Lewis and Clark's fifty-member "corps of discovery" set out from St. Louis on the most famous exploring party in American history. They were accompanied by a fifteen-year-old Shoshone Indian woman, Sacajawea, the wife of a French fur trader, who served as their guide and interpreter. After crossing the Rocky Mountains, the expedition reached the Pacific Ocean in present-day Oregon. They returned in 1806, bringing an immense amount of information about the region as well as numerous plant and animal specimens. The success of their journey helped to strengthen the idea that American territory was destined to reach all the way to the Pacific.

Incorporating Louisiana

The only part of the Louisiana Purchase with a significant non-Indian population in 1803 was the region around New Orleans. When the United States took control, the city had around 8,000 inhabitants, including nearly 3,000 slaves and 1,300 free persons of color. Incorporating this diverse population into the United States was by no means easy. French and Spanish law accorded free blacks, many of whom were the offspring of unions between white military officers and slave women, nearly all the rights of white citizens. Moreover, Spain made it easy for slaves to obtain their freedom through purchase or voluntary emancipation by the owners.

The treaty that transferred Louisiana to the United States promised that all free inhabitants would enjoy "the rights, advantages, and immunities of citizens." Spanish and French civil codes, unlike British and American law, recognized women as co-owners of family property. Under American rule, Louisiana retained this principle of "community property" within marriage. But free blacks suffered a steady decline in status. And the local legislature soon adopted one of the most sweeping slave codes in the South. Louisiana's slaves had enjoyed far more freedom under the rule of tyrannical Spain than as part of the liberty-loving United States.

The Barbary Wars

Jefferson hoped to avoid foreign entanglements, but he found it impossible as president to avoid being drawn into the continuing wars of Europe. Even as he sought to limit the power of the national government, foreign relations compelled him to expand it. The first war fought by the United States was to protect American commerce in a dangerous world.

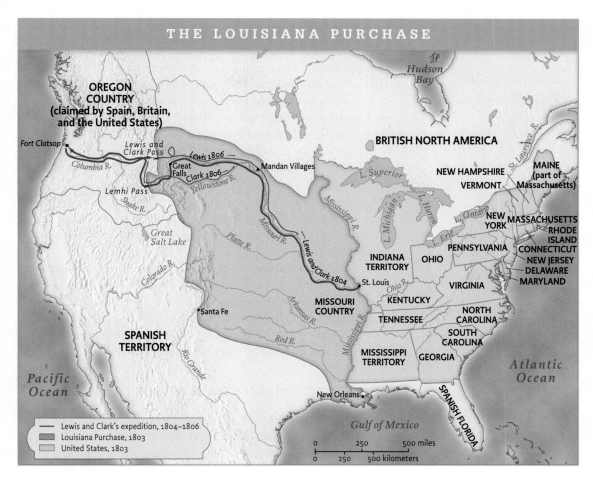

THE LOUISIANA PURCHASE

The Barbary states on the northern coast of Africa had long preyed on shipping in the Mediterranean and Atlantic, receiving tribute from several countries, including the United States, to protect their vessels. In 1801, Jefferson refused demands for increased payments, and the pasha of Tripoli, in modern-day Libya, declared war on the United States. The naval conflict lasted until 1804, when an American squadron won a victory at Tripoli harbor (a victory commemorated in the official hymn of the Marine Corps, which mentions fighting on "the shores of Tripoli").

The **Barbary Wars** were the new nation's first encounter with the Islamic world. In the 1790s, as part of an attempt to establish peaceful relations, the federal government declared that the United States was "not, in any sense, founded on the Christian religion." But the conflicts helped to establish a long-lasting pattern in which many Americans viewed Muslims as an exotic people whose way of life did not adhere to Western standards.

The Louisiana Purchase of 1803 doubled the land area of the United States.

Defending American shipping

The Embargo

Blockades by Britain and France

Far more serious in its impact on the United States was warfare between Britain and France, which resumed in 1803 after a brief lull. By 1806, each combatant had declared the other under blockade, seeking to deny trade with America to its rival. The Royal Navy resumed the practice of impressment. By the end of 1807, it had seized more than 6,000 American sailors (claiming they were British citizens and deserters).

To Jefferson, the economic health of the United States required freedom of trade with which no foreign government had a right to interfere. American farmers needed access to markets in Europe and the Caribbean. Deciding to use trade as a weapon, in December 1807 he persuaded Congress to enact the **Embargo Act**, a ban on all American vessels sailing for foreign ports. For a believer in limited government, this was an amazing exercise of federal power.

Effects of the Embargo

In 1808, American exports plummeted by 80 percent. Unfortunately, neither Britain nor France took much notice. But the Embargo devastated the economies of American port cities. Just before his term ended, in March 1809, Jefferson signed the Non-Intercourse Act, banning trade only with Britain and France but providing that if either side rescinded its edicts against American shipping, commerce with that country would resume.

Madison and Pressure for War

Jefferson left office at the lowest point of his career. He had won a sweeping reelection in 1804, receiving 162 electoral votes to only 14 for the Federalist candidate, Charles C. Pinckney. With the exception of Connecticut, he even carried the Federalist stronghold of New England. Four years later, his handpicked successor, James Madison, also won an easy victory. The Embargo, however, failed to achieve its aims and was increasingly violated by American shippers. In 1810, Madison adopted a new policy.

Macon's Bill No. 2

Congress enacted a measure known as Macon's Bill No. 2, which allowed trade to resume but provided that if either France or Britain ceased interfering with American rights, the president could reimpose an embargo on the other. With little to lose, since Britain controlled the seas, the French emperor Napoleon announced that he had repealed his decrees against neutral shipping. But the British continued to attack American vessels. In the spring of 1812, Madison reimposed the embargo on trade with Britain.

Meanwhile, a group of younger congressmen, mostly from the West, were calling for war with Britain. Known as the War Hawks, this new generation of political leaders had come of age after the winning of independence and were ardent nationalists. Their leaders included Henry Clay of Kentucky, elected Speaker of the House of Representatives in 1810, and John

C. Calhoun of South Carolina. The War Hawks spoke passionately of defending the national honor against British insults, but they also had more practical goals in mind, notably the annexation of Canada and the conquest of Florida, a haven for fugitive slaves owned by Britain's ally Spain. Members of Congress also spoke of the necessity of upholding the principle of free trade and liberating the United States once and for all from European infringements on its independence.

THE "SECOND WAR OF INDEPENDENCE"

War Party at Fort Douglas, a watercolor by the Swiss-born Canadian artist Peter Rindisbacher. Painted in 1823, it depicts an incident during the War of 1812 when Indian allies of Great Britain fired rifles into the air to greet their commander, Captain Andrew Bulger, pictured on the far right.

The growing crisis between the United States and Britain took place against the background of deteriorating Indian relations in the West, which also helped propel the United States down the road to war. Jefferson had long favored the removal beyond the Mississippi River of Indian tribes that refused to cooperate in "civilizing" themselves. He encouraged traders to lend money to Indians, in the hope that accumulating debt would force them to sell some of their holdings west of the Appalachian Mountains, thus freeing up more land for "our increasing numbers." On the other hand, the government continued President Washington's policy of promoting settled farming among the Indians.

The Indian Response

By 1800, nearly 400,000 American settlers lived west of the Appalachian Mountains. They far outnumbered the remaining Indians, whose seemingly irreversible decline in power led some to rethink their opposition to assimilation. Among the Creek and Cherokee, a group led by men of mixed Indian-white ancestry like Major Ridge and John Ross enthusiastically endorsed the federal policy of promoting "civilization." Many had established businesses as traders and slaveowning farmers with the help of their white fathers. Their views, in turn, infuriated "nativists," who strongly opposed assimilation.

The period from 1800 to 1812 was an "age of prophecy" among the Indians, as many tribal leaders sought to revitalize Native American life. A militant message was expounded by two Shawnee brothers,

An "age of prophecy"

WHO IS AN AMERICAN?

From Tecumseh, Speech to the Osage (1810)

While some Native Americans claimed rights as Americans, others asserted a pan-Indian identity, insisting that all Indian nations shared a common set of values and a common future of freedom and autonomy rather than assimilation or removal. The Shawnee leader Tecumseh sought to rally Indians to unite as one people. This speech, to Osage Indians, was recorded by John P. Hunter, who had been held captive by the Osage since childhood.

Brothers—We all belong to one family; we are all children of the Great Spirit; we walk in the same path; slake our thirst at the same spring; and now affairs of the greatest concern lead us to smoke the pipe around the same council fire!

Brothers—we are friends; we must assist each other to bear our burdens. The blood of many of our fathers and brothers has run like water on the ground, to satisfy the avarice of the white men. We, ourselves, are threatened with a great evil; nothing will pacify them but the destruction of all the red men.

Brothers—The white men are not friends to the Indians: at first, they only asked for land sufficient for a wigwam; now, nothing will satisfy them but the whole of our hunting grounds, from the rising to the setting sun. . . .

Brothers—My people are brave and numerous; but the white people are too strong for them alone. I wish you to take up the tomahawk with them. If we all unite, we will cause the rivers to stain the great waters with their blood.

Brothers—if you do not unite with us, they will first destroy us, and then you will fall an easy prey to them. They have destroyed many nations of red men because they were not united. . . . They wish to make us enemies,

that they may sweep over and desolate our hunting grounds, like devastating winds, or rushing waters.

Brothers—Our Great Father over the great waters [the king of England] is angry with the white people, our enemies. He will send his brave warriors against them; he will send us rifles, and whatever else we want—he is our friend, and we are his children.

Brothers—We must be united; we must smoke the same pipe; we must fight each other's battles; and more than all, we must love the Great Spirit; he is for us; he will destroy our enemies, and make his red children happy.

QUESTIONS

1. *How does Tecumseh's understanding of national identity compare with that of most white Americans of his era?*

2. *Why does he claim that the king of England is the Indians' ally, and what does this suggest about his attitudes toward white people?*

Tecumseh and Tenskwatawa. Tecumseh was a chief who had refused to sign the Treaty of Greenville in 1795, and Tenskwatawa was a religious prophet who called for complete separation from whites, the revival of traditional Indian culture, and resistance to federal policies. White people, Tenskwatawa preached, were the source of all evil in the world, and Indians should abandon American alcohol, clothing, food, and manufactured goods. His followers gathered at Prophetstown, located in Indiana.

Tecumseh meanwhile traversed the Mississippi Valley, pressing the argument that the alternative to Indian resistance was extermination. He repudiated chiefs who had sold land to the federal government: "Sell a country! Why not sell the air, the great sea, as well as the earth? Did not the Great Spirit make them all for the use of his children?" In 1810, Tecumseh called for attacks on American frontier settlements. In November 1811, while he was absent, American forces under William Henry Harrison destroyed Prophetstown in the Battle of Tippecanoe.

Tenskwatawa (the Prophet), in a portrait by the American artist Charles Bird King, who painted numerous Indian leaders.

The War of 1812

In 1795, James Madison had written that war is the greatest enemy of "true liberty." Nonetheless, Madison became a war president. Reports that the British were encouraging Tecumseh's efforts contributed to the coming of the **War of 1812**. In June 1812, with assaults on American shipping continuing, Madison asked Congress for a declaration of war. American nationality, the president declared, was at stake—would Americans remain "an independent people" or become "colonists and vassals" of Great Britain? The vote revealed a deeply divided country. Both Federalists and Republicans representing the states from New Jersey northward, where most of the mercantile and financial resources of the country were concentrated, voted against war. The South and West were strongly in favor. The bill passed the House by a vote of 79–49 and the Senate by 19–13. It was the first time the United States declared war on another country, and it was approved by the smallest margin of any declaration of war in American history.

In retrospect, it seems remarkably foolhardy for a disunited and militarily unprepared nation to go to war with one of the world's two major powers. Fortunately for the United States, Great Britain at the outset was preoccupied with the struggle in Europe. But it easily repelled two feeble American invasions of Canada and imposed a blockade that all but destroyed American commerce. In 1814, having finally defeated Napoleon,

An engraving depicting the burning of Washington, D.C., by the British during the War of 1812, from an 1817 book by the antislavery Philadelphia physician Jesse Torrey. Torrey suggests that the event is divine punishment for the practice of slave trading in the nation's capital. The image includes children among the group of chained slaves at the right, to emphasize the breakup of slave families. At the top is a heavenly image of liberty.

Britain invaded the United States. Its forces seized Washington, D.C., and burned the Capitol and the White House, while the government fled for safety.

Americans did enjoy a few military successes. In August 1812, the American frigate *Constitution* defeated the British warship *Guerriere*. Commodore Oliver H. Perry defeated a British naval force in September 1813 on Lake Erie. In the following year, a British assault on Baltimore was repulsed when **Fort McHenry** at the entrance to the harbor withstood a British bombardment. This was the occasion when Francis Scott Key composed "The Star-Spangled Banner," an ode to the "land of the free and home of the brave" that became the national anthem during the 1930s.

Fighting the British and the Indians

Like the War of Independence, the War of 1812 was a two-front struggle—against the British and against the Indians. The war produced significant victories over western Indians who sided with the British. In 1813, pan-Indian forces led by Tecumseh (who had been commissioned a general in the British army) were defeated, and he himself was killed, at the Battle of the Thames, near Detroit, by an American force led by William Henry Harrison. In March 1814, an army of Americans and pro-assimilation Cherokees and Creeks under the command of Andrew Jackson defeated hostile Creeks known as the Red Sticks at the Battle of Horseshoe Bend in Alabama, killing more than 800. Jackson dictated terms of surrender that required the Indians, hostile and friendly alike, to cede more than half their land, over 23 million acres in all, to the federal government.

Jackson then proceeded to New Orleans, where he engineered the war's greatest American victory, fighting off a British invasion in January 1815. Although a slaveholder, Jackson recruited the city's free men of color into his forces, appealing to them as "sons of freedom" and promising them the same pay and land bounties as white recruits.

Treaty of Ghent

With neither side wishing to continue the conflict, the United States and Britain signed the Treaty of Ghent, ending the war. Although the treaty was signed in December 1814, ships carrying news of the agreement did not reach America until after the **Battle of New Orleans** had been fought. The treaty restored the previous status quo. No territory changed hands, nor did any provisions relate to impressment or neutral shipping rights.

The War's Aftermath

A number of contemporaries called the War of 1812 the Second War of Independence. Jackson's victory at New Orleans not only made him a national hero but also became a celebrated example of the ability of virtuous citizens of a republic to defeat the forces of despotic Europe.

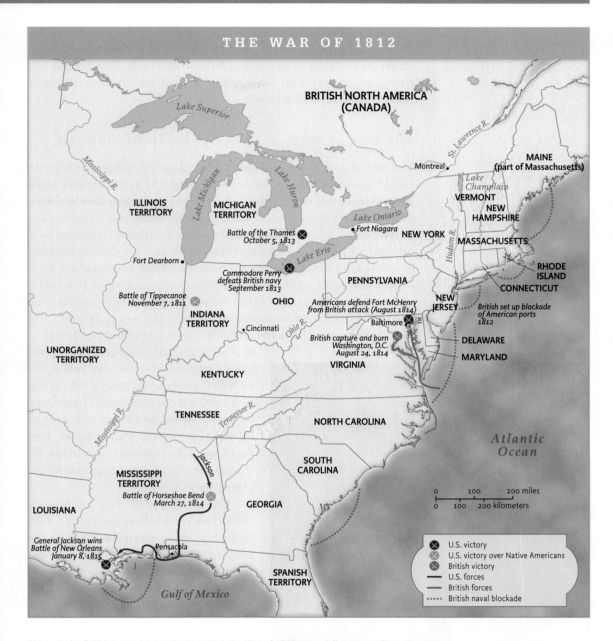

THE WAR OF 1812

BRITISH NORTH AMERICA (CANADA)

Lake Superior

Mississippi R.

Lake Michigan

Lake Huron

St. Lawrence R.

Montreal

MAINE (part of Massachusetts)

Lake Champlain

VERMONT

NEW HAMPSHIRE

ILLINOIS TERRITORY

MICHIGAN TERRITORY

Lake Ontario

■ Fort Niagara

NEW YORK

Fort Dearborn ■

Battle of the Thames October 5, 1813

Lake Erie

MASSACHUSETTS

RHODE ISLAND

Hudson R.

CONNECTICUT

Commodore Perry defeats British navy September 1813

PENNSYLVANIA

NEW JERSEY

British set up blockade of American ports 1812

Battle of Tippecanoe November 7, 1811

OHIO

Americans defend Fort McHenry from British attack (August 1814)

INDIANA TERRITORY

● Cincinnati

Ohio R.

Baltimore

DELAWARE

British capture and burn Washington, D.C. August 24, 1814

MARYLAND

UNORGANIZED TERRITORY

KENTUCKY

VIRGINIA

Mississippi R.

TENNESSEE

Tennessee R.

NORTH CAROLINA

Atlantic Ocean

SOUTH CAROLINA

MISSISSIPPI TERRITORY

Jackson

Battle of Horseshoe Bend March 27, 1814

GEORGIA

0   100   200 miles

0   100   200 kilometers

LOUISIANA

General Jackson wins Battle of New Orleans January 8, 1815

Pensacola

⊗ U.S. victory

⊗ U.S. victory over Native Americans

⊗ British victory

— U.S. forces

— British forces

···· British naval blockade

SPANISH TERRITORY

Gulf of Mexico

Although the British burned the nation's capital, the War of 1812 essentially was a military draw.

Moreover, the war completed the conquest of the area east of the Mississippi River, which had begun during the Revolution. Never again would the British or Indians pose a threat to American control of this vast region. In its aftermath, white settlers poured into Indiana, Michigan, Alabama, and Mississippi.

American control east of the Mississippi

The War of 1812 and the Canadian Borderland

The War of 1812 had a profound impact along the border between the United States and Canada, further solidifying it as a dividing line. Much of the fighting took place in the long-contested region near Detroit and on the Great Lakes. A great deal of trade had developed between Vermont and Quebec, and across the lakes, which became a flourishing smuggling business during Jefferson's embargo. When war broke out, Canadians began to see American traders as spies. The unsuccessful American attacks on Canada during the war (some led by Irish immigrants resentful at British rule over their country of birth) strengthened anti-Americanism even among Canadians not connected to revolutionary-era Loyalists. To be sure, as in so many borderland regions, many people had family ties on both sides and the exchange of goods and ideas continued after the war ended. But for both Canadians and Americans, the war reaffirmed a sense of national identity, and both came to see the conflict as a struggle for freedom—for the United States, freedom from dependence on Great Britain; for Canada, freedom from domination by the United States.

Britain's defeat of Napoleon inaugurated a long period of peace in Europe. With diplomatic affairs playing less and less of a role in American public life, Americans' sense of separateness from the Old World grew ever stronger.

This colorful painting by the artist John Archibald Woodside from around the time of the War of 1812 contains numerous symbols of freedom, among them the goddess of liberty with her liberty cap, a broken chain at the sailor's feet, the fallen crown (under his left foot), a broken royal scepter, and the sailor himself, because English interference with American shipping was one of the war's causes.

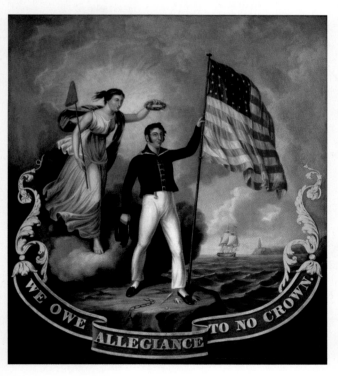

The End of the Federalist Party

Jefferson and Madison succeeded in one major political aim—the elimination of the Federalist Party. At first, the war led to a revival of Federalist fortunes. With antiwar sentiment at its peak in 1812, Madison was reelected by the relatively narrow margin of 128 electoral votes to 89 over his Federalist opponent, DeWitt Clinton of New York. But then came a self-inflicted blow. In December 1814, a group of New England Federalists gathered at Hartford, Connecticut, to give voice to their party's long-standing grievances, especially the domination of the federal government by Virginia presidents and their region's declining influence as new western states entered the Union. The **Hartford Convention** did not call for secession or disunion. But it affirmed the right of a state to "interpose" its authority if the federal government violated the Constitution.

The Hartford Convention had barely adjourned before Jackson electrified the nation with his victory at New Orleans. In speeches and sermons, political and religious leaders alike proclaimed that Jackson's triumph revealed, once again, that a divine hand oversaw America's destiny. The Federalists could not free themselves from the charge of lacking patriotism. Within a few years, their party no longer existed. *Demise of the Federalists* Yet in their dying moments Federalists had raised an issue—southern domination of the national government—that would long outlive their political party. And the country stood on the verge of a profound economic and social transformation that strengthened the very forces of commercial development that Federalists had welcomed and many Republicans feared.

CHAPTER REVIEW AND ONLINE RESOURCES

REVIEW QUESTIONS

1. *Identify the major parts of Hamilton's financial plan, who supported these proposals, and why they aroused such passionate opposition.*

2. *How did the French Revolution and the ensuing global struggle between Great Britain and France shape early American politics?*

3. *How did the United States become involved in foreign affairs in this period?*

4. *How did the expansion of the public sphere and a new language of rights offer opportunities to women?*

5. *What caused the demise of the Federalists?*

6. *What impact did the Haitian Revolution have on the United States?*

7. *How did the Louisiana Purchase affect the situation of Native Americans in that region?*

8. *Whose status was changed the most by the War of 1812—that of Great Britain, the United States, or Native Americans?*

KEY TERMS

Bank of the United States (p. 223)
impressment (p. 225)
Jay's Treaty (p. 225)
Federalists and Republicans (p. 226)
Whiskey Rebellion (p. 226)
Democratic-Republican societies (p. 227)
Judith Sargent Murray (p. 230)
XYZ affair (p. 231)
Alien and Sedition Acts (p. 231)
Virginia and Kentucky resolutions (p. 232)
Revolution of 1800 (p. 233)
Haitian Revolution (p. 234)
Gabriel's Rebellion (p. 235)
Marbury v. Madison (p. 236)
Louisiana Purchase (p. 237)
Lewis and Clark expedition (p. 238)
Barbary Wars (p. 239)
Embargo Act (p. 240)
Tecumseh and Tenskwatawa (p. 243)
War of 1812 (p. 243)
Fort McHenry (p. 244)
Battle of New Orleans (p. 244)
Hartford Convention (p. 247)

Go to 📖 INQUIZITIVE

To see what you know—and learn what you've missed—with personalized feedback along the way.

Visit the *Give Me Liberty!* **Student Site** for primary source documents and images, interactive maps, author videos featuring Eric Foner, and more.

CHAPTER 9

THE MARKET REVOLUTION

★

1800–1840

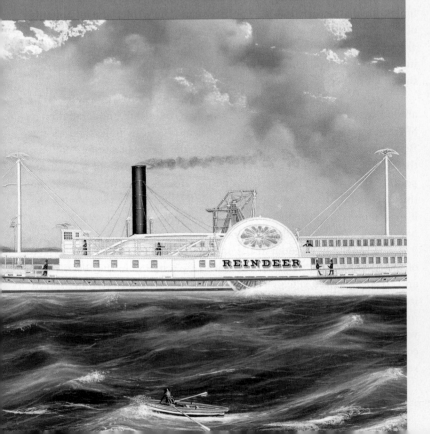

A painting from 1850 of the steamboat *Reindeer*, by the artist John Bard. Steamboats, able to travel against the current on rivers and across the Great Lakes, played an essential role in opening large parts of the nation's interior to commercial agriculture, an essential component of the market revolution.

In 1824, the Marquis de Lafayette visited the United States. Nearly fifty years had passed since, as a youth of twenty, the French nobleman fought at Washington's side in the War of Independence. Since 1784, when he last journeyed to the United States, the nation's population had tripled to nearly 12 million, its land area had more than doubled, and its political institutions had thrived. The thirteen states of 1784 had grown to twenty-four, and Lafayette visited every one. He traveled up the Mississippi and Ohio rivers by steamboat, a recent invention that was helping to bring economic development to the trans-Appalachian West, and crossed upstate New York via the Erie Canal, the world's longest man-made waterway, which linked the region around the Great Lakes with the Atlantic coast via the Hudson River.

Americans in the first half of the nineteenth century were fond of describing liberty as the defining quality of their new nation, the unique genius of its institutions. Likenesses of the goddess of liberty, a familiar figure in eighteenth-century British visual imagery, became even more common in the United States, appearing in paintings and sculpture and on folk art from weather vanes to quilts and tavern signs. In *Democracy in America*, the French historian and politician Alexis de Tocqueville wrote of the "holy cult of freedom" he encountered on his own visit to the United States during the early 1830s. "For fifty years," he wrote, "the inhabitants of the United States have been repeatedly and constantly told that they are the only religious, enlightened, and free people. They . . . have an immensely high opinion of themselves and are not far from believing that they form a species apart from the rest of the human race."

Even as Lafayette, Tocqueville, and numerous other visitors from abroad toured the United States, however, Americans' understandings of freedom were changing. Three historical processes unleashed by the Revolution accelerated after the War of 1812: the spread of market relations, the westward movement of the population, and the rise of a vigorous political democracy. (The first two will be discussed in this chapter, the third in Chapter 10.) All helped to reshape the idea of freedom, identifying it ever more closely with economic opportunity, physical mobility, and participation in a vibrantly democratic political system.

But American freedom also continued to be shaped by the presence of slavery. Lafayette, who had purchased a plantation in the West Indies and freed its slaves, once wrote, "I would never have drawn my sword in the cause of America if I could have conceived that thereby I was founding a land of slavery." Yet slavery was moving westward with the young republic. Half a century after the winning of independence, the coexistence of liberty and slavery, and their simultaneous expansion, remained the central contradiction of American life.

A NEW ECONOMY

In the first half of the nineteenth century, an economic transformation known to historians as the market revolution swept over the United States. Its catalyst was a series of innovations in transportation and communication. The market revolution was an acceleration of developments already under way in the colonial era. As noted in previous chapters, southern planters were selling the products of slave labor in the international market as early as the seventeenth century. By the eighteenth, many colonists had been drawn into Britain's commercial empire. Consumer goods like sugar and tea and market-oriented tactics like the boycott of British goods had been central to the political battles leading up to independence.

An economic transformation

Nonetheless, as Americans moved across the Appalachian Mountains and into interior regions of the states along the Atlantic coast, they found themselves more and more isolated from markets. In 1800, American farm families produced at home most of what they needed, from clothing to farm implements. What they could not make themselves, they obtained by bartering with their neighbors or purchasing from local stores and from rural craftsmen like blacksmiths and shoemakers. Those farmers not located near cities or navigable waterways found it almost impossible to market their produce. Many Americans devoted their energies to solving the technological problems that inhibited commerce within the country.

Roads and Steamboats

In the first half of the nineteenth century, in rapid succession, the steamboat, canal, railroad, and telegraph wrenched America out of its economic past. These innovations opened new land to settlement, lowered transportation costs, and made it far easier for economic enterprises to sell their products. They linked farmers to national and world markets and made them major consumers of manufactured goods. Americans, wrote Tocqueville, had "annihilated space and time."

A watercolor from 1829 depicts the Erie Canal five years after it opened. Boats carrying passengers and goods traverse the waterway, along whose banks farms and villages have sprung up.

In 1806, Congress authorized the construction of the paved National Road from Cumberland, Maryland, to the Old Northwest. It reached Wheeling, on the Ohio River, in 1818 and by 1838 extended to Illinois, where it ended. But it was improved water transportation

A view of New York City, in 1849, by the noted lithographer Nathaniel Currier. Steamships and sailing vessels of various sizes crowd the harbor of the nation's largest city and busiest port.

that most dramatically increased the speed and lowered the expense of commerce.

Robert Fulton, a Pennsylvania-born artist and engineer, had experimented with **steamboat** designs while living in France during the 1790s. But not until 1807, when Fulton's ship the *Clermont* navigated the Hudson River from New York City to Albany, was the steamboat's technological and commercial feasibility demonstrated. The invention made possible upstream commerce (that is, travel against the current) on the country's major rivers as well as rapid transport across the Great Lakes and, eventually, the Atlantic Ocean. By 1811, the first steamboat had been introduced on the Mississippi River; twenty years later some 200 plied its waters.

Advantages of the steamboat

The Erie Canal

The completion in 1825 of the 363-mile **Erie Canal** across upstate New York (a remarkable feat of engineering at a time when America's next-largest canal was only twenty-eight miles long) allowed goods to flow between the Great Lakes and New York City. Almost instantaneously, the canal attracted an influx of farmers migrating from New England, giving birth to cities like Buffalo, Rochester, and Syracuse along its path.

Connecting New York City and the Old Northwest

New York governor DeWitt Clinton, who oversaw the construction of the state-financed canal, predicted that it would make New York City "the granary of the world, the emporium of commerce, the seat of manufactures, the focus of great moneyed operations." And, indeed, the canal gave

THE MARKET REVOLUTION: ROADS AND CANALS, 1840

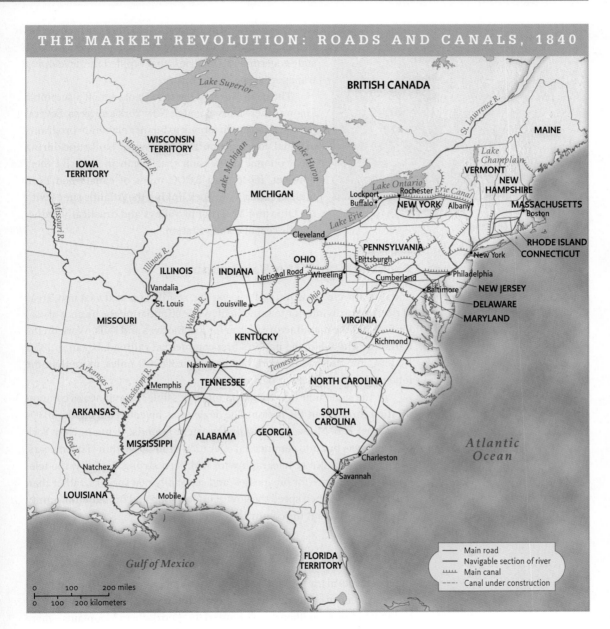

The improvement of existing roads and building of new roads and canals sharply reduced transportation times and costs and stimulated the growth of the market economy.

This "diploma" issued in the 1850s by the Delaware County (Pennsylvania) Society for the Promotion of Agriculture, Horticulture, Manufactures, and the Mechanic and Household Arts depicts scenes of an integrated diversified economy, including farming, manufacturing, and household labor. Farmers plow and reap the fields and transport produce; women work at sewing machines and a power loom; a ship is under construction; and a water-powered factory is also visible.

New York City primacy over competing ports in access to trade with the Old Northwest. In its financing by the state government, the Erie Canal typified the developing transportation infrastructure.

The completion of the Erie Canal set off a scramble among other states to match New York's success. Several borrowed so much money to finance elaborate programs of canal construction that they went bankrupt during the economic depression that began in 1837. By then, however, more than 3,000 miles of canals had been built, creating a network linking the Atlantic states with the Ohio and Mississippi Valleys and drastically reducing the cost of transportation.

Railroads and the Telegraph

Canals connected existing waterways. The railroad opened vast new areas of the American interior to settlement, while stimulating the mining of coal for fuel and the manufacture of iron for locomotives and rails. Work on the Baltimore and Ohio, the nation's first commercial railroad, began in 1828. By 1860, the railroad network had grown to 30,000 miles, more than the total in the rest of the world combined.

At the same time, the telegraph made possible instantaneous communication throughout the nation. The device was invented during the 1830s by Samuel F. B. Morse, an artist and amateur scientist living in New York City, and was put into commercial operation in 1844. Within sixteen years, some 50,000 miles of telegraph wire had been strung. Initially, the telegraph was a service for businesses, and especially newspapers, rather than individuals. It helped speed the flow of information and brought uniformity to prices throughout the country.

The Rise of the West

Improvements in transportation and communication made possible the rise of the West as a powerful, self-conscious region of the new nation. Between 1790 and 1840, some 4.5 million people crossed the Appalachian Mountains—more than the entire U.S. population at the time of Washington's first inauguration. Most of this migration took place after the War of 1812, which unleashed a flood

Migration west

of land-hungry settlers moving from eastern states. In the six years following the end of the war in 1815, six new states entered the Union (Indiana, Illinois, Missouri, Alabama, Mississippi, and Maine—the last an eastern frontier for New England).

Few Americans moved west as lone pioneers. More frequently, people traveled in groups and, once they arrived in the West, cooperated with each other to clear land, build houses and barns, and establish communities. One stream of migration, including both small farmers and planters with their slaves, flowed out of the South to create the new Cotton Kingdom of Alabama, Mississippi, Louisiana, and Arkansas. Many farm families from the Upper South crossed into southern Ohio, Indiana, and Illinois. A third population stream moved from New England across New York to the Upper Northwest—northern Ohio, Indiana, and Illinois, and Michigan and Wisconsin.

An 1884 watercolor, *Locomotive DeWitt Clinton*, recalls the early days of rail travel. The train is driven by a steam-powered locomotive and the cars strongly resemble horse-drawn stagecoaches.

Some western migrants became "squatters," setting up farms on unoccupied land without a clear legal title. Those who purchased land acquired it either from the federal government, at the price, after 1820, of $1.25 per acre payable in cash or from land speculators on long-term credit. The West became the home of regional cultures very much like those the migrants had left behind. Upstate New York and the Upper Northwest resembled New England, with its small towns, churches, and schools, while the Lower South replicated the plantation-based society of the southern Atlantic states.

National boundaries made little difference to territorial expansion— in Florida, and later in Texas and Oregon, American settlers rushed in to claim land under the jurisdiction of foreign countries (Spain, Mexico, and Britain) or Indian tribes, confident that American sovereignty would soon follow in their wake. In 1810, American residents of West Florida rebelled and seized Baton Rouge, and the United States soon annexed the area. The drive for the acquisition of East Florida was spurred by Georgia and Alabama planters who wished to eliminate a refuge for fugitive slaves and hostile Seminole Indians. Andrew Jackson led troops into the area in 1818. While on foreign soil, he created an international crisis by executing two British traders and a number of Indian chiefs. Although Jackson withdrew, Spain, aware that it could not defend the territory, sold it to the United States in the Adams-Onís Treaty of 1819 negotiated by John Quincy Adams.

Expansion across national boundaries

Adams-Onis Treaty of 1819

Successive censuses told the remarkable story of western growth. In 1840, by which time the government had sold to settlers and land companies nearly 43 million acres of land, 7 million Americans—two-fifths of

A NEW ECONOMY

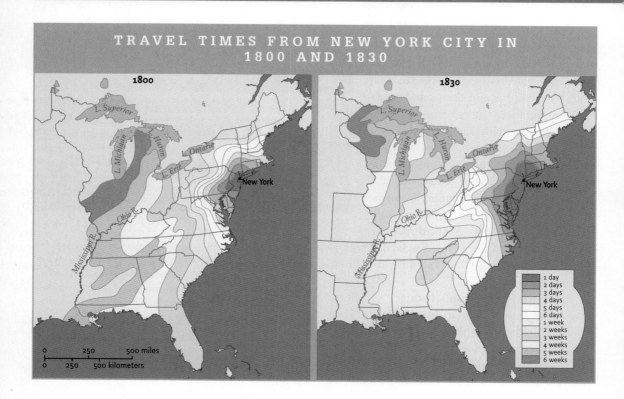

TRAVEL TIMES FROM NEW YORK CITY IN 1800 AND 1830

1800

1830

L. Superior
L. Michigan
L. Huron
L. Ontario
L. Erie
Ohio R.
Mississippi R.
New York

0   250   500 miles
0   250   500 kilometers

1 day
2 days
3 days
4 days
5 days
6 days
1 week
2 weeks
3 weeks
4 weeks
5 weeks
6 weeks

These maps illustrate how the transportation revolution of the early nineteenth century made possible much more rapid travel within the United States.

the total population—lived beyond the Appalachian Mountains. Between 1810 and 1830, Ohio's population grew from 231,000 to more than 900,000. It reached nearly 2 million in 1850, when it ranked third among all the states. The careers of the era's leading public figures reflected the westward movement. Andrew Jackson, Henry Clay, and many other statesmen were born in states along the Atlantic coast but made their mark in politics after moving west.

An Internal Borderland

Before the War of 1812, the Old Northwest was a prime example of a borderland, a meeting-ground of Native Americans and various people of English, French, and American descent, where cultural boundaries remained unstable and political authority uncertain. The American victory over the British and Indians erased any doubt over who would control the region. But a new, internal borderland region quickly developed.

Ohio River as boundary

Because the Northwest Ordinance of 1787 prohibited slavery in the Old Northwest, the Ohio River came to mark a boundary between free and slave societies. But for many years it was easier for people and goods to travel between the slave state Kentucky and the southern counties of Ohio, Indiana, and Illinois than to the northern parts of those states. The region stretching northward from the Ohio River retained much of the cultural flavor of the Upper South. Its food, speech, settlement patterns, family ties, and economic relations had more in common with Kentucky and Tennessee than with the northern counties of their own states, soon to be settled by New Englanders. Until the 1850s, farmers in the southern counties of Ohio, Indiana, and Illinois were far more likely to ship their produce southward via the Ohio and Mississippi Rivers than northward or to the East. The large concentration of people of southern ancestry would make Indiana and Illinois key political battlegrounds as the slavery controversy developed.

TABLE 9.1 Population Growth of Selected Western States, 1810–1850 (Excluding Indians)

STATE	1810	1830	1850
Alabama	9,000	310,000	772,000
Illinois	12,000	157,000	851,000
Indiana	25,000	343,000	988,000
Louisiana	77,000	216,000	518,000
Mississippi	31,000	137,000	607,000
Missouri	20,000	140,000	682,000
Ohio	231,000	938,000	1,980,000

The Cotton Kingdom

Although the market revolution and westward expansion occurred simultaneously in the North and the South, their combined effects heightened the nation's sectional divisions. In some ways, the most dynamic feature of the American economy in the first thirty years of the nineteenth century was the rise of the **Cotton Kingdom**. The early industrial revolution, which began in England and soon spread to parts of the North, centered on factories producing cotton textiles with water-powered spinning and weaving machinery. These factories generated an immense demand for cotton, a crop the Lower South was particularly suited to growing because of its climate and soil fertility. Until 1793, the marketing of cotton had been slowed by the laborious task of removing seeds from the plant itself. But in that year, Eli Whitney, a Yale graduate working in Georgia as a private tutor, invented the **cotton gin**. A fairly simple device consisting of rollers and brushes, the gin quickly separated the seed from the cotton. Coupled with rising demand for cotton and the opening of new lands in the West, Whitney's invention revolutionized American slavery, an institution that many Americans had expected to die out because its major crop, tobacco, exhausted the soil.

Cotton and industry

Whitney's cotton gin

After the War of 1812, the federal government moved to consolidate American control over the Deep South, forcing defeated Indians to cede land, encouraging white settlement, and acquiring Florida. Settlers from

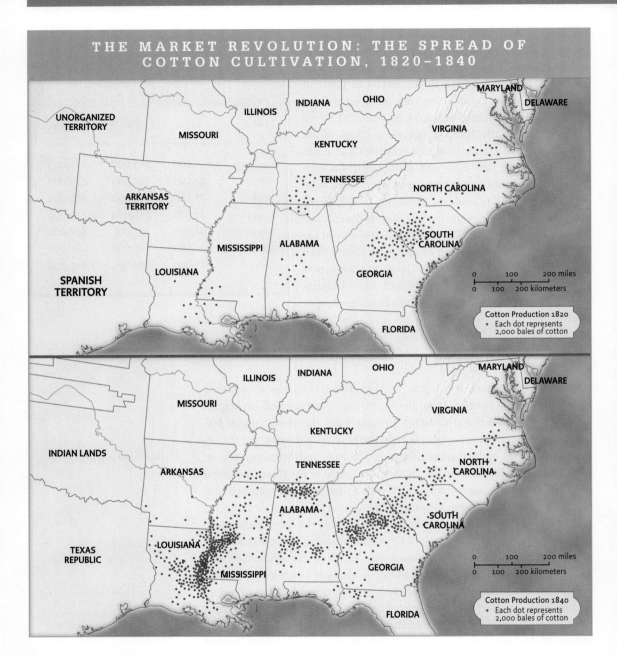

THE MARKET REVOLUTION: THE SPREAD OF COTTON CULTIVATION, 1820–1840

Cotton Production 1820
- Each dot represents 2,000 bales of cotton

Cotton Production 1840
- Each dot represents 2,000 bales of cotton

Maps of cotton production graphically illustrate the rise of the Cotton Kingdom stretching from South Carolina to Louisiana.

the older southern states flooded into the region. Planters monopolized the most fertile land, whereas poorer farmers were generally confined to less productive and less accessible areas in the "hill country" and piney woods. After Congress prohibited the Atlantic slave trade in 1808, a massive trade in slaves developed within the United States, supplying the labor force required by the new Cotton Kingdom.

Slave trading became a well-organized business, with firms gathering slaves in Maryland, Virginia, and South Carolina and shipping them to markets in Mobile, Natchez, and New Orleans. Slave coffles—groups chained to one another on forced marches to the Lower South—became a common sight. Indeed, historians estimate that around 1 million slaves were shifted from the older slave states to the Lower South between 1800 and 1860. A source of greater freedom for many whites, the westward movement meant to African-Americans the destruction of family ties, the breakup of long-standing communities, and receding opportunities for liberty.

In 1793, when Whitney designed his invention, the United States produced 5 million pounds of cotton. By 1820, the crop had grown to nearly 170 million pounds.

MARKET SOCIETY

Since cotton was produced solely for sale in national and international markets, the South was in some ways the most commercially oriented region of the United States. Yet rather than spurring economic change, the South's expansion westward simply reproduced the agrarian, slave-based social order of the older states. The region remained overwhelmingly rural. In 1860, roughly 80 percent of southerners worked the land—the same proportion as in 1800.

Commercial Farmers

In the North, however, the market revolution and westward expansion set in motion changes that transformed the region into an integrated economy of commercial farms and manufacturing cities. As the Old Northwest became a more settled society, bound by a web of transportation and credit to eastern centers of commerce and banking, farmers found themselves drawn into the new market economy. They increasingly concentrated on growing crops and raising livestock for sale, while purchasing at stores goods previously produced at home.

Western farmers found in the growing cities of the East a market for their produce and a source of credit. Loans originating with eastern banks and insurance companies financed the acquisition of land and supplies and, in the 1840s and 1850s, the purchase of fertilizer and new agricultural machinery to expand production. The steel plow, invented by John Deere in 1837 and mass-produced by the 1850s, made possible the rapid subduing of the western prairies. The reaper, a horse-drawn machine that greatly increased the amount of wheat a farmer could harvest, was invented by Cyrus McCormick in 1831 and produced in large quantities soon afterward. Eastern farmers, unable to grow wheat and corn as cheaply as their western counterparts, increasingly concentrated on producing dairy products, fruits, and vegetables for nearby urban centers.

Technology and western farming

The Growth of Cities

From the beginning, cities formed part of the western frontier. Cincinnati was known as **Porkopolis**, after its slaughterhouses, where hundreds of thousands of pigs were butchered each year and processed for shipment to eastern consumers of meat. The greatest of all the western cities was Chicago. In the early 1830s, it was a tiny settlement on the shore of Lake Michigan. By 1860, thanks to the railroad, Chicago had become the nation's fourth-largest city, where farm products from throughout the Northwest were gathered to be sent east.

Western cities

Like rural areas, urban centers witnessed dramatic changes due to the market revolution. Urban merchants, bankers, and master craftsmen took advantage of the economic opportunities created by the expanding market among commercial farmers. The drive among these businessmen to increase production and reduce labor costs fundamentally altered the nature of work. Traditionally, skilled artisans had manufactured goods at home, where they controlled the pace and intensity of their own labor. Now, entrepreneurs gathered artisans into large workshops in order to oversee their work and subdivide their tasks. Craftsmen who traditionally produced an entire pair of shoes or piece of furniture saw the labor process broken down into numerous steps requiring far less skill and training. They found themselves subjected to constant supervision by their employers and relentless pressure for greater output and lower wages.

A trade card depicts the interior of a chair-manufacturing workshop in New York City. The owner stands at the center, dressed quite differently from his employees. The men are using traditional hand tools; furniture manufacturing had not yet been mechanized.

The Factory System

In some industries, most notably textiles, the factory superseded traditional craft production altogether. Factories gathered large groups of workers under central supervision and replaced hand tools with power-driven machinery. Samuel Slater, an immigrant from England, established America's first factory in 1790 at Pawtucket, Rhode Island. Since British law made it illegal to export the plans for industrial machinery, Slater, a skilled mechanic, built from memory a power-driven spinning jenny, one of the key inventions of the early industrial revolution.

A painting of Cincinnati, self-styled Queen City of the West, from 1835. Steamboats line the Ohio River waterfront.

Spinning factories such as Slater's produced yarn, which was then sent to traditional hand-loom weavers and farm families to be woven into cloth. This "outwork" system, in which rural men and women earned money by taking in jobs from factories, typified early industrialization. Eventually, however, the entire manufacturing process in textiles, shoes, and many other products was brought under a single factory roof.

The cutoff of British imports because of the Embargo of 1807 and the War of 1812 stimulated the establishment of the first large-scale American factory utilizing power looms for weaving cotton cloth. This was constructed in 1814 at Waltham, Massachusetts, by a group of merchants who came to be called the Boston Associates. In the 1820s, they expanded their enterprise by creating an entirely new factory town (incorporated as the city of Lowell in 1836) on the Merrimack River, twenty-seven miles from Boston. Here they built a group of modern textile factories that brought together all phases of production from the spinning of thread to the weaving and finishing of cloth.

A broadside from 1853 illustrates the long hours of work (from 5 AM to 6:30 PM with brief breaks for meals) in the textile mills of Holyoke, Massachusetts. Factory labor was strictly regulated by the clock.

The earliest factories, including those at Pawtucket, Waltham, and Lowell, were located along the "fall line," where waterfalls and river rapids could be harnessed to provide power for spinning and weaving machinery. By the 1840s, steam power made it possible for factory owners to locate in towns like New Bedford that were nearer to the coast, and in large cities like Philadelphia and Chicago with their immense local markets. In 1850, manufacturers produced in factories not only textiles but also a wide variety of other goods, including tools, firearms, shoes, clocks, ironware, and agricultural machinery. What came to be called the **American system of manufactures** relied on the mass production of interchangeable parts that could be rapidly assembled into standardized finished products. More impressive, in a way, than factory production was the wide dispersion of mechanical skills throughout northern society. Every town, it seemed, had its sawmill, paper mill, iron works, shoemaker, hatmaker, tailor, and a host of other such small enterprises.

Time Table of the Holyoke Mills,

To take effect on and after Jan. 3d, 1853.

The standard being that of the Western Rail Road, which is the Meridian time at Cambridge.

MORNING BELLS.

First Bell ring at 4.40, A. M.   Second Bell ring in at 5, A. M.

YARD GATES

Will be opened at ringing of Morning Bells, of Meal Bells, and of Evening Bells, and kept open ten minutes.

WORK COMMENCES

At ten minutes after last Morning Bell, and ten minutes after Bell which "rings in" from Meals.

BREAKFAST BELLS.

October 1st, to March 31st, inclusive, ring out at 7, A. M. ; ring in at 7.30, A. M.

April 1st, to Sept. 30th, inclusive, ring out at 6.30, A. M.; ring in at 7, A. M.

DINNER BELLS.

Ring out at 12.30, P. M. ; ring in at 1, P. M.

EVENING BELLS.

Ring out at 6.30,* P. M.

* Excepting on Saturdays when the Sun sets previous to 6.30.   At such times, ring out at Sunset.

In all cases, the first stroke of the Bell is considered as marking the time.

The "Mill Girls"

Although some factories employed entire families, the early New England textile mills relied largely on female and child labor. At Lowell, the most famous center of early textile manufacturing, young unmarried women from Yankee farm families dominated the workforce that tended the spinning machines. To persuade parents to allow their daughters to leave home to work in the mills, Lowell owners set up boarding houses with strict rules regulating personal behavior. They also established lecture halls and churches to occupy the women's free time.

Women at work tending machines in the Lowell textile mills.

This was the first time in history that large numbers of women left their homes to participate in the public world. Many **mill girls** complained about low wages and long hours. Others valued the opportunity to earn money independently at a time when few other jobs were open to women. But these women did not become a permanent class of factory workers. They typically remained in the factories for only a few years, after which they left to return home, marry, or move west.

The Growth of Immigration

Economic expansion fueled a demand for labor, which was met, in part, by increased immigration from abroad. Between 1790 and 1830, immigrants contributed only marginally to American population growth. But between 1840 and 1860, over 4 million people (more than the entire population in 1790) entered the United States, the majority from Ireland and Germany. About 90 percent headed for the northern states, where job opportunities were most abundant and the new arrivals would not have to compete with slave labor. In 1860, the 814,000 residents of New York City, the major port of entry, included more than 384,000 immigrants, and one-third of the population of Wisconsin was foreign-born.

Numerous factors inspired this massive flow of population across the Atlantic. In Europe, the modernization of agriculture and the industrial revolution disrupted centuries-old patterns of life, pushing peasants off the land and eliminating the jobs of traditional craft workers. The introduction of the oceangoing steamship and the railroad made long-distance travel more practical. Moreover, America's political and religious freedoms attracted Europeans, including political refugees from the failed revolutions of 1848, who chafed under the continent's repressive governments and rigid social hierarchies.

The largest number of immigrants, however, were refugees from disaster—Irish men and women fleeing the Great Famine of

TABLE 9.2 Total Number of Immigrants by Five-Year Period

YEARS	NUMBER OF IMMIGRANTS
1841–1845	430,000
1846–1850	1,283,000
1851–1855	1,748,000
1856–1860	850,000

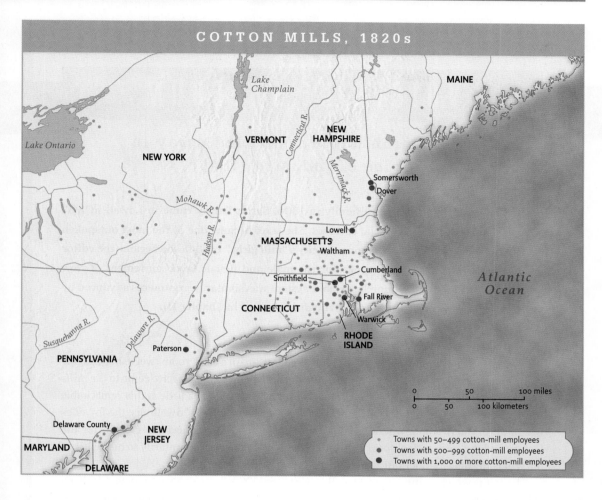

COTTON MILLS, 1820s

MAINE

Lake Champlain

VERMONT

NEW HAMPSHIRE

NEW YORK

Lake Ontario

Connecticut R.

Merrimack R.

Somersworth

Dover

Mohawk R.

Lowell

MASSACHUSETTS

Waltham

Hudson R.

Cumberland

Smithfield

Fall River

CONNECTICUT

Warwick

RHODE ISLAND

Atlantic Ocean

Susquehanna R.

Delaware R.

Paterson

PENNSYLVANIA

| 0 | 50 | 100 miles |
| 0 | 50 | 100 kilometers |

Delaware County

NEW JERSEY

MARYLAND

DELAWARE

· Towns with 50–499 cotton-mill employees
● Towns with 500–999 cotton-mill employees
● Towns with 1,000 or more cotton-mill employees

1845–1851, when a blight destroyed the potato crop on which the island's diet relied. An estimated 1 million persons starved to death and another million emigrated in those years, most of them to the United States. Lacking industrial skills and capital, these impoverished agricultural laborers and small farmers ended up filling the low-wage unskilled jobs native-born Americans sought to avoid. Male Irish immigrants built America's railroads, dug canals, and worked as common laborers, servants, longshoremen, and factory operatives. Irish women frequently went to work as servants in the homes of native-born Americans, although some preferred factory work to domestic service. By the end of the 1850s, the Lowell textile mills had largely replaced Yankee farm women with immigrant Irish families. Four-fifths of Irish immigrants remained in the Northeast.

The early industrial revolution was concentrated in New England, where factories producing textiles from raw cotton sprang up along the region's many rivers, taking advantage of water power to drive their machinery.

VOICES OF FREEDOM

From Sarah Bagley, untitled essay in *Voice of Industry* (1845)

Born to a New Hampshire farm family in 1806, Sarah Bagley came to Lowell in 1837 after her father suffered financial reverses. She soon became one of the most outspoken leaders of the labor movement among the city's "mill girls." In 1845 she became the editor of the *Voice of Industry*, which spoke for the male and female labor movement of New England. Her critique of the northern labor system was similar to arguments advanced by proslavery thinkers such as George Fitzhugh (discussed in Chapter 11).

Whenever I raise the point that it is immoral to shut us up in a close room twelve hours a day in the most monotonous and tedious of employment, I am told that we have come to the mills voluntarily and we can leave when we will. Voluntary! Let us look a little at this remarkable form of human freedom. Do we from mere choice leave our fathers' dwellings, the firesides where all of our friends, where too our earliest and fondest recollections cluster, for the factory and the corporation's boarding house? . . . A slave too goes voluntarily to his task, but his will is in some manner quickened by the whip of the overseer.

The whip which brings us to Lowell is NECESSITY. We must have money; a father's debts are to be paid, an aged mother to be sup ported, a brother's ambition to be aided, and so the factories are supplied. Is this to act from free will? . . . Is any one such a fool as to suppose that out of six thousand factory girls of Lowell, sixty would be there if they could help it? Everybody knows that it is necessity alone, in some form or other, that takes us to Lowell and keeps us there. Is this freedom? To my mind it is slavery quite as really as any in Turkey or Carolina. It matters little as to the fact of slavery, whether the slave be compelled to his task by the whip of the over-seer or the wages of the Lowell Corporation. In either case it is not free will, leading the laborer to work, but an outward necessity that puts free will out of the question.

From Letter of Margaret McCarthy to Her Family (1850)

Between 1840 and 1860, over 4 million people (more than the entire population of 1790) entered the United States, the majority from Ireland and Germany. Many sent money home to help family members join them, a process today sometimes called chain migration. In this letter, Margaret McCarthy, a young immigrant writing from New York City, offers advice to her family in Ireland.

My dear father I must only say that this is a good place and a good country for if one place does not suit a man he can go to another and can very easy please himself. . . . [But] I would advise no one to come to America that would not have some money after landing here that [will] enable them to go west in case they would get no work to do here. But any man or woman without a family are fools that would not venture and come to this plentiful country where no man or woman ever hungered or ever will. . . .

Come you all together courageously and bid adieu to that lovely place the land of our birth. . . . But alas I am now told it's the gulf of misery, oppression, degradation and ruin. . . . This, my dear father induces me to remit to you in this letter 20 dollars. . . . Dan Keliher tells me that you knew more of house carpentry than he did himself and he can earn from twelve to fourteen shilling a day and he also tells me that Florence will do very well and that Michael can get a place right off. . . . It is not for slavery I want you to come here no its for affording my brothers and sisters and I an opportunity of showing our kindness and gratitude and coming on your senior days . . . [so] that you my dear father and mother could walk about leisurely and independently . . . .

Oh how happy I feel [that] the Lord had not it destined for me to get married . . . at home [and] after a few months he and I may be an encumbrance on you or perhaps in the poor house.

QUESTIONS

1. *Why does Sarah Bagley compare the situation of female factory workers with slavery?*

2. *What aspirations seem to be uppermost in Margaret McCarthy's mind?*

3. *What do these documents suggest about how Americans of different backgrounds experienced and responded to economic conditions during the first half of the nineteenth century?*

A lithograph by an anonymous artist depicts the city of Lowell, Massachusetts, an early center of textile manufacturing, around 1850. Factories line the banks of the Merrimack River, which provided power for spinning machines and power looms. By this time, the original workforce of young New England women was being replaced by Irish immigrant families.

The second-largest group of immigrants, Germans, included a considerably larger number of skilled craftsmen than the Irish. Germans also settled in tightly knit neighborhoods in eastern cities, but many were able to move to the West, where they established themselves as craftsmen, shopkeepers, and farmers. The "German triangle," as the cities of Cincinnati, St. Louis, and Milwaukee were sometimes called, attracted large German populations.

Some 40,000 Scandinavians also emigrated to the United States in these years, most of whom settled on farms in the Old Northwest.

The Rise of Nativism

The idea of the United States as a refuge for those seeking economic opportunity or as an escape from oppression has always coexisted with suspicion of and hostility to foreign newcomers. American history has witnessed periods of intense anxiety over immigration. The Alien Act of 1798 reflected fear of immigrants with radical political views. During the early twentieth century, as will be discussed below, there was widespread hostility to the "new immigration" from southern and eastern Europe. In the early twenty-first century, the question of how many persons should be allowed to enter the United States, and under what circumstances, remains a volatile political issue.

Archbishop John Hughes of New York City made the Catholic Church a more assertive institution. He condemned the use of the Protestant King James Bible in the city's public schools, pressed Catholic parents to send their children to an expanding network of parochial schools, and sought

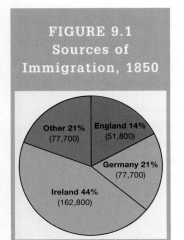

FIGURE 9.1
Sources of
Immigration, 1850

Other 21%
(77,700)
England 14%
(51,800)
Germany 21%
(77,700)
Ireland 44%
(162,800)

government funding to pay for them. He aggressively sought to win converts from Protestantism.

In the eyes of many Protestants, the newly assertive activities of the Catholic Church raised anew the question of national identity—the question, Who is an American, and its close relative, what kinds of immigrants should the country welcome. Catholicism, they feared, threatened American institutions and American freedom. In 1834, Lyman Beecher, a prominent Presbyterian minister (and father of the religious leader Henry Ward Beecher and the writers Harriet Beecher Stowe and Catharine Beecher), delivered a sermon in Boston, soon published as "A Plea for the West." Beecher warned that Catholics were seeking to dominate the American West, where the future of Christianity in the world would be worked out. His sermon inspired a mob to burn a Catholic convent in the city.

The Irish influx of the 1840s and 1850s thoroughly alarmed many native-born Americans. Those who feared the impact of immigration on American political and social life were called "nativists." They blamed immigrants for urban crime, political corruption, and a fondness for intoxicating liquor, and accused them of undercutting native-born skilled laborers by working for starvation wages. Stereotypes similar to those directed at blacks flourished regarding the Irish as well—seen as childlike, lazy, and slaves of their passions, they were said to be unsuited for republican freedom.

Nativism would not become a national political movement until the 1850s, as we will see in Chapter 13. But in the 1840s, nativism found expression both in the streets and at the ballot box. New York City and Philadelphia witnessed violent anti-immigrant, anti-Catholic riots.

Riot in Philadelphia, an 1844 lithograph, depicts street battles between nativists and Irish Catholics that left fifteen persons dead. The violence originated in a dispute over the use of the Protestant King James Bible in the city's public schools.

Nativist stereotypes

The Transformation of Law

American law increasingly supported the efforts of entrepreneurs to participate in the market revolution, while shielding them from interference by local governments and liability for some of the less desirable results of economic growth. The corporate form of business organization became central to the new market economy. A corporate firm enjoys special privileges and powers granted in a charter from the government, among them that investors and directors are not personally liable for the company's debts. Unlike companies owned by an individual, family, or limited partnership, in other words, a corporation can fail without ruining its directors and stockholders.

Corporations

A song written in 1845 offers a satire of the widely held image of the West as "the land of the free," a place where the "humblest" American can achieve economic success. The pictures surrounding the text offer a somewhat different image of westerners, and the verses go on to complain about illness and hardship. But the opening words reflect the ways in which Americans have always viewed the West.

Many Americans distrusted corporate charters as a form of government-granted special privilege. But the courts upheld their validity, while opposing efforts by established firms to limit competition from newcomers. In *Dartmouth College v. Woodward* (1819), John Marshall's Supreme Court defined corporate charters issued by state legislatures as contracts, which future lawmakers could not alter or rescind. Five years later, in *Gibbons v. Ogden*, the Court struck down a monopoly the New York legislature had granted for steamboat navigation. And in 1837, with Roger B. Taney now the chief justice, the Court ruled that the Massachusetts legislature did not infringe the charter of an existing company that had constructed a bridge over the Charles River when it empowered a second company to build a competing bridge. The community, Taney declared, had a legitimate interest in promoting transportation and prosperity.

THE FREE INDIVIDUAL

By the 1830s, the market revolution and westward expansion had produced a society that amazed European visitors: energetic, materialistic, and seemingly in constant motion. Alexis de Tocqueville was struck by Americans' restless energy and apparent lack of attachment to place. "No sooner do you set foot on American soil," he observed, "than you find yourself in a sort of tumult. All around you, everything is on the move."

The West and Freedom

Westward expansion and the market revolution reinforced some older ideas of freedom and helped to create new ones. American freedom, for example, had long been linked with the availability of land in the West. A New York journalist, John L. O'Sullivan, first employed the phrase "**manifest destiny**," meaning that the United States had a divinely appointed mission, so obvious as to be beyond dispute, to occupy all of North America. Americans, he proclaimed, had a far better title to western lands than could be provided by any international treaty, right of discovery, or long-term settlement.

O'Sullivan wrote these words in 1845, but the essential idea was familiar much earlier. Many Americans believed that the settlement and economic exploitation of the West would prevent the United States from following the path of Europe and becoming a society with fixed social classes and a large group of wage-earning poor. In the West, where land was more readily available and oppressive factory labor far less common than in the East, there continued to be the chance to achieve economic independence, the social condition of freedom. In national myth and ideology, the West would long remain, as the writer Wallace Stegner later put it, "the last home of the freeborn American."

Westward expansion and freedom

The Transcendentalists

The restless, competitive world of the market revolution strongly encouraged the identification of American freedom with the absence of restraints on self-directed individuals seeking economic advancement and personal development. The "one important revolution" of the day, the philosopher Ralph Waldo Emerson wrote in the 1830s, was "the new value of the private man." In Emerson's definition, rather than a preexisting set of rights or privileges, freedom was an open-ended process of self-realization by which individuals could remake themselves and their own lives.

Emerson was perhaps the most prominent member of a group of New England intellectuals known as the **transcendentalists**, who insisted on the primacy of individual judgment over existing social traditions and institutions. Emerson's Concord, Massachusetts, neighbor, the writer Henry David Thoreau, echoed his call for individual self-reliance. "Any man more right than his neighbors," Thoreau wrote, "is a majority of one."

In his own life, Thoreau illustrated Emerson's point about the primacy of individual conscience in matters political, social, and personal, and the need to find one's own way rather than following the crowd. Thoreau became persuaded that modern society stifled individual judgment by making men "tools of their tools," trapped in stultifying jobs by their obsession with acquiring wealth. Even in "this comparatively free country," he wrote, most persons were so preoccupied with material things that they had no time to contemplate the beauties of nature.

To escape this fate, Thoreau retreated for two years to a cabin on Walden Pond near Concord, where he could enjoy the freedom of isolation from the "economical and moral tyranny" he believed ruled American society. He subsequently published *Walden* (1854), an account of his experiences and a critique of how the market revolution was, in his opinion, degrading both Americans' values and the natural environment. An area

The daguerreotype, an early form of photography, required the sitter to remain perfectly still for twenty seconds or longer, meaning that the subject usually looked rather stiff. Nonetheless, Henry David Thoreau, pictured here in 1856, wrote, "my friends think it is pretty good though better looking than I."

that had been covered with dense forest in his youth, he observed, had been so transformed by woodcutters and farmers that it was almost completely devoid of trees and wild animals. Thoreau appealed to Americans to "simplify" their lives rather than become obsessed with the accumulation of wealth. Genuine freedom, he insisted, lay within.

The Second Great Awakening

The popular religious revivals that swept the country during the **Second Great Awakening** added a religious underpinning to the celebration of personal self-improvement, self-reliance, and self-determination. These revivals, which began at the turn of the century, were originally organized by established religious leaders alarmed by low levels of church attendance in the young republic (perhaps as few as 10 percent of white Americans regularly attended church during the 1790s). But they quickly expanded far beyond existing churches. They peaked in the 1820s and early 1830s, when the Reverend Charles Grandison Finney held months-long revival meetings in upstate New York and New York City. Like the evangelists (traveling preachers) of the first Great Awakening of the mid-eighteenth century discussed in Chapter 4, Finney warned of hell in vivid language while offering the promise of salvation to converts who abandoned their sinful ways.

Religious revivals

The Second Great Awakening democratized American Christianity, making it a truly mass enterprise. At the time of independence, fewer than 2,000 Christian ministers preached in the United States. In 1845, they numbered 40,000. Evangelical denominations such as the Methodists and Baptists enjoyed explosive growth in membership, and smaller sects proliferated. By the 1840s, Methodism, with more than 1 million members, had become the country's largest denomination. At large camp meetings, especially prominent on the frontier, fiery revivalist preachers rejected the idea that man is a sinful creature with a preordained fate, promoting instead the doctrine of human free will. At these gatherings, rich and poor, male and female, and in some instances whites and blacks worshiped alongside one another and pledged to abandon worldly sins in favor of the godly life.

Das neue Jerusalem (The New Jerusalem), an early nineteenth-century watercolor, in German, illustrates the narrow gateway to heaven and the fate awaiting sinners in hell. These were common themes of preachers in the Second Great Awakening.

The Awakening's Impact

Even more than its predecessor of several decades earlier, the Second Great Awakening stressed the right of private judgment in spiritual matters and the possibility of universal salvation through faith and good works. Every person, Finney insisted, was a "moral free agent"—that is, a person free to choose between a Christian life and sin.

Revivalist ministers seized the opportunities offered by the market revolution to spread their message. They raised funds, embarked on lengthy preaching tours by canal, steamboat, and railroad, and flooded the country with mass-produced, inexpensive religious tracts. The revivals' opening of religion to mass participation and their message that ordinary Americans could shape their own spiritual destinies resonated with the spread of market values.

Mass religion

To be sure, evangelical preachers can hardly be described as cheer-leaders for a market society. They regularly railed against greed and indifference to the welfare of others as sins. Yet the revivals thrived in areas caught up in the rapid expansion of the market economy, such as the region of upstate New York along the path of the Erie Canal. Most of Finney's converts here came from the commercial and professional classes. Evangelical ministers promoted what might be called a controlled **individualism** as the essence of freedom. In stressing the importance of industry, sobriety, and self-discipline as examples of freely chosen moral behavior, evangelical preachers promoted the very qualities necessary for success in a market culture.

The Awakening and market society

The Emergence of Mormonism

The end of governmental support for established churches promoted competition among religious groups that kept religion vibrant and promoted the emergence of new denominations. Among the most successful of the religions that sprang up was the **Church of Jesus Christ of Latter-Day Saints**, or Mormons, which hoped to create a Kingdom of God on earth. The Mormons were founded in the 1820s by Joseph Smith, a farmer in upstate New York who as a youth began to experience religious visions. He claimed to have been led by an angel to a set of golden plates covered with strange writing. Smith translated and published them as *The Book of Mormon*, after a fourth-century prophet.

The Book of Mormon tells the story of three families who traveled from the ancient Middle East to the Americas, where they eventually evolved into Native American tribes. Jesus Christ plays a prominent role in the book, appearing to one of the family groups in the

The Book of Mormon

In this 1846 photograph, the massive Mormon temple in Nauvoo, Illinois, towers over the ramshackle wooden buildings of this town along the Mississippi River.

Brigham Young

Western Hemisphere after his death and resurrection. The second coming of Christ would take place in the New World, where Smith was God's prophet.

Mormonism emerged in a center of the Second Great Awakening, upstate New York. The church founded by Smith shared some features with other Christian denominations including a focus on the family and community as the basis of social order and a rejection of alcohol. Gradually, however, Smith began to receive visions that led to more controversial doctrines, notably polygamy, which allows one man to have more than one wife. By the end of his life, Smith had married no fewer than thirty women. Along with the absolute authority Smith exercised over his followers, this doctrine outraged the Mormons' neighbors. Mobs drove Smith and his followers out of New York, Ohio, and Missouri before they settled in 1839 in Nauvoo, Illinois. There, five years later, Smith was arrested on the charge of inciting a riot that destroyed an anti-Mormon newspaper. While in jail awaiting trial, Smith was murdered by a group of intruders. In 1847, his successor as Mormon leader, Brigham Young, led more than 2,000 followers across the Great Plains and Rocky Mountains to the shores of the Great Salt Lake in present-day Utah. By 1852, the number of Mormons in various settlements in Utah reached 16,000. The Mormons' experience revealed the limits of religious toleration in nineteenth-century America but also the opportunities offered by religious pluralism. Today, Mormons constitute the fourth largest church in the United States, and *The Book of Mormon* has been translated into over 100 languages.

THE LIMITS OF PROSPERITY

Liberty and Prosperity

As the market revolution progressed, the right to compete for economic advancement became a touchstone of American freedom. Americans celebrated the opportunities open to the "self-made man," a term that came into use at this time. According to this idea, those who achieved success in America did so not as a result of hereditary privilege or government favoritism as in Europe, but through their own intelligence and hard work. The market revolution enriched numerous bankers, merchants, industrialists, and planters. It produced a new middle class—an army of clerks, accountants, and other office employees who staffed businesses in Boston, New York, and elsewhere. It created new opportunities for farmers who profited from the growing demand at home and abroad for American agricultural products, and for skilled craftsmen such as Thomas Rodgers, a machine builder who established a successful locomotive factory in Paterson, New Jersey. New opportunities for talented men opened in professions such as law, medicine, and teaching. By the early 1820s, there were an estimated 10,000 physicians in the United States.

Pat Lyon at the Forge, an 1826–1827 painting of a prosperous blacksmith. Proud of his accomplishments as a self-made man who had achieved success through hard work and skill rather than inheritance, Lyon asked the artist to paint him in his shop wearing his work clothes.

Race and Opportunity

The market revolution affected the lives of all Americans. But not all were positioned to take advantage of its benefits. Most blacks, of course, were slaves, but even free blacks found themselves excluded from the new economic opportunities. The 220,000 blacks living in the free states on the eve of the Civil War (less than 2 percent of the North's population) suffered discrimination in every phase of their lives. The majority of blacks lived in the poorest, unhealthiest sections of cities like New York, Philadelphia, and Cincinnati. And even these neighborhoods were subject to occasional violent assault by white mobs, like the armed bands that attacked blacks and destroyed their homes and businesses in Cincinnati in 1829.

Barred from schools and other public facilities, free blacks laboriously constructed their own institutional life, centered on mutual-aid and educational societies, as well as independent churches, most notably the African Methodist Episcopal Church. Richard Allen of Philadelphia, a Methodist preacher, had been spurred to found it after being forcibly removed from his former church for praying at the altar rail, a place reserved for whites.

Black institutions

Whereas many white Americans could look forward to a life of economic accumulation and individual advancement, large numbers of free blacks experienced downward mobility. At the time of abolition in the North, because of widespread slave ownership among eighteenth-century artisans, a considerable number of northern blacks possessed craft skills. But it became more and more difficult for blacks to utilize these skills once they became free. Although many white artisans criticized slavery, most viewed the freed slaves as low-wage competitors and sought to bar them from skilled employment.

Downward mobility of free blacks

Hostility from white craftsmen, however, was only one of many obstacles that kept blacks confined to the lowest ranks of the labor market. White employers refused to hire them in anything but menial positions, and white customers did not wish to be served by them. The result was a rapid decline in economic status until by mid-century, the vast majority of northern blacks labored for wages in unskilled jobs and as domestic servants. The state census of 1855 revealed 122 black barbers and 808 black servants in New York City, but only 1 lawyer and 6 doctors. Nor could free blacks take advantage of the opening of the West to improve their economic status, a central component of American freedom. Federal law barred them from access to public land, and by 1860 four states—Indiana, Illinois, Iowa, and Oregon—prohibited them from entering their territory altogether.

The Cult of Domesticity

Women, too, found many of the opportunities opened by the market revolution closed to them. As the household declined as a center of economic production, many women saw their traditional roles undermined by the availability of mass-produced goods previously made at home. Some women, as noted above, followed work as it moved from household to factory. Others embraced a new definition of femininity, which glorified not a woman's contribution to the family's economic well-being, but her ability to create a private environment shielded from the competitive tensions of the market economy. Woman's "place" was in the home, a site increasingly emptied of economically productive functions as work moved from the household to workshops and factories. Her role was to sustain nonmarket values like love, friendship, and mutual obligation, providing men with a shelter from the competitive marketplace.

The earlier ideology of "republican motherhood," which allowed women a kind of public role as mothers of future citizens, subtly evolved into the mid-nineteenth-century **cult of domesticity**. "In whatever situation of life a woman is placed from her cradle to her grave," declared *The Young Lady's Book*, one of numerous popular magazines addressed to female audiences of the 1820s and 1830s, "a spirit of obedience and submission, pliability of temper, and humility of mind, are required from her."

With more and more men leaving the home for work, women did exercise considerable power over personal affairs within the family. The rapid decline in the American birthrate during the nineteenth century (from an average of seven children per woman in 1800 to four in 1900) cannot be explained except by the conscious decision of millions of women to limit the number of children they bore. But the idea of domesticity minimized women's even indirect participation in the outside world. Men moved freely between the public

The Industrious Man, a lithograph from a book produced for children by the American Sunday School Union in the 1840s, depicts an ideal family scene. The father, a laborer, returns home carrying his lunch pail to find his wife and children awaiting him in a comfortable although hardly extravagant home. The scene exemplifies the idea of separate spheres according to which men worked outside the home and women's role was to fulfill their family responsibilities.

THE INDUSTRIOUS MAN.

and private "spheres"; women were supposed to remain cloistered in the private realm of the family.

Women and Work

Prevailing ideas concerning gender bore little relation to the experience of those women who worked for wages at least some time in their lives. They did so despite severe disadvantages. Women could not compete freely for employment, since only low-paying jobs were available to them. Married women still could not sign independent contracts or sue in their own names, and not until after the Civil War did they, not their husbands, control the wages they earned. Nonetheless, for poor city dwellers and farm families, the labor of all family members was essential to economic survival. Thousands of poor women found jobs as domestic servants, factory workers, and seamstresses.

This nineteenth-century wood sculpture of a woman at a spinning wheel depicts a form of labor practiced by millions of American women in their homes—despite the advent of machines that did the same work—producing thread or yarn from fibers such as wool and cotton.

For the expanding middle class, however, it became a badge of respectability for wives to remain at home, outside the disorderly new market economy, while husbands conducted business in their offices, shops, and factories. In larger cities, where families of different social classes had previously lived alongside one another, fashionable middle-class neighborhoods populated by merchants, factory owners, and professionals like lawyers and doctors began to develop. Work in middle-class homes was done by domestic servants, the largest employment category for women in nineteenth-century America. The freedom of the middle-class woman—defined in part as freedom from labor—rested on the employment of other women within her household.

Even though most women were anything but idle, in a market economy where labor increasingly meant work that created monetary value, it became more and more difficult to think of labor as encompassing anyone but men. Discussions of labor rarely mentioned housewives, domestic servants, and female outworkers, except as an indication of how the spread of capitalism was degrading men. The idea that the male head of household should command a **family wage** that enabled him to support his wife and children became a popular definition of social justice. It sank deep roots not only among middle-class Americans but among working-class men as well.

Discussions of labor excluding women

The Early Labor Movement

Although many Americans welcomed the market revolution, others felt threatened by its consequences. Surviving members of the revolutionary generation feared that the obsession with personal economic gain was undermining devotion to the public good.

"The Intelligence Office," an 1849 painting by the artist William Henry Burr, depicts a female employment office. The two women at the left are responding to an ad for a domestic worker printed in a New York City newspaper, which lies crumpled on the ground. The seated woman is the prospective employer, and in the middle is the agent who runs the office. Domestic work was the largest category of female employment throughout the nineteenth century.

Many Americans experienced the market revolution not as an enhancement of the power to shape their own lives, but as a loss of freedom. The period between the War of 1812 and 1840 witnessed a sharp economic downturn in 1819, a full-fledged depression starting in 1837, and numerous ups and downs in between, during which employment was irregular and numerous businesses failed. The economic transformation significantly widened the gap between wealthy merchants and industrialists on the one hand and impoverished factory workers, unskilled dockworkers, and seamstresses laboring at home on the other. In Massachusetts, the most industrialized state in the country, the richest 5 percent of the population owned more than half the wealth.

Alarmed at the erosion of traditional skills and the threat of being reduced to the status of dependent wage earners, skilled craftsmen in the late 1820s created the world's first Workingmen's Parties, short-lived political organizations that sought to mobilize lower-class support for candidates who would press for free public education, an end to imprisonment for debt, and legislation limiting work to ten hours per day. In the 1830s, a time of rapidly rising prices, union organization spread and strikes became commonplace. Along with demands for higher wages and shorter hours, the early labor movement called for free homesteads for settlers on public land and an end to the imprisonment of union leaders for conspiracy.

The "Liberty of Living"

But over and above these specific issues, workers' language of protest drew on older ideas of freedom linked to economic autonomy, public-spirited virtue, and social equality. The conviction of twenty New York tailors in 1835 under the common law of conspiracy for combining to seek higher wages inspired a public procession marking the "burial of liberty." Such actions and language were not confined to male workers. The young mill women of Lowell walked off their jobs in 1834 to protest a reduction in wages and again two years later when employers raised rents at their boardinghouses. They carried banners affirming their rights as "daughters of free men," and, addressing the factory owners, charged that "the oppressive hand of avarice [greed] would enslave us."

Labor actions

Rooted in the traditions of the small producer and the identification of freedom with economic independence, labor's critique of the market economy directly challenged the idea that individual improvement—Emerson's "self-trust, self-reliance, self-control, self-culture"—offered an adequate response to social inequality. Orestes Brownson, in his influential essay "The Laboring Classes" (1840), argued that the solution to workers' problems did not require a more complete individualism. What was needed instead, he believed, was a "radical change [in] existing social arrangements" so as to produce "equality between man and man." Here lay the origins of the idea, which would become far more prominent in the late nineteenth and twentieth centuries, that economic security—a standard of life below which no person would fall—formed an essential part of American freedom.

The Shoemakers' Strike in Lynn—Procession in the Midst of a Snow-Storm, of Eight Hundred Women Operatives, an engraving from *Frank Leslie's Illustrated Newspaper*, March 17, 1860. The striking women workers carry a banner comparing their condition to that of slaves.

Thus, the market revolution transformed and divided American society and its conceptions of freedom. It encouraged a new emphasis on individualism and physical mobility among white men while severely limiting the options available to women and African-Americans. It opened new opportunities for economic freedom for many Americans while leading others to fear that their traditional economic independence was being eroded. In a democratic society, it was inevitable that the debate over the market revolution and its consequences for freedom would be reflected in American politics.

CHAPTER REVIEW AND ONLINE RESOURCES

REVIEW QUESTIONS

1. *Identify the major transportation improvements in this period, and explain how they influenced the market economy.*

2. *How did state and local governments promote the national economy in this period?*

3. *How did the market economy and westward expansion entrench the institution of slavery?*

4. *How did westward expansion and the market revolution drive each other?*

5. *What role did immigrants play in the new market society?*

6. *How did changes in the law promote development in the economic system?*

7. *As it democratized American Christianity, the Second Great Awakening both took advantage of the market revolution and criticized its excesses. Explain.*

8. *How did the market revolution change women's work and family roles?*

9. *Give some examples of the rise of individualism in these years.*

10. *How did immigration and nativism address the question of who is an American?*

KEY TERMS

steamboat (p. 252)
Erie Canal (p. 252)
Cotton Kingdom (p. 257)
cotton gin (p. 257)
Porkopolis (p. 260)
American system of manufactures (p. 261)
mill girls (p. 262)
nativism (p. 267)
Dartmouth College v. Woodward (p. 268)
Gibbons v. Ogden (p. 268)
manifest destiny (p. 268)
transcendentalists (p. 269)
Second Great Awakening (p. 270)
individualism (p. 271)
Church of Jesus Christ of Latter-Day Saints (p. 271)
cult of domesticity (p. 274)
family wage (p. 275)

Go to INQUIZITIVE

To see what you know—and learn what you've missed—with personalized feedback along the way.

Visit the *Give Me Liberty!* **Student Site** for primary source documents and images, interactive maps, author videos featuring Eric Foner, and more.

CHAPTER 10

DEMOCRACY IN AMERICA

★

1815–1840

"Militia Training," an 1841 painting by the British-born artist James G. Clonney, depicts the Fourth of July celebration of an all-white militia company. Black dancers perform in the foreground while militia members socialize. A handful of women are also present.

The inauguration of Andrew Jackson on March 4, 1829, made it clear that something had changed in American politics. The swearing-in of the president had previously been a small, dignified event. Jackson's inauguration attracted a crowd of some 20,000 people who poured into the White House after the ceremony, ruining furniture and breaking china and glassware in the crush. It was "the reign of King Mob," lamented Justice Joseph Story of the Supreme Court.

Jackson's career embodied the major developments of his era—the market revolution, the westward movement, the expansion of slavery, and the growth of democracy. He was a symbol of the self-made man. Unlike previous presidents, Jackson rose to prominence from a humble background, reflecting his era's democratic opportunities. Born in 1767 on the South Carolina frontier, he had been orphaned during the American Revolution. While still a youth, he served as a courier for patriotic forces during the War of Independence. His military campaigns against the British and Indians during the War of 1812 helped to consolidate American control over the Lower South, making possible the rise of the Cotton Kingdom. He himself acquired a large plantation in Tennessee. But more than anything else, to this generation of Americans Andrew Jackson symbolized one of the most crucial features of national life—the triumph of political democracy.

Americans pride themselves on being the world's oldest democracy. New Zealand, whose constitution of 1893 gave women and Maoris (the native population) the right to vote, may have a better claim. Europe, however, lagged far behind. Britain did not achieve universal male suffrage until the 1880s. France instituted it in 1793, abandoned it in 1799, reintroduced it in 1848, and abandoned it again a few years later. More to the point, perhaps, democracy became a central part of the definition of American nationality and the American idea of freedom.

THE TRIUMPH OF DEMOCRACY

Property and Democracy

The market revolution and territorial expansion were intimately connected with a third central element of American freedom—political democracy. The challenge to property qualifications for voting, begun during the American Revolution, reached its culmination in the early nineteenth century. Not a single state that entered the Union after the original thirteen required ownership of property to vote. In the older states, by 1860 all but one had ended property requirements for voting (though several continued to bar persons accepting poor relief, on the grounds that they lacked genuine independence). The personal independence necessary in the citizen now rested not on ownership of property but on ownership of one's self—a reflection of the era's individualism.

The Dorr War

The lone exception to the trend toward democratization was Rhode Island, which required voters to own real estate valued at $134 or rent property for at least $7 per year. A center of factory production, Rhode Island had a steadily growing population of propertyless wage earners unable to vote. In October 1841, proponents of democratic reform organized a People's Convention, which drafted a new state constitution. It enfranchised all adult white men while eliminating entirely blacks (although in a subsequent referendum, blacks' right to vote was restored). When the reformers ratified their constitution in an extralegal referendum and proceeded to inaugurate Thomas Dorr, a prominent Rhode Island lawyer, as governor, President John Tyler dispatched federal troops to the state. The movement collapsed, and Dorr subsequently served nearly two years in prison for treason. **The Dorr War** demonstrated the passions aroused by the continuing exclusion of any group of white men from voting.

An anti-Jackson cartoon from 1832 portrays Andrew Jackson as an aspiring monarch, wielding the veto power while trampling on the Constitution.

Tocqueville on Democracy

By 1840, more than 90 percent of adult white men were eligible to vote. A flourishing democratic system had been consolidated. American politics was boisterous, highly partisan, and sometimes violent, and it engaged the energies of massive numbers of citizens. In a country that lacked more traditional bases of nationality—a powerful and menacing neighbor, historic ethnic, religious, or cultural unity—democratic political institutions came to define the nation's sense of its own identity.

White male suffrage

Alexis de Tocqueville, the French writer who visited the United States in the early 1830s, returned home to produce ***Democracy in America***, a classic account of a society in the midst of a political transformation. Tocqueville had come to the United States to study prisons. But he soon realized that to understand America, he must understand democracy (which as a person of aristocratic background he rather disliked). His key insight was that democracy by this time meant far more than either the right to vote or a particular set of political institutions. It was a "habit of the heart," a culture that encouraged individual initiative, belief in equality, and an active public sphere populated by numerous voluntary

Alexis de Tocqueville

Democratic culture

Justice's Court in the Back Woods, an 1852 painting by Tompkins Harrison Matteson, depicts the expansion of the public sphere to include ordinary Americans. A court is in session in a local tavern. The justice of the peace, who presides, is a shoemaker who has set aside his tools but still wears his leather work apron. A lawyer appeals to the jury, composed of average (male) citizens. The case has to do with an assault. The plaintiff, his head bandaged, leans on the table at the right.

organizations that sought to improve society. Democracy, Tocqueville saw, had become an essential attribute of American freedom.

Popular sovereignty

As Tocqueville recognized, the idea that sovereignty belongs to the mass of ordinary citizens was a profound shift in political thought. The founders of the republic, who believed that government must rest on the consent of the governed, also sought to shield political authority from excessive influence by ordinary people (hence the Electoral College, Supreme Court, and other undemocratic features of the Constitution). Nonetheless, thanks to persistent pressure from those originally excluded from political participation, democracy—for white males—triumphed by the Age of Jackson.

The Information Revolution

The rise of the mass-circulation press

The market revolution and political democracy produced a large expansion of the public sphere and an explosion in printing sometimes called the "information revolution." The application of steam power to newspaper printing led to a great increase in output and the rise of the mass-circulation "penny press," priced at one cent per issue instead of the traditional six. Newspapers such as the *New York Sun* and *New York Herald* introduced a new style of journalism, appealing to a mass audience by emphasizing sensationalism, crime stories, and exposés of official misconduct. By 1840, according to one estimate, the total weekly circulation of newspapers in the United States, with a population of 17 million, exceeded that of Europe, with 233 million people.

Alternative journalism

The reduction in the cost of printing also made possible the appearance of "alternative" newspapers in the late 1820s and early 1830s, including

Freedom's Journal (the first black newspaper), *Philadelphia Mechanic's Advocate* and other labor publications, the abolitionist weekly *The Liberator*, and *Cherokee Phoenix*, the first Native American newspaper.

The Limits of Democracy

By the 1830s, the time of Andrew Jackson's presidency, the axiom that "the people" ruled had become a universally accepted part of American politics. Those who opposed this principle, wrote Tocqueville, "hide their heads." But the very centrality of democracy to the definition of both freedom and nationality made it all the more necessary to define the boundaries of the political nation. As older economic exclusions fell away, others survived and new ones were added.

The "principle of universal suffrage," declared the *United States Magazine and Democratic Review* in 1851, meant that "white males of age constituted the political nation." How could the word "universal" be reconciled with barring blacks and women from political participation? As democracy triumphed, the intellectual grounds for exclusion shifted from economic dependency to natural incapacity. Gender and racial differences were widely understood as part of a single, natural hierarchy of innate endowments. White males were considered inherently superior in character and abilities to non-whites and women. The debate over which people are and are not qualified to take part in American democracy has lasted well into the twenty-first century. Not until 1920 was the Constitution amended to require states to allow women to vote. The Voting Rights Act of 1965 swept away restrictions on black voting imposed by many southern states.

"Universal suffrage"

Democracy, gender, and race

A Racial Democracy

If the exclusion of women from political freedom continued a long-standing practice, the increasing identification of democracy and whiteness marked something of a departure. Blacks were increasingly considered a group apart. Racist imagery became the stock-in-trade of popular theatrical presentations like minstrel shows, in which white actors in blackface entertained the audience by portraying African-Americans as stupid, dishonest, and altogether ridiculous. With the exception of Herman Melville, who portrayed complex, sometimes heroic black characters in works like *Moby Dick* and *Benito Cereno* (the latter a fictionalized account of a shipboard slave rebellion), American authors either ignored blacks entirely or presented them as stereotypes—happy slaves prone to superstition or long-suffering but devout Christians. Meanwhile, the somewhat tentative thinking of the revolutionary era about the status of non-whites

Racist imagery

Jim Crow, a piece of sheet music from 1829. Minstrel shows were a form of nineteenth-century entertainment in which white actors impersonated blacks. One of the most popular characters was Jim Crow, the happy, childlike plantation slave created by the performer Thomas D. Rice. Years later, "Jim Crow" would come to mean the laws and customs of southern segregation.

flowered into an elaborate ideology of racial superiority and inferiority, complete with "scientific" underpinnings. These developments affected the boundaries of the political nation.

In the revolutionary era, only Virginia, South Carolina, and Georgia explicitly confined the vote to whites, although elsewhere, custom often made it difficult for free blacks to exercise the **franchise**. As late as 1800, no northern state barred blacks from voting. But every state that entered the Union after that year, with the single exception of Maine, limited the right to vote to white males. And, beginning with Kentucky in 1799 and Maryland two years later, several states that had allowed blacks to vote rescinded the privilege. By 1860, blacks could vote on the same basis as whites in only five New England states, which contained only 4 percent of the nation's free black population.

In effect, race had replaced class as the boundary between those American men who were entitled to enjoy political freedom and those who were not. Even as this focus on race limited America's political community as a whole, it helped to solidify a sense of national identity among the diverse groups of European origin. In a country where the right to vote had become central to the meaning of freedom, it is difficult to overstate the importance of the fact that white male immigrants could vote in some states almost from the moment they landed in America, whereas nearly all free blacks (and, of course, slaves), whose ancestors had lived in the country for centuries, could not vote at all.

NATIONALISM AND ITS DISCONTENTS

The American System

The War of 1812, which the United States and Great Britain—the world's foremost military power—fought to a draw, inspired an outburst of nationalist pride. But the war also revealed how far the United States still was from being a truly integrated nation. With the Bank of the United States having gone out of existence when its charter expired in 1811, the country lacked a uniform currency and found it almost impossible to raise funds for the war effort. Given the primitive state of transportation, it proved very difficult to move men and goods around the country. One shipment of supplies from New England had taken seventy-five days to reach New Orleans. With the coming of peace, the manufacturing enterprises that sprang up while trade with Britain had been suspended faced intense competition from low-cost imported goods. A younger generation of Republicans, including Henry Clay

War of 1812 and American nationalism

and John C. Calhoun, who had led the call for war in 1812, believed these "infant industries" deserved national protection.

In his annual message (now known as the State of the Union address) to Congress in December 1815, President James Madison put forward a blueprint for government-promoted economic development that came to be known as the **American System**, a label coined by Henry Clay. The plan rested on three pillars: a new national bank, a tariff on imported manufactured goods to protect

American industry, and federal financing of improved roads and canals. The last was particularly important to those worried about the dangers of disunity. "Let us bind the nation together, with a perfect system of roads and canals," John C. Calhoun implored Congress in 1815. "Let us conquer space."

Congress enacted an internal improvements program drafted by Calhoun, only to be astonished when the president, on the eve of his retirement from office in March 1817, vetoed the bill. Since calling for its enactment, Madison had become convinced that allowing the national government to exercise powers not mentioned in the Constitution would prove dangerous to individual liberty and southern interests. The other two parts of his plan, however, became law. The **tariff of 1816** offered protection to goods that could be produced in the United States, especially cheap cotton textiles, while admitting tax-free those that could not be manufactured at home. Many southerners supported the tariff, believing that it would enable their region to develop a manufacturing base to rival New England's. And in 1816, a new Bank of the United States was created, with a twenty-year charter from Congress.

An image from a broadside from the campaign of 1824, promoting the American System of government-sponsored economic development. The illustrations represent industry, commerce, and agriculture. The ship at the center is named the *John Quincy Adams*. Its flag, "No Colonial Subjection," suggests that without a balanced economy, the United States will remain economically dependent on Great Britain.

Bank of the United States

Banks and Money

The Second Bank of the United States soon became the focus of public resentment. Like its predecessor, it was a private, profit-making corporation that acted as the government's financial agent, issuing paper money, collecting taxes, and paying the government's debts. It was also charged with ensuring that paper money issued by local banks had real value. In the nineteenth century, paper money consisted of notes promising to pay the bearer on demand a specified amount of "specie" (gold or silver). Since banks often printed far more money than the specie in their vaults, the value of paper currency fluctuated wildly. The Bank of the United States was supposed to correct this problem by preventing the overissuance of money.

Regulating local banks

The Panic of 1819

But instead of effectively regulating the currency and loans issued by local banks, the Bank of the United States participated in a speculative fever that swept the country after the end of the War of 1812. The resumption of trade with Europe created a huge overseas market for American cotton and grain. Coupled with the rapid expansion of settlement into the West, this stimulated demand for loans to purchase land, which local banks and branches of the Bank of the United States were only too happy to meet by printing more money. The land boom was especially acute in the South, where the Cotton Kingdom was expanding.

Land boom

Early in 1819, as European demand for American farm products declined to normal levels, the economic bubble burst. The Bank of the United States, followed by state banks, began asking for payments from those to whom it had loaned money. Farmers and businessmen who could not repay declared bankruptcy, and unemployment rose in eastern cities.

The economic bubble bursts

The **Panic of 1819** lasted little more than a year, but it severely disrupted the political harmony of the previous years. To the consternation of creditors, many states, especially in the West, suspended the collection of debts. Kentucky went even further, establishing a state bank that flooded the state with paper money that creditors were required to accept in repayment of loans. This eased the burden on indebted farmers but injured those who had loaned them the money. Overall, the panic deepened many Americans' traditional distrust of banks. It undermined the reputation of the Second Bank of the United States, which was widely blamed for causing the panic. Several states retaliated against the national bank by taxing its local branches.

These tax laws produced another of John Marshall's landmark Supreme Court decisions, in the case of ***McCulloch v. Maryland*** (1819). Reasserting his broad interpretation of governmental powers, Marshall declared the Bank a legitimate exercise of congressional authority under the Constitution's clause that allowed Congress to pass "necessary and proper" laws. Marshall's interpretation of the Constitution directly contradicted the "strict construction" view that limited Congress to powers specifically granted in the Constitution.

The House of Representatives in 1822, in a painting by Samuel F. B. Morse (who also invented the telegraph). By this time, most adult white men could vote for members of the House, a far wider franchise than was known in Europe at the time.

The Missouri Controversy

In 1816, James Monroe handily defeated the Federalist candidate Rufus King, becoming the last of the Virginia presidents. By 1820,

THE MISSOURI COMPROMISE, 1820

Legend:
- Territory closed to slavery by the Missouri Compromise
- Free states and territories
- Territory opened to slavery by the Missouri Compromise
- Slave states and territories

the Federalists fielded electoral tickets in only two states, and Monroe carried the entire country. Monroe's two terms in office were years of one-party government, sometimes called the **Era of Good Feelings**. Plenty of bad feelings, however, surfaced during his presidency. In the absence of two-party competition, politics was organized along lines of competing sectional interests.

In 1819, Congress considered a request from Missouri, an area carved out of the Louisiana Purchase, to draft a constitution in preparation for admission to the Union as a state. Missouri's slave population already exceeded 10,000. James Tallmadge, a Republican congressman from New York, moved that the introduction of further slaves be prohibited and that children of those already in Missouri be freed at age twenty-five.

Tallmadge's proposal sparked two years of controversy, during which Republican unity shattered along sectional lines. His restriction passed the House, where most northern congressmen supported it over the objections of southern representatives. It died in the Senate, however. When Congress reconvened in 1820, Senator Jesse Thomas of Illinois proposed a compromise. Missouri would be authorized to draft a constitution without

The Missouri Compromise temporarily settled the question of the expansion of slavery by dividing the Louisiana Purchase into free and slave areas.

Tallmadge's restriction. Maine, which prohibited slavery, would be admitted to the Union to maintain the sectional balance between free and slave states. And slavery would be prohibited in all remaining territory within the Louisiana Purchase north of latitude 36°30' (Missouri's southern boundary). Congress adopted Thomas's plan as the **Missouri Compromise**.

Westward expansion of slavery

The Missouri controversy raised for the first time what would prove to be a fatal issue—the westward expansion of slavery. The sectional division it revealed aroused widespread feelings of dismay. "This momentous question," wrote Jefferson, "like a fire bell in the night, awakened and filled me with terror. I considered it at once as the knell of the union." For the moment, however, the slavery issue faded once again from national debate.

NATION, SECTION, AND PARTY

The United States and the Latin American Wars of Independence

The new Latin American republics

Between 1810 and 1822, Spain's Latin American colonies rose in rebellion and established a series of independent nations, including Mexico, Venezuela, Ecuador, and Peru. By 1825, Spain's once vast American empire had been reduced to the islands of Cuba and Puerto Rico. The uprisings inspired a wave of sympathy in the United States. In 1822, the Monroe administration became the first government to extend diplomatic recognition to the new Latin American republics.

Parallels existed between the Spanish-American revolutions and the one that had given birth to the United States. In both cases, the crisis of empire was precipitated by programs launched by the imperial country aimed in large measure at making the colonies contribute more to its finances. As had happened in British North America, local elites demanded status and treatment equal to residents of the imperial power. The Spanish-American declarations of independence borrowed directly from that of the United States. The first, issued in 1811, declared that the "United Provinces" of Venezuela now enjoyed "among the sovereign nations of the earth the rank which the Supreme Being and nature has assigned us"—language strikingly similar to Jefferson's.

Latin American constitutions

In some ways, the new Latin American constitutions—adopted by seventeen different nations—were more democratic than that of the United States. Most sought to implement the transatlantic ideals of rights and freedom by creating a single national "people" out of the diverse populations that made up the Spanish empire. To do so, they extended the right to vote to Indians and free blacks. The Latin American wars of independence, in which black soldiers participated on both sides, also set in motion the gradual abolition of slavery. But the Latin American wars of independence lasted longer—sometimes more than a decade—and were more destructive than the one in the United States had been. As a result, it proved far more difficult for the new Latin American republics to achieve economic development than for the United States.

The Monroe Doctrine

John Quincy Adams, who was serving as James Monroe's secretary of state, was devoted to consolidating the power of the national government at home and abroad. Adams feared that Spain would try to regain its Latin American colonies. In 1823, he drafted a section of the president's annual message to Congress that became known as the **Monroe Doctrine**. It expressed three principles. First, the United States would oppose any further efforts at colonization by European powers in the Americas. Second, the United States would abstain from involvement in the wars of Europe. Finally, Monroe warned European powers not to interfere with the newly independent states of Latin America.

John Quincy Adams

The Monroe Doctrine is sometimes called America's diplomatic declaration of independence. For many decades, it remained a cornerstone of American foreign policy. Based on the assumption that the Old and New Worlds formed separate political and diplomatic systems, it claimed for the United States the role of dominant power in the Western Hemisphere.

America's diplomatic declaration of independence

The Election of 1824

The Monroe Doctrine reflected a rising sense of American nationalism. But sectionalism seemed to rule domestic politics. As the election of 1824 approached, only Andrew Jackson could claim truly national support. Jackson's popularity rested not on any specific public policy—few voters knew his views—but on military victories over the British at the Battle of New Orleans, and over the Creek and Seminole Indians. Other candidates included John Quincy Adams, Secretary of the Treasury William H. Crawford of Georgia, and Henry Clay of Kentucky. Adams's support was concentrated in New England and, more generally, in the North, where Republican leaders insisted the time had come for the South to relinquish the presidency. Crawford represented the South's Old Republicans, who wanted the party to reaffirm the principles of states' rights and limited government. Clay was one of the era's most popular politicians, but his support in 1824 lay primarily in the West.

Sectionalism and domestic politics

Jackson received 153,544 votes and carried states in all the regions outside of New England. But with four candidates in the field, none

A split election

NATION, SECTION, AND PARTY | 289

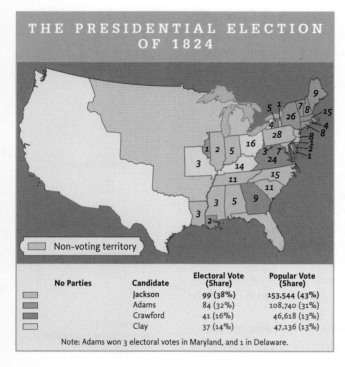

THE PRESIDENTIAL ELECTION OF 1824

Non-voting territory

No Parties	Candidate	Electoral Vote (Share)	Popular Vote (Share)
	Jackson	99 (38%)	153,544 (43%)
	Adams	84 (32%)	108,740 (31%)
	Crawford	41 (16%)	46,618 (13%)
	Clay	37 (14%)	47,136 (13%)

Note: Adams won 3 electoral votes in Maryland, and 1 in Delaware.

received a majority of the electoral votes. As required by the Constitution, Clay, who finished fourth, was eliminated, and the choice among the other three fell to the House of Representatives. Sincerely believing Adams to be the most qualified candidate and the one most likely to promote the American System, and probably calculating that the election of Jackson, a westerner, would impede his own presidential ambitions, Clay gave his support to Adams, helping to elect him. He soon became secretary of state in Adams's cabinet. The charge that he had made a "corrupt bargain"—bartering critical votes in the presidential contest for a public office—clung to Clay for the rest of his career, making it all but impossible for him to reach the White House. The election of 1824 laid the groundwork for a new system of political parties. Supporters of Jackson and Crawford would soon unite in the Democratic Party. The alliance of Clay and Adams became the basis for the Whig Party of the 1830s.

John Quincy Adams in an 1843 daguerreotype.

The Nationalism of John Quincy Adams

John Quincy Adams enjoyed one of the most distinguished pre-presidential careers of any American president. The son of John Adams, he had witnessed the Battle of Bunker Hill at age eight and at fourteen had worked as private secretary and French interpreter for an American envoy in Europe. He had gone on to serve as ambassador to Prussia, the Netherlands, Britain, and Russia, and as a senator from Massachusetts.

Adams was not an engaging figure. He described himself as "a man of cold, austere, and foreboding manners." But he had a clear vision of national greatness. At home, he strongly supported the American System of government-sponsored economic development. Abroad, he hoped to encourage American commerce throughout the world and, as illustrated by his authorship of the Monroe Doctrine, enhance American influence in the Western Hemisphere. An ardent expansionist, Adams was certain that the United States would eventually, and peacefully, absorb Canada, Cuba, and at least part of Mexico.

"Liberty Is Power"

Adams held a view of federal power far more expansive than did most of his contemporaries. In his first message to Congress, in December 1825, he set forth a comprehensive program for an activist national state. "The spirit of improvement is abroad in the land," Adams announced, and the federal government should be its patron. He called for legislation promoting agriculture, commerce, manufacturing, and "the mechanical and elegant arts." His plans included the establishment of a national university, an astronomical observatory, and a naval academy. At a time when many Americans felt that governmental authority posed the greatest threat to freedom, Adams astonished many listeners with the bold statement "Liberty is power."

Adams's nationalism

Adams's proposals alarmed all believers in strict construction of the Constitution. His administration spent more on internal improvements than those of his five predecessors combined, and it enacted a steep increase in tariff rates in 1828. But the rest of Adams's ambitious ideas received little support in Congress.

Martin Van Buren and the Democratic Party

Adams's program handed his political rivals a powerful weapon. With individual liberty, states' rights, and limited government as their rallying cries, Jackson's supporters began to organize for the election of 1828 almost as soon as Adams assumed office. Martin Van Buren, a senator from New York, supervised the task. The clash between Adams and Van Buren demonstrated how democracy was changing the nature of American politics. Adams typified the old politics—he was the son of a president and, like Jefferson and Madison, a man of sterling intellectual accomplishments. Van Buren represented the new political era. The son of a tavern keeper, he was a talented party manager, not a person of great vision or intellect.

The new politics

But Van Buren did have a compelling idea. Rather than being dangerous and divisive, as the founding generation had believed, political parties, he insisted, were necessary and desirable. Party competition provided a check on those in power and offered voters a real choice in elections. And by bringing together political leaders from different regions in support of common candidates and principles, national parties could counteract the sectionalism that had reared its head during the 1820s. National political parties, Van Buren realized, formed a bond of unity in a divided nation. He set out to reconstruct the Jeffersonian political alliance between "the planters of the South and the plain republicans [the farmers and urban workers] of the North."

Political parties as desirable

VOICES OF FREEDOM

By the 1820s, as political democracy expanded, only North Carolina, Rhode Island, and Virginia still required property qualifications for voting for white men. When Virginia held a constitutional convention in 1829–1830, "non-freeholders" of Richmond—men who did not possess enough property—petitioned for the right to vote. The major slaveholders who dominated Virginia politics resisted their demand; not until 1850 did the state eliminate the property qualification.

Your memorialists . . . belong to that class of citizens, who, not having the good fortune to possess a certain portion of land, are, for that cause only, debarred from the enjoyment of the right of suffrage. . . . Comprising a very large part, probably a majority of male citizens of mature age, they have been passed by, like aliens or slaves, as if . . . unworthy of a voice, in the measures involving their future political destiny. . . .

The existing regulation of the suffrage . . . creates an odious distinction between members of the same community; robs of all share, in the enactment of the laws, a large portion of the citizens, . . . and vests in a favored class, not in consideration of their public services, but of their private possessions, the highest of all privileges. . . . [We] cannot discern in the possession of land any evidence of peculiar merit, or superior title [to] moral or intellectual endowments. . . . Such possession no more proves him who has it, wiser or better, than it proves him taller or stronger, than him who has it not. . . .

Let us concede that the right of suffrage is a social right; that it must of necessity be regulated by society. . . . For obvious reasons, by almost universal consent, women and children, aliens and slaves, are excluded. . . . But the exclusion of these classes for reasons peculiarly applicable to them, is no argument for excluding others. . . .

They alone deserve to be called free, or have a guarantee for their rights, who participate in the formation of their political institutions, and in control of those who make and administer the law.

From Appeal of Forty Thousand Citizens Threatened with Disfranchisement (1838)

In many states, the expansion of political democracy for white men went hand in hand with the elimination of democratic participation for blacks. In 1837, a constitutional convention in Pennsylvania stripped black men of the right to vote. A large gathering in Philadelphia issued a protest to "fellow citizens" of Pennsylvania.

Fellow Citizens:—We appeal to you from the decision of the "Reform Convention," which has stripped us of a right peaceably enjoyed during forty-seven years under the Constitution of this commonwealth. We honor Pennsylvania and her noble institutions too much to part with our birthright, as her free citizens, without a struggle. To all her citizens the right of suffrage is valuable in proportion as she is free; but surely there are none who can so ill afford to spare it as ourselves. . . .

When a distinct class of the community, already sufficiently the objects of prejudice, are wholly, and for ever, disfranchised and excluded, to the remotest posterity, from the possibility of a voice in regard to the laws under which they are to live—it is the same thing as if their abode were transferred to the dominions of the Russian Autocrat, or of the Grand Turk. They have lost their check upon oppression, their wherewith to buy friends, their panoply of manhood; in short, they are thrown upon the mercy of a despotic majority. . . .

It was said in the Convention, that this government belongs to the Whites. We have already shown this to be false, as to the past. Those who established our present government designed it equally for all. It is for you to decide whether it shall be confined to the European complexion in future. Why should you exclude us from a fair participation in the benefits of the republic? . . . We put it to the conscience of every Pennsylvanian, whether there is, or ever has been, in the commonwealth, either a political party or religious sect which has less deserved than ourselves to be thus disfranchised. . . . If we are bad citizens let them apply the proper remedies. . . . Fair protection is all that we aspire to.

QUESTIONS

1. *What "obvious reasons" exclude women, children, noncitizens, and slaves from the right to vote?*

2. *How do the Philadelphia memorialists link their claims to the legacy of the American Revolution?*

3. *How similar are the definitions of political freedom in the two documents?*

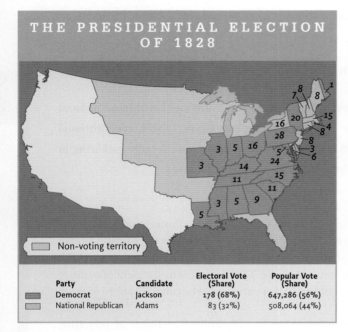

THE PRESIDENTIAL ELECTION OF 1828

Non-voting territory

Party	Candidate	Electoral Vote (Share)	Popular Vote (Share)
Democrat	Jackson	178 (68%)	647,286 (56%)
National Republican	Adams	83 (32%)	508,064 (44%)

The Election of 1828

By 1828, Van Buren had established the political apparatus of the Democratic Party, complete with local and state party units overseen by a national committee and a network of local newspapers devoted to the party and to the election of Andrew Jackson. Apart from a general commitment to limited government, Jackson's supporters made few campaign promises, relying on their candidate's popularity and the workings of party machinery to get out the vote. The 1828 election campaign was scurrilous. Jackson's supporters praised their candidate's frontier manliness and ridiculed Adams's intellectual attainments. ("Vote for Andrew Jackson who can fight, not John Quincy Adams who can write," declared one campaign slogan.) Jackson's opponents condemned him as a murderer for having executed army deserters and killing men in duels. They questioned the morality of his wife, Rachel, because she had married Jackson before her divorce from her first husband had become final.

Nearly 57 percent of the eligible electorate cast ballots, more than double the percentage four years earlier. Jackson won a resounding victory, carrying the entire South and West, along with Pennsylvania. His election was the first to demonstrate how the advent of universal white male voting, organized by national political parties, had transformed American politics. For better or worse, the United States had entered the Age of Jackson.

"The Old Democrat," a painting by Edward Hicks, illustrates the association of Andrew Jackson with nationalism and democracy.

THE AGE OF JACKSON

Andrew Jackson was a man of many contradictions. Although he had little formal education, Jackson was capable of genuine eloquence in his public statements. A self-proclaimed champion of the common man, he held a vision of democracy that excluded any role for Indians, whom he believed should be pushed west of the Mississippi River, and African-Americans, who should remain as slaves or be freed and sent abroad. A strong nationalist, Jackson nonetheless believed that the states, not Washington, D.C., should be the focal point of governmental activity.

The Party System

By the time of Jackson's presidency, politics had become more than a series of political contests—it was a spectacle, a form of mass entertainment, a part of Americans' daily lives. Every year witnessed elections to some office—local, state, or national—and millions took part in the parades and rallies organized by the parties. Politicians were popular heroes with mass followings and popular nicknames. Jackson was Old Hickory, Clay Harry of the West, and Van Buren the Little Magician (or, to his critics, the Sly Fox). Thousands of Americans willingly attended lengthy political orations and debates.

Politics and public life

Party machines, headed by professional politicians, reached into every neighborhood, especially in cities. They provided benefits like jobs to constituents and ensured that voters went to the polls on election day. Government posts, Jackson declared, should be open to the people, not reserved for a privileged class of permanent bureaucrats. He introduced the principle of rotation in office (called the **spoils system** by opponents) into national government, making loyalty to the party the main qualification for jobs like postmaster and customs official.

Professional politicians

Large national conventions where state leaders gathered to hammer out a platform now chose national candidates. Newspapers played a greater and greater role in politics. Every significant town, it seemed, had its Democratic and Whig papers whose job was not so much to report the news as to present the party's position on issues of the day. Jackson's Kitchen Cabinet—an informal group of advisers who helped to write his speeches and supervise communication between the White House and local party officials—mostly consisted of newspaper editors.

Role of newspapers

Democrats and Whigs

There was more to party politics, however, than spectacle and organization. Jacksonian politics revolved around issues spawned by the market revolution and the continuing tension between national and sectional loyalties.

Democrats on the issues

Democrats tended to be alarmed by the widening gap between social classes. They warned that "nonproducers"—bankers, merchants, and speculators—were seeking to use connections with government to enhance their wealth to the disadvantage of the "producing classes" of farmers, artisans, and laborers. They believed the government should adopt a hands-off attitude toward the economy and not award special favors to entrenched economic interests. This would enable ordinary Americans to test their abilities in the fair competition of the self-regulating market. The Democratic Party attracted aspiring entrepreneurs who resented government aid to established businessmen, as well as large numbers of farmers and city workingmen suspicious of new corporate enterprises. Poorer farming regions isolated from markets, like the lower Northwest and the southern backcountry, tended to vote Democratic.

Whigs on the issues

Whigs united behind the American System, believing that via a protective tariff, a national bank, and aid to internal improvements, the federal government could guide economic development. They were strongest in the Northeast, the most rapidly modernizing region of the country. Most established businessmen and bankers supported their program of government-promoted economic growth, as did farmers in regions near rivers, canals, and the Great Lakes, who benefited from economic changes or hoped to do so. The counties of upstate New York along the Erie Canal, for example, became a Whig stronghold, whereas more isolated rural communities tended to vote Democratic. Many slaveholders supported the Democrats, believing states' rights to be slavery's first line of defense. But like well-to-do merchants and industrialists in the North, the largest southern planters generally voted Whig.

Public and Private Freedom

The party battles of the Jacksonian era reflected the clash between "public" and "private" definitions of American freedom and their relationship to governmental power, a persistent tension in the nation's history. For Democrats, liberty was a set of private rights best secured by local governments and endangered by powerful national authority. "The limitation of power, in every branch of our government," wrote a Democratic newspaper in 1842, The Democrats: power a threat to liberty "is the only safeguard of liberty." During Jackson's presidency, Democrats reduced expenditures, lowered the tariff, killed the national bank, and refused pleas for federal aid to internal improvements. By 1835, Jackson even managed to pay off the national debt. As a result, states replaced the federal government as the country's main economic actors, planning systems of canals and roads and chartering banks and other corporations.

Democrats, moreover, considered individual morality a private matter, not a public concern. They opposed attempts to impose a unified moral vision on society, such as "temperance" legislation, which restricted or outlawed the production and sale of liquor, and laws prohibiting various kinds of entertainment on Sundays. "In this country," declared the New York *Journal of Commerce* in 1848, "liberty is understood to be the *absence* of government from private affairs."

Whigs, for their part, insisted that liberty and power reinforced each other. An activist national government could enhance the realm of freedom. The government, Whigs believed, should create the conditions for balanced and regulated economic development, thereby promoting a prosperity in which all classes and regions would share.

The Whigs: power allied with liberty

Whigs, moreover, rejected the premise that the government must not interfere in private life. To function as free—that is, self-directed and self-disciplined—moral agents, individuals required certain character traits, which government could help to instill. Many evangelical Protestants supported the Whigs, convinced that via public education, the building of schools and asylums, temperance legislation, and the like, democratic governments could inculcate the "principles of morality." And during the Jacksonian era, popularly elected local authorities enacted numerous laws, ordinances, and regulations that tried to shape public morals by banning prostitution and the consumption of alcohol, and regulating other kinds of personal behavior.

Government and private life

Shaping public morals

South Carolina and Nullification

Andrew Jackson, it has been said, left office with many more principles than he came in with. Elected as a military hero backed by an efficient party machinery, he was soon forced to define his stance on public issues. Despite his commitment to states' rights, Jackson's first term was dominated by a battle to uphold the supremacy of federal over state law. The tariff of 1828, which raised taxes on imported manufactured goods made of wool as well as on raw materials such as iron, had aroused considerable opposition in the South, nowhere more than in South Carolina, where it was called the **tariff of abominations**. The state's leaders no longer believed it possible or desirable to compete with the North in industrial development. Insisting that the tariff on imported manufactured goods raised the prices paid by southern consumers to benefit the North, the legislature threatened to "nullify" it—that is, declare it null and void within their state.

The south and the "tariff of abominations"

The state with the largest proportion of slaves in its population (55 percent in 1830), South Carolina was controlled by a tightly knit group of large planters. They maintained their grip on power by a state constitution that gave plantation counties far greater representation in the legislature than their population warranted, as well as through high property qualifications for officeholders. Behind their economic complaints

John C. Calhoun, who evolved from a nationalist into the most prominent spokesman for state sovereignty and the right of nullification, in an 1845 portrait by George P. A. Healy.

against the tariff lay the conviction that the federal government must be weakened lest it one day take action against slavery.

Calhoun's Political Theory

John C. Calhoun soon emerged as the leading theorist of nullification. As the South began to fall behind the rest of the country in population, Calhoun had evolved from the nationalist of 1812 into a powerful defender of southern sectionalism. Having been elected vice president in 1828, Calhoun at first remained behind the scenes, secretly drafting the *Exposition and Protest* in which the South Carolina legislature justified nullification. The national government, Calhoun insisted, had been created by an agreement, or compact, among sovereign states, each of which retained the right to prevent the enforcement within its borders of acts of Congress that exceeded the powers specifically spelled out in the Constitution.

Almost from the beginning of Jackson's first term, Calhoun's influence in the administration waned, while Secretary of State Martin Van Buren emerged as the president's closest adviser. One incident that helped set Jackson against Calhoun occurred a few weeks after the inauguration. Led by Calhoun's wife, Floride, Washington society women ostracized Peggy Eaton, the wife of Jackson's secretary of war, because she was the daughter of a Washington tavern keeper and, allegedly, a woman of "easy virtue." Jackson identified the criticism of Peggy Eaton with the abuse his own wife had suffered during the campaign of 1828.

Far weightier matters soon divided Jackson and Calhoun. Debate over nullification raged in Washington. In a memorable exchange in the Senate in January 1830 that came to be known as the **Webster-Hayne debate**, Daniel Webster, a senator from Massachusetts, responded to South Carolina senator Robert Y. Hayne, a disciple of Calhoun. The people, not the states, declared Webster, created the Constitution, making the federal government sovereign. He called nullification illegal, unconstitutional, and treasonous. Webster's ending was widely hailed throughout the country—"Liberty *and* Union, now and forever, one and inseparable." A few weeks later, at a White House dinner, Jackson delivered a toast while fixing his gaze on Calhoun: "Our Federal Union—it must be preserved." Calhoun's reply came immediately: "The Union—next to our liberty most dear." By 1831, Calhoun had publicly emerged as the leading theorist of states' rights.

Webster-Hayne debate

The Nullification Crisis

Nullification was not a purely sectional issue. South Carolina stood alone during the **nullification crisis**, and several southern states passed resolutions condemning its action. Nonetheless, the elaboration of the compact theory of the Constitution gave the South a well-developed political philosophy to which it would turn when sectional conflict became more intense.

To Jackson, nullification amounted to nothing less than disunion. He dismissed Calhoun's constitutional arguments out of hand: "Can anyone of common sense believe the absurdity, that a faction of any state, or a state, has a right to secede and destroy this union, and the liberty of the country with it?" The issue came to a head in 1832, when a new tariff was enacted. Despite a reduction in rates, South Carolina declared the tax on imported goods null and void in the state after the following February. In response, Jackson persuaded Congress to pass a Force Act authorizing him to use the army and navy to collect customs duties. To avert a confrontation, Henry Clay, with Calhoun's assistance, engineered the passage of a new tariff, in 1833, further reducing duties. South Carolina then rescinded the ordinance of nullification, although it proceeded to "nullify" the **Force Act**. Calhoun abandoned the Democratic Party for the Whigs, where, with Clay and Webster, he became part of a formidable trio of political leaders (even though the three agreed on virtually nothing except hostility toward Jackson).

Jackson's stance

South Carolina and the tariff of 1832

Indian Removal

The nullification crisis underscored Jackson's commitment to the sovereignty of the nation. His exclusion of Indians from the era's assertive democratic nationalism led to the final act in the centuries-long conflict between white Americans and Indians east of the Mississippi River. In the slave states, the onward march of cotton cultivation placed enormous pressure on remaining Indian holdings. One of the early laws of Jackson's administration, the **Indian Removal Act** of 1830, provided funds for uprooting the so-called Five Civilized Tribes—the Cherokee, Chickasaw, Choctaw, Creek, and Seminole—with a population of around 60,000 living in North Carolina, Georgia, Florida, Alabama, and Mississippi.

Indian Removal Act of 1830

The law marked a repudiation of the Jeffersonian idea that "civilized" Indians could be assimilated into the American population. These tribes had made great efforts to become everything republican citizens should be. The Cherokee had taken the lead, establishing schools, adopting written laws and a constitution modeled on that of the United States, and becoming successful farmers, many of whom owned slaves. But in his messages to Congress, Jackson repeatedly referred to them as "savages" and supported Georgia's effort to seize Cherokee land and nullify the tribe's laws.

Shift in Indian policy

In 1832, the "headmen and warriors of the Creek nation" sent a memorial to Congress that dwelled on the meaning of freedom and what they considered oppression by Alabama's lawmakers. "We never have been

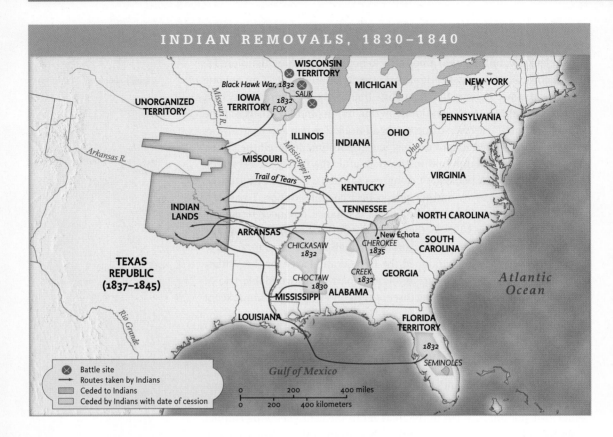

INDIAN REMOVALS, 1830–1840

The removal of the so-called Five Civilized Tribes from the Southeast all but ended the Indian presence east of the Mississippi River.

slaves," they proclaimed, "we have been born free. As freemen we have assisted in fighting the battles of our white brethren." Yet now their people were being "subjected to the penalties of forfeiture" of their land. The Creeks were claiming a place in the nation's life, but unlike their white contemporaries, identification with their own "nation" came before identity as Americans. And freedom meant maintaining their cultural independence, which, in turn, required keeping possession of ancestral lands.

In good American fashion, Cherokee leaders went to court to protect their rights, guaranteed in treaties with the federal government. Their appeals forced the Supreme Court to clarify the unique status of American Indians.

The Supreme Court and the Indians

In a crucial case involving Indians in 1823, *Johnson v. M'Intosh*, the Court had proclaimed that Indians were not in fact owners of their land but merely had a "right of occupancy." Chief Justice John Marshall declared that from the early

"Right of occupancy"

colonial era, Indians had lived as nomads and hunters, not farmers. Entirely inaccurate as history, the decision struck a serious blow against Indian efforts to retain their lands. In *Cherokee Nation v. Georgia* (1831), Marshall described Indians as "wards" of the federal government. They deserved paternal regard and protection, but they lacked the standing as citizens that would allow the Supreme Court to enforce their rights. The justices could not, therefore, block Georgia's effort to extend its jurisdiction over the tribe.

Marshall, however, believed strongly in the supremacy of the federal government over the states. In 1832, in **Worcester v. Georgia**, the Court seemed to change its mind, holding that Indian nations were a distinct people with the right to maintain a separate political identity. They must be dealt with by the federal government, not the states, and Georgia's actions violated the Cherokees' treaties with Washington. Jackson, however, refused to recognize the validity of the *Worcester* ruling. "John Marshall has made his decision," he supposedly declared, "now let him enforce it."

With legal appeals exhausted, one faction of the tribe agreed to cede their lands, but the majority, led by John Ross, who had been elected "principal chief" under the Cherokee constitution, adopted a policy of passive resistance. Federal soldiers forcibly removed them during the presidency of Jackson's successor, Martin Van Buren. The army herded 18,000 Cherokee men, women, and children into stockades and then forced them to move west. At least one-quarter perished during the winter of 1838–1839 on the **Trail of Tears**, as the removal route from Georgia to present-day Oklahoma came to be called. (In the Cherokee language, it literally meant "the trail on which we cried.")

During the 1830s, most of the other southern tribes bowed to the inevitable and departed peacefully. But with the assistance of escaped slaves, the Seminoles of sparsely settled Florida resisted. In the Second Seminole War, which lasted from 1835 to 1842 (the first had preceded American acquisition of Florida in 1819), some 1,500 American soldiers and the same number of Seminoles were killed, and perhaps 3,000 Indians and 500 blacks were forced to move to the West. A small number of Seminoles managed to remain in Florida, a tiny remnant of the once sizable Indian population east of the Mississippi River.

Removal of the Indians powerfully reinforced the racial definition of American nationhood and freedom. At the time of independence, Indians had been a familiar presence in many parts of the United States. But by 1840, in the eyes of most whites east of the Mississippi River, they were simply a curiosity, a relic of an earlier period of American history. Although Indians still dominated

A lithograph from 1836 depicts Sequoia, with the alphabet of the Cherokee language that he developed. Because of their written language and constitution, the Cherokee were considered by many white Americans to be a "civilized tribe."

John Mix Stanley painted Native Americans engaged in a buffalo hunt on the western prairies in 1845.

The Last of the Race, by Tompkins Harrison Matteson, depicts a Native American family looking out at the Pacific Ocean, having been pushed westward by the inexorable tide of white settlement. Matteson, like Stanley, saw himself as recording a vanishing way of life.

the trans-Mississippi West, as American settlement pushed relentlessly westward it was clear that their days of freedom there also were numbered.

THE BANK WAR AND AFTER

Biddle's Bank

The central political struggle of the Age of Jackson was the president's war on the Bank of the United States. The Bank symbolized the hopes and fears inspired by the market revolution. The expansion of banking helped to finance the nation's economic development. But many Americans, including Jackson, distrusted bankers as "nonproducers" who contributed nothing to the nation's wealth but profited from the labor of others. The tendency of banks to overissue paper money, whose deterioration in value reduced the real income of wage earners, reinforced this conviction.

Distrust of banks

Heading the Bank was Nicholas Biddle of Pennsylvania, who during the 1820s had effectively used the institution's power to curb the overissuing of money by local banks and to create a stable currency throughout the nation. A snobbish, aristocratic Philadelphian, Biddle was as strong-willed as Jackson and as unwilling to back down in a fight. In 1832, he told a congressional committee that his Bank had the ability to "destroy" any state bank. He hastened to add that he had never "injured" any of them. But Democrats wondered whether any

Nicholas Biddle

The Downfall of Mother Bank, a Democratic cartoon celebrating the destruction of the Second Bank of the United States. President Andrew Jackson topples the building by brandishing his order removing federal funds from the Bank. Led by Nicholas Biddle, with the head of a demon, the Bank's corrupt supporters flee, among them Henry Clay, Daniel Webster, and newspaper editors allegedly paid by the institution.

institution, public or private, ought to possess such power. Many called it the Monster Bank, an illegitimate union of political authority and entrenched economic privilege. The issue of the Bank's future came to a head in 1832. Although the institution's charter would not expire until 1836, Biddle's allies persuaded Congress to approve a bill extending it for another twenty years. Jackson saw the tactic as a form of blackmail—if he did not sign the bill, the Bank would use its considerable resources to oppose his reelection.

Jackson's veto message is perhaps the central document of his presidency. In a democratic government, Jackson insisted, it was unacceptable for Congress to create a source of concentrated power and economic privilege unaccountable to the people. "It is to be regretted," he declared, "that the rich and powerful too often bend the acts of government to their selfish purposes." Exclusive privileges like the Bank's charter widened the gap between the wealthy and "the humble members of society—the farmers, mechanics, and laborers." Jackson presented himself as the defender of these "humble" Americans.

Jackson's veto of the bank bill

The **Bank War** reflected how Jackson enhanced the power of the presidency during his eight years in office, proclaiming himself the symbolic representative of all the people. He was the first president to use the veto power as a major weapon and to appeal directly to the public for political support, over the head of Congress. Whigs denounced him for usurping the power of the legislature. But Jackson's effective appeal to democratic popular sentiments helped him win a sweeping reelection victory in 1832 over the Whig candidate, Henry Clay. His victory ensured the death of the Bank of the United States.

Enhancing the power of the presidency

Pet Banks, the Economy, and the Panic of 1837

What, however, would take the Bank's place? Two very different groups applauded Jackson's veto—state bankers who wished to free themselves from Biddle's regulations and issue more paper currency (called **soft money**), **and hard money** advocates who opposed all banks and believed that gold and silver formed the only reliable currency. Not content to wait for the charter of the Bank of the United States to expire in 1836, Jackson authorized the removal of federal funds from its vaults and their deposit in select local banks. Not surprisingly, political and personal connections often determined the choice of these **pet banks**. Two secretaries of the Treasury refused to transfer federal money to the pet banks, since the law creating the Bank had specified that government funds could not be removed except for a good cause as communicated to Congress. Jackson finally appointed Attorney General Roger B. Taney, a loyal Maryland Democrat, to the Treasury post, and he carried out the order. When John Marshall died in 1835, Jackson rewarded Taney by appointing him chief justice.

Jackson's pet banks

Without government deposits, the Bank of the United States lost its ability to regulate the activities of state banks. The value of bank notes in circulation rose from $10 million in 1833 to $149 million in 1837. As prices rose dramatically, "real wages"—the actual value of workers' pay—declined. Numerous labor unions emerged, which attempted to protect the earnings of urban workers. Meanwhile, speculators hastened to cash in on rising land prices. Using paper money, they bought up huge blocks of public land, which they resold to farmers or to eastern purchasers of lots in entirely nonexistent western towns.

Consequences of the removal of federal deposits

Inevitably, the speculative boom collapsed. The government sold 20 million acres of federal land in 1836, ten times the amount sold in 1830, nearly all of it paid for in paper money, often of questionable value. In July 1836, the Jackson administration issued the Specie Circular, declaring that henceforth it would only accept gold and silver as payment for public land. At the same time, the Bank of England, increasingly suspicious about the value of American bank notes, demanded that American merchants pay their creditors in London in gold or silver. Then, an economic downturn in Britain dampened demand for American cotton, the country's major export.

The Specie Circular

Taken together, these events triggered an economic collapse in the United States, the **Panic of 1837**, followed by a depression that lasted to 1843. Businesses throughout the country failed, and many farmers, unable to meet mortgage payments because of declining income, lost their land. Tens of thousands of urban workers saw their jobs disappear. The fledgling labor movement collapsed as strikes became impossible, given the surplus of unemployed labor.

Economic collapse

The Times, an 1837 engraving that blames Andrew Jackson's policies for the economic depression. The Custom House is idle, while next door a bank is mobbed by worried depositors. Beneath Jackson's hat, spectacles, and clay pipe (with the ironic word "glory"), images of hardship abound.

Van Buren in Office

The president forced to deal with the depression was Martin Van Buren, who had been elected in 1836 over three regional candidates put forward by the Whigs. Under Van Buren, the hard-money, anti-bank wing of the Democratic Party came to power. In 1837, the administration announced its intention to remove federal funds from the pet banks and hold them in the Treasury Department in Washington, under the control of government officials. Not until 1840 did Congress approve the new policy, known as the Independent Treasury, which completely separated the federal government from the nation's banking system. It would be repealed in 1841 when the Whigs returned to power, but it was reinstated under President James K. Polk in 1846.

The Independent Treasury

The Election of 1840

Despite his reputation as a political magician, Van Buren found that without Jackson's personal popularity he could not hold the Democratic coalition together. In 1840, he also discovered that his Whig opponents had mastered the political techniques he had helped to pioneer. Confronting an unprecedented opportunity for victory because of the continuing economic depression, the Whigs abandoned their most prominent leader, Henry Clay, and nominated William Henry Harrison. Harrison's main claim to fame was military success against the British and Indians during the War of 1812.

The party nominated Harrison without a platform. In a flood of publications, banners, parades, and mass meetings, they promoted him as

THE ALMIGHTY LEVER

A political cartoon from the 1840 presidential campaign shows public opinion as the "almighty lever" of politics in a democracy. Under the gaze of the American eagle, "Loco-Foco" Democrats slide into an abyss, while the people are poised to lift William Henry Harrison, the Whig candidate, to victory.

the "log cabin" candidate, the champion of the common man. This tactic proved enormously effective, even though it bore little relationship to the actual life of the wealthy Harrison. His running mate was John Tyler, a states'-rights Democrat from Virginia who had joined the Whigs after the nullification crisis and did not follow Calhoun back to the Democrats. On almost every issue of political significance, Tyler held views totally opposed to those of other Whigs. But party leaders hoped he could expand their base in the South.

By 1840, the mass democratic politics of the Age of Jackson had absorbed the logic of the marketplace. Selling candidates and their images was as important as the positions for which they stood. With two highly organized parties competing throughout the country, voter turnout soared to 80 percent of those eligible. Harrison won a sweeping victory. "We have taught them how to conquer us," lamented a Democratic newspaper.

Whig success proved short-lived. Immediately on assuming office, Harrison contracted pneumonia. He died a month later, and John Tyler succeeded him. When the Whig majority in Congress tried to enact the American System into law, Tyler vetoed nearly every measure, including a new national bank and higher tariff. Most of the cabinet resigned, and his party repudiated him. Tyler's four years in office were nearly devoid of accomplishment. If the campaign that resulted in the election of Harrison demonstrated how a flourishing system of democratic politics had come into existence, Tyler's lack of success showed that political parties had become central to American government. Without a party behind him, a president could not govern. But a storm was now gathering that would test the stability of American democracy and the statesmanship of its political leaders and of the party system itself.

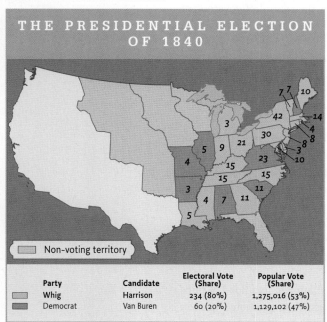

THE PRESIDENTIAL ELECTION OF 1840

Non-voting territory

Party	Candidate	Electoral Vote (Share)	Popular Vote (Share)
Whig	Harrison	234 (80%)	1,275,016 (53%)
Democrat	Van Buren	60 (20%)	1,129,102 (47%)

CHAPTER REVIEW AND ONLINE RESOURCES

REVIEW QUESTIONS

1. *What global changes prompted the Monroe Doctrine? What were its key provisions? How does it show America's growing international presence?*

2. *How did Andrew Jackson represent the major developments of the era: westward movement, the market revolution, and the expansion of democracy for some alongside the limits on it for others?*

3. *How did the expansion of white male democracy run counter to the ideals of the founders, who believed government should be sheltered from excessive influence by ordinary people?*

4. *What were the components of the American System, and how were they designed to promote the national economy under the guidance of the federal government?*

5. *How did the Missouri Compromise and the nullification crisis demonstrate increasing sectional competition and disagreements over slavery?*

6. *According to Martin Van Buren, why were political parties a desirable element of public life? What did he do to build the party system?*

7. *What rights did the Creek nation seek to confirm in its 1832 memorial to Congress?*

8. *What were the major economic, humanitarian, political, and social arguments for and against Indian Removal?*

9. *What were the key issues that divided the Democratic and Whig Parties? Where did each party stand on those issues?*

10. *Explain the causes and effects of the Panic of 1837.*

KEY TERMS

the Dorr War (p. 281)
Democracy in America (p. 281)
franchise (p. 284)
American System (p. 285)
tariff of 1816 (p. 285)
Panic of 1819 (p. 286)
McCulloch v. Maryland (p. 286)
Era of Good Feelings (p. 287)
Missouri Compromise (p. 288)
Monroe Doctrine (p. 289)
spoils system (p. 295)
tariff of abominations (p. 297)
Exposition and Protest (p. 298)
Webster-Hayne debate (p. 298)
nullification crisis (p. 298)
Force Act (p. 299)
Indian Removal Act (p. 299)
Worcester v. Georgia (p. 301)
Trail of Tears (p. 301)
Bank War (p. 303)
soft money and hard money
   (p. 304)
pet banks (p. 304)
Panic of 1837 (p. 304)

Go to **INQUIZITIVE**

To see what you know—and learn what you've missed—with personalized feedback along the way.

Visit the *Give Me Liberty!* **Student Site** for primary source documents and images, interactive maps, author videos featuring Eric Foner, and more.

CHAPTER 11

THE PECULIAR INSTITUTION

★

This image of the Portuguese slave ship *Diligente* was painted by an officer on a British naval vessel in 1838. By this time, the *Diligente*'s voyage—with 600 slaves on board—was illegal. The international agreement outlawing the Atlantic slave trade was largely enforced by British ships.

I

n an age of "self-made" men, no American rose more dramatically from humble origins to national and international distinction than Frederick Douglass. Born into slavery in 1818, he became a major figure in the crusade for abolition, the drama of emancipation, and the effort during Reconstruction to give meaning to black freedom.

Douglass was the son of a slave mother and an unidentified white man, possibly his owner. As a youth in Maryland, he gazed out at the ships in Chesapeake Bay, seeing them as "freedom's swift-winged angels." In violation of Maryland law, Douglass learned to read and write, initially with the assistance of his owner's wife and then, after her husband forbade her to continue, with the help of local white children. "From that moment," he later wrote, he understood that knowledge was "the pathway from slavery to freedom." In 1838, having borrowed the free papers of a black sailor, he escaped to the North.

Frederick Douglass went on to become the most influential African-American of the nineteenth century and the nation's preeminent advocate of racial equality. He also published a widely read autobiography that offered an eloquent condemnation of slavery and racism. Indeed, his own accomplishments testified to the incorrectness of prevailing ideas about blacks' inborn inferiority. Douglass was also active in other reform movements, including the campaign for women's rights. Douglass argued that in their desire for freedom, the slaves were truer to the nation's underlying principles than the white Americans who annually celebrated the Fourth of July while allowing the continued existence of slavery.

FOCUS QUESTIONS

• *How did slavery shape social and economic relations in the Old South?*

• *What were the legal and material constraints on slaves' lives and work?*

• *How did a distinct slave culture emerge in the Old South?*

• *What were the major forms of resistance to slavery?*

THE OLD SOUTH

When Frederick Douglass was born, slavery was already an old institution in America. Two centuries had passed since the first twenty Africans were landed in Virginia from a Dutch ship. After abolition in the North, slavery had become **the "peculiar institution"** of the South—that is, an institution unique to southern society. The Mason-Dixon Line, drawn by two surveyors in the eighteenth century to settle a boundary dispute between Maryland and Pennsylvania, eventually became the dividing line between slavery and freedom.

Mason-Dixon Line

Despite the hope of some of the founders that slavery might die out, in fact the institution survived the crisis of the American Revolution and rapidly expanded westward. On the eve of the Civil War, the slave population had risen to nearly 4 million, its high rate of natural increase more than making up for the prohibition in 1808 of further slave imports from Africa. In the South as a whole, slaves made up one-third of the total population,

The expansion of slavery

and in the cotton-producing states of the Lower South, around half. By the 1850s, slavery had crossed the Mississippi River and was expanding rapidly in Arkansas, Louisiana, and eastern Texas.

Cotton Is King

Rise of cotton

In the nineteenth century, cotton replaced sugar as the world's major crop produced by slave labor. And although slavery survived in Brazil and the Spanish and French Caribbean, its abolition in the British empire in 1833 made the United States indisputably the center of New World slavery.

Because the early industrial revolution centered on factories using cotton as the raw material to manufacture cloth, cotton became by far the most important commodity in international trade. And three-fourths of the world's cotton supply came from the southern United States. Textile manufacturers in places as far flung as Massachusetts, Lancashire in Great Britain, Normandy in France, and the suburbs of Moscow depended on a regular supply of American cotton.

Cotton sales earned the money from abroad that allowed the United States to pay for imported manufactured goods. On the eve of the Civil War, cotton accounted for well over half of the total value of American exports.

Economic value of slavery

In 1860, the economic investment represented by the slave population exceeded the value of the nation's factories, railroads, and banks combined.

The Second Middle Passage

As noted in Chapter 9, to replace the slave trade from Africa, which had been prohibited by Congress in 1808, a massive trade in slaves developed within the United States. More than 2 million slaves were sold between 1820 and 1860, resulting in what came to be known as the **Second Middle Passage**. The main commercial districts of southern cities contained the offices of slave traders, complete with signs reading "Negro Sales" or "Negroes Bought Here." Auctions of slaves took place at public slave markets, as in New Orleans, or at courthouses. Southern newspapers carried advertisements

Texan Farm in Montgomery County, a drawing from 1843, depicts a cotton farm on the Texas frontier. The owner's house is at the center, flanked by slave cabins and, on the far right, a cotton gin and press. At this point, two years before its annexation by the United States, Texas was an independent republic.

HAULING THE WHOLE WEEK8 'PICKING

In this painting from 1842, slaves—men, women, and children—accompany an oxcart carrying the week's cotton crop to New Orleans.

for slave sales, southern banks financed slave trading, southern ships and railroads carried slaves from buyers to sellers, and southern states and municipalities earned revenue by taxing the sale of slaves.

Slave trade in the South

Slavery and the Nation

Slavery shaped the lives of all Americans, white as well as black. It helped to determine where they lived, how they worked, and under what conditions they could exercise their freedoms of speech, assembly, and the press.

Northern merchants and manufacturers participated in the slave economy and shared in its profits. Money earned in the cotton trade helped to finance industrial development and internal improvements in the North. Northern ships carried cotton to New York and Europe, northern bankers financed cotton plantations, northern companies insured slave property, and northern factories turned cotton into cloth. New York City's rise to commercial prominence depended as much on the establishment of shipping lines that gathered the South's cotton and transported it to Europe as on the Erie Canal.

The Southern Economy

There was no single South before the Civil War. In the eight slave states of the Upper South, slaves and slaveowners made up a smaller percentage of the total population than in the seven Lower South states, which stretched from South Carolina west to Texas. The Upper South had major centers of industry in Baltimore, Richmond, and St. Louis, and its economy was more diversified than that of the Lower South, which was heavily dependent on cotton.

TABLE 11.1 Growth of the Slave Population

YEAR	SLAVE POPULATION
1790	697,624
1800	893,602
1810	1,191,362
1820	1,538,022
1830	2,009,043
1840	2,487,355
1850	3,204,313
1860	3,953,760

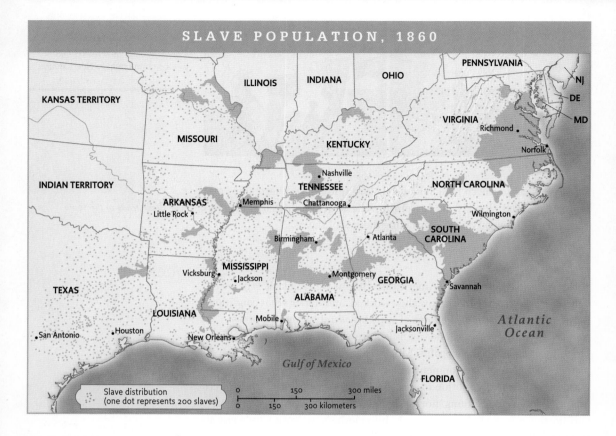

SLAVE POPULATION, 1860

Slave distribution
(one dot represents 200 slaves)

0   150   300 miles
0   150   300 kilometers

Rather than being evenly distributed throughout the South, the slave population was concentrated in areas with the most fertile soil and easiest access to national and international markets. By 1860, a significant percentage of the slave population had been transported from the Atlantic coast to the Lower South via the internal slave trade.

Not surprisingly, during the secession crisis of 1860–1861, the Lower South states were the first to leave the Union.

Nonetheless, slavery led the South down a very different path of economic development than the North's, limiting the growth of industry, discouraging immigrants from entering the region, and inhibiting technological progress. The South did not share in the urban growth experienced by the rest of the country. In the Cotton Kingdom, the only city of significant size was New Orleans. With a population of 168,000 in 1860, New Orleans ranked as the nation's sixth-largest city. As the gathering point for cotton grown along the Mississippi River and sugar from the plantations of southeastern Louisiana, it was the world's leading exporter of slave-grown crops.

In 1860, the South produced less than 10 percent of the nation's manufactured goods. Many northerners viewed slavery as an obstacle to American economic progress. But as New Orleans showed, slavery and economic growth could go hand in hand. In general, the southern economy was hardly stagnant, and slavery proved very profitable for most owners. The profits produced by slavery for the South and the nation as a whole

This 1860 view of New Orleans captures the size and scale of the cotton trade in the South's largest city. More than 3,500 steamboats arrived in New Orleans in 1860.

formed a powerful obstacle to abolition. Senator James Henry Hammond of South Carolina declared, "No power on earth dares to make war upon it. **Cotton is king**."

Plain Folk of the Old South

The foundation of the Old South's economy, slavery powerfully shaped race relations, politics, religion, and the law. Its influence was pervasive: "Nothing escaped," writes one historian, "nothing and no one." This was true despite the fact that the majority of white southerners—three out of four white families—owned no slaves. Many southern farmers lived outside the plantation belt in hilly areas unsuitable for cotton production. Using family labor, they raised livestock and grew food for their own use, purchasing relatively few goods at local stores. Unlike northern farmers, therefore, they did not provide a market for manufactured goods. This was one of the main reasons that the South did not develop an industrial base.

Some poorer whites resented the power and privileges of the great planters. Politicians such as Andrew Johnson of Tennessee and Joseph Brown of Georgia rose to power as self-proclaimed spokesmen of the common man against the "slavocracy." But most poor whites made their peace with the planters in whose hands economic and social power was concentrated. Racism, kinship ties, common participation in a democratic political culture, and regional loyalty in the face

An upcountry family, dressed in homespun, in Cedar Mountain, Virginia. Many white families in the pre–Civil War South were largely isolated from the market economy. This photograph was taken in 1862 but reflects the prewar way of life.

of outside criticism all served to cement bonds between planters and the South's "plain folk." Like other white southerners, most small farmers believed their economic and personal freedom rested on slavery.

The Planter Class

Even among slaveholders, the planter was far from typical. In 1850, a majority of slaveholding families owned five or fewer slaves. Fewer than 40,000 families possessed the twenty or more slaves that qualified them as planters. Fewer than 2,000 families owned a hundred slaves or more. Nonetheless, the planter's values and aspirations dominated southern life. The plantation, wrote Frederick Douglass, was "a little nation by itself, with its own language, its own rules, regulations, and customs." These rules and customs set the tone for southern society.

Slave ownership and status

Ownership of slaves provided the route to wealth, status, and influence. Planters not only held the majority of slaves but also controlled the most fertile land, enjoyed the highest incomes, and dominated state and local offices and the leadership of both political parties. Slavery, of course, was a profit-making system, and slaveowners kept close watch on world prices for their products, invested in enterprises such as railroads and canals, and carefully supervised their plantations. Their wives—the "plantation mistresses" idealized in southern lore for femininity, beauty, and dependence on men—were hardly idle. They cared for sick slaves, directed the domestic servants, and supervised the entire plantation when their husbands were away. Of course, owners' sexual exploitation of slave women produced deep resentment among their wives, who sometimes took it out on the slaves themselves.

On the cotton frontier, many planters lived in crude log homes. But in the older slave states, and as settled society developed in the Lower South, they constructed elegant mansions adorned with white columns in the Greek Revival style of architecture.

The Paternalist Ethos

The slave plantation was deeply embedded in the world market, and planters sought to accumulate land, slaves, and profits. However, planters' values glorified not the competitive capitalist marketplace but a hierarchical, agrarian society in which slaveholding gentlemen took personal responsibility for the physical and moral well-being of their dependents—women, children, and slaves.

This outlook, known as **paternalism** (from the Latin word for "father"), had been a feature of American slavery even in the eighteenth century. But it became more ingrained after the closing of the African slave

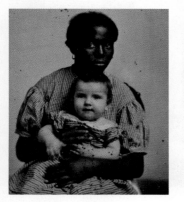

Louisa, a slave woman, with her charge in an 1858 photograph. The slave had been purchased at age twenty-two at a slave auction in New Orleans to serve as a nursemaid. Because of a death in the white family, the child was her legal owner.

trade in 1808, which narrowed the cultural gap between master and slave. Unlike the absentee planters of the West Indies, many of whom resided in Great Britain, southern slaveholders lived on their plantations and thus had year-round contact with their slaves.

The paternalist outlook both masked and justified the brutal reality of slavery. It enabled slaveowners to think of themselves as kind, responsible masters even as they bought and sold their human property—a practice at odds with the claim that slaves formed part of the master's "family."

The Proslavery Argument

In the thirty years before the outbreak of the Civil War, even as northern criticism of the "peculiar institution" began to deepen, proslavery thought came to dominate southern public life. Even those who had no direct stake in slavery shared with planters a deep commitment to white supremacy. Indeed, racism—the belief that blacks were innately inferior to whites and unsuited for life in any condition other than slavery—formed one pillar of the **proslavery argument**. Most slaveholders also found legitimation for slavery in biblical passages such as the injunction that servants should obey their masters. Others argued that slavery was essential to human progress. Without slavery, they believed, planters would be unable to cultivate the arts, sciences, and other civilized pursuits.

White southerners thought slavery was "modern," in tune with the times. Despite British emancipation, other forms of unfree labor were spreading in the world. The products of slave labor, especially cotton, were essential to the nineteenth-century economy. Southern planters were hardly parochial. They took a deep interest in international affairs. They felt a community of interest with owners in Cuba and Brazil and used their power in the federal government to insist that American foreign policy promote the interests of slavery throughout the hemisphere.

Still other defenders of slavery insisted that the institution guaranteed equality for whites by preventing the growth of a class doomed to a life of unskilled labor. Like

A slave dealer's place of business in Alexandria, Virginia, then part of the District of Columbia, the nation's capital. The buying and selling of slaves was a regularized part of the southern economy, and such businesses were a common sight in every southern city. This building contained a "slave pen" that typically contained over 300 slaves being kept before their sale.

TABLE 11.2 Slaveholding, 1850 (in Round Numbers)	
NUMBER OF SLAVES OWNED	SLAVEHOLDERS
1	68,000
2–4	105,000
5–9	80,000
10–19	55,000
20–49	30,000
50–99	6,000
100–199	1,500
200+	250

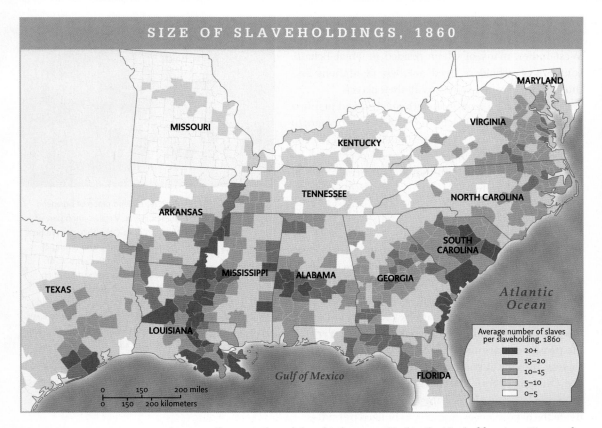

SIZE OF SLAVEHOLDINGS, 1860

Average number of slaves
per slaveholding, 1860
- 20+
- 15–20
- 10–15
- 5–10
- 0–5

Most southern slaveholders owned fewer than five slaves. The largest plantations were concentrated in coastal South Carolina and along the Mississippi River.

northerners, they claimed to be committed to the ideal of freedom. Slavery for blacks, they declared, was the surest guarantee of "perfect equality" among whites, liberating them from the "low, menial" jobs such as factory labor and domestic service performed by wage laborers in the North.

Abolition in the Americas

American slaveowners were well aware of developments in slave systems elsewhere in the Western Hemisphere. They observed carefully the results of the wave of emancipations that swept the hemisphere in the first four decades of the century. In these years, slavery was abolished in most of Spanish America and in the British empire.

The experience of emancipation in other parts of the hemisphere strongly affected debates over slavery in the United States. Southern slaveowners judged the vitality of the Caribbean economy by how much sugar and other crops it produced for the world market. Since many former slaves preferred to grow food for their own families, defenders of slavery in the United States charged that British emancipation had been a failure.

Abolitionists disagreed, pointing to the rising standard of living of freed slaves, the spread of education among them, and other improvements in their lives. In a hemispheric perspective, slavery was a declining institution. At mid-century, significant New World slave systems remained only in Cuba, Puerto Rico, Brazil—and the United States.

Slavery and Liberty

Many white southerners declared themselves the true heirs of the American Revolution. They claimed to be inspired by "the same spirit of freedom and independence" that motivated the founding generation. Beginning in the 1830s, however, proslavery writers began to question the ideals of liberty, equality, and democracy so widely shared elsewhere in the nation. South Carolina, where a majority of white families owned slaves, became the home of an aggressive defense of slavery that repudiated the idea that freedom and equality were universal entitlements. The language of the Declaration of Independence—that all men were created equal and entitled to liberty—was "the most false and dangerous of all political errors," insisted John C. Calhoun.

The Virginia writer George Fitzhugh took the argument to its most radical conclusion. Far from being the natural condition of mankind, Fitzhugh wrote, "universal liberty" was the exception, an experiment carried on "for a little while" in "a corner of Europe" and the northern United States. Taking the world and its history as a whole, slavery, "without regard to race and color," was "the general, . . . normal, natural" basis of "civilized society."

After 1830, southern writers, newspaper editors, politicians, and clergymen increasingly devoted themselves to spreading the defense of slavery. The majority of white southerners came to believe that freedom for whites rested on the power to command the labor of blacks. In the words of the Richmond *Enquirer*, "freedom is not possible without slavery."

A plate manufactured in England to celebrate emancipation in the British empire. After a brief period of apprenticeship, all slaves were freed on August 1, 1838. At the center, a family of former slaves celebrates outside their cabin.

Spreading defense of slavery

LIFE UNDER SLAVERY

Slaves and the Law

For slaves, the "peculiar institution" meant a life of incessant toil, brutal punishment, and the constant fear that their families would be destroyed by sale. Under the law, slaves were property. Although they had a few

Slaves as property

legal rights (all states made it illegal to kill a slave except in self-defense, and slaves accused of serious crimes were entitled to their day in court, before all-white judges and juries), these were haphazardly enforced. Slaves could be sold or leased by their owners at will and lacked any voice in the governments that ruled over them. They could not testify in court against a white person, sign contracts or acquire property, own firearms, hold meetings unless a white person was present, or leave the farm or plantation without the permission of their owner. By the 1830s, it was against the law to teach a slave to read or write.

Legal restrictions on slaves

Not all of these laws were rigorously enforced. Some members of slaveholding families taught slave children to read (although rather few, since well over 90 percent of the slave population was illiterate in 1860). It was quite common throughout the South for slaves to gather without white supervision at crossroads villages and country stores on Sunday, their day of rest.

The slave, declared a Louisiana law, "owes to his master . . . a respect without bounds, and an absolute obedience." No aspect of slaves' lives, from the choice of marriage partners to how they spent their free time, was immune from his interference. The entire system of southern justice, from the state militia and courts down to armed patrols in each locality, was designed to enforce the master's control over the persons and labor of his slaves.

In one famous case, a Missouri court considered the case of Celia, a slave who had killed her master in 1855 while resisting a sexual assault. State law deemed "any woman" in such circumstances to be acting in self-defense. But Celia, the court ruled, was not a "woman" in the eyes of the law. She was a slave, whose master had complete power over her person. The court sentenced her to death. However, since Celia was pregnant, her execution was postponed until the child was born, so as not to deprive her owner's heirs of their property rights.

A poster advertising the raffle of a horse and a slave, treated as equivalents, at a Missouri store.

Conditions of Slave Life

Compared with their counterparts in the West Indies and Brazil, American slaves enjoyed better diets, lower rates of infant mortality, and longer life expectancies. Many factors contributed to improving material conditions. Most of the South lies outside the geographical area where tropical diseases like malaria, yellow fever, and typhoid fever flourish, so health among all southerners was better than in the Caribbean. And with the price of slaves rising dramatically after the closing of the African slave trade, it made economic sense for owners to become concerned with the health and living conditions of their human property.

Although slaves in the United States enjoyed better material lives than elsewhere in the Western Hemisphere, they had far less access to freedom. In Brazil, it was not uncommon for an owner to free slaves as a form of celebration—on the occasion of a wedding in the owner's family, for example—or to allow slaves to purchase their freedom. In the nineteenth-century South, however, more and more states set limits on voluntary manumission, requiring that such acts be approved by the legislature. Few slave societies in history have so systematically closed off all avenues to freedom as the Old South.

Slaves outside their cabin on a South Carolina plantation, probably photographed in the 1850s. They had brought their furniture outdoors to be included in the photo.

Free Blacks in the Old South

The existence of slavery helped to define the status of those blacks who did enjoy freedom. On the eve of the Civil War, nearly half a million free blacks lived in the United States, a majority in the South. Most were the descendants of slaves freed by southern owners in the aftermath of the Revolution or by the gradual emancipation laws of the northern states. Their numbers were supplemented by slaves who had been voluntarily liberated by their masters, who had been allowed to purchase their freedom, or who succeeded in running away.

When followed by "black" or "Negro," the word "free" took on an entirely new meaning. Free blacks in the South could legally own property and marry and, of course, could not be bought and sold. But many regulations restricting the lives of slaves also applied to them. Free blacks had no voice in selecting public officials. They were not allowed to testify in court against whites or serve on juries, and they had to carry at all times a certificate of freedom. Poor free blacks who required public assistance could be bound out to labor alongside slaves. By the 1850s, most southern states prohibited free blacks from entering their territory. A few states even moved to expel them altogether, offering the choice of enslavement or departure.

Restrictions on free blacks

In New Orleans and Charleston, on the other hand, relatively prosperous free black communities developed, mostly composed of mixed-race descendants of unions between white men and slave women. Many free blacks in these cities acquired an education and worked as skilled craftsmen such as tailors, carpenters, and mechanics. They established churches for their communities and schools for their children. In the Upper South, where the large majority of southern free blacks lived, they generally worked for wages as farm laborers. Overall, in the words of Willis A. Hodges, a member of a free Virginia family that helped runaways reach the North, free blacks and slaves were "one man of sorrow."

Slave Labor

A system of labor

First and foremost, slavery was a system of labor; "from sunup to first dark," with only brief interruptions for meals, work occupied most of the slaves' time. Large plantations were diversified communities, where slaves performed all kinds of work. The 125 slaves on one plantation, for instance, included a butler, two waitresses, a nurse, a dairymaid, a gardener, ten carpenters, and two shoemakers. Other plantations counted among their slaves engineers, blacksmiths, and weavers, as well as domestic workers from cooks to coachmen.

The large majority of slaves—75 percent of women and nearly 90 percent of men, according to one study—worked in the fields. The precise organization of their labor varied according to the crop and the size of the holding. On small farms, the owner often toiled side by side with his slaves. The largest concentration of slaves, however, lived and worked on plantations in the Cotton Belt, where men, women, and children labored in gangs, often under the direction of an overseer and perhaps a slave "driver" who assisted him. Among slaves, overseers had a reputation for meting out brutal treatment.

In this undated photograph, men, women, and children pick cotton under the watchful eye of an overseer. Unlike sugarcane, cotton does not grow to a great height, allowing an overseer to supervise a large number of slaves.

The 150,000 slaves who worked in the sugar fields of southern Louisiana also labored in large gangs. Conditions here were among the harshest in the South, for the late fall harvest season required round-the-clock labor to cut and process the sugarcane before it spoiled. On the rice plantations of South Carolina and Georgia, the system of task labor, which had originated in the colonial era, prevailed. With few whites willing to venture into the malaria-infested swamps, slaves were assigned daily tasks and allowed to set their own pace of work. Once a slave's task had been completed, he or she could spend the rest of the day hunting, fishing, or cultivating garden crops.

Slavery in the Cities

Businessmen, merchants, lawyers, and civil servants owned slaves, and by 1860 some

200,000 worked in industry, especially in the iron-works and tobacco factories of the Upper South. Most city slaves were servants, cooks, and other domestic laborers. But owners sometimes allowed those with craft skills to "hire their own time." This meant that they could make work arrangements individually with employers, with most of the wages going to the slave's owner. Many urban slaves even lived on their own. But slaveholders increasingly became convinced that, as one wrote, the growing independence of skilled urban slaves "exerts a most injurious influence upon the relation of master and servant." For this reason, many owners in the 1850s sold city slaves to the countryside and sought replacements among skilled white labor.

Detail from *Rice Culture on the Ogeechee*. Published in January 1867 in *Harper's Weekly*, this engraving illustrates work on a rice plantation divided into a checkerboard pattern by irrigation ditches. Although a white person is present, most slaves in the rice fields worked under the task system, without daily oversight.

Maintaining Order

Slaveowners employed a variety of means in their attempts to maintain order and discipline among their human property and persuade them to labor productively. At base, the system rested on force. Masters had almost complete discretion in inflicting punishment, and rare was the slave who went through his or her life without experiencing a whipping. Any infraction of plantation rules, no matter how minor, could be punished by the lash. One Georgia planter recorded in his journal that he had whipped a slave "for not bringing over milk for my coffee, being compelled to take it without."

Subtler means of control supplemented violence. Owners encouraged and exploited divisions among the slaves, especially between field hands and house servants. They created systems of incentives that rewarded good work with time off or even money payments. Probably the most powerful weapon wielded by slaveowners was the threat of sale, which separated slaves from their immediate families and from the communities that, despite overwhelming odds, African-Americans created on plantations throughout the South.

A Public Whipping of Slaves in Lexington, Missouri, in 1856, an illustration from the abolitionist publication *The Suppressed Book about Slavery*. Whipping was a common form of punishment for slaves.

SLAVE CULTURE

Slaves never abandoned their desire for freedom or their determination to resist total white control over their lives. In the face of grim realities, they succeeded in forging a

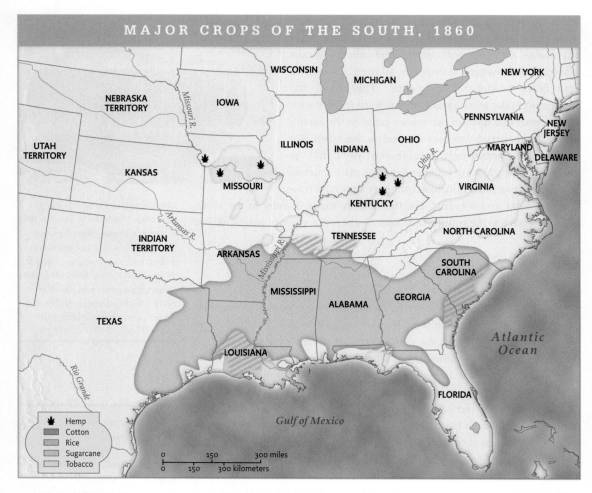

MAJOR CROPS OF THE SOUTH, 1860

Hemp
Cotton
Rice
Sugarcane
Tobacco

Gulf of Mexico

0   150   300 miles
0   150   300 kilometers

Cotton was the major agricultural crop of the South and, indeed, the nation, but slaves also grew rice, sugarcane, tobacco, and hemp.

semi-independent culture, centered on the family and church. This enabled them to survive the experience of bondage without surrendering their self-esteem and to pass from generation to generation a set of ideas and values fundamentally at odds with those of their masters.

Slave culture drew on the African heritage. African influences were evident in the slaves' music and dances, their style of religious worship, and the use of herbs by slave healers to combat disease. Slave culture was a new creation, shaped by African traditions and American values and experiences.

The Slave Family

At the center of the slave community stood the family. On the sugar plantations of the West Indies, the number of males far exceeded that of females, the workers lived in barracks-type buildings, and settled family life was nearly impossible. The United States, where the slave population grew from natural increase rather than continued importation from Africa, had an even male-female ratio, making the creation of families far more possible. To be sure, the law did not recognize the legality of slave marriages. The master had to consent before a man and woman could "jump over the broomstick" (the slaves' marriage ceremony), and families stood in constant danger of being broken up by sale.

Nonetheless, most adult slaves married, and their unions, when not disrupted by sale, typically lasted for a lifetime. To solidify a sense of family continuity, slaves frequently named children after cousins, uncles, grandparents, and other relatives. Because of constant sales, the slave community had a significantly higher number of female-headed households than among whites, as well as families in which grandparents, other relatives, or even non-kin assumed responsibility for raising children.

This 1842 engraving depicts an estate sale in New Orleans. At the center, a family of slaves is being sold. On the extreme right and left, auctioneers sell other property, including paintings.

The Threat of Sale

As noted above, the threat of sale, which disrupted family ties, was perhaps the most powerful disciplinary weapon slaveholders possessed. As the domestic slave trade expanded with the rise of the Cotton Kingdom, about one slave marriage in three in slave-selling states like Virginia was broken by sale. Many children were separated from their parents by sale.

Slave traders gave little attention to preserving family ties. A public notice, "Sale of Slaves and Stock," announced the 1852 auction of property belonging to a recently deceased Georgia planter. It listed thirty-six individuals ranging from an infant to a sixty-nine-year-old woman and ended with the proviso: "Slaves will be sold separate, or in lots, as best suits the purchaser." Sales like this were a human tragedy.

A broadside advertising the public sale of slaves, along with horses, mules, and cattle, after the death of their owner. The advertisement notes that the slaves will be sold individually or in groups "as best suits the purchaser," an indication that families were likely to be broken up. The prices are based on each slave's sex, age, and skill.

Gender Roles among Slaves

In some ways, gender roles under slavery differed markedly from those in the larger society. Slave men and women experienced, in a sense, the equality of powerlessness. The nineteenth century's "cult of domesticity," which defined the home as a woman's proper sphere, did

Sale of Slaves and Stock.

The Negroes and Stock listed below, are a Prime Lot, and belong to the ESTATE OF THE LATE LUTHER McGOWAN, and will be sold on Monday, Sept. 22nd, 1852, at the Fair Grounds, in Savannah, Georgia, at 1:00 P. M. The Negroes will be taken to the grounds two days previous to the Sale, so that they may be inspected by prospective buyers.

On account of the low prices listed below, they will be sold for cash only, and must be taken into custody within two hours after sale.

No.	Name.	Age.	Remarks.
1	Lunesta	27	Prime Rice Planter,
2	Violet	16	Housework and Nursemaid,
3	Lizzie	30	Rice, Unsound,
4	Minda	27	Cotton, Prime Woman,
5	Adam	28	Cotton, Prime Young M
6	Abel	41	Rice Hand, Eyesight P
7	Tanney	22	Prime Cotton Hand,
8	Flementina	39	Good Cook. Stiff Kn
9	Lanney	34	Prime Cottom Man
10	Sally	10	Handy in Kitchen

Virginian Luxuries. Originally painted on the back panel of a formal portrait, this image illustrates two "luxuries" of a Virginia slaveowner—the power to sexually abuse slave women and to whip slaves.

Plantation Burial, a painting from around 1860 by John Antrobus, an English artist who emigrated to New Orleans in 1850 and later married the daughter of a plantation owner. A slave preacher conducts a funeral service while black men, women, and children look on. This is a rare eyewitness depiction of black culture under slavery.

not apply to slave women, who regularly worked in the fields. Slave men could not act as the economic providers for their families. Nor could they protect their wives from physical or sexual abuse by owners and overseers (a frequent occurrence on many plantations) or determine when and under what conditions their children worked.

When slaves worked "on their own time," however, more conventional gender roles prevailed. Slave men chopped wood, hunted, and fished, while women washed, sewed, and assumed primary responsibility for the care of children. Some planters allowed their slaves small plots of land on which to grow food to supplement the rations provided by the owner; women usually took charge of these "garden plots."

Slave Religion

A distinctive version of Christianity also offered solace to slaves in the face of hardship and hope for liberation from bondage. Some blacks, free and slave, had taken part in the Great Awakening of the colonial era, and even more were swept into the South's Baptist and Methodist churches during the religious revivals of the late eighteenth and early nineteenth centuries. As one preacher recalled of the great camp meeting that drew thousands of worshipers to Cane Ridge, Kentucky, in 1801, no distinctions were made "as to age, sex, color, or anything of a temporary nature; old and young, male and female, black and white, had equal privilege to minister the light which they received, in whatever way the Spirit directed."

Even though the law prohibited slaves from gathering without a white person present, every plantation, it seemed, had its own black preacher. Usually the preacher was a "self-called" slave who possessed little or no formal education but whose rhetorical abilities and familiarity with the Bible made him one of the most respected members of the slave community. Especially in southern cities, slaves also worshiped in biracial congregations with white ministers, where they generally were required to sit in the back pews or in the balcony. Urban free blacks established their own churches, sometimes attended by slaves.

To masters, Christianity offered another means of social control. Many required slaves to attend services conducted by white ministers, who preached that theft was immoral and that the Bible required servants to obey their masters. One slave later recalled being told in a white minister's sermon "how good God was in bringing us over to this country from dark and benighted Africa, and permitting us to listen to the sound of the gospel."

In their own religious gatherings, slaves transformed the Christianity they had embraced, turning it to their own purposes. The biblical story of Exodus, for example, in which God chose Moses to lead the enslaved Jews of Egypt into a promised land of freedom, played a central role in black Christianity. Slaves identified themselves as a chosen people whom God in the fullness of time would deliver from bondage. At the same time, the figure of Jesus Christ represented to slaves a personal redeemer, one who truly cared for the oppressed. And in the slaves' eyes, the Christian message of brotherhood and the equality of all souls before the Creator offered an irrefutable indictment of the institution of slavery.

Transforming Christianity

The Desire for Liberty

Despite their masters' elaborate ideology defending the South's "peculiar institution," slave culture rested on a conviction of the injustices of bondage and the desire for freedom. When slaves sang, "I'm bound for the land of Canaan," they meant not only relief from worldly woes in an afterlife but also escaping to the North or witnessing the breaking of slavery's chains.

Most slaves, however, fully understood the impossibility of directly confronting such an entrenched system. Their folk tales had no figures equivalent to Paul Bunyan, the powerful, larger-than-life backwoodsman popular in white folklore. Slaves' folklore, such as the Brer Rabbit stories, glorified the weak hare who outwitted stronger foes like the bear and fox, rather than challenging them outright. Their religious songs, or spirituals, spoke of lives of sorrow ("I've been 'buked and I've been scorned"), while holding out hope for ultimate liberation ("Didn't my Lord deliver Daniel?").

Folk tales

Owners attempted to prevent slaves from learning about the larger world. But slaves created neighborhood networks that transmitted information between plantations. Skilled craftsmen, preachers, pilots on ships, and other privileged slaves spread news of local and national events. James Henry Hammond of South Carolina was "astonished and shocked" to find that his slaves understood the political views of the presidential candidates of 1844, Henry Clay and James K. Polk, and knew "most of what the abolitionists are doing."

Neighborhood networks

The world of most rural slaves was bounded by their local communities and kin. Nor could slaves remain indifferent to the currents of thought unleashed by the American Revolution or to the language of freedom in

Language of free

the society around them. "I am in a land of liberty," wrote Joseph Taper, a Virginia slave who escaped to Canada around 1840. "Man is as God intended he should be."

RESISTANCE TO SLAVERY

Revolts and resistance

Confronted with federal, state, and local authorities committed to preserving slavery, and outnumbered within the South as a whole by the white population, slaves could only rarely express their desire for freedom by outright rebellion. Compared with revolts in Brazil and the West Indies, which experienced numerous uprisings, involving hundreds or even thousands of slaves, revolts in the United States were smaller and less frequent. Resistance to slavery took many forms in the Old South, from individual acts of defiance to occasional uprisings. These actions posed a constant challenge to the slaveholders' self-image as benign paternalists and their belief that slaves were obedient subjects grateful for their owners' care.

Forms of Resistance

The most widespread expression of hostility to slavery was "day-to-day resistance" or "silent sabotage"—doing poor work, breaking tools, abusing animals, and in other ways disrupting the plantation routine. Then there was the theft of food, a form of resistance so common that one southern physician diagnosed it as a hereditary disease unique to blacks. Less frequent, but more dangerous, were serious crimes committed by slaves, including arson, poisoning, and armed assaults against individual whites.

Runaway slaves

Even more threatening to the stability of the slave system were slaves who ran away. Formidable obstacles confronted the prospective **fugitive slaves**. Patrols were constantly on the lookout for runaway slaves. Slaves had little or no knowledge of geography, apart from understanding that following the north star led to freedom. Not surprisingly, most of those who succeeded lived, like Frederick Douglass, in the Upper South, especially Maryland, Virginia, and Kentucky, which bordered on the free states. Douglass, who escaped at age twenty, was also typical in that the large majority of fugitives were young men. Most slave women were not willing to leave children behind, and taking them along on the arduous escape journey was nearly impossible.

Fugitive destinations

In the Lower South, fugitives tended to head for cities like New Orleans or Charleston, where they hoped to lose themselves in the free black community. Other escapees fled to remote areas like the Great Dismal Swamp of Virginia or the Florida Everglades, where the Seminole

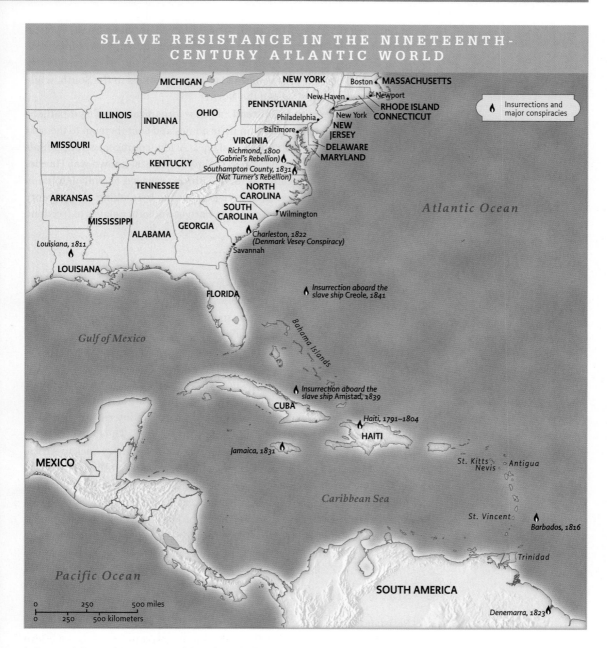

SLAVE RESISTANCE IN THE NINETEENTH-CENTURY ATLANTIC WORLD

Instances of slave resistance occurred throughout the Western Hemisphere, on land and at sea. This map shows the location of major events in the nineteenth century.

The top part of a typical broadside offering a reward for the capture of four runaway slaves. This was distributed in Mississippi County, Missouri, in 1852. The high reward for George, $1,000, suggests that he is an extremely valued worker.

Uprising on ship

Indians offered refuge before they were forced to move west. Even in Tennessee, a study of newspaper advertisements for runaways finds that around 40 percent were thought to have remained in the local neighborhood and 30 percent to have headed to other locations in the South, while only 25 percent tried to reach the North.

The **Underground Railroad**, a loose organization of sympathetic abolitionists who hid fugitives in their homes and sent them on to the next "station," assisted some runaway slaves. A few courageous individuals made forays into the South to liberate slaves. The best known was **Harriet Tubman**. Born in Maryland in 1820, Tubman escaped to Philadelphia in 1849 and during the next decade risked her life by making some twenty trips back to her state of birth to lead relatives and other slaves to freedom.

The *Amistad*

In a few instances, large groups of slaves collectively seized their freedom. The most celebrated instance involved fifty-three slaves who in 1839 took control of **the *Amistad***, a ship transporting them from one port in Cuba to another, and tried to force the navigator to steer it to Africa. The *Amistad* wended its way up the Atlantic coast until an American vessel seized it off the coast of Long Island. President Martin Van Buren favored returning the slaves to Cuba. But abolitionists brought their case to the Supreme Court, where the former president John Quincy Adams argued that since they had been recently brought from Africa in violation of international treaties banning the slave trade, the captives should be freed. The Court accepted Adams's reasoning, and most of the captives made their way back to Africa.

The *Amistad* case had no legal bearing on slaves within the United States. But it may well have inspired a similar uprising in 1841, when 135 slaves being transported by sea from Norfolk, Virginia, to New Orleans seized control of the ship *Creole* and sailed for Nassau in the British Bahamas. Their leader had the evocative name Madison Washington. To the dismay of the Tyler administration, the British gave refuge to the *Creole* slaves.

Slave Revolts

Resistance to slavery occasionally moved beyond such individual and group acts of defiance to outright rebellion. The four largest conspiracies in American history occurred within the space of thirty-one years in the early nineteenth century. The first, organized by the Virginia slave Gabriel in 1800, was discussed in Chapter 8. It was followed eleven years later by an uprising on sugar plantations upriver from New Orleans. Some 500 men and women, armed with sugarcane knives, axes, clubs, and a few guns, marched toward the city, destroying property as they proceeded. The white population along the route fled in panic to New Orleans. Within two days, the militia and regular army troops met the rebels and dispersed them in a pitched battle, killing sixty-six.

The next major conspiracy was organized in 1822 by Denmark Vesey, a slave carpenter in Charleston, South Carolina, who had purchased his freedom after winning a local lottery. **Denmark Vesey's conspiracy** reflected the combination of American and African influences then circulating in the Atlantic world and coming together in black culture. "He studied the Bible a great deal," recalled one of his followers, "and tried to prove from it that slavery and bondage is against the Bible." Vesey also quoted the Declaration of Independence, pored over newspaper reports of the debates in Congress regarding the Missouri Compromise, and made pronouncements like "all men had equal rights, blacks as well as whites." And he read to his conspirators accounts of the successful slave revolution in Haiti. The African heritage was present in the person of Vesey's lieutenant Gullah Jack, a religious "conjurer" from Angola who claimed to be able to protect the rebels against injury or death. The plot was discovered before it could reach fruition.

As with many slave conspiracies, evidence about the Vesey plot is contradictory and disputed. Much of it comes from a series of trials in which the court operated in secret and failed to allow the accused to confront those who testified against them.

Nat Turner's Rebellion

The best known of all slave rebels was Nat Turner, a slave preacher and religious mystic in Southampton County, Virginia, who came to believe that God had chosen him to lead a black uprising. Turner traveled widely in the county, conducting religious services. He told of seeing black and white angels fighting in the sky and the heavens running red with blood. Perhaps from a sense of irony, Turner initially chose July 4, 1831, for his rebellion, only to fall ill on the appointed day. On August 22, he and a handful of followers marched from farm to farm assaulting the white inhabitants. By the time the militia put down the uprising, about eighty slaves had joined Turner's band, and some sixty whites had been killed. Turner was subsequently captured and, with seventeen other rebels, condemned to die. Asked before his execution whether he regretted what he had done, Turner responded, "Was not Christ crucified?"

Nat Turner's Rebellion sent shock waves through the entire South. "A Nat Turner," one white Virginian warned, "might be in any family." In the panic that followed the revolt, hundreds of innocent slaves were whipped, and scores

Cinque, a leader of the slave revolt on the *Amistad*, in an 1839 painting by Nathaniel Jocelyn, a prominent Connecticut artist.

In one of the most celebrated escapes of the antebellum years, Henry Brown, a slave in Richmond, had himself concealed in a crate and shipped to the antislavery office in Philadelphia. This lithograph from 1851 shows three white abolitionists, including J. Miller McKim, with a hatchet, as well as the African-American William Still, a leader of the underground railroad in the city, who holds the top of the crate as Brown emerges.

VOICES OF FREEDOM

From Letter by Joseph Taper to Joseph Long (1840)

No one knows how many slaves succeeded in escaping from bondage before the Civil War. Some settled in northern cities like Boston, Cincinnati, and New York. But because the Constitution required that fugitives be returned to slavery, many continued northward until they reached Canada.

One successful fugitive was Joseph Taper, a slave in Frederick County, Virginia, who in 1837 ran away to Pennsylvania with his wife and children. Two years later, learning that a "slave catcher" was in the neighborhood, the Tapers fled to Canada. In 1840, Taper wrote to a white acquaintance in Virginia recounting some of his experiences.

The biblical passage to which Taper refers reads: "And I will come near to you to judgment; and I will be a swift witness against the sorcerers, and against the adulterers, and against false swearers, and against those that oppress the hireling in his wages, the widow, and the fatherless, and that turn aside the stranger from his right, and fear not me, saith the Lord of hosts."

Dear sir,

I now take the opportunity to inform you that I am in a land of liberty, in good health. . . . Since I have been in the Queen's dominions I have been well contented, Yes well contented for Sure, man is as God intended he should be. That is, all are born free and equal. This is a wholesome law, not like the Southern laws which puts man made in the image of God, on level with brutes. O, what will become of the people, and where will they stand in the day of Judgment. Would that the 5th verse of the 3d chapter of Malachi were written as with the bar of iron, and the point of a diamond upon every oppressor's heart that they might repent of this evil, and let the oppressed go free. . . .

We have good schools, and all the colored population supplied with schools. My boy Edward who will be six years next January, is now reading, and I intend keeping him at school until he becomes a good scholar.

I have enjoyed more pleasure within one month here than in all my life in the land of bondage. . . . My wife and self are sitting by a good comfortable fire happy, knowing that there are none to molest [us] or make [us] afraid. God save Queen Victoria. The Lord bless her in this life, and crown her with glory in the world to come is my prayer,

Yours With much respect

most obt, Joseph Taper

From "Slavery and the Bible" (1850)

White southerners developed an elaborate set of arguments defending slavery in the period before the Civil War. One pillar of proslavery thought was the idea that the institution was sanctioned by the Bible, as in this essay from the influential southern magazine *De Bow's Review.*

A very large party in the United States believe that holding slaves is morally wrong; this party founds its belief upon precepts taught in the Bible, and takes that book as the standard of morality and religion.

. . . We think we can show, that the Bible teaches clearly and conclusively that the holding of slaves is right; and if so, no deduction from general principles can make it wrong, if that book is true. . . .

Slavery has existed in some form or under some name, in almost every country of the globe. It existed in every country known, even by name, to any one of the sacred writers, at the time of his writing; yet none of them condemns it in the slightest degree. Would this have been the case had it been wrong in itself? Would not some one of the host of sacred writers have spoken of this alleged crime, in such terms as to show, in a manner not to be misunderstood, that God wished all men to be equal?

Abraham, the chosen servant of God, had his bond servants, whose condition was similar to, or worse than, that of our slaves. He considered them as his property, to be bought and sold as any other property which he owned. . . .

We find . . . that both the Old and New Testaments speak of slavery—that they do not condemn the relation, but, on the contrary, expressly allow it or create it; and they give commands and exhortations, which are based upon its legality and propriety. It can not, then, be wrong.

QUESTIONS

1. *How does Taper's letter reverse the rhetoric, common among white Americans, which saw the United States as a land of freedom and the British empire as lacking in liberty?*

2. *Why does De Bow feel that it is important to show that the Bible sanctions slavery?*

3. *How do Taper and De Bow differ in their understanding of the relationship of slavery and Christianity?*

An engraving depicting Nat Turner's slave rebellion of 1831, from a book published soon after the revolt.

executed. For one last time, Virginia's leaders openly debated whether steps ought to be taken to do away with the "peculiar institution." But a proposal for gradual emancipation and the removal of the black population from the state failed to win legislative approval.

Instead of moving toward emancipation, the Virginia legislature of 1832 decided to fasten even more tightly the chains of bondage. New laws prohibited blacks, free or slave, from acting as preachers (a measure that proved impossible to enforce), strengthened the militia and patrol systems, banned free blacks from owning firearms, and prohibited teaching slaves to read. Other southern states followed suit.

A turning point

In some ways, 1831 marked a turning point for the Old South. In that year, Parliament debated a program for abolishing slavery throughout the British empire, underscoring the South's growing isolation. Turner's rebellion, following only a few months after the appearance in Boston of William Lloyd Garrison's abolitionist journal, *The Liberator*, suggested that American slavery faced enemies both within and outside the South. The proslavery argument increasingly permeated southern intellectual and political life, while dissenting opinions were suppressed. Some states made membership in an abolitionist society a criminal offense, while mobs drove critics of slavery from their homes. The South's "great reaction" produced one of the most thoroughgoing suppressions of freedom of speech in American history. Even as reform movements arose in the North that condemned slavery as contrary to Christianity and to basic American values, and national debate over the peculiar institution intensified, southern society closed in defense of slavery.

An intensifying debate

CHAPTER REVIEW AND ONLINE RESOURCES

REVIEW QUESTIONS

1. *Given that most northern states had abolished slavery by the 1830s, how is it useful to think of slavery as a national—rather than regional—economic and political system?*

2. *Although some poor southern whites resented the dominance of the "slavocracy," most supported the institution and accepted the power of the planter class. Why did the "plain folk" continue to support slavery?*

3. *How did the planters' paternalism serve to justify the system of slavery? How did it hide the reality of life for slaves?*

4. *Identify the basic elements of the proslavery defense and those points aimed especially at non-southern audiences.*

5. *In what sense did southern slaveholders consider themselves forward-looking?*

6. *Compare slaves in the Old South with those elsewhere in the world, focusing on health, diet, and opportunities for freedom.*

7. *Describe the difference between gang labor and task labor for slaves, and explain how slaves' tasks varied by region across the Old South.*

8. *How did enslaved people create community and a culture that allowed them to survive in an oppressive society?*

9. *Identify the different types of resistance to slavery. Which ones were the most common, the most effective, and the most demonstrative?*

KEY TERMS

the "peculiar institution" (p. 309)

Second Middle Passage (p. 310)

"Cotton is king" (p. 313)

paternalism (p. 314)

proslavery argument (p. 315)

fugitive slaves (p. 326)

Underground Railroad (p. 328)

Harriet Tubman (p. 328)

the *Amistad* (p. 328)

Denmark Vesey's conspiracy (p. 329)

Nat Turner's Rebellion (p. 329)

Go to INQUIZITIVE

To see what you know—and learn what you've missed—with personalized feedback along the way.

Visit the *Give Me Liberty!* **Student Site** for primary source documents and images, interactive maps, author videos featuring Eric Foner, and more.

CHAPTER 12

AN AGE OF REFORM

★

1820–1840

A Woman's Rights Quilt. Made by an unknown woman only a few years after the Seneca Falls Convention of 1848, this quilt embodies an unusual form of political expression. It includes scenes visualizing a woman engaged in various activities that violated the era's cult of domesticity, and it illustrates some of the demands of the early women's rights movement. The individual blocks show a woman driving her own buggy and a banner advocating "woman rights," another dressing to go out while her husband remains at home wearing an apron, and a third addressing a public meeting with a mixed male-female audience.

A mong the many Americans who devoted their lives to the crusade against slavery, few were as selfless or courageous as Abby Kelley. As a teacher in Lynn, Massachusetts, she joined the Female Anti-Slavery Society and, like thousands of other northern women, threw herself into the abolitionist movement. In 1838, Kelley began to give public speeches about slavery. Her first lecture outside of Lynn was literally a baptism of fire. Enraged by reports that abolitionists favored "amalgamation" of the races—that is, sexual relations between whites and blacks—residents of Philadelphia stormed the meeting hall and burned it to the ground.

For two decades, Kelley traveled throughout the North, speaking almost daily in churches, public halls, and antislavery homes on "the holy cause of human rights." Her career illustrated the interconnections of the era's reform movements. In addition to abolitionism, she was active in pacifist organizations—which opposed the use of force, including war, to settle disputes—and was a pioneer in the early struggle for women's rights. She forthrightly challenged her era's assumption that a woman's "place" was in the home. More than any other individual, remarked Lucy Stone, another women's rights advocate, Kelley "earned for us all the right of free speech."

Abby Kelley's private life was as unconventional as her public career. Happily married to the ardent abolitionist Stephen S. Foster, she gave birth to a daughter in 1847 but soon returned to lecturing. When criticized for not devoting herself to the care of her infant, Kelley replied: "I have done it for the sake of the mothers whose babies are sold away from them. The most precious legacy I can leave my child is a free country."

FOCUS QUESTIONS

- *What were the major movements and goals of antebellum reform?*

- *What were the different varieties of abolitionism?*

- *How did abolitionism challenge barriers to racial equality and free speech?*

- *What were the diverse sources of the antebellum women's rights movement and its significance?*

THE REFORM IMPULSE

"In the history of the world," wrote Ralph Waldo Emerson in 1841, "the doctrine of reform has never had such hope as at the present hour." Abolitionism was only one of this era's numerous efforts to improve American society. Americans established voluntary organizations that worked to prevent the manufacture and sale of liquor, end public entertainments and the delivery of the mail on Sunday, improve conditions in prisons, expand public education, uplift the condition of wage laborers, and reorganize society on the basis of cooperation rather than competitive individualism.

Goals of reformers

Nearly all these groups worked to convert public opinion to their cause. They sent out speakers, gathered signatures on petitions, and published pamphlets. Some reform movements, like restraining the consumption of liquor and alleviating the plight of the blind and insane, flourished throughout the nation. Others, including women's rights, labor

A rare photograph of an abolitionist meeting in New York State around 1850. Frederick Douglass is to the left of the woman at the center.

unionism, and educational reform, were weak or nonexistent in the South, where they were widely associated with antislavery sentiment. Reform was an international crusade. Peace, temperance, women's rights, and antislavery advocates regularly crisscrossed the Atlantic to promote their ideas.

Reformers adopted a wide variety of tactics to bring about social change. Some relied on "moral suasion" to convert people to their cause. Others, such as opponents of "demon rum," sought to use the power of the government to force sinners to change their ways. Some reformers decided to withdraw altogether from the larger society and establish their own cooperative settlements. They hoped to change American life by creating "heavens on earth," where they could demonstrate by example the superiority of a collective way of life.

Utopian Communities

Thomas More

About 100 reform communities were established in the decades before the Civil War. Historians call them "utopian" after Thomas More's sixteenth-century novel *Utopia*, an outline of a perfect society. (The word has also come to imply that such plans are impractical and impossible to realize.) Most communities arose from religious conviction, but others were inspired by the secular desire to counteract the social and economic changes set in motion by the market revolution.

Social harmony

Nearly all the communities set out to reorganize society on a cooperative basis, hoping to restore social harmony to a world of excessive individualism and to narrow the widening gap between rich and poor. Through their efforts, the words "socialism" and "communism," meaning a social organization in which productive property is owned by the community rather than private individuals, entered the language of politics. Most **utopian communities** also tried to find substitutes for conventional gender relations and marriage patterns. Some prohibited sexual relations between men and women altogether; others allowed them to change partners at will. But nearly all insisted that the abolition of private property must be accompanied by an end to men's "property" in women.

The Shakers

Religious communities attracted those who sought to find a retreat from a society permeated by sin. But the **Shakers**, the most successful of the

An engraving of a Shaker dance, drawn by Benson Lossing, an artist who visited a Shaker community and reported on life there for *Harper's Magazine* in 1857.

religious communities, also had a significant impact on the outside world. At their peak during the 1840s, cooperative Shaker settlements, which stretched from Maine to Kentucky, included more than 5,000 members.

God, the Shakers believed, had a "dual" personality, both male and female, and thus the two sexes were spiritually equal. "Virgin purity" formed a pillar of the Shakers' faith. They completely abandoned traditional family life. Men and women lived separately in large dormitory-like structures and ate in communal dining rooms. They increased their numbers by attracting converts and adopting children from orphanages, rather than through natural increase. Although they rejected the individual accumulation of private property, the Shakers proved remarkably successful economically. They were among the first to market vegetable and flower seeds and herbal medicines commercially and to breed cattle for profit. Their beautifully crafted furniture is still widely admired today.

Shaker beliefs

Oneida

Another influential and controversial community was **Oneida**, founded in 1848 in upstate New York by John Humphrey Noyes, the Vermont-born son of a U.S. congressman. In 1836, Noyes and his disciples formed a small community in Putney, Vermont. The community became notorious for what Noyes called "complex marriage," whereby any man could propose sexual relations to any woman, who had the right to reject or accept his invitation, which would then be registered in a public record book. The great danger was "exclusive affections," which, Noyes felt, destroyed social harmony.

John Humphrey Noyes

"Complex marriage"

UTOPIAN COMMUNITIES, MID-NINETEENTH CENTURY

In the first half of the nineteenth century, dozens of utopian communities were established in the United States, where small groups of men and women attempted to establish a more perfect social order within the larger society.

After being indicted for adultery by local officials, Noyes in 1848 moved his community to Oneida, where it survived until 1881. Oneida was an extremely dictatorial environment. To become a member of the community, one had to demonstrate command of Noyes's religious teachings and live according to his rules.

Worldly Communities

Longevity of utopian communities

To outside observers, utopian communities like Oneida seemed cases of "voluntary slavery." But because of their members' selfless devotion to the teachings and rules laid down by their leader, spiritually oriented communities often achieved remarkable longevity. The Shakers survived well into the twentieth century. Communities with a more worldly orientation tended to be beset by internal divisions and therefore lasted for much shorter periods.

The most important secular communitarian (meaning a person who plans or lives in a cooperative community) was Robert Owen, a British factory owner. Appalled by the degradation of workers in the early industrial revolution, Owen created a model factory village at New Lanark, Scotland, which combined strict rules of work discipline with comfortable housing and free public education. Around 1815, its 1,500 employees made New Lanark the largest center of cotton manufacturing in the world. Owen promoted **communitarianism** as a peaceful means of ensuring that workers received the full value of their labor. In 1824, he purchased the Harmony community in Indiana—originally founded by the German Protestant religious leader George Rapp, who had emigrated to America with his followers at the beginning of the nineteenth century. Here, Owen established **New Harmony**, where he hoped to create a "new moral world."

In Owen's scheme, children would be removed at an early age from the care of their parents to be educated in schools where they would be trained to subordinate individual ambition to the common good. Owen also defended women's rights, especially access to education and the right to divorce. At New Harmony, he promised, women would no longer be "enslaved" to their husbands, and "false notions" about innate differences between the sexes would be abandoned.

Harmony eluded the residents of New Harmony. They squabbled about everything from the community's constitution to the distribution of property. Owen's settlement survived for only a few years, but it strongly influenced the labor movement, educational reformers, and women's rights advocates. Owen's vision resonated with the widely held American belief that a community of equals could be created in the New World.

The Crisis, a publication by the communitarian Robert Owen and his son, Robert Dale Owen. The cover depicts Owen's vision of a planned socialist community.

Religion and Reform

Most Americans saw the ownership of property as the key to economic independence—and, therefore, to freedom—and marriage as the foundation of the social order. Few were likely to join communities that required them to surrender both. Far more typical of the reform impulse were movements that aimed at liberating men and women either from restraints external to themselves, such as slavery and war, or from forms of internal "servitude" like drinking, illiteracy, and a tendency toward criminality. Many of these reform movements drew their inspiration from the religious revivalism of the Second Great Awakening, discussed in Chapter 9. If, as the revivalist preachers maintained, God had created man as a "free moral agent," sinners could not only reform themselves but could also remake the world.

Mainstream reform

The revivals popularized the outlook known as **perfectionism**, which saw both individuals and society at large as capable of indefinite improvement. Under the impact of the revivals, older reform efforts moved in a new, radical direction. Temperance (which literally means moderation in the consumption of liquor) was transformed into a crusade to eliminate drinking entirely, known as the **temperance movement**. Criticism of war became outright pacifism. And, as will be related below, critics of

Temperance

slavery now demanded not gradual emancipation but immediate and total abolition.

To members of the North's emerging middle-class culture, reform became a badge of respectability, an indication that individuals had taken control of their own lives and had become morally accountable. The American Temperance Society, founded in 1826, sought to redeem not only habitual drunkards but also the occasional drinker. It claimed by the 1830s to have persuaded hundreds of thousands of Americans to renounce liquor. By 1840, the consumption of alcohol per person had fallen to less than half the level of a decade earlier. (It had peaked in 1830 at seven gallons per person per year, compared with around two gallons today.)

A temperance banner from around 1850 depicts a young man torn between a woman in white, who illustrates female purity, and a temptress, who offers him a drink of liquor.

Critics of Reform

Many Americans saw the reform impulse as an attack on their own freedom. Taverns were popular meeting places for workingmen, sites not only of drinking but also of political discussions, organizational meetings, and recreation. Drinking was a prominent feature of festive celebrations and events like militia gatherings. A "Liberty Loving Citizen" of Worcester, Massachusetts, wondered what gave one group of citizens the right to dictate to others how to conduct their personal lives.

Catholics on reform

American Catholics, their numbers growing because of Irish and German immigration, proved hostile to the reform impulse. Catholics understood freedom in ways quite different from how Protestant reformers did. They viewed sin as an inescapable burden of individuals and society. The perfectionist idea that evil could be banished from the world struck them as an affront to genuine religion, and they bitterly opposed what they saw as reformers' efforts to impose their own version of Protestant morality on their neighbors. Whereas reformers spoke of man as a free moral agent, Catholics tended to place less emphasis on individual independence and more on the importance of communities centered on family and church.

Reformers and Freedom

Tension between liberation and control

Reformers had to reconcile their desire to create moral order with their quest to enhance personal freedom. They did this through a vision of freedom that was liberating and controlling at the same time. On the one hand, reformers insisted that their goal was to enable Americans to enjoy genuine liberty. In a world in which personal freedom increasingly meant the opportunity to compete for economic gain and individual self-improvement, they spoke of liberating Americans from various forms of "slavery" that made it impossible to succeed—slavery to drink, to poverty, to sin.

On the other hand, reformers insisted that self-fulfillment came through self-discipline. Their definition of the free individual was the person who internalized the practice of self-control. In some ways, reformers believed, American society suffered from an excess of liberty—the anarchic "natural liberty" John Winthrop had warned against in the early days of Puritan Massachusetts, as opposed to the "Christian liberty" of the morally upright citizen.

Self-discipline

Many religious groups in the East worried that settlers in the West and immigrants from abroad lacked self-control and led lives of vice, exhibited by drinking, violations of the Sabbath, and lack of Protestant devotion. They formed the American Tract Society, the American Bible Society, and other groups that flooded eastern cities and the western frontier with copies of the gospel and pamphlets promoting religious virtue. Between 1825 and 1835, the pamphlets distributed by the Tract Society amounted to more than 500 million pages.

American Tract Society

The Invention of the Asylum

The tension between liberation and control in the era's reform movements was vividly evident in the proliferation of new institutions that reformers hoped could remake human beings into free, morally upright citizens. In colonial America, crime had mostly been punished by whipping, fines, or banishment. The poor received relief in their own homes, orphans lived with neighbors, and families took care of mentally ill members.

During the 1830s and 1840s, Americans embarked on a program of institution building—jails for criminals, poorhouses for the destitute, asylums for the insane, and orphanages for children without families. These institutions differed in many respects, but they shared with believers in "perfectionism" the idea that social ills once considered incurable could in fact be eliminated. Today, prisons and asylums have become overcrowded places where rehabilitating the inmates seems less important than simply holding them at bay, away from society. At the outset, however, these institutions were inspired by the conviction that those who passed through their doors could eventually be released to become productive, self-disciplined citizens.

Reform institutions

The Common School

The largest effort at institution building before the Civil War came in the movement to establish **common schools**—that is, tax-supported state school systems open to all children. In the early nineteenth century, most children were educated in locally supported schools, private academies, charity schools, or at home. Many had no access to learning at all. School reform reflected the numerous purposes that came together in the era's reform impulse. Horace Mann, a Massachusetts lawyer and Whig politician who served as director of the state's board of education, was the era's leading educational reformer. He hoped that universal public education could restore equality to a fractured society by bringing the children of all classes together in a common learning experience and equipping the less fortunate to advance in the social scale.

Horace Mann

With labor organizations, factory owners, and middle-class reformers all supporting the idea, every northern state by 1860 had established tax-supported school systems for its children. The common-school movement created the first real career opportunity for women, who quickly came to dominate the ranks of teachers. The South, where literate blacks were viewed as a danger to social order and planters had no desire to tax themselves to pay for education for poor white children, lagged far behind. This was one of many ways in which North and South seemed to be growing apart.

The rise of public education

THE CRUSADE AGAINST SLAVERY

Compared with drinking, Sabbath-breaking, and illiteracy, the greatest evil in American society at first appeared to attract the least attention from reformers. For many years, it seemed that the only Americans willing to challenge the existence of slavery were Quakers, slaves, and free blacks.

Colonization

Before the 1830s, those white Americans willing to contemplate an end to bondage almost always coupled calls for abolition with the "colonization" of freed slaves—their deportation to Africa, the Caribbean, or Central America. In 1816, proponents of this idea founded the **American Colonization Society**, which promoted the gradual abolition of slavery and the settlement of black Americans in Africa. It soon established Liberia on the coast of West Africa, an outpost of American influence whose capital, Monrovia, was named for President James Monroe.

Liberia

Colonization struck many observers as totally impractical. Nonetheless, numerous prominent political leaders of the Jacksonian era—including Henry Clay, John Marshall, and Jackson himself—supported the Colonization Society. Many colonizationists believed that slavery and

Supporters of colonization

racism were so deeply embedded in American life that blacks could never achieve equality if freed and allowed to remain in the country. Like Indian removal, colonization rested on the premise that America is fundamentally a white society.

In the decades before the Civil War, several thousand black Americans did emigrate to Liberia with the aid of the Colonization Society. Some were slaves emancipated by their owners on the condition that they depart, while others left voluntarily, motivated by a desire to spread Christianity in Africa or to enjoy rights denied them in the United States. Having experienced "the legal slavery of the South and the social slavery of the North," wrote one emigrant on leaving for Liberia, he knew he could "never be a free man in this country."

But most African-Americans adamantly opposed the idea of colonization. In fact, the formation of the American Colonization Society galvanized free blacks to claim their rights as Americans. Early in 1817, some 3,000 free blacks assembled in Philadelphia for the first national black convention. Their resolutions insisted that blacks were Americans, entitled to the same freedom and rights enjoyed by whites.

An abolitionist banner. Antislavery organizations adopted the Liberty Bell as a symbol of their campaign to extend freedom to black Americans. Previously, the bell, forged in Philadelphia in the eighteenth century, had simply been known as the Old State House Bell.

Militant Abolitionism

The abolitionist movement that arose in the 1830s differed profoundly from its genteel, conservative predecessor. Drawing on the religious conviction that slavery was an unparalleled sin and the secular one that it contradicted the values enshrined in the Declaration of Independence, a new generation of reformers rejected the traditional approach of gradual emancipation and demanded immediate abolition. Also unlike their predecessors, they directed explosive language against slavery and slaveholders and insisted that blacks, once free, should be incorporated as equal members of the republic rather than being deported. Perfecting American society, they insisted, meant rooting out not just slavery, but racism in all its forms.

The first indication of the new spirit of abolitionism came in 1829 with the appearance of *An Appeal to the Coloured Citizens of the World* by David Walker, a free black who had been born in North Carolina and now operated a used-clothing store in Boston. A passionate indictment of slavery and racial prejudice, the *Appeal* warned whites that the nation faced divine punishment if it did not mend its sinful ways. Walker called on blacks to

David Walker

William Lloyd Garrison, editor of *The Liberator* and one of the country's most prominent abolitionists, in an undated portrait by Edwin T. Billings.

take pride in the achievements of ancient African civilizations and to claim all their rights as Americans.

Walker died in mysterious circumstances in 1830. Not until the appearance in 1831 of *The Liberator*, William Lloyd Garrison's weekly journal published in Boston, did the new breed of abolitionism find a permanent voice. "I will be as harsh as truth," Garrison announced, "and as uncompromising as justice. On this subject, I do not wish to think, or speak, or write, with moderation. . . . I will not equivocate—I will not excuse—I will not retreat a single inch—and I will be heard."

And heard he was. Some of Garrison's ideas, such as his suggestion that the North abrogate the Constitution and dissolve the Union to end its complicity in the evil of slavery, were rejected by most abolitionists. But his call for the immediate abolition of slavery echoed throughout antislavery circles. Garrison's pamphlet *Thoughts on African Colonization* persuaded many foes of slavery that blacks must be recognized as part of American society, not viewed as aliens to be shipped overseas.

Spreading the Abolitionist Message

Beginning with a handful of activists, the abolitionist movement expanded swiftly throughout the North. Antislavery leaders took advantage of the rapid development of print technology and the expansion of literacy due to common-school education to spread their message. Like radical pamphleteers of the American Revolution and evangelical ministers of the Second Great Awakening, they recognized the democratic potential in the production of printed material. Abolitionists seized on the recently invented steam printing press to produce millions of copies of pamphlets, newspapers, petitions, novels, and broadsides. Between the formation of the **American Anti-Slavery Society** in 1833 and the end of the decade, some 100,000 northerners joined local groups devoted to abolition. Most were ordinary citizens—farmers, shopkeepers, craftsmen, and laborers, along with a few prominent businessmen like the merchants Arthur and Lewis Tappan of New York.

Pamphlets, broadsides, newspapers

Theodore Weld

If Garrison was the movement's most notable propagandist, Theodore Weld, a young minister who had been converted by the evangelical preacher Charles G. Finney, helped to create its mass constituency. A brilliant orator, Weld trained a band of speakers who brought the abolitionist message into the heart of the rural and small-town North. Their methods were those of the revivals—fervent preaching, calls for individuals to renounce their immoral ways—and their message was a simple one: slavery is a sin.

A is an Abolitionist—
A man who wants to free
The wretched slave—and give to all
An equal liberty.

B is a Brother with a skin
Of somewhat darker hue,
But in our Heavenly Father's sight,
He is as dear as you.

5

C is the Cotton-field, to which
This injured brother's driven,
When, as the white man's *slave*, he toils
From early morn till even.

D is the Driver, cold and stern,
Who follows, whip in hand,
To punish those who dare to rest,
Or disobey command.

Pages from an abolitionist book for children. Abolitionists sought to convince young and old of the evils of slavery.

Slavery and Moral Suasion

Many southerners feared that the abolitionists intended to spark a slave insurrection, a belief strengthened by the outbreak of Nat Turner's Rebellion a few months after *The Liberator* made its appearance. Yet not only was Garrison completely unknown to Turner, but nearly all abolitionists, despite their militant language, rejected violence as a means of ending slavery. Many were pacifists or "non-resistants," who believed that coercion should be eliminated from all human relationships and institutions. Their strategy was **moral suasion** and their arena the public sphere. Slaveholders must be convinced of the sinfulness of their ways, and the North of its complicity in the peculiar institution.

"Non-resistants"

Among the first to appreciate the key role of public opinion in a mass democracy, abolitionists focused their efforts not on infiltrating the existing political parties, but on awakening the nation to the moral evil of slavery. Their language was deliberately provocative, calculated to seize public attention. "Slavery," said Garrison, "will not be overthrown without excitement, without a most tremendous excitement." Abolitionists argued that the inherent, natural, and absolute right to personal liberty, regardless of race, took precedence over other forms of freedom, such as the right of citizens to accumulate and hold property or self-government by local political communities.

Slave Market of America, an engraving produced by the American Anti-Slavery Society in 1836, illustrates how abolitionists sought to identify their cause with American traditions, even as they mocked the nation's claim to be a "land of the free."

"Colored citizens"

Birthright Citizenship

The crusade against slavery gave birth to a new understanding of citizenship and the rights it entailed, a new answer to the question, Who is an American? Long before the Civil War, abolitionists black and white developed a definition of national citizenship severed from the concept of race, with citizens' rights enforced by the federal government. Abolitionists campaigned for northern free blacks' right to vote, access to education, and equal treatment by transportation companies and public accommodations such as hotels and theaters. They put forward ideas that would be incorporated into the laws and Constitution after the Civil War: that any person born in the United States was entitled to American citizenship and that citizens should enjoy full equality, regardless of race.

The antislavery conventions organized by free blacks promoted the principle of "birthright citizenship," commonly describing themselves as gatherings of "colored citizens." "Nothing could be plainer," declared the National Convention of Colored Citizens in 1843, "than that native free born men must be citizens." Black leaders insistently claimed the same civil and political rights as enjoyed by white citizens, as well as what they called "public rights," which encompassed equal access to businesses serving the public such as hotels, theaters, streetcars, steamships, and railroads, which regularly excluded blacks. Free blacks and their white allies used a variety of tactics to press for citizenship rights. They launched campaigns for the right to vote, sued streetcar companies that excluded black passengers, and challenged discriminatory laws in local, state, and federal courts. Their efforts were usually unsuccessful, but they did win a few victories, such as the repeal of Ohio's discriminatory Black Laws in

1849 and the racial integration of Boston's public schools in 1855. These campaigns helped to establish a new discourse of citizens' rights.

A New Vision of America

In a society in which the rights of citizenship had become more and more closely associated with whiteness, the antislavery movement sought to reinvigorate the idea of freedom as a truly universal entitlement. The origin of the idea of an American people unbounded by race lies not with the founders, who by and large made their peace with slavery, but with the abolitionists. The antislavery crusade viewed slaves and free blacks as members of the national community, a position summarized in the title of Lydia Maria Child's popular treatise of 1833, *An Appeal in Favor of That Class of Americans Called Africans*.

An American people unbounded by race

The crusade against slavery, wrote Angelina Grimké, who became a leading abolitionist speaker, was the nation's preeminent "school in which human rights are . . . investigated." Abolitionists debated the Constitution's relationship to slavery. William Lloyd Garrison burned the document, calling it a covenant with the devil; Frederick Douglass came to believe that it offered no national protection to slavery. But despite this difference of opinion, abolitionists developed an alternative, rights-oriented view of constitutional law, grounded in their universalistic understanding of liberty. Seeking to define the core rights to which all Americans were entitled—the meaning of freedom in concrete legal terms—abolitionists invented the concept of equality before the law regardless of race, one all but unknown in American life before the Civil War. Abolitionist literature also helped to expand the definition of cruelty. The graphic descriptions of the beatings, brandings, and other physical sufferings of the slaves helped to popularize the idea of bodily integrity as a basic right that slavery violated.

Abolitionism and the Constitution

Despite being denounced by their opponents as enemies of American principles, abolitionists consciously identified their movement with the revolutionary heritage. The Declaration of Independence was not as fundamental to public oratory in the early republic as it would later become. Abolitionists seized upon it, interpreting the document's preamble as a condemnation of slavery. The Liberty Bell, later one of the nation's most venerated emblems of freedom, did not achieve that status until abolitionists adopted it as a symbol and gave it its name as part of an effort to identify their principles with those of the founders. Of course, Americans of all regions and political beliefs claimed the Revolution's legacy. Abolitionists never represented more than a small part of the North's population. But as the slavery controversy intensified, the belief spread far beyond abolitionist circles that slavery contradicted the nation's heritage of freedom.

Abolitionism and the revolutionary heritage

PERILOUS ESCAPE OF ELIZA AND CHILD.

One of many popular lithographs illustrating scenes from Harriet Beecher Stowe's novel *Uncle Tom's Cabin*, the most widely read of all antislavery writings. This depicts the slave Eliza escaping with her child across the ice floes of the Ohio River.

A photograph of Frederick Douglass, the fugitive slave who became a prominent abolitionist, taken between 1847 and 1852. As a fellow abolitionist noted at the time, "The very look and bearing of Douglass are an irresistible logic against the oppression of his race."

BLACK AND WHITE ABOLITIONISM

Black Abolitionists

Blacks played a leading role in the antislavery movement. Frederick Douglass was only one among many former slaves who published accounts of their lives in bondage; these works convinced thousands of northerners of the evils of slavery. Indeed, the most effective piece of antislavery literature of the entire period, Harriet Beecher Stowe's novel *Uncle Tom's Cabin*, was to some extent modeled on the autobiography of the fugitive slave Josiah Henson. Serialized in 1851 in a Washington antislavery newspaper and published as a book the following year, **Uncle Tom's Cabin** sold more than 1 million copies by 1854, and it also inspired numerous stage versions. By portraying slaves as sympathetic men and women, and as Christians at the mercy of slaveholders who split up families and set bloodhounds on innocent mothers and children, Stowe's melodrama gave the abolitionist message a powerful human appeal.

By the 1840s, black abolitionists sought an independent role within the movement, regularly holding their own conventions. The black abolitionist Henry Highland Garnet, who as a child had escaped from slavery in Maryland with his father, proclaimed at one such gathering in 1843 that slaves should rise in rebellion to throw off their shackles. His position was so at odds with the prevailing belief in moral suasion that the published proceedings entirely omitted the speech.

At every opportunity, black abolitionists rejected the nation's pretensions as a land of liberty. Free black communities in the North devised an alternative calendar of "freedom celebrations" centered on January 1, the date in 1808 on which the slave trade became illegal, and August 1, the anniversary of West Indian emancipation, rather than July 4. Even more persistently than their white counterparts, black abolitionists articulated the ideal of color-blind citizenship.

The greatest oration on American slavery and American freedom was delivered in Rochester in 1852 by Frederick Douglass. Speaking just after the annual Independence Day celebration, Douglass posed the question, "What, to the Slave, Is the Fourth of July?" He answered that Fourth of July festivities revealed the hypocrisy of a nation that proclaimed its belief in liberty yet daily committed "practices more shocking and bloody" than did any other country on earth. Like other abolitionists, however, Douglass also laid claim to the founders' legacy. The Revolution had left a "rich inheritance of justice, liberty, prosperity, and independence" from which subsequent generations had tragically strayed. Only by abolishing slavery and freeing the "great doctrines" of the Declaration of Independence from the "narrow bounds" of race could the United States recapture its original mission.

Gentlemen of Property and Standing

At first, abolitionism aroused violent hostility from northerners who feared that the movement threatened to disrupt the Union, interfere with profits wrested from slave labor, and overturn white supremacy. Led by "**gentlemen of property and standing**" (often merchants with close commercial ties to the South), mobs disrupted abolitionist meetings in northern cities.

In 1837, antislavery editor Elijah P. Lovejoy became the movement's first martyr when he was killed by a mob in Alton, Illinois, while defending his press. In 1838, a mob in Philadelphia burned to the ground Pennsylvania Hall, which abolitionists had built to hold their meetings. Before starting the fire, however, the mob patriotically carried a portrait of George Washington to safety.

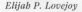

Elijah P. Lovejoy

Elsewhere, crowds of southerners, with the unspoken approval of Andrew Jackson's postmaster general, Amos Kendall, burned abolitionist literature that they had removed from the mails. In 1836, when abolitionists began to flood Washington with petitions calling for emancipation in the nation's capital, the House of Representatives adopted the notorious **gag rule**, which prohibited their consideration. The rule was repealed in 1844, thanks largely to the tireless opposition of former president John Quincy Adams, who from 1831 represented Massachusetts in the House.

Burning abolitionist literature

Far from stemming the movement's growth, however, mob attacks and attempts to limit abolitionists' freedom of speech convinced many northerners that slavery was incompatible with the democratic liberties of white Americans. "We commenced the present struggle," announced

Destruction by Fire of Pennsylvania Hall, a lithograph depicting the burning of the abolitionist meeting hall by a Philadelphia mob in 1838.

BLACK AND WHITE ABOLITIONISM | 349

abolitionist William Jay, "to obtain the freedom of the slave; we are compelled to continue it to preserve our own. We are now contending . . . for the liberty of speech, of the press, and of conscience."

The abolitionist movement now broadened its appeal so as to win the support of northerners who cared little about the rights of blacks but could be convinced that slavery endangered their own cherished freedoms. The gag rule aroused considerable resentment in the North. "If the government once begins to discriminate as to what is orthodox and what heterodox in opinion," wrote the *New York Evening Post*, hardly a supporter of abolitionism, "farewell, a long farewell to our freedom."

Am I Not a Man and a Brother? The most common abolitionist depiction of a slave, this image not only presents African-Americans as unthreatening individuals seeking white assistance but also calls upon white Americans to recognize blacks as fellow men unjustly held in bondage.

THE ORIGINS OF FEMINISM

The Rise of the Public Woman

"When the true history of the antislavery cause shall be written," Frederick Douglass later recalled, "women will occupy a large space in its pages." Much of the movement's grassroots strength derived from northern women, who joined by the thousands. Most were evangelical Protestants, New England Congregationalists, or Quakers convinced, as Martha Higginson of Vermont wrote, that slavery was "a disgrace in this land of Christian light and liberty."

Women and politics

The public sphere was open to women in ways government and party politics were not. Women's letters and diaries reveal a keen interest in political issues, from slavery to presidential campaigns. Long before they could vote, women circulated petitions, attended mass meetings, marched in political parades, delivered public lectures, and raised money for political causes. They became active in the temperance movement, the building of asylums, and other reform activities. **Dorothea Dix**, a Massachusetts schoolteacher, was the leading advocate of more humane treatment of the insane, who at the time generally were placed in jails alongside debtors and hardened criminals. Thanks to her efforts, twenty-eight states constructed mental hospitals before the Civil War.

Women and Free Speech

Abolitionism and women's rights

All these activities enabled women to carve out a place in the public sphere. But it was participation in abolitionism that inspired the early movement for women's rights. In working for the rights of the slave, not a few women developed a new understanding of their own subordinate status. The daughters of a prominent South Carolina slaveholder, Angelina and Sarah Grimké had been converted first to Quakerism and then to abolitionism while visiting Philadelphia. During the 1830s, they began to deliver popular lectures that offered a scathing condemnation of slavery from the perspective of those who had witnessed its evils firsthand.

Outraged by the sight of females sacrificing all "modesty and delicacy" by appearing on the public lecture platform, a group of Massachusetts clergymen denounced the sisters. In reply, they forthrightly defended not only the right of women to take part in political debate but also their right to share the social and educational privileges enjoyed by men. "Since I engaged in the investigation of the rights of the slave," declared Angelina Grimké, "I have necessarily been led to a better understanding of my own." Her sister Sarah proceeded to publish *Letters on the Equality of the Sexes* (1838), a powerful call for equal rights for women. The book raised numerous issues familiar even today, including what later generations would call "equal pay for equal work." Why, Sarah Grimké wondered, did male teachers invariably receive higher wages than women, and a male tailor earn "two or three times as much" as a female counterpart "although the work done by each may be equally good?"

Letters on the Equality of the Sexes

Women's Rights

The Grimké sisters were the first to apply the abolitionist doctrine of universal freedom and equality to the status of women. Although they soon retired from the fray, unwilling to endure the intense criticism to which they were subjected, their writings helped to spark the movement for women's rights, which arose in the 1840s.

Elizabeth Cady Stanton and Lucretia Mott, the key organizers of the Seneca Falls Convention of 1848, were veterans of the antislavery crusade. In 1840, they had traveled to London as delegates to the World Anti-Slavery Convention, only to be barred from participating because of their sex. The Seneca Falls Convention, a gathering on behalf of women's rights held in the upstate New York town where Stanton lived, raised the issue of **woman suffrage** for the first time. Stanton, the principal author, modeled the Seneca Falls Declaration of Sentiments on the Declaration of Independence (see the Appendix for the full text). But the document added "women" to Jefferson's axiom "all men are created equal," and in place of a list of injustices committed by George III, it condemned the "injuries and usurpations on the part of man toward woman." The first was denying her the right to vote. As Stanton told the convention, only the vote would make woman "free as man is free," since in a democratic society, freedom was impossible without access to the ballot. The argument was simple and irrefutable: in the words of Lydia Maria Child, "either the theory of our government is *false*, or women have a right to vote."

The Seneca Falls Convention

The Declaration of Sentiments

From Declaration of Sentiments of the Seneca Falls Convention (1848)

The Seneca Falls Convention is best known as the beginning of the seventy-year struggle for woman suffrage. Modeled on the Declaration of Independence and mainly written by Elizabeth Cady Stanton, the Declaration of Sentiments began by demanding the right to vote but went on to denounce numerous forms of inequality that prevented women from enjoying full participation in American life.

We hold these truths to be self-evident: that all men and women are created equal; that they are endowed by their Creator with certain inalienable rights; that among these are life, liberty, and the pursuit of happiness. . . .

The history of mankind is a history of repeated injuries and usurpations on the part of man toward woman, having in direct object the establishment of an absolute tyranny over her. To prove this, let facts be submitted to a candid world.

He has never permitted her to exercise her inalienable right to the elective franchise. . . .

He has made her, if married, in the eye of the law, civilly dead.

He has taken from her all right in property, even to the wages she earns. . . . In the covenant of marriage, she is compelled to promise obedience to her husband, he becoming, to all intents and purposes, her master—the law giving him power to deprive her of her liberty, and to administer chastisement. . . .

He has monopolized nearly all the profitable employments, and from those she is permitted to follow, she receives but a scanty remuneration. He closes against her all the avenues to wealth and distinction which he considers most honorable to himself. As a teacher of theology, medicine, or law, she is not known. He has denied her the facilities of obtaining a thorough education, all colleges being closed against her. . . .

He has endeavored, in every way that he could, to destroy her confidence in her own powers, to lessen her self-respect, and to make her willing to lead a dependent and abject life.

Now, in view of the unjust laws mentioned above, and because women do feel themselves aggrieved, oppressed, and fraudulently deprived of their most sacred rights, we insist that they have immediate admission to all the rights and privileges which belong to them as citizens of the United States.

QUESTIONS

1. *Other than denial of the right to vote, what are the key grievances of these women?*

2. *Why does the document model itself on the Declaration of Independence?*

Seneca Falls marked the beginning of the seventy-year struggle for woman suffrage. The vote, however, was hardly the only issue raised at the convention. The Declaration of Sentiments condemned the entire structure of inequality that denied women access to education and employment, gave husbands control over the property and wages of their wives and custody of children in the event of divorce, deprived women of independent legal status after they married, and restricted them to the home as their "sphere of action." Equal rights became the rallying cry of the early movement for women's rights, and equal rights meant claiming access to all the prevailing definitions of freedom.

Start of the struggle for suffrage

Feminism and Freedom

Like abolitionism, temperance, and other reforms, **feminism** was an international movement. Lacking broad backing at home, early feminists found allies abroad. "Women alone will say what freedom they want," declared an article in *The Free Woman*, a journal established in Paris in 1832.

Women, wrote Margaret Fuller, had the same right as men to develop their talents, to "grow . . . to live freely and unimpeded." The daughter of a Jeffersonian congressman, Fuller was educated at home. (She learned Latin before the age of six.) She became part of New England's transcendentalist circle (discussed in Chapter 9) and from 1840 to 1842 edited *The Dial*, a magazine that reflected the group's views. In 1844, Fuller became literary editor of the *New York Tribune*, the first woman to achieve so important a position in American journalism.

In *Woman in the Nineteenth Century*, published in 1845, Fuller sought to apply to women the transcendentalist idea that freedom meant a quest for personal development. "Every path" to self-fulfillment, she insisted, should be "open to woman as freely as to man." Fuller traveled to Europe as a correspondent for the *Tribune*, and there she married an Italian patriot. Along with her husband and baby, she died in a shipwreck in 1850 while returning to the United States.

The artist Thomas Hicks painted this portrait of the feminist writer and editor Margaret Fuller in 1848, two years before she died in a shipwreck as she was returning from a sojourn in Europe.

Women and Work

Women also demanded the right to participate in the market revolution. At an 1851 women's rights convention, the black abolitionist Sojourner Truth insisted that the movement devote attention to the plight of poor and working-class women and repudiate the idea that women were too delicate to engage in work outside the home. Born a slave in New York State around 1799, Truth did not obtain her freedom until slavery finally ended in the state in 1827. A listener at her 1851 speech (which was not recorded at the time) later recalled that Truth had spoken of her years of hard physical labor, flexed her arm to show her strength, and exclaimed, "And aren't I a woman?"

VOICES OF FREEDOM

From Angelina Grimké, Letter in
The Liberator (August 2, 1837)

The daughters of a prominent South Carolina slaveholder, Angelina and Sarah Grimké became abolitionists after being sent to Philadelphia for education. In this article, Angelina Grimké explains how participation in the movement against slavery led her to a greater recognition of women's lack of basic freedoms.

Since I engaged in the investigation of the rights of the slave, I have necessarily been led to a better understanding of my own; for I have found the Anti-Slavery cause to be . . . the school in which human rights are more fully investigated, and better understood and taught, than in any other [reform] enterprise. . . . Here we are led to examine why human beings have any rights. It is because they are moral beings. . . . Now it naturally occurred to me, that if rights were founded in moral being, then the circumstance of sex could not give to man higher rights and responsibilities, than to woman. . . .

When I look at human beings as moral beings, all distinction in sex sinks to insignificance and nothingness; for I believe it regulates rights and responsibilities no more than the color of the skin or the eyes. My doctrine, then is, that whatever it is morally right for man to do, it is morally right for woman to do. . . . This regulation of duty by the mere circumstance of sex . . . has led to all that [numerous] train of evils flowing out of the anti-christian doctrine of masculine and feminine virtues. By this doctrine, man has been converted into the warrior, and clothed in sternness . . . whilst woman has been taught to lean upon an arm of flesh, to . . . be admired for her personal charms, and caressed and humored like a spoiled child, or converted into a mere drudge to suit the convenience of her lord and master. . . . It has robbed woman of . . . the right to think and speak and act on all great moral questions, just as men think and speak and act. . . .

The discussion of the wrongs of slavery has opened the way for the discussion of other rights, and the ultimate result will most certainly be . . . the letting of the oppressed of every grade and description go free.

From Catharine Beecher, *An Essay on Slavery and Abolitionism* (1837)

Most men, and many women, did not approve of women taking part in public debate. The prominent writer Catharine Beecher responded to the activities of the Grimké sisters by urging them to accept the fact that "heaven" had designated man "the superior" and woman "the subordinate."

I have . . . been informed, that you contemplate a tour, during the ensuing year, for the purpose of exerting your influence to form Abolition Societies among ladies of the non-slave-holding States. . . . The object I have in view, is to present some reasons why it seems unwise and inexpedient for ladies of the non-slave-holding States to unite themselves in Abolition Societies; and thus, at the same time, to exhibit the inexpediency of the course you propose to adopt. . . .

Heaven has appointed to one sex the superior, and to the other the subordinate station, and this without any reference to the character or conduct of either. It is therefore as much for the dignity as it is for the interest of females, in all respects to conform to the duties of this relation. . . . But while woman holds a subordinate relation in society to the other sex, it is not because it was designed that her duties or her influence should be any the less important, or all-pervading. But it was designed that the mode of gaining influence and of exercising power should be altogether different and peculiar. . . . Woman is to win every thing by peace and love; by making herself so much respected, esteemed and loved, that to yield to her opinions and to gratify her wishes, will be the free-will offering of the heart. But this is to be all accomplished in the domestic and social circle. . . . The moment woman begins to feel the promptings of ambition, or the thirst for power, her ægis of defence is gone. All the sacred protection of religion, all the generous promptings of chivalry, all the poetry of romantic gallantry, depend upon woman's retaining her place as dependent and defenceless, and making no claims, and maintaining no right but what are the gifts of honour, rectitude and love.

A woman may seek the aid of co-operation and combination among her own sex, to assist her in her appropriate offices of piety, charity, maternal and domestic duty; but whatever, in any measure, throws a woman into the attitude of a combatant, either for herself or others—whatever binds her in a party conflict—whatever obliges her in any way to exert coercive influences, throws her out of her appropriate sphere. . . . In this country, petitions to congress, in reference to the official duties of legislators, seem, IN ALL CASES, to fall entirely without the sphere of female duty. Men are the proper persons to make appeals to the rulers whom they appoint, and if their female friends, by arguments and persuasions, can induce them to petition, all the good that can be done by such measures will be secured.

QUESTIONS

1. *What consequences does Grimké believe follow from the idea of rights being founded in the individual's "moral being"?*

2. *How does Beecher believe women should exert power within American society?*

3. *How do the two definitions of women's freedom differ from one another?*

Although those who convened at Seneca Falls were predominantly from the middle class—no representatives of the growing number of "factory girls" and domestic servants took part—the participants rejected the identification of the home as woman's "sphere." During the 1850s, some feminists tried to popularize a new style of dress, devised by Amelia Bloomer, consisting of a loose-fitting tunic and trousers. The target of innumerable male jokes, the "bloomer" costume attempted to make a serious point—that the long dresses, tight corsets, and numerous petticoats considered to be appropriate female attire were so confining that they made it almost impossible for women to claim a place in the public sphere or to work outside the home.

Amelia Bloomer and female attire

The Slavery of Sex

The dichotomy between freedom and slavery powerfully shaped early feminists' political language. Just as the idea of "wage slavery" enabled northern workers to challenge the inequalities of the market revolution, the concept of the "slavery of sex" empowered the women's movement to develop an all-encompassing critique of male authority and their own subordination. Feminists of the 1840s and 1850s pointed out that the law of marriage made nonsense of the description of the family as a "private" institution independent of public authority. When the abolitionists and women's rights activists Lucy Stone and Henry Blackwell married, they felt obliged to repudiate New York's laws that clothed the husband "with legal powers which . . . no man should possess." The analogy between free women and slaves gained prominence as it was swept up in the accelerating debate over slavery. For their part, southern defenders of slavery frequently linked slavery and marriage as natural and just forms of inequality. Eliminating the former institution, they charged, would threaten the latter.

Marriage and slavery

Marriage was not, literally speaking, equivalent to slavery. The married woman, however, did not enjoy the fruits of her own labor—a central element of freedom. Beginning with Mississippi in 1839, numerous states enacted married women's property laws, shielding from a husband's creditors property brought into a marriage by his wife. Such laws initially aimed not to expand women's rights so much as to prevent families from losing their property during the depression that began in 1837. But in 1860, New York enacted a more far-reaching measure, allowing married women to sign contracts, buy and sell property, and keep their

Woman's Emancipation, a satirical engraving from *Harper's Monthly*, August 1851, illustrating the much-ridiculed "bloomer" costume.

own wages. In most states, however, property accumulated after marriage, as well as wages earned by the wife, still belonged to the husband.

"Social Freedom"

Influenced by abolitionism, women's rights advocates turned another popular understanding of freedom—self-ownership, or control over one's own person—in an entirely new direction. The law of domestic relations presupposed the husband's right of sexual access to his wife and to inflict corporal punishment on her. Courts proved reluctant to intervene in cases of physical abuse so long as it was not "extreme" or "intolerable." "Women's Rights," declared a Boston meeting in 1859, included "freedom and equal rights in the family." The demand that women should enjoy the rights to regulate their own sexual activity and procreation and to be protected by the state against violence at the hands of their husbands challenged the notion that claims for justice, freedom, and individual rights should stop at the household's door.

Self-ownership

Rights within the family

The issue of women's private freedom revealed underlying differences within the movement for women's rights. Belief in equality between the sexes and in the sexes' natural differences coexisted in antebellum feminist thought. Even as they entered the public sphere and thereby challenged some aspects of the era's "cult of domesticity" (discussed in Chapter 9), many early feminists accepted other elements. Allowing women a greater role in the public sphere, many female reformers argued, would bring their "inborn" maternal instincts to bear on public life, to the benefit of the entire society.

Even feminists critical of the existing institution of marriage generally refrained from raising in public the explosive issue of women's "private" freedom. Not until the twentieth century would the demand that freedom be extended to intimate aspects of life inspire a mass movement. But the dramatic fall in the birthrate over the course of the nineteenth century suggests that many women were quietly exercising "personal freedom" within their families.

Women's private freedom

The Abolitionist Schism

Even in reform circles, the demand for a greater public role for women remained extremely controversial. Massachusetts physician Samuel Gridley Howe pioneered humane treatment of the blind and educational reform, and he was an ardent abolitionist. But Howe did not support his wife's participation in the movement for female suffrage, which, he complained, caused her to "neglect domestic relations." When abolitionism split into two wings in 1840, the immediate cause was a dispute over the proper role of women in antislavery work. Abby Kelley's election to the business committee of the

The role of women in abolitionism

This image appeared on the cover of the sheet music for "Get Off the Track!," a song popularized by the Hutchinson singers, who performed antislavery songs. The trains *Immediate Emancipation* (with *The Liberator* as its front wheel) and *Liberty Party* pull into a railroad station. *The Herald of Freedom* and *American Standard* were antislavery newspapers. The song's lyrics praised William Lloyd Garrison and criticized various politicians, among them Henry Clay. The chorus went: "Roll it along! Through the nation / Freedom's car, Emancipation."

American Anti-Slavery Society sparked the formation of a rival abolitionist organization, the American and Foreign Anti-Slavery Society, which believed it wrong for a woman to occupy so prominent a position. The antislavery poet John Greenleaf Whittier compared Kelley to Eve, Delilah, and Helen of Troy, women who had sown the seeds of male destruction.

Behind the split lay the fear among some abolitionists that Garrison's radicalism on issues like women's rights, as well as his refusal to support the idea of abolitionists voting or running for public office, impeded the movement's growth. Determined to make abolitionism a political movement, the seceders formed the **Liberty Party**, which nominated James G. Birney as its candidate for president. He received only 7,000 votes (about one-third of 1 percent of the total). In 1840, antislavery northerners saw little wisdom in "throwing away" their ballots.

Achievements of feminism and abolitionism

While the achievement of most of their demands lay far in the future, the women's rights movement succeeded in making "the woman question" a permanent part of the transatlantic discussion of social reform. As for abolitionism, although it remained a significant presence in northern public life until emancipation was achieved, by 1840 the movement had accomplished its most important work. More than 1,000 local antislavery societies were now scattered throughout the North, representing a broad constituency awakened to the moral issue of slavery. The "great duty of freedom," Ralph Waldo Emerson had declared in 1837, was "to open our halls to discussion of this question." The abolitionists' greatest achievement lay in shattering the conspiracy of silence that had sought to preserve national unity by suppressing public debate over slavery.

CHAPTER REVIEW AND ONLINE RESOURCES

REVIEW QUESTIONS

1. *How did the utopian communities challenge existing ideas about property and marriage?*

2. *How did the supporters and opponents of temperance understand the meaning of freedom differently?*

3. *What were the similarities and differences between the common school and the institutions like asylums, orphanages, and prisons that were created by reformers?*

4. *Why did so many prominent white Americans, from both the North and South, support the colonization of freed slaves?*

5. *How was the abolition movement affected by other social and economic changes such as the rise in literacy, new print technology, and ideas associated with the market revolution?*

6. *How was racism evident even in the abolitionist movement? What steps did some abolitionists take to fight racism in American society?*

7. *How could antebellum women participate in the public sphere even though they were excluded from government and politics?*

8. *How did white women's participation in the abolitionist movement push them to a new understanding of their own rights and oppression?*

9. *How did advocates for women's rights in these years both accept and challenge existing gender beliefs and social roles?*

10. *To what degree was antebellum reform international in scope?*

11. *How did the antislavery movement give rise to a new understanding of citizenship and the rights it afforded?*

KEY TERMS

Go to **INQUIZITIVE**

To see what you know—and learn what you've missed—with personalized feedback along the way.

Visit the *Give Me Liberty!* **Student Site** for primary source documents and images, interactive maps, author videos featuring Eric Foner, and more.

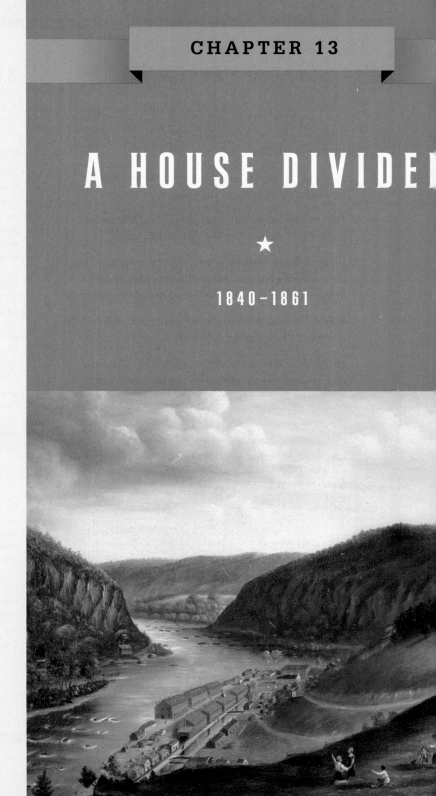

CHAPTER 13

A HOUSE DIVIDED

★

1840–1861

An 1835 painting of the federal arsenal at Harpers Ferry, Virginia (now West Virginia). John Brown's raid on Harpers Ferry in October 1859 helped to bring on the Civil War.

I n 1855, Thomas Crawford, one of the era's most prominent American sculptors, was asked to design a statue to adorn the Capitol's dome, still under construction in Washington, D.C. He proposed a statue of Freedom, a female figure wearing a liberty cap. Secretary of War Jefferson Davis of Mississippi, one of the country's largest slaveholders, objected to Crawford's plan. Ancient Romans, he noted, regarded the cap as "the badge of the freed slave." Its use, he feared, might suggest that there was a connection between the slaves' longing for freedom and the liberty of freeborn Americans. Davis ordered the liberty cap replaced with a less controversial military symbol, a feathered helmet.

In 1863, the colossal Statue of Freedom was installed atop the Capitol, where it can still be seen today. By the time it was put in place, the country was immersed in the Civil War and Jefferson Davis had become president of the Confederate States of America. The dispute over the Statue of Freedom offers a small illustration of how, by the mid-1850s, nearly every public question was being swept up into the gathering storm over slavery.

FRUITS OF MANIFEST DESTINY

Continental Expansion

In the 1840s, slavery moved to the center stage of American politics. It did so not in the moral language or with the immediatist program of

FOCUS QUESTIONS

- *What were the major factors contributing to U.S. territorial expansion in the 1840s?*

- *Why did the expansion of slavery become the most divisive political issue in the 1840s and 1850s?*

- *What combination of issues and events fueled the creation of the Republican Party in the 1850s?*

- *What enabled Lincoln to emerge from the divisive party politics of the 1850s?*

- *What were the final steps on the road to secession?*

The original and final designs for Thomas Crawford's *Statue of Freedom* for the dome of the Capitol building. Secretary of War Jefferson Davis of Mississippi insisted that the liberty cap in the first design, a symbol of the emancipated slave in ancient Rome, be replaced.

abolitionism, but as a result of the nation's territorial expansion. Between 1840 and 1860, nearly 300,000 men, women, and children braved disease, starvation, the natural barrier of the Rocky Mountains, and occasional Indian attacks to travel overland to Oregon and California.

During most of the 1840s, the United States and Great Britain jointly administered Oregon, and Utah was part of Mexico. This did not stop Americans from settling in either region. National boundaries meant little to those who moved west. The 1840s witnessed an intensification of the old belief that God intended the American nation to reach all the way to the Pacific Ocean. As noted in Chapter 9, the term that became a shorthand for this expansionist spirit was "manifest destiny."

"Manifest destiny"

The Mexican Frontier: New Mexico and California

Settlement of Oregon did not directly raise the issue of slavery, although the prospect of new states in a region that did not seem hospitable to slavery alarmed some southerners. But the nation's acquisition of part of Mexico did. When Mexico achieved its independence from Spain in 1821, it was nearly as large as the United States, and its population of 6.5 million was about two-thirds that of its northern neighbor. However, Mexico's northern provinces—California, New Mexico, and Texas—were isolated and sparsely settled outposts surrounded by Indian country. California's non-Indian population in 1821, some 3,200 missionaries, soldiers, and settlers, was vastly outnumbered by about 20,000 Indians living and working on land owned by religious missions and by 150,000 members of unsubdued tribes in the interior. By 1840, California was already linked commercially with the United States, and New England ships were trading with the region. In 1846, Alfred Robinson, who had moved from Boston, published *Life in California*. "In this age of annexation," he wondered, "why not extend the 'area of freedom' by the annexation of California?"

Mexican California

A scene on a California ranch in 1849, with *Californios* (on horseback) and Native Americans at work.

The Texas Revolt

The first part of Mexico to be settled by significant numbers of Americans was Texas, whose non-Indian population of Spanish origin (called ***Tejanos***)

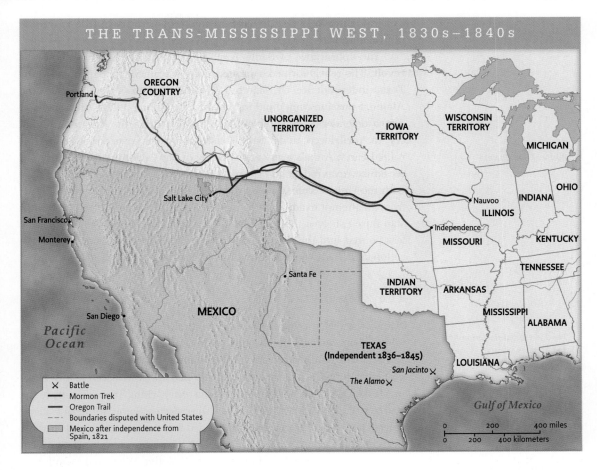

THE TRANS-MISSISSIPPI WEST, 1830s–1840s

Legend:
- **X** Battle
- Mormon Trek
- Oregon Trail
- --- Boundaries disputed with United States
- Mexico after independence from Spain, 1821

numbered only about 2,000 when Mexico became independent. In order to develop the region, the Spanish government had accepted an offer by Moses Austin, a Connecticut-born farmer, to colonize it with Americans. In 1820, Austin received a large land grant. He died soon afterward, and his son Stephen continued the plan, now in independent Mexico, reselling land in smaller plots to American settlers at twelve cents per acre.

Alarmed that its grip on the area was weakening, the Mexican government in 1830 annulled existing land contracts and barred future emigration from the United States. Led by Stephen Austin, American settlers demanded greater autonomy within Mexico. Part of the area's tiny *Tejano* elite joined them. Mostly ranchers and large farmers, they had welcomed the economic boom that accompanied the settlers and had formed economic alliances with American traders. The issue of slavery further exacerbated matters. Mexico had abolished slavery, but local authorities allowed American settlers to bring slaves with them. Mexico's ruler,

Westward migration in the early and mid-1840s took American settlers across Indian country into the Oregon Territory, ownership of which was disputed with Great Britain. The Mormons migrated west to Salt Lake City, then part of Mexico.

Reasons for the Texas revolt

General **Antonio López de Santa Anna**, sent an army in 1835 to impose central authority.

The appearance of Santa Anna's army sparked the chaotic **Texas revolt**. The rebels formed a provisional government that soon called for Texan independence. On March 6, 1836, Santa Anna's army stormed the Alamo, a mission compound in San Antonio, killing its 187 American and *Tejano* defenders. "Remember the Alamo" became the Texans' rallying cry. In April, forces under Sam Houston, a former governor of Tennessee, routed Santa Anna's army at the Battle of San Jacinto and forced him to recognize Texas independence. In 1837, the Texas Congress called for union with the United States. But fearing the political disputes certain to result from an attempt to add another slave state to the Union, President Martin Van Buren shelved the question. Settlers from the United States nonetheless poured into the region, many of them slaveowners taking up fertile cotton land. By 1845, the population of Texas reached nearly 150,000.

Battle of San Jacinto

The Election of 1844

The Tyler administration and Texas

Texas annexation remained on the political back burner until President John Tyler revived it in the hope of rescuing his failed administration and securing southern support for renomination in 1844. In April 1844, a letter by John C. Calhoun, whom Tyler had appointed secretary of state, was leaked to the press. It linked the idea of absorbing Texas directly to the goal of strengthening slavery in the United States. Some southern leaders, indeed, hoped that Texas could be divided into several states, thus further enhancing the South's power in Congress. Late that month, Henry Clay and former president Van Buren, the prospective Whig and Democratic candidates for president and two of the party system's most venerable leaders, met at Clay's Kentucky plantation. They agreed to issue letters rejecting immediate annexation on the grounds that it might provoke war with Mexico.

Slavery and expansion

The plaza in San Antonio not long after the United States annexed Texas in 1845.

Clay went on to receive the Whig nomination, but for Van Buren the letters proved to be a disaster. At the Democratic convention, southerners bent on annexation deserted Van Buren's cause, and he failed to receive the two-thirds majority necessary for nomination. The delegates then turned to the little-known James K. Polk, a former governor of Tennessee whose main assets were his support for annexation and his close association with Andrew Jackson, still the party's most popular figure. To soothe injured feelings among northern Democrats over the rejection of Van Buren, the party platform called for not only the "reannexation" of Texas (implying that Texas had been part of the Louisiana Purchase and therefore had once belonged to the United States) but also the "reoccupation" of all of Oregon. "Fifty-four forty or fight"—American control of Oregon all the way to its northern boundary at north latitude 54°40'—became a popular campaign slogan.

Polk was the first "dark horse" candidate for president—that is, one whose nomination was completely unexpected. In the fall, he defeated Clay in an extremely close election. Polk's margin in the popular vote was less than 2 percent. Had not James G. Birney, running again as the Liberty Party candidate, received 16,000 votes in New York, mostly from antislavery Whigs, Clay would have been elected. In March 1845, only days before Polk's inauguration, Congress declared Texas part of the United States.

The Road to War

James K. Polk may have been virtually unknown, but he assumed the presidency with a clearly defined set of goals: to reduce the tariff, reestablish the Independent Treasury system, settle the dispute over ownership of Oregon, and bring California into the Union. Congress soon enacted the

A campaign handkerchief from 1844 depicts the Whig candidate for president, Henry Clay, surrounded by images of national unity and the economic progress that, Whigs argued, would follow from the enactment of a protective tariff. Clay and his running mate, Theodore Frelinghuysen, were narrowly defeated by the Democrat James K. Polk.

This 1853 watercolor by Sarah Ann Lillie Hardinge depicts a river crossing in Texas. Before bridges were built, a ferryman (in this case, a slave) brought people and goods across a river by pulling on a rope.

first two goals, and the third was accomplished in an agreement with Great Britain dividing Oregon at the forty-ninth parallel.

Acquiring California

Acquiring California proved more difficult. Polk dispatched an emissary to Mexico offering to purchase the region, but the Mexican government refused to negotiate. By the spring of 1846, Polk was planning for military action. In April, American soldiers under Zachary Taylor moved into the region between the Nueces River and the Rio Grande, land claimed by both countries on the disputed border between Texas and Mexico. This action made conflict with Mexican forces inevitable. When fighting broke out, Polk claimed that the Mexicans had "shed blood upon American soil" and called for a declaration of war.

The War and Its Critics

The **Mexican War** was the first American conflict to be fought primarily on foreign soil and the first in which American troops occupied a foreign capital. Inspired by the expansionist fervor of manifest destiny, a majority of Americans supported the war. But a significant minority in the North dissented, fearing that far from expanding the "great empire of liberty," the administration's real aim was to acquire new land for the expansion of slavery. Henry David Thoreau was jailed in Massachusetts in 1846 for refusing to pay taxes as a protest against the war. Defending his action, Thoreau wrote

"On Civil Disobedience"

an important essay, "On Civil Disobedience," which inspired such later advocates of nonviolent resistance to unjust laws as Martin Luther King Jr.

Among the war's critics was Abraham Lincoln, who had been elected to Congress in 1846 from Illinois. Like many Whigs, Lincoln questioned whether the Mexicans had actually inflicted casualties on American soil, as Polk claimed. Lincoln's stance proved unpopular in Illinois. He had

Lincoln as war critic

already agreed to serve only one term in Congress, but when Democrats captured his seat in 1848, many blamed the result on Lincoln's criticism of the war. Nonetheless, the concerns he raised regarding the president's power to "make war at pleasure" would continue to echo in the twentieth and twenty-first centuries.

Combat in Mexico

More than 60,000 volunteers enlisted and did most of the fighting. Combat took place on three fronts. In June 1846, a band of American insurrectionists proclaimed California freed from Mexican control and named Captain John C. Frémont, head of a small scientific expedition in the West, its ruler. Their aim was California's incorporation into the United States, but for the moment they adopted a flag depicting a large bear as the symbol of the area's independence. A month later, the U.S. Navy sailed into Monterey and San Francisco harbors, raised the American flag, and put an end to the "bear flag republic." At almost the same time, 1,600 American troops under General Stephen W. Kearney occupied Sante Fe without resistance and then set out for southern California, where they helped to put down a Mexican uprising against American rule.

The bulk of the fighting occurred in central Mexico. In February 1847, Taylor defeated Santa Anna's army at the Battle of Buena Vista. When the Mexican government still refused to negotiate, Polk ordered American forces under Winfield Scott to march inland from the port of Veracruz toward Mexico City. Scott's forces routed Mexican defenders and in September occupied the country's capital. In February 1848, the two governments agreed to the Treaty of Guadalupe Hidalgo, which confirmed the annexation of Texas and ceded California and present-day New Mexico, Arizona, Nevada, and Utah to the United States.

War News from Mexico, an 1848 painting by Richard C. Woodville, shows how Americans received war news through the popular press.

The Mexican War is only a footnote in most Americans' historical memory. Unlike for other wars, few public monuments celebrate the conflict. Mexicans, however, regard the war (or "the dismemberment," as it is called) as a central event of their national history and a source of resentment over a century and a half after it was fought.

With the end of the Mexican War, the United States absorbed half a million square miles of Mexico's territory, one-third of that nation's total area. A region that for centuries had been united was suddenly split in two, dividing families and severing trade routes. An estimated 75,000 to 100,000 Spanish-speaking Mexicans and more than 150,000 Indians inhabited the land annexed from Mexico, known as the Mexican Cession. The Treaty of Guadalupe Hidalgo guaranteed to "male citizens" of the area "the free enjoyment of their liberty and property" and "all the rights" of Americans—a provision designed to protect the property of large Mexican landowners in California. Thus, in the first half of the nineteenth century, some residents of the area went from being Spaniards to Mexicans to Americans. Although not newcomers, they had to adjust to a new identity as if they were immigrants. As for Indians whose homelands and hunting grounds suddenly became part of the United States, the treaty referred to them only as "savage tribes" whom the United States must prevent from launching incursions into Mexico across the new border.

The Mexican Cession

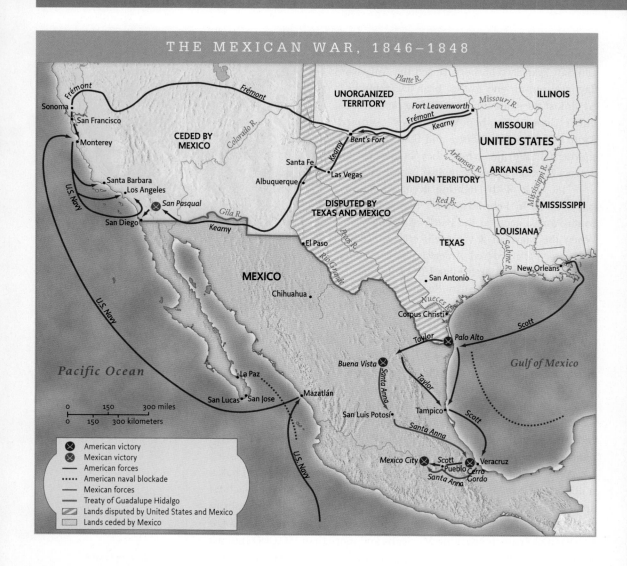

THE MEXICAN WAR, 1846–1848

The Mexican War was the first in which an American army invaded another country and occupied its capital. As a result of the war, the United States acquired a vast new area in the modern-day Southwest.

The Texas Borderland

After achieving independence in 1836, Texas became a prime example of a western borderland. *Anglos* (white settlers from the East) and *Tejanos* had fought together to achieve independence, but soon relations between them soured. *Anglos* in search of land and resources expelled some Mexicans, including former allies, now suspected of loyalty to Mexico. Juan Seguín, a *Tejano*, had played an active role in the revolt and served for a time as mayor of San Antonio. In 1842, still mayor, he was driven from the town by vigilantes. He had become, he lamented, "a foreigner in my native land."

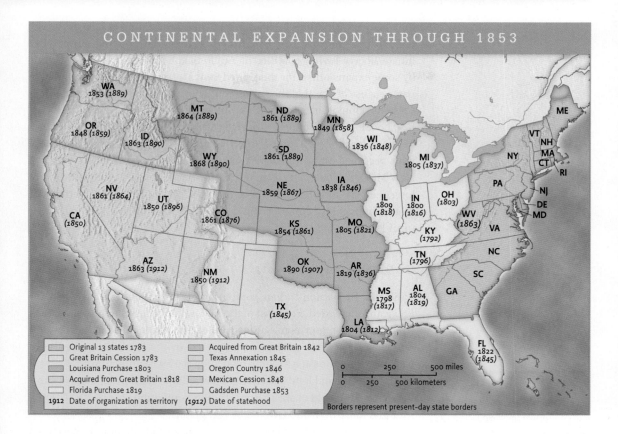

CONTINENTAL EXPANSION THROUGH 1853

Legend:
- Original 13 states 1783
- Great Britain Cession 1783
- Louisiana Purchase 1803
- Acquired from Great Britain 1818
- Florida Purchase 1819
- Acquired from Great Britain 1842
- Texas Annexation 1845
- Oregon Country 1846
- Mexican Cession 1848
- Gadsden Purchase 1853
- **1912** Date of organization as territory *(1912)* Date of statehood

Borders represent present-day state borders

Increasingly, *Tejanos* were confined to unskilled agricultural or urban labor. Some *Tejanos* used their ambiguous identities to their own advantage. During the Civil War, some *Tejano* men avoided the Confederate draft by claiming to be citizens of Mexico.

Meanwhile, in southern Texas, the disputed territory between the Nueces River and the Rio Grande, claimed by both Texas and Mexico but actually controlled by Comanche Indians, became a site of continual conflict. Authority in the area remained contested until Texas became part of the much more powerful United States and even then, Comanche power would not be broken until the 1860s and 1870s.

By 1853, with the Gadsden Purchase, the present boundaries of the United States in North America, with the exception of Alaska, had been created.

Race and Manifest Destiny

During the 1840s, territorial expansion came to be seen as proof of the innate superiority of the "Anglo-Saxon race" (a mythical construct defined largely by its opposites: blacks, Indians, Hispanics, and Catholics). "*Race*," declared John L. O'Sullivan's *Democratic Review*, was the "key" to the "history of nations." Newspapers, magazines, and scholarly works popularized the link between American freedom and the supposedly innate liberty-loving qualities of Anglo-Saxon Protestants. Indeed, calls by some expansionists for the United States to annex all of Mexico failed in part because of fear that the nation could not assimilate its large non-white Catholic population, supposedly unfit for citizenship in a republic.

"Spanish" Mexicans as white

Local circumstances affected racial definitions in the former Mexican territories. Texas defined "Spanish" Mexicans, especially those who occupied important social positions, as white. The residents of New Mexico of both Mexican and Indian origin, on the other hand, were long deemed "too Mexican" for democratic self-government. With white migration lagging, Congress did not allow New Mexico to become a state until 1912.

Gold-Rush California

Sutter's mill

California had a non-Indian population of fewer than 15,000 when the Mexican War ended. For most of the 1840s, five times as many Americans emigrated to Oregon as to California. But this changed dramatically after January 1848, when gold was discovered in the foothills of the Sierra Nevada Mountains at a sawmill owned by the Swiss immigrant Johann A. Sutter. By ship and land, newcomers poured into California, in what came to be called the **gold rush**. The non-Indian population rose to 200,000 by 1852 and more than 360,000 eight years later.

California's gold-rush population was incredibly diverse. Experienced miners flooded in from Mexico and South America. Tens of thousands of Americans who had never seen a mine arrived from the East, and from overseas came Irish, Germans, Italians, and Australians. Nearly 25,000 Chinese landed between 1849 and 1852. Unlike the families who settled farming frontiers, most of the gold-rush migrants were young men. Women played many roles in western mining communities, running restaurants and boardinghouses and working as laundresses, cooks, and prostitutes. But as late as 1860, California's male population outnumbered females by nearly three to one.

A hand-colored engraving from the 1850s advertises the sale of a sixteen-year-old Southern California Native American woman. The price, listed in French, is a pound of gunpowder and a bottle of brandy. Slavery had been abolished in California law but persisted in some parts of the state.

As early surface mines quickly became exhausted, they gave way to underground mining that required a large investment of capital. This economic development worsened conflicts among California's many racial and ethnic groups engaged in fierce competition for gold. White miners organized extralegal groups that expelled "foreign miners"—Mexicans, Chileans, Chinese, French, and American Indians—from areas with gold. The state legislature imposed a tax of twenty dollars per month on foreign miners, driving many of them from the state.

For California's Indians, the gold rush and absorption into the United States proved to be disastrous. Gold seekers overran Indian communities. Miners, ranchers, and vigilantes murdered thousands of Indians. Determined to reduce the native population, state officials paid millions in bounties to private militias that launched attacks on the state's Indians. Although California was a free state, thousands of Indian children, declared orphans or vagrants by local courts, were bought and sold as slaves. By 1860, California's Indian population, nearly 150,000 when the Mexican War ended, had been reduced to around 30,000.

Opening Japan

The Mexican War ended with the United States in possession of the magnificent harbors of San Diego and San Francisco, long seen as jumping-off points for trade with the Far East. Between 1848 and 1860 American trade with China tripled. In the 1850s, the United States took the lead in opening Japan, a country that had closed itself to nearly all foreign contact for more than two centuries. In 1853 and 1854, American warships under the command of **Commodore Matthew Perry** (the younger brother of Oliver Perry, a hero of the War of 1812) sailed into Tokyo Harbor. Perry, who had been sent by President Millard Fillmore to negotiate a trade treaty, demanded that the Japanese deal with him. Alarmed by European intrusions into China and impressed by Perry's armaments as well as a musical pageant he presented that included a blackface minstrel show, Japanese leaders agreed to do so. In 1854, they opened two ports to American shipping. Japan soon launched a process of modernization that transformed it into the region's major military power.

A DOSE OF ARSENIC

Victory over Mexico added more than 1 million square miles to the United States—an area larger than the Louisiana Purchase. But the acquisition of this vast territory raised the fatal issue that would disrupt the political system and

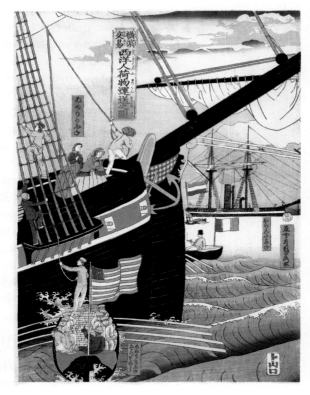

Transportation of Cargo by Westerners at the Port of Yokohama, 1861, by the Japanese artist Utagawa Sadahide, depicts ships in port, including an American one on the left, eight years after Commodore Perry's first voyage to Japan.

plunge the nation into civil war—whether slavery should be allowed to expand into the West. Events soon confirmed Ralph Waldo Emerson's prediction that if the United States gobbled up part of Mexico, "it will be as the man who swallows arsenic. . . . Mexico will poison us."

Already, the bonds of union were fraying. In 1844 and 1845, the Methodists and Baptists, the two largest evangelical churches, divided into northern and southern branches. But it was the entrance of the slavery issue into the heart of American politics as the result of the Mexican War that eventually dissolved perhaps the strongest force for national unity—the two-party system.

The Wilmot Proviso

Before 1846, the status of slavery in all parts of the United States had been settled, either by state law or by the Missouri Compromise, which determined slavery's status in the Louisiana Purchase. The acquisition of new land reopened the question of slavery's expansion. The divisive potential of this issue became clear in 1846, when Congressman David Wilmot of Pennsylvania proposed a resolution prohibiting slavery from all territory acquired from Mexico. Party lines crumbled as every northerner, Democrat and Whig alike, supported what came to be known as the **Wilmot Proviso**, while nearly all southerners opposed it. The measure passed the House, where the more populous North possessed a majority, but failed in the Senate, with its even balance of free and slave states.

In 1848, opponents of slavery's expansion organized the **Free Soil Party** and nominated Martin Van Buren for president and Charles Francis Adams, the son of John Quincy Adams, as his running mate. Democrats nominated Lewis Cass of Michigan, who proposed that the decision on whether to allow slavery should be left to settlers in the new territories (an idea later given the name "popular sovereignty"). Van Buren was motivated in part by revenge against the South for jettisoning him in 1844. But his campaign struck a chord among northerners opposed to the expansion of slavery, and he polled some 300,000 votes, 14 percent of the northern total. Victory in 1848 went to the Whig candidate, Zachary Taylor, a hero of the Mexican War and a Louisiana sugar planter. But the fact that one former president and the son of another abandoned their parties to run on a Free Soil platform showed that antislavery sentiment had spread far beyond abolitionist ranks.

The Free Soil Appeal

The Free Soil position had a popular appeal in the North that far exceeded the abolitionists' demand for immediate emancipation and equal rights for blacks. Many northerners had long resented what they considered southern domination of the federal government. The idea of preventing the creation of new slave states appealed to those who favored policies, such as the protective tariff and government aid to internal improvements, that the majority of southern political leaders opposed.

For thousands of northerners, moreover, the ability to move to the new western territories held out the promise of economic betterment. "Freedom of the soil," declared George Henry Evans, the editor of a pro-labor newspaper, offered the only alternative to permanent economic dependence for American workers.

Economic betterment

Such views merged easily with opposition to the expansion of slavery. If slave plantations were to occupy the fertile lands of the West, northern migration would be effectively blocked. The term "free soil" had a double meaning. The Free Soil platform of 1848 called both for barring slavery from western territories and for the federal government to provide free homesteads to settlers in the new territories. Unlike abolitionism, the "free soil" idea also appealed to the racism so widespread in northern society. Wilmot himself insisted that his controversial proviso was motivated to advance "the cause and rights of the free white man," in part by preventing him from having to compete with "black labor."

The Free Soil platform of 1848

To white southerners, the idea of barring slavery from territory acquired from Mexico seemed a violation of their equal rights as members of the Union. Just as northerners believed westward expansion essential to their economic well-being, southern leaders became convinced that slavery must expand or die. Moreover, the admission of new free states would overturn the delicate political balance between the sections and make the South a permanent minority. Southern interests would not be secure in a Union dominated by non-slaveholding states.

The view of southern leaders

Crisis and Compromise

In world history, the year 1848 is remembered as the "springtime of nations," a time of democratic uprisings against the monarchies of Europe and demands by ethnic minorities for national independence. American principles of liberty and self-government appeared to be triumphing in the Old World. The Chartist movement in Great Britain organized massive demonstrations in support of democratic reforms. The French replaced their monarchy with a republic. Hungarians proclaimed their independence from Austrian rule. Patriots in Italy and Germany, both divided into numerous states, demanded national unification. But the revolutionary tide receded. Chartism faded away, Emperor Napoleon III soon restored the French monarchy, and revolts in Budapest, Rome, and other cities

"Springtime of nations"

Developments in Europe

Senator Daniel Webster of Massachusetts in a daguerreotype from 1850, the year his speech in support of the Compromise of 1850 contributed to its passage.

This daguerreotype of Henry Clay, by the studio of the photographer Matthew Brady, was taken between 1850—when Clay became the chief author of the Compromise of 1850— and his death two years later.

were crushed. Would their own experiment in self-government, some Americans wondered, suffer the same fate as the failed revolutions of Europe?

With the slavery issue appearing more and more ominous, established party leaders moved to resolve differences between the sections. In 1850, California asked to be admitted to the Union as a free state. Many southerners opposed the measure, fearing that it would upset the sectional balance in Congress. Senator Henry Clay offered a plan with four main provisions that came to be known as the **Compromise of 1850**. California would enter the Union as a free state. The slave trade, but not slavery itself, would be abolished in the nation's capital. A stringent new law would help southerners reclaim runaway slaves. And the status of slavery in the remaining territories acquired from Mexico would be left to the decision of the local white inhabitants. The United States would also agree to pay off the massive debt Texas had accumulated while independent.

The Great Debate

In the Senate debate on the Compromise, powerful leaders spoke for and against compromise. Daniel Webster of Massachusetts announced his willingness to abandon the Wilmot Proviso and accept a new fugitive slave law if this were the price of sectional peace. John C. Calhoun, again representing South Carolina, was too ill to speak. A colleague read his remarks rejecting the very idea of compromise. The North must yield, Calhoun insisted, or the Union could not survive. William H. Seward of New York also opposed compromise. To southerners' talk of their constitutional rights, Seward responded that a "higher law" than the Constitution condemned slavery—the law of morality. Here was the voice of abolitionism, now represented in the U.S. Senate.

President Zachary Taylor, like Andrew Jackson a southerner but a strong nationalist, insisted that all Congress needed to do was admit California to the Union. But Taylor died suddenly of an intestinal infection on July 9, 1850. His successor, Millard Fillmore of New York, threw his support to Clay's proposals. Fillmore helped to break the impasse in Congress and secure adoption of the Compromise of 1850.

The Fugitive Slave Issue

For one last time, political leaders had removed the dangerous slavery question from congressional debate. The new **Fugitive Slave Act**, however, made further controversy inevitable. The law allowed special federal commissioners to determine the fate of alleged fugitives without benefit of a jury trial or even testimony by the accused individual. It prohibited local authorities from interfering with the capture of fugitives and required individual citizens to assist in such capture when called upon by federal agents. Thus, southern leaders, usually strong defenders of states' rights and local autonomy, supported a measure that brought federal agents into communities throughout the North, armed with the power to override local law enforcement and judicial procedures to secure the return of runaway slaves. The security of slavery was more important to them than states'-rights consistency.

THE FUGITIVE SLAVE LAW.....HAMLET IN CHAINS.

During the 1850s, federal tribunals heard more than 300 cases throughout the free states and ordered 157 fugitives returned to the South, many at the government's expense. The law further widened sectional divisions and reinvigorated the Underground Railroad. In a series of dramatic confrontations, fugitives, aided by abolitionist allies, violently resisted recapture. A large crowd in 1851 rescued the escaped slave Jerry from jail in Syracuse, New York, and spirited him off to Canada. In the same year, an owner who attempted to recapture a fugitive was killed in Christiana, Pennsylvania.

Less dramatically, the men and women involved in the Underground Railroad redoubled their efforts to assist fugitives. Thanks to the consolidation of the railroad network in the North, it was now possible for escaping slaves who reached the free states to be placed on trains that would take them to safety in Canada in a day or two. In 1855 and 1856, Sydney Howard Gay, an abolitionist editor in New York City and a key Underground Railroad operative, recorded in a notebook the arrival of over 200 fugitives—men, women, and children—a majority of whom had been sent by train from Philadelphia. Gay dispatched them to upstate New York and Canada.

Overall, several thousand fugitives and freeborn blacks, worried that they might be swept up in the stringent provisions of the Fugitive Slave Act, fled to safety in Canada. The sight of so many refugees seeking liberty in a foreign land challenged the familiar image of the United States as an asylum for freedom.

An engraving from the *National Anti-Slavery Standard*, October 17, 1850, depicts James Hamlet, the first person returned to slavery under the Fugitive Slave Act of 1850, in front of City Hall in New York. Flags fly from the building, emblazoned with popular American maxims violated by Hamlet's rendition. By the time this appeared in print, New Yorkers had raised the money to purchase Hamlet's freedom and he was back in the city.

Fleeing to Canada

Douglas and Popular Sovereignty

At least temporarily, the Compromise of 1850 seemed to restore sectional peace and party unity. In the 1852 presidential election, Democrat Franklin

Pierce won a sweeping victory over the Whig Winfield Scott on a platform that recognized the Compromise as a final settlement of the slavery controversy.

In 1854, the party system finally succumbed to the disruptive pressures of sectionalism. Early in that year, Illinois senator Stephen A. Douglas introduced a bill to provide territorial governments for Kansas and Nebraska, located within the Louisiana Purchase. A strong believer in western development, he hoped that a transcontinental railroad could be constructed through Kansas or Nebraska. Southerners in Congress, however, seemed adamant against allowing the organization of new free territories that might further upset the sectional balance. Douglas hoped to satisfy them by applying the principle of **popular sovereignty**, whereby the status of slavery would be determined by the votes of local settlers, not Congress. To Douglas, popular sovereignty embodied the idea of local self-government and offered a middle ground between the extremes of North and South.

The Kansas-Nebraska Act opened a vast area in the nation's heartland to the possible spread of slavery by repealing the Missouri Compromise and providing that settlers would determine the status of slavery in these territories.

THE KANSAS-NEBRASKA ACT, 1854

WASHINGTON TERRITORY

OREGON TERRITORY

BRITISH CANADA

ME

MINNESOTA TERRITORY

NEBRASKA TERRITORY

WI

MI

VT
NH

NY

MA

RI
CT

IA

PA

Mason-Dixon Line

NJ

UTAH TERRITORY

IL

IN

OH

DE

CA

KANSAS TERRITORY

see inset

MO

VA

MD

Missouri Compromise Line 36°30′N

KY

NEW MEXICO TERRITORY

INDIAN TERRITORY

AR

TN

NC

SC

MS

AL

GA

TX

LA

FL

BLEEDING KANSAS

Atchison
Leavenworth
Lecompton
Lawrence
KANSAS TERRITORY
Pottawatomie Massacre
Osawatomie
Missouri R.
MISSOURI

0   250   500 miles
0   250   500 kilometers

Free states and territories
Slave states
Indian territory (unorganized)
Open to slavery by popular sovereignty under the Compromise of 1850
Open to slavery by popular sovereignty under the Kansas-Nebraska Act, 1854

The Kansas-Nebraska Act

Unlike the lands taken from Mexico, Kansas and Nebraska lay in the nation's heartland, directly in the path of westward migration. Slavery, moreover, was prohibited there under the terms of the Missouri Compromise, which Douglas's bill would repeal. In response, a group of antislavery congressmen issued the *Appeal of the Independent Democrats*. It arraigned Douglas's bill as a "gross violation of a sacred pledge," part and parcel of "an atrocious plot" to convert free territory into a "dreary region of despotism, inhabited by masters and slaves." It helped to convince millions of northerners that southern leaders aimed at nothing less than extending their peculiar institution throughout the West.

Appeal of Independent Democrats

Thanks to Douglas's energetic leadership, the **Kansas-Nebraska Act** became law in 1854. But it shattered the Democratic Party's unity and sparked a profound reorganization of American politics. During the next two years, the Whig Party, unable to develop a unified response to the political crisis, collapsed. The South became solidly Democratic. Most northern Whigs, augmented by thousands of disgruntled Democrats, joined a new organization, the Republican Party, dedicated to preventing the further expansion of slavery.

The collapse of the Whig Party

THE RISE OF THE REPUBLICAN PARTY

The Northern Economy

The disruptive impact of slavery on the traditional parties was the immediate cause of political transformation in the mid-1850s. But the rise of the Republican Party also reflected underlying economic and social changes, notably the completion of the market revolution and the beginning of mass immigration from Europe.

The period from 1843 to 1857 witnessed explosive economic growth, especially in the North. The catalyst was the completion of the railroad network. From 5,000 miles in 1848, railroad track mileage grew to 30,000 by 1860, with most of the construction occurring in Ohio, Illinois, and other states of the Old Northwest. Four great trunk railroads now linked eastern cities with western farming and commercial centers. The railroads completed the reorientation of the Northwest's trade from the South to the East. As late as 1850, most western farmers still shipped their produce down the Mississippi River. Ten years later, however, railroads transported nearly all their crops to the East, at a fraction of the previous cost. Eastern industrialists marketed manufactured goods to the com-

The railroad network in the North

THE RAILROAD NETWORK, 1850s

The rapid expansion of the railroad network in the 1850s linked the Northeast and Old Northwest in a web of commerce. The South's rail network was considerably less developed, accounting for only 30 percent of the nation's track mileage.

mercial farmers of the West, while residents of the region's growing cities consumed the food westerners produced. The economic integration of the Northwest and Northeast created the groundwork for their political unification in the Republican Party.

Integration of Northwest and Northeast

Although most northerners still lived in small towns and rural areas, the majority of the workforce no longer labored in agriculture. Two great areas of industrial production had arisen. One, along the Atlantic coast, stretched from Boston to Philadelphia and Baltimore. A second was centered on or near the Great Lakes, in inland cities like Buffalo, Cleveland, Pittsburgh, and Chicago. Driven by railroad expansion, coal mining and iron manufacturing were growing rapidly. Chicago, the Old Northwest's major rail center and the jumping-off place for settlers heading for the Great Plains, had become a complex manufacturing center. Although the southern economy was also growing and the continuing expansion of cotton production brought wealth to slaveholders, the South did not share in these broad economic changes.

Industrial manufacturing in the North

The Rise and Fall of the Know-Nothings

Nativism—hostility to immigrants, especially Catholics—became a national political movement with the sudden appearance in 1854 of the American, or Know-Nothing, Party (so called because it began as a secret organization whose members, when asked about its existence, were supposed to respond, "I know nothing"). The **Know-Nothing Party** trumpeted its dedication to reserving political office for native-born Americans and to resisting the "aggressions" of the Catholic Church, such as its supposed

Nativism

The Propagation Society—More Free than Welcome, an anti-Catholic cartoon from the 1850s, illustrates the nativist fear that the Catholic Church poses a threat to American society. Pope Pius IX, cross in hand, steps ashore from a boat that also holds five bishops. Addressing "Young America," who holds a Bible, he says that he has come to "take charge of your spiritual welfare." A bishop adds, "I cannot bear to see that boy, with that horrible book."

efforts to undermine public school systems. The Know-Nothings swept the 1854 state elections in Massachusetts, electing the governor, all of the state's congressmen, and nearly every member of the state legislature. In many states, nativists emerged as a major component of victorious "anti-Nebraska" coalitions of voters opposed to the Kansas-Nebraska Act. In the North, the Know-Nothings' appeal combined anti-Catholic and antislavery sentiment, with opposition to the sale of liquor often added to the equation.

Immigrant suffrage

Despite severe anti-Irish discrimination in jobs, housing, and education, however, it is remarkable how little came of demands that immigrants be barred from the political nation. All European immigrants benefited from being white. The newcomers had the good fortune to arrive after white male suffrage had become the norm and automatically received the right to vote.

The Free Labor Ideology

The Republican Party

By 1856, it was clear that the Republican Party—a coalition of anti-slavery Democrats, northern Whigs, Free Soilers, and Know-Nothings opposed to the further expansion of slavery—would become the major alternative to the Democratic Party in the North. The party's appeal rested on the idea of "free labor." In Republican hands, the antithesis between "free society" and "slave society" coalesced into a comprehensive worldview that glorified the North as the home of progress, opportunity, and freedom.

Slavery versus free labor

The defining quality of northern society, Republicans declared, was the opportunity it offered each laborer to move up to the status of land-owning farmer or independent craftsman, thus achieving the economic independence essential to freedom. Slavery, by contrast, spawned a social order consisting of degraded slaves, poor whites with no hope of advancement, and idle aristocrats. If slavery were to spread into the West, northern free laborers would be barred, and their chances for social advancement severely diminished. Slavery, Republicans insisted, must be kept out of the territories so that free labor could flourish.

Republicans were not abolitionists—they focused on preventing the spread of slavery, not attacking it where it existed. Nonetheless, many party leaders viewed the nation's division into free and slave societies as an "irrepressible conflict," as Senator William H. Seward of New York put it in 1858, that eventually would have to be resolved.

"Bleeding Kansas" and the Election of 1856

Their free labor outlook, which resonated so effectively with deeply held northern values, helps to explain the Republicans' rapid rise to prominence.

But dramatic events also fueled the party's growth. When Kansas held elections in 1854 and 1855, hundreds of proslavery Missourians crossed the border to cast fraudulent ballots. President Franklin Pierce recognized the legitimacy of the resulting proslavery legislature. Settlers from free states soon established a rival government. A sporadic civil war broke out in Kansas in which some 200 persons eventually lost their lives. In one incident, in May 1856, a proslavery mob attacked the free-soil stronghold of Lawrence, burning public buildings and pillaging private homes.

SOUTHERN CHIVALRY— ARGUMENT versus CLUB'S.

"**Bleeding Kansas**" seemed to discredit Douglas's policy of leaving the decision on slavery up to the local population, thus aiding the Republicans. The party also drew strength from an unprecedented incident in the halls of Congress. South Carolina representative Preston Brooks, wielding a gold-tipped cane, beat the antislavery senator Charles Sumner of Massachusetts unconscious.

A contemporary print denounces South Carolina congressman Preston S. Brooks's assault on Massachusetts senator Charles Sumner in May 1856. The attack on the floor of the Senate was in retaliation for Sumner's speech accusing Senator Andrew P. Butler (Brooks's distant cousin) of having taken "the harlot slavery" as his mistress.

In the election of 1856, the Republican Party chose as its candidate John C. Frémont and drafted a platform that strongly opposed the further expansion of slavery. Stung by the northern reaction to the Kansas-Nebraska Act, the Democrats nominated James Buchanan, who had been minister to Great Britain in 1854 and thus had no direct connection with that divisive measure. The Democratic platform endorsed the principle of popular sovereignty as the only viable solution to the slavery controversy. Meanwhile, the Know-Nothings presented ex-president Millard Fillmore as their candidate. Frémont outpolled Buchanan in the North, carrying eleven of sixteen free states—a remarkable achievement for an organization that had existed for only two years. But Buchanan won the entire South and the key northern states of Illinois, Indiana, and Pennsylvania, enough to ensure his victory. Fillmore carried only Maryland. The 1856 election returns made starkly clear that political parties had reoriented themselves along sectional lines. One major party had been destroyed, another was seriously weakened, and a new one had arisen, devoted entirely to the interests of the North.

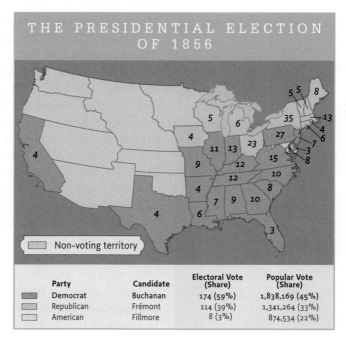

THE PRESIDENTIAL ELECTION OF 1856

Non-voting territory

Party	Candidate	Electoral Vote (Share)	Popular Vote (Share)
Democrat	Buchanan	174 (59%)	1,838,169 (45%)
Republican	Frémont	114 (39%)	1,341,264 (33%)
American	Fillmore	8 (3%)	874,534 (22%)

THE EMERGENCE OF LINCOLN

The final collapse of the party system took place during the administration of a president who epitomized the old political order. Born during George Washington's presidency, James Buchanan had served in Pennsylvania's legislature, in both houses of Congress, and as secretary of state under James K. Polk. A staunch believer in the Union, he committed himself to pacifying inflamed sectional emotions. Few presidents have failed more disastrously in what they set out to accomplish.

The Dred Scott Decision

Even before his inauguration, Buchanan became aware of an impending Supreme Court decision that held out the hope of settling the slavery controversy once and for all. This was the case of ***Dred Scott v. Sandford***. During the 1830s, Scott had accompanied his owner, Dr. John Emerson of Missouri, to Illinois, where slavery had been prohibited by the Northwest Ordinance of 1787 and by state law, and to Wisconsin Territory, where it was barred by the Missouri Compromise. After returning to Missouri, Scott sued for his freedom, claiming that residence on free soil had made him free.

The Dred Scott decision, one of the most famous—or infamous—rulings in the long history of the Supreme Court, was announced in March 1857, two days after Buchanan's inauguration. Speaking for the majority, Chief Justice Roger B. Taney declared that only white persons could be citizens of the United States. The nation's founders, Taney insisted, believed that blacks "had no rights which the white man was bound to respect." Ironically, one reason for Taney's ruling was his robust understanding of what citizenship entailed. Being a citizen, he declared, meant freedom from legal discrimination and full enjoyment of the rights specified in the Constitution, among them the ability to travel anywhere in the country and the right "to keep and carry arms wherever they [citizens] went." These were not rights he thought black people, free or slave, should enjoy.

As for Scott's residence in Wisconsin, the ruling stated that Congress possessed no power under the Constitution to bar slavery from a territory. The Missouri Compromise, recently repealed by the Kansas-Nebraska Act, had been unconstitutional, and so was any measure interfering with southerners' right to bring slaves into the western territories. The decision in effect declared unconstitutional the Republican platform of restricting slavery's expansion. It also seemed to undermine Douglas's doctrine of popular sovereignty. For if Congress lacked the power to prohibit slavery in a territory, how could a territorial legislature created by Congress do so?

Dred Scott as painted in 1857, the year the Supreme Court ruled that he and his family must remain in slavery.

WHO IS AN AMERICAN?

From Opinion of the Court, Chief Justice Roger B. Taney, The Dred Scott Decision (1857)

In the Dred Scott decision, the Supreme Court attempted to resolve a divisive question: were free African-Americans citizens of the United States? The Court answered "no." For the majority, Chief Justice Roger B. Taney insisted that American citizenship was for white persons alone.

The words "people of the United States" and "citizens" are synonymous terms, and mean the same thing. They both describe the political body who, according to our republican institutions, form the sovereignty, and who hold the power and conduct the government through their representatives. They are what we familiarly call the "sovereign people," and every citizen is one of this people and a constituent member of this sovereignty. The question before us is, whether the class of persons described in the plea . . . compose a portion of this people, and are constituent members of this sovereignty? We think they are not, and that they are not included, and were not intended to be included, under the word "citizens" in the Constitution, and can therefore claim none of the rights and privileges which that instrument provides for and secures to citizens of the United States. On the contrary, they were at that time considered as a subordinate and inferior class of beings, who had been subjugated by the dominant race, and, whether emancipated or not, yet remained subject to their authority, and had no rights or privileges but such as those who held the power and the government might choose to grant them. . . .

They had for more than a century before been regarded as beings of an inferior order, and altogether unfit to associate with the white race, either in social or political relations; and so far inferior, that they had no rights which the white man was bound to respect. . . .

The general words [of the Declaration of Independence] would seem to embrace the whole human family, . . . but it is too clear for dispute, that the enslaved African race were not intended to be included. [The authors] perfectly understood the meaning of the language they used, and they knew that it would not in any part of the civilized world be supposed to embrace the Negro race.

> ### QUESTIONS
>
> 1. *What evidence does Taney present that blacks were not considered citizens by the authors of the Declaration of Independence and the Constitution?*
>
> 2. *Why do you think he bases his argument on what he says were the intentions of the founders rather than the situation of free blacks in the 1850s?*

The Dred Scott decision caused a furor in the North and put the question of black citizenship on the national political agenda. James McCune Smith, a black physician, author, and antislavery activist, carefully dissected Taney's reasoning, citing legal precedents going back to "the annals of lofty Rome" to demonstrate that all free persons born in the United States, black as well as white, "must be citizens." Many Republicans also rejected Taney's reasoning. In a stinging dissent, Justice John McLean of Ohio insisted that regardless of race, "birth on the soil of a country both creates the duties and confers the rights of citizenship." Ohio's legislature adopted a resolution declaring that "every free person, born within the limits of any state of this Union, is a citizen thereof."

Slavery, announced President Buchanan, henceforth existed in all the territories, "by virtue of the Constitution." In 1858, his administration attempted to admit Kansas as a slave state under the Lecompton Constitution, which had been drafted by a pro-southern convention and never submitted to a popular vote. Outraged by this violation of popular sovereignty, Douglas formed an unlikely alliance with congressional Republicans to block the attempt. The Lecompton battle convinced southern Democrats that they could not trust their party's most popular northern leader.

The Lecampton battle

Lincoln and Slavery

The depth of Americans' divisions over slavery was brought into sharp focus in 1858 in one of the most storied election campaigns in the nation's history. Seeking reelection to the Senate as both a champion of popular sovereignty and the man who had prevented the administration from forcing slavery on the people of Kansas, Douglas faced an unexpectedly strong challenge from Abraham Lincoln, then little known outside of Illinois. Born into a modest farm family in Kentucky in 1809, Lincoln had moved as a youth to frontier Indiana and then Illinois. He had served four terms as a Whig in the state legislature and one in Congress from 1847 to 1849.

Lincoln developed a critique of slavery and its expansion that gave voice to the central values of the emerging Republican Party and the millions of northerners whose loyalty it commanded. His speeches combined the moral fervor of the abolitionists with the respect for order and the Constitution of more conservative northerners.

"I want every man to have the chance," said Lincoln, "and I believe a black man is entitled to it, in which he *can* better his condition." Blacks might not be the equal of whites in all respects, but in their "natural right" to the fruits of their labor, they were "my equal and the equal of all others."

Abraham Lincoln's nickname, "The Railsplitter," recalled his humble origins. An unknown artist created this larger-than-life portrait. The White House is visible in the distance. The painting is said to have been displayed during campaign rallies in 1860.

The Lincoln-Douglas Campaign

The campaign against Douglas, the North's preeminent political leader, created Lincoln's national reputation. Accepting his party's nomination for the Senate in June 1858, Lincoln announced, "A house divided against itself cannot stand. I believe this government cannot endure, permanently half *slave* and half *free*." Lincoln's point was not that civil war was imminent, but that Americans must choose between favoring and opposing slavery.

The **Lincoln-Douglas debates**, held in seven Illinois towns and attended by tens of thousands of listeners, remain classics of American political oratory. Clashing definitions of freedom lay at their heart. To Lincoln, freedom meant opposition to slavery. Douglas argued, on the other hand, that the essence of freedom lay in local self-government and individual self-determination. A large and diverse nation could only survive by respecting the right of each locality to determine its own institutions. In response to a question posed by Lincoln during the Freeport debate, Douglas insisted that popular sovereignty was not incompatible with the Dred Scott decision. Although territorial legislatures could no longer exclude slavery directly, he argued, if the people wished to keep slaveholders out, all they needed to do was refrain from giving the institution legal protection.

Lincoln shared many of the racial prejudices of his day. He opposed giving Illinois blacks the right to vote or serve on juries and spoke frequently of colonizing blacks overseas as the best solution to the problems of slavery and race. Yet, unlike Douglas, Lincoln did not use appeals to racism to garner votes. And he refused to exclude blacks from the human family. No less than whites, they were entitled to the inalienable rights of the Declaration of Independence, which applied to "all men, in all lands, everywhere," not merely to Europeans and their descendants.

The 1858 Illinois election returns revealed a state sharply divided, like the nation itself. Southern Illinois, settled from the South, voted strongly Democratic, while the rapidly growing northern part of the state was firmly in the Republican column. Douglas was reelected. His victory was remarkable because elsewhere in the North Republicans swept to victory in 1858.

John Brown at Harpers Ferry

An armed assault by the abolitionist John Brown on the federal arsenal at **Harpers Ferry**, **Virginia**, further heightened sectional tensions. During

Abraham Lincoln in 1858, the year of the Lincoln-Douglas debates.

Stephen A. Douglas, in a daguerreotype from around 1853.

the civil war in Kansas, Brown traveled to the territory. In May 1856, after the attack on Lawrence, he and a few followers murdered five proslavery settlers at Pottawatomie Creek. For the next two years, he traveled through the North and Canada, raising funds and enlisting followers for a war against slavery.

On October 16, 1859, with twenty-one men, five of them black, Brown seized Harpers Ferry. The plan made little military sense. Brown's band was soon surrounded and killed or captured by a detachment of federal soldiers headed by Colonel Robert E. Lee. Placed on trial for treason against the state of Virginia, Brown conducted himself with dignity and courage. When Virginia's governor, Henry A. Wise, spurned pleas for clemency and ordered Brown executed, he turned Brown into a martyr to much of the North.

To the South, the failure of Brown's assault seemed less significant than the adulation he seemed to arouse from much of the northern public. His raid and execution further widened the breach between the sections. Brown's last letter was a brief, prophetic statement: "I, John Brown, am quite certain that the crimes of this guilty land will never be purged away but with blood."

Two years after the end of the Civil War in 1867, the artist Thomas Satterwhite Noble, a veteran of the Confederate army, painted *John Brown's Blessing*, commemorating an apocryphal incident in which a slave woman presented her child to Brown as he was being led to the gallows. Two white children, accompanied by their black nurse, look on.

The Rise of Southern Nationalism

With the Republicans continuing to gain strength in the North, Democrats might have been expected to put a premium on party unity as the election of 1860 approached. By this time, however, a sizable group of southerners viewed their region's prospects as more favorable outside the Union than within it. To remain in the Union, secessionists argued, meant to accept "bondage" to the North. But an independent South could become the foundation of a slave empire ringing the Caribbean and embracing Cuba, other West Indian islands, Mexico, and parts of Central America.

More and more southerners were speaking openly of southward expansion. In 1854, Pierre Soulé of Louisiana, the

American ambassador to Spain, persuaded the ministers to Britain and France to join him in signing the Ostend Manifesto, which called on the United States to purchase or seize Cuba, where slavery was still legal, from Spain. Meanwhile, the military adventurer William Walker led a series of "filibustering" expeditions (the term derived from the Spanish word for pirate, *filibustero*) in Central America.

William Walker

By the late 1850s, southern leaders were bending every effort to strengthen the bonds of slavery. "Slavery is our king," declared a South Carolina politician in 1860. "Slavery is our truth, slavery is our divine right." By early 1860, seven states of the Lower South had gone on record demanding that the Democratic platform pledge to protect slavery in all the territories that had not yet been admitted to the Union as states. Virtually no northern politician could accept this position. For southern leaders to insist on it would guarantee the destruction of the Democratic Party as a national institution. But southern nationalists, known as "fire-eaters," hoped to split the party and the country and form an independent southern Confederacy.

The "fire-eaters"

The Election of 1860

When the Democratic convention met in April 1860, Douglas's supporters commanded a majority but not the two-thirds required for a presidential nomination. When the convention adopted a platform reaffirming the doctrine of popular sovereignty, delegates from the seven slave states of the Lower South walked out, and the gathering recessed in confusion. Six weeks later, it reconvened, replaced the bolters with Douglas supporters, and nominated him for president. In response, southern Democrats placed their own ticket in the field, headed by John C. Breckinridge of Kentucky. Breckinridge insisted that slavery must be protected in the western territories.

The Democratic Party, the last great bond of national unity, had been shattered. National conventions had traditionally been places where party

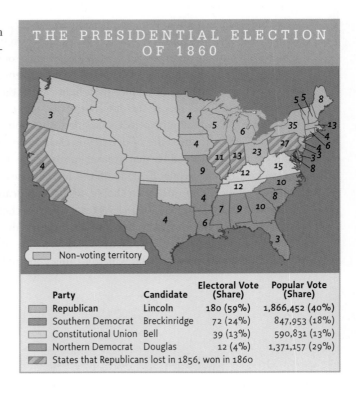

THE PRESIDENTIAL ELECTION OF 1860

Non-voting territory

Party	Candidate	Electoral Vote (Share)	Popular Vote (Share)
Republican	Lincoln	180 (59%)	1,866,452 (40%)
Southern Democrat	Breckinridge	72 (24%)	847,953 (18%)
Constitutional Union	Bell	39 (13%)	590,831 (13%)
Northern Democrat	Douglas	12 (4%)	1,371,157 (29%)
States that Republicans lost in 1856, won in 1860			

VOICES OF FREEDOM

From William Lyman and Others, Letter to the *Middletown Sentinel and Witness* (1850)

The passage of the Fugitive Slave Act in 1850 raised in the most direct way the relationship between law and liberty. Six residents of Middletown, Connecticut, in a letter to the local newspaper, explained why they would not obey the new law.

The undersigned are friends of law. We reverence law. We are of the party of law and order...Even an imperfect law we will respect and bear with, till we can obtain its modification or repeal. But all is not law which calls itself law. When iniquity frames itself into law, the sacredness of law is gone. When an enactment, falsely calling itself law, is imposed upon us, which disgraces our country, which invades our conscience, which dishonors our religion, which is an outrage upon our sense of justice, we take our stand against the imposition.

The Fugitive Slave Law commands all good citizens to be slave catchers. Good citizens *cannot* be slave catchers, any more than light can be darkness. You tell us, the Union will be endangered if we oppose this law. We reply, that greater things than the Union will be endangered, if we submit to it: Conscience, Humanity, Self-respect are greater than the Union . . . . When our sense of decency is clean gone forever, we will turn slave catchers; till then, never. You tell us that great men made this law. If great men choose to disgrace themselves, choose to put off all manliness, and plunge all over into meanness and dishonor, it does not follow that small men should do so too. If Beacon Street [a chief commercial street in Boston] and Marshfield [Daniel Webster's estate] choose to turn slave catchers, let them. We farmers and working men choose to stay by our plows and mills . . . . We are not yet ready to give ourselves over to all manner of villainy. Be the consequence what it may, come fines, come imprisonment, come what will, this thing you call law *we will not obey.*

From Declaration of the Immediate Causes of Secession (1860)

In December 1860, South Carolina declared its secession from the Union. Like the American Revolutionaries of 1776, the legislature issued a document explaining to the world why the state had taken this step.

The non-slaveholding States . . . have assumed the right of deciding upon the propriety of our domestic institutions; and have denied the rights of property established in fifteen of the States and recognized by the Constitution; they have denounced as sinful the institution of slavery; they have permitted open establishment among them of societies, whose avowed object is to disturb the peace and to eloign [take away] the property of the citizens of other States. They have encouraged and assisted thousands of our slaves to leave their homes; and those who remain, have been incited by emissaries, books and pictures to servile insurrection.

For twenty-five years this agitation has been steadily increasing, until it has now secured to its aid the power of the common Government . . . . A geographical line has been drawn across the Union, and all the States north of that line have united in the election of a man to the high office of President of the United States, whose opinions and purposes are hostile to slavery. He is to be entrusted with the administration of the common Government, because he has declared that that "government cannot endure permanently half slave, half free," and that the public mind must rest in the belief that slavery is in the course of ultimate extinction. . . .

On the 4th of March next this party will take possession of the Government. It has announced that the South shall be excluded from the common territory, that the Judicial tribunal shall be made sectional, and that a war must be waged against slavery until it shall cease throughout the United States.

The guarantees of the Constitution will then no longer exist; the equal rights of the states will be lost. The slaveholding states will no longer have the power of self-government, or self-protection, and the federal government will have become their enemy.

QUESTIONS

1. *Whom do the Connecticut writers seem to blame for the Fugitive Slave Act?*

2. *What is the main motivation for South Carolina's secession?*

3. *What do these documents indicate about the rule of law in the nineteenth-century United States?*

managers, mindful of the need for unity in the fall campaign, reconciled their differences. But in 1860, neither northern nor southern Democrats were interested in conciliation. Southern Democrats no longer trusted their northern counterparts. Douglas's backers, for their part, would not accept a platform that doomed their party to certain defeat in the North.

Meanwhile, Republicans gathered in Chicago and chose Lincoln as their standard-bearer. The party platform denied the validity of the Dred Scott decision, reaffirmed Republicans' opposition to slavery's expansion, and added economic planks designed to appeal to a broad array of northern voters—free homesteads in the West, a protective tariff, and government aid in building a transcontinental railroad.

Two presidential campaigns

In effect, two presidential campaigns took place in 1860. In the North, Lincoln and Douglas were the combatants. In the South, the Republicans had no presence, and three candidates contested the election—Douglas, Breckinridge, and John Bell of Tennessee, the candidate of the hastily organized Constitutional Union Party. A haven for Unionist former Whigs, this new party adopted a platform consisting of a single pledge—to preserve "the Constitution as it is [that is, with slavery] and the Union as it was [without sectional discord]."

Sectional results

The most striking thing about the election returns was their sectional character. Lincoln carried all of the North except New Jersey, receiving 1.8 million popular votes (54 percent of the regional total and 40 percent of the national) and 180 electoral votes (a clear majority). Breckinridge captured most of the slave states, although Bell carried three Upper South states and about 40 percent of the southern vote as a whole. Douglas placed first only in Missouri, but he was the only candidate with significant support in all parts of the country. His failure to carry either section, however, suggested that a traditional political career based on devotion to the Union was no longer possible. Without a single vote in ten southern states, Lincoln was elected the nation's sixteenth president. But because of the North's superiority in population, Lincoln would still have carried the electoral college and thus been elected president even if the votes of his three opponents had all been cast for a single candidate.

THE IMPENDING CRISIS

The Secession Movement

Southern response to Lincoln's victory

In the eyes of many white southerners, Lincoln's victory placed their future at the mercy of a party avowedly hostile to their region's values and interests. Those advocating secession did not believe Lincoln's administration would take immediate steps against slavery in the states. But if, as seemed quite possible, the election of 1860 marked a fundamental shift in power, the beginning of a long period of Republican rule, who could say what the North's antislavery sentiment would demand in five years, or ten? Slaveowners, moreover, feared Republican efforts to extend their party into the South by appealing to non-slaveholders. Rather than accept permanent minority status, Lower South political leaders boldly struck for their region's independence.

In the months that followed Lincoln's election, seven states stretching from South Carolina to Texas seceded from the Union. These were the states of the Cotton Kingdom, where slaves represented a larger part of the total population than in the Upper South. First to secede was South Carolina, the state with the highest percentage of slaves in its population and a long history of political radicalism. On December 20, 1860, the legislature unanimously voted to leave the Union. Its *Declaration of the Immediate Causes of Secession* placed the issue of slavery squarely at the center of the crisis.

South Carolina

The Secession Crisis

As the Union unraveled, President Buchanan seemed paralyzed. He denied that a state could secede, but he also insisted that the federal government had no right to use force against it. Other political leaders struggled to find a formula to resolve the crisis. Senator John J. Crittenden of Kentucky, a slave state on the border between North and South, offered the most

widely supported compromise plan of the secession winter. Embodied in a series of unamendable constitutional amendments, Crittenden's proposal would have guaranteed the future of slavery in the states where it existed and extended the Missouri Compromise line to the Pacific Ocean, dividing between slavery and free soil all territories "now held, or hereafter acquired." The seceding states rejected the compromise as too little, too late. But many in the Upper South and North saw it as a way to settle sectional differences and prevent civil war.

Crittenden's plan, however, foundered on the opposition of Abraham

An 1860 engraving of a mass meeting in Savannah, Georgia, shortly after Lincoln's election as president, which called for the state to secede from the Union. The banner on the obelisk at the center reads, "Our Motto Southern Rights, Equality of the States, Don't Tread on Me"—the last a slogan from the American Revolution.

Lincoln. Willing to conciliate the South on issues like the return of fugitive slaves, Lincoln took an unyielding stand against the expansion of slavery. "We have just carried an election," he wrote, "on principles fairly stated to the people. Now we are told in advance that the government shall be broken up unless we surrender to those we have beaten, before we take the offices. . . . If we surrender, it is the end of us and the end of the government."

The Confederate States of America

Before Lincoln assumed office on March 4, 1861, the seven seceding states formed the Confederate States of America, adopted a constitution, and chose as their president Jefferson Davis of Mississippi. With a few alterations—the president served a single six-year term; cabinet members, as in Britain, could sit in Congress—the Confederate constitution was modeled closely on that of the United States. It departed from the federal Constitution, however, in explicitly guaranteeing slave property both in the states and in any territories the new nation acquired. The "cornerstone" of the Confederacy, announced Davis's vice president, Alexander H. Stephens of Georgia, was "the great truth that the negro is not equal to the white man, that slavery, subordination to the superior race, is his natural and normal condition." Confederates were confident their new nation would thrive on the global stage. They looked forward to aggressively pursuing a pro-slavery foreign policy in the Caribbean and annexing new areas.

Inauguration of Mr. Lincoln, a photograph taken on March 4, 1861. The unfinished dome of the Capitol building symbolizes the precarious state of the Union at the time Lincoln assumed office.

And the War Came

In his inaugural address, Lincoln tried to be conciliatory. He rejected the right of secession but denied any intention of interfering with slavery in the states. He said nothing of retaking the forts, arsenals, and customs houses the Confederacy had seized, although he did promise to "hold" remaining federal property in the seceding states. But Lincoln also issued a veiled warning: "In your hands, my dissatisfied fellow countrymen, and not in mine, is the momentous issue of civil war."

In his first month as president, Lincoln walked a tightrope. He avoided any action that might drive more states from the Union, encouraged southern Unionists to assert themselves within the Confederacy, and sought to quiet a growing clamor

An Allegory of the North and the South, painted in 1858 by the Connecticut-born artist Luther Terry, offers a symbolic portrait of the United States on the eve of the Civil War. At the center is a female figure representing the nation and wearing a cap of liberty, with a horn of plenty at her feet. The figure of the South, on the left, is seated on a bale of cotton, with slaves visible in the fields behind her. The North, on the right, holds a book, Useful Arts and Sciences, and sits before a New England town with a church and a textile mill. The sectional harmony portrayed here would soon be replaced by bloody warfare.

in the North for forceful action against secession. Knowing that the risk of war existed, Lincoln strove to ensure that if hostilities did break out, the South, not the Union, would fire the first shot. And that is precisely what happened on April 12, 1861, at **Fort Sumter**, an enclave of Union control in the harbor of Charleston, South Carolina.

A few days earlier, Lincoln had notified South Carolina's governor that he intended to replenish the garrison's dwindling food supplies. Viewing Fort Sumter's presence as an affront to southern nationhood and perhaps hoping to force the wavering Upper South to join the Confederacy, Jefferson Davis ordered batteries to fire on the fort. On April 14, its commander surrendered. The following day, Lincoln proclaimed that an insurrection existed in the South and called for 75,000 troops to suppress it. Civil war had begun. Within weeks, Virginia, North Carolina, Tennessee, and Arkansas joined the Confederacy. "Both sides deprecated war," Lincoln later said, "but one of them would *make* war rather than let the nation survive; and the other would *accept* war rather than let it perish. And the war came."

The Union created by the founders lay in ruins. The struggle to rebuild it would bring about a new birth of American freedom.

Fort Sumter

CHAPTER REVIEW AND ONLINE RESOURCES

REVIEW QUESTIONS

1. *Explain the justifications for the doctrine of manifest destiny, including material and idealistic motivations.*

2. *Why did many Americans criticize the Mexican War? How did they see expansion as a threat to American liberties?*

3. *How did the concept of "race" develop by the mid-nineteenth century? How did it enter into the manifest destiny debate?*

4. *How did western expansion affect the sectional tensions between the North and South?*

5. *How did the market revolution contribute to the rise of the Republican Party? How did those economic and political factors serve to unite groups in the Northeast and in the Northwest, and why was that unity significant?*

6. *How did the Dred Scott decision spark new debates over citizenship for African-Americans?*

7. *Based on the Lincoln-Douglas debates, how did the two differ on the expansion of slavery, equal rights, and the role of the national government? Use examples of their words to illustrate your points.*

8. *Why did Stephen Douglas, among others, believe that "popular sovereignty" could resolve sectional divisions of the 1850s? Why did the idea not work out?*

9. *Explain how sectional voting patterns in the 1860 presidential election allowed southern "fire-eaters" to justify secession.*

10. *What do the California gold rush and the opening of Japan reveal about the United States' involvement in a global economic system?*

KEY TERMS

Tejanos (p. 362)

Antonio López de Santa Anna (p. 364)

Texas revolt (p. 364)

Mexican War (p. 366)

gold rush (p. 370)

Commodore Matthew Perry (p. 371)

Wilmot Proviso (p. 372)

Free Soil Party (p. 372)

Compromise of 1850 (p. 374)

Fugitive Slave Act (p. 374)

popular sovereignty (p. 376)

Kansas-Nebraska Act (p. 377)

Know-Nothing Party (p. 379)

"Bleeding Kansas" (p. 381)

Dred Scott v. Sandford (p. 382)

Lincoln-Douglas debates (p. 385)

Harpers Ferry, Virginia (p. 385)

Fort Sumter (p. 393)

Go to INQUIZITIVE

To see what you know—and learn what you've missed—with personalized feedback along the way.

Visit the *Give Me Liberty! Student Site* for primary source documents and images, interactive maps, author videos featuring Eric Foner, and more.

CHAPTER 14

A NEW BIRTH OF FREEDOM

★

THE CIVIL WAR, 1861–1865

Departure of the 7th Regiment, a lithograph from 1861 illustrating the departure of a unit of the New York State militia for service in the Civil War. A contemporary writer captured the exuberant spirit of the early days of the war: "New York was certainly raving mad with excitement. The ladies laughed, smiled, sighed, sobbed, and wept. The men cheered and shouted as never men cheered and shouted before."

FOCUS
QUESTIONS

- *Why is the Civil War considered the first modern war?*

- *How did a war to preserve the Union become a war to end slavery?*

- *How did the Civil War transform the national economy and create a stronger nation-state?*

- *How did the war effort affect the society and economy of the Confederacy?*

- *What were the military and political turning points of the war?*

- *What were the most important wartime "rehearsals for Reconstruction"?*

Like hundreds of thousands of other Americans, Marcus M. Spiegel volunteered in 1861 to fight in the Civil War. Born into a Jewish family in Germany in 1829, Spiegel emigrated to Ohio, where he married the daughter of a local farmer. When the Civil War broke out, the nation's 150,000 Jews represented less than 1 percent of the total population. But Spiegel shared wholeheartedly in American patriotism. He went to war, he wrote to his brother-in-law, to defend "the flag that was ever ready to protect you and me and every one who sought its protection from oppression." He never wavered in his commitment to the "glorious cause" of preserving the Union and its heritage of freedom.

What one Pennsylvania recruit called "the magic word *Freedom*" shaped how many Union soldiers understood the conflict. But as the war progressed, prewar understandings of liberty gave way to something new. Millions of northerners who had not been abolitionists became convinced that preserving the Union required the destruction of slavery. Marcus Spiegel's changing views mirrored this transformation. Spiegel was an ardent Democrat. He shared the era's racist attitudes and thought Lincoln's Emancipation Proclamation a serious mistake. Yet as the Union army penetrated the heart of the Lower South, Spiegel became increasingly opposed to slavery. "Since I am here," he wrote to his wife from Louisiana in January 1864, "I have learned and seen . . . the horrors of slavery. . . . Never hereafter will I either speak or vote in favor of slavery."

Marcus Spiegel was killed in a minor engagement in Louisiana in May 1864, one of hundreds of thousands of Americans to perish in the Civil War.

THE FIRST MODERN WAR

The American Civil War is often called the first modern war. Never before had mass armies confronted each other on the battlefield with the deadly weapons created by the industrial revolution. The resulting casualties dwarfed anything in the American experience. Beginning as a battle of army versus army, the war became a conflict of society against society, in which the distinction between military and civilian targets often disappeared. In a war of this kind, the effectiveness of political leadership, the ability to mobilize economic resources, and a society's willingness to keep up the fight despite setbacks are as crucial to the outcome as success or failure on individual battlefields.

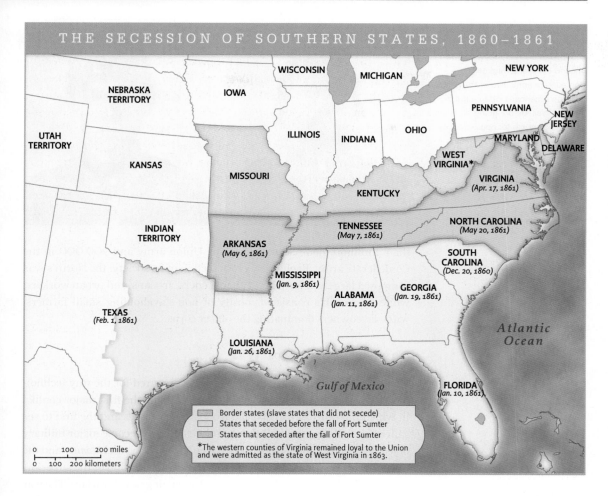

THE SECESSION OF SOUTHERN STATES, 1860–1861

VIRGINIA
(Apr. 17, 1861)

NORTH CAROLINA
(May 20, 1861)

TENNESSEE
(May 7, 1861)

SOUTH
CAROLINA
(Dec. 20, 1860)

ARKANSAS
(May 6, 1861)

MISSISSIPPI
(Jan. 9, 1861)

ALABAMA
(Jan. 11, 1861)

GEORGIA
(Jan. 19, 1861)

TEXAS
(Feb. 1, 1861)

LOUISIANA
(Jan. 26, 1861)

FLORIDA
(Jan. 10, 1861)

*Atlantic
Ocean*

Gulf of Mexico

Border states (slave states that did not secede)
States that seceded before the fall of Fort Sumter
States that seceded after the fall of Fort Sumter

*The western counties of Virginia remained loyal to the Union and were admitted as the state of West Virginia in 1863.

0   100   200 miles
0   100   200 kilometers

The Two Combatants

Almost any comparison between Union and Confederacy seemed to favor the Union. The population of the North and the loyal border slave states numbered 22 million in 1860, whereas only 9 million persons lived in the Confederacy, 3.5 million of them slaves. In manufacturing, railroad mileage, and financial resources, the Union far outstripped its opponent. On the other hand, the Union confronted by far the greater task. To restore the shattered nation, it had to invade and conquer an area larger than western Europe. Moreover, Confederate soldiers were highly motivated fighters, defending their homes and families.

On both sides, the outbreak of war stirred powerful feelings of patriotism. Recruits rushed to enlist, expecting a short, glorious war. Later, as enthusiasm waned, both sides resorted to a draft. By 1865, more

By the time secession ran its course, eleven slave states had left the Union.

Advantages of the North and South

Patriotism

Sergeant James W. Travis, Thirty-eighth Illinois Infantry, Union army, and Private Edwin Francis Jemison, Second Louisiana Regiment, Confederate army, two of the nearly 3 million Americans who fought in the Civil War. Before going off to war, many soldiers sat for photographs like these, reproduced on small cards called *cartes de visite*, which they distributed to friends and loved ones. Jemison was killed in the Battle of Malvern Hill in July 1862.

Soldiers North and South

than 2 million men had served in the Union army and 900,000 in the Confederate army. Each was a cross section of its society: the North's was composed largely of farm boys, shopkeepers, artisans, and urban workers, while the South's consisted mostly of non-slaveholding small farmers, with slaveowners dominating the officer corps.

The Technology of War

Neither the soldiers nor their officers were prepared for the way technology had transformed warfare. The Civil War was the first major conflict in which the railroad transported troops and supplies and the first to see railroad junctions such as Atlanta and Petersburg become major military objectives. The famous sea battle between the Union vessel *Monitor* and the Confederate *Merrimac* in 1862 was the first demonstration of the superiority of ironclads over wooden ships, revolutionizing naval warfare. The war saw the use of the telegraph for military communication, the introduction of observation balloons to view enemy lines, and even primitive hand grenades and submarines.

Ironclad ships

Perhaps most important, a revolution in arms manufacturing had replaced the traditional musket, accurate at only a short range, with the more modern rifle, deadly at 600 yards or more because of its grooved (or "rifled") barrel. This development changed the nature of combat, emphasizing the importance of heavy fortifications and elaborate trenches and giving those on the defensive—usually southern armies—a significant advantage over attacking forces. The war of rifle and trench produced the appalling casualty statistics of Civil War battles. The most recent estimate of those who perished in the war—around 750,000 men—represents the equivalent, in terms of today's population, of more than 7 million. The death toll in the Civil War exceeds the total number of Americans who died in all the nation's

The rifle

other wars, from the Revolution to the wars in Iraq and Afghanistan.

Nor was either side ready for other aspects of modern warfare. Medical care remained primitive. Diseases such as measles, dysentery, malaria, and typhus swept through army camps, killing more men than did combat. The Civil War was the first war in which large numbers of Americans were captured by the enemy and held in dire conditions in military prisons. Some 50,000 men died in these prisons, victims of starvation and disease, including 13,000 Union soldiers at Andersonville, Georgia.

An eight-inch cannon, one of the weapons forged in the industrial revolution and deployed in the Civil War.

The Public and the War

Another modern feature of the Civil War was that both sides employed a vast propaganda effort to mobilize public opinion. In the Union, an outpouring of lithographs, souvenirs, sheet music, and pamphlets issued by patriotic organizations and the War Department reaffirmed northern values, tarred the Democratic Party with the brush of treason, and accused the South of numerous crimes against Union soldiers and loyal civilians. Comparable items appeared in the Confederacy.

War Spirit at Home, an 1866 painting by the New Jersey artist Lilly M. Spencer, depicts a family reading the news of the Union capture of Vicksburg in 1863. The household is now composed of women and children; the husband may be off in the army. While the children play as soldiers, the cross in the folds of the newspaper suggests a less celebratory reflection on the conflict. Newspapers brought news of the war into American homes.

FIGURE 14.1 Resources for War: Union versus Confederacy

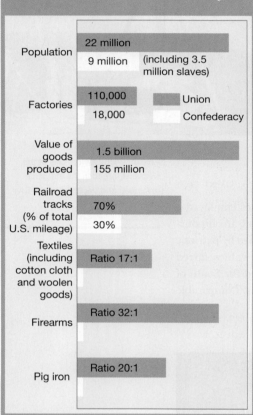

Population	22 million	
	9 million	(including 3.5 million slaves)
Factories	110,000	■ Union
	18,000	□ Confederacy
Value of goods produced	1.5 billion	
	155 million	
Railroad tracks (% of total U.S. mileage)	70%	
	30%	
Textiles (including cotton cloth and woolen goods)	Ratio 17:1	
Firearms	Ratio 32:1	
Pig iron	Ratio 20:1	

In nearly every resource for warfare, the Union enjoyed a distinct advantage. But this did not make Union victory inevitable; as in the War of Independence, the stronger side sometimes loses.

Southern strategy

At the same time, the war's brutal realities were brought home with unprecedented immediacy to the public at large. War correspondents accompanied the armies, and newspapers reported the results of battles on the following day and quickly published long lists of casualties. The infant art of photography carried images of war into millions of American living rooms.

Mobilizing Resources

The outbreak of the war found both sides unprepared. In 1861, there was no national railroad gauge (the distance separating the two rails), so trains built for one line could not run on another. There was no national banking system, no tax system capable of raising the enormous funds needed to finance the war, and not even accurate maps of the southern states. Soon after the firing on Fort Sumter, Lincoln proclaimed a naval blockade of the South, part of the so-called Anaconda Plan, which aimed to strangle the South economically. But the navy, charged with patrolling the 3,500-mile coastline, consisted of only ninety vessels, fewer than half of them steam powered. Not until late in the war did the blockade become effective.

Then there was the problem of purchasing and distributing the food, weapons, and other supplies required by the soldiers. The Union army eventually became the best-fed and best-supplied military force in history. By the war's third year, on the other hand, southern armies were suffering from acute shortages of food, uniforms, and shoes.

Military Strategies

Each side tried to find ways to maximize its advantages. Essentially, the Confederacy adopted a defensive strategy, with occasional thrusts into the North. General Robert E. Lee, the leading southern commander, was a brilliant battlefield tactician who felt confident of his ability to fend off attacks by larger Union forces. He hoped that a series of defeats would weaken the North's resolve and lead it eventually to abandon the conflict and recognize southern independence.

Lincoln's early generals initially concentrated on occupying southern territory and attempting to capture Richmond, the Confederate capital. They attacked sporadically and withdrew after a battle, thus sacrificing the

North's manpower superiority and allowing the South to concentrate its smaller forces when an engagement impended. Well before his generals, Lincoln realized that simply capturing and occupying territory would not win the war, and that defeating the South's armies, not capturing its capital, had to be the North's battlefield objective. And when he came to adopt the policy of emancipation, Lincoln acknowledged that to win the war, the Union must make the institution that lay at the economic and social foundation of southern life a military target.

Changing northern strategy

The War Begins

In the East, most of the war's fighting took place in a narrow corridor between Washington and Richmond—a distance of only 100 miles—as a succession of Union generals led the Army of the Potomac (as the main northern force in the East was called) toward the Confederate capital, only to be turned back by southern forces. The first significant engagement, the **first Battle of Bull Run**, took place in northern Virginia on July 21, 1861. It ended with the chaotic retreat of the Union soldiers, along with the sightseers and politicians who had come to watch the battle.

First Bull Run

In the wake of Bull Run, George B. McClellan, an army engineer who had recently won a minor engagement with Confederate troops in western Virginia, assumed command of the Union's Army of the Potomac. A brilliant organizer, McClellan succeeded in welding his men into a superb fighting force. He seemed reluctant, however, to commit them to battle, since he tended to overestimate the size of enemy forces. And as a Democrat, he hoped that compromise might end the war without large-scale loss of life or a weakening of slavery. Months of military inactivity followed.

McClellan

The War in the East, 1862

Not until the spring of 1862, after a growing clamor for action by Republican newspapers, members of Congress, and an increasingly impatient Lincoln, did McClellan lead his army of more than 100,000 men into Virginia. Here they confronted the smaller Army of Northern Virginia under the command of the Confederate general Joseph E. Johnston, and after he was wounded, Robert E. Lee. In the Seven Days' Campaign, a series of engagements in June 1862 on the peninsula south of Richmond, Lee blunted McClellan's attacks and forced him to withdraw to the vicinity of Washington, D.C. In August 1862, Lee again emerged victorious at the **second Battle of Bull Run** against Union forces under the command of General John Pope.

The Seven Days' Campaign

Successful on the defensive, Lee now launched an invasion of the North. At the **Battle of Antietam**, in Maryland, McClellan and the Army

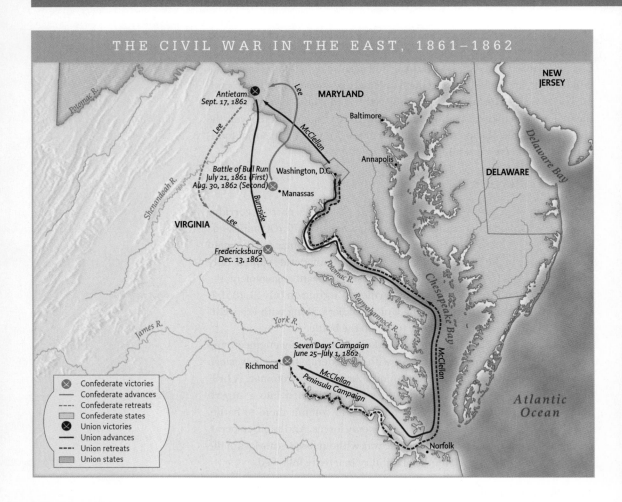

Legend:
- ⊗ Confederate victories
- Confederate advances
- ---- Confederate retreats
- ☐ Confederate states
- ⊗ Union victories
- Union advances
- ---- Union retreats
- ▨ Union states

During the first two years of the war, most of the fighting took place in Virginia and Maryland.

of the Potomac repelled Lee's advance. In a single day of fighting, nearly 4,000 men were killed and 18,000 wounded (2,000 of whom later died of their injuries). More Americans died on September 17, 1862, when the Battle of Antietam was fought, than on any other day in the nation's history, including Pearl Harbor and D-Day in World War II and the terrorist attacks of September 11, 2001.

The War in the West

Emergence of Grant

While the Union accomplished little in the East in the first two years of the war, events in the West followed a different course. Here, the architect of early success was Ulysses S. Grant. A West Point graduate who had resigned from the army in 1854, Grant had been notably unsuccessful in civilian life. When the war broke out, he was working as a clerk in his

Union General George B. McClellan
drilling his troops during the winter of
1861–1862, a painting by an unknown
artist.

brother's leather store in Galena, Illinois. But after being commissioned as a colonel in an Illinois regiment, Grant quickly displayed the daring, the logical mind, and the grasp of strategy he would demonstrate throughout the war.

In February 1862, Grant won the Union's first significant victory when he captured Forts Henry and Donelson in Tennessee. In April, naval forces under Admiral David G. Farragut steamed into New Orleans, giving the Union control of the South's largest city and the rich sugar plantation parishes to its south and west. At the same time, Grant withstood a surprise Confederate attack at Shiloh, Tennessee. But Union momentum in the West then stalled.

Union victories in the West

THE COMING OF EMANCIPATION

Slavery and the War

War, it has been said, is the midwife of revolution. And the Civil War produced far-reaching changes in American life. The most dramatic of these was the destruction of slavery, the central institution of southern society. In numbers, scale, and the economic power of the institution of slavery, American emancipation dwarfed that of any other country (although far more people were liberated in 1861 when Czar Alexander II abolished serfdom in the Russian empire).

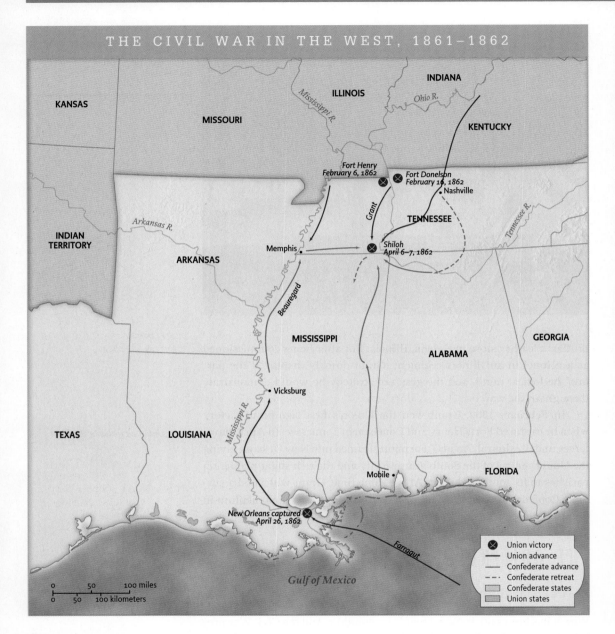

THE CIVIL WAR IN THE WEST, 1861–1862

KANSAS

MISSOURI

ILLINOIS

INDIANA

Mississippi R.

Ohio R.

KENTUCKY

Fort Henry
February 6, 1862

Fort Donelson
February 16, 1862

Nashville

Arkansas R.

Grant

TENNESSEE

Tennessee R.

INDIAN
TERRITORY

ARKANSAS

Memphis

Shiloh
April 6–7, 1862

Beauregard

MISSISSIPPI

ALABAMA

GEORGIA

Vicksburg

TEXAS

LOUISIANA

Mississippi R.

Mobile

FLORIDA

New Orleans captured
April 26, 1862

Farragut

Gulf of Mexico

⊗	Union victory
—	Union advance
—	Confederate advance
---	Confederate retreat
	Confederate states
	Union states

0   50   100 miles
0   50   100 kilometers

Most of the Union's victories in the first two years of the war occurred in the West, especially at Shiloh and New Orleans.

Lincoln initially insisted that slavery was irrelevant to the conflict. In the war's first year, his paramount concerns were to keep the border slave states—Delaware, Maryland, Kentucky, and Missouri—in the Union and to build the broadest base of support in the North for the war effort. Action against slavery, he feared, would drive the border, with its white population of 2.6 million and nearly 500,000 slaves, into the Confederacy and alienate conservative northerners.

Thus, in the early days of the war, a nearly unanimous Congress adopted a resolution proposed by Senator John J. Crittenden of Kentucky, which affirmed that the Union had no intention of interfering with slavery. Northern military commanders even returned fugitive slaves to their owners, a policy that raised an outcry in antislavery circles. Yet as the Confederacy set slaves to work as military laborers and blacks began to escape to Union lines, the policy of ignoring slavery unraveled. By the end of 1861, the military had adopted the plan, begun in Virginia by General Benjamin F. Butler, of treating escaped blacks as contraband of war—that is, property of military value subject to confiscation. Butler's order added a word to the war's vocabulary. Escaping slaves (**"the contrabands"**) were housed by the army in "contraband camps" and educated in new "contraband schools."

Meanwhile, slaves took actions that helped propel a reluctant white America down the road to emancipation. Well before Lincoln made emancipation a war aim, blacks, in the North and the South, were calling the conflict the "freedom war." In 1861 and 1862, as the federal army occupied Confederate territory, slaves by the thousands headed for Union lines. Unlike fugitives before the war, these runaways included large numbers of women and children, as entire families abandoned the plantations. Not a few passed along military intelligence and detailed knowledge of the South's terrain. In southern Louisiana, the arrival of the Union army in 1862 led slaves to sack plantation houses and refuse to work unless wages were paid. Slavery there, wrote a northern reporter, "is forever destroyed and worthless, no matter what Mr. Lincoln or anyone else may say on the subject."

A Civil War photograph depicts African-American men, women, and children who have escaped to Union lines in a mule-drawn covered wagon. The actions of fugitives like these helped propel the nation down the road to emancipation.

Fortress Monroe, Virginia, a Union installation near Norfolk, where the process of emancipation began early in the Civil War when General Benjamin F. Butler refused to return runaway slaves to their owners.

THE COMING OF

Steps toward Emancipation

Fighting for emancipation

The most uncompromising opponents of slavery before the war, abolitionists and **Radical Republicans**, quickly concluded that the institution must become a target of the Union war effort. Outside of Congress, few pressed the case for emancipation more eloquently than Frederick Douglass. From the outset, he insisted that it was futile to "separate the freedom of the slave from the victory of the government."

Congressional policy against slavery

These appeals won increasing support in a Congress frustrated by lack of military success. In March 1862, Congress prohibited the army from returning fugitive slaves. Then came abolition in the District of Columbia (with monetary compensation for slaveholders) and the territories, followed in July by the Second Confiscation Act, which liberated slaves of disloyal owners in Union-occupied territory, as well as slaves who escaped to Union lines.

Lincoln's evolving policy

Throughout these months, Lincoln struggled to retain control of the emancipation issue. In August 1861, John C. Frémont, commanding Union forces in Missouri, a state racked by a bitter guerrilla war between pro-northern and pro-southern bands, decreed the freedom of its slaves. Fearful of the order's impact on the border states, Lincoln swiftly rescinded it. In November, the president proposed that the border states embark on a program of gradual emancipation with the federal government paying owners for their loss of property. He also revived the idea of colonization. In August 1862, Lincoln met at the White House with a delegation of black leaders and urged them to promote emigration from the United States. "You and we are different races," he declared. "It is better for us both to be separated." As late as December 1862, the president signed an agreement with a shady entrepreneur to settle former slaves on an island off the coast of Haiti.

Abe Lincoln's Last Card, an engraving from the British magazine *Punch*, October 18, 1862, portrays the Preliminary Emancipation Proclamation as the last move of a desperate gambler.

Lincoln's Decision

During the summer of 1862, Lincoln concluded that emancipation had become a political and military necessity. Many factors contributed to his decision—lack of military success, hope that emancipated slaves might help meet the army's growing manpower needs, changing northern public opinion, and the calculation that making slavery a target of the war effort would counteract sentiment in Britain for recognition of the Confederacy. But on the advice of

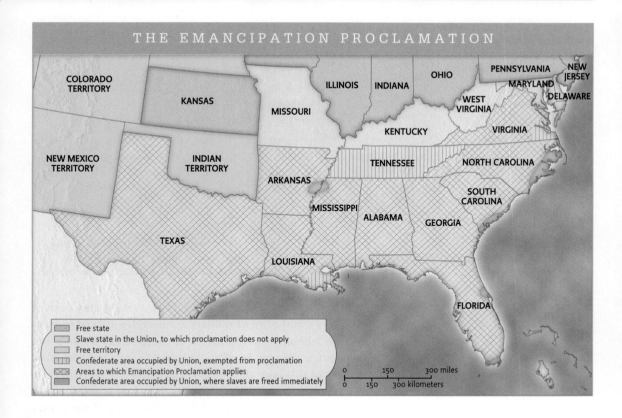

THE EMANCIPATION PROCLAMATION

Legend:
- Free state
- Slave state in the Union, to which proclamation does not apply
- Free territory
- Confederate area occupied by Union, exempted from proclamation
- Areas to which Emancipation Proclamation applies
- Confederate area occupied by Union, where slaves are freed immediately

0   150   300 miles
0   150   300 kilometers

Secretary of State William H. Seward, Lincoln delayed his announcement until after a Union victory, lest it seem an act of desperation. On September 22, 1862, five days after McClellan's army forced Lee to retreat at Antietam, Lincoln issued the Preliminary Emancipation Proclamation. It warned that unless the South laid down its arms by the end of 1862, he would decree abolition.

The initial northern reaction was not encouraging. In the fall elections of 1862, Democrats made opposition to emancipation the centerpiece of their campaign. The Republicans suffered sharp reverses. In his annual message to Congress, early in December, Lincoln tried to calm northerners' racial fears: "In giving freedom to the slave, we assure freedom to the free—honorable alike in what we give, and what we preserve."

With the exception of a few areas, the Emancipation Proclamation applied only to slaves in parts of the Confederacy not under Union control on January 1, 1863. Lincoln did not "free the slaves" with a stroke of his pen, but the proclamation did change the nature of the Civil War.

The Emancipation Proclamation

On January 1, 1863, after greeting visitors at the annual White House New Year's reception, Lincoln retired to his study to sign the **Emancipation Proclamation**. The document did not liberate all the slaves—indeed, on

THE COMING OF

Freed Negroes Celebrating President Lincoln's Decree of Emancipation, a fanciful engraving from the French periodical *Le Monde Illustré*, March 21, 1863.

the day it was issued, it applied to very few. Because its legality derived from the president's authority as military commander-in-chief to combat the South's rebellion, the proclamation exempted areas firmly under Union control (where the war, in effect, had already ended). Thus, it did not apply to the loyal border slave states that had never seceded or to areas of the Confederacy occupied by Union soldiers, such as Tennessee and parts of Virginia and Louisiana. But the vast majority of the South's slaves—more than 3 million men, women, and children—it declared "henceforward shall be free." Since most of these slaves were still behind Confederate lines, however, their liberation would have to await Union victories.

Despite its limitations, the proclamation set off scenes of jubilation among free blacks and abolitionists in the North and "contrabands" and slaves in the South. "Sound the loud timbrel o'er Egypt's dark sea," intoned a black preacher at a celebration in Boston. "Jehovah hath triumphed, his people are free." By making the Union army an agent of emancipation and wedding the goals of Union and abolition, the proclamation sounded the eventual death knell of slavery.

Not only did the Emancipation Proclamation alter the nature of the Civil War and the course of American history, but it also marked a turning point in Lincoln's own thinking. For the first time, it committed the government to enlisting black soldiers in the Union army. He would later refuse suggestions that he rescind or modify the proclamation in the interest of peace. Were he to do so, he told one visitor, "I should be damned in time and eternity."

Enlisting Black Troops

Of the proclamation's provisions, few were more radical in their implications than the enrollment of blacks into military service. Since sailor had been one of the few occupations open to free blacks before the war, Secretary of the Navy Gideon Welles had already allowed African-Americans to serve on Union warships. But at the outset, the administration feared that whites would not be willing to fight alongside blacks and that enlisting black soldiers would alienate the border slave states that remained in the Union.

By the end of the war, however, more than 180,000 black men had served in the Union army and 24,000 in the navy. One-third died in battle, or of wounds or disease. Some black units won considerable renown, among them the Fifty-fourth Massachusetts Volunteers, a company of free blacks from throughout the North commanded by Robert Gould Shaw, a young reformer from a prominent Boston family. The bravery of the Fifty-fourth in the July 1863 attack on Fort Wagner, South Carolina, where nearly half the unit, including Shaw, perished, helped to dispel widespread doubts about blacks' ability to withstand the pressures of the Civil War battlefield.

Most black soldiers were emancipated slaves who joined the army in the South. After Union forces in 1863 seized control of the rich plantation lands of the Mississippi Valley, General Lorenzo Thomas raised fifty regiments of black soldiers—some 76,000 men in all. Another large group hailed from the border states exempted from the Emancipation Proclamation, where enlistment was, for most of the war, the only route to freedom. Here black military service undermined slavery, for Congress expanded the Emancipation Proclamation to liberate the families of black soldiers.

A photograph of a black washerwoman for the Union army wearing a small American flag reflects how the war and emancipation led African-Americans to identify strongly with the nation.

This is the only known photograph of a black Union soldier with his family.

The Black Soldier

For black soldiers themselves, military service proved to be a liberating experience. Out of the army came many of the leaders of the Reconstruction era. At least 130 former soldiers served in political office after the Civil War. In time, the memory of black military service would fade from white America's collective memory. Of the hundreds of Civil War monuments that still dot the northern landscape, fewer than a dozen contain an image of a black soldier. But well into the twentieth century, it remained a point of

THE COMING OF

THE AMERICAN FLAG,
A NEW NATIONAL LYRIC.

The illustration accompanying *The American Flag*, a piece of patriotic Civil War sheet music, exemplifies how the war united the ideals of liberty and nationhood.

A songbook compiled and illustrated by a Union soldier includes "John Brown's Body," sung to the melody of a Methodist hymn.

pride in black families throughout the United States that their fathers and grandfathers had fought for freedom.

Within the army, however, black soldiers received treatment that was anything but equal to that of their white counterparts. Organized into segregated units under sometimes abusive white officers, they initially received lower pay (ten dollars per month, compared to sixteen dollars for white soldiers). They were disproportionately assigned to labor rather than combat, and they could not rise to the rank of commissioned officer until the very end of the war. In a notorious incident in 1864, 200 of 262 black soldiers died when southern troops under the command of Nathan B. Forrest overran Fort Pillow in Tennessee. Some of those who perished had been killed after surrendering.

Nonetheless, black soldiers played a crucial role not only in winning the Civil War but also in defining the war's consequences. Thanks in part to black military service, many Republicans in the last two years of the war came to believe that emancipation must bring with it equal protection of the laws regardless of race. One of the first acts of the federal government to recognize this principle was the granting of retroactive equal pay to black soldiers early in 1865.

The service of black soldiers affected Lincoln's own outlook. In 1864, Lincoln, who before the war had never supported suffrage for African-Americans, urged the governor of Union-occupied Louisiana to work for the partial enfranchisement of blacks, singling out soldiers as especially deserving. At some future time, he observed, they might again be called upon to "keep the *jewel of Liberty* in the family of freedom."

THE SECOND AMERICAN REVOLUTION

The changing status of black Americans was only one dramatic example of what some historians call the **Second American Revolution**—the transformation of American government and society brought about by the Civil War.

Liberty, Union, and Nation

Never was freedom's contested nature more evident than during the Civil War. "We all declare for liberty," Lincoln observed in 1864, "but in using the same *word* we do not all mean the same *thing*." To the North, he continued, freedom meant for "each man" to enjoy "the product of his labor." To southern whites, it conveyed mastership—the power to do "as they please with other men, and the product of other men's labor." The Union's triumph consolidated the northern understanding of freedom as the national norm.

But it was Lincoln himself who linked the conflict with the deepest beliefs of northern society. It is sometimes said that the American Civil War was part of a broader nineteenth-century process of nation building. Throughout the world, powerful, centralized nation-states developed in old countries, and new nations emerged where none had previously existed. The Civil War took place as modern states were consolidating their power and reducing local autonomy. Lincoln has been called the American equivalent of Giuseppe Mazzini or Otto von Bismarck, who during this same era created nation-states in Italy and Germany from disunited collections of principalities. But Lincoln's nation was different from those being constructed in Europe. They were based on the idea of unifying a particular people with a common ethnic, cultural, and linguistic heritage. To Lincoln, the American nation embodied, instead, a set of universal ideas, centered on political democracy and human liberty.

Nation building

Lincoln summarized his conception of the war's meaning in November 1863 in brief remarks at the dedication of a military cemetery at the site of the war's greatest battle. The Gettysburg Address is considered his finest speech (see the Appendix for the full text). In less than three minutes, he identified the nation's mission with the principle that "all men are created equal," spoke of the war as bringing about a "new birth of freedom," and defined the essence of democratic government. The sacrifices of Union soldiers, he declared, would ensure that "government of the people, by the people, for the people, shall not perish from the earth."

The Gettysburg Address

The mobilization of the Union's resources for modern war brought into being a new American nation-state with greatly expanded powers and responsibilities. The United States remained a federal republic with sovereignty divided between the state and national governments. But the war forged a new national self-consciousness, reflected in the increasing use of the word "nation"—a unified political entity—in place of the older "Union" of separate states. In his inaugural address in 1861, Lincoln used the word "Union" twenty times, while making no mention of the "nation." By 1863, "Union" does not appear at all in the 269-word Gettysburg Address, while Lincoln referred five times to the "nation."

Lincoln and the Female Slave, by the free black artist David B. Bowser. Working in Philadelphia, Bowser painted flags for a number of black Civil War regiments. Lincoln confers freedom on a kneeling slave, an image that downplays blacks' role in their own emancipation.

The War and American Religion

The upsurge of patriotism, and of national power, was reflected in many aspects of American life. Even as the war produced unprecedented casualties, the northern Protestant clergy strove to provide it with a religious

412 | Chapter 14

The Sisters of Charity, an order of nuns, photographed with doctors and soldiers at a hospital in Philadelphia in 1863. Many of the wounded from the Battle of Gettysburg were sent here for treatment. The Catholic contribution to the Union war effort mitigated the nativist bias so prominent in the 1850s.

Religious justification

justification and to reassure their congregations that the dead had not died in vain. The religious press now devoted more space to military and political developments than to spiritual matters. In numerous wartime sermons, Christianity and patriotism were joined in a civic religion that saw the war as God's mechanism for ridding the United States of slavery and enabling it to become what it had never really been—a land of freedom. Of course, the southern clergy was equally convinced that the Confederate cause represented God's will.

Religious beliefs enabled Americans to cope with mass death. Coping with death, moreover, required unprecedented governmental action, from notifying next of kin to accounting for the dead and missing. Both the Union and Confederacy established elaborate systems for gathering statistics and maintaining records of dead and wounded soldiers, an effort supplemented by private philanthropic organizations. After the war ended, the federal government embarked on a program to locate and re-bury hundreds of thousands of Union soldiers in national military cemeteries. Between 1865 and 1871, the government reinterred more than 300,000 Union (but not Confederate) soldiers—including black soldiers, who were buried in segregated sections of military cemeteries.

Liberty in Wartime

This intense new nationalism made criticism of the war effort—or of the policies of the Lincoln administration—seem to Republicans equivalent to treason. During the conflict, declared the Republican *New York Times*, "the

A girl in mourning dress holds a framed photograph of her father, a cavalryman.

safety of the nation is the supreme law." Arbitrary arrests numbered in the thousands. They included opposition newspaper editors, Democratic politicians, individuals who discouraged enlistment in the army, and ordinary civilians like the Chicago man briefly imprisoned for calling the president a "damned fool." With the Constitution unclear as to who possessed the power to suspend the writ of habeas corpus (thus allowing prisoners to be held without charge), Lincoln claimed the right under the presidential war powers and twice suspended the writ throughout the entire Union for those accused of "disloyal activities." Not until 1866, after the fighting had ended, did the Supreme Court, in the case ***Ex parte Milligan***, declare it unconstitutional to bring accused persons before military tribunals where civil courts were operating. The Constitution, declared Justice David Davis, is not suspended in wartime—it remains "a law for rulers and people, equally in time of war and peace."

Arbitrary arrests and the suspension of habeas corpus

Lincoln was not a despot. Most of those arrested were quickly released, the Democratic press continued to flourish, and contested elections were held throughout the war. But the policies of the Lincoln administration offered proof—to be repeated during later wars—of the fragility of civil liberties in the face of assertive patriotism and wartime demands for national unity.

Sheet music for two of the best-known patriotic songs written during the Civil War.

The North's Transformation

Even as he invoked traditional values, Lincoln presided over far-reaching changes in northern life. The effort to mobilize the resources of the Union greatly enhanced the power not only of the federal government but also of a rising class of capitalist entrepreneurs. Unlike the South, which suffered economic devastation, the North experienced the war as a time of prosperity.

Nourished by wartime inflation and government contracts, the profits of industry boomed. New England mills worked day and night to supply the army with blankets and uniforms, and Pennsylvania coal mines and ironworks rapidly expanded their production. Mechanization proceeded apace in many industries, especially those, such as boot and shoe production and meatpacking, that supplied the army's ever-increasing needs. Agriculture also flourished, for even as farm boys by the hundreds of thousands joined the army, the frontier of cultivation pushed westward, with machinery and immigrants replacing lost labor.

Government and the Economy

The new American nation-state that emerged during the Civil War was committed to rapid economic development. Congress adopted policies that promoted economic growth and permanently altered the nation's financial system. To spur agricultural development, the **Homestead Act**

offered 160 acres of free public land to settlers in the West. It took effect on January 1, 1863, the same day as the Emancipation Proclamation, and like the proclamation, tried to implement a vision of freedom. By the 1930s, more than 400,000 families had acquired farms under its provisions. In addition, the Morrill Land Grant College Act, named for Justin S. Morrill of Vermont, who introduced the measure, assisted the states in establishing "agricultural and mechanic colleges."

Congress also made huge grants of money and land for internal improvements, including up to 100 million acres to the Union Pacific and Central Pacific, two companies chartered in 1862 and charged with building a railroad from the Missouri River to the Pacific coast. (These were the first corporate charters issued by the federal government since the Second Bank of the United States in 1816.) It required some 20,000 men to lay the tracks across prairies and mountains, a substantial number of them immigrant Chinese contract laborers, called "coolies" by many Americans. Hundreds of Chinese workers died blasting tunnels and building bridges through this treacherous terrain. When it was completed in 1869, the **transcontinental railroad**, which ran from Omaha, Nebraska, to San Francisco, reduced the time of a cross-country journey from four or five months to six days. It expanded the national market, facilitated the spread of settlement and investment in the West, and heralded the doom of the Plains Indians.

This photograph from 1861 depicts Native American volunteer soldiers being enrolled in the Union army. Indian soldiers were recruited well before the army admitted blacks.

The West and the War

Most accounts of the Civil War say little or nothing about the West. Yet the conflict engulfed Missouri, Kansas, and Indian Territory, and spread into the Southwest borderlands. The war divided western communities as residents flocked to both armies.

Since the beginning of the republic, the question of slavery had been tied up with the status of new western lands. Jefferson Davis had long been interested in the expansion of slavery into the Southwest. In pursuit of this goal, in October 1861, Confederate units from Texas launched an invasion of New Mexico (which Texans had long claimed as part of their state). They hoped to conquer the region as a gateway to acquisition of southern California and northern Mexico, a continuation of a southern version of manifest destiny, evidenced before the war in filibustering expeditions in the Caribbean. But the Confederates were defeated at Glorieta Pass in March 1862 by a small Union army contingent reinforced by volunteers from Colorado and California. With their retreat to Texas died the dream of a slave empire in the Far West.

The war had a profound impact on western Indians. One of Lincoln's first orders as president was to withdraw federal troops from the West so that they could protect Washington, D.C. Recognizing that this would make it impossible for the army to keep white interlopers from intruding on Indian land, as treaties required it to do, Indian leaders begged Lincoln to reverse this decision, but to no avail. Inevitably, conflict flared in

A lithograph depicts the hanging of thirty-eight Sioux Indians in December 1862, the largest mass execution in American history.

the West between Native Americans and white settlers, with disastrous results. During the Civil War, the Sioux killed hundreds of white farmers in Minnesota before being subdued by the army. After a military court sentenced more than 300 Indians to death, Lincoln commuted the sentences of all but 38. But their hanging in December 1862 remains the largest official execution in American history.

In November 1864, Colorado militiamen attacked a group of around 700 Cheyennes and Arapahos camped along Sand Creek in Colorado. Led by Colonel John Chivington, an abolitionist and a former Methodist minister, the soldiers were bent on punishing Indians responsible for raids on nearby settlements. They failed to locate the hostile Indians, but chose to assault the peaceful encampment with rifles and artillery, killing more than 150 men, women, and children. The incident sparked intensified warfare on the southern plains, as Cheyennes and Arapahos retaliated with attacks of their own.

The Union army also launched a series of campaigns in the Southwest against tribes like the Kiowas and Comanches, whose violent raids on ranches and settlements had been an essential, although disruptive, part of the borderlands economy, organized around trading and exchanging captives (usually women), livestock, and horses. The army also made war on the Navajo, who were more victims than perpetrators of these raids. Indian raiding parties had stolen more than 50,000 sheep from their settlements in 1860 alone. Union forces destroyed Navajo orchards and sheep and

Union campaigns against Indians

forced 8,000 people to move to a reservation set aside by the government.
The **Navajo's Long Walk** became as central to their historical experience
as the Trail of Tears to the Cherokee (see Chapter 10). Unlike the eastern
Indians, however, the Navajo were eventually allowed to return to a portion of their lands. The wars against Native Americans, a small part of the
violence that engulfed the nation during the Civil War, would continue for
more than two decades after the sectional conflict ended.

Navajo's Long Walk

Some tribes that owned slaves, like the Cherokee, sided with the
Confederacy. After 1865, they were forced to cede much of their land to the
federal government and to accept former slaves into the Cherokee nation
and give them land (the only slaveowners required to do so). Their status
remains a point of controversy to this day. The Cherokee constitution was
recently amended to exclude descendants of slaves from citizenship, leading to lawsuits that have yet to be resolved.

Cherokee nation and slavery

A New Financial System

The need to pay for the war produced dramatic changes in financial
policy. To raise money, the government increased the tariff to unprecedented heights (thus promoting the further growth of northern industry),
imposed new taxes on the production and consumption of goods, and
enacted the nation's first income tax. It also borrowed more than $2 billion
by selling interest-bearing bonds, thus creating an immense national debt.
And it printed more than $400 million worth of paper money, called
"greenbacks," declared to be legal tender—that is, money that must be
accepted for nearly all public and private payments and debts. To rational-
ize banking, Congress established a system of nationally chartered banks,
which were required to purchase government bonds and were given the
right to issue bank notes as currency.

Financing the war

Numerous Americans who would take the lead in reshaping the
nation's postwar economy created or consolidated their fortunes during the Civil War, among them the iron and steel entrepreneur Andrew
Carnegie, the oil magnate John D. Rockefeller, the financiers Jay Gould
and J. P. Morgan, and Philip D. Armour, who earned millions supplying
beef to the Union army. These and other "captains of industry" managed
to escape military service, sometimes by purchasing exemptions or hiring
substitutes, as allowed by the draft law.

"Captains of industry"

Taken together, the Union's economic policies vastly increased the
power and size of the federal government. The federal budget for 1865
exceeded $1 billion—nearly twenty times that of 1860. With its new army
of clerks, tax collectors, and other officials, the government became the
nation's largest employer. And although much of this expansion proved

THE CIVIL WAR IN THE WESTERN TERRITORIES, 1862–1864

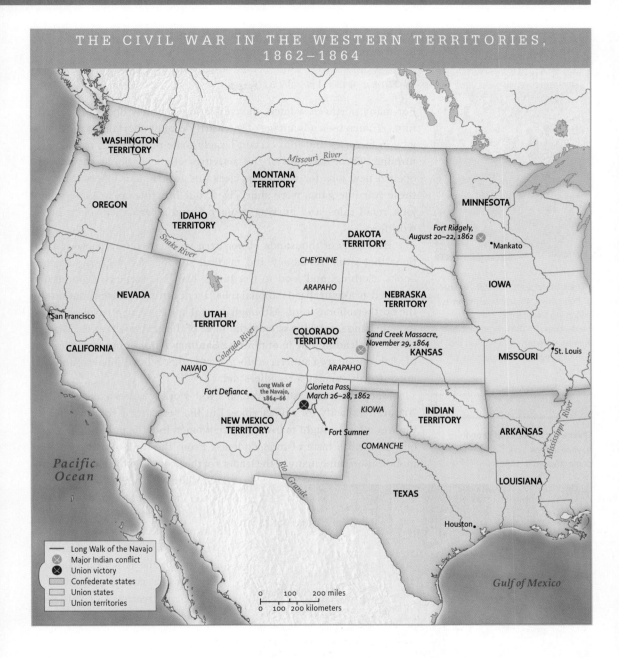

WASHINGTON TERRITORY

OREGON

IDAHO TERRITORY

Missouri River

MONTANA TERRITORY

MINNESOTA

Snake River

DAKOTA TERRITORY

Fort Ridgely, August 20–22, 1862

•Mankato

CHEYENNE

ARAPAHO

NEVADA

UTAH TERRITORY

NEBRASKA TERRITORY

IOWA

•San Francisco

Colorado River

COLORADO TERRITORY

Sand Creek Massacre, November 29, 1864

CALIFORNIA

KANSAS

MISSOURI

•St. Louis

NAVAJO

ARAPAHO

Long Walk of the Navajo, 1864–66

Glorieta Pass, March 26–28, 1862

Fort Defiance •

KIOWA

INDIAN TERRITORY

NEW MEXICO TERRITORY

•Fort Sumner

ARKANSAS

Mississippi River

COMANCHE

Pacific Ocean

LOUISIANA

Rio Grande

TEXAS

Houston•

Legend:
— Long Walk of the Navajo
⊗ Major Indian conflict
⊗ Union victory
Confederate states
Union states
Union territories

0   100   200 miles
0 100 200 kilometers

Gulf of Mexico

HARPER'S WEEKLY
JOURNAL OF CIVILIZATION

Filling Cartridges at the U.S. Arsenal of Watertown, Massachusetts, an engraving from *Harper's Weekly*, September 21, 1861. Both men and women were drawn to work in the booming war-related industries of the North.

Children at the Colored Orphan Asylum in New York City, photographed in 1862.

temporary, the government would never return to its weak and fragmented condition of the prewar period.

Women and the War

For many northern women, the conflict opened new doors of opportunity. Women took advantage of the wartime labor shortage to move into jobs in factories and into certain largely male professions, particularly nursing. The expansion of the activities of the national government opened new jobs for women as clerks in government offices. Many of these wartime gains were short lived, but in white-collar government jobs, retail sales, and nursing, women found a permanent place in the workforce.

Hundreds of thousands of northern women took part in organizations that gathered money and medical supplies for soldiers and sent books, clothing, and food to freedmen. The U.S. Sanitary Commission emerged as a centralized national relief agency to coordinate donations on the northern home front. Although control at the national level remained in male hands, patriotic women did most of the grassroots work. Women played the leading role in organizing **Sanitary Fairs**—grand bazaars that displayed military banners, uniforms, and other relics of the war and sold goods to raise money for soldiers' aid.

Many men understood women's war work as an extension of their "natural" capacity for self-sacrifice. But the very act of volunteering for the war effort brought many northern women into the public sphere and offered them a taste of independence. From the ranks of this wartime mobilization came many of the leaders of the postwar movement for women's rights. Clara Barton organized supply lines and nursed wounded soldiers in northern Virginia. After the war, she became not only an advocate of woman suffrage but also, as president of the American National Red Cross, a strong proponent of the humane treatment of battlefield casualties.

The Divided North

Despite Lincoln's political skills, the war and his administration's policies divided northern society. Republicans labeled those opposed to the war Copperheads, after a poisonous snake that strikes without warning. Mounting casualties and rapid societal changes divided the North. Disaffection was strongest among the large southern-born population of states like Ohio, Indiana, and Illinois and working-class Catholic immigrants in eastern cities.

As the war progressed, it heightened existing social tensions and created new ones. The growing power of the federal government challenged traditional notions of local autonomy. The Union's draft law, which allowed individuals to provide a substitute or buy their way out of the army, caused widespread indignation. Workers resented manufacturers and financiers who reaped large profits while their own real incomes dwindled because of inflation. The prospect of a sweeping change in the status of blacks called forth a racist reaction in many parts of the North. Throughout the war, the Democratic Party subjected Lincoln's policies to withering criticism, although it remained divided between "War Democrats," who supported the military effort while criticizing emancipation and the draft, and those who favored immediate peace.

On occasion, dissent degenerated into outright violence. In July 1863, the introduction of the draft provoked four days of rioting in New York City. The mob, composed largely of Irish immigrants, assaulted symbols of the new order being created by the war—draft offices, the mansions of wealthy Republicans, industrial establishments, and the city's black

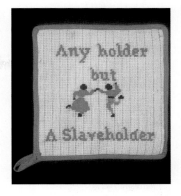

Whimsical potholders expressing hope for a better life for emancipated slaves were sold at the Chicago Sanitary Fair of 1865 to raise money for soldiers' aid.

Rioting in New York City

THE RIOTS IN NEW YORK : DESTRUCTION OF THE COLOURED ORPHAN ASYLUM.

The burning of the Colored Orphan Asylum during the New York City draft riots of 1863. The children were evacuated before the mob destroyed the building.

population, many of whom fled to New Jersey or took refuge in Central Park. Only the arrival of Union troops quelled the uprising, but not before more than 100 persons had died.

THE CONFEDERATE NATION

Leadership and Government

Jefferson Davis

The man charged with the task of rallying public support for the Confederacy proved unequal to the task. Jefferson Davis moved to Mississippi as a youth, attended West Point, and acquired a large plantation. Aloof and stubborn, Davis lacked Lincoln's political flexibility and ability to communicate the war's meaning effectively to ordinary men and women.

Centralizing the South

Under Davis, the Confederate nation became far more centralized than the Old South had been. The government raised armies from scratch, took control of southern railroads, and built manufacturing plants. But it failed to find an effective way of utilizing the South's major economic resource, cotton. In the early part of the war, the administration tried to suppress cotton production, urging planters to grow food instead and banning cotton exports. This, it was hoped, would promote economic self-sufficiency and force Great Britain, whose textile mills could not operate without southern cotton, to intervene on the side of the Confederacy.

The international dimension

"**King Cotton diplomacy**" turned out to be ineffective. But the Confederate policy had far-reaching global consequences. Recognizing their overdependence on southern cotton, other nations moved to expand production. Britain promoted cultivation of the crop in Egypt and India, and Russia did the same in parts of Central Asia. As a result, the resumption of American cotton production after the war led directly to a worldwide crisis of overproduction that drove down the price of cotton, impoverishing farmers around the world.

The Inner Civil War

Social change in the South

As the war progressed, social change and internal turmoil engulfed much of the Confederacy. At the outset, most white southerners rallied to the Confederate cause. No less fervently than northern troops, southern soldiers spoke of their cause in the language of freedom. "We are fighting for our liberty," wrote one volunteer, without any sense of contradiction, "against tyrants of the North . . . who are determined to destroy slavery."

The centrality of slavery to the Confederacy is illustrated by the paper money issued by state governments and private banks, which frequently juxtaposed scenes of slaves at work with other revered images. The ten-dollar note of the Eastern Bank of Alabama depicts slaves working in the field and at a port, along with an idealized image of southern white womanhood. Alabama's five-dollar bill includes an overseer directing slaves in the field and a symbol of liberty.

But even as it waged a desperate struggle for independence, the South found itself increasingly divided. One grievance was the draft. Like the Union, the Confederacy allowed individuals to provide a substitute. Because of the accelerating disintegration of slavery, it also exempted one white male for every twenty slaves on a plantation (thus releasing many overseers and planters' sons from service). The "twenty-negro" provision convinced many yeomen that the struggle for southern independence had become "a rich man's war and a poor man's fight."

"Twenty-negro" provision

Economic Problems

Economic deprivation also sparked disaffection. As the blockade tightened, areas of the Confederacy came under Union occupation, and production by slaves declined, shortages arose of essential commodities such as salt, corn, and meat. The war left countless farms, plantations, businesses, and railroads in ruins. The economic crisis, which stood in glaring contrast to the North's boom, was an unavoidable result of the war. But Confederate policies exaggerated its effects. War requires sacrifice, and civilian support for war depends, in part, on the belief that sacrifice is being fairly shared. Many non-slaveholders, however, became convinced that they were bearing an unfair share of the war's burdens.

Declining southern production

VOICES OF FREEDOM

From Letter of Thomas F. Drayton (1861)

A South Carolina plantation owner and ardent supporter of secession, Thomas F. Drayton explained the Confederate cause in this letter to his brother Percival, an officer in the U.S. Navy, written from Charleston in April 1861, shortly after the firing on Fort Sumter. Drayton went on to serve as a brigadier general in the Confederate army.

My dear Percy

And so Sumter is at last ours, and this too without the loss of a *single* life upon either side. . . . Before this dispute is over however, I look for abundance of death & blood. . . .

You say I don't yet understand the position you have taken. I do fully, but certainly differ from you when you say that to side with us, would be "battling for slavery against freedom." On the contrary, by siding with us, you likewise defend yourselves at the North against a far greater danger than we are threatened with, which is the enslavement of the *whites*; for the tendency with you is towards consolidation & the abrogation of State rights. . . . All these evils & horrors will be laid to your doors, because you have encouraged . . . in the form of abolition lecturers, fanatical preachers, unscrupulous editors, selfish politicians; . . . and by voting for men . . . with the *avowed object* of abolishing slavery throughout the Southern States . . . who made a merit of John Brown's murderous invasion; set at defiance all fugitive slave laws, . . . and whose clergy denounced us indiscriminately as barbarians. . . .

We are fighting for home & liberty. Can the North say as much? Good night. And don't say again, that in siding for us, you would be defending slavery and fighting for what is abhorrent to your feelings & convictions. On the contrary, in fighting on our side, you will be battling for law & order & against abstract fanatical ideas which will certainly bring about vastly greater evils upon our race, then could possibly result from the perpetuation of slavery among us.

From Abraham Lincoln, Address at a Sanitary Fair, Baltimore (1864)

Abraham Lincoln's speech at a Sanitary Fair (a grand bazaar that raised money for the care of Union soldiers) offers a dramatic illustration of the contested meaning of freedom during the Civil War.

The world has never had a good definition of the word liberty, and the American people, just now, are much in want of one. We all declare for liberty; but in using the same *word* we do not all mean the same *thing*. With some the word liberty may mean for each man to do as he pleases with himself, and the product of his labor; while with others the same word may mean for some men to do as they please with other men, and the product of other men's labor. Here are two, not only different, but incompatible things, called by the same name—liberty. And it follows that each of the things is, by the respective parties, called by two different and incompatible names—liberty and tyranny.

The shepherd drives the wolf from the sheep's throat, for which the sheep thanks the shepherd as a *liberator*, while the wolf denounces him for the same act as the destroyer of liberty, especially as the sheep was a black one. Plainly the sheep and the wolf are not agreed upon a definition of the word liberty; and precisely the same difference prevails today among us human creatures, even in the North, and all professing to love liberty. Hence we behold the process by which thousands are daily passing from under the yoke of bondage, hailed by some as the advance of liberty, and bewailed by others as the destruction of all liberty. Recently, as it seems, the people of Maryland have been doing something to define liberty [abolishing slavery in the state]; and thanks to them that, in what they have done, the wolf's dictionary, has been repudiated.

QUESTIONS

1. *Why does Drayton deny that the Confederacy is fighting to defend slavery?*

2. *What does Lincoln identify as the essential difference between northern and southern definitions of freedom?*

3. *How do Drayton and Lincoln differ in their definitions of liberty and whether it applies to African-Americans?*

An engraving in the *New York Illustrated News* depicts the bread riot that took place in Mobile, Alabama, in the fall of 1863.

Like the Union, the Confederacy borrowed heavily to finance the war. Unlike federal lawmakers, however, the planter-dominated Confederate Congress proved unwilling to levy heavy taxes that planters would have to pay. It relied on paper money, of which it issued $1.5 billion, far more than the North's greenbacks. The Confederate Congress also authorized military officers to seize farm goods to supply the army, paying with increasingly worthless Confederate money. Small farmers deeply resented this practice, known as "impressment." Food riots broke out in many places, including Richmond, Virginia, and Mobile, Alabama, where in 1863 large crowds of women plundered army food supplies. As the war progressed, desertion became what one officer called a "crying evil" for the southern armies. By the war's end, more than 100,000 men had deserted, almost entirely from among "the poorest class of nonslaveholders whose labor is indispensable to the daily support of their families."

By 1864, organized peace movements had appeared in several southern states, and secret pro-Union societies such as the Heroes of America were actively promoting disaffection.

Women and the Confederacy

Even more than in the North, the war placed unprecedented burdens on southern white women. Left alone on farms and plantations, they were often forced to manage business affairs and discipline slaves, previously the responsibility of men. As in the North, women mobilized to support soldiers in the field and stepped out of their traditional "sphere" to run commercial establishments and work in arms factories. In Richmond, "government girls" staffed many of the clerkships in the new Confederate bureaucracy.

Wartime roles for women in the Confederacy

All Confederate women struggled to cope as their loved ones were drawn off into the army. The war led to the political mobilization, for the first time, of non-slaveholding white women. Lacking the aid of slave labor, they found that the absence of their husbands from their previously self-sufficient farms made it impossible to feed their families. They flooded Confederate authorities with petitions seeking assistance, not as charity but as a right. Politicians could not ignore the pleas of soldiers' wives, and state governments began to distribute supplies to needy families.

Women mobilizing for assistance

Painted in 1864 by the Virginia artist William D. Washington, *The Burial of Latané* depicts a common wartime scene. The deceased is Confederate cavalry officer William Latané. The work illustrates how women, children, and slaves predominated on the southern home front. The painting was displayed in Richmond accompanied by a bucket into which viewers were urged to deposit contributions to the southern cause.

Southern women's self-sacrificing devotion to the cause became legendary. But as the war went on and the death toll mounted, increasing numbers of women came to believe that the goal of independence was not worth the cost. The growing disaffection of southern white women, conveyed in letters to loved ones at the front, contributed to the decline in civilian morale and encouraged desertion from the army.

Decline in morale among women

Black Soldiers for the Confederacy

The growing shortage of white manpower eventually led Confederate authorities to a decision no one could have foreseen when the war began: they authorized the arming of slaves to fight for the South. Many slaveholders fiercely resisted this idea, and initially, the Confederate Senate rejected it. Not until March 1865, after Robert E. Lee had endorsed the plan, did the Confederate Congress authorize the arming of slaves.

Southern debate over arming the slaves

The war ended before the recruitment of black soldiers actually began. But the Confederate army did employ numerous blacks, nearly all of them slaves, as laborers. This later led to some confusion over whether blacks actually fought for the Confederacy—apart from a handful who "passed" for white, none in fact did. But the South's decision to raise black troops illustrates how the war undermined not only slavery but also the proslavery ideology. Declared Howell Cobb, a Georgia planter and politician, "If slaves make good soldiers, our whole theory of slavery is wrong."

Employing blacks as laborers

TURNING POINTS

Gettysburg and Vicksburg

Despite the accelerating demise of slavery and the decline of morale in the South, the war's outcome remained very much in doubt for much of its third and fourth years. In April 1863, "Fighting Joe" Hooker, who had succeeded Ambrose E. Burnside as the Union commander in the East, brought the Army of the Potomac into central Virginia to confront Lee. Outnumbered two to one, Lee repelled Hooker's attack at Chancellorsville, although he lost his ablest lieutenant, "Stonewall" Jackson, mistakenly killed by fire from his own soldiers.

Generals Robert E. Lee and Ulysses S. Grant, leaders of the opposing armies in the East, 1864–1865.

Lee now gambled on another invasion of the North, although his strategic objective remains unclear. Perhaps he believed a defeat on its own territory would destroy the morale of the northern army and public. In any event, the two armies, with Union soldiers now under the command of General George G. Meade, met at Gettysburg, Pennsylvania, on the first three days of July 1863. With 165,000 troops involved, the **Battle of Gettysburg** remains the largest battle ever fought on the North American continent. On July 3, Confederate forces, led by Major General George E. Pickett's crack division, marched across an open field toward Union forces. Withering artillery and rifle fire met the charge, and most of Pickett's soldiers never reached Union lines. Pickett's Charge was Lee's greatest blunder. His army retreated to Virginia, never again to set foot on northern soil.

On the same day that Lee began his retreat from Gettysburg, the Union achieved a significant victory in the West at the **Battle of Vicksburg**. Late in 1862, Grant had moved into Mississippi toward the city of Vicksburg. From its heights, defended by miles of trenches and earthworks, the Confederacy commanded the central Mississippi River. When direct attacks failed, Grant launched a siege. On July 4, 1863, Vicksburg surrendered, and with it John C. Pemberton's army of 30,000 men, a loss the Confederacy could ill afford. The entire Mississippi Valley now lay in Union hands.

1864

Nearly two years, however, would pass before the war ended. Brought east to take command of Union forces, Grant in 1864 began a war of attrition against Lee's army in Virginia. That is, he was willing to accept high numbers of casualties, knowing that the North could replace its manpower losses, whereas the South could not. Grant understood that to bring the North's manpower advantage into play, he must attack continuously "all along the line," thereby preventing the enemy from concentrating its forces or retreating to safety after an engagement.

THE CIVIL WAR, 1863

In May 1864, the 115,000-man Army of the Potomac crossed the Rapidan River to do battle with Lee's forces in Virginia. At the end of six weeks of fighting, Grant's casualties stood at 60,000—almost the size of Lee's entire army—while Lee had lost 30,000 men. The sustained fighting in Virginia was a turning point in modern warfare. With daily combat and a fearsome casualty toll, it had far more in common with the trench warfare of World War I (discussed in Chapter 19) than the almost gentlemanly fighting with which the Civil War began.

Grant had become the only Union general to maintain the initiative against Lee, but at a cost that led critics to label him a "butcher of men." Victory still eluded him. Grant attempted to capture Petersburg, which controlled the railway link to Richmond, but Lee got to Petersburg first, and Grant settled in for a prolonged siege. Meanwhile, General William T. Sherman, who had moved his forces into Georgia from

In July 1863. the Union won major victories at Gettysburg and Vicksburg.

Tennessee, encountered dogged resistance from Confederate troops. Not until September 1864 did he finally enter Atlanta, seizing Georgia's main railroad center.

As casualty rolls mounted in the spring and summer of 1864, northern morale sank to its lowest point of the war. Lincoln for a time believed he would be unable to win reelection. In May, hoping to force Lincoln to step aside, Radical Republicans nominated John C. Frémont on a platform calling for a constitutional amendment to abolish slavery, federal protection of the freedmen's rights, and confiscation of the land of leading Confederates. The Democratic candidate for president, General George B. McClellan, was hampered from the outset of the campaign by a platform calling for an immediate cease-fire and peace conference—a plan that even war-weary northerners viewed as equivalent to surrender. In the end, Frémont withdrew, and buoyed by Sherman's capture of Atlanta, Lincoln won a sweeping victory. He captured every state but Kentucky, Delaware, and New Jersey. The result ensured that the war would continue until the Confederacy's defeat.

General Grant's Council of War, an unusual candid photograph taken in Virginia in 1864 from the upper floor of a nearby church, shows Grant leaning over the shoulder of General George G. Meade to examine a map. Other generals and staff sit on pews removed from the church.

REHEARSALS FOR RECONSTRUCTION AND THE END OF THE WAR

A political cartoon from 1864 suggests the difficulty faced by the Democratic candidate, George B. McClellan, in reconciling the party's war and peace wings.

LITTLE MAC, IN HIS GREAT TWO HORSE ACT, IN THE PRESIDENTIAL CANVASS OF 1864.

As the war drew toward a close and more and more parts of the Confederacy came under Union control, federal authorities found themselves presiding over the transition from slavery to freedom. In South Carolina, Louisiana, and other parts of the South, debates took place over issues—access to land, control of labor, and the new structure of political power—that would reverberate in the postwar world.

The Sea Islands Experiment

The most famous "rehearsal for Reconstruction" took place on the Sea Islands just off the coast of South Carolina. The war was only a few months old when, in November 1861, the Union navy occupied the islands. Nearly the entire white population fled, leaving behind some 10,000 slaves. The navy was soon followed by other northerners—army officers, Treasury agents, prospective investors in cotton land, and a group known as Gideon's Band, which included black and white reformers and teachers committed to uplifting the freed slaves. Northern-born teachers like Charlotte Forten, a member of one of Philadelphia's most prominent black families, and Laura M. Towne, a white native of Pittsburgh, devoted themselves to teaching the freed blacks.

Gideon's Band

Forten and Towne

Many northerners believed that the transition from slave to free labor meant enabling blacks to work for wages in more humane conditions than under slavery. When the federal government put land on the islands up for sale, most was acquired not by former slaves but by northern investors bent on demonstrating the superiority of free wage labor and turning a tidy profit at the same time. By 1865, the **Sea Islands experiment** was widely held to be a success. But the experiment also bequeathed to postwar Reconstruction the contentious issue of whether landownership should accompany black freedom.

Wartime Reconstruction in the West

A very different rehearsal for Reconstruction, involving a far larger area and population than the Sea Islands, took place in Louisiana and the Mississippi Valley. After the capture of Vicksburg, the Union army established regulations for plantation labor. Military authorities insisted that the emancipated slaves must sign labor contracts with plantation owners who took an oath of loyalty. But, unlike before the war, the laborers would be paid wages and provided with education, physical punishment was prohibited, and their families were safe from disruption by sale.

Neither side was satisfied with the new labor system. Blacks resented having to resume working for whites and being forced to sign labor contracts. Planters complained that their workers were insubordinate. But only occasionally did army officers seek to implement a different vision of freedom. At Davis Bend, Mississippi, site of the cotton plantations of Jefferson Davis and his brother Joseph, the emancipated slaves saw the land divided among themselves. In addition, a system of government was established that allowed the former slaves to elect their own judges and sheriffs.

A school for freedpeople established in 1862 on St. Helena Island, South Carolina, by an aid association in Pennsylvania.

The Politics of Wartime Reconstruction

As the Civil War progressed, the future political status of African-Americans emerged as a key dividing line in public debates. Events in Union-occupied Louisiana brought the issue to national attention. Hoping to establish a functioning civilian government in the state, Lincoln in 1863 announced his **Ten-Percent Plan of Reconstruction**. He essentially offered an amnesty and full restoration of rights, including property except for slaves, to nearly all white southerners who took an oath affirming loyalty to the Union and support for emancipation. When 10 percent of the voters of 1860 had taken the oath, they could elect a new state government, which would be required to abolish slavery. Lincoln's plan offered no role to blacks in shaping the post-slavery order.

Lincoln's Ten-Percent Plan

Another group now stepped onto the stage of politics—the free blacks of New Orleans, who saw the Union occupation as a golden opportunity to press for equality before the law and a role in government for themselves. Their complaints at being excluded under Lincoln's Reconstruction plan won a sympathetic hearing from Radical Republicans in Congress. By the summer of 1864, dissatisfaction with events in Louisiana helped to inspire the **Wade-Davis Bill**, named for two leading Republican members of Congress. This bill required a majority (not one-tenth) of white male southerners to pledge support for the Union before Reconstruction could begin in any state, and it guaranteed blacks equality before the law, although not the right to vote. The bill passed Congress only to die when Lincoln refused to sign it and Congress adjourned. As the war drew to a close, it was clear that although slavery was dead, no agreement existed as to what social and political system should take its place.

Wade-Davis Bill

Victory at Last

After Lincoln's reelection, the war hastened to its conclusion. In November 1864, Sherman and his army of 60,000 set out from Atlanta on their March to the Sea. Cutting a sixty-mile-wide swath through the heart of Georgia, they destroyed railroads, buildings, and all the food and supplies they could not use. His aim, Sherman wrote, was "to whip the rebels, to humble their pride, to follow them to their innermost recesses, and make them fear and dread us." Here was modern war in all its destructiveness, even though few civilians were physically harmed. In January 1865, after capturing Savannah, Sherman moved into South Carolina, bringing even greater destruction.

On January 31, 1865, Congress approved the **Thirteenth Amendment**, which abolished slavery throughout the entire Union—and in so doing, introduced the word "slavery" into the Constitution for the first time. In

General William T. Sherman, photographed in 1864.

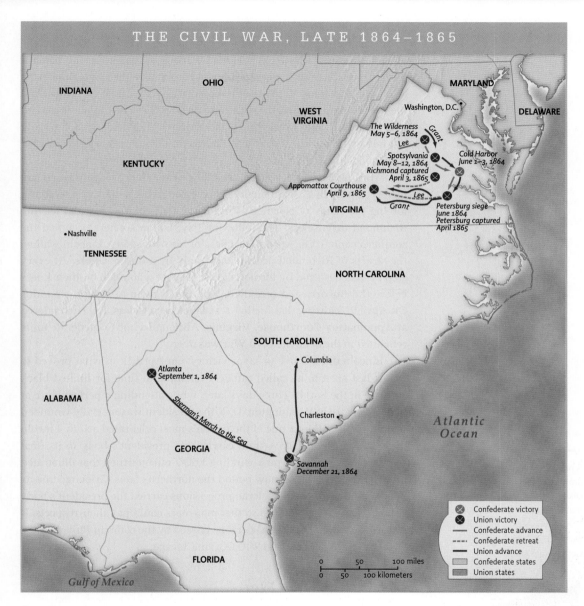

THE CIVIL WAR, LATE 1864–1865

INDIANA

OHIO

MARYLAND

DELAWARE

WEST VIRGINIA

Washington, D.C.

KENTUCKY

The Wilderness
May 5–6, 1864

Grant

Lee

Spotsylvania
May 8–12, 1864

Cold Harbor
June 1–3, 1864

Richmond captured
April 3, 1865

Appomattox Courthouse
April 9, 1865

Lee

VIRGINIA

Grant

Petersburg siege
June 1864
Petersburg captured
April 1865

Nashville

TENNESSEE

NORTH CAROLINA

SOUTH CAROLINA

Columbia

Atlanta
September 1, 1864

ALABAMA

Sherman's March to the Sea

Charleston

Atlantic Ocean

GEORGIA

Savannah
December 21, 1864

FLORIDA

Gulf of Mexico

⊗	Confederate victory
⊗	Union victory
—	Confederate advance
---	Confederate retreat
—	Union advance
	Confederate states
	Union states

0   50   100 miles
0   50   100 kilometers

The military defeat of the Confederacy came in the East, with Sherman's March to the Sea, Grant's occupation of Richmond, and the surrender of Robert E. Lee's army.

March, in his second inaugural address, Lincoln called for reconciliation: "With malice toward none, with charity for all, . . . let us . . . bind up the nation's wounds." Yet he also leveled a harsh judgment on the nation's past. Perhaps, Lincoln suggested, God had brought on the war to punish the entire nation, not just the South, for the sin of slavery. And if God willed that the war continue until all the wealth created by 250 years of slave labor had been destroyed, and "every drop of blood drawn with the lash shall be paid by another drawn with the sword," this too would be an act of justice (see the Appendix for the full text).

April 1865 brought some of the most momentous events in American history. On April 2, Grant finally broke through Lee's lines at Petersburg, forcing the Army of Northern Virginia to abandon the city and leaving Richmond defenseless. The following day, Union soldiers occupied the southern capital. On April 4, heedless of his own safety, Lincoln walked the streets of Richmond accompanied only by a dozen sailors. At every step he was besieged by former slaves, some of whom fell on their knees before the embarrassed president, who urged them to remain standing. On April 9, realizing that further resistance was useless, Lee surrendered at **Appomattox Courthouse, Virginia**. Although some Confederate units remained in the field, the Civil War was over.

Lincoln did not live to savor victory. On April 11, in what proved to be his last speech, he called publicly for the first time for limited black suffrage in the South. Three days later, while attending a performance at Ford's Theatre in Washington, D.C., the president was mortally wounded by John Wilkes Booth, one of the nation's most celebrated actors. Lincoln died the next morning. A train carried the president's body to its final resting place in Illinois on a winding 1,600-mile journey that illustrated how tightly the railroad now bound the northern states. Grieving crowds lined the train route, and solemn processions carried the president's body to lie in state in major cities so that mourners could pay their respects. It was estimated that 300,000 persons passed by the coffin in Philadelphia, 500,000 in New York, and 200,000 in Chicago.

Occupation at Richmond

Surrender at Appomattox

A redesign of the American flag proposed in 1863 illustrates the linkage of nationalism and freedom that was solidified by the Civil War. The thirty-five stars forming the word "FREE" include the eleven Confederate states.

The War and the World

In 1877, soon after retiring as president, Ulysses S. Grant embarked with his wife on a two-year tour of the world. At almost every location, he was greeted as a modern-day hero. What did America in the aftermath of the Civil War represent to the world? In England, the son of the duke of Wellington greeted Grant as a military genius. In Newcastle, parading English workers hailed him as the man whose military prowess had saved the world's leading experiment in democratic government and as a "Hero of

Freedom." In Berlin, Otto von Bismarck, the chancellor of Germany, welcomed Grant as a nation-builder, who had accomplished on the battlefield something—national unity—that Bismarck was attempting to create for his own people.

The War in American History

The Civil War laid the foundation for modern America, guaranteeing the Union's permanence, destroying slavery, and shifting power in the nation from the South to the North (and, more specifically, from slaveowning planters to northern capitalists). It dramatically increased the power of the federal government and accelerated the modernization of the northern economy. And it placed on the postwar agenda the challenge of defining and protecting African-American freedom. "Verily," as Frederick Douglass declared, "the work does not *end* with the abolition of slavery, but only *begins*."

Paradoxically, both sides lost something they had gone to war to defend. Slavery was the cornerstone of the Confederacy, but the war led inexorably to slavery's destruction. In the North, the war hastened the transformation of Lincoln's America—the world of free labor, of the small shop and independent farmer—into an industrial giant. Americans, in the words of the abolitionist Wendell Phillips, would "never again . . . see the republic in which we were born."

Some of the more than 200,000 victorious soldiers who paraded in Washington on May 23 and 24, 1865, in the Grand Review of the Union Armies. In the background stands the Capitol, its dome, unfinished when the war began, now complete.

Winslow Homer's painting *The Veteran in a New Field*, completed in the fall of 1865, offers a reflection on the Civil War and its legacy. The former Union soldier, whose army jacket lies in the right corner, is at work cutting wheat. The scythe brings to mind the grim reaper, a symbol of death, perhaps a reference not only to war casualties but also to Lincoln's assassination. But the bountiful field suggests national regeneration.

CHAPTER REVIEW AND ONLINE RESOURCES

REVIEW QUESTIONS

1. *What made the American Civil War the first modern war?*

2. *How was the North's victory over the South tied to the different ways the market revolution had developed in the North and South?*

3. *Describe how President Lincoln's war aims evolved between 1861 and 1863, changing from simply preserving the Union to also ending slavery.*

4. *How did the actions of slaves themselves, northern military strategy, and the Emancipation Proclamation combine to end slavery?*

5. *What role did blacks play in winning the Civil War and in defining the war's consequences?*

6. *How did federal policies undertaken during the Civil War transform the United States into a stronger nation-state—economically, politically, and ideologically?*

7. *What was the impact of the Civil War on civil liberties?*

8. *Compare and contrast women's efforts in the North and South to support the war effort and their families.*

9. *In what ways did the outcome of the Civil War change the United States' status in the world?*

KEY TERMS

first Battle of Bull Run (p. 401)
second Battle of Bull Run (p. 401)
Battle of Antietam (p. 401)
"the contrabands" (p. 405)
Radical Republicans (p. 406)
Emancipation Proclamation (p. 407)
Second American Revolution (p. 410)
Ex parte Milligan (p. 413)
Homestead Act (p. 413)
transcontinental railroad (p. 414)
Navajo's Long Walk (p. 416)
Sanitary Fairs (p. 418)
"King Cotton diplomacy" (p. 420)
Battle of Gettysburg (p. 426)
Battle of Vicksburg (p. 426)
Sea Islands experiment (p. 429)
Ten-Percent Plan of Reconstruction (p. 430)
Wade-Davis Bill (p. 430)
Thirteenth Amendment (p. 430)
Appomattox Courthouse, Virginia (p. 432)

Go to 🐰 INQUIZITIVE

To see what you know—and learn what you've missed—with personalized feedback along the way.

Visit the *Give Me Liberty!* **Student Site** for primary source documents and images, interactive maps, author videos featuring Eric Foner, and more.

CHAPTER 15

"WHAT IS FREEDOM?"

★

RECONSTRUCTION, 1865–1877

The Shackle Broken—by the Genius of Freedom. This 1874 lithograph depicts Robert B. Elliott, a black congressman from South Carolina, delivering a celebrated speech supporting the bill that became the Civil Rights Act of 1875.

On the evening of January 12, 1865, less than a month after Union forces captured Savannah, Georgia, twenty leaders of the city's black community gathered for a discussion with General William T. Sherman and Secretary of War Edwin M. Stanton. The conversation revealed that the black leaders brought out of slavery a clear definition of freedom. Asked what he understood by slavery, Garrison Frazier, a Baptist minister chosen as the group's spokesman, responded that it meant one person's "receiving by irresistible power the work of another man, and not by his consent." Freedom he defined as "placing us where we could reap the fruit of our own labor, and take care of ourselves." The way to accomplish this was "to have land, and turn it and till it by our own labor."

Sherman's meeting with the black leaders foreshadowed some of the radical changes that would take place during the era known as Reconstruction (meaning, literally, the rebuilding of the shattered nation). In the years following the Civil War, former slaves and their white allies, North and South, would seek to redefine the meaning and boundaries of American freedom and citizenship. Previously an entitlement of whites, these would be expanded to include black Americans. The laws and Constitution would be rewritten to guarantee African-Americans, for the first time in the nation's history, recognition as citizens and equality before the law. Black men would be granted the right to vote, ushering in a period of interracial democracy throughout the South. Black schools, churches, and other institutions would flourish, laying the foundation for the modern African-American community. Many of the advances of Reconstruction would prove temporary, swept away during a campaign of violence in the South and the North's retreat from the ideal of equality. But Reconstruction laid the foundation for future struggles to extend freedom to all Americans.

Four days after the meeting, Sherman responded to the black delegation by issuing Special Field Order 15. This set aside the Sea Islands and a large area along the South Carolina and Georgia coasts for the settlement of black families on forty-acre plots of land. He also offered them broken-down mules that the army could no longer use. In Sherman's order lay the origins of the phrase "forty acres and a mule," which would reverberate across the South in the next few years. Among the emancipated slaves, Sherman's order raised hopes that the end of slavery would be accompanied by the economic independence that they, like other Americans, believed essential to genuine freedom.

THE MEANING OF FREEDOM

"What is freedom?" asked Congressman James A. Garfield in 1865. "Is it the bare privilege of not being chained? If this is all, then freedom is a bitter mockery, a cruel delusion." Did freedom mean simply the absence of slavery, or did it imply other rights for the former slaves, and if so, which ones? Equal civil rights, the vote, ownership of property? During Reconstruction, freedom became a terrain of conflict, its substance open to different, often contradictory interpretations.

Conflicts over freedom

African-Americans' understanding of freedom was shaped by their experiences as slaves and their observation of the free society around them. To begin with, freedom meant escaping the numerous injustices of slavery—punishment by the lash, the separation of families, denial of access to education, the sexual exploitation of black women by their owners—and sharing in the rights and opportunities of American citizens. "If I cannot do like a white man," Henry Adams, an emancipated slave in Louisiana, told his former master in 1865, "I am not free."

Families in Freedom

With slavery dead, institutions that had existed before the war, like the black family, free blacks' churches and schools, and the secret slave church, were strengthened, expanded, and freed from white supervision. The family was central to the postemancipation black community. Former slaves made remarkable efforts to locate loved ones from whom they had been separated under slavery. One northern reporter in 1865 encountered a freedman who

Marriage of a Colored Soldier at Vicksburg, a sketch of a wedding ceremony by Alfred R. Waud soon after the end of the Civil War.

Five Generations of a Black Family, an 1862 photograph that suggests the power of family ties among emancipated slaves.

Mother and Daughter Reading, Mt. Meigs, Alabama, an 1890 photograph by Rudolph Eickemeyer. During Reconstruction and for years thereafter, former slaves exhibited a deep desire for education, and learning took place outside of school as well as within.

had walked more than 600 miles from Georgia to North Carolina, searching for the wife and children from whom he had been sold away before the war.

While freedom helped to stabilize family life, it also subtly altered relationships within the family. Immediately after the Civil War, planters complained that freedwomen had "withdrawn" from field labor and work as house servants. Many black women preferred to devote more time to their families than had been possible under slavery, and men considered it a badge of honor to see their wives remain at home. Eventually, the dire poverty of the black community would compel a far higher proportion of black women than white women to go to work for wages.

Church and School

At the same time, blacks abandoned white-controlled religious institutions to create churches of their own. On the eve of the Civil War, 42,000 black Methodists worshiped in biracial South Carolina churches; by the end of Reconstruction, only 600 remained. As the major institution independent of white control, the church played a central role in the black community. A place of worship, it also housed schools, social events, and political gatherings. Black ministers came to play a major role in politics. Some 250 held public office during Reconstruction.

Another striking example of the freedpeople's quest for individual and community improvement was their desire for education. The thirst for learning sprang from many sources—a desire to read the Bible, the need to prepare for the economic marketplace, and the opportunity, which arose in 1867, to take part in politics. Blacks of all ages flocked to the schools established by northern missionary societies, the Freedmen's Bureau, and groups of ex-slaves. Reconstruction also witnessed the creation of the nation's first black colleges, including Fisk University in Tennessee, Hampton Institute in Virginia, and Howard University in the nation's capital.

Political Freedom

In a society that had made political participation a core element of freedom, the right to vote inevitably became central to the former slaves' desire for empowerment and equality. As Frederick Douglass put it soon after the South's surrender in 1865, "Slavery is not abolished until the black man has the ballot." In a "monarchial government," Douglass explained, no "special" disgrace applied to those denied the right to vote. But in a

The First African Church, Richmond, as depicted in *Harper's Weekly*, June 27, 1874. The establishment of independent black churches was an enduring accomplishment of Reconstruction.

democracy, "where universal suffrage is the rule," excluding any group meant branding them with "the stigma of inferiority." Anything less than full citizenship, black spokesmen insisted, would betray the nation's democratic promise and the war's meaning.

Land, Labor, and Freedom

Like those of rural people throughout the world, former slaves' ideas of freedom were directly related to landownership. On the land they would develop independent communities free of white control. Many former slaves insisted that through their unpaid labor, they had acquired a right to the land. "The property which they hold," declared an Alabama black convention, "was nearly all earned by the sweat of *our* brows." In some parts of the South, blacks in 1865 seized property, insisting that it belonged to them.

Freedom and landownership

In its individual elements and much of its language, former slaves' definition of freedom resembled that of white Americans—self-ownership, family stability, religious liberty, political participation, and economic autonomy. But these elements combined to form a vision very much their own. For whites, freedom, no matter how defined, was a given, a birthright to be defended. For African-Americans, it was an open-ended process, a transformation of every aspect of their lives and of the society and culture that had sustained slavery in the first place. Although the freedpeople failed to achieve full freedom as they understood it, their definition did much to shape national debate during the turbulent era of Reconstruction.

Freedom's meaning for former slaves

Masters without Slaves

Most white southerners reacted to military defeat and emancipation with dismay, not only because of the widespread devastation but also because

The southern white reaction to emancipation

Two maps of the Barrow plantation illustrate the effects of emancipation on rural life in the South. In 1860, slaves lived in communal quarters near the owner's house. Twenty-one years later, former slaves working as sharecroppers lived scattered across the plantation and had their own church and school.

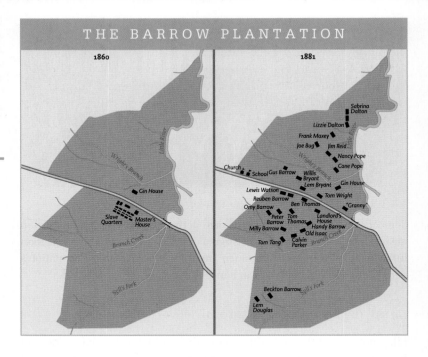

THE BARROW PLANTATION

1860

1881

they must now submit to northern demands. "The demoralization is complete," wrote a Georgia girl. "We are whipped, there is no doubt about it." The appalling loss of life, a disaster without parallel in the American experience, affected all classes of southerners. Nearly 260,000 men died for the Confederacy—more than one-fifth of the South's adult male white population. The wholesale destruction of work animals, farm buildings, and machinery ensured that economic revival would be slow and painful. In 1870, the value of property in the South, not counting that represented by slaves, was 30 percent lower than before the war.

Confederate deaths

Planter families faced profound changes in the war's aftermath. Many lost not only their slaves but also their life savings, which they had patriotically invested in now-worthless Confederate bonds. Some, whose slaves departed the plantation, for the first time found themselves compelled to do physical labor.

Planters

Southern planters sought to implement an understanding of freedom quite different from that of the former slaves. As they struggled to accept the reality of emancipation, most planters defined black freedom in the narrowest manner. As journalist Sidney Andrews discovered late in 1865, "The whites seem wholly unable to comprehend that freedom for the negro means the same thing as freedom for them."

Narrow understanding of freedom

The Free Labor Vision

Along with former slaves and former masters, the victorious Republican North tried to implement its own vision of freedom. Central to its definition was the antebellum principle of free labor, now further strengthened as a definition of the good society by the Union's triumph. In the free labor vision of a reconstructed South, emancipated blacks, enjoying the same opportunities for advancement as northern workers, would labor more productively than they had as slaves. At the same time, northern capital and migrants would energize the economy. The South would eventually come to resemble the "free society" of the North, complete with public schools, small towns, and independent farmers.

Free labor and the good society

With planters seeking to establish a labor system as close to slavery as possible, and former slaves demanding economic autonomy and access to land, a long period of conflict over the organization and control of labor followed on plantations throughout the South. It fell to **the Freedmen's Bureau**, an agency established by Congress in March 1865, to attempt to establish a working free labor system.

The Freedmen's Bureau

Under the direction of O. O. Howard, a graduate of Bowdoin College in Maine and a veteran of the Civil War, the bureau took on responsibilities that can only be described as daunting. The bureau was an experiment in government social policy that seems to belong more comfortably to the New Deal of the 1930s or the Great Society of the 1960s (see Chapters 21 and 25, respectively) than to nineteenth-century America. Bureau agents were supposed to establish schools, provide aid to the poor and aged, settle disputes between whites and blacks and among the freed-people, and secure for former slaves and white Unionists equal treatment before the courts. "It is not . . . in your power to fulfill one-tenth of the expectations of those who framed the Bureau," General William T. Sherman wrote to Howard. "I fear you have Hercules' task."

The bureau lasted from 1865 to 1870. Even at its peak, there were fewer than 1,000 agents in the entire South.

Winslow Homer's 1876 painting *A Visit from the Old Mistress* depicts an imaginary meeting between a southern white woman and her former slaves. Their stance and gaze suggest the tensions arising from the birth of a new social order. Despite the clear class difference suggested by their clothing, Homer places his subjects on an equal footing, yet maintains a space of separation between them. He exhibited the painting to acclaim at the Paris Universal Exposition in 1878.

The Freedmen's Bureau, an engraving from *Harper's Weekly*, July 25, 1868, depicts the bureau agent as a promoter of racial peace in the violent postwar South.

Nonetheless, the bureau's achievements in some areas, notably education and health care, were striking. By 1869, nearly 3,000 schools, serving more than 150,000 pupils in the South, reported to the bureau. Bureau agents also assumed control of hospitals established during the war and provided medical care to both black and white southerners.

The Failure of Land Reform

Andrew Johnson and land reform

One provision of the law establishing the bureau gave it the authority to divide abandoned and confiscated land into forty-acre plots for rental and eventual sale to the former slaves. In the summer of 1865, however, President Andrew Johnson, who had succeeded Lincoln, ordered nearly all land in federal hands returned to its former owners. A series of confrontations followed, notably in South Carolina and Georgia, where the army forcibly evicted blacks who had settled on "Sherman land." When O. O. Howard, head of the Freedmen's Bureau, traveled to the Sea Islands to inform blacks of the new policy, he was greeted with disbelief and protest. A committee of former slaves drew up petitions to Howard and President Johnson. Land, the freedmen insisted, was essential to the meaning of freedom. Without it, they declared, "we have not bettered our condition" from the days of slavery—"you will see, this is not the condition of really free men."

Because no land distribution took place, the vast majority of rural freedpeople remained poor and without property during Reconstruction. They had no alternative but to work on white-owned plantations, often for their former owners. Far from being able to rise in the social scale through hard work, black men were largely confined to farm work, unskilled labor, and service jobs, and black women to positions in private homes as cooks and maids. The failure of land reform produced a deep sense of betrayal that survived among the former slaves and their descendants long after the end of Reconstruction. "No sir," Mary Gaffney, an elderly ex-slave, recalled in the 1930s, "we were not given a thing but freedom."

Out of the conflict on the plantations, new systems of labor emerged in the different regions of the South. **Sharecropping** came to dominate the Cotton Belt and much of the Tobacco Belt of Virginia and North Carolina. Sharecropping initially arose as a compromise between blacks' desire for land and planters' demand for labor discipline. The system allowed each black family to rent a part of a plantation, with the crop divided between worker and owner at the end of the year. Sharecropping guaranteed the planters a stable resident labor force. Former slaves preferred it to gang labor because it offered them the prospect of working without day-to-day white supervision. But as the years went on, sharecropping became more and more oppressive. Sharecroppers' economic opportunities were severely limited by a world market in which the price of farm products suffered a prolonged decline.

A nursemaid and her charge, from a daguerreotype around 1865.

The White Farmer

The plight of the small farmer was not confined to blacks in the postwar South. Wartime devastation set in motion a train of events that permanently altered the independent way of life of white yeomen, leading to what they considered a loss of freedom. To obtain supplies from merchants, farmers were forced to take up the growing of cotton and pledge a part of the crop as collateral (property the creditor can seize if a debt is not paid). This system became known as the **crop lien**. Since interest rates were extremely high and the price of cotton fell steadily, many farmers found themselves still in debt after marketing their portion of the crop at year's end. They had no choice but to continue to plant cotton to obtain new loans. By the mid-1870s, white farmers, who cultivated only 10 percent of the South's cotton crop in 1860, were growing 40 percent, and many who had owned their land had fallen into dependency as sharecroppers who now rented land owned by others.

The crop-lien system

Both black and white farmers found themselves caught in the sharecropping and crop-lien systems. The workings of sharecropping and the crop-lien system are illustrated by the case of Matt Brown, a Mississippi farmer who borrowed money each year from a local merchant. He began 1892 with a debt of $226 held over from the previous year. By 1893,

The burden of debt

VOICES OF FREEDOM

From Petition of Committee in Behalf
of the Freedmen to Andrew Johnson (1865)

In the summer of 1865, President Andrew Johnson ordered land that had been distributed to freed slaves in South Carolina and Georgia returned to its former owners. A committee of freedmen drafted a petition asking for the right to obtain land. Johnson did not, however, change his policy.

We the freedmen of Edisto Island, South Carolina, have learned from you through Major General O. O. Howard . . . with deep sorrow and painful hearts of the possibility of [the] government restoring these lands to the former owners. We are well aware of the many perplexing and trying questions that burden your mind, and therefore pray to god (the preserver of all, and who has through our late and beloved President [Lincoln's] proclamation and the war made us a free people) that he may guide you in making your decisions and give you that wisdom that cometh from above to settle these great and important questions for the best interests of the country and the colored race.

Here is where secession was born and nurtured. Here is where we have toiled nearly all our lives as slaves and treated like dumb driven cattle. This is our home, we have made these lands what they were, we are the only true and loyal people that were found in possession of these lands. We have been always ready to strike for liberty and humanity, yea to fight if need be to preserve this glorious Union. Shall not we who are freedmen and have always been true to this Union have the same rights as are enjoyed by others? . . . Are not our rights as a free people and good citizens of these United States to be considered before those who were found in rebellion against this good and just government? . . .

[Are] we who have been abused and oppressed for many long years not to be allowed the privilege of purchasing land but be subject to the will of these large land owners? God forbid. Land monopoly is injurious to the advancement of the course of freedom, and if government does not make some provision by which we as freedmen can obtain a homestead, we have not bettered our condition. . . .

We look to you . . . for protection and equal rights with the privilege of purchasing a homestead—a homestead right here in the heart of South Carolina.

From a Sharecropping Contract (1866)

Few former slaves were able to acquire land in the post–Civil War South. Most ended up as sharecroppers, working on white-owned land for a share of the crop at the end of the growing season. This contract, typical of thousands of others, originated in Tennessee. The laborers signed with an X, as they were illiterate.

Thomas J. Ross agrees to employ the Freedmen to plant and raise a crop on his Rosstown Plantation. . . . On the following Rules, Regulations and Remunerations.

The said Ross agrees to furnish the land to cultivate, and a sufficient number of mules & horses and feed them to make and house said crop and all necessary farming utensils to carry on the same and to give unto said Freedmen whose names appear below one half of all the cotton, corn and wheat that is raised on said place for the year 1866 after all the necessary expenses are deducted out that accrues on said crop. Outside of the Freedmen's labor in harvesting, carrying to market and selling the same the said Freedmen . . . covenant and agrees to and with said Thomas J. Ross that for and in consideration of one half of the crop before mentioned that they will plant, cultivate, and raise under the management control and Superintendence of said Ross, in good faith, a cotton, corn and oat crop under his management for the year 1866. And we the said Freedmen agrees to furnish ourselves & families in provisions, clothing, medicine and medical bills and all, and every kind of other expenses that we may incur on said plantation for the year 1866 free of charge to said Ross. Should the said Ross furnish us any of the above supplies or any other kind of expenses, during said year, [we] are to settle and pay him out of the net proceeds of our part of the crop the retail price of the county at time of sale or any price we may agree upon—The said Ross shall keep a regular book account, against each and every one or the head of every family to be adjusted and settled at the end of the year.

We furthermore bind ourselves to and with said Ross that we will do good work and labor ten hours a day on an average, winter and summer. . . . We further agree that we will lose all lost time, or pay at the rate of one dollar per day, rainy days excepted. In sickness and women lying in childbed are to lose the time and account for it to the other hands out of his or her part of the crop. . . .

We furthermore bind ourselves that we will obey the orders of said Ross in all things in carrying out and managing said crop for said year and be docked for disobedience . . . and are also responsible to said Ross if we carelessly, maliciously maltreat any of his stock for said year to said Ross for damages to be assessed out of our wages.

Samuel (X) Johnson, Thomas (X) Richard, Tinny (X) Fitch, Jessie (X) Simmons, Sophe (X) Pruden, Henry (X) Pruden, Frances (X) Pruden, Elijah (X) Smith.

QUESTIONS

1. *Why do the black petitioners believe that owning land is essential to the enjoyment of freedom?*

2. *In what ways does the contract limit the freedom of the laborers?*

3. *What do these documents suggest about competing definitions of black freedom in the aftermath of slavery?*

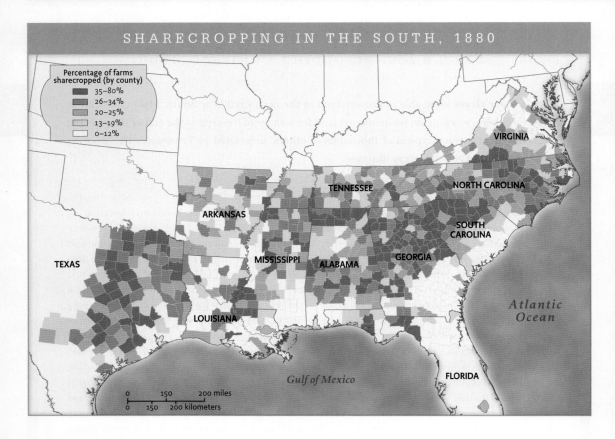

Percentage of farms
sharecropped (by county)
- 35–80%
- 26–34%
- 20–25%
- 13–19%
- 0–12%

VIRGINIA

TENNESSEE

NORTH CAROLINA

ARKANSAS

SOUTH
CAROLINA

TEXAS

MISSISSIPPI   ALABAMA

GEORGIA

LOUISIANA

*Atlantic
Ocean*

Gulf of Mexico   FLORIDA

| 0 | 150 | 200 miles |
| 0 | 150 | 200 kilometers |

By 1880, sharecropping had become the dominant form of agricultural labor in large parts of the South. The system involved both white and black farmers.

Growth of southern cities

although he produced cotton worth $171, Brown's debt had increased to $402, because he had borrowed $33 for food, $29 for clothing, $173 for supplies, and $112 for other items. Brown never succeeded in getting out of debt. He died in 1905; the last entry under his name in the merchant's account book is a coffin.

Even as the rural South stagnated economically, southern cities experienced remarkable growth after the Civil War. As railroads penetrated the interior, they enabled merchants in market centers like Atlanta to trade directly with the North, bypassing coastal cities that had traditionally monopolized southern commerce. A new urban middle class of merchants, railroad promoters, and bankers reaped the benefits of the spread of cotton production in the postwar South.

Aftermath of Slavery

The United States, of course, was not the only society to confront the transition from slavery to freedom. Indeed, many parallels exist between the debates during Reconstruction and struggles that followed slavery in other parts of the Western Hemisphere over the same issues of land, control of labor, and political power. Planters elsewhere held the same stereotypical views of black laborers as were voiced by their counterparts in the United States—former slaves were supposedly lazy and lacking in ambition, and thought that freedom meant an absence of labor.

For their part, former slaves throughout the hemisphere tried to carve out as much independence as possible, both in their daily lives and in their labor. In many places, the plantations either fell to pieces, as

Chinese laborers at work on a Louisiana plantation during Reconstruction.

in Haiti, or continued operating with a new labor force composed of indentured servants from India and China, as in Jamaica, Trinidad, and British Guiana. Southern planters in the United States brought in a few Chinese laborers in an attempt to replace freedmen, but since the federal government opposed such efforts, the Chinese remained only a tiny proportion of the southern workforce.

But if struggles over land and labor united its postemancipation experience with that of other societies, in one respect the United States was unique. Only in the United States were former slaves, within two years of the end of slavery, granted the right to vote and, thus, given a major share of political power. Few anticipated this development when the Civil War ended. It came about as the result of one of the greatest political crises of American history—the battle between President Andrew Johnson and Congress over Reconstruction. The struggle resulted in profound changes in the nature of citizenship, the structure of constitutional authority, and the meaning of American freedom.

Emancipation and the right to vote

THE MAKING OF RADICAL RECONSTRUCTION

Andrew Johnson

To Lincoln's successor, Andrew Johnson, fell the task of overseeing the restoration of the Union. Born in poverty in North Carolina, as a youth Johnson worked as a tailor's apprentice. Becoming a successful politician after moving to Tennessee, Johnson identified himself as the champion of his state's "honest yeomen" and a foe of large planters, whom he described as a "bloated, corrupted aristocracy." A strong defender of the Union, he

Johnson's background

became the only senator from a seceding state to remain at his post in Washington, D.C., when the Civil War began. When northern forces occupied Tennessee, Abraham Lincoln named him military governor. In 1864, Republicans nominated him to run for vice president as a symbol of the party's hope of extending its organization into the South.

Outlook

In personality and outlook, Johnson proved unsuited for the responsibilities he shouldered after Lincoln's death. A lonely, stubborn man, he was intolerant of criticism and unable to compromise. He lacked Lincoln's political skills and keen sense of public opinion. Moreover, while Johnson had supported emancipation once Lincoln made it a goal of the war effort, he held deeply racist views. African-Americans, Johnson believed, had no role to play in Reconstruction.

The Failure of Presidential Reconstruction

A little over a month after Lee's surrender at Appomattox, and with Congress out of session until December, Johnson in May 1865 outlined his plan for reuniting the nation. He issued a series of proclamations that began the period of Presidential Reconstruction (1865–1867). Johnson

Johnson's program

offered a pardon (which restored political and property rights, except for slaves) to nearly all white southerners who took an oath of allegiance to the Union. He excluded Confederate leaders and wealthy planters whose prewar property had been valued at more than $20,000. Most of those exempted, however, soon received individual pardons from the president. Johnson also appointed provisional governors and ordered them to call state conventions, elected by whites alone, that would establish loyal governments in the South. Apart from the requirement that they abolish slavery, repudiate secession, and refuse to pay the Confederate debt—all unavoidable consequences of southern defeat—he granted the new governments a free hand in managing local affairs.

Republicans against Johnson

The conduct of the southern governments elected under Johnson's program turned most of the Republican North against the president. By and large, white voters returned prominent Confederates and members of the old elite to power. Reports of violence directed against former slaves and northern visitors in the South further alarmed Republicans.

The Black Codes

But what aroused the most opposition to Johnson's Reconstruction policy were the **Black Codes**, laws passed by the new southern governments that attempted to regulate the lives of the former slaves. These laws granted

Regulating former slaves

blacks certain rights, such as legalized marriage, ownership of property,

Selling a Freedman to Pay His Fine at Monticello, Florida, an engraving from *Frank Leslie's Illustrated Newspaper,* January 19, 1867. Under the Black Codes enacted by southern legislatures immediately after the Civil War, blacks convicted of "vagrancy"—often because they refused to sign contracts to work on plantations—were fined and, if unable to pay, auctioned off to work for the person who paid the fine.

and limited access to the courts. But they denied them the rights to testify against whites, to serve on juries or in state militias, or to vote. And in response to planters' demands that the freedpeople be required to work on the plantations, the Black Codes declared that those who failed to sign yearly labor contracts could be arrested and hired out to white landowners.

Clearly, the death of slavery did not automatically mean the birth of freedom. But the Black Codes so completely violated free labor principles that they called forth a vigorous response from the Republican North. In general, few groups of rebels in history have been treated more leniently than the defeated Confederates. A handful of southern leaders were arrested, but most were quickly released. Only one was executed—Henry Wirz, the commander of Andersonville prison, where thousands of Union prisoners of war had died. Most of the Union army was swiftly demobilized. What motivated the North's turn against Johnson's policies was not a desire to "punish" the white South, but the inability of the South's political leaders to accept the reality of emancipation as evidenced by the Black Codes.

Reaction to Black Codes

The Radical Republicans

When Congress assembled in December 1865, Johnson announced that with loyal governments functioning in all the southern states, the nation had been reunited. In response, Radical Republicans, who had grown increasingly disenchanted with Johnson during the summer and fall, called for the dissolution of these governments and the establishment of new ones with "rebels" excluded from power and black men guaranteed the right to vote.

Thaddeus Stevens, leader of the Radical Republicans in the House of Representatives during Reconstruction.

The Civil Rights Bill of 1866

Radicals shared the conviction that Union victory created a golden opportunity to institutionalize the principle of equal rights for all, regardless of race.

The most prominent Radicals in Congress were Charles Sumner, a senator from Massachusetts, and Thaddeus Stevens, a lawyer and iron manufacturer who represented Pennsylvania in the House of Representatives. Before the Civil War, both had been outspoken foes of slavery and defenders of black rights. Stevens's most cherished aim was to confiscate the land of disloyal planters and divide it among former slaves and northern migrants to the South. But his plan to make "small independent landholders" of the former slaves proved too radical even for many of his Radical colleagues and failed to pass.

The Origins of Civil Rights

With the South unrepresented, Republicans enjoyed an overwhelming majority in Congress. Most Republicans were moderates, not Radicals. Moderates believed that Johnson's plan was flawed, but they desired to work with the president to modify it. They feared that neither northern nor southern whites would accept black suffrage. Moderates and Radicals joined in refusing to seat the southerners recently elected to Congress, but moderates broke with the Radicals by leaving the Johnson governments in place.

Early in 1866, Senator Lyman Trumbull of Illinois proposed two bills that reflected the moderates' belief that Johnson's policy required modification. The first extended the life of the Freedmen's Bureau, which had originally been established for only one year. The second, the **Civil Rights Bill of 1866**, was described by one congressman as "one of the most important bills ever presented to the House for its action." It defined all persons born in the United States as citizens and spelled out rights they were to enjoy without regard to race. Equality before the law was central to the measure—no longer could states enact laws like the Black Codes discriminating between white and black citizens. So were free labor values. According to the law, no state could deprive any citizen of the right to make contracts, bring lawsuits, or enjoy equal protection of one's person and property. These, said Trumbull, were the "fundamental rights belonging to every man as a free man." The bill made no mention of the right to vote for blacks. In constitutional terms, the Civil Rights Bill represented the first attempt to define in law the essence of freedom.

To the surprise of Congress, Johnson vetoed both bills. Both, he said, would centralize power in the national government and deprive the states of the authority to regulate their own affairs. Moreover, he argued, blacks did not deserve the rights of citizenship. Congress failed by a single vote to muster the two-thirds majority necessary to override the veto of the Freedmen's Bureau Bill (although later in 1866, it did extend the bureau's life to 1870). But in April 1866, the Civil Rights Bill became the first major law in American history to be passed over a presidential veto.

The Fourteenth Amendment

Congress now proceeded to adopt its own plan of Reconstruction. In June, it approved and sent to the states for ratification the **Fourteenth Amendment**, which placed in the Constitution the principle of birthright citizenship, except for Native Americans subject to tribal authority, and which empowered the federal government to protect the rights of all Americans. The amendment prohibited the states from abridging the "privileges or immunities" of citizens or denying any person the "equal protection of the laws." This broad language opened the door for future Congresses and the federal courts to breathe meaning into the guarantee of legal equality.

In a compromise between the radical and moderate positions on black suffrage, the amendment did not grant blacks the right to vote. But it did provide that if a state denied the vote to any group of men, that state's representation in Congress would be reduced. (This provision did not apply when states barred women from voting.) The abolition of slavery threatened to increase southern political power, since now all blacks, not merely three-fifths as in the case of slaves, would be counted in determining a state's representation in Congress. The Fourteenth Amendment offered the leaders of the white South a choice—allow black men to vote and keep their state's full representation in the House of Representatives, or limit the vote to whites and sacrifice part of their political power.

By writing into the Constitution the principle that equality before the law regardless of race is a fundamental right of all American citizens, the amendment made the most important change in that document since the adoption of the Bill of Rights.

The Reconstruction Act

The Fourteenth Amendment became the central issue of the political campaign of 1866. Johnson embarked on a speaking tour of the North. Denouncing his critics, the president made wild accusations that the Radicals were plotting to assassinate him. His behavior further undermined public support for his policies, as did riots that broke out in Memphis and New Orleans, in which white policemen and citizens killed dozens of blacks.

In the northern congressional elections that fall, Republicans opposed to Johnson's policies won a sweeping victory. Nonetheless, at the president's urging, every southern state but Tennessee refused to ratify the Fourteenth Amendment. The intransigence of Johnson and the bulk of the white South pushed moderate Republicans toward the Radicals. In March 1867, over

President Andrew Johnson, in an 1868 lithograph by Currier and Ives. Because of Johnson's stubborn opposition to the congressional Reconstruction policy, one disgruntled citizen drew a crown on his head with the words, "I am King."

Significance of the fourteenth amendment

Johnson's speaking tour

A Democratic Party broadside from the election of 1866 in Pennsylvania uses racist imagery to argue that government assistance aids lazy former slaves at the expense of hardworking whites.

Johnson's veto, Congress adopted the **Reconstruction Act**, which temporarily divided the South into five military districts and called for the creation of new state governments, with black men given the right to vote. Thus began the period of Radical Reconstruction, which lasted until 1877.

Radical Reconstruction

Impeachment and the Election of Grant

In March 1867, Congress adopted the **Tenure of Office Act**, barring the president from removing certain officeholders, including cabinet members, without the consent of the Senate. Johnson considered this an unconstitutional restriction on his authority. In February 1868, he dismissed Secretary of War Edwin M. Stanton, an ally of the Radicals. The House of Representatives responded by approving articles of **impeachment**—that is, it presented charges against Johnson to the Senate, which had to decide whether to remove him from office.

First impeachment trial

That spring, for the first time in American history, a president was placed on trial before the Senate for "high crimes and misdemeanors." By this point, virtually all Republicans considered Johnson a failure as president. But some moderates feared that conviction would damage the constitutional separation of powers between Congress and the executive. Johnson's lawyers assured moderate Republicans that, if acquitted, he would stop interfering with Reconstruction policy. The final tally was 35-19 to convict Johnson, one vote short of the two-thirds necessary to remove him. Seven Republicans joined the Democrats in voting to acquit the president.

Reconstruction, an elaborate allegory of national reconciliation, equality, and progress, designed by Horatio Bateman and printed in 1867. The overall message is that Reconstruction, grounded in liberty and equality, will restore good will between the sections and races. The structure at the center symbolizes the federal government; it is being rebuilt as black and white men carry new pillars, representing the states, to support it. The old bases of some of the columns, called "Foundations of Slavery" are being replaced by new ones representing Liberty, Justice, and Education. Under the dome, former rivals shake hands, including Generals Grant and Lee, and Republican editor Horace Greeley and Jefferson Davis. Scenes surrounding it include a schoolyard, men and women voting, and Indians and whites sitting together. At the top are the heads of great figures of American history, as well as other historical characters including Joan of Arc, John Milton, and Jesus Christ. The eagle at the center carries a streamer reading: "All men are born free and equal."

A few days after the vote, Republicans nominated Ulysses S. Grant, the Union's most prominent military hero, as their candidate for president. Grant's Democratic opponent was Horatio Seymour, the former governor of New York. Reconstruction became the central issue of the bitterly fought 1868 campaign. Democrats denounced Reconstruction as unconstitutional and condemned black suffrage as a violation of America's political traditions. They appealed openly to racism. Seymour's running mate, Francis P. Blair Jr., charged Republicans with placing the South under the rule of "a semi-barbarous race" who longed to "subject the white women to their unbridled lust."

The Fifteenth Amendment

Grant won the election of 1868, although by a margin—300,000 of 6 million votes cast—that many Republicans found uncomfortably slim. The result led Congress to adopt the **Fifteenth Amendment**, which prohibited the federal and state governments from denying any citizen the right to vote because of race. Bitterly opposed by the Democratic Party, it was ratified in 1870.

Although the Fifteenth Amendment left the door open to suffrage restrictions not explicitly based on race—literacy tests, property qualifications, and poll taxes—and did not extend the right to vote to women, it marked the culmination of four decades of abolitionist agitation. "Nothing in all history," exclaimed veteran abolitionist William Lloyd Garrison,

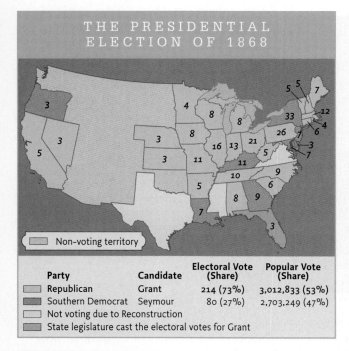

THE PRESIDENTIAL ELECTION OF 1868

Party	Candidate	Electoral Vote (Share)	Popular Vote (Share)
Republican	Grant	214 (73%)	3,012,833 (53%)
Southern Democrat	Seymour	80 (27%)	2,703,249 (47%)
Not voting due to Reconstruction			
State legislature cast the electoral votes for Grant			

Non-voting territory

equaled "this wonderful, quiet, sudden transformation of four millions of human beings from . . . the auction-block to the ballot-box."

The Second Founding

The laws and amendments of Reconstruction reflected the intersection of two products of the Civil War era—a newly empowered national state, and the idea of a national citizenry enjoying equality before the law. What Republican leader Carl Schurz called the "great Constitutional revolution" of Reconstruction transformed the federal system and with it, the language of freedom so central to American political culture.

Race and citizenship

But the laws and amendments of Reconstruction repudiated the pre–Civil War idea that citizenship was an entitlement of whites alone. As one congressman noted, the amendments expanded the liberty of whites as well as blacks, including "the millions of people of foreign birth who will flock to our shores."

The new amendments also transformed the relationship between the federal government and the states. The Bill of Rights had linked civil liberties to the autonomy of the states. Its language—"Congress shall make

National power

no law"—reflected the belief that concentrated national power posed the greatest threat to freedom. The authors of the Reconstruction amendments assumed that rights required national power to enforce them. Rather than a threat to liberty, the federal government, in Charles Sumner's words, had become "the custodian of freedom."

Constitutional significance

The Reconstruction amendments transformed the Constitution from a document primarily concerned with federal-state relations and the rights of property into a vehicle through which members of vulnerable minorities could stake a claim to freedom and seek protection against misconduct by all levels of government. In the twentieth century, many of the Supreme Court's most important decisions expanding the rights of American citizens were based on the Fourteenth Amendment, including the 1954 *Brown* ruling that outlawed school segregation and the decision in 2015 preventing states from discriminating against gay Americans in the right to marry.

Together with far-reaching congressional legislation meant to secure to former slaves access to the courts, ballot box, and public accommodations, and to protect them against violence, the Reconstruction amendments transferred much of the authority to define citizens' rights from the states to the nation. They were crucial in creating the world's first biracial democracy, in which people only a few years removed from slavery exercised significant political power. Introducing into the Constitution for the first time the words "equal protection of the law" and "the right to vote" (along with "male," to the outrage of the era's advocates of women's rights), the amendments both reflected and reinforced a new era of individual rights consciousness among Americans of all races and backgrounds. They forged a new constitutional relationship between individual Americans and the national government and created a new definition of citizenship.

Biracial democracy

Today, the legal doctrine of birthright citizenship sets the United States apart. Most countries, including every one in Europe, limit automatic access to citizenship via ethnicity, culture, or religion. Birthright citizenship remains an eloquent statement about the nature of American society, and a repudiation of a long history of equating citizenship with whiteness.

Birthright citizenship

So profound were these changes that the amendments are frequently seen not simply as an alteration of an existing structure but as a second founding, which created a fundamentally new document with a new definition of both the status of blacks and the rights of all Americans.

The Rights of Women

"The contest with the South that destroyed slavery," wrote the Philadelphia lawyer Sidney George Fisher in his diary, "has caused an immense increase in the popular passion for liberty and equality." But advocates of women's rights encountered the limits of the Reconstruction commitment to equality. Women activists saw Reconstruction as the moment to claim their own emancipation. The rewriting of the Constitution, declared suffrage leader Olympia Brown, offered the opportunity to sever the blessings of freedom from sex as well as race and to "bury the black man and the woman in the citizen."

Women and the limits of equality

Even Radical Republicans insisted that Reconstruction was the "Negro's hour" (the hour, that is, of the black male). The Fourteenth Amendment for the first time introduced the word "male" into the Constitution, in its clause penalizing a state for denying any group of men the right to vote. The Fifteenth Amendment outlawed discrimination in voting based on race but not gender. These measures produced a bitter split both between feminists and Radical Republicans, and within feminist circles. Some leaders, like Elizabeth Cady Stanton and Susan B. Anthony, denounced their former

WHO IS AN AMERICAN?

From Frederick Douglass, "The Composite Nation" (1869)

In a remarkable speech delivered in Boston, Frederick Douglass condemned anti-Asian discrimination and called for giving Chinese immigrants all the rights of other Americans, including the right to vote. Douglass's vision of a country made up of people of all races and national origins enjoying equal rights was too radical for the time, and remains controversial today.

We are a country of all extremes, ends and opposites; the most conspicuous example of composite nationality in the world. Our people defy all the ethnological and logical classifications. In races we range all the way from black to white, with intermediate shades which . . . no man can name a number. . . . Our land is capable of supporting one fifth of all the globe. Here, labor is abundant and here labor is better remunerated that anywhere else. All moral, social and geographical causes conspire to bring to us the peoples of all other over-populated countries.

Europe and Africa are already here, and the Indian was here before either. . . . Heretofore the policy of our government has been governed by race pride, rather than by wisdom. . . . Before the relations of [blacks and Indians] are satisfactorily settled, and in spite of all opposition, a new race is making its appearance within our borders, and claiming attention [the Chinese]. . . . Do you ask, if I favor such immigration. I answer *I would*. Would you have them naturalized, and have them invested with all the rights of American citizenship? *I would*. Would you allow them to hold office? *I would*. . . .

There are such things in the world as human rights. They rest upon no conventional foundation, but are external, universal, and indestructible. Among these, is the right of locomotion; the right of migration; the right which belongs to no particular race, but belongs alike to all. . . . We shall mold them all . . . into Americans; Indian and Celt, Negro and Saxon, Latin and Teuton, Mongolian and Caucasian, Jew and Gentile, all shall here bow to the same law, speak the same language, support the same government, enjoy the same liberty.

QUESTIONS

1. *What is Douglass's answer to the question, "Who is an American?"*

2. *Why does he believe that being able to move freely from one country to another should be considered a universal human right?*

abolitionist allies and moved to sever the women's rights movement from its earlier moorings in the antislavery tradition.

Thus, even as it rejected the racial definition of freedom that had emerged in the first half of the nineteenth century, Reconstruction left the gender boundary largely intact. When women tried to use the rewritten legal code and Constitution to claim equal rights, they found the courts unreceptive. Myra Bradwell invoked the idea of free labor in challenging an Illinois rule limiting the practice of law to men, but the Supreme Court in 1873 rebuffed her claim. Free labor principles, the justices declared, did not apply to women, since "the law of the Creator" had assigned them to "the domestic sphere."

A Delegation of Advocates of Woman Suffrage Addressing the House Judiciary Committee, an engraving from *Frank Leslie's Illustrated Newspaper,* February 4, 1871. The group includes Elizabeth Cady Stanton, seated just to the right of the speaker, and Susan B. Anthony, at the table on the extreme right.

Despite their limitations, the Fourteenth and Fifteenth Amendments and the Reconstruction Act of 1867 marked a radical departure in American history. The Reconstruction Act of 1867 inaugurated America's first real experiment in interracial democracy.

RADICAL RECONSTRUCTION IN THE SOUTH

"The Tocsin of Freedom"

Among the former slaves, the passage of the Reconstruction Act inspired an outburst of political organization. At mass political meetings—community gatherings attended by men, women, and children—African-Americans staked their claim to equal citizenship. Blacks, declared an Alabama meeting, deserved "exactly the same rights, privileges and immunities as are enjoyed by white men. We ask for nothing more and will be content with nothing less."

Political action by African-Americans

Determined to exercise their new rights as citizens, thousands joined the Union League, an organization closely linked to the Republican Party, and the vast majority of eligible African-Americans registered to vote. James K. Green, a former slave in Hale County, Alabama, and a League organizer, went on to serve eight years in the Alabama legislature. In the 1880s, Green looked back on his political career. Before the war, he declared, "I was entirely ignorant; I knew nothing more than to obey my master; and there were thousands of us in the same attitude. . . . But the tocsin

The Union League

Electioneering at the South, an engraving from *Harper's Weekly*, July 25, 1868, depicts a speaker at a political meeting in the rural South. Women as well as men took part in these grassroots gatherings.

From the Plantation to the Senate, an 1883 lithograph celebrating African-American progress during Reconstruction. Among the black leaders pictured at the top are Reconstruction congressmen Benjamin S. Turner, Josiah T. Walls, and Joseph H. Rainey; Hiram Revels of Mississippi, the first African-American senator; religious leader Richard Allen; and abolitionists Frederick Douglass and William Wells Brown. At the center emancipated slaves work in the cotton fields, and below children attend school and a black family stands outside its home.

[warning bell] of freedom sounded and knocked at the door and we walked out like free men and shouldered the responsibilities."

By 1870, all the former Confederate states had been readmitted to the Union, and in a region where the Republican Party had not existed before the war, nearly all were under Republican control. Their new state constitutions, drafted in 1868 and 1869 by the first public bodies in American history with substantial black representation, marked a considerable improvement over those they replaced. The constitutions established the region's first state-funded systems of free public education, and they created new penitentiaries, orphan asylums, and homes for the insane. They guaranteed equality of civil and political rights and abolished practices of the antebellum era such as whipping as a punishment for crime, property qualifications for officeholding, and imprisonment for debt. A few states initially barred former Confederates from voting, but this policy was quickly abandoned by the new state governments.

The Black Officeholder

Throughout Reconstruction, black voters provided the bulk of the Republican Party's support. But African-Americans did not control Reconstruction politics, as their opponents frequently charged. The highest offices remained almost entirely in white hands, and only in South Carolina, where blacks made up 60 percent of the population, did they form a majority of the legislature. Nonetheless, the fact that some 2,000 African-Americans held public office during Reconstruction marked a fundamental shift of power in the South and a radical departure in American government.

African-Americans were represented at every level of government. Fourteen were elected to the national House of Representatives. Two blacks served in the U.S. Senate during Reconstruction, both representing Mississippi. Hiram Revels, who had been born free in North Carolina, in 1870 became the first black senator in American history. The second, Blanche K. Bruce, a former slave, was elected in 1875. At state and local levels, the presence of black officeholders and their white allies made a real difference in southern life, ensuring that blacks accused of crimes would be tried before juries of their peers and enforcing fairness in such aspects of local government as road repair, tax assessment, and poor relief.

In South Carolina and Louisiana, homes of the South's wealthiest and best-educated free black communities, most prominent Reconstruction officeholders had never experienced slavery. In addition, a number of black Reconstruction officials, like Pennsylvania-born Jonathan J. Wright, who served on the South Carolina Supreme Court, had come from the North after the Civil War. The majority, however, were former slaves who had established their leadership in the black community by serving in the Union army; working as ministers, teachers, or skilled craftsmen; or engaging in Union League organizing.

The First Vote, an engraving from *Harper's Weekly*, November 16, 1867, depicts the first biracial elections in southern history. The voters represent key sources of the black political leadership that emerged during Reconstruction—the artisan carrying his tools, the well-dressed city person (probably free before the war), and the soldier.

Carpetbaggers and Scalawags

The new southern governments also brought to power new groups of whites. Many Reconstruction officials were northerners who for one reason or another made their homes in the South after the war. Their opponents dubbed them **carpetbaggers**, implying that they had packed all their belongings in a suitcase and left their homes in order to reap the spoils of office in the South. Some carpetbaggers were undoubtedly corrupt adventurers. The large majority, however, were former Union soldiers who decided to remain in the South when the war ended, before there was any prospect of going into politics.

White northerners in the South

Most white Republicans had been born in the South. Former Confederates reserved their greatest scorn for these **scalawags**, whom they considered traitors to their race and region. Some southern-born Republicans were men of stature and wealth, like James L. Alcorn, the owner of one of Mississippi's largest plantations and the state's first Republican governor. Most scalawags, however, were non-slaveholding white farmers from the southern upcountry. Many had been wartime Unionists, and they now cooperated with the Republicans in order to prevent "rebels" from returning to power.

Southern Republicans in Power

In view of the daunting challenges they faced, the remarkable thing is not that Reconstruction governments in some respects failed, but how much they did accomplish. Perhaps their greatest achievement lay in establishing the South's first state-supported public schools. The new educational systems served both black and white children, although generally in schools segregated by race. Only in New Orleans were the public schools integrated during Reconstruction, and only in South Carolina did the state university admit black students (elsewhere, separate colleges were established). The new governments also pioneered civil rights legislation. Their laws made it illegal for railroads, hotels, and other institutions to discriminate on the basis of race. Enforcement varied considerably from locality to locality, but Reconstruction established for the first time at the state level a standard of equal citizenship and a recognition of blacks' right to a share of public services.

Republican governments also took steps to strengthen the position of rural laborers and promote the South's economic recovery. They passed laws to ensure that agricultural laborers and sharecroppers had the first claim on harvested crops, rather than merchants to whom the landowner owed money. South Carolina created a state Land Commission, which by 1876 had settled 14,000 black families and a few poor whites on their own farms.

A portrait of Hiram Revels, the first black U.S. senator, by Theodore Kaufmann, a German-born artist who immigrated to the United States in 1855. Lithograph copies sold widely in the North during Reconstruction. Frederick Douglass, commenting on the dignified image, noted that African-Americans "so often see ourselves described and painted as monkeys, that we think it a great piece of fortune to find an exception to this general rule."

The Quest for Prosperity

Economic development during Reconstruction

Rather than on land distribution, however, the Reconstruction governments pinned their hopes for southern economic growth and opportunity for African-Americans and poor whites alike on regional economic development. Railroad construction, they believed, was the key to transforming the South into a society of booming factories, bustling towns, and diversified agriculture. Every state during Reconstruction helped to finance railroad construction, and through tax reductions and other incentives tried to attract northern manufacturers to invest in the region. The program had mixed results. Economic development in general remained weak.

To their supporters, the governments of Radical Reconstruction presented a complex pattern of disappointment and accomplishment. A revitalized southern economy failed to materialize, and most African-Americans remained locked in poverty. On the other hand, biracial democratic government, a thing unknown in American history, for the first time functioned effectively in many parts of the South. The conservative elite that had dominated southern government from colonial times to 1867

A group of black students and their teacher in a picture taken by an amateur photographer, probably a Union army veteran, while touring Civil War battlefields.

found itself excluded from political power, while poor whites, newcomers from the North, and former slaves cast ballots, sat on juries, and enacted and administered laws. It is a measure of how far change had progressed that the reaction against Reconstruction proved so extreme.

THE OVERTHROW OF RECONSTRUCTION

Reconstruction's Opponents

The South's traditional leaders—planters, merchants, and Democratic politicians—bitterly opposed the new governments. "Intelligence, virtue, and patriotism" in public life, declared a protest by prominent southern Democrats, had given way to "ignorance, stupidity, and vice." Corruption did exist during Reconstruction, but it was confined to no race, region, or party. The rapid growth of state budgets and the benefits to be gained from public aid led in some states to a scramble for influence that produced bribery, insider dealing, and a get-rich-quick atmosphere. Southern frauds, however, were dwarfed by those practiced in these years by the Whiskey Ring, which involved high officials of the Grant administration, and by New York's Tweed Ring, controlled by the Democrats, whose thefts ran into the tens of millions of dollars. (These are discussed in the next chapter.) The rising taxes needed to pay for schools and other new public facilities and to assist railroad development were another cause of opposition to Reconstruction. Many poor whites who had initially supported the Republican Party turned against it when it became clear that their economic situation was not improving.

Sources of opposition

Practical Illustration of the Virginia Constitution.

WHITE MAN THE BOTTOM RAIL.

MIXED SCHOOL SYSTEM.

NEGRO COURT AND JURY.

A cartoon from around 1870 illustrates a key theme of the racist opposition to Reconstruction—that blacks had forced themselves upon whites and gained domination over them. A black schoolteacher inflicts punishment on a white student in an integrated classroom, and a racially mixed jury judges a white defendant.

A terrorist organization

The most basic reason for opposition to Reconstruction, however, was that most white southerners could not accept the idea of former slaves voting, holding office, and enjoying equality before the law. Opponents launched a campaign of violence in an effort to end Republican rule. Their actions posed a fundamental challenge both for Reconstruction governments in the South and for policymakers in Washington, D.C.

"A Reign of Terror"

The Civil War ended in 1865, but violence remained widespread in large parts of the postwar South. In the early years of Reconstruction, violence was mostly local and unorganized. Blacks were assaulted and murdered for refusing to give way to whites on city sidewalks, using "insolent" language, challenging end-of-year contract settlements, and attempting to buy land. The violence that greeted the advent of Republican governments after 1867, however, was far more pervasive and more directly motivated by politics. In wide areas of the South, secret societies sprang up with the aim of preventing blacks from voting and destroying the organization of the Republican Party by assassinating local leaders and public officials.

The most notorious such organization was the **Ku Klux Klan**, which in effect served as a military arm of the Democratic Party in the South. The Klan was a terrorist organization. It committed some of the most brutal criminal acts in American history. In many counties throughout the South, it launched what one victim called a "reign of terror" against Republican leaders, black and white.

The Klan's victims included white Republicans, among them wartime Unionists and local officeholders, teachers, and party organizers. But African-Americans—local political leaders, those who managed to acquire land, and others who in one way or another defied the norms of white supremacy—bore the brunt of the violence. On occasion, violence escalated from assaults on individuals to mass terrorism and even local insurrections. The bloodiest act of violence during Reconstruction took place in Colfax, Louisiana, in 1873, where armed whites assaulted the town with a small cannon. Scores of former slaves were murdered, including fifty members of a black militia unit after they had surrendered.

In 1870 and 1871, Congress adopted three **Enforcement Acts**, outlawing terrorist societies and allowing the president to use the army against them. These laws continued the expansion of national authority during Reconstruction. In 1871, President Grant dispatched federal marshals, backed up by troops in some areas, to arrest hundreds of accused Klansmen. Many Klan leaders fled the South. After a series of well-publicized trials, the Klan went out of existence. In 1872, for the first time since before the Civil War, peace reigned in most of the former Confederacy.

A Prospective Scene in the City of Oaks, a cartoon in the September 1, 1868, issue of the *Independent Monitor*, a Democratic newspaper published in Tuscaloosa, Alabama. The cartoon sent a warning to the Reverend A. S. Lakin, who had moved from Ohio to become president of the University of Alabama, and Dr. N. B. Cloud, a southern-born Republican serving as Alabama's superintendent of public education. The Ku Klux Klan forced both men from their positions. While most of the Klan's victims were black, the two men pictured here are white.

The Liberal Republicans

Despite the Grant administration's effective response to Klan terrorism, the North's commitment to Reconstruction waned during the 1870s. Northerners increasingly felt that the South should be able to solve its own problems without constant interference from Washington. The federal government had freed the slaves, made them citizens, and given them the right to vote. Now, blacks should rely on their own resources, not demand further assistance.

In 1872, an influential group of Republicans, alienated by corruption within the Grant administration and believing that the growth of federal power during and after the war needed to be curtailed, formed their own party. They included Republican founders like Lyman Trumbull and prominent editors and journalists such as E. L. Godkin of *The Nation*. Calling themselves Liberal Republicans, they nominated Horace Greeley, editor of the *New York Tribune*, for president.

Democratic criticisms of Reconstruction found a receptive audience among the Liberals. As in the North, they became convinced, the "best men" of the South had been excluded from power while "ignorant" voters controlled politics, producing corruption and misgovernment. Greeley had spent most of his career, first as a Whig and then as a Republican, denouncing the Democratic Party. But with the Republican split presenting an opportunity to repair their political fortunes, Democratic leaders endorsed Greeley as their candidate. But many rank-and-file Democrats, unable to bring themselves to vote for Greeley, stayed at home on election day. As a result, Greeley suffered a devastating defeat by Grant, whose margin of more than 700,000 popular votes was the largest in a

Horace Greeley

Changes in graphic artist Thomas Nast's depiction of blacks in *Harper's Weekly* mirrored the evolution of Republican sentiment in the North. *And Not This Man?*, August 5, 1865, shows the black soldier as an upstanding citizen deserving of the vote. *Colored Rule in a Reconstructed (?) State*, March 14, 1874, suggests that Reconstruction legislatures had become travesties of democratic government.

A bankbook issued by the Freedman's Savings and Trust Company, a private corporation established by Congress to promote thrift among the former slaves. Black individuals, families, church groups, and civic organizations deposited nearly $2 million in branches scattered across the South. The bank failed in 1874 because of mismanagement, and thousands of depositors lost their savings.

nineteenth-century presidential contest. But Greeley's campaign placed on the northern agenda the one issue on which the Liberal reformers and the Democrats could agree—a new policy toward the South.

The North's Retreat

The Liberal attack on Reconstruction, which continued after 1872, contributed to a resurgence of racism in the North. Journalist James S. Pike, a leading Greeley supporter, in 1874 published *The Prostrate State*, an influential account of a visit to South Carolina. The book depicted a state engulfed by political corruption and under the control of "a mass of black barbarism." Resurgent racism offered blacks' alleged incapacity as a convenient explanation for the "failure" of Reconstruction. The solution, for many, was to restore leading whites to political power.

Other factors also weakened northern support for Reconstruction. In 1873, the country plunged into a severe economic depression. Distracted by economic problems, Republicans were in no mood to devote further attention to the South. The depression dealt the South a severe blow and further weakened the prospect that Republicans could revitalize the region's economy. Democrats made substantial gains throughout the nation in the elections of 1874. For the first time since the Civil War, their party took control of the House of Representatives. Before the new Congress met, the old one enacted a final piece of Reconstruction legislation, the **Civil Rights Act of 1875**. This outlawed

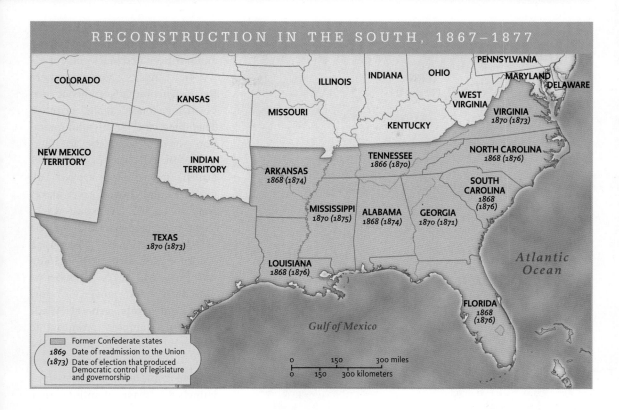

RECONSTRUCTION IN THE SOUTH, 1867–1877

Former Confederate states

1869 Date of readmission to the Union

(1873) Date of election that produced Democratic control of legislature and governorship

racial discrimination in places of public accommodation like hotels and theaters. But it was clear that the northern public was retreating from Reconstruction.

The Supreme Court whittled away at the guarantees of black rights Congress had adopted. In the *Slaughterhouse Cases* (1873), the justices ruled that the Fourteenth Amendment had not altered traditional federalism. Most of the rights of citizens, it declared, remained under state control. Three years later, in *United States v. Cruikshank*, the Court gutted the Enforcement Acts by throwing out the convictions of some of those responsible for the Colfax Massacre of 1873.

The Supreme Court and Reconstruction

The Triumph of the Redeemers

By the mid-1870s, Reconstruction was clearly on the defensive. Democrats had already regained control of states with substantial white voting majorities such as Tennessee, North Carolina, and Texas. The victorious Democrats called themselves **Redeemers**, since they claimed to have "redeemed" the white South from corruption, misgovernment, and northern and black control.

In those states where Reconstruction governments survived, violence again erupted. This time, the Grant administration showed no desire to intervene. In Mississippi, in 1875, armed Democrats destroyed ballot boxes and drove former slaves from the polls. The result was a Democratic landslide and the end of Reconstruction in Mississippi. Similar events took place in South Carolina in 1876. Democrats nominated for governor former Confederate general Wade Hampton. Hampton promised to respect the rights of all citizens of the state, but his supporters, inspired by Democratic tactics in Mississippi, launched a wave of intimidation. Democrats intended to carry the election, one planter told a black official, "if we have to wade in blood knee-deep."

The Disputed Election and Bargain of 1877

"The Ignorant Vote," a famous cartoon by Thomas Nast in *Harper's Weekly*, December 9, 1876, equates blacks and Irish immigrants as unworthy of participation in democracy. It reflects a growing reaction against universal manhood suffrage in both North and South.

Events in South Carolina directly affected the outcome of the presidential campaign of 1876. To succeed Grant, the Republicans nominated Governor Rutherford B. Hayes of Ohio. The Democrats chose as his opponent New York's governor, Samuel J. Tilden. By this time, only South Carolina, Florida, and Louisiana remained under Republican control in the South. The election turned out to be so close that whoever captured these states—which both parties claimed to have carried—would become the next president.

Unable to resolve the impasse on its own, Congress in January 1877 appointed a fifteen-member Electoral Commission, composed of senators, representatives, and Supreme Court justices. Republicans enjoyed an 8-7 majority on the commission, and to no one's surprise, the members decided by that margin that Hayes had carried the disputed southern states and had been elected president.

Even as the commission deliberated, however, behind-the-scenes negotiations took place between leaders of the two parties. Hayes's representatives agreed to recognize Democratic control of the entire South and to avoid further intervention in local affairs. For their part, Democrats promised not to dispute Hayes's right to office and to respect the civil and political rights of blacks.

Thus was concluded the **Bargain of 1877**. Hayes became president and quickly ordered federal troops to stop guarding the state houses in Louisiana and South Carolina, allowing Democratic claimants to become governors. (Contrary to legend, Hayes did not remove the last soldiers from the South—he simply ordered them to return to their barracks.) The triumphant southern Democrats failed to live up to their pledge to recognize blacks as equal citizens.

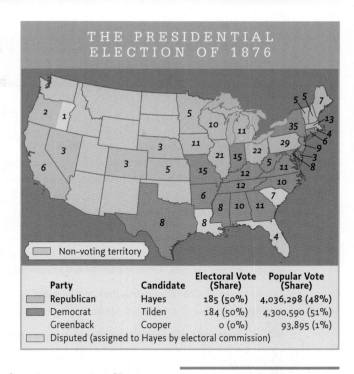

THE PRESIDENTIAL ELECTION OF 1876

Non-voting territory

Party	Candidate	Electoral Vote (Share)	Popular Vote (Share)
Republican	Hayes	185 (50%)	4,036,298 (48%)
Democrat	Tilden	184 (50%)	4,300,590 (51%)
Greenback	Cooper	0 (0%)	93,895 (1%)
Disputed (assigned to Hayes by electoral commission)			

The End of Reconstruction

As a historical process—the nation's adjustment to the destruction of slavery—Reconstruction continued well after 1877. Blacks continued to vote and, in some states, hold office into the 1890s. But as a distinct era of national history—when Republicans controlled much of the South, blacks exercised significant political power, and the federal government accepted the responsibility for protecting the fundamental rights of all American citizens—Reconstruction had come to an end. Despite its limitations, Reconstruction was a remarkable chapter in the story of American freedom. Nearly a century would pass before the nation again tried to bring equal rights to the descendants of slaves. The civil rights era of the 1950s and 1960s would sometimes be called the Second Reconstruction.

Is This a Republican Form of Government?, a cartoon by Thomas Nast in *Harper's Weekly*, September 2, 1876, illustrates his conviction that the overthrow of Reconstruction meant that the United States was not prepared to live up to its democratic ideals or protect the rights of black citizens threatened by violence.

CHAPTER REVIEW AND ONLINE RESOURCES

REVIEW QUESTIONS

1. In 1865, the former Confederate general Robert Richardson remarked that "the emancipated slaves own nothing, because nothing but freedom has been given to them." Explain whether this would be an accurate assessment of Reconstruction twelve years later.

2. The women's movement split into two separate national organizations in part because the Fifteenth Amendment did not give women the vote. Explain why the two groups split.

3. In what sense did the Reconstruction amendments mark a second founding of the United States?

4. What is birthright citizenship, and why is it important?

5. How did black families, churches, schools, and other institutions contribute to the development of African-American culture and political activism in this period?

6. Why did ownership of land and control of labor become major points of contention between former slaves and whites in the South?

7. By what methods did southern whites seek to limit African-American civil rights and liberties? How did the federal government respond?

8. How did the failure of land reform and continued poverty lead to new forms of servitude for both blacks and whites?

9. What caused the confrontation between President Johnson and Congress over Reconstruction policies?

10. What national issues and attitudes combined to bring an end to Reconstruction by 1877?

11. By 1877, how did the condition of former slaves in the United States compare with that of freedpeople around the globe?

KEY TERMS

the Freedmen's Bureau (p. 441)
sharecropping (p. 443)
crop lien (p. 443)
Black Codes (p. 448)
Civil Rights Bill of 1866 (p. 450)
Fourteenth Amendment (p. 451)
Reconstruction Act (p. 452)
Tenure of Office Act (p. 452)
impeachment (p. 452)
Fifteenth Amendment (p. 453)
carpetbaggers (p. 459)
scalawags (p. 459)
Ku Klux Klan (p. 462)
Enforcement Acts (p. 463)
Civil Rights Act of 1875 (p. 464)
Redeemers (p. 465)
Bargain of 1877 (p. 466)

Go to 🐇 INQUIZITIVE

To see what you know—and learn what you've missed—with personalized feedback along the way.

Visit the *Give Me Liberty!* **Student Site** for primary source documents and images, interactive maps, author videos featuring Eric Foner, and more.

★

APPENDIX

★

THE DECLARATION OF INDEPENDENCE (1776)

When in the course of human events, it becomes necessary for one people to dissolve the political bands which have connected them with another, and to assume among the Powers of the earth, the separate and equal station to which the Laws of Nature and of Nature's God entitle them, a decent respect to the opinions of mankind requires that they should declare the causes which impel them to the separation.

We hold these truths to be self-evident, that all men are created equal, that they are endowed by their Creator with certain unalienable rights, that among these are Life, Liberty, and the pursuit of Happiness. That to secure these rights, Governments are instituted among Men, deriving their just powers from the consent of the governed. That whenever any Form of Government becomes destructive of these ends, it is the Right of the People to alter or to abolish it, and to institute new Government, laying its foundation on such principles and organizing its powers in such form, as to them shall seem most likely to effect their Safety and Happiness. Prudence, indeed, will dictate that Governments long established should not be changed for light and transient causes; and accordingly all experience hath shown, that mankind are more disposed to suffer, while evils are sufferable, than to right themselves by abolishing the forms to which they are accustomed. But when a long train of abuses and usurpations, pursuing invariably the same Object evinces a design to reduce them under absolute Despotism, it is their right, it is their duty, to throw off such Government, and to provide new Guards for their future security.—Such has been the patient sufferance of these Colonies; and such is now the necessity which constrains them to alter their former Systems of Government. The history of the present King of Great Britain is a history of repeated injuries and usurpations, all having in direct object the establishment of an absolute Tyranny over these States. To prove this, let Facts be submitted to a candid world.

He has refused his Assent to Laws, the most wholesome and necessary for the public good.

He has forbidden his Governors to pass Laws of immediate and pressing importance, unless suspended in their operation till his Assent should be obtained; and when so suspended, he has utterly neglected to attend to them.

He has refused to pass other Laws for the accommodation of large districts of people, unless those people would relinquish the right of Representation in the Legislature, a right inestimable to them and formidable to tyrants only.

He has called together legislative bodies at places unusual, uncomfortable, and distant from the depository of their public Records, for the sole purpose of fatiguing them into compliance with his measures.

He has dissolved Representative Houses repeatedly, for opposing with manly firmness his invasions on the rights of the people.

He has refused for a long time, after such dissolutions, to cause others to be elected; whereby the Legislative powers, incapable of Annihilation, have returned to the People at large for their exercise; the State remaining in the mean time exposed to all dangers of invasion from without, and convulsions within.

He has endeavoured to prevent the population of these States; for that purpose obstructing the Laws of Naturalization of Foreigners; refusing to pass others to encourage their migrations hither, and raising the conditions of new Appropriations of Lands.

He has obstructed the Administration of Justice, by refusing his Assent to Laws for establishing Judiciary powers.

He has made Judges dependent on his Will alone, for the tenure of their offices, and the amount and payment of their salaries.

He has erected a multitude of New Offices, and sent hither swarms of Officers to harass our People, and eat out their substance.

He has kept among us, in times of peace, Standing Armies without the Consent of our legislatures.

He has affected to render the Military independent of and superior to the Civil Power.

He has combined with others to subject us to a jurisdiction foreign to our constitution, and unacknowledged by our laws; giving his Assent to their Acts of pretended Legislation:

For quartering large bodies of armed troops among us:

For protecting them, by a mock Trial, from Punishment for any Murders which they should commit on the Inhabitants of these States:

For cutting off our Trade with all parts of the world:

For imposing taxes on us without our Consent:

For depriving us of many cases, of the benefits of Trial by jury:

For transporting us beyond Seas to be tried for pretended offences:

For abolishing the free System of English Laws in a neighbouring Province, establishing therein an Arbitrary government, and enlarging its Boundaries so as to render it at once an example and fit instrument for introducing the same absolute rule into these Colonies:

For taking away our Charters, abolishing our most valuable Laws, and altering fundamentally the Forms of our Governments:

For suspending our own Legislatures, and declaring themselves invested with Power to legislate for us in all cases whatsoever.

He has abdicated Government here, by declaring us out of his Protection and waging War against us.

He has plundered our seas, ravaged our Coasts, burnt our towns, and destroyed the lives of our people.

He is at this time transporting large armies of foreign mercenaries to compleat the works of death, desolation, and tyranny, already begun with circumstances of Cruelty & perfidy scarcely paralleled in the most barbarous ages, and totally unworthy the Head of a civilized nation.

He has constrained our fellow Citizens taken Captive on the high Seas to bear Arms against their Country, to become the executioners of their friends and Brethren, or to fall themselves by their Hands.

He has excited domestic insurrections amongst us, and has endeavoured to bring on the inhabitants of our frontiers, the merciless Indian Savages, whose known rule of warfare, is an undistinguished destruction of all ages, sexes, and conditions.

In every stage of these Oppressions We have Petitioned for Redress in the most humble terms: Our repeated Petitions have been answered only by repeated injury. A Prince, whose character is thus marked by every act which may define a Tyrant, is unfit to be the ruler of a free people.

Nor have We been wanting in attention to our British brethren. We have warned them from time to time of attempts by their legislature to extend an unwarrantable jurisdiction over us. We have reminded them of the circumstances of our emigration and settlement here. We have appealed to their native justice and magnanimity, and we have conjured them by the ties of our common kindred to disavow these usurpations, which, would inevitably interrupt our connections and correspondence. They too must have been deaf to the voice of justice and of consanguinity. We must, therefore, acquiesce in the necessity, which denounces our Separation, and hold them, as we hold the rest of mankind, Enemies in War, in Peace Friends.

WE, THEREFORE, the Representatives of the UNITED STATES OF AMERICA, in General Congress, Assembled, appealing to the Supreme Judge of the world for the rectitude of our intentions, do, in the Name, and by Authority of the good People of these Colonies, solemnly publish and declare, That these United Colonies are, and of Right ought to be FREE AND INDEPENDENT STATES; that they are Absolved from all Allegiance to the British Crown, and that all political connection between them and the State of Great Britain, is and ought to be totally dissolved; and that as Free and Independent States, they have full Power to levy War, conclude Peace, contract Alliances, establish Commerce, and to do all other Acts and Things which Independent States may of right do. And for the support of this Declaration, with a firm reliance on the Protection of Divine Providence, we mutually pledge to each other our Lives, our Fortunes, and our sacred Honor.

The foregoing Declaration was, by order of Congress, engrossed, and signed by the following members:

John Hancock

NEW HAMPSHIRE
Josiah Bartlett
William Whipple
Matthew Thornton

MASSACHUSETTS BAY
Samuel Adams
John Adams
Robert Treat Paine
Elbridge Gerry

RHODE ISLAND
Stephen Hopkins
William Ellery

CONNECTICUT
Roger Sherman
Samuel Huntington
William Williams
Oliver Wolcott

NEW YORK
William Floyd
Philip Livingston
Francis Lewis
Lewis Morris

NEW JERSEY
Richard Stockton
John Witherspoon
Francis Hopkinson
John Hart
Abraham Clark

PENNSYLVANIA
Robert Morris
Benjamin Rush
Benjamin Franklin
John Morton
George Clymer
James Smith
George Taylor
James Wilson
George Ross

DELAWARE
Caesar Rodney
George Read
Thomas M'Kean

MARYLAND
Samuel Chase
William Paca
Thomas Stone
Charles Carroll, of Carrollton

VIRGINIA
George Wythe
Richard Henry Lee
Thomas Jefferson
Benjamin Harrison
Thomas Nelson, Jr.
Francis Lightfoot Lee
Carter Braxton

NORTH CAROLINA
William Hooper
Joseph Hewes
John Penn

SOUTH CAROLINA
Edward Rutledge
Thomas Heyward, Jr.
Thomas Lynch, Jr.
Arthur Middleton

GEORGIA
Button Gwinnett
Lyman Hall
George Walton

Resolved, That copies of the Declaration be sent to the several assemblies, conventions, and committees, or councils of safety, and to the several commanding officers of the continental troops; that it be proclaimed in each of the United States, at the head of the army.

THE CONSTITUTION OF THE UNITED STATES (1787)

We the People of the United States, in order to form a more perfect Union, establish Justice, insure domestic Tranquility, provide for the common defence, promote the general Welfare, and secure the Blessings of Liberty to ourselves and our Posterity, do ordain and establish this Constitution for the United States of America.

ARTICLE. I.

Section. 1. All legislative Powers herein granted shall be vested in a Congress of the United States, which shall consist of a Senate and House of Representatives.

Section. 2. The House of Representatives shall be composed of Members chosen every second Year by the People of the several States, and the Electors in each State shall have the Qualifications requisite for Electors of the most numerous Branch of the State Legislature.

No Person shall be a Representative who shall not have attained to the Age of twenty five Years, and been seven Years a Citizen of the United States, and who shall not, when elected, be an Inhabitant of that State in which he shall be chosen.

Representatives and direct Taxes shall be apportioned among the several States which may be included within this Union, according to their respective Numbers, which shall be determined by adding to the whole Number of free Persons, including those bound to Service for a Term of Years, and excluding Indians not taxed, three fifths of all other Persons. The actual Enumeration shall be made within three Years after the first Meeting of the Congress of the United States, and within every subsequent Term of ten Years, in such Manner as they shall by Law direct. The Number of Representatives shall not exceed one for every thirty Thousand, but each State shall have at Least one Representative; and until such enumeration

shall be made, the State of New Hampshire shall be entitled to chuse three, Massachusetts eight, Rhode-Island and Providence Plantations one, Connecticut five, New York six, New Jersey four, Pennsylvania eight, Delaware one, Maryland six, Virginia ten, North Carolina five, South Carolina five, and Georgia three.

When vacancies happen in the Representation from any state, the Executive Authority thereof shall issue Writs of Election to fill such Vacancies.

The House of Representatives shall chuse their Speaker and other Officers; and shall have the sole Power of Impeachment.

Section. 3. The Senate of the United States shall be composed of two Senators from each State, chosen by the legislature thereof, for six Years; and each Senator shall have one Vote.

Immediately after they shall be assembled in Consequence of the first Election, they shall be divided as equally as may be into three Classes. The Seats of the Senators of the first Class shall be vacated at the Expiration of the second Year, of the second Class at the Expiration of the fourth Year, and of the third Class at the Expiration of the sixth Year, so that one third may be chosen every second Year; and if Vacancies happen by Resignation, or otherwise, during the Recess of the Legislature of any State, the Executive thereof may make temporary Appointments until the next Meeting of the Legislature, which shall then fill such Vacancies.

No Person shall be a Senator who shall not have attained to the Age of thirty Years, and been nine Years a Citizen of the United States, and who shall not, when elected, be an Inhabitant of that State for which he shall be chosen.

The Vice President of the United States shall be President of the Senate, but shall have no Vote, unless they be equally divided.

The Senate shall chuse their other Officers, and also a President pro tempore, in the Absence of the Vice President, or when he shall exercise the Office of President of the United States.

The Senate shall have the sole Power to try all Impeachments. When sitting for that Purpose, they shall be on Oath or Affirmation. When the President of the United States is tried, the Chief Justice shall preside: And no Person shall be convicted without the Concurrence of two thirds of the Members present.

Judgment in Cases of Impeachment shall not extend further than to removal from Office, and disqualification to hold and enjoy any Office of honor, Trust or Profit under the United States: but the Party convicted shall nevertheless be liable and subject to Indictment, Trial, Judgment and Punishment, according to Law.

Section. 4. The Times, Places and Manner of holding Elections for Senators and Representatives, shall be prescribed in each State by the Legislature thereof; but the Congress may at any time by Law make or alter such Regulations, except as to the Places of chusing Senators.

The Congress shall assemble at least once in every Year, and such Meeting shall be on the first Monday in December, unless they shall by Law appoint a different Day.

Section. 5. Each House shall be the Judge of the Elections, Returns and Qualifications of its own Members, and a Majority of each shall constitute a Quorum to do Business; but a smaller Number may adjourn from day to day, and may be authorized to compel the Attendance of absent Members, in such Manner, and under such Penalties as each House may provide.

Each House may determine the Rules of its Proceedings, punish its Members for disorderly Behaviour, and, with the Concurrence of two thirds, expel a Member.

Each House shall keep a Journal of its Proceedings, and from time to time publish the same, excepting such Parts as may in their Judgment require Secrecy; and the Yeas and Nays of the Members of either House on any question shall, at the Desire of one fifth of those Present, be entered on the Journal.

Neither House, during the Session of Congress, shall, without the Consent of the other, adjourn for more than three days, not to any other Place than that in which the two Houses shall be sitting.

Section. 6. The Senators and Representatives shall receive a Compensation for their Services, to be ascertained by Law, and paid out of the Treasury of the United States. They shall in all Cases, except Treason, Felony and Breach of the Peace, be privileged from Arrest during their Attendance at the Session of their respective Houses, and in going to and returning from the same; and for any Speech or Debate in either House, they shall not be questioned in any other Place.

No Senator or Representative shall, during the Time for which he was elected, be appointed to any civil Office under the Authority of the United States, which shall have been created, or the Emoluments whereof shall have been encreased during such time; and no Person holding any Office under the United States, shall be a Member of either House during his Continuance in Office.

Section. 7. All Bills for raising Revenue shall originate in the House of Representatives; but the Senate may propose or concur with Amendments as on other Bills.

Every Bill which shall have passed the House of Representatives and the Senate shall, before it become a Law, be presented to the President of the United States; If he approve he shall sign it, but if not he shall return it, with his Objections to that House in which it shall have originated, who shall enter the Objections at large on their Journal, and proceed to reconsider it. If after such Reconsideration two thirds of that House shall agree to pass the Bill, it shall be sent, together with the Objections, to the other House, by which it shall likewise be reconsidered, and if approved by two thirds of that House, it shall become a Law. But in all such Cases the Votes of both Houses shall be determined by Yeas and Nays, and the Names of the Persons voting for and against the Bill shall be entered on the Journal of each House respectively. If any Bill shall not be returned by the President within ten Days (Sundays excepted) after it shall have been presented to him, the Same shall be a Law, in like Manner as if he had signed it, unless the

Congress by their Adjournment prevent its Return, in which Case it shall not be a Law.

Every Order, Resolution, or Vote to which the Concurrence of the Senate and House of Representatives may be necessary (except on a question of Adjournment) shall be presented to the President of the United States; and before the Same shall take Effect, shall be approved by him, or being disapproved by him, shall be repassed by two thirds of the Senate and House of Representatives, according to the Rules and Limitations prescribed in the Case of a Bill.

Section. 8. The Congress shall have Power To lay and collect Taxes, Duties, Imposts and Excises, to pay the Debts and provide for the common Defence and general Welfare of the United States; but all Duties, Imposts and Excises shall be uniform throughout the United States;

To borrow Money on the credit of the United States;

To regulate Commerce with foreign Nations, and among the several States, and with the Indian Tribes;

To establish an uniform Rule of Naturalization, and uniform Laws on the subject of Bankruptcies throughout the United States;

To coin Money, regulate the Value thereof, and of foreign Coin, and fix the Standard of Weights and Measures;

To provide for the Punishment of counterfeiting the Securities and current Coin of the United States;

To establish Post Offices and Post Roads;

To promote the Progress of Science and useful Arts, by securing for limited Times to Authors and Inventors the exclusive Right to their respective Writings and Discoveries;

To constitute Tribunals inferior to the supreme Court;

To define and punish Piracies and Felonies committed on the high Seas, and Offences against the Law of Nations;

To declare War, grant Letters of Marque and Reprisal, and make Rules concerning Captures on Land and Water;

To raise and support Armies, but no Appropriation of Money to that Use shall be for a longer Term than two Years;

To provide and maintain a Navy;

To make Rules for the Government and Regulation of the land and naval Forces;

To provide for calling forth the Militia to execute the Laws of the Union, suppress Insurrections and repel Invasions;

To provide for organizing, arming, and disciplining, the Militia, and for governing such Part of them as may be employed in the Service of the United States, reserving to the States respectively, the Appointment of the Officers, and the Authority of training the Militia according to the discipline prescribed by Congress;

To exercise exclusive Legislation in all Cases whatsoever, over such District (not exceeding ten Miles square) as may, by Cession of Particular States, and the Acceptance of Congress, become the Seat of the Government of the United States, and to exercise like Authority over all Places purchased by the Consent of the Legislature of the State in which the Same shall be, for the Erection of Forts, Magazines, Arsenals, dock-Yards, and other needful Buildings;—And

To make all Laws which shall be necessary and proper for carrying into Execution the foregoing Powers, and all other Powers vested by this Constitution in the Government of the United States, or in any Department or Officer thereof.

Section. 9. The Migration or Importation of such Persons as any of the States now existing shall think proper to admit, shall not be prohibited by the Congress prior to the Year one thousand eight hundred and eight, but a Tax or duty may be imposed on such Importation, not exceeding ten dollars for each Person.

The Privilege of the Writ of Habeas Corpus shall not be suspended, unless when in Cases of Rebellion or Invasion the public Safety may require it.

No Bill of Attainder or ex post facto Law shall be passed.

No Capitation, or other direct, Tax shall be laid, unless in Proportion to the Census or Enumeration herein before directed to be taken.

No Tax or Duty shall be laid on Articles exported from any State.

No Preference shall be given by any Regulation of Commerce or Revenue to the Ports of one State over those of another: nor shall Vessels bound to, or from, one State, be obliged to enter, clear, or pay Duties in another.

No Money shall be drawn from the Treasury, but in Consequence of Appropriations made by Law; and a regular Statement and Account of the Receipts and Expenditures of all public Money shall be published from time to time.

No Title of Nobility shall be granted by the United States: And no Person holding any Office of Profit or Trust under them, shall, without the Consent of the Congress, accept of any present, Emolument, Office, or Title, of any kind whatever, from any King, Prince, or foreign State.

Section. 10. No State shall enter into any Treaty, Alliance, or Confederation; grant Letters of Marque and Reprisal; coin Money; emit Bills of Credit; make any Thing but gold and silver Coin a Tender in Payment of Debts; pass any Bill of Attainder, ex post facto Law, or Law impairing the Obligation of Contracts, or grant any Title of Nobility.

No State shall, without the Consent of the Congress, lay any Imposts or Duties on Imports or Exports, except what may be absolutely necessary for executing its inspection Laws: and the net Produce of all Duties and Imposts, laid by any State on Imports or Exports, shall be for the Use of the Treasury of the United States; and all such Laws shall be subject to the Revision and Controul of the Congress.

No State shall, without the Consent of Congress, lay any Duty of Tonnage, keep Troops, or Ships of War in time of Peace, enter into any Agreement or Compact with another State, or with a foreign Power, or engage in War, unless actually invaded, or in such imminent Danger as will not admit of delay.

ARTICLE. II.

Section. 1. The executive Power shall be vested in a President of the United States of America. He shall hold his Office during the term of four Years, and, together with the Vice President, chosen for the same Term, be elected, as follows:

Each State shall appoint, in such Manner as the Legislature thereof may direct, a Number of Electors, equal to the whole Number of Senators and Representatives to which the State may be entitled in the Congress: but no Senator or Representative, or Person holding an Office of Trust or Profit under the United States, shall be appointed an Elector.

The Electors shall meet in their respective States, and vote by Ballot for two Persons, of whom one at least shall not be an Inhabitant of the same State with themselves. And they shall make a List of all the Persons voted for, and of the Number of Votes for each; which List they shall sign and certify, and transmit sealed to the Seat of the Government of the United States, directed to the President of the Senate. The President of the Senate shall, in the Presence of the Senate and House of Representatives, open all the Certificates, and the Votes shall then be counted. The Person having the greatest Number of Votes shall be the President, if such Number be a Majority of the whole Number of Electors appointed; and if there be more than one who have such Majority, and have an equal Number of Votes, then the House of Representatives shall immediately chuse by Ballot one of them for President; and if no Person have a Majority, then from the five highest on the List the said House shall in like Manner chuse the President. But in chusing the President, the Votes shall be taken by States, the Representation from each State having one Vote; A quorum for this Purpose shall consist of a Member or Members from two thirds of the States, and a Majority of all the States shall be necessary to a Choice. In every Case, after the Choice of the President, the Person having the greatest Number of Votes of the Electors shall be the Vice President. But if there should remain two or more who have equal Votes, the Senate shall chuse from them by Ballot the Vice President.

The Congress may determine the Time of chusing the Electors, and the Day on which they shall give their Votes; which Day shall be the same throughout the United States.

No Person except a natural born Citizen, or a Citizen of the United States, at the time of the Adoption of this Constitution, shall be eligible to the Office of President; neither shall any Person be eligible to that Office who shall not have attained to the Age of thirty five Years, and been fourteen Years a Resident within the United States.

In Case of the Removal of the President from Office, or of his Death, Resignation, or Inability to discharge the Powers and Duties of the said Office, the Same shall devolve on the Vice President, and the Congress may by Law provide for the Case of Removal, Death, Resignation or Inability, both of the President and Vice President, declaring what Officer shall then act as President, and such Officer shall act accordingly, until the Disability be removed, or a President shall be elected.

The President shall, at stated Times, receive for his Services, a Compensation, which shall neither be encreased or diminished during the Period for which he shall have been elected, and he shall not receive within that Period any other Emolument from the United States, or any of them.

Before he enters on the Execution of his Office, he shall take the following Oath or Affirmation:—"I do solemnly swear (or affirm) that I will faithfully execute the Office of President of the United States, and will to the best of my Ability, preserve, protect and defend the Constitution of the United States."

Section. 2. The President shall be Commander in Chief of the Army and Navy of the United States, and of the Militia of the several States, when called into the actual Service of the United States; he may require the Opinion, in writing, of the principal Officer in each of the executive Departments, upon any Subject relating to the Duties of their respective Offices, and he shall have Power to grant Reprieves and Pardons for Offences against the United States, except in Cases of Impeachment.

He shall have Power, by and with the Advice and Consent of the Senate, to make Treaties, provided two thirds of the Senators present concur; and he shall nominate, and by and with the Advice and Consent of the Senate, shall appoint Ambassadors, other public Ministers and Consuls, Judges of the supreme Court, and all other Officers of the United States, whose Appointments are not herein otherwise provided for, and which shall be established by Law; but the Congress may by Law vest the Appointment of such inferior Officers, as they think proper, in the

President alone, in the Courts of Law, or in the Heads of Departments.

The President shall have Power to fill up all Vacancies that may happen during the Recess of the Senate, by granting Commissions which shall expire at the End of their next Session.

Section. 3. He shall from time to time give to the Congress Information of the State of the Union, and recommend to their Consideration such Measures as he shall judge necessary and expedient; he may, on extraordinary Occasions, convene both Houses, or either of them, and in Case of Disagreement between them, with Respect to the Time of Adjournment, he may adjourn them to such Time as he shall think proper; he shall receive Ambassadors and other public Ministers; he shall take Care that the Laws be faithfully executed, and shall Commission all the Officers of the United States.

Section. 4. The President, Vice President and all civil Officers of the United States, shall be removed from Office on Impeachment for, and Conviction of, Treason, Bribery, or other high Crimes and Misdemeanors.

ARTICLE. III.

Section. 1. The judicial Power of the United States, shall be vested in one supreme Court, and in such inferior Courts as the Congress may from time to time ordain and establish. The Judges, both of the supreme and inferior Courts, shall hold their Offices during good Behavior, and shall, at stated Times, receive for their Services, a Compensation, which shall not be diminished during their Continuance in Office.

Section. 2. The judicial Power shall extend to all Cases, in Law and Equity, arising under this Constitution, the Laws of the United States, and Treaties made, or which shall be made, under their Authority;—to all Cases affecting Ambassadors, other public Ministers and Consuls;—to all Cases of admiralty and maritime Jurisdiction;—the Controversies to which the United States shall be a Party;—to Controversies between two or more States;—between a State and Citizens of another State;—between Citizens of different States;—

between Citizens of the same State claiming Lands under Grants of different States, and between a State, or the Citizens thereof, and foreign States, Citizens or Subjects.

In all cases affecting Ambassadors, other public Ministers and Consuls, and those in which a State shall be Party, the supreme Court shall have original Jurisdiction. In all the other Cases before mentioned, the supreme Court shall have appellate Jurisdiction, both as to Law and Fact, with such Exceptions, and under such Regulations as the Congress shall make.

The Trial of all Crimes, except in Cases of Impeachment, shall be by Jury; and such Trial shall be held in the State where the said Crimes shall have been committed; but when not committed within any State, the Trial shall be at such Place or Places as the Congress may by Law have directed.

Section. 3. Treason against the United States, shall consist only in levying War against them, or in adhering to their Enemies, giving them Aid and Comfort. No Person shall be convicted of Treason unless on the Testimony of two Witnesses to the same overt Act, or on Confession in open Court.

The Congress shall have Power to declare the Punishment of Treason, but no Attainder of Treason shall work Corruption of Blood, or Forfeiture except during the Life of the Person attainted.

ARTICLE. IV.

Section. 1. Full Faith and Credit shall be given in each State to the public Acts, Records, and judicial Proceedings of every other State. And the Congress may by general Laws prescribe the Manner in which such Acts, Records and Proceedings shall be proved, and the Effect thereof.

Section. 2. The Citizens of each State shall be entitled to all Privileges and Immunities of Citizens in the several States.

A Person charged in any State with Treason, Felony, or other Crime, who shall flee from Justice, and be found in another State, shall on Demand of the executive Authority of the State from which he fled,

be delivered up, to be removed to the State having Jurisdiction of the Crime.

No Person held to Service or Labour in one State, under the Laws thereof, escaping into another, shall, in Consequence of any Law or Regulation therein, be discharged from such Service or Labour, but shall be delivered up on Claim of the Party to whom such Service or Labour may be due.

Section. 3. New States may be admitted by the Congress into this Union; but no new State shall be formed or erected within the Jurisdiction of any other State; nor any State be formed by the Junction of two or more States, or Parts of States, without the consent of the Legislatures of the States concerned as well as of the Congress.

The Congress shall have Power to dispose of and make all needful Rules and Regulations respecting the Territory or other Property belonging to the United States; and nothing in this Constitution shall be so construed as to Prejudice any Claims of the United States, or of any particular States.

Section. 4. The United States shall guarantee to every State in this Union a Republican Form of Government, and shall protect each of them against Invasion; and on Application of the Legislature, or of the Executive (when the Legislature cannot be convened) against domestic Violence.

ARTICLE. V.

The Congress, whenever two thirds of both Houses shall deem it necessary, shall propose Amendments to this Constitution, or, on the Application of the Legislatures of two thirds of the several States, shall call a Convention for proposing Amendments, which, in either Case, shall be valid to all Intents and Purposes, as Part of this Constitution, when ratified by the Legislatures of three fourths of the several States, or by Conventions in three fourths thereof, as the one or the other Mode of Ratification may be proposed by the Congress; Provided that no Amendment which may be made prior to the Year One thousand eight hundred and eight shall in any Manner affect the first and fourth Clauses in the Ninth Section of the first Article; and that no State, without its Consent, shall be deprived of its equal Suffrage in the Senate.

ARTICLE. VI.

All Debts contracted and Engagements entered into, before the Adoption of this Constitution, shall be as valid against the United States under this Constitution, as under the Confederation.

This Constitution, and the Laws of the United States which shall be made in Pursuance thereof; and all Treaties made, or which shall be made, under the Authority of the United States, shall be the supreme Law of the Land; and the Judges in every State shall be bound thereby, any Thing in the Constitution or Laws of any State to the Contrary notwithstanding.

The Senators and Representatives before mentioned, and the Members of the several State Legislatures, and all executive and judicial Officers, both of the United States and of the several States, shall be bound by Oath or Affirmation, to support this Constitution; but no religious Test shall ever be required as a Qualification to any Office or public Trust under the United States.

ARTICLE. VII.

The Ratification of the Conventions of nine States, shall be sufficient for the Establishment of this Constitution between the States so ratifying the Same.

Done in Convention by the Unanimous Consent of the States present the Seventeenth Day of September in the Year of our Lord one thousand seven hundred and Eighty seven and of the Independence of the United States of America the Twelfth. In witness thereof We have hereunto subscribed our Names,

G⁰. WASHINGTON—Presdᵗ.
and deputy from Virginia

NEW HAMPSHIRE
John Langdon
Nicholas Gilman

MASSACHUSETTS
Nathaniel Gorham
Rufus King

CONNECTICUT
Wm Saml Johnson
Roger Sherman

NEW YORK
Alexander Hamilton

NEW JERSEY
Wil: Livingston
David A. Brearley
Wm Paterson
Jona: Dayton

PENNSYLVANIA
B Franklin
Thomas Mifflin
Robt Morris
Geo. Clymer
Thos FitzSimons
Jared Ingersoll
James Wilson
Gouv Morris

DELAWARE
Geo: Read
Gunning Bedford jun
John Dickinson
Richard Bassett
Jaco: Broom

MARYLAND
James McHenry
Dan of St Thos Jenifer
Danl Carroll

VIRGINIA
John Blair—
James Madison Jr.

NORTH CAROLINA
Wm Blount
Richd Dobbs Spaight
Hu Williamson

SOUTH CAROLINA
J. Rutledge
Charles Cotesworth
Pinckney
Charles Pinckney
Pierce Butler

GEORGIA
William Few
Abr Baldwin

AMENDMENTS TO THE CONSTITUTION

Articles in addition to, and Amendment of the Constitution of the United States of America, proposed by Congress, and ratified by the Legislatures of the several States, pursuant to the fifth Article of the original Constitution.

AMENDMENT I.*
Congress shall make no law respecting an establishment of religion, or prohibiting the free exercise thereof; or abridging the freedom of speech, or of the press; or the right of the people peaceably to assemble, and to petition the Government for a redress of grievances.

AMENDMENT II.
A well regulated Militia, being necessary to the security of a free State, the right of the people to keep and bear Arms, shall not be infringed.

AMENDMENT III.
No Soldier shall, in time of peace be quartered in any house, without the consent of the Owner, nor in time of war, but in a manner to be prescribed by law.

AMENDMENT IV.
The right of the people to be secure in their persons, houses, papers, and effects, against unreasonable searches and seizures, shall not be violated, and no Warrants shall issue, but upon probable cause, supported by Oath or affirmation, and particularly describing the place to be searched, and the persons or things to be seized.

AMENDMENT V.
No person shall be held to answer for a capital, or otherwise infamous crime, unless on a presentment or indictment of a Grand Jury, except in cases arising in the land or naval forces, or in the Militia, when in actual service in time of War or public danger; nor shall any person be subject for the same offence to be twice put in jeopardy of life or limb; nor shall be compelled in any criminal case to be a witness against himself, nor be deprived of life, liberty, or property, without due process of law; nor shall private property be taken for public use, without just compensation.

AMENDMENT VI.
In all criminal prosecutions, the accused shall enjoy the right to a speedy and public trial, by an impartial jury of the State and district wherein the crime shall have been committed, which district shall have been previously ascertained by law, and to be informed of the nature and cause of the accusation; to be confronted with the witnesses against him; to have compulsory process for obtaining witnesses in his favor, and to have the Assistance of Counsel for his defence.

AMENDMENT VII.
In Suits at common law, where the value in controversy shall exceed twenty dollars, the right of trial by jury shall be preserved, and no fact tried by a jury, shall be otherwise re-examined in any Court of the United States, than according to the rules of the common law.

AMENDMENT VIII.
Excessive bail shall not be required, nor excessive fines imposed, nor cruel and unusual punishments inflicted.

AMENDMENT IX.
The enumeration in the Constitution, of certain rights, shall not be construed to deny or disparage others retained by the people.

AMENDMENT X.
The powers not delegated to the United States by the Constitution, nor prohibited by it to the States, are reserved to the States respectively, or to the people.

AMENDMENT XI.
The Judicial power of the United States shall not be construed to extend to any suit in law or equity, commenced or prosecuted against one of the United States by Citizens of another State, or by Citizens or Subjects of any Foreign State. [January 8, 1798]

*The first ten Amendments (the Bill of Rights) were ratified in 1791.

AMENDMENT XII.

The Electors shall meet in their respective states, and vote by ballot for President and Vice-President, one of whom, at least, shall not be an inhabitant of the same state with themselves; they shall name in their ballots the person voted for as President, and in distinct ballots the person voted for as Vice-President, and they shall make distinct lists of all persons voted for as President, and of all persons voted for as Vice President, and of the number of votes for each, which lists they shall sign and certify, and transmit sealed to the seat of the government of the United States, directed to the President of the Senate;—The President of the Senate shall, in the presence of the Senate and House of Representatives, open all the certificates and the votes shall then be counted;—The person having the greatest number of votes for President, shall be the President, if such number be a majority of the whole number of Electors appointed; and if no person have such majority, then from the persons having the highest numbers not exceeding three on the list of those voted for as President, the House of Representatives shall choose immediately, by ballot, the President. But in choosing the President, the votes shall be taken by states, the representation from each state having one vote; a quorum for this purpose shall consist of a member or members from two-thirds of the states, and a majority of all the states shall be necessary to a choice. And if the House of Representatives shall not choose a President whenever the right of choice shall devolve upon them, before the fourth day of March next following, then the Vice-President shall act as President, as in the case of the death or other constitutional disability of the President.—The person having the greatest number of votes as Vice-President, shall be the Vice-President, if such number be a majority of the whole number of Electors appointed, and if no person have a majority, then from the two highest numbers on the list, the Senate shall choose the Vice-President; a quorum for the purpose shall consist of two-thirds of the whole number of Senators, and a majority of the whole number shall be necessary to a choice. But no person constitutionally ineligible to the office of President shall be eligible to that of Vice-President of the United States. [September 25, 1804]

AMENDMENT XIII.

Section 1. Neither slavery nor involuntary servitude, except as a punishment for crime whereof the party shall have been duly convicted, shall exist within the United States, or any place subject to their jurisdiction.

Section 2. Congress shall have power to enforce this article by appropriate legislation. [December 18, 1865]

AMENDMENT XIV.

Section 1. All persons born or naturalized in the United States, and subject to the jurisdiction thereof, are citizens of the United States and of the State wherein they reside. No State shall make or enforce any law which shall abridge the privileges or immunities of citizens of the United States; nor shall any State deprive any person of life, liberty, or property, without due process of law; nor deny to any person within its jurisdiction the equal protection of the laws.

Section 2. Representatives shall be apportioned among the several States according to their respective numbers, counting the whole number of persons in each State, excluding Indians not taxed. But when the right to vote at any election for the choice of electors for President and Vice President of the United States, Representatives in Congress, the Executive and Judicial officers of a State, or the members of the Legislature thereof, is denied to any of the male inhabitants of such State, being twenty-one years of age, and citizens of the United States, or in any way abridged, except for participation in rebellion, or other crime, the basis of representation therein shall be reduced in the proportion which the number of such male citizens shall bear to the whole number of male citizens twenty-one years of age in such State.

Section 3. No person shall be a Senator or Representative in Congress, or elector of President and Vice President, or hold any office, civil or military, under the United States, or under any State, who, having previously taken an oath, as a member of Congress, or as an officer of the United States, or as a member of any State legislature, or as an executive or judicial officer of any State, to support the Constitution of the United

States, shall have engaged in insurrection or rebellion against the same, or given aid or comfort to the enemies thereof. But Congress may by a vote of two-thirds of each House, remove such disability.

Section 4. The validity of the public debt of the United States, authorized by law, including debts incurred for payment of pensions and bounties for services in suppressing insurrection or rebellion, shall not be questioned. But neither the United States nor any State shall assume or pay any debt or obligation incurred in aid of insurrection or rebellion against the United States, or any claim for the loss or emancipation of any slave; but all such debts, obligations and claims shall be held illegal and void.

Section 5. The Congress shall have power to enforce, by appropriate legislation, the provisions of this article. [July 28, 1868]

AMENDMENT XV.

Section 1. The right of citizens of the United States to vote shall not be denied or abridged by the United States or by any State on account of race, color, or previous condition of servitude—

Section 2. The Congress shall have power to enforce this article by appropriate legislation. [March 30, 1870]

AMENDMENT XVI.

The Congress shall have power to lay and collect taxes on incomes, from whatever source derived, without apportionment among the several States, and without regard to any census or enumeration. [February 25, 1913]

AMENDMENT XVII.

The Senate of the United States shall be composed of two senators from each State, elected by the people thereof, for six years; and each Senator shall have one vote. The electors in each State shall have the qualifications requisite for electors of the most numerous branch of the State legislatures.

When vacancies happen in the representation of any State in the Senate, the executive authority of such State shall issue writs of election to fill such vacancies: *Provided,* That the legislature of any State may empower the executive thereof to make temporary appointments until the people fill the vacancies by election as the legislature may direct.

This amendment shall not be so construed as to affect the election or term of any senator chosen before it becomes valid as part of the Constitution. [May 31, 1913]

AMENDMENT XVIII.

After one year from the ratification of this article, the manufacture, sale, or transportation of intoxicating liquors within, the importation thereof into, or the exportation thereof from the United States and all territory subject to the jurisdiction thereof for beverage purposes is hereby prohibited.

The Congress and the several States shall have concurrent power to enforce this article by appropriate legislation.

This article shall be inoperative unless it shall have been ratified as an amendment to the Constitution by the legislatures of the several States, as provided in the Constitution, within seven years from the date of the submission thereof to the States by Congress. [January 29, 1919]

AMENDMENT XIX.

The right of citizens of the United States to vote shall not be denied or abridged by the United States or by any State on account of sex.

The Congress shall have power by appropriate legislation to enforce the provisions of this article. [August 26, 1920]

AMENDMENT XX.

Section 1. The terms of the President and Vice-President shall end at noon on the twentieth day of January, and the terms of Senators and Representatives at noon on the third day of January, of the years in which such terms would have ended if this article had not been ratified; and the terms of their successors shall then begin.

Section 2. The Congress shall assemble at least once in every year, and such meeting shall begin at noon on the third day of January, unless they shall by law appoint a different day.

Section 3. If, at the time fixed for the beginning of the term of the President, the President-elect shall have died, the Vice-President-elect shall become President. If a President shall not have been chosen before the time fixed for the beginning of his term, or if the President-elect shall have failed to qualify, then the Vice-President-elect shall act as President until a President shall have qualified; and the Congress may by law provide for the case wherein neither a President-elect nor a Vice-President-elect shall have qualified, declaring who shall then act as President, or the manner in which one who is to act shall be selected, and such person shall act accordingly until a President or Vice-President shall have qualified.

Section 4. The Congress may by law provide for the case of the death of any of the persons from whom the House of Representatives may choose a President whenever the right of choice shall have devolved upon them, and for the case of the death of any of the persons from whom the Senate may choose a Vice-President whenever the right of choice shall have devolved upon them.

Section 5. Sections 1 and 2 shall take effect on the 15th day of October following the ratification of this article.

Section 6. This article shall be inoperative unless it shall have been ratified as an amendment to the Constitution by the legislatures of three-fourths of the several States within seven years from the date of its submission. [February 6, 1933]

AMENDMENT XXI.

Section 1. The eighteenth article of amendment to the Constitution of the United States is hereby repealed.

Section 2. The transportation or importation into any State, Territory or possession of the United States for delivery or use therein of intoxicating liquors, in violation of the laws thereof, is hereby prohibited.

Section 3. This article shall be inoperative unless it shall have been ratified as an amendment to the Constitution by convention in the several States, as provided in the Constitution, within seven years from the date of the submission thereof to the States by the Congress. [December 5, 1933]

AMENDMENT XXII.

Section 1. No person shall be elected to the office of the President more than twice, and no person who has held the office of President, or acted as President, for more than two years of a term to which some other person was elected President shall be elected to the office of the President more than once. But this Article shall not apply to any person holding the office of President when this Article was proposed by the Congress, and shall not prevent any person who may be holding the office of President, or acting as President, during the term within which this Article becomes operative from holding the office of President or acting as President during the remainder of such term.

Section 2. This article shall be inoperative unless it shall have been ratified as an amendment to the Constitution by the legislatures of three-fourths of the several States within seven years from the date of its submission to the States by the Congress. [February 27, 1951]

AMENDMENT XXIII.

Section 1. The District constituting the seat of government of the United States shall appoint in such manner as the Congress may direct:

A number of electors of President and Vice-President equal to the whole number of Senators and Representatives in Congress to which the District would be entitled if it were a State, but in no event more than the least populous State; they shall be in addition to those appointed by the States, but they shall be considered, for the purposes of the election of President and Vice-President, to be electors appointed by a State; and they shall meet in the District and perform such duties as provided by the twelfth article of amendment.

Section 2. The Congress shall have the power to enforce this article by appropriate legislation. [March 29, 1961]

AMENDMENT XXIV.

Section 1. The right of citizens of the United States to vote in any primary or other election for President or Vice President, for electors for President or Vice President, or for Senator or Representative in Congress, shall not be denied or abridged by the United States or any State by reason of failure to pay any poll tax or other tax.

Section 2. The Congress shall have power to enforce this article by appropriate legislation. [January 23, 1964]

AMENDMENT XXV.

Section 1. In case of the removal of the President from office or of his death or resignation, the Vice President shall become President.

Section 2. Whenever there is a vacancy in the office of Vice President, the President shall nominate a Vice President who shall take office upon confirmation by a majority vote of both Houses of Congress.

Section 3. Whenever the President transmits to the President pro tempore of the Senate and the Speaker of the House of Representatives his written declaration that he is unable to discharge the powers and duties of his office, and until he transmits to them a written declaration to the contrary, such powers and duties shall be discharged by the Vice President as Acting President.

Section 4. Whenever the Vice President and a majority of either the principal officers of the executive departments or of such other body as Congress may by law provide, transmit to the President pro tempore of the Senate and the Speaker of the House of Representatives their written declaration that the President is unable to discharge the powers and duties of his office, the Vice President shall immediately assume the powers and duties of the office as Acting President.

Thereafter, when the President transmits to the President pro tempore of the Senate and the Speaker of the House of Representatives his written declaration that no inability exists, he shall resume the powers and duties of his office unless the Vice President and a majority of either the principal officers of the executive departments or of such other body as Congress may by law provide, transmit within four days to the President pro tempore of the Senate and the Speaker of the House of Representatives their written declaration that the President is unable to discharge the powers and duties of his office. Thereupon Congress shall decide the issue, assembling within forty-eight hours for that purpose if not in session. If the Congress, within twenty-one days after receipt of the latter written declaration, or, if Congress is not in session, within twenty-one days after Congress is required to assemble, determines by two-thirds vote of both Houses that the President is unable to discharge the powers and duties of his office, the Vice-President shall continue to discharge the same as Acting President; otherwise, the President shall resume the powers and duties of his office. [February 10, 1967]

AMENDMENT XXVI.

Section 1. The right of citizens of the United States, who are eighteen years of age or older, to vote shall not be denied or abridged by the United States or by any State on account of age.

Section 2. The Congress shall have power to enforce this article by appropriate legislation. [June 30, 1971]

AMENDMENT XXVII.

No law, varying the compensation for the services of the Senators and Representatives shall take effect, until an election of Representatives shall have intervened. [May 8, 1992]

SUGGESTED READING

CHAPTER 1: A NEW WORLD
Books

Bender, Thomas. *A Nation among Nations: America's Place in World History* (2006). Attempts to place American history in an international context; the opening chapters offer a global portrait of the age of exploration and conquest.

Crosby, Alfred J. *The Columbian Exchange: Biological and Cultural Consequences of 1492* (1972). Examines the flow of goods and diseases across the Atlantic and their consequences.

Fernández-Armesto, Felipe. *Pathfinders: A Global History of Exploration* (2006). A history of explorations throughout the centuries, including those of the fifteenth and sixteenth centuries.

Fischer, David H. *Champlain's Dream* (2008). A lively account of Samuel de Champlain's effort to build a French colony in North America based on toleration and mutual respect between settlers and Native Americans.

Gutiérrez, Ramón A. *When Jesus Came, the Corn Mothers Went Away: Marriage, Sexuality, and Power in New Mexico, 1500–1846* (1991). Discusses the changes in Indian life in New Mexico as a result of Spanish colonization.

Haefeli, Evan. *New Netherland and the Dutch Origins of American Religious Liberty* (2012). Explores the complex conditions of religious life in New Netherland.

Knaut, Andrew L. *The Pueblo Revolt of 1680: Conquest and Resistance in Seventeenth-Century New Mexico* (1997). A recent account of the largest revolt of native peoples.

Mann, Charles C. *1491: New Revelations of the Americas before Columbus* (2005). A comprehensive portrait of life in the Western Hemisphere before the arrival of Europeans.

Richter, Daniel K. *Facing East from Indian Country* (2001). Examines the era of exploration and settlement as viewed through the experience of Native Americans.

Rodriguez, Jaime E. *Political Culture in Spanish America, 1500–1830* (2017). Political ideas and practices from colonization through Spanish-American independence.

Witgen, Michael. *An Infinity of Nations: How the Native New World Shaped Early North America* (2012). An imaginative account of how native peoples and Europeans interacted in the Great Lakes region.

Websites

Archive of Early American Images: www.brown.edu /academics/libraries/john-carter-brown/jcb -online/image-collections/archive-early-american -images

Cahokia Mounds: http://cahokiamounds.org

Exploring the Early Americas: www.loc.gov/exhibits /earlyamericas/

France in America: http://international.loc.gov/intldl /fiahtml

Jamestown, Quebec, Santa Fe: Three North American Beginnings: http://americanhistory.si.edu /jamestown-quebec-santafe/en/introduction

CHAPTER 2: BEGINNINGS OF ENGLISH AMERICA, 1607–1660
Books

Anderson, Virginia. *Creatures of Empire: How Domestic Animals Transformed Early America* (2006). Shows how livestock brought by English settlers helped to transform the colonial landscape and provoked conflict with Native Americans.

Banner, Stuart. *How the Indians Lost Their Land: Law and Power on the Frontier* (2005). Argues that most Indian land came into settlers' hands by legal processes rather than conquest.

Brown, Kathleen. *Good Wives, Nasty Wenches, and Anxious Patriarchs: Gender, Race, and Power in Colonial Virginia* (1996). A pioneering study of gender relations and their impact on Virginia society.

Cronon, William. *Changes in the Land: Colonists and the Ecology of New England* (1983). A pathbreaking examination of how English colonization affected the natural environment in New England.

Gaskill, Malcolm. *Between Two Worlds: How the English Became Americans* (2014). Traces the slow development of a distinctive American identity in the mainland British colonies.

Gleach, Frederic W. *Powhatan's World and Colonial Virginia: A Conflict of Cultures* (1997). A study of Indian culture and the impact of European colonization upon it.

Noll, Mark. *The Old Religion in a New World: The History of North American Christianity* (2001). Relates how the transplantation of European religions to America changed religious institutions and practices.

Norton, Mary Beth. *Founding Mothers and Fathers: Gendered Power and the Forming of American Society* (2011). An examination of legal cases that illuminate the power relations involving colonial women and men.

Pestana, Carla G. *The English Atlantic in an Age of Revolution, 1640–1661* (2001). Analyzes how the English Civil War reverberated in the American colonies.

Philbrick, Nathaniel. *Mayflower* (2006). An account of one of the most celebrated voyages of the colonial era and the early history of the Plymouth colony.

Price, David A. *Love and Hate in Jamestown: John Smith, Pocahontas, and the Start of a New Nation* (2003). Presents the legend and reality of John Smith, Pocahontas, and early Virginia.

Rees, John. *The Leveller Revolution: Radical Political Organization in England, 1640–1650* (2017). The most recent study of history's first democratic popular movement.

Taylor, Alan. *American Colonies* (2001). A comprehensive survey of the history of North American colonies from their beginnings to 1763.

Websites

The Plymouth Colony Archive Project: www.histarch.illinois.edu/plymouth

Virtual Jamestown: www.virtualjamestown.org

CHAPTER 3: CREATING ANGLO-AMERICA, 1660–1750

Books

Bailyn, Bernard. *The Peopling of British North America* (1986). A brief survey of the movement of peoples across the Atlantic.

Berlin, Ira. *Many Thousands Gone: The First Two Centuries of Slavery in North America* (1998). The most extensive study of the origins and development of colonial slavery.

Bushman, Richard. *The Refinement of America: Persons, Houses, Cities* (1992). A study of how a more "refined" lifestyle emerged in the eighteenth-century colonies.

Dayton, Cornelia H. *Women before the Bar: Gender, Law, and Society in Connecticut, 1639–1789* (1995). Examines the changing legal status of women in one American colony.

Kidd, Thomas S. *The Great Awakening* (2007). An account of the religious movement that swept the American colonies in the eighteenth century.

Lipman, Andrew. *The Saltwater Frontier: Indians and the Contest for the American Coast* (2015). Explores how the sea was an area of conflict between Native American fishermen and merchants and European colonizers.

Morgan, Edmund S. *American Slavery, American Freedom: The Ordeal of Colonial Virginia* (1975). An influential study of the slow development of slavery in seventeenth-century Virginia.

Norton, Mary Beth. *In the Devil's Snare: The Salem Witchcraft Crisis of 1692* (2002). A study of the witch trials that places them in the context of anxieties over Indian warfare on the Massachusetts frontier.

Pestana, Carla G. *Protestant Empire: Religion and the Making of the British Atlantic World* (2009). Discusses the role of Protestantism in inspiring and justifying British overseas expansion.

Silver, Peter. *Our Savage Neighbors: How Indian War Transformed Early America* (2008). Argues that hostility to Indians provided a way of unifying the diverse population of European origin that made up colonial America.

Website

Afro-Louisiana History and Genealogy: www.ibiblio.org/laslave/

CHAPTER 4: SLAVERY, FREEDOM, AND THE STRUGGLE FOR EMPIRE, TO 1763

Books

Anderson, Fred. *Crucible of War: The Seven Years' War and the Fate of Empire in British North America, 1754–1766* (2000). A general history of the Seven Years' War and its consequences.

Beeman, Richard R. *Varieties of Political Experience in Eighteenth-Century America* (2004). Explores how political life differed from colony to colony and what characteristics they had in common.

Calloway, Colin G. *The Scratch of a Pen: 1763 and the Transformation of North America* (2006). Examines the impact of the Peace of Paris on North America, especially the Native American population.

Colley, Linda. *Britons: Forging the Nation, 1707–1837* (1992). An influential study of the rise of a sense of national identity in Great Britain, relevant also for the American colonies.

Newman, Simon P. *A New World of Labor: The Development of Plantation Slavery in the British Atlantic* (2013). The most recent account of how slavery emerged and was consolidated in the British empire.

Noll, Mark. *The Rise of Evangelicalism: The Age of Edwards, Whitefield, and the Wesleys* (2004). Explores the Great Awakening on both sides of the Atlantic and its impact on religious life.

Rediker, Marcus. *The Slave Ship: A Human History* (2007). A fascinating and disturbing account of the Atlantic slave trade that focuses on the captains, sailors, and slaves aboard the slave ships.

Reséndez, Andrés. *The Other Slavery: The Uncovered Story of Indian Enslavement in America* (2016). A careful analysis of the development and extent of Indian slavery in the early colonies.

Rucker, Walter C. *The River Flows On: Black Resistance, Culture, and Identity Formation in Early America* (2006). Traces the emergence of a new African-American identity and how it affected modes of slave resistance.

Smith, Barbara Clark. *The Freedoms We Lost: Consent and Resistance in Revolutionary America* (2010). Examines the ways colonial Americans participated in public life and sought to defend their concepts of freedom.

Valerio-Jiménez, Omar S. *River of Hope: Forging Identity and Nation in the Rio Grande Borderlands* (2013). Traces the processes of cultural interaction and the establishment of national power in a major borderlands region.

White, Richard. *The Middle Ground: Indians, Empires, and Republics in the Great Lakes Region, 1650–1815* (1991). The book that developed the idea of a middle ground where Europeans and Indians both exercised authority.

Websites

Africans in America: www.pbs.org/wgbh/aia/

Web de Anza: http://anza.uoregon.edu

CHAPTER 5: THE AMERICAN REVOLUTION, 1763–1783

Books

Armitage, David. *The Declaration of Independence: A Global History* (2007). Traces the international impact of the Declaration of Independence in the years since it was written.

Bailyn, Bernard. *The Ideological Origins of the American Revolution* (1967; 2nd ed., 1992). A classic study of the ideas that shaped the movement for independence.

Bloch, Ruth. *Visionary Republic: Millennial Themes in American Thought, 1756–1800* (1988). Explores how the religious vision of a more perfect society contributed to the coming of the Revolution.

Breen, T. H. *Marketplace of Revolution: How Consumer Politics Shaped American Independence* (2004). An examination of how the colonists' very dependence on British consumer goods led them to resent interference with trade.

Countryman, Edward. *The American Revolution* (rev. ed., 2002). A brief summary of the Revolution's causes, conduct, and consequences.

Foner, Eric. *Tom Paine and Revolutionary America* (1976). Examines the ideas of the era's greatest pamphleteer of revolution and how they contributed to the struggle for independence.

Maier, Pauline. *American Scripture: Making the Declaration of Independence* (1997). The most detailed study of the writing of the Declaration and of previous calls for independence within the colonies.

Nash, Gary. *The Urban Crucible: Social Change, Political Consciousness, and the Origins of the American Revolution* (1979). Explores how the social history of American cities contributed to the coming of the Revolution.

Neimeyer, Charles. *America Goes to War: A Social History of the Continental Army* (1995). A history of Washington's army that stresses the role of nonelite Americans in the fighting and the impact of military service on the soldiers.

Polansky, Janet. *Revolutions without Borders: The Call to Liberty in the Atlantic World* (2015). Explores both the revolutions of the late eighteenth century and the kinds of sources historians use to study them.

Raphael, Ray. *A People's History of the American Revolution* (2001). A study of grassroots resistance to Britain before and during the War of Independence.

Saunt, Claudio. *West of the Revolution: An Uncommon History of 1776* (2014). An account of events in North America among Indians, Spanish colonists, and others in the year of the Declaration of Independence.

Taylor, Alan. *American Revolutions: A Continental History, 1750–1804* (2015). An excellent history of the Revolution as a continental event.

Websites

The American Revolution and Its Era: Maps and Charts of North America and the West Indies: http://memory.loc.gov/ammem/gmdhtml/armhtml/armhome.html

The Coming of the American Revolution: www.masshist.org/revolution/

CHAPTER 6: THE REVOLUTION WITHIN
Books

Berkin, Carol. *Revolutionary Mothers: Women in the Struggle for American Independence* (2005). Presents profiles of women who took part in the movement for independence.

Boulton, Terry. *Taming Democracy: "The People," the Founders, and the Troubled Ending of the American Revolution* (2007). Argues that the democratic impulse unleashed by the War of Independence was to some extent reversed by the events of the 1780s.

Calloway, Colin. *The American Revolution in Indian Country* (1995). Examines how the Revolution affected Indians in each region of the United States.

Davis, David Brion. *The Problem of Slavery in the Age of Revolution* (1975). An influential study of the emergence of slavery as a major public issue in the Atlantic world.

DuVal, Kathleen. *Independence Lost: Lives on the Edge of the American Revolution* (2015). A study of the Revolution as a borderlands conflict on the Gulf Coast, in which European empires and Native Americans fought for their own ideas of power and liberty.

Frey, Sylvia R. *Water from the Rock: Black Resistance in a Revolutionary Age* (1991). A study of the many ways blacks sought to gain freedom for themselves during the Revolution.

Hatch, Nathan O. *The Democratization of American Christianity* (1989). A comprehensive account of the Revolution's impact on religion, and its aftermath.

Jasanoff, Maya. *Liberty's Exiles: American Loyalists in the Revolutionary World* (2011). A study of Americans who remained loyal to Great Britain during the War of Independence.

Kruman, Marc. *Between Authority and Liberty: State Constitution Making in Revolutionary America* (1997). The most detailed account of how state constitutions were changed during the era.

Parkinson, Robert G. *The Common Cause: Creating Race and Nation in the American Revolution* (2016). How hostility to Native Americans and slaves helped to create a sense of shared identity among white patriots fighting for American independence.

Taylor, Alan. *The Divided Ground: Indians, Settlers, and the Northern Borderland of the American Revolution* (2006). Examines the Revolution and its consequence in the Iroquois region of upstate New York.

Wood, Gordon. *The Radicalism of the American Revolution* (1992). An influential work that sees the Revolution as transforming a hierarchical society into a democratic one.

Websites

Creating the United States: www.loc.gov/exhibits/creating-the-united-states

The Geography of Slavery in Virginia: www2.vcdh.virginia.edu/gos/

CHAPTER 7: FOUNDING A NATION, 1783–1791
Books

Cornell, Saul. *The Other Founders: Anti-Federalism and the Dissenting Tradition in America, 1788–1828* (1999). A careful examination of the ideas of those who opposed ratification of the Constitution.

Dowd, Gregory E. *A Spirited Resistance: The North American Indian Struggle for Unity, 1745–1815* (1992). Contains an important discussion of the place of Indians in the new American nation.

Dunbar, Eric Armstrong. *Never Caught: The Washingtons' Relentless Pursuit of Their Runaway Slave Ona Judge* (2017). Uses the fascinating story of one of George and Martha Washington's slaves to illuminate the dilemma of slavery and freedom in the early republic.

Holton, Woody. *Unruly Americans and the Origins of the Constitution* (2007). Argues that the political activities of ordinary Americans helped to shape the Constitution.

Kettner, James T. *The Development of American Citizenship, 1608–1870* (1978). Traces the development of the definition of American citizenship from early colonization to the aftermath of the Civil War.

Klarman, Michael. *The Framers' Coup: The Making of the United States Constitution* (2016). Unlike many other books on the Constitutional Convention, emphasizes the deep divides among the delegates rather than eventual consensus.

Levy, Leonard. *The Establishment Clause: Religion and the First Amendment* (1994). A historical account of one of the key components of the Bill of Rights.

Maier, Pauline. *Ratification: The People Debate the Constitution, 1787–1788* (2010). The most complete account of the state-by-state debates over ratification of the Constitution.

Nash, Gary. *The Forgotten Fifth: African Americans in the Age of Revolution* (2006). A comprehensive survey of the Revolution's impact on blacks, slave and free.

Rakove, Jack. *Original Meanings: Politics and Ideas in the Making of the Constitution* (1996). An influential interpretation of the ideas that went into the drafting of the Constitution.

Wilentz, Sean. *No Property in Man: Slavery and Antislavery at the Nation's Founding* (2018). Emphasizes the long-term consequences of the framers' refusal to include a direct national acknowledgment of property in man in the Constitution.

Websites

Creating the United States: www.loc.gov/exhibits/creating-the-united-states

Explore the Constitution: http://constitutioncenter.org

The Presidency: http://americanhistory.si.edu/presidency/home.html

CHAPTER 8: SECURING THE REPUBLIC, 1791–1815

Books

Egerton, Douglas R. *Gabriel's Rebellion: The Virginia Slave Conspiracies of 1800 and 1802* (1993). The most comprehensive account of one of the most important slave conspiracies in American history.

Elkins, Stanley, and Eric L. McKitrick. *The Age of Federalism* (1993). A detailed account of the politics of the 1790s.

Kerber, Linda K. *Women of the Republic: Intellect and Ideology in Revolutionary America* (1980). A study of prevailing ideas about women's place in the new republic.

Lambert, Frank. *The Barbary Wars: American Independence in the Atlantic World* (2005). An account of the first foreign military conflict conducted by the newly independent United States.

McCoy, Drew. *The Elusive Republic: Political Economy in Jeffersonian America* (1980). An influential study of the economic and political outlooks and policies of Federalists and Jeffersonians.

Perl-Rosenthal, Nathan. *Citizen Sailors: Becoming American in the Age of Revolution* (2015). How sailors, white and black, asserted their rights as American citizens in the decades after the Revolution.

Ronda, James P. *Lewis and Clark among the Indians* (1984). An account of the most famous exploring party in American history.

Rothman, Adam. *Slave Country: American Expansion and the Origins of the Deep South* (2005). A pioneering study of how the United States secured control of what are now the Gulf states, opening the door for the expansion of slavery.

Taylor, Alan. *The Civil War of 1812* (2010). An account of the War of 1812 that stresses how divided Americans were during the conflict.

Waldstreicher, David. *In the Midst of Perpetual Fetes: The Making of American Nationalism, 1776–1820* (1997). Explores how Americans celebrated and thought about their nation's independence in the years of the early republic.

Websites

Rivers, Edens, Empires: Lewis and Clark and the Revealing of America: www.loc.gov/exhibits/lewisandclark/lewisandclark.html

CHAPTER 9: THE MARKET REVOLUTION, 1800–1840

Books

Bergmann, William H. *The American National State and the Early West* (2014). Demonstrates how governmental action was crucial to early western development.

Boydston, Jeanne. *Home and Work: Housework, Wages, and the Ideology of Work in the Early Republic* (1990). Examines how the market revolution affected ideas relating to women's work.

Deyle, Steven. *Carry Me Back: The Domestic Slave Trade in American Life* (2005). The most comprehensive history of the internal slave trade, by which millions of slaves were transported to the Lower South.

Harris, Leslie. *In the Shadow of Slavery: African-Americans in New York City, 1626–1863* (2003). A study that emphasizes the exclusion of African-Americans from the economic opportunities offered by the market revolution.

Haselby, Sam. *The Origins of American Religious Nationalism* (2015). Explores how the battle between frontier evangelists and more traditional New England ministers shaped religion and politics in the early republic.

Howe, Daniel W. *What Hath God Wrought: The Transformation of America, 1815–1848* (2007). A comprehensive account of social and political changes in this era, emphasizing the significance of the communications revolution.

Johnson, Paul E. *A Shopkeeper's Millennium: Society and Revivals in Rochester, New York, 1815–1837* (1978). Explores the impact of religious revivals on a key city of upstate New York.

Larson, John L. *The Market Revolution in America: Liberty, Ambition, and the Eclipse of the Common Good* (2010). The most recent account of the market revolution and its impact on American society and values.

Miller, Kerby A. *Exiles and Emigrants: Ireland and the Irish Exodus to North America* (1985). An examination of Irish immigration over the course of American history.

Ryan, Mary P. *Cradle of the Middle Class: The Family in Oneida County, New York, 1790–1865* (1981). Examines how economic change helped to produce a new kind of middle-class family structure centered on women's dominance of the household.

Wilentz, Sean. *Chants Democratic: New York City and the Rise of the American Working Class, 1788–1850* (1984). A study of the early labor movement in one of its key centers in antebellum America.

Zakim, Michael. *Accounting for Capitalism: The World the Clerks Made* (2018). How a new generation of clerks arose in the early nineteenth century and how they personified and helped to shape the market revolution.

Websites

American Transcendentalism: www.vcu.edu/engweb/transcendentalism/

Women in America, 1820–1842: http://xroads.virginia.edu/~hyper/detoc/fem/home.htm

CHAPTER 10: DEMOCRACY IN AMERICA, 1815–1840

Books

Balogh, Brian. *A Government Out of Sight: The Mystery of National Authority in Nineteenth-Century America* (2009). Examines the paradox of widespread belief in limited government yet frequent energetic use of federal authority.

Fitz, Caitlin. *Our Sister Republics: The United States in an Age of American Revolutions* (2016). Traces changes in responses in the United States to the Latin American Wars of Independence, from initial enthusiasm to skepticism as the new nations moved to end slavery.

Forbes, Robert. *The Missouri Compromise and Its Aftermath: Slavery and the Meaning of America* (2007). Places the Missouri controversy in the context of the long national debate over slavery.

Guyatt, Nicholas. *Bind Us Apart: How Enlightened Americans Invented Racial Segregation* (2016). Compares the movements for Indian removal and colonization of African-Americans outside the country as precursors to later racial segregation laws.

Howe, Daniel W. *The Political Culture of the American Whigs* (1979). Illuminates the key ideas that held the Whig Party together.

Keyssar, Alexander. *The Right to Vote: The Contested History of Democracy in the United States* (2000). The most up-to-date history of the right to vote in America from the colonial era to the present.

Schlesinger, Arthur M., Jr. *The Age of Jackson* (1945). An influential account of Jacksonian ideas and politics, which shaped debate among a generation of historians.

Starr, Paul. *Creation of the Media: Political Origins of Modern Communications* (2004). Contains an illuminating account of the "information revolution" in Jacksonian America.

Wallace, Anthony. *The Long, Bitter Trail: Andrew Jackson and the Indians* (1993). A brief history of Jackson's Indian policies, especially Indian Removal in the southern states.

Watson, Harry. *Liberty and Power: The Politics of Jacksonian America* (1990). A valuable brief account of the politics of the 1820s and 1830s.

Wilentz, Sean. *The Rise of American Democracy: Jefferson to Lincoln* (2005). A comprehensive history of democratic ideas and politics from the American Revolution to the Civil War.

Websites

Democracy in America, Alexis de Tocqueville: http://xroads.virginia.edu/~hyper/detoc/home.html

Legacy: Spain and the United States in the Age of Independence, 1763–1848: http://latino.si.edu/SpainLegacy/Archive/index.html

CHAPTER 11: THE PECULIAR INSTITUTION

Books

Beckert, Sven. *The Empire of Cotton* (2014). A history of one of the world's most important commodities, placing the Old South in an international context.

Berlin, Ira. *Slaves without Masters: The Free Negro in the Antebellum South* (1974). A careful study of the status of free blacks, stressing differences between the Upper and Lower South.

Breen, Patrick H. *The Land Shall Be Deluged in Blood: A New History of the Nat Turner Revolt* (2016). The most recent account of the most famous slave rebellion in American history.

Davis, David Brion. *Inhuman Bondage: The Rise and Fall of Slavery in the New World* (2006). Places the history of slavery in the United States firmly in a hemispheric context.

Foner, Eric. *Gateway to Freedom: The Hidden History of the Underground Railroad* (2015). A study of the operations of the Underground Railroad, focusing on New York City, and of the fugitives it assisted.

Genovese, Eugene D. *Roll, Jordan, Roll: The World the Slaves Made* (1974). A classic study of the paternalist ethos and the culture that developed under slavery.

Gutman, Herbert G. *The Black Family in Slavery and Freedom* (1976). A pioneering examination of how slaves created and sustained families under the harsh conditions of slavery.

Johnson, Walter. *Soul by Soul: Life inside the Antebellum Slave Market* (1999). Considers the operations of the New Orleans slave market as a window into slavery as a whole.

Karp, Matthew. *This Vast Southern Empire: Slaveholders at the Helm of American Foreign Policy* (2016). Explores how slaveholders tried to use the power of the federal government to protect slavery in the United States and the rest of the Western Hemisphere.

Kaye, Anthony E. *Joining Places: Slave Neighborhoods in the Old South* (2007). Emphasizes the importance of the local networks established by slaves in Mississippi.

Kolchin, Peter. *American Slavery, 1619–1877* (rev. ed., 2003). A careful, up-to-date survey of the history of slavery in North America from its beginning through emancipation.

McCurry, Stephanie. *Masters of Small Worlds: Yeoman Households, Gender Relations, and the Political Culture of Antebellum South Carolina* (1995). Studies the lives of men and women in non-slaveholding families to explore their links with the planter class.

Stevenson, Brenda. *Life in Black and White: Family and Community in the Slave South* (1996). Focusing on Virginia, an examination of how slaves adapted to the rise of the interstate slave trade.

Websites

Born in Slavery: Slave Narratives from the Federal Writers' Project: http://lcweb2.loc.gov/ammem /snhtml/snhome.html

Documenting the American South: http://docsouth.unc .edu

Slaves and the Courts, 1740–1860: http://memory.loc.gov /ammem/sthtml/sthome.html

CHAPTER 12: AN AGE OF REFORM, 1820–1840

Books

Bestor, Arthur E. *Backwoods Utopias: The Sectarian and Owenite Phases of Communitarian Socialism in America* (1948). An account of some of the numerous communitarian experiments in pre–Civil War America.

Boylan, Anne M. *The Origins of Women's Activism: New York and Boston, 1797–1840* (2002). Considers how middle-class urban women organized numerous associations for social improvement and thereby gained a place in the public sphere.

Goodman, Paul. *Of One Blood: Abolitionists and the Origins of Racial Equality* (1998). Explores the origins of racial egalitarianism in the movement against slavery.

Jeffrey, Julie R. *The Great Silent Army of Abolitionism: Ordinary Women in the Antislavery Movement* (1998). The role of women as the grassroots foot soldiers of the abolitionist movement.

Jones, Martha S. *Birthright Citizens: A History of Race and Rights in Antebellum America* (2018). Examines how free black activists before the Civil War struggled to gain recognition as American citizens in the face of legal inequality and demands that they be "colonized" outside the country.

Kantrowitz, Stephen. *More Than Freedom: Fighting for Black Citizenship in a White Republic, 1829–1889* (2012). A study of the black abolitionists of Boston and their struggle for an expansive understanding of freedom.

McGreevy, John T. *Catholicism and American Freedom* (2003). Contains an illuminating discussion of how

Catholics responded to Protestant-based reform movements.

Sinha, Manisha. *The Slave's Cause: A History of Abolition* (2016). A comprehensive history of the antislavery movement from the colonial era through the Civil War.

Tyrrell, Ian. *Sobering Up: From Temperance to Prohibition in Antebellum America, 1800–1860* (1979). Traces the movement against the sale and use of liquor and how it changed in the first part of the nineteenth century.

Zboray, Ronald J., and Mary Zboray. *Voices without Votes: Women and Politics in Antebellum New England* (2010). Shows how women took part in Jacksonian-era politics in ways other than voting.

Websites

Samuel J. May Anti-Slavery Collection: http://dlxs.library.cornell.edu/m/mayantislavery/

Women and Social Movements in the United States, 1600–2000: http://asp6new.alexanderstreet.com/wam2/wam2.index.map.aspx

CHAPTER 13: A HOUSE DIVIDED, 1840–1861
Books

Cronon, William. *Nature's Metropolis: Chicago and the Great West* (1992). An influential account of the rise of Chicago and the city's relationship to its agricultural hinterland.

Dean, Adam W. *An Agrarian Republic: Farming, Antislavery Politics, and Nature Parks in the Civil War Era* (2015). Challenges the idea of the coming of the Civil War as a clash between an agricultural South and an industrialized North by stressing the agrarian origins of political antislavery.

DeLay, Brian. *War of a Thousand Deserts: Indian Raids and the U.S.-Mexican War* (2008). A history of the Mexican war that emphasizes its impact on Native Americans.

Foner, Eric. *Free Soil, Free Labor, Free Men: The Ideology of the Republican Party before the Civil War* (1970). A discussion of the basic ideas that united Republicans in the 1850s, especially their "free labor ideology."

Freeman, Joanne B. *The Field of Blood: Violence in Congress and the Road to Civil War* (2018). How fistfights, assaults, and other violence among members of Congress (of which the assault on Charles Sumner was the most prominent example, but by no means the only one) reflected and contributed to the growing divide between the sections.

Haas, Lisbeth. *Conquests and Historical Identities in California, 1769–1936* (1995). Contains a detailed description of how California's acquisition by the United States affected the state's diverse population groups.

Levine, Bruce. *Half Slave and Half Free: The Roots of the Civil War* (1992). A survey of the coming of the Civil War, stressing irreconcilable differences between North and South.

Maizlish, Stephen E. *A Strife of Tongues: The Compromise of 1850 and the Ideological Foundations of the American Civil War* (2018). A careful account of the long congressional debate over the Compromise of 1850, showing how it revealed the hardening of sectional ideologies.

Montejano, David. *Anglos and Mexicans in the Making of Texas* (1987). A history of cultural relations among the varied populations of Texas.

Potter, David M. *The Impending Crisis, 1848–1861* (1976). Still the standard account of the nation's history in the years before the Civil War.

Sinha, Manisha. *The Counterrevolution of Slavery: Politics and Ideology in Antebellum South Carolina* (2002). A detailed study of how a vigorous defense of slavery developed in South Carolina, which justified the decision for secession.

Stephanson, Anders. *Manifest Destiny: American Expansionism and the Empire of Right* (1995). Considers how the idea of an American mission to spread freedom and democracy has affected American foreign policy throughout the country's history.

Websites

Gold Rush!: www.museumca.org/goldrush/

The Mexican-American War and the Media, 1845–1858: www.history.vt.edu/MxAmWar/Index.htm

The Oregon Trail: http://oregontrail101.com

Record of Fugitives: https://exhibitions.cul.columbia.edu/exhibits/show/fugitives/record_fugitives

Uncle Tom's Cabin and American Culture: http://jefferson.village.virginia.edu/utc/

CHAPTER 14: A NEW BIRTH OF FREEDOM: THE CIVIL WAR, 1861–1865
Books

Ayers, Edward L. *In the Presence of Mine Enemies: War in the Heart of America, 1859–1863* (2003), and *The Thin Light of Freedom: The Civil War and Emancipation in the Heart of America* (2017). A two-volume study of the experiences of Americans in two counties—one in

Pennsylvania, one in Virginia—in the early years of the Civil War.

Foner, Eric. *The Fiery Trial: Abraham Lincoln and American Slavery* (2010). A study of the evolution of Lincoln's ideas and policies relating to slavery over the course of his life.

Glatthaar, Joseph T. *Forged in Battle: The Civil War Alliance of Black Soldiers and White Officers* (1990). Relates the complex experience of black Civil War soldiers and their officers.

Lawson, Melinda. *Patriot Fires: Forging a New Nationalism in the Civil War North* (2002). Considers how both public and private groups, in order to mobilize support for the war effort, promoted a new idea of American nationalism.

McCurry, Stephanie. *Confederate Reckoning: Power and Politics in the Civil War South* (2010). A pioneering study of the political mobilization of poorer white women and slaves in the Confederacy.

McPherson, James M. *Battle Cry of Freedom: The Civil War Era* (1988). The standard account of the coming of the war, its conduct, and its consequences.

Mitchell, Reid. *Civil War Soldiers* (1988). A look at the Civil War from the point of view of the experience of ordinary soldiers.

Neely, Mark E. *The Fate of Liberty: Abraham Lincoln and Civil Liberties* (1991). Explores how the Lincoln administration did and did not meet the challenge of preserving civil liberties while fighting the war.

Oakes, James. *Freedom National: The Destruction of Slavery in the United States* (2012). A careful account of the complex path to emancipation.

Richardson, Heather C. *Greatest Nation of the Earth: Republican Economic Policies during the Civil War* (1997). Considers the far-reaching impact of the economic measures adopted by the Union during the war.

Silber, Nina. *Daughters of the Union: Northern Women Fight the Civil War* (2005). Examines the participation of northern women in the war effort and how this did and did not alter their lives.

Websites

Civil War Photographs: http://memory.loc.gov/ammem /cwphtml/cwphome.html

A House Divided: America in the Age of Lincoln: www .digitalhistory.uh.edu/exhibits/ahd/index.html

The Valley of the Shadow: Two Communities in the American Civil War: http://valley.vcdh.virginia.edu

CHAPTER 15: "WHAT IS FREEDOM?": RECONSTRUCTION, 1865–1877

Books

Bottoms, D. Michael. *An Aristocracy of Color: Race and Reconstruction in California and the West, 1850–1890* (2013). A study of changing race relations, and definitions of race, in the western states.

Butchart, Ronald E. *Schooling the Freed People: Teaching, Learning, and the Struggle for Black Freedom* (2010). Relates the efforts of black and white teachers to educate the former slaves and some of the conflicts that arose over the purposes of such education.

Downs, Gregory. *Declarations of Dependence: The Long Reconstruction of Popular Politics in the South, 1861–1908* (2011). Traces the changing ways black and white southerners sought aid and protection from the government during and after the Civil War and Reconstruction.

Downs, James. *Sick from Freedom: The Deadly Consequences of Emancipation* (2012). How disease shaped the experience of freedom and how the Freedmen's Bureau and other agencies sought to cope with widespread illness among former slaves.

DuBois, Ellen C. *Feminism and Suffrage: The Emergence of an Independent Women's Movement in America, 1848–1869* (1978). Explores how the split over the exclusion of women from the Fourteenth and Fifteenth Amendments gave rise to a movement for woman suffrage no longer tied to the abolitionist tradition.

Edwards, Laura. *A Nation of Rights: A Legal History of the Civil War and Reconstruction* (2015). A careful analysis of how this era changed American law and the Constitution.

Fields, Barbara J. *Slavery and Freedom on the Middle Ground: Maryland during the Nineteenth Century* (1985). A study of slavery and emancipation in a key border state.

Foner, Eric. *Nothing but Freedom: Emancipation and Its Legacy* (1983). Includes a comparison of the emancipation experience in different parts of the Western Hemisphere.

Foner, Eric. *Reconstruction: America's Unfinished Revolution, 1863–1877* (1988). A comprehensive account of the Reconstruction era.

Hahn, Steven. *A Nation under Our Feet: Black Political Struggles in the Rural South from Slavery to the Great Migration* (2003). A detailed study of black political activism, stressing nationalist consciousness and emigration movements.

Hahn, Steven. *A Nation without Borders: The United States and Its World in an Age of Civil Wars, 1830–1910* (2016). The chapters on Reconstruction emphasize the role of the West during that period.

Litwack, Leon F. *Been in the Storm So Long: The Aftermath of Slavery* (1979). A detailed look at the immediate aftermath of the end of slavery and the variety of black and white responses to emancipation.

Parsons, Elaine F. *Ku-Klux: The Birth of the Klan during Reconstruction* (2016). Emphasizes both the Klan's terrorism and how discourse about it helped to shape politics and culture, North and South.

Rodrigue, John C. *Reconstruction in the Cane Fields: From Slavery to Free Labor in Louisiana's Sugar Parishes, 1862–1880* (2001). A study of how an often-neglected part of the South experienced the aftermath of slavery.

Websites

America's Reconstruction: People and Politics after the Civil War: www.digitalhistory.uh.edu/exhibits/reconstruction/index.html

Freedmen and Southern Society Project: www.history.umd.edu/Freedmen/

Freedmen's Bureau Online: http://www.freedmensbureau.com/

GLOSSARY

abolition Social movement of the pre–Civil War era that advocated the immediate emancipation of the slaves and their incorporation into American society as equal citizens.

Act Concerning Religion (or Maryland Toleration Act) 1649 law that granted free exercise of religion to all Christian denominations in colonial Maryland.

Adkins v. Children's Hospital 1923 Supreme Court case that reversed *Muller v. Oregon*, the 1908 case that permitted states to set maximum hours to protect working women. Justices ruled in *Adkins* that women no longer deserved special treatment because they could vote.

affirmative action Policy efforts to promote greater employment opportunities for minorities.

Agricultural Adjustment Act New Deal legislation passed in 1933 that established the Agricultural Adjustment Administration (AAA) to improve agricultural prices by limiting market supplies; declared unconstitutional in *United States v. Butler* (1936).

Albany Plan of Union A failed 1754 proposal by the seven northern colonies in anticipation of the French and Indian War, urging the unification of the colonies under one crown-appointed president.

Alien and Sedition Acts Four measures passed in 1798 during the undeclared war with France that limited the freedoms of speech and press and restricted the liberty of noncitizens.

American Anti-Slavery Society Founded in 1833, the organization that sought an immediate end to slavery and the establishment of equality for black Americans. It split in 1840 after disputes about the role of women within the organization and other issues.

American Civil Liberties Union Organization founded during World War I to protest the suppression of freedom of expression in wartime; played a major role in court cases that achieved judicial recognition of Americans' civil liberties.

American Colonization Society Organized in 1816 to encourage colonization of free blacks to Africa; West African nation of Liberia founded in 1822 to serve as a homeland for them.

American exceptionalism The belief that the United States has a special mission to serve as a refuge from tyranny, a symbol of freedom, and a model for the rest of the world.

American Federation of Labor A federation of trade unions founded in 1881, composed mostly of skilled, white, native-born workers; its long-term president was Samuel Gompers.

American Indian Movement (AIM) Movement founded in 1963 by Native Americans who were fed up with the poor conditions on Indian reservations and the federal government's unwillingness to help. In 1973, AIM led 200 Sioux in the occupation of Wounded Knee. After a ten-week standoff with the federal authorities, the government agreed to reexamine Indian treaty rights and the occupation ended.

"American standard of living" The Progressive-era idea that American workers were entitled to a wage high enough to allow them full participation in the nation's mass consumption economy.

American System Program of internal improvements and protective tariffs promoted by Speaker of the House Henry Clay in his presidential campaign of 1824; his proposals formed the core of Whig ideology in the 1830s and 1840s.

American system of manufactures A system of production that relied on the mass production of interchangeable parts that could be rapidly assembled into standardized finished products. First perfected in Connecticut by clockmaker Eli Terry and by small-arms producer Eli Whitney in the 1840s and 1850s.

Americans with Disabilities Act 1990 law that prohibited the discrimination against persons with disabilities in both hiring and promotion. It also mandated accessible entrances for public buildings.

the *Amistad* Ship that transported slaves from one port in Cuba to another, seized by the slaves in 1839. They made their way northward to the United States, where the status of the slaves became the subject of a celebrated court case; eventually most were able to return to Africa.

Anglican Church The established state church of England, formed by Henry VIII after the pope refused to annul his marriage to Catherine of Aragon.

annuity system System of yearly payments to Native American tribes by which the federal government justified and institutionalized its interference in Indian tribal affairs.

Antietam, Battle of One of the bloodiest battles of the Civil War, fought to a standoff on September 17, 1862, in western Maryland.

Anti-Federalists Opponents of the Constitution who saw it as a limitation on individual and states' rights; their demands led to the addition of a Bill of Rights to the document.

Anti-Imperialist League Coalition of anti-imperialist groups united in 1899 to protest American territorial expansion, especially in the Philippine Islands; its membership included prominent politicians, industrialists, labor leaders, and social reformers.

Appomattox Courthouse, Virginia Site of the surrender of Confederate general Robert E. Lee to Union general Ulysses S. Grant on April 9, 1865, marking the end of the Civil War.

Army-McCarthy hearings Televised U.S. Senate hearings in 1954 on Senator Joseph McCarthy's charges of disloyalty in the army; his tactics contributed to his censure by the Senate.

Arnold, Benedict A traitorous American commander who planned to sell out the American garrison at West Point to the British. His plot was discovered before it could be executed, and he joined the British army.

Articles of Confederation First frame of government for the United States; in effect from 1781 to 1788, it provided for a weak central authority and was soon replaced by the Constitution.

Atlanta Compromise Speech to the Cotton States and International Exposition in 1895 by educator Booker T. Washington, the leading black spokesman of the day; black scholar W. E. B. Du Bois gave the speech its derisive name and criticized Washington for encouraging blacks to accommodate segregation and disenfranchisement.

Atlantic slave trade The systematic importation of African slaves from their native continent across the Atlantic Ocean to the New World, largely fueled by rising demand for sugar, rice, coffee, and tobacco.

Attucks, Crispus During the Boston Massacre, the individual who was supposedly at the head of the crowd of hecklers and who baited the British troops. He was killed when the British troops fired on the crowd.

Axis powers In World War II, the nations of Germany, Italy, and Japan.

Aztec Mesoamerican people who were conquered by the Spanish under Hernan Cortes, 1519–1528.

baby boom Markedly higher birthrate in the years following World War II; led to the biggest demographic "bubble" in American history.

backcountry In colonial America, the area stretching from central Pennsylvania southward through the Shenandoah Valley of Virginia and into upland North and South Carolina.

Bacon's Rebellion Unsuccessful 1676 revolt led by planter Nathaniel Bacon against Virginia governor William Berkeley's administration because of governmental corruption and because Berkeley had failed to protect settlers from Indian raids and did not allow them to occupy Indian lands.

Balkan crisis A series of ethnic and political crises that arose following the dissolution of Yugoslavia in the 1990s. Many atrocities were committed during the conflict, and NATO, the United Nations, and the United States intervened several times.

Bank of the United States Proposed by the first secretary of the treasury, Alexander Hamilton, the bank that opened in 1791 and operated until 1811 to issue a uniform currency, make business loans, and collect tax monies. The Second Bank of the United States was chartered in 1816 but President Andrew Jackson vetoed the recharter bill in 1832.

Bank War Political struggle in the early 1830s between President Jackson and financier Nicholas Biddle over the renewing of the Second Bank's charter.

Barbary Wars The first wars fought by the United States, and the nation's first encounter with the Islamic world. The wars were fought from 1801 to 1805 against plundering pirates off the Mediterranean coast of Africa after President Thomas Jefferson's refusal to pay them tribute to protect American ships.

Bargain of 1877 Deal made by a Republican and Democratic special congressional commission to resolve the disputed presidential election of 1876; Republican Rutherford B. Hayes, who had lost the popular vote, was declared the winner in exchange for the withdrawal of federal troops from involvement in politics in the South, marking the end of Reconstruction.

Bay of Pigs Invasion U.S. mission in which the CIA, hoping to inspire a revolt against Fidel Castro, sent 1,500 Cuban exiles to invade their homeland on April 17, 1961; the mission was a spectacular failure.

the Beats A term coined by Jack Kerouac for a small group of poets and writers who railed against 1950s mainstream culture.

Bill for Establishing Religious Freedom A Virginia law, drafted by Thomas Jefferson in 1777 and enacted in 1786, that guarantees freedom of, and from, religion.

Bill of Rights First ten amendments to the U.S. Constitution, adopted in 1791 to guarantee individual rights against infringement by the federal government.

birth-control movement An offshoot of the early twentieth-century feminist movement that saw access to birth control and "voluntary motherhood" as essential to women's freedom. The birth-control movement was led by Margaret Sanger.

Black Codes Laws passed from 1865 to 1866 in southern states to restrict the rights of former slaves; to nullify the codes, Congress passed the Civil Rights Act of 1866 and the Fourteenth Amendment.

Black Legend Idea that the Spanish New World empire was more oppressive toward the Indians than other European empires; was used as a justification for English imperial expansion.

Black Lives Matter Civil rights movement sparked by a series of incidents of police brutality and lethal force against people of color.

Black Power Post-1966 rallying cry of a more militant civil rights movement.

"Bleeding Kansas" Violence between pro- and antislavery settlers in the Kansas Territory, 1856.

bonanza farms Large farms that covered thousands of acres and employed hundreds of wage laborers in the West in the late nineteenth century.

borderland A place between or near recognized borders where no group of people has complete political control or cultural dominance.

Boston Massacre Clash between British soldiers and a Boston mob, March 5, 1770, in which five colonists were killed.

Boston Tea Party The incident on December 16, 1773, in which the Sons of Liberty, dressed as Indians, dumped hundreds of chests of tea into Boston Harbor to protest the Tea Act of 1773. Under the Tea Act, the British exported to the colonies millions of pounds of cheap—but still taxed—tea, thereby undercutting the price of smuggled tea and forcing payment of the tea duty.

***bracero* program** System agreed to by Mexican and American governments in 1942 under which tens of thousands of Mexicans entered the United States to work temporarily in agricultural jobs in the Southwest; lasted until 1964 and inhibited labor organization among farm workers since *braceros* could be deported at any time.

Bretton Woods conference International meeting held in the town of Bretton Woods, New Hampshire, in 1944 in which participants agreed that the American dollar would replace the British pound as the most important international currency. The conference also created the World Bank and International Monetary Fund to promote rebuilding after World War II and to ensure that countries did not devalue their currencies.

Brown v. Board of Education 1954 U.S. Supreme Court decision that struck down racial segregation in public education and declared "separate but equal" unconstitutional.

Bull Run, first Battle of The first land engagement of the Civil War, which took place on July 21, 1861, at Manassas Junction, Virginia, and at which Union troops quickly retreated.

Bull Run, second Battle of Civil War engagement that took place one year after the first Battle of Bull Run, on August 29–30, during which Confederates captured the federal supply depot at Manassas Junction, Virginia, and forced Union troops back to Washington.

Bunker Hill, Battle of First major battle of the Revolutionary War; it actually took place at nearby Breed's Hill, Massachusetts, on June 17, 1775.

Bush Doctrine President George W. Bush's foreign policy principle wherein the United States would launch a war on terrorism.

Bush v. Gore U.S. Supreme Court case that determined the winner of the disputed 2000 presidential election.

busing The means of transporting students via buses to achieve school integration in the 1970s.

Camp David Accords Peace agreement between the leaders of Israel and Egypt, brokered by President Jimmy Carter in 1978.

captivity narratives Accounts written by colonists after their time in Indian captivity, often stressing the captive's religious convictions.

caravel A fifteenth-century European ship capable of long-distance travel.

carpetbaggers Derisive term for northern emigrants who participated in the Republican governments of the Reconstruction South.

checks and balances A systematic balance to prevent any one branch of the national government from dominating the other two.

Chinese Exclusion Act 1882 law that halted Chinese immigration to the United States.

Church of Jesus Christ of Latter-Day Saints Religious sect founded in 1830 by Joseph Smith; it was a product of the intense revivalism of the "burned-over district" of New York. Smith's successor Brigham Young led 15,000 followers to Utah in 1847 to escape persecution.

Civil Rights Act (1964) Law that outlawed discrimination in public accommodations and employment.

Civil Rights Act of 1875 The last piece of Reconstruction legislation, which outlawed racial discrimination in places of public accommodation such as hotels and theaters. Many parts of it were ruled unconstitutional by the Supreme Court in 1883.

Civil Rights Bill of 1866 Along with the Fourteenth Amendment, legislation that guaranteed the rights of citizenship to former slaves.

Civil Service Act of 1883 Law that established the Civil Service Commission and marked the end of the spoils system.

Civilian Conservation Corps (CCC) 1933 New Deal public work relief program that provided outdoor manual work for unemployed men, rebuilding infrastructure and implementing conservation programs. The program cut the unemployment rate, particularly among young men.

Cold War Term for tensions, 1945–1989, between the Soviet Union and the United States, the two major world powers after World War II.

collective bargaining The process of negotiations between an employer and a group of employees to regulate working conditions.

Columbian Exchange The transatlantic flow of goods and people that began with Columbus's voyages in 1492.

Committee of Correspondence Group organized by Samuel Adams in retaliation for the *Gaspée* incident to address American grievances, assert American rights, and form a network of rebellion.

common school Tax-supported state schools of the early nineteenth century open to all children.

Common Sense A pamphlet anonymously written by Thomas Paine in January 1776 that attacked the English principles of hereditary rule and monarchical government.

communitarianism Social reform movement of the nineteenth century driven by the belief that by establishing small communities based on common ownership of property, a less competitive and less individualistic society could be developed.

Compromise of 1850 Complex compromise devised by Senator Henry Clay that admitted California as a free state, included a stronger fugitive slave law, and delayed determination of the slave status of the New Mexico and Utah territories.

Congress of Industrial Organizations Umbrella organization of semiskilled industrial unions, formed in 1935 as the Committee for Industrial Organization and renamed in 1938.

conquistadores Spanish term for "conquerors," applied to Spanish and Portuguese soldiers who conquered lands held by indigenous peoples in central and southern America as well as the current states of Texas, New Mexico, Arizona, and California.

conservation movement A progressive reform movement focused on the preservation and sustainable management of the nation's natural resources.

Constitutional Convention Meeting in Philadelphia, May 25–September 17, 1787, of representatives from twelve colonies—excepting Rhode Island—to revise the existing Articles of Confederation; the convention soon resolved to produce an entirely new constitution.

containment General U.S. strategy in the Cold War that called for containing Soviet expansion; originally devised by U.S. diplomat George F. Kennan.

Continental army Army authorized by the Continental Congress in 1775 to fight the British; commanded by General George Washington.

Continental Congress First meeting of representatives of the colonies, held in Philadelphia in 1774 to formulate actions against British policies; in the Second Continental Congress (1775–1789), the colonial representatives conducted the war and adopted the Declaration of Independence and the Articles of Confederation.

"the contrabands" Slaves who sought refuge in Union military camps or who lived in areas of the Confederacy under Union control.

Contract with America A list of conservatives' promises in response to the supposed liberalism of the Clinton administration, that was drafted by Speaker of the House Newt Gingrich and other congressional Republicans as the GOP platform for the 1994 midterm elections. It was more a campaign tactic than a practical program; few of its proposed items ever became law.

cotton gin Invented by Eli Whitney in 1793, the machine that separated cotton seed from cotton fiber, speeding cotton processing and making profitable the cultivation of the more hardy, but difficult to clean, short-staple cotton; led directly to the dramatic nineteenth-century expansion of slavery in the South.

"Cotton is king" Phrase from Senator James Henry Hammond's speech extolling the virtues of cotton, and, implicitly, the slave system of production that led to its bounty for the South. "King Cotton" became a shorthand for Southern political and economic power.

Cotton Kingdom Cotton-producing region, relying predominantly on slave labor, that spanned from North Carolina west to Louisiana and reached as far north as southern Illinois.

counterculture "Hippie" youth culture of the 1960s, which rejected the values of the dominant culture in favor of illicit drugs, communes, free sex, and rock music.

Court packing President Franklin D. Roosevelt's failed 1937 attempt to increase the number of U.S. Supreme Court justices from nine to fifteen in order to save his Second New Deal programs from constitutional challenges.

Covenant Chain Alliance formed in the 1670s between the English and the Iroquois nations.

coverture Principle in English and American law that a married woman lost her legal identity, which became "covered" by that of her husband, who therefore controlled her person and the family's economic resources.

Coxey's Army A march on Washington organized by Jacob Coxey, an Ohio member of the People's Party. Coxey believed in abandoning the gold standard and printing enough legal tender to reinvigorate the economy. The marchers demanded that Congress create jobs and pay workers in paper currency not backed by gold.

creoles Persons born in the New World of European ancestry.

crop lien Credit extended by merchants to tenants based on their future crops; under this system, high interest rates and the uncertainties of farming often led to inescapable debts.

Cuban missile crisis Tense confrontation caused when the United States discovered Soviet offensive missile sites in Cuba in October 1962; the U.S.-Soviet confrontation was the Cold War's closest brush with nuclear war.

cult of domesticity The nineteenth-century ideology of "virtue" and "modesty" as the qualities that were essential to proper womanhood.

Culture Wars Battles over moral values that occurred throughout the 1990s. The Culture Wars touched many areas of American life—from popular culture to academia. Flashpoints included the future of the nuclear family and the teaching of evolution.

Dartmouth College v. Woodward 1819 U.S. Supreme Court case in which the Court upheld the original charter of the college against New Hampshire's attempt to alter the board of trustees; set the precedent of support of contracts against state interference.

Dawes Act Law passed in 1887 meant to encourage adoption of white norms among Indians; broke up tribal holdings into small farms for Indian families, with the remainder sold to white purchasers.

D-Day June 6, 1944, when an Allied amphibious assault landed on the Normandy coast and established a foothold in Europe, leading to the liberation of France from German occupation.

Declaration of Independence Document adopted on July 4, 1776, that made the break with Britain official; drafted by a committee of the Second Continental Congress, including principal writer Thomas Jefferson.

decolonization The process by which African and Asian colonies of European empires became independent in the years following World War II.

deindustrialization Term describing decline of manufacturing in old industrial areas in the late twentieth century as companies shifted production to low-wage centers in the South and West or in other countries.

Deism Enlightenment thought applied to religion; emphasized reason, morality, and natural law.

Democracy in America Two works, published in 1835 and 1840, by the French thinker Alexis de Tocqueville on the subject of American democracy. Tocqueville stressed the cultural nature of American democracy, and the importance and prevalence of equality in American life.

Democratic-Republican societies Organizations created in the mid-1790s by opponents of the policies of the Washington administration and supporters of the French Revolution.

Denmark Vesey's conspiracy An 1822 failed slave uprising in Charleston, South Carolina, purported to have been led by Denmark Vesey, a free black man.

deregulation Legislation of the Reagan-Clinton era that removed regulations on many industries, including finance and air travel.

détente Period of improving relations between the United States and Communist nations, particularly China and the Soviet Union, during the Nixon administration.

disenfranchisement Depriving a person or persons of the right to vote; in the United States, exclusionary policies were used to deny groups, especially African-Americans and women, their voting rights.

Dissenters Protestants who belonged to denominations outside of the established Anglican Church.

division of powers The division of political power between the state and federal governments under the U.S. Constitution (also known as federalism).

Dix, Dorothea An important figure in increasing the public's awareness of the plight of the mentally ill. After a two-year investigation of the treatment of the mentally ill in Massachusetts, she presented her findings and won the support of leading reformers. She eventually convinced twenty states to reform their treatment of the mentally ill.

Dixiecrats Lower South delegates who walked out of the 1948 Democratic national convention in protest of the party's support for civil rights legislation and later formed the States' Rights Democratic (Dixiecrat) Party, which nominated Strom Thurmond of South Carolina for president.

Dollar Diplomacy A foreign policy initiative under President William Howard Taft that promoted the spread of American influence through loans and economic investments from American banks.

Dominion of New England Consolidation into a single colony of the New England colonies—and later New York and New Jersey—by royal governor Edmund Andros in 1686; dominion reverted to individual colonial governments three years later.

"Don't ask, don't tell" President Clinton's compromise measure that allowed gay people to serve in the military incognito, as officers could no longer seek them out for dismissal but they could not openly express their identity. "Don't ask, don't tell" was ended under the Obama administration, when gay military service was allowed.

the Dorr War A movement in Rhode Island against property qualifications for voting. The movement formed an extralegal constitutional convention for the state and elected Thomas Dorr as a governor, but was quashed by federal troops dispatched by President John Tyler.

double-V Led by *the Pittsburgh Courier*, the movement that pressed for victory over fascism abroad and over racism at home. It argued that since African-Americans were risking their lives abroad, they should receive full civil rights at home.

dower rights In colonial America, the right of a widowed woman to inherit one-third of her deceased husband's property.

Dred Scott v. Sandford 1857 U.S. Supreme Court decision in which Chief Justice Roger B. Taney ruled that Congress could not prohibit slavery in the territories, on the grounds that such a prohibition would violate the Fifth Amendment rights of slaveholders, and that no black person could be a citizen of the United States.

Dust Bowl Great Plains counties where millions of tons of topsoil were blown away from parched farmland in the 1930s; massive migration of farm families followed.

Eighteenth Amendment Prohibition amendment passed in 1919 that made illegal the manufacture, sale, or transportation of alcoholic beverages; repealed in 1933.

Ellis Island Reception center in New York Harbor through which most European immigrants to America were processed from 1892 to 1954.

Emancipation Proclamation Declaration issued by President Abraham Lincoln; the preliminary proclamation on September 22, 1862, freed the slaves in areas under Confederate control as of January 1, 1863, the date of the final proclamation, which also authorized the enrollment of black soldiers into the Union army.

Embargo Act Attempt in 1807 to exert economic pressure by prohibiting all exports from the United States, instead of waging war in reaction to continued British impressment of American sailors; smugglers easily circumvented the embargo, and it was repealed two years later.

Emergency Banking Act Passed in 1933, the First New Deal measure that provided for reopening the banks under strict conditions and took the United States off the gold standard.

empire of liberty The idea, expressed by Jefferson, that the United States would not rule its new territories as colonies, but rather would eventually admit them as full member states.

enclosure movement A legal process that divided large farm fields in England that were previously collectively owned by groups of peasants into smaller, individually owned plots. The enclosure movement took place over several centuries, and resulted in eviction for many peasants.

Enforcement Acts Three laws passed in 1870 and 1871 that tried to eliminate the Ku Klux Klan by outlawing it and other such terrorist societies; the laws allowed the president to deploy the army for that purpose.

English Bill of Rights A series of laws enacted in 1689 that inscribed the rights of Englishmen into law and enumerated parliamentary powers such as taxation.

English liberty The idea that English people were entitled to certain liberties, including trial by jury, habeas corpus, and the right to face one's accuser in court. These rights meant that even the English king was subject to the rule of law.

English Toleration Act A 1690 act of Parliament that allowed all English Protestants to worship freely.

Enlightenment Revolution in thought in the eighteenth century that emphasized reason and science over the authority of traditional religion.

Equal Rights Amendment Amendment to guarantee equal rights for women, introduced in 1923 but not passed by Congress until 1972; it failed to be ratified by the states.

Era of Good Feelings Contemporary characterization of the administration of popular Republican president James Monroe, 1817–1825.

Erie Canal Most important and profitable of the canals of the 1820s and 1830s; stretched from Buffalo to Albany, New York, connecting the Great Lakes to the East Coast and making New York City the nation's largest port.

Espionage Act 1917 law that prohibited spying and interfering with the draft as well as making "false statements" that hurt the war effort.

ethnic cleansing The systematic removal of an ethnic group from a territory through violence or intimidation in order to create a homogeneous society; the term was popularized by the Yugoslav policy brutally targeting Albanian Muslims in Kosovo.

Ex parte Milligan 1866 Supreme Court case that declared it unconstitutional to bring accused persons before military tribunals where civil courts were operating.

Exposition and Protest Document written in 1828 by Vice President John C. Calhoun of South Carolina to protest the so-called Tariff of Abominations, which seemed to favor northern industry; introduced the concept of state interposition and became the basis for South Carolina's Nullification Doctrine of 1833.

Fair Deal Domestic reform proposals of the Truman administration; included civil rights legislation, national health insurance, and repeal of the Taft-Hartley Act, but only extensions of some New Deal programs were enacted.

family values Set of beliefs usually associated with conservatism that stressed the superiority of nuclear family, heterosexual marriage, and traditional gender roles.

family wage Idea that male workers should earn a wage sufficient to enable them to support their entire family without their wives having to work outside the home.

Federal Housing Administration (FHA) A government agency created during the New Deal to guarantee mortgages, allowing lenders to offer long-term (usually thirty-year) loans with low down payments (usually 10 percent of the asking price). The FHA seldom underwrote loans in racially mixed or minority neighborhoods.

Federal Trade Commission (FTC) Independent agency created by the Wilson administration that replaced the Bureau of Corporations as an even more powerful tool to combat unfair trade practices and monopolies.

federalism A system of government in which power is divided between the central government and the states.

The Federalist Collection of eighty-five essays that appeared in the New York press in 1787–1788 in support of the Constitution; written by Alexander Hamilton, James Madison, and John Jay and published under the pseudonym "Publius."

Federalists and Republicans The two increasingly coherent political parties that appeared in Congress by the mid-1790s. The Federalists, led by George Washington, John Adams, and Alexander Hamilton, favored a strong central government. The Republicans, first identified during the early nineteenth century, supported a strict interpretation of the Constitution, which they believed would safeguard individual freedoms and states' rights from the threats posed by a strong central government.

The Feminine Mystique The book widely credited with sparking second-wave feminism in the United States. Author Betty Friedan focused on college-educated women, arguing that they would find fulfillment by engaging in paid labor outside the home.

feminism Term that entered the lexicon in the early twentieth century to describe the movement for full equality for women, in political, social, and personal life.

Fifteenth Amendment Constitutional amendment ratified in 1870, which prohibited states from discriminating in voting privileges on the basis of race.

flappers Young women of the 1920s whose rebellion against prewar standards of femininity included wearing shorter dresses, bobbing their hair, dancing to jazz music, driving cars, smoking cigarettes, and indulging in illegal drinking and gambling.

Force Act 1833 legislation, sparked by the nullification crisis in South Carolina, that authorized the president's use of the army to compel states to comply with federal law.

Fordism Early twentieth-century term describing the economic system pioneered by Ford Motor Company based on high wages and mass consumption.

Fort McHenry Fort in Baltimore Harbor unsuccessfully bombarded by the British in September 1814; Francis Scott Key, a witness to the battle, was moved to write the words to "The Star-Spangled Banner."

Fort Sumter First battle of the Civil War, in which the federal fort in Charleston (South Carolina) Harbor was captured by the Confederates on April 14, 1861, after two days of shelling.

Four Freedoms Freedom of speech, freedom of worship, freedom from want, and freedom from fear, as described by President Franklin D. Roosevelt during his January 6, 1941, State of the Union address.

Fourteen Points President Woodrow Wilson's 1918 plan for peace after World War I; at the Versailles peace conference, however, he failed to incorporate all of the points into the treaty.

Fourteenth Amendment 1868 constitutional amendment that guaranteed rights of citizenship to former slaves, in words similar to those of the Civil Rights Act of 1866.

franchise The right to vote.

free blacks African-American persons not held in slavery; immediately before the Civil War, there were nearly a half million in the United States, split almost evenly between North and South.

Free Soil Party Political organization formed in 1848 to oppose slavery in the territory acquired in the Mexican War; nominated Martin Van Buren for president in 1848. By 1854 most of the party's members had joined the Republican Party.

free trade The belief that economic development arises from the exchange of goods between different countries without governmental interference.

the Freedmen's Bureau Reconstruction agency established in 1865 to protect the legal rights of former slaves and to assist with their education, jobs, health care, and landowning.

freedom petitions Arguments for liberty presented to New England's courts and legislatures in the early 1770s by enslaved African-Americans.

Freedom Rides Bus journeys challenging racial segregation in the South in 1961.

French and Indian War The last—and most important—of four colonial wars fought between England and France for control of North America east of the Mississippi River.

Fugitive Slave Act 1850 law that gave the federal government authority in cases involving runaway slaves; aroused considerable opposition in the North.

fugitive slaves Slaves who escaped from their owners.

fundamentalism Anti-modernist Protestant movement started in the early twentieth century that proclaimed the literal truth of the Bible; the name came from *The Fundamentals*, published by conservative leaders.

Gabriel's Rebellion An 1800 uprising planned by Virginian slaves to gain their freedom. The plot was led by a blacksmith named Gabriel, but was discovered and quashed.

gag rule Rule adopted by the House of Representatives in 1836 prohibiting consideration of abolitionist petitions; opposition, led by former president John Quincy Adams, succeeded in having it repealed in 1844.

Garvey, Marcus The leading spokesman for Negro Nationalism, which exalted blackness, black cultural expression, and black exclusiveness. He called upon African-Americans to liberate themselves from the surrounding white culture and create their own businesses, cultural centers, and newspapers. He was also the founder of the Universal Negro Improvement Association.

Geneva Accords A 1954 document that had promised elections to unify Vietnam and established the Seventeenth Parallel demarcation line that divided North and South Vietnam.

"gentlemen of property and standing" Well-to-do merchants who often had commercial ties to the South and resisted abolitionism, occasionally inciting violence against its adherents.

Gettysburg, Battle of Battle fought in southern Pennsylvania, July 1–3, 1863; the Confederate defeat and the simultaneous loss at Vicksburg marked the military turning point of the Civil War.

Ghost Dance A spiritual and political movement among Native Americans whose followers performed a ceremonial "ghost dance" intended to connect the living with the dead and make the Indians bulletproof in battles intended to restore their homelands.

GI Bill of Rights The 1944 legislation that provided money for education and other benefits to military personnel returning from World War II.

Gibbons v. Ogden 1824 U.S. Supreme Court decision reinforcing the "commerce clause" (the federal government's right to regulate interstate commerce) of the Constitution; Chief Justice John Marshall ruled against the State of New York's granting of steamboat monopolies.

the Gilded Age The popular but derogatory name for the period from the end of the Civil War to the turn of the century, after the title of the 1873 novel by Mark Twain and Charles Dudley Warner.

globalization Term that became prominent in the 1990s to describe the rapid acceleration of international flows of commerce, financial resources, labor, and cultural products.

Glorious Revolution A coup in 1688 engineered by a small group of aristocrats that led to William of Orange taking the British throne in place of James II.

gold rush The massive migration of Americans into California territory in the late 1840s and 1850s in pursuit of gold, which was discovered there in 1848.

gold standard Policy at various points in American history by which the value of a dollar is set at a fixed price in terms of gold (in the post–World War II era, for example, $35 per ounce of gold).

Good Neighbor Policy Policy proclaimed by President Franklin D. Roosevelt in his first inaugural address in 1933 that sought improved diplomatic relations between the United States and its Latin American neighbors.

gradual emancipation A series of acts passed in state legislatures throughout the North in the years following the Revolution that freed slaves after they reached a certain age, following lengthy "apprenticeships."

grandfather clause Loophole created by southern disenfranchising legislatures of the 1890s for illiterate white males whose grandfathers had been eligible to vote before the Civil War.

Great Awakening Fervent religious revival movement in the 1720s through the 1740s that was spread throughout the colonies by ministers like New England Congregationalist Jonathan Edwards and English revivalist George Whitefield.

Great Depression Worst economic depression in American history; it was spurred by the stock market crash of 1929 and lasted until World War II.

Great League of Peace An alliance of the Iroquois tribes, originally formed sometime between 1450 and 1600, that used their combined strength to pressure Europeans to work with them in the fur trade and to wage war across what is today eastern North America.

Great Migration Large-scale migration of southern blacks during and after World War I to the North, where jobs had become available during the labor shortage of the war years.

Great Migration (1630s) The migration of approximately 21,000 English Puritans to the Massachusetts Bay Colony.

Great Railroad Strike A series of demonstrations, some violent, held nationwide in support of striking railroad workers in Martinsburg, West Virginia, who refused to work due to wage cuts.

Great Recession A period of major economic stagnation across the United States and western Europe, characterized by rising unemployment and inflation and a 37 percent decline in the stock market between March and December 1974.

Great Society Term coined by President Lyndon B. Johnson in his 1965 State of the Union address, in which he proposed legislation to address problems of voting rights, poverty, diseases, education, immigration, and the environment.

Griswold v. Connecticut Supreme Court decision that, in overturning Connecticut law prohibiting the use of contraceptives, established a constitutional right to privacy.

Guantánamo Bay A detention center at the American naval base at Guantánamo Bay, Cuba, where beginning in 2002 suspected terrorists and war prisoners were held indefinitely and tried by extrajudicial military tribunals. During his 2008 presidential campaign, Senator Barack Obama pledged to close the prison, but as of 2015 it remained open.

Gulf of Tonkin resolution Legislation passed by Congress in 1964 in reaction to supposedly unprovoked attacks on American warships off the coast of North Vietnam; it gave the president unlimited authority to defend U.S. forces and members of the Southeast Asia Treaty Organization (SEATO).

Gulf War Military action in 1991 in which an international coalition led by the United States drove Iraq from Kuwait, which it had occupied the previous year.

hacienda Large-scale farm in the Spanish New World empire worked by Indian laborers.

Haitian Revolution A slave uprising that led to the establishment of Haiti as an independent country in 1804.

Half-Way Covenant A 1662 religious compromise that allowed baptism and partial church membership to colonial New Englanders whose parents were not among the Puritan elect.

Harlem Renaissance African-American literary and artistic movement of the 1920s centered in New York City's Harlem neighborhood; writers Langston Hughes, Jean Toomer, Zora Neale Hurston, and Countee Cullen were among those active in the movement.

Harpers Ferry, Virginia Site of abolitionist John Brown's failed raid on the federal arsenal, October 16–17, 1859; Brown became a martyr to his cause after his capture and execution.

Hart-Celler Act 1965 law that eliminated the national origins quota system for immigration established by laws in 1921 and 1924; led to radical change in the origins of immigrants to the United States, with Asians and Latin Americans outnumbering Europeans.

Hartford Convention Meeting of New England Federalists on December 15, 1814, to protest the War of 1812; proposed seven constitutional amendments (limiting embargoes and changing requirements for officeholding, declaration of war, and admission of new states), but the war ended before Congress could respond.

Haymarket Affair Violence during an anarchist protest at Haymarket Square in Chicago on May 4, 1886; the deaths of eight, including seven policemen, led to the trial of eight anarchist leaders for conspiracy to commit murder.

Haynes, Lemuel A black member of the Massachusetts militia and celebrated minister who urged that Americans extend their conception of freedom to enslaved Africans during the Revolutionary era.

headright system A land-grant policy that promised fifty acres to any colonist who could afford passage to Virginia, as well as fifty more for any accompanying servants. The headright policy was eventually expanded to include any colonists—and was also adopted in other colonies.

Helsinki Accords 1975 agreement between the USSR and the United States that recognized the post–World War II boundaries of Europe and guaranteed the basic liberties of each nation's citizens.

Hessians German soldiers, most from Hesse-Cassel principality (hence, the name), paid to fight for the British in the Revolutionary War.

Hollywood Ten A group called before the House Un-American Activities Committee who refused to speak about their political leanings or "name names"—that is, identify communists in Hollywood. Some were imprisoned as a result.

Holocaust Systematic racist attempt by the Nazis to exterminate the Jews of Europe, resulting in the murder of over 6 million Jews and more than a million other "undesirables."

Homestead Act 1862 law that authorized Congress to grant 160 acres of public land to a western settler, who had to live on the land for five years to establish title.

horizontal expansion The process by which a corporation acquires or merges with its competitors.

House of Burgesses The first elected assembly in colonial America, established in 1619 in Virginia. Only wealthy landowners could vote in its elections.

House Un-American Activities Committee (HUAC) Committee formed in 1938 to investigate subversives in the government and holders of radical ideas more generally; best-known investigations were of Hollywood notables and of former State Department official Alger Hiss, who was accused in 1948 of espionage and Communist Party membership. Abolished in 1975.

Hundred Days Extraordinarily productive first three months of President Franklin D. Roosevelt's administration in which a special session of Congress enacted fifteen of his New Deal proposals.

Hurricane Katrina 2005 hurricane that devastated much of the Gulf Coast, especially New Orleans. The Bush administration's response was widely criticized as inadequate.

illegal alien A new category established by the Immigration Act of 1924 that referred to immigrants crossing U.S. borders in excess of the new immigration quotas.

Immigration Restriction League A political organization founded in 1894 that called for reducing immigration to the United States by requiring a literacy test for immigrants.

impeachment Bringing charges against a public official; for example, the House of Representatives can impeach a president for "treason, bribery, or other high crimes and misdemeanors" by majority vote, and after the trial the Senate can remove the president by a vote of two-thirds. Two presidents, Andrew Johnson and Bill Clinton, have been impeached and tried before the Senate; neither was convicted.

impressment The British navy's practice of using press-gangs to kidnap men in British and colonial ports who were then forced to serve in the British navy.

"In God We Trust" Phrase placed on all new U.S. currency as of 1954.

indentured servants Settlers who signed on for a temporary period of servitude to a master in exchange for passage to the New World; Virginia and Pennsylvania were largely peopled in the seventeenth and eighteenth centuries by English and German indentured servants.

Indian New Deal Phrase that refers to the reforms implemented for Native Americans during the New Deal era. John Collier, the commissioner of the Bureau of Indian Affairs (BIA), increased the access Native Americans had to relief programs and employed more Native Americans at the BIA. He worked to pass the Indian Reorganization Act. However, the version of the act passed by Congress was a much diluted version of Collier's original proposal and did not greatly improve the lives of Native Americans.

Indian Removal Act 1830 law signed by President Andrew Jackson that permitted the negotiation of treaties to obtain the Indians' lands in exchange for their relocation to what would become Oklahoma.

individualism Term that entered the language in the 1820s to describe the increasing emphasis on the pursuit of personal advancement and private fulfillment free of outside interference.

Industrial Workers of the World Radical union organized in Chicago in 1905 and nicknamed the Wobblies; its opposition to World War I led to its destruction by the federal government under the Espionage Act.

inflation An economic condition in which prices rise continuously.

initiative A Progressive-era reform that allowed citizens to propose and vote on laws, bypassing state legislatures.

Insular Cases Series of cases between 1901 and 1904 in which the Supreme Court ruled that constitutional protection of individual rights did not fully apply to residents of "insular" territories acquired by the United States in the Spanish-American War, such as Puerto Rico and the Philippines.

Interstate Commerce Commission Organization established by Congress, in reaction to the U.S. Supreme Court's ruling in *Wabash Railroad v. Illinois* (1886), in order to curb abuses in the railroad industry by regulating rates.

interstate highway system National network of interstate superhighways; its construction began in the late 1950s for the purpose of commerce and defense. The interstate highways would enable the rapid movement of military convoys and the evacuation of cities after a nuclear attack.

Intolerable Acts Four parliamentary measures in reaction to the Boston Tea Party that forced payment for the tea, disallowed colonial trials of British soldiers, forced their quartering in private homes, and reduced the number of elected officials in Massachusetts.

Iran-Contra Affair Scandal of the second Reagan administration involving sales of arms to Iran in partial exchange for release of hostages in Lebanon and use of the arms money to aid the Contras in Nicaragua, which had been expressly forbidden by Congress.

Iraq War Military campaign in 2003 in which the United States, unable to gain approval by the United Nations, unilaterally occupied Iraq and removed dictator Saddam Hussein from power.

iron curtain Term coined by Winston Churchill to describe the Cold War divide between western Europe and the Soviet Union's eastern European satellites.

ISIS An insurgency that emerged from the sectarian civil wars that destabilized Syria and post–Saddam Hussein Iraq. Beginning in 2014, ISIS forces attacked towns and cities in Iraq, Syria, and Libya, systematically murdering members of ethnic and religious minorities.

isolationism The desire to avoid foreign entanglements that dominated the U.S. Congress in the 1930s; beginning in 1935, lawmakers passed a series of Neutrality Acts that banned travel on belligerents' ships and the sale of arms to countries at war.

Japanese-American internment Policy adopted by the Roosevelt administration in 1942 under which 110,000 persons of Japanese descent, most of them American citizens, were removed from the West Coast and forced to spend most of World War II in internment camps; it was the largest violation of American civil liberties in the twentieth century.

Jay's Treaty Treaty with Britain negotiated in 1794 by Chief Justice John Jay; Britain agreed to vacate forts in the Northwest Territories, and festering disagreements (border with Canada, prewar debts, shipping claims) would be settled by commission.

Kansas Exodus A migration in 1879 and 1880 by some 40,000–60,000 blacks to Kansas to escape the oppressive environment of the New South.

Kansas-Nebraska Act 1854 law sponsored by Illinois senator Stephen A. Douglas to allow settlers in newly organized territories north of the Missouri border to decide the slavery issue for themselves; fury over the resulting repeal of the Missouri Compromise of 1820 led to violence in Kansas and to the formation of the Republican Party.

"King Cotton diplomacy" An attempt during the Civil War by the South to encourage British intervention by banning cotton exports.

King Philip's War A multiyear conflict that began in 1675 with an Indian uprising against white colonists. Its end result was broadened freedoms for white New Englanders and the dispossession of the region's Indians.

Knights of Labor Founded in 1869, the first national union; lasted, under the leadership of Terence V. Powderly, only into the 1890s; supplanted by the American Federation of Labor.

Know-Nothing Party Nativist, anti-Catholic third party organized in 1854 in reaction to large-scale German and Irish immigration; the party's only presidential candidate was Millard Fillmore in 1856.

Korean War Conflict touched off in 1950 when Communist North Korea invaded South Korea; fighting, largely by U.S. forces, continued until 1953.

Korematsu v. United States 1944 Supreme Court case that found Executive Order 9066 to be constitutional. Fred Korematsu, an American-born citizen of Japanese descent, defied the military order that banned all persons of Japanese ancestry from designated western coastal areas. The Court upheld Korematsu's arrest and internment.

Ku Klux Klan Group organized in Pulaski, Tennessee, in 1866 to terrorize former slaves who voted and held political offices during Reconstruction; a revived organization in the 1910s and 1920s that stressed white, Anglo-Saxon, fundamentalist Protestant supremacy; revived a third time to fight the civil rights movement of the 1950s and 1960s in the South.

Las Casas, Bartolomé de A Catholic missionary who renounced the Spanish practice of coercively converting Indians and advocated their better treatment. In 1552, he wrote *A Brief Relation of the Destruction of the Indies*, which described the Spanish's cruel treatment of the Indians.

League of Nations Organization of nations to mediate disputes and avoid war, established after World War I as part of the Treaty of Versailles; President Woodrow Wilson's "Fourteen Points" speech to Congress in 1918 proposed the formation of the league, which the United States never joined.

League of United Latin American Citizens Often called LULAC, an organization that challenged restrictive housing, employment discrimination, and other inequalities faced by Latino Americans.

Lend-Lease Act 1941 law that permitted the United States to lend or lease arms and other supplies to the Allies, signifying increasing likelihood of American involvement in World War II.

Levittown Low-cost, mass-produced developments of suburban tract housing built by William Levitt after World War II on Long Island and elsewhere.

Lewis and Clark expedition Led by Meriwether Lewis and William Clark, a mission to the Pacific coast commissioned for the purposes of scientific and geographical exploration.

Lexington and Concord, Battles of The first shots fired in the Revolutionary War, on April 19, 1775, near Boston; approximately 100 minutemen and 250 British soldiers were killed.

liberal internationalism Woodrow Wilson's foreign policy theory, which rested on the idea that economic and political freedom went hand in hand, and encouraged American intervention abroad in order to secure these freedoms globally.

liberalism Originally, political philosophy that emphasized the protection of liberty by limiting the power of government to interfere with the natural rights of citizens; in the twentieth century, belief in an activist government promoting greater social and economic equality.

liberty of contract A judicial concept of the late nineteenth and early twentieth centuries whereby the courts overturned laws regulating labor conditions as violations of the economic freedom of both employers and employees.

Liberty Party Abolitionist political party that nominated James G. Birney for president in 1840 and 1844; merged with the Free Soil Party in 1848.

Lincoln-Douglas debates Series of senatorial campaign debates in 1858 focusing on the issue of slavery in the territories; held in Illinois between Republican Abraham Lincoln, who made a national reputation for himself, and incumbent Democratic senator Stephen A. Douglas, who managed to hold on to his seat.

the Little Bighorn, Battle of Most famous battle of the Great Sioux War; took place in 1876 in the Montana Territory; combined Sioux and Cheyenne warriors massacred a vastly outnumbered U.S. Cavalry commanded by Lieutenant Colonel George Armstrong Custer.

Long Telegram A telegram by American diplomat George Kennan in 1946 outlining his views of the Soviet Union that eventually inspired the policy of containment.

Lord Dunmore's proclamation A proclamation issued in 1775 by the earl of Dunmore, the British governor of Virginia, that offered freedom to any slave who fought for the king against the rebelling colonists.

Lords of Trade An English regulatory board established to oversee colonial affairs in 1675.

the Lost Cause A romanticized view of slavery, the Old South, and the Confederacy that arose in the decades following the Civil War.

Louisiana Purchase President Thomas Jefferson's 1803 purchase from France of the important port of New Orleans and 828,000 square miles west of the Mississippi River to the Rocky Mountains; it more than doubled the territory of the United States at a cost of only $15 million.

Loyalists Colonists who remained loyal to Great Britain during the War of Independence.

Lusitania British passenger liner sunk by a German U-boat, May 7, 1915, creating a diplomatic crisis and public outrage at the loss of 128 Americans (roughly 10 percent of the total aboard); Germany agreed to pay reparations, and the United States waited two more years to enter World War I.

lynching Practice, particularly widespread in the South between 1890 and 1940, in which persons (usually black) accused of a crime were murdered by mobs before standing trial. Lynchings often took place before large crowds, with law enforcement authorities not intervening.

Manhattan Project Secret American program during World War II to develop an atomic bomb; J. Robert Oppenheimer led the team of physicists at Los Alamos, New Mexico.

manifest destiny Phrase first used in 1845 to urge annexation of Texas; used thereafter to encourage American settlement of European colonial and Indian lands in the Great Plains and the West and, more generally, as a justification for American empire.

Marbury v. Madison First U.S. Supreme Court decision to declare a federal law—the Judiciary Act of 1801—unconstitutional.

March for Our Lives Student-led protest on March 24, 2018, against gun violence and for gun control legislation in the United States.

March on Washington Civil rights demonstration on August 28, 1963, where the Reverend Martin Luther King Jr. gave his "I Have a Dream" speech on the steps of the Lincoln Memorial.

Marshall Plan U.S. program for the reconstruction of post–World War II Europe through massive aid to former enemy nations as well as allies; proposed by General George C. Marshall in 1947.

massive retaliation Strategy that used the threat of nuclear warfare as a means of combating the global spread of communism.

maternalist reforms Progressive-era reforms that sought to encourage women's child-bearing and -rearing abilities and to promote their economic independence.

Mayflower Compact Document signed in 1620 aboard the *Mayflower* before the Pilgrims landed at Plymouth; the document committed the group to majority-rule government.

McCarran-Walter Act Immigration legislation passed in 1952 that allowed the government to deport immigrants who had been identified as communists, regardless of whether they were citizens.

McCarthyism Post–World War II Red Scare focused on the fear of Communists in U.S. government positions; peaked during the Korean War; most closely associated with Joseph McCarthy, a major instigator of the hysteria.

McCulloch v. Maryland 1819 U.S. Supreme Court decision in which Chief Justice John Marshall, holding that Maryland could not tax the Second Bank of the United States, supported the authority of the federal government versus the states.

mercantilism Policy of Great Britain and other imperial powers of regulating the economies of colonies to benefit the mother country.

mestizos Spanish word for persons of mixed Native American and European ancestry.

Metacom The chief of the Wampanoags, whom the colonists called King Philip. He resented English efforts to convert Indians to Christianity and waged a war against the English colonists, one in which he was killed.

métis Children of marriages between Indian women and French traders and officials.

Me Too movement Social movement founded in 2006 by Tarana Burke to help survivors of sexual violence and oppose sexual harassment and assault, particularly in the workplace. In October 2017 it spread virally on social media with the hashtag #MeToo.

Mexican War Controversial war with Mexico for control of California and New Mexico, 1846–1848; the Treaty of Guadalupe Hidalgo fixed the border at the Rio Grande and extended the United States to the Pacific coast, annexing more than a half-million square miles of Mexican territory.

middle ground A borderland between European empires and Indian sovereignty where various native peoples and Europeans lived side by side in relative harmony.

Middle Passage The hellish and often deadly middle leg of the transatlantic "Triangular Trade" in which European ships carried manufactured goods to Africa, then transported enslaved Africans to the Americas and the Caribbean, and finally conveyed American agricultural products back to Europe; from the late sixteenth to the early nineteenth century, some 12 million Africans were transported via the Middle Passage, unknown millions more dying en route.

military-industrial complex The concept of "an immense military establishment" combined with a "permanent arms industry," which President Eisenhower warned against in his 1961 Farewell Address.

mill girls Women who worked at textile mills during the Industrial Revolution who enjoyed new freedoms and independence not seen before.

missile gap The claim, raised by John F. Kennedy during his campaign for president in 1960, that the Soviet Union had developed a technological and military advantage during Eisenhower's presidency.

Missouri Compromise Deal proposed by Kentucky senator Henry Clay in 1820 to resolve the slave/free imbalance in Congress that would result from Missouri's admission as a slave state; Maine's admission as a free state offset Missouri, and slavery was prohibited in the remainder of the Louisiana Territory north of the southern border of Missouri.

Monroe Doctrine President James Monroe's declaration to Congress on December 2, 1823, that the American continents would be thenceforth closed to European colonization, and that the United States would not interfere in European affairs.

Montgomery bus boycott Sparked by Rosa Parks's arrest on December 1, 1955, for refusing to surrender her seat to a white passenger, a successful yearlong boycott protesting segregation on city buses; led by the Reverend Martin Luther King Jr.

moral imperialism The Wilsonian belief that U.S. foreign policy should be guided by morality, and should teach other peoples about democracy. Wilson used this belief to both repudiate Dollar Diplomacy and justify frequent military interventions in Latin America.

moral suasion The abolitionist strategy that sought to end slavery by persuading both slaveowners and complicit northerners that the institution was evil.

muckraking Writing that exposed corruption and abuses in politics, business, meatpacking, child labor, and more, primarily in the first decade of the twentieth century; included popular books and magazine articles that spurred public interest in reform.

Muller v. Oregon 1908 Supreme Court decision that held that state interest in protecting women could override liberty of contract. Louis D. Brandeis, with help from his sister-in-law Josephine Goldmark of the National Consumers League, filed a brief in *Muller* that used statistics about women's health to argue for their protection.

multiculturalism Term that became prominent in the 1990s to describe a growing emphasis on group racial and ethnic identity and demands that jobs, education, and politics reflect the increasingly diverse nature of American society.

Murray, Judith Sargent A writer and early feminist thinker prominent in the years following the American Revolution.

My Lai massacre Massacre of 347 Vietnamese civilians in the village of My Lai by Lieutenant William Calley and troops under his command. U.S. army officers covered up the massacre for a year until an investigation uncovered the events. Eventually twenty-five army officers were charged with complicity in the massacre and its cover-up, but only Calley was convicted. He served little time for his crimes.

Nat Turner's Rebellion Most important slave uprising in nineteenth-century America, led by a slave preacher who, with his followers, killed about sixty white persons in Southampton County, Virginia, in 1831.

National Association for the Advancement of Colored People Founded in 1910, the civil rights organization that brought lawsuits against discriminatory practices and published *The Crisis*, a journal edited by African-American scholar W. E. B. Du Bois.

National Defense Education Act 1958 law passed in reaction to America's perceived inferiority in the space race; encouraged education in science and modern languages through student loans, university research grants, and aid to public schools.

National Industrial Recovery Act 1933 law passed on the last of the Hundred Days; it created public-works jobs through the Federal Emergency Relief Administration and established a system of self-regulation for industry through the National Recovery Administration, which was ruled unconstitutional in 1935.

National Organization for Women Organization founded in 1966 by writer Betty Friedan and other feminists; it pushed for abortion rights, nondiscrimination in the workplace, and other forms of equality for women.

National Recovery Administration (NRA) Controversial federal agency created in 1933 that brought together business and labor leaders to create "codes of fair competition" and "fair labor" policies, including a national minimum wage.

nativism Anti-immigrant and anti-Catholic feeling especially prominent from the 1830s through the 1850s; the largest group of its proponents was New York's Order of the Star-Spangled Banner, which expanded into the American (Know-Nothing) Party in 1854.

Navajo's Long Walk The forced removal of 8,000 Navajos from their lands by Union forces to a reservation in the 1860s.

Navigation Act Law passed by the English Parliament to control colonial trade and bolster the mercantile system, 1650–1775; enforcement of the act led to growing resentment by colonists.

neoconservatives The leaders of the conservative insurgency of the early 1980s. Their brand of conservatism was personified in Ronald Reagan, who believed in less government, supply-side economics, and "family values."

Neolin A Native American religious prophet who, by preaching pan-Indian unity and rejection of European technology and commerce, helped inspire Pontiac's Rebellion.

Neutrality Acts Series of laws passed between 1935 and 1939 to keep the United States from becoming involved in war by prohibiting American trade and travel to warring nations.

New Deal Franklin D. Roosevelt's campaign promise, in his speech to the Democratic National Convention of 1932, to combat the Great Depression with a "new deal for the American people"; the phrase became a catchword for his ambitious plan of economic programs.

new feminism A new aspect of the women's rights movement that arose in the early part of the twentieth century. New feminism added a focus on individual and sexual freedom to the movement, and introduced the word "feminism" into American life.

New Freedom Democrat Woodrow Wilson's political slogan in the presidential campaign of 1912; Wilson wanted to improve the banking system, lower tariffs, and, by breaking up monopolies, give small businesses freedom to compete.

New Harmony Community founded in Indiana by British industrialist Robert Owen in 1825; the short-lived New Harmony Community of Equality was one of the few nineteenth-century communal experiments not based on religious ideology.

new immigrants Wave of newcomers from southern and eastern Europe, including many Jews, who became a majority among immigrants to America after 1890.

New Jersey Plan New Jersey's delegation to the Constitutional Convention's plan for one legislative body with equal representation for each state.

New Left Radical youth protest movement of the 1960s, named by leader Tom Hayden to distinguish it from the Old (Marxist-Leninist) Left of the 1930s.

New Nationalism Platform of the Progressive Party and slogan of former president Theodore Roosevelt in the presidential campaign of 1912; stressed government activism, including regulation of trusts, conservation, and recall of state court decisions that had nullified progressive programs.

New Negro Term used in the 1920s, in reference to a slow and steady growth of black political influence that occurred in northern cities, where African-Americans were freer to speak and act. This political activity created a spirit of protest that expressed itself culturally in the Harlem Renaissance and politically in "new Negro" nationalism.

New Orleans, Battle of Last battle of the War of 1812, fought on January 8, 1815, weeks after the peace treaty was signed but prior to the news' reaching America; General Andrew Jackson led the victorious American troops.

New South *Atlanta Constitution* editor Henry W. Grady's 1886 term for the prosperous post–Civil War South he envisioned: democratic, industrial, urban, and free of nostalgia for the defeated plantation South.

new world order President George H. W. Bush's term for the post–Cold War world.

Ninety-Five Theses The list of moral grievances against the Catholic Church by Martin Luther, a German priest, in 1517.

"No taxation without representation" The rallying cry of opponents to the 1765 Stamp Act. The slogan decried the colonists' lack of representation in Parliament.

North American Free Trade Agreement (NAFTA) Approved in 1993, the agreement with Canada and Mexico that allowed goods to travel across their borders free of tariffs. Critics of the agreement argued that American workers would lose their jobs to cheaper Mexican labor.

North Atlantic Treaty Organization (NATO) Alliance founded in 1949 by ten western European nations, the United States, and Canada to deter Soviet expansion in Europe.

Northwest Ordinance of 1787 Law that created the Northwest Territory (area north of the Ohio River and west of Pennsylvania), established conditions for self-government and statehood, included a Bill of Rights, and permanently prohibited slavery.

Notes on the State of Virginia Thomas Jefferson's 1785 book that claimed, among other things, that black people were incapable of becoming citizens and living in harmony alongside white people due to the legacy of slavery and what Jefferson believed were the "real distinctions that nature has made" between races.

NSC-68 Top-secret policy paper approved by President Truman in 1950 that outlined a militaristic approach to combating the spread of global communism.

nullification crisis The 1832 attempt by the State of South Carolina to nullify, or invalidate within its borders, the 1832 federal tariff law. President Jackson responded with the Force Act of 1833.

Obergefell v. Hodges 2015 Supreme Court decision that allowed same-sex couples to marry throughout the United States.

Occupy Wall Street A grassroots movement in 2011 against growing economic inequality, declining opportunity, and the depredations of Wall Street banks.

oil embargo Prohibition on trade in oil declared by the Organization of Petroleum Exporting Countries, dominated by Middle Eastern producers, in October 1973 in response to U.S. and western European support for Israel in the 1973 Yom Kippur War. The rise in gas prices and fuel shortages resulted in a global economic recession and profoundly affected the American economy.

Oneida Utopian community founded in 1848; the Perfectionist religious group practiced "complex marriage" under leader John Humphrey Noyes.

Open Door Policy Demand in 1899 by Secretary of State John Hay, in hopes of protecting the Chinese market for U.S. exports, that Chinese trade be open to all nations.

Operation Dixie CIO's largely ineffective post–World War II campaign to unionize southern workers.

Ordinance of 1784 A law drafted by Thomas Jefferson that regulated land ownership and defined the terms by which western land would be marketed and settled; it established stages of self-government for the West. First Congress would govern a territory; then the territory would be admitted to the Union as a full state.

Ordinance of 1785 A law that regulated land sales in the Old Northwest. The land surveyed was divided into 640-acre plots and sold at $1 per acre.

Panama Canal Zone The small strip of land on either side of the Panama Canal. The Canal Zone was under U.S. control from 1903 to 1979 as a result of Theodore Roosevelt's assistance in engineering a coup in Colombia that established Panama's independence.

Panic of 1819 Financial collapse brought on by sharply falling cotton prices, declining demand for American exports, and reckless western land speculation.

Panic of 1837 Beginning of major economic depression lasting about six years; touched off by a British financial crisis and made worse by falling cotton prices, credit and currency problems, and speculation in land, canals, and railroads.

Paris Agreement 2016 agreement within the United Nations Framework Convention on Climate Change, concerned with mitigating greenhouse gas emissions.

paternalism A moral position developed during the first half of the nineteenth century that claimed that slaves were deprived of liberty for their own "good." Such a rationalization was adopted by some slaveowners to justify slavery.

the "peculiar institution" A phrase used by whites in the antebellum South to refer to slavery without using the word "slavery."

Pentagon Papers Informal name for the Defense Department's secret history of the Vietnam conflict; leaked to the press by former official Daniel Ellsberg and published in the *New York Times* in 1971.

Pequot War An armed conflict in 1637 that led to the destruction of one of New England's most powerful Indian groups.

perfectionism The idea that social ills once considered incurable could in fact be eliminated, popularized by the religious revivalism of the nineteenth century.

Perry, Commodore Matthew U.S. naval officer who negotiated the Treaty of Kanagawa in 1854. That treaty was the first step in starting a political and commercial relationship between the United States and Japan.

pet banks Local banks that received deposits while the charter of the Bank of the United States was about to expire in 1836. The choice of these banks was influenced by political and personal connections.

Philippine War American military campaign that suppressed the movement for Philippine independence after the Spanish-American War; America's death toll was over 4,000, and the Philippines' was far higher.

Pilgrims Puritan separatists who broke completely with the Church of England and sailed to the New World aboard the *Mayflower*, founding Plymouth Colony on Cape Cod in 1620.

plantation An early word for a colony, a settlement "planted" from abroad among an alien population in Ireland or the New World. Later, a large agricultural enterprise that used unfree labor to produce a crop for the world market.

Platt Amendment 1901 amendment to the Cuban constitution that reserved the United States' right to intervene in Cuban affairs and forced newly independent Cuba to host American naval bases on the island.

Plessy v. Ferguson U.S. Supreme Court decision supporting the legality of Jim Crow laws that permitted or required "separate but equal" facilities for blacks and whites.

Pontiac's Rebellion An Indian attack on British forts and settlements after France ceded to the British its territory east of the Mississippi River, as part of the Treaty of Paris in 1763, without consulting France's Indian allies.

Popular Front A period during the mid-1930s when the Communist Party sought to ally itself with socialists and New Dealers in movements for social change, urging reform of the capitalist system rather than revolution.

popular sovereignty Program that allowed settlers in a disputed territory to decide the slavery issue for themselves; most closely associated with Senator Stephen A. Douglas of Illinois.

Populists Founded in 1892, a group that advocated a variety of reform issues, including free coinage of silver, income tax, postal savings, regulation of railroads, and direct election of U.S. senators.

Porkopolis Nickname of Cincinnati, coined in the mid-nineteenth century, after its numerous slaughter houses.

Port Huron Statement A manifesto by Students for a Democratic Society that criticized institutions ranging from political parties to corporations, unions, and the military-industrial complex, while offering a new vision of social change.

Potsdam conference Last meeting of the major Allied powers; the conference that took place outside Berlin from July 17 to August 2, 1945, at which U.S. president Harry Truman, Soviet dictator Joseph Stalin, and British prime minister Clement Attlee finalized plans begun at Yalta.

Proclamation of 1763 Royal directive issued after the French and Indian War prohibiting settlement, surveys, and land grants west of the Appalachian Mountains; caused considerable resentment among colonists hoping to move west.

Progressive Party Political party created when former president Theodore Roosevelt broke away from the Republican Party to run for president again in 1912; the party supported progressive reforms similar to those of the Democrats but stopped short of seeking to eliminate trusts. Also the name of the party backing Robert La Follette for president in 1924.

Progressivism Broad-based reform movement, 1900–1917, that sought governmental action in solving problems in many areas of American life, including education, public health, the economy, the environment, labor, transportation, and politics.

proslavery argument The series of arguments defending the institution of slavery in the South as a positive good, not a necessary evil. The arguments included the racist belief that black people were inherently inferior to white people, as well as the belief that slavery, in creating a permanent underclass of laborers, made freedom possible for whites. Other elements of the argument included biblical citations.

Public Works Administration A New Deal agency that contracted with private construction companies to build roads, bridges, schools, hospitals, and other public facilities.

Pueblo Revolt Uprising in 1680 in which Pueblo Indians temporarily drove Spanish colonists out of modern-day New Mexico.

Pure Food and Drug Act Passed in 1906, the first law to regulate manufacturing of food and medicines; prohibited dangerous additives and inaccurate labeling.

Puritans English religious group that sought to purify the Church of England; founded the Massachusetts Bay Colony under John Winthrop in 1630.

Radical Republicans Group within the Republican Party in the 1850s and 1860s that advocated strong resistance to the expansion of slavery, opposition to compromise with the South in the secession crisis of 1860–1861, emancipation and arming of black soldiers during the Civil War, and equal civil and political rights for blacks during Reconstruction.

Reagan Revolution The rightward turn of American politics following the 1980 election of Ronald Reagan. The Reagan Revolution made individual "freedom" a rallying cry for the right.

Reaganomics Popular name for President Ronald Reagan's philosophy of "supply side" economics, which combined tax cuts with an unregulated marketplace.

recall A Progressive-era reform that allowed the removal of public officials by popular vote.

reconquista The "reconquest" of Spain from the Moors completed by King Ferdinand and Queen Isabella in 1492.

Reconstruction Act 1867 law that established temporary military governments in ten Confederate states—excepting Tennessee—and required that the states ratify the Fourteenth Amendment and permit freedmen to vote.

Reconstruction Finance Corporation Federal program established in 1932 under President Herbert Hoover to loan money to banks and other institutions to help them avert bankruptcy.

Red Scare of 1919–1920 Fear among many Americans after World War I of Communists in particular and noncitizens in general, a reaction to the Russian Revolution, mail bombs, strikes, and riots.

Redeemers Post–Civil War Democratic leaders who supposedly saved the South from Yankee domination and preserved the primarily rural economy.

redemptioners Indentured families or persons who received passage to the New World in exchange for a promise to work off their debt in America.

referendum A Progressive-era reform that allowed public policies to be submitted to popular vote.

Regulators Groups of backcountry Carolina settlers who protested colonial policies.

repartimiento **system** Spanish labor system under which Indians were legally free and able to earn wages but were also required to perform a fixed amount of labor yearly. Replaced the *encomienda* system.

republic Representative political system in which citizens govern themselves by electing representatives, or legislators, to make key decisions on the citizens' behalf.

republican motherhood The ideology that emerged as a result of American independence where women played an indispensable role by training future citizens.

republicanism Political theory in eighteenth-century England and America that celebrated active participation in public life by economically independent citizens as central to freedom.

reverse discrimination Belief that affirmative action programs discriminate against white people.

Revolution of 1800 First time that an American political party surrendered power to the opposition party; Jefferson, a Republican, had defeated incumbent Adams, a Federalist, for president.

Roanoke colony English expedition of 117 settlers, including Virginia Dare, the first English child born in the New World; the colony disappeared from Roanoke Island in the Outer Banks sometime between 1587 and 1590.

robber barons Also known as "captains of industry"; Gilded-Age industrial figures who inspired both admiration, for their economic leadership and innovation, and hostility and fear, due to their unscrupulous business methods, repressive labor practices, and unprecedented economic control over entire industries.

Roe v. Wade 1973 U.S. Supreme Court decision requiring states to permit first-trimester abortions.

Roosevelt Corollary 1904 announcement by President Theodore Roosevelt, essentially a corollary to the Monroe Doctrine, that the United States could intervene militarily to prevent interference from European powers in the Western Hemisphere.

Rwandan genocide 1994 genocide conducted by the Hutu ethnic group upon the Tutsi minority in Rwanda.

Sacco-Vanzetti case A case held during the 1920s in which two Italian-American anarchists were found guilty and executed for a crime in which there was very little evidence linking them to the particular crime.

Salem witch trials A crisis of trials and executions in Salem, Massachusetts, in 1692 that resulted from anxiety over witchcraft.

salutary neglect Informal British policy during the first half of the eighteenth century that allowed the American colonies considerable freedom to pursue their economic and political interests in exchange for colonial obedience.

Sanitary Fairs Fund-raising bazaars led by women on behalf of Civil War soldiers. The fairs offered items such as uniforms and banners, as well as other emblems of war.

Santa Anna, Antonio López de The military leader who, in 1834, seized political power in Mexico and became a dictator. In 1835, Texans rebelled against him, and he led his army to Texas to crush their rebellion. He captured the missionary called the Alamo and killed all of its defenders, which inspired Texans to continue their resistance and Americans to volunteer to fight for Texas. The Texans captured Santa Anna during a surprise attack, and he bought his freedom by signing a treaty recognizing Texas's independence.

Saratoga, Battle of Major defeat of British general John Burgoyne and more than 5,000 British troops at Saratoga, New York, on October 17, 1777.

scalawags Southern white Republicans—some former Unionists—who supported Reconstruction governments.

Schenck v. United States 1919 U.S. Supreme Court decision upholding the wartime Espionage and Sedition Acts; in the opinion he wrote for the case, Justice Oliver Wendell Holmes set the now-familiar "clear and present danger" standard.

scientific management Management campaign to improve worker efficiency using measurements like "time and motion" studies to achieve greater productivity; introduced by Frederick Winslow Taylor in 1911.

Scopes trial 1925 trial of John Scopes, Tennessee teacher accused of violating state law prohibiting teaching of the theory of evolution; it became a nationally celebrated confrontation between religious fundamentalism and civil liberties.

Scottsboro case Case in which nine black youths were convicted of raping two white women; in overturning the verdicts of this case, the Court established precedents in *Powell v. Alabama* (1932) that adequate counsel must be appointed in capital cases, and in *Norris v. Alabama* (1935) that African-Americans cannot be excluded from juries.

Sea Islands experiment The 1861 pre-Reconstruction social experiment that involved converting slave plantations into places where former slaves could work for wages or own land. Former slaves also received education and access to improved shelter and food.

Second American Revolution The transformation of American government and society brought about by the Civil War.

Second Great Awakening Religious revival movement of the early decades of the nineteenth century, in reaction to the growth of secularism and rationalist religion; began the predominance of the Baptist and Methodist Churches.

second Great Migration The movement of black migrants from the rural South to the cities of the North and West, which occurred from 1941 through World War II, that dwarfed the Great Migration of World War I.

Second Middle Passage The massive trade of slaves from the upper South (Virginia and the Chesapeake) to the lower South (the Gulf states) that took place between 1820 and 1860.

Sedition Act 1918 law that made it a crime to make spoken or printed statements that criticized the U.S. government or encouraged interference with the war effort.

Selective Service Act Law passed in 1917 to quickly increase enlistment in the army for the United States' entry into World War I; required men to register with the draft.

"separate but equal" Principle underlying legal racial segregation, upheld in *Plessy v. Ferguson* (1896) and struck down in *Brown v. Board of Education* (1954).

separation of powers Feature of the U.S. Constitution, sometimes called "checks and balances," in which power is divided between executive, legislative, and judicial branches of the national government so that no one can dominate the other two and endanger citizens' liberties.

Serra, Father Junípero Missionary who began and directed the California mission system in the 1770s and 1780s. Serra presided over the conversion of many Indians to Christianity, but also engaged them in forced labor.

settlement house Late-nineteenth-century movement to offer a broad array of social services in urban immigrant neighborhoods; Chicago's Hull House was one of hundreds of settlement houses that operated by the early twentieth century.

Seven Years' War The last—and most important—of four colonial wars fought between England and France for control of North America east of the Mississippi River.

Seventeenth Amendment Progressive reform passed in 1913 that required U.S. senators to be elected directly

by voters; previously, senators were chosen by state legislatures.

Shakers Religious sect founded by Mother Ann Lee in England. The United Society of Believers in Christ's Second Appearing settled in Watervliet, New York, in 1774, and subsequently established eighteen additional communes in the Northeast, Indiana, and Kentucky.

Share Our Wealth movement Program offered by Huey Long as an alternative to the New Deal. The program proposed to confiscate large personal fortunes, which would be used to guarantee every poor family a cash grant of $5,000 and every worker an annual income of $2,500. It also promised to provide pensions, reduce working hours, and pay veterans' bonuses and ensured a college education to every qualified student.

sharecropping Type of farm tenancy that developed after the Civil War in which landless workers—often former slaves—farmed land in exchange for farm supplies and a share of the crop.

Shays's Rebellion Attempt by Massachusetts farmer Daniel Shays and 1,200 compatriots, seeking debt relief through issuance of paper currency and lower taxes, to prevent courts from seizing property from indebted farmers.

Sherman Antitrust Act Passed in 1890, first law to restrict monopolistic trusts and business combinations; extended by the Clayton Antitrust Act of 1914.

Silent Spring A 1962 book by biologist Rachel Carson about the destructive impact of the widely used insecticide DDT that launched the modern environmentalist movement.

single tax Concept of taxing only landowners as a remedy for poverty, promulgated by Henry George in *Progress and Poverty* (1879).

sit-down strike Tactic adopted by labor unions in the mid- and late 1930s, whereby striking workers refused to leave factories, making production impossible; proved highly effective in the organizing drive of the Congress of Industrial Organizations.

sit-in Tactic adopted by young civil rights activists, beginning in 1960, of demanding service at lunch counters or public accommodations and refusing to leave if denied access; marked the beginning of the most militant phase of the civil rights struggle.

Sixteenth Amendment Constitutional amendment passed in 1913 that legalized the federal income tax.

Smith, John A swashbuckling soldier of fortune with rare powers of leadership and self-promotion who was appointed to the resident council to manage Jamestown.

Smoot-Hawley Tariff 1930 act that raised tariffs to an unprecedented level and worsened the Great Depression by raising prices and discouraging foreign trade.

Snowden, Edward An NSA contractor turned whistleblower, who released classified information relating to the United States' intelligence gathering both at home and abroad.

social contract Agreement hammered out between labor and management in leading industries; called a new "social contract." Unions signed long-term agreements that left decisions regarding capital investment, plant location, and output in management's hands, and they agreed to try to prevent unauthorized "wildcat" strikes.

Social Darwinism Application of Charles Darwin's theory of natural selection to society; used the concept of the "survival of the fittest" to justify class distinctions and to explain poverty.

Social Gospel Ideals preached by liberal Protestant clergymen in the late nineteenth and early twentieth centuries; advocated the application of Christian principles to social problems generated by industrialization.

Social Security Act 1935 law that created the Social Security system with provisions for a retirement pension, unemployment insurance, disability insurance, and public assistance (welfare).

Socialist Party Political party demanding public ownership of major economic enterprises in the United States as well as reforms like recognition of labor unions and woman suffrage; reached peak of influence in 1912 when presidential candidate Eugene V. Debs received over 900,000 votes.

Society of American Indians Organization founded in 1911 that brought together Native American intellectuals of many tribal backgrounds to promote discussion of the plight of Indian peoples.

Society of Friends (Quakers) Religious group in England and America whose members believed all persons possessed the "inner light" or spirit of God; they were early proponents of abolition of slavery and equal rights for women.

soft money and hard money In the 1830s, "soft money" referred to paper currency issued by banks. "Hard money" referred to gold and silver currency—also called specie.

Sons of Liberty Organization formed by Samuel Adams, John Hancock, and other radicals in response to the Stamp Act.

Sotomayor, Sonia First Supreme Court Justice of Hispanic descent. Justice Sotomayor was appointed by President Barack Obama in 2009.

Southern Christian Leadership Conference (SCLC) Civil rights organization founded in 1957 by the Reverend Martin Luther King Jr. and other civil rights leaders.

Southern Manifesto A document written in 1956 that repudiated the Supreme Court decision in *Brown v. Board of Education* and supported the campaign against racial integration in public places.

spoils system The term meaning the filling of federal government jobs with persons loyal to the party of the president; originated in Andrew Jackson's first term.

Sputnik First artificial satellite to orbit the earth; launched October 4, 1957, by the Soviet Union.

stagflation A combination of stagnant economic growth and high inflation present during the 1970s.

Stamp Act Parliament's 1765 requirement that revenue stamps be affixed to all colonial printed matter, documents, and playing cards; the Stamp Act Congress met to formulate a response, and the act was repealed the following year.

staple crops Important cash crops;—for example, cotton or tobacco.

steamboats Paddlewheelers that could travel both up- and down-river in deep or shallow waters; they became commercially viable early in the nineteenth century and soon developed into America's first inland freight and passenger service network.

stock market crash Also known as Black Tuesday, a stock market panic in 1929 that resulted in the loss of more than $10 billion in market value (worth approximately ten times more today). One among many causes of the Great Depression.

Stonewall Inn A gathering place for New York's gay community, the site of the 1969 police raids and resulting riots that launched the modern gay rights movement.

Stono Rebellion A slave uprising in 1739 in South Carolina that led to a severe tightening of the slave code and the temporary imposition of a prohibitive tax on imported slaves.

Strategic Arms Limitation Talks 1972 talks between President Nixon and Secretary Brezhnev that resulted in the Strategic Arms Limitation Treaty (or SALT), which limited the quantity of nuclear warheads each nation could possess, and prohibited the development of missile defense systems.

Student Nonviolent Coordinating Committee (SNCC) Organization founded in 1960 to coordinate civil rights sit-ins and other forms of grassroots protest.

Students for a Democratic Society (SDS) Major organization of the New Left, founded at the University of Michigan in 1960 by Tom Hayden and Al Haber.

suffrage The right to vote.

Sugar Act 1764 decision by Parliament to tax refined sugar and many other colonial products.

Sunbelt The label for an arc that stretched from the Carolinas to California. During the postwar era, much of the urban population growth occurred in this area.

Taft-Hartley Act 1947 law passed over President Harry Truman's veto; the law contained a number of provisions to weaken labor unions, including the banning of closed shops.

tariff of abominations Tariff passed in 1828 by Parliament that taxed imported goods at a very high rate; it aroused strong opposition in the South.

tariff of 1816 First true protective tariff, intended to protect certain American goods against foreign competition.

Tea Party A grassroots Republican movement that emerged in 2009 named for the Boston Tea Party of the 1770s. The Tea Party opposed the Obama administration's sweeping legislative enactments and advocated for a more stringent immigration policy.

Teapot Dome Harding administration scandal in which Secretary of the Interior Albert B. Fall profited from secret leasing to private oil companies of government oil reserves at Teapot Dome, Wyoming, and Elk Hills, California.

Tecumseh and Tenskwatawa Tecumseh—a leader of the Shawnee tribe who tried to unite all Indians into a confederation to resist white encroachment on their lands. His beliefs and leadership made him seem dangerous to the American government. He was killed at the Battle of the Thames. His brother, Tenskwatawa—a religious prophet who called for complete separation from whites, the revival of traditional Indian culture, and resistance to federal policies.

Tejanos Texas settlers of Spanish or Mexican descent.

temperance movement A widespread reform movement, led by militant Christians, focused on reducing the use of alcoholic beverages.

Tennessee Valley Authority Administrative body created in 1933 to control flooding in the Tennessee River valley, provide work for the region's unemployed, and produce inexpensive electric power for the region.

Tenochtitlán The capital city of the Aztec Empire. The city was built on marshy islands on the western side of Lake Tetzcoco, which is the site of present-day Mexico City.

Ten-Percent Plan of Reconstruction President Lincoln's proposal for reconstruction, issued in 1863, in which southern states would rejoin the Union if 10 percent of the 1860 electorate signed loyalty pledges, accepted emancipation, and had received presidential pardons.

Tenure of Office Act 1867 law that required the president to obtain Senate approval to remove any official whose appointment had also required Senate approval; President Andrew Johnson's violation of the law by firing Secretary of War Edwin Stanton led to Johnson's impeachment.

Tet offensive Surprise attack by the Viet Cong and North Vietnamese during the Vietnamese New Year of 1968; turned American public opinion strongly against the war in Vietnam.

Texas revolt The 1830s rebellion of residents of the territory of Texas—many of them American emigrants—against Mexican control of the region.

Thirteenth Amendment Constitutional amendment adopted in 1865 that irrevocably abolished slavery throughout the United States.

Three Mile Island Nuclear power plant near Harrisburg, Pennsylvania, site of a 1979 accident that released radioactive steam into the air; public reaction ended the nuclear power industry's expansion.

three-fifths clause A provision signed into the Constitution in 1787 that three-fifths of the slave population would be counted in determining each state's representation in the House of Representatives and its electoral votes for president.

Title IX Part of the Educational Amendments Act of 1972 that banned gender discrimination in higher education.

totalitarianism The term that describes aggressive, ideologically driven states that seek to subdue all of civil society to their control, thus leaving no room for individual rights or alternative values.

Townshend Acts 1767 parliamentary measures (named for the chancellor of the Exchequer) that taxed tea and other commodities, and established a Board of Customs Commissioners and colonial vice-admiralty courts.

Trail of Tears Cherokees' own term for their forced removal, 1838–1839, from the Southeast to Indian lands (later Oklahoma); of 15,000 forced to march, 4,000 died on the way.

transcendentalists Philosophy of a small group of mid-nineteenth-century New England writers and thinkers, including Ralph Waldo Emerson, Henry David Thoreau, and Margaret Fuller; they stressed personal and intellectual self-reliance.

transcontinental railroad First line across the continent from Omaha, Nebraska, to Sacramento, California, established in 1869 with the linkage of the Union Pacific and Central Pacific railroads at Promontory, Utah.

Treaty of Greenville 1795 treaty under which twelve Indian tribes ceded most of Ohio and Indiana to the federal government, and that also established the "annuity" system.

Treaty of Paris Signed on September 3, 1783, the treaty that ended the Revolutionary War, recognized American independence from Britain, established the border between Canada and the United States, fixed the western border at the Mississippi River, and ceded Florida to Spain.

Truman Doctrine President Harry S. Truman's program announced in 1947 of aid to European countries—particularly Greece and Turkey—threatened by communism.

trusts Companies combined to limit competition.

Tubman, Harriet Abolitionist who was born a slave, escaped to the North, and then returned to the South nineteen times and guided 300 slaves to freedom.

Tulsa riot A race riot in 1921—the worst in American history—that occurred in Tulsa, Oklahoma, after a group of black veterans tried to prevent a lynching. Over 300 African-Americans were killed, and 10,000 lost their homes in fires set by white mobs.

Uncle Tom's Cabin Harriet Beecher Stowe's 1852 antislavery novel that popularized the abolitionist position.

Underground Railroad Operating in the decades before the Civil War, a clandestine system of routes and safehouses through which slaves were led to freedom in the North.

United Nations Organization of nations to maintain world peace, established in 1945 and headquartered in New York.

Uprising of 1622 Unsuccessful uprising of Virginia Native Americans that wiped out one-quarter of the settler population, but ultimately led to the settlers' gaining supremacy.

urban renewal A series of policies supported by all levels of government that allowed local governments and housing authorities to demolish so-called blighted areas in urban centers to replace them with more valuable real estate usually reserved for white people.

USA Patriot Act A 2001 mammoth bill that conferred unprecedented powers on law-enforcement agencies charged with preventing domestic terrorism, including the power to wiretap, read private messages, and spy on citizens.

U.S.S. *Maine* Battleship that exploded in Havana Harbor on February 15, 1898, resulting in 266 deaths; the American public, assuming that the Spanish had mined the ship, clamored for war, and the Spanish-American War was declared two months later.

utopian communities Ideal communities that offered innovative social and economic relationships to those who were interested in achieving salvation.

V-E Day May 8, 1945, the day World War II officially ended in Europe.

Versailles Treaty The treaty signed at the Versailles peace conference after World War I that established President Woodrow Wilson's vision of an international regulating body, redrew parts of Europe and the Middle East, and assigned economically crippling war reparations to Germany, but failed to incorporate all of Wilson's Fourteen Points.

vertical integration Company's avoidance of middlemen by producing its own supplies and providing for distribution of its product.

Vicksburg, Battle of The fall of Vicksburg, Mississippi, to General Ulysses S. Grant's army on July 4, 1863, after

two months of siege; a turning point in the war because it gave the Union control of the Mississippi River.

Vietnam Syndrome The belief that the United States should be extremely cautious in deploying its military forces overseas that emerged after the end of the Vietnam War.

Virginia and Kentucky resolutions Legislation passed in 1798 and 1799 by the Virginia and the Kentucky legislatures; written by James Madison and Thomas Jefferson in response to the Alien and Sedition Acts, the resolutions advanced the state-compact theory of the Constitution. Virginia's resolution called on the federal courts to protect free speech. Jefferson's draft for Kentucky stated that a state could nullify federal law, but this was deleted.

Virginia Company A joint-stock enterprise that King James I chartered in 1606. The company was to spread Christianity in the New World as well as find ways to make a profit in it.

Virginia Plan Virginia's delegation to the Constitutional Convention's plan for a strong central government and a two-house legislature apportioned by population.

virtual representation The idea that the American colonies, although they had no actual representative in Parliament, were "virtually" represented by all members of Parliament.

Voting Rights Act Law passed in the wake of Martin Luther King Jr.'s Selma-to-Montgomery March in 1965; it authorized federal protection of the right to vote and permitted federal enforcement of minority voting rights in individual counties, mostly in the South.

Wade-Davis Bill Radical Republicans' 1864 plan for reconstruction that required loyalty oaths, abolition of slavery, repudiation of war debts, and denial of political rights to high-ranking Confederate officials; President Lincoln refused to sign the bill.

Wagner Act Law that established the National Labor Relations Board and facilitated unionization by regulating employment and bargaining practices.

Walking Purchase An infamous 1737 purchase of Indian land in which Pennsylvanian colonists tricked the

Lenni Lanape Indians. The Lanape agreed to cede land equivalent to the distance a man could walk in thirty-six hours, but the colonists marked out an area using a team of runners.

war in Afghanistan War fought against the Taliban and Al Qaeda in Afghanistan following the attacks of September 11, 2001. It remains the longest war in American history.

War Industries Board Board run by financier Bernard Baruch that planned production and allocation of war materiel, supervised purchasing, and fixed prices, 1917–1919.

War of 1812 War fought with Britain, 1812–1814, over issues that included impressment of American sailors, interference with shipping, and collusion with Northwest Territory Indians; settled by the Treaty of Ghent in 1814.

War on Poverty Plan announced by President Lyndon B. Johnson in his 1964 State of the Union address; under the Economic Opportunity Bill signed later that year, Head Start, VISTA, and the Jobs Corps were created, and programs were created for students, farmers, and businesses in efforts to eliminate poverty.

war on terrorism Global crusade to root out anti-American, anti-Western Islamist terrorist cells; launched by President George W. Bush as a response to the 9/11 attacks.

War Powers Act Law passed in 1973, reflecting growing opposition to American involvement in the Vietnam War; it required congressional approval before the president sent troops abroad.

Watergate Washington office and apartment complex that lent its name to the 1972–1974 scandal of the Nixon administration; when his knowledge of the break-in at the Watergate and subsequent cover-up were revealed, Nixon resigned the presidency under threat of impeachment.

The Wealth of Nations The 1776 work by economist Adam Smith that argued that the "invisible hand" of the free market directed economic life more effectively and fairly than governmental intervention.

Webster-Hayne debate U.S. Senate debate of January 1830 between Daniel Webster of Massachusetts and Robert Hayne of South Carolina over nullification and states' rights.

welfare state A term that originated in Britain during World War II to refer to a system of income assistance, health coverage, and social services for all citizens.

Whiskey Rebellion Violent protest by western Pennsylvania farmers against the federal excise tax on whiskey, 1794.

Wilmot Proviso Proposal to prohibit slavery in any land acquired in the Mexican War; it was defeated by southern senators, led by John C. Calhoun of South Carolina, in 1846 and 1847.

Winthrop, John Puritan leader and governor of the Massachusetts Bay Colony who resolved to use the colony as a refuge for persecuted Puritans and as an instrument of building a "wilderness Zion" in America.

woman suffrage Movement to give women the right to vote through a constitutional amendment, spearheaded by Susan B. Anthony and Elizabeth Cady Stanton's National Woman Suffrage Association.

Women's March International protest on January 21, 2017 for women's rights, LGBT rights, gender equality, and racial equality following the inauguration of President Donald Trump, and the biggest single-day protest in U.S. history.

Worcester v. Georgia 1832 Supreme Court case that held that the Indian nations were distinct peoples who could not be dealt with by the states—instead, only the federal government could negotiate with them. President Jackson refused to enforce the ruling.

Works Progress Administration (WPA) Part of the Second New Deal; it provided jobs for millions of the unemployed on construction and arts projects.

Wounded Knee massacre Last incident of the Indian Wars; it took place in 1890 in the Dakota Territory, where the U.S. Cavalry killed over 200 Sioux men, women, and children.

writs of assistance One of the colonies' main complaints against Britain; the writs allowed unlimited search warrants without cause to look for evidence of smuggling.

XYZ affair Affair in which French foreign minister Talleyrand's three anonymous agents demanded payments to stop French plundering of American ships in 1797; refusal to pay the bribe was followed by two years of undeclared sea war with France (1798–1800).

Yalta conference Meeting of Franklin D. Roosevelt, Winston Churchill, and Joseph Stalin at a Crimean resort to discuss the postwar world on February 4–11, 1945; Joseph Stalin claimed large areas in eastern Europe for Soviet domination.

Yamasee uprising Revolt of Yamasee and Creek Indians, aggravated by rising debts and slave traders' raids, against Carolina settlers. It resulted in the expulsion of many Indians to Florida.

yellow press Sensationalism in newspaper publishing that reached a peak in the circulation war between Joseph Pulitzer's *New York World* and William Randolph Hearst's *New York Journal* in the 1890s; the papers' accounts of events in Havana Harbor in 1898 led directly to the Spanish-American War.

yeoman farmers Small landowners (the majority of white families in the Old South) who farmed their own land and usually did not own slaves.

Yorktown, Battle of Last battle of the Revolutionary War; General Lord Charles Cornwallis along with over 7,000 British troops surrendered at Yorktown, Virginia, on October 17, 1781.

Zimmermann Telegram Telegram from the German foreign secretary to the German minister in Mexico, February 1917, instructing the minister to offer to recover Texas, New Mexico, and Arizona for Mexico if it would fight the United States to divert attention from Germany in the event that the United States joined the war.

zoot suit riots 1943 riots in which sailors on leave attacked Mexican-American youths.

CREDITS

PHOTOS

Front Matter: In order of appearance: Library of Congress; **(top left and right):** Granger Collection; **(bottom left):** Museum of the City of New York / Bridgeman Images; **(bottom right):** Dorothea Lange / National Archives; Photo by Erin Silber; Art Collection 4 / Alamy Stock Photo; Collection of the New-York Historical Society / Bridgeman Images; Archivart / Alamy Stock Photo; Abby Aldrich Rockefeller Folk Art Museum, museum purchase of the Friends of Colonial Williamsburg Collections Fund; Huntington Library and Art Gallery, San Marino, CA / © The Huntington Library, Art Collections & Botanical Gardens / Bridgeman Images; Collection of the New-York Historical Society / Bridgeman Images; Smithsonian American Art Museum, Washington, DC / Art Resource, NY; Gift of Constance Fuller Threinen, great-granddaughter of Margaret Fuller's brother, the Rev. Arthur Buckminster Fuller, who was a Unitarian minister in Boston, a chaplain in the Civil War, and was killed at the Battle of Fredericksburg in 1862. National Portrait Gallery, Smithsonian; Wisconsin Historical Society, WHS- 6909; Chicago History Museum, ICHi-022125; Granger Collection. **Chapter 1: Page 1:** Art Collection 4 / Alamy Stock Photo; **p. 5:** Cahokia Mounds State Historic Site, painting by William R. Iseminger; **p. 6:** Georg Gerster / Science Source; **p. 7:** Bridgeman Images; **p. 9:** Library of Congress; **p. 10:** Courtesy of the John Carter Brown Library at Brown University; **p. 11 (top):** Library of Congress; **(bottom):** Courtesy Lilly Library, Indiana University, Bloomington, IN; **p. 16:** Granger Collection; **p. 17:** Granger Collection; **p. 20:** Unknown artist, Young Woman With a Harpsichord, 1735–50. Denver Art Museum: Gift of the Collection of Frederick and Jan Mayer, 2014.209. Photo courtesy of Denver Art Museum; **p. 21:** DeA Picture Library / Art Resource, NY; **p. 23:** Library of Congress; **p. 27:** National Museum of American History, Smithsonian Institution, Behring Center; **p. 33 (top):** Bettmann / Corbis / Getty

Images; **(bottom):** Bibliotheque Nationale, Paris / Bridgeman Images; **p. 35:** Granger Collection; **p. 36:** Collection of the New-York Historical Society / Bridgeman Images. **Chapter 2: Page 38:** © The Trustees of the British Museum / Art Resource, NY; **p. 40:** The London Art Archive / Alamy; **p. 41:** Woburn Abbey, Bedfordshire, UK / The Bridgeman Art Library; **p. 45:** Museum of Art, Rhode Island School of Design. Gift of Robert Winthrop. Photography by Erik Gould; **p. 46:** The Picture Art Collection / Alamy Stock Photo; **p. 48 (top):** Granger Collection; **(bottom):** National Portrait Gallery, Smithsonian Institution; transfer from the National Gallery of Art; gift of the A.W. Mellon Educational and Charitable Trust, 1942; **p. 50:** The New York Public Library / Art Resource, NY; **p. 51:** MPI / Getty Images; **p. 54:** Courtesy of the John Carter Brown Library at Brown University; **p. 55:** Courtesy of the Massachusetts Archives; **p. 56:** Worcester Art Museum, Worcester, Massachusetts, Gift of William A. Savage / Bridgeman Images; **p. 57:** Massachusetts Historical Society; **p. 60:** The New York Public Library / Art Resource, NY; **p. 64:** Annenberg Rare Book and Manuscript Library, Van Pelt-Dietrich Library Center, U Penn; **p. 65:** Library of Congress; **p. 66:** Mrs. Elizabeth Freake and Baby Mary, unknown artist, 1963.134, Worcester Art Museum / Bridgeman Images; **p. 67:** Private Collection / Bridgeman Images; **p. 68:** British Library Board / Robana / Art Resource, NY. **Chapter 3: Page 72:** Emmet Collection, Miriam and Ira D. Wallach Division of Art, Prints and Photographs, The New York Public Library; **p. 76:** Library of Congress; **p. 78:** Unidentified artist, British, 18th century or first quarter 19th century; Quaker Meeting; Oil on canvas; 64.1 x 76.2cm (25 1/4 x 30in.); Museum of Fine Arts, Boston; Bequest of Maxim Karolik; 64.456; **p. 80:** Free Women of Color with Their Children and Servants in a Landscape, 1770–1796 (oil on canvas), Brunias, Agostino (1728–96) / Brooklyn Museum of Art, New York, USA / Gift of

Mrs. Carl H. de Silver in memory of her husband, by exchange and gift of George S. Hellman, by exchange / Bridgeman Images; **p. 81:** © British Library Board. All Rights Reserved / The Bridgeman Art Library; **p. 83:** © National Maritime Museum, Greenwich, London; **p. 87:** Courtesy of the John Carter Brown Library at Brown University; **p. 90:** The New York Public Library / Art Resource, NY; **p. 95:** Library of Congress; **p. 96:** Eileen Tweedy / REX / Shutterstock; **p. 98:** Collection of the New-York Historical Society / Bridgeman Images; **p. 99:** National Portrait Gallery, Smithsonian Institution; **p. 100:** Private Collection. Photograph by Alex Jamison, courtesy the National Portrait Gallery, Smithsonian Institution; **p. 101:** Gift of Edgar William and Bernice Chrysler Garbisch, Image © 2006 Board of Trustees, National Gallery of Art, Washington. **Chapter 4: Page 104:** Barry Lawrence Ruderman Antique Maps Inc. www.raremaps.com; **p. 106:** Library of Congress; **p. 109:** Chateau des ducs de Bretagne, Musee d'histoire de Nantes; **p. 112:** Jamestown-Yorktown Foundation; **p. 113:** The Colonial Williamsburg Foundation. Gift of Abby Aldrich Rockefeller; **p. 114:** Image copyright © The Metropolitan Museum of Art. Image source: Art Resource, NY; **p. 115:** Schomburg Center for Research in Black Culture, Photographs and Prints Division, The New York Public Library; **p. 116:** Chicago History Museum, ICHi-032162; **p. 117:** Library of Congress; **p. 119:** The Library Company of Philadelphia; **p. 122:** Archivart / Alamy Stock Photo; **p. 124:** National Portrait Gallery, London; **p. 125:** Library of Congress; **p. 126:** Granger Collection; **p. 127:** Album / Alamy Stock Photo; **p. 129:** Library of Congress; **p. 130:** Library of Congress. **Chapter 5: Page 138:** Library of Congress; **p. 140:** Library of Congress; **p. 142:** The Colonial Williamsburg Foundation. Museum Purchase; **p. 146:** Library of Congress; **p. 147:** Library of Congress; **p. 149:** Chicago History Museum, ICHi-076663; **p. 151:** American Philosophical Society; **p. 153:** Courtesy, American

p. **328**: GLC07238 $2,500 Reward! Mississippi Co., Missouri broadside advertising runaway slaves, August 23, 1852 / Courtesy of The Gilder Lehrman Institute of American History; **p. 329: (top):** New Haven Museum; **(bottom):** The Library Company of Philadelphia; **p. 332:** Library of Congress. **Chapter 12: Page 334:** Collection of Dr. and Mrs. John Livingston and Mrs. Elizabeth Livingston Jaeger, Photo: Hearts and Hands Media Arts. Photography courtesy of Hearts & Hands Media Arts, from the book and film "Hearts and Hands: A Social History of 19th Century Women and their Quilts" (New Day Films); **p. 336:** Granger Collection; **p. 337:** Library of Congress; **p. 339:** Bibliotheque Nationale, Paris, France / Archives Charmet / The Bridgeman Art Library; **p. 340:** Library of Congress; **p. 343:** Massachusetts Historical Society. Banner, William Lloyd Garrison (1805-1879) "Proclaim Liberty Throughout all the Land unto all the inhabitants thereof." MHS image #332; **p. 344:** Collection of the New-York Historical Society / Purchase, The Louis Durr Fund / Bridgeman Images; **p. 345:** Boston Athenaeum; **p. 346:** Library of Congress; **p. 348 (top):** Chicago History Museum; **(bottom):** Samuel J. Miller, Frederick Douglass, 1847–52, cased half-plate daguerreotype, plate: 14 x 10.6 cm, Major Acquisitions Centennial Endowment, The Art Institute of Chicago; **p. 349:** The Library Company of Philadelphia; **p. 350:** Library of Congress; **p. 353:** Gift of Constance Fuller Threinen, great-granddaughter of Margaret Fuller's brother, the Rev. Arthur Buckminster Fuller, who was a Unitarian minister in Boston, a chaplain in the Civil War, and was killed at the Battle of Fredericksburg in 1862. National Portrait Gallery, Smithsonian; **p. 356:** Bettmann / Corbis / Getty Images; **p. 358:** Library of Congress. **Chapter 13: Page 360:** Courtesy of the Maryland Historical Society; **p. 361 (left):** Library of Congress; **(right):** Architect of the Capitol; p. 362: A65.43 Alfred Sully, Monterey, California Rancho Scene, circa 1849. Watercolor on paper, 15.25 x 18 in. Collection of the Oakland Museum of California. The Oakland Museum of California Kahn Collection; **p. 364:** Bettmann / Corbis / Getty Images; **p. 365 (top):** Collection of the New-York Historical Society / Gift of George K. Higgins / Bridgeman Images; **(bottom):** Sarah Ann Lillie Hardinge (1824–1913) View on the Guadalupe, Seguin, Texas 1853, transparent and opaque watercolor over

graphite on paper, 4 3/4 x 7 1/2 in. Amon Carter Museum of American Art, Fort Worth, Texas, Gift of Natalie K. Shastid, 1984.3.14; **p. 367:** Granger Collection; **p. 370:** The Bancroft Library, University of California, Berkeley; **p. 371:** Image copyright (c) The Metropolitan Museum of Art / Art Resource, NY; **p. 374 (top):** © The Metropolitan Museum of Art / Art Resource, NY; **(bottom):** Library of Congress; **p. 375:** Fugitive slave law . . . Hamlet in chains. National antislavery standard. Vol. 21 (Oct. 17, 1850), page 82, Rare Book & Manuscript Library, Columbia University in the City of New York; **p. 379:** Library of Congress; **p. 381:** Bettmann / Corbis / Getty Images; **p. 382:** Collection of the New-York Historical Society / Bridgeman Images; **p. 384:** Bettmann / Corbis / Getty Images; **p. 385 (top):** Chicago History Museum, ICHi-022206; Christopher S. German, photographer; **(bottom):** George Eastman House / Getty Images; **p. 386:** Collection of the New-York Historical Society / Bridgeman Images; **p. 391:** Library of Congress; **p. 39:** Greenville County Museum of Art, Greenville, SC. **Chapter 14: Page 395:** Museum of Fine Arts, Boston / M. and M. Karolik Collection of American Watercolors and / Drawings, 1800–75 / The Bridgeman Art Library; **p. 398 (both):** Library of Congress; **p. 399 (top):** Library of Congress; **(bottom):** Newark Museum / Art Resource, NY; **p. 403:** Artist/maker unknown, American, Fourth Pennsylvania Cavalry After 1861 Oil on canvas. The Collection of Edgar William and Bernice Chrysler Garbisch, 1968 1968-222-3 Philadelphia Museum of Art; **p. 405 (both):** Library of Congress; **p. 406:** Granger Collection; **p. 408:** The Print Collector / Alamy Stock Photo; **p. 409 (top):** Smithsonian Institution, Photographic History Collection, Division of Information Technology; **(bottom):** Library of Congress; **p. 410 (top):** Library of Congress; **(bottom):** GLC00968 Unknown (Civil War Songbook). November 24, 1862 / Courtesy of The Gilder Lehrman Institute of American History; **p. 411:** David Bustill Bowser. Untitled (Lincoln and the Female Slave) 1863. Oil on canvas 1987.1.83. Simpson Collection, The Amistad Center for Art & Culture. Photo: John Groo / The Amistad Center for Art & Culture; **p. 412 (top):** Courtesy, Daughters of Charity, Province of St. Louise, St. Louis, MO; **(bottom):** Library of Congress; **p. 413 (top):** Chicago History Museum, ICHi-016764; **(bottom):** Chicago History Museum,

ICHi-027442; **p. 414:** Wisconsin Historical Society, WHS- 6909; **p. 415:** Granger Collection; **p. 418 (top):** Library of Congress; **(bottom):** Collection of the New-York Historical Society / Bridgeman Images; **p. 419 (top):** Chicago History Museum, ICHi-068078; **(bottom):** The New York Public Library Digital Collections; **p. 421 (both):** Louisiana State University Special Collections From the U.S. Civil War Center exhibit Beyond Face Value, courtesy of Jules d'Hemecourt; **p. 424:** provided courtesy (c) HarpWeek., LLC; **p. 425:** William Washington (1831–1870), The Burial of Latané, 1864, oil on canvas, 38 x 48 inches. The Johnson Collection, Spartanburg, South Carolina; **p. 426 (both):** Library of Congress; **p. 428 (both):** Library of Congress; **p. 429:** Library of Congress; **p. 430:** National Archives; **p. 432 (top):** provided courtesy © HarpWeek LLC; **p. 433 (top):** Library of Congress; **(bottom):** © The Metropolitan Museum of Art / Art Resource, NY. **Chapter 15: Page 435:** Chicago History Museum, ICHi-022125; **p. 437:** Pictures Now / Alamy Stock Photo; **p. 438:** Library of Congress; **(bottom):** Photographic History Collection, Division of Information Technology and Communications, National Museum of American History, Smithsonian Institution; **p. 439:** Granger Collection; **p. 441:** Smithsonian American Art Museum, Washington, DC / Art Resource, NY; **p. 442:** Library of Congress; **p. 443:** The Valentine; **p. 447:** Niday Picture Library / Alamy Stock Photo; **p. 449 (both):** Library of Congress; **p. 450:** Library of Congress; **p. 451:** Museum of Political Life, University of Hartford; **p. 452:** Library of Congress; **p. 453:** Library of Congress; **p. 457:** Library of Congress; **p. 458 (both):** Library of Congress; **p. 459 (both):** Library of Congress; **p. 460:** Granger Collection; **p. 461:** Clements Library Collection, University of Michigan; **p. 462:** Granger Collection; **p. 463:** Wikimedia, public domain; **p. 464 (top both):** Library of Congress; **(bottom):** National Archives; p. 466: Library of Congress; **p. 467:** Library of Congress.

TEXT

Chapter 1: Bartolomé de las Casas: "History of the Indies [1528]", excerpt from *History of the Indies*, translated and edited by Andrée Collard (New York: Harper & Row, 1971), pp. 82, 112–115. Copyright © 1971 by Andrée M. Collard, renewed © 1999 by

Joyce J. Contrucci. Reprinted by permission of Joyce J. Contrucci. **Chapter 2: Thomas Hutchinson**: "The Examination of Mrs. Ann Hutchinson at the court of Newtown." Reprinted by permission of the publisher from *The History of the Colony and Province of Massachusetts Bay, Vol. II* by Thomas Hutchinson, edited by Lawrence Shaw Mayo, pp. 366–391, Cambridge, Mass.: Harvard University Press, Copyright © 1963 by the President and Fellows of Harvard College. Copyright © renewed 1964 by Lawrence Shaw Mayo. **Chapter 6: Abigail Adams**: "Abigail Adams to John Adams, 31 March 1776." Reprinted by permission of the publisher from *The Adams Papers: Adams Family Correspondence, Volume I and II: December 1761–March 1778*, edited by L. H. Butterfield, Cambridge, Mass.: The Belknap Press of Harvard University Press, Copyright © 1963 by the Massachusetts Historical Society. **Chapter 8: Democratic-Republican Society of Pennsylvania**: Excerpt from minutes of The Democratic Society of Pennsylvania, December 18, 1794. The Historical Society of Pennsylvania (HSP), Collection # Am. 315/3150. Reprinted with permission. **Chapter 9: Margaret McCarthy**: "Letter of Margaret McCarthy to Her Family (1850") From "State-Aided Emigration Schemes from Crown Estates in Ireland c. 1850" by Eilish Ellis. *Analecta Hibernica 22* (1960), pp. 390–393. Reprinted by permission of the estate of Eilish Ellis. **Chapter 11: Joseph Taper**: Excerpt from "Letter from Joseph Taper to Joseph Long, November 11, 1840" in the Joseph Long Papers located in the Rare Book, Manuscript, and Special Collections Library, Duke University.

INDEX

Page numbers in *italics* refer to illustrations.

proprietorship, 57, 77–78, 88, 89, 98
    Maryland as, 52
Prospective Scene in the City of Oaks, A, 463
Prostrate State, The (Pike), 464
Protestant Association, 89
Protestant Reformation, 34
Protestants, *23*, *40*, 136, 297, 339, 341, 350,
    370, 411–12
    in American colonies, 88–90, 92, 95
    in Amsterdam, 33–34
    Catholics *vs.*, 267
    Dissenters, and, 60, 88
    in England, 40, 69, 70
    French, 26, 32
    Indians and, 23
    in Maryland colony, 52, 69–70, 89
    in New York colony, 77
    planter class, 70
    and spread of Protestantism, 41–42
    tax support of, 174
    voting rights and, 172–73
    see also Christianity; *specific*
        denominations
Prussia, 290
public goods, 177
Public Whipping of Slaves in Lexington,
    Missouri, in 1856, A, *321*
"Publius," 207
Pueblo Bonita, 6, *6*
Pueblo Indians, 6, 27, 102, 126
Pueblo Revolt, *27*, 27–30, 87
pueblos, 6
Puerto Rico, 24, 288
Punch, *406*
Puritans, Puritanism, 54–55, 89–90, 341
    beliefs of, 52–53, 57, 60–61, 63
    church and state and, 58–59
    emigration to New England, 54
    families of, 55–56, *56*, 63
    Indians and, 61–64
    intolerance in, 58–61, 63, 69
    liberties of, 58
    rise of, 52–54
    sermons of, 52–53
    slavery and, 58
    women's role in, 55–56, 63, 65
    worldly success as viewed by, 53, 66
pyramids, Egyptian, 5

quadrant, 14
Quaker Meeting, A, *78*
Quakers, 69, *78*, 95, 106, 136, 179, 185
    Gabriel's Rebellion and, 234–35
    liberty of, 78–79
    as pacifists, 78–79
    slavery repudiated by, 78, 342, 350
Quebec, 30, *140*
Quebec Act (1774), 147, 172
Quito, Ecuador, 21

race, racism
    Andrew Johnson and, 447–48
    and class, 283
    lack of opportunities and, 273–74
    as pillar of slavery, 315
    Reconstruction and, 462, 464–65
    riots and, 273
    theories of, 369–70
    see also segregation
Radical Reconstruction, 447–51
Radical Republicans, 406, 428, 430,
    449–50, *450*, 451–52
railroads, 254, *255*, 260, 262–63, *378*, 443
    in Civil War, 398, 400, 414, 420
    in Northwest, 377, 379
    in Reconstruction, 460
    Southern, 314
    transcontinental, 376, 390, 414
"Railsplitter, The," *384*
Rainey, Joseph H., *458*
Raleigh, Walter (1554–1618), *7*, 40–42
Ramsay, David (1749–1815), 210
Randolph, Richard, 185
Rapp, George (1757–1847), 339
"re-Africanization," 112
reaper, 260
reconquista, 16–17
Reconstruction, 309, 409, 428–30,
    435–67, *465*
    African-Americans in, 52, *435*, 446–47,
        449–51, *452*, 453–57, *459*
    battle over, 447–48
    black officeholders during, 458–59
    Chinese laborers during, 447
    Johnson's policies in, 442, 447–51, *451*,
        451–52
    overthrow of, 461–67, *467*
    public schools in, 460, *461*, *462*
    radical, 447–51
    railroads built during, 460
    violence in, 462–63
    white farmers in, 442–46
    women's rights and, 455, 457
    see also Presidential Reconstruction;
        Radical Reconstruction; Second
        Reconstruction
Reconstruction (Baterman), *453*
Reconstruction Act (1867), 451–52, 457
Redeemers, 465–66
redemptioners, 92
    see also indentured servitude
Red Scare, 209
Red Sticks (Creeks), 244
reform, 334–59
    freedom and, 340–41
    religion and, 339–40
    temperance and, 339–40
    utopian communities and, 336–39
Reformation, 22, 40, 41–42, 52

Regulators, 143–44, 199
religion
    from Africa, 113
    of African-Americans, rise in, 438, *440*
    and attempted conversions of Indians,
        9, 22–24, 27, 32
    Bible and, 23, 52–53, 56, 59
    Bible Commonwealth and, 58, 59, 89
    Enlightenment and, 123
    and founding of Connecticut, 60
    in Maryland, 52, 69–70
    missionaries and, 22–24, 27, 32, 120,
        127
    Native American, 7, 7–9, *11*
    reform and, 339–40
    Salem witch trials and, 90–91
    and separation of church and state, 58,
        92–93, 95, 173–75
    slaves and, 113
    Thomas Jefferson and, 123, 173, 174
    witchcraft and, 90–91
    see also Great Awakening; Great
        Awakening, Second; *specific*
        denominations
religious freedom
    in American colonies, 3, 89–90, 92–93,
        95
    in Carolina, 77
    in early U.S., 123–24, 172–75
    in England, 68
    First Amendment and, 213
    in Maryland colony, 52, 89
    in New England colonies, 89–90
    in New Netherland, 34–35
    in New York City, *172*
    in New York colony, 76, 77
    in Pennsylvania, 171
    in Pennsylvania colony, 78–79
    in Rhode Island, 60
    voting rights and, 173–74
    see also diversity
repartimiento system, 24
Report on Manufactures (Hamilton), 223
republicanism, 116, 117
    Christian, 174–75
republican motherhood, 189, 274
Republican Party (Jeffersonian), 226, 230,
    231, *233*
    in election of 1824, 289
    platform of, 226–27
    press of, 232–33
Republican Party (modern), 38, 385–86,
    407, 418–19
    as antislavery, 380
    black voters and, 457–58
    Johnson's impeachment and, 452–53
    Liberal, 463–64
    and Lincoln's nomination, 390
    press of, 401, 412–13